MARRINER S. ECCLES

Marriner S. Eccles,
with portrait of his father.

MARRINER S. ECCLES

Private Entrepreneur
and
Public Servant

SIDNEY HYMAN

With a Foreword by G. L. Bach

GRADUATE SCHOOL OF BUSINESS

STANFORD UNIVERSITY

STANFORD, CALIFORNIA

Stanford University Graduate School of Business
Stanford, California 94305

© 1976 by the Board of Trustees of the Leland Stanford Junior University
All rights reserved. Published 1976
Printed in the United States of America

Library of Congress Catalog Card Number: 76-46152

To Fredda, My Wife

Contents

IV   IN DUBIOUS BATTLE

V   THE ECONOMICS OF WAR

VI   THE PUBLIC CITIZEN

Foreword

FEW MEN MAKE A DIFFERENCE in the course of human history. Marriner Eccles, deeply involved in the affairs of the nation as a private citizen and public servant during this tumultuous century, did. Sidney Hyman, in different parts of this biography, cites Eccles' major role in selling active government fiscal policy to fight the Great Depression in Franklin Roosevelt's New Deal, in bringing bank deposit insurance and banking reform to speed the recovery and avoid future financial debacles, in restoring Federal Reserve independence from the Treasury after it had become an "engine of inflation" during the war years. He notes, too, Eccles' extraordinary record of running ahead of economic and social change—not only during the New Deal years (where Hyman correctly emphasizes that Eccles' vigorous support of counter-depression government spending predated by several years the much-discussed "Keynesian revolution"), but also in more recent years where he early forecast the national malaise that would follow escalation of Vietnam intervention, and the core role of the international population explosion in the growing tensions between the United States and the less-developed "Third World."

One could go on. Eccles was, indeed, a perceptive observer of the rapidly changing plight of mankind, and a courageous, feisty battler for what he thought was right, whatever the odds of success. But the thing that makes this biography, like Eccles' (1951) autobiographical *Beckoning Frontiers,* so fascinating is the extraordinary encapsulation in one man of the explosive changes in American economic history. Marriner Eccles *was* American economic history.

Eccles' father grew up in the slums of Glasgow, in the shadow of Adam Smith's famous *Wealth of Nations* (which, so far as I know, Eccles never read). The family, headed by a blind father, was desperately poor. David Eccles attended no school, and went to work, earning literally pennies a day, at the age of eight. When the family emigrated to America in 1863 this was still a land of the open frontier, and the Mormon Eccles family came among the early settlers to Utah, where Marriner Eccles was born into a family no longer poor but deeply imbued with the spirit of thriftiness, initiative, self-reliance, and hard work. Although David Eccles' shrewd business dealings gradually accumulated the wealth that would one day make the family one of the richest in Utah, Marriner was raised on a Mormon diet of hard work, honesty, respect for money, and service to the Church. At twenty-two, his father's death thrust him into responsibility for the family undertakings and into a business career that within two decades had made the Eccles banking and sugar interests among the largest in the West. He was shrewd, tough, thrifty, concerned to expand the family fortune, successful.

The collapse of the American economy in the 1930s, and especially the massive failure of the banks, led Eccles to question the conventional wisdom that thrift, saving and a balanced budget would right the nation. With some fascinatingly fast footwork, he managed to save the Eccles chain of banks, and no depositor lost a penny. But the experience was a vivid one, and after it, unlike most of his business and banking friends, he could no longer believe that merely adhering to the traditional business virtues would bring order out of chaos. There was little the individual banker could do to halt economy-wide pressures of deflation. Only the government could do that. Thus when a largely chance invitation brought him to Washington in 1933 to testify before a Senate committee on how to rescue the nation from depression, he came with a challenging program of government action, stimulated partly by his reading of Foster and Catchings (not Keynes) and partly by his own insatiable curiosity.

His ideas, which later developed into the New Deal program of unbalanced-budget government spending to fight the depression, found sympathetic listeners in the small group around Franklin Roosevelt. Eccles, the "liberal" millionaire, came increasingly to challenge the business orthodoxy that dominated the nation's economic thinking. From 1933 on, he persistently advocated in the inner circles of the New Deal the ideas later to be called "Keynesian economics," long before the voice of Keynes himself was heard in Washington.

Eccles came to Washington in 1934 for a brief stay as a special assistant to Henry Morgenthau, then Secretary of the Treasury, and only a few months later was appointed governor of the Federal Reserve Board by President Roosevelt. The Fed became the base of his operations for seventeen years to come. Just as his inquiring mind challenged the conventional fiscal wisdom, so it questioned the banking orthodoxy of the day, and his biggest battle in Washington was to reorganize the Federal Reserve and indeed the entire private banking system to make the Federal Reserve more responsive to the Congress, the White House and the people, and to make the whole banking system a more effective agency for restoration and preservation of national prosperity. He was one of the prime movers in establishing nationwide deposit insurance.

But Eccles did not fit any of the standard molds. Though a radical in the eyes of some, he wrote in 1934: "The main concern of the American economy must be to assure maximum employment to its members. Under capitalism, private enterprise must be the main means to that end. Government can and should insist on minimum standards of decency in the mode and conditions of life for its people. Within the limits of its resources, it can and should insist on minimum income for its families; a minimum age for schooling and employment; a maximum age for retirement; decent and safe working conditions; increasing benefits for labor as productivity increases; adequate protection for the aged and unemployed; and adequate educational, health and recreational facilities. But in the final analysis, these must, under capitalism, be enforced and supported by the productivity of the business community itself."

After World War II, this pragmatic, conservative liberal single-handedly tackled the Treasury and President Truman to restore the independence of the Federal Reserve to fight inflation rather than pegging Treasury bond yields. And as he worried more about the growing problem of inflation, he, long before the recent preoccupation with wage-push and incomes policies, focussed on union monopoly power in labor markets as a basic cause of the new inflation.

Returning to private life and the family business and financial interests after his battle for Federal Reserve independence, his flair for turning a profit proved in no way diminished by his long stay in Washington. And his flair for running against the tide of the conventional wisdom was no more diminished. As one of the nation's business and financial leaders, he was one of the first to stress the need for slowing population growth in the third-world nations as the prerequisite to higher living standards there and peaceful coexistence between them and the affluent West in a shrinking world. He mounted a major charge against "the establishment" on the short-sightedness of American involvement in Vietnam. He was one of the first vigorously to advocate reopening economic and diplomatic relations with mainland China.

How different a career from what one would predict for a successful, self-reliant, thrifty financier and business executive! Reading the tale of Marriner Eccles' battle against orthodoxy in business and finance, in Washington and New York and San Francisco, one sees the mores and the patterns of the industrial and commercial revolutions challenged and giving way, with bitter resistance, to the more complex, interactive economic patterns of the 20th century. Eccles epitomized, as perhaps no other man does, the success stories of the old regime, and the new look of business, government and the changing society in the modern world.

Sidney Hyman has written his tale from Marriner Eccles' point of view, and properly so. Somehow, without intending to do so, he makes it all sound too easy. The battles were bitter and divisive. Eccles had enemies with sharp knives and sharp tongues, and it would be well to hear more of their viewpoints if one is to understand both the bitterness of the battles, the significance of the struggles, and the remarkable batting average Eccles compiled in his running challenge to convention, ranging across the whole sweep of the modern economy.

But be that as it may, it is a fascinating life story which illumines the sweep of the economic and financial history of the past century. Stanford's

Graduate School of Business is proud to sponsor its publication. Whether one agrees or disagrees with the positions Eccles took throughout his long and distinguished private and public careers, it will be a better world that has more such men to speak their views and to fight for what they believe is right.

G. L. BACH
Stanford, April 1976

Introduction

EMERSON ONCE LAID IT DOWN as a rule that when old friends meet after a time apart, they should greet each other by asking, "Has anything become clear to you since we were last together?" In 1971, two decades after I had last seen Marriner Stoddard Eccles, we met again, and I put the Emersonian question to him. The protracted reply led to the birth of this biography and accounts for its purpose.

When we came together in Salt Lake City, Eccles was eighty-one. Then, and even now when he is eighty-five, he was spared the bite time itself extracts from a person as the price of longevity. He was spared the spectacle where a lifetime of work yields in the end only a harvest of dead leaves. He was spared the shock of disillusion when the passing years reveal what the days hide. He was spared, above all, the decay of the mind and will.

—As a pillar of the Western business establishment, the enterprises he founded or rebuilt in banking, mining and sugar refining are presently among the corporations which dominate the economic skyline of the American West.

—As the first Westerner ever to head the Federal Reserve Board, he lived to see how major aspects of our present-day national life were prefigured by the results of the policy and institutional battles he won or lost between 1934 and 1951.

—As a free-standing "public citizen" after he returned from Washington to his native Utah in 1951, he aged in ways which fell outside the natural order of things. Though his sight in one eye was eventually impaired, his vision, previously focused mainly on domestic matters, was enlarged to take in a world in which the traditional divisions between internal and external affairs had become as indistinct as a line drawn through water. Though a "pacer" was eventually implanted above his heart to stimulate its beat, his force of will grew stronger whenever he glanced at the clock and was reminded anew that with every tick he had less time left to do what he believed was urgent.

His sense of urgency extended to many things. In one direction, for example, he was in the advance guard of the people who saw that a population explosion threatened to overshoot the carrying capacity of the earth. In a second direction, as a witness before congressional committees and as member of the National Commission on Money and Credit, he repeatedly stressed the growing misfit between the aims of American economic policy and the structure of the public and private institutions which were expected to realize those aims. In a related direction, he repeatedly warned that the American economy was being imperiled by monopoly labor practices which priced American products out of world markets. In yet another direction, starting in mid-1965, Eccles emerged as the first major figure in the American business world publicly to oppose the nation's involvement in the Vietnam conflict. Afterward, from one year to the next, and into his eighties, he spoke to the American business community with the voice of an apostle of the bitter truth, saying over and again that the only thing to expect from America's massive intervention in Vietnam would be the carnage of lives lost in vain and an American economic order shaken to its roots.

II

But the immediate point of the question I put to Eccles went back to the time when I helped prepare and edit his brief memoir, *Beckoning Frontiers,* published in 1951. Work on the book had begun in anticipation of his planned resignation from government, and proceeded amid the shot and shell of his last fight in Washington. Without regard to personal consequences, he had waged that fight with two indivisible objectives in view. The first was to rescue the Federal Reserve System from a war-born condition carried over into the years after VJ Day—a condition whereby the System was independent in name only but in fact was the captive of the Treasury Department. The second was to compel the Treasury to stop the kind of debt management policies that pushed the Reserve System, against its will, into the role of an "engine of inflation."

Because of the demands of the battle, it was not possible for Eccles to spend long hours poring over the records in his files bearing on what he wanted to say in his memoir, and only a fraction of his papers were accessible to me as an editor. A number of documents provided the texts that were woven into his narrative, but much of what he wrote in the first person singular was drawn from the archives of his memory. In doing so, moreover, he deliberately ruled out all except the barest details of his private life, contending that more would not be of interest to the reader. He was mainly concerned with public acts, without regard to the way in which the private and the public man interacted.

Because of the limits Eccles placed its scope, *Beckoning Frontiers* amounted to an argument in summation of all the arguments that had brought him to Washington and kept him there for more than seventeen years at no small personal price. He first explained how he got hold of the concept of a "compensatory economy" in 1931—some years before its theoretical underpinnings were fully set forth by John Maynard Keynes. He then showed the changing implications that concept had for governmental policy in the context of the Great Depression, the Second World War, and the years of adjustment to peacetime conditions. Along with this, he dwelt on the shortfall between the policies actually pursued and what he believed the circumstances special to each case demanded. The cutoff date of the narrative was the spring of 1951, when he resigned from government and returned to his home in Utah.

The book was well received by critics in the United States and abroad. It was widely used as source material for historians and as a text in college courses on contemporary economic thought. In publishing terms, it was a "long distance runner" until it ran out of print twenty years after it first appeared. All this was gratifying, but it was also a source of unease. During the preparation of the memoir, Eccles' version of "what happened" could not be tested against the testimony of other men who had been coactors in the events he recalled.

The diaries of Henry Morgenthau and Harold Ickes, for example, were not yet in print; the diaries of secondary but important figures such as Charles S. Hamlin and George L. Harrison were not as yet open for study; and the memoirs of Harry S. Truman still lay in the future. Further, professional economists such as Milton Friedman, Herbert Stein and John Kenneth Galbraith had not yet analyzed the decisions to which Eccles was a party. Professional historians such as Frank Friedel, Arthur Schlesinger, Jr., and James McGregor Burns had not as yet drawn their full-scale portraits of the Roosevelt years in whose light one could see more clearly the place and value of what Eccles personally tried to do. What was not available in 1951 for use in cross-examining Eccles' version of "what happened" became available in the years following the publication of *Beckoning Frontiers*.

III

In 1971, when I was reunited with Eccles, conditions in the nation and in the world had radically changed since I saw him last. In 1951, for example, despite many internal strains including the commotions over the course of the Korean War, most Americans still viewed the United States itself, a "nation with the soul of a church," as the object of their "civil religion." Most of them, that is, shared in some degree the old Puritan conviction that America itself comprised the "winnowing of the winnowed." It was a New Israel, a chosen people, the steward of divine righteousness and the carrier of divine destiny. Its history was part of holy history, and its future was properly viewed in millennial terms.

In 1971, however, this psychic outlook seemed to be fast losing strength. It was a time when merely to be an American was to have one's inherited system of thought brought under siege, when self-flagellation and paranoia threatened to crack the social frame, when the old faith in America's divine mission was decried as a mask for the use of brute force in the world arena. It was a time when the old vaunts about the glories of American power were answered by voices inveighing against the shame of American power, when the old Party of Hope to which most Americans once belonged, seemingly lost millions of defectors to an emergent new Party of Despair.

In 1951, when Americans admitted that there were blemishes on the face of the nation, they tended to use cosmetic words which concealed from their own eyes the underlying cancers. Crime, for example, seemed to mean only "organized crime." Political corruption seemed to imply only "dollar" corruption. Racial discrimination seemed to imply a disease "endemic only in the rural South." Meanwhile, though the air in 1951 rang with political counterbattery fire bearing on the impending presidential election, the targets in view tended to be persons, not institutions. The targets were *a* president and *his* methods, *a* congressional leadership and *their* methods, *a* political faction and *its* methods—and not *the* presidency, *the* Congress, or *the* American party system. Despite the enormities associated with the name of Senator Joseph McCarthy, the nation's inherited constitutional structure still seemed in such vigorous health that most Americans would have answered "yes" if asked whether Heaven itself was governed under the American Constitution.

In 1971, however, painful doubts about the capacity of American institutions to serve as instruments of responsible power led to anguished questions. What was the true state of the nation's constitutional morality? Had it become so lax that success itself cleansed any means by which success was achieved? Did that laxness extend to "the national interest?" Did the mere assertion of the "national interest" justify all the grabbing and getting done in its name? Did it transform every lie into a higher truth, every deception into a higher fidelity, every evasion into a higher candor?

One more example. In 1951 the U.S. dollar, though already under siege, was still the versatile workhorse of the international monetary system hinged to the 1944 Bretton Woods Agreements creating the International Monetary Fund (IMF) and the World Bank. The dollar, for example, was the *key* currency, because the United States was the sole country which still pegged its currency to gold. It was the primary *intervention* currency, since other countries pegged their own currency to the dollar, either directly or indirectly. Further, because the dollar was widely used by central bankers as an international asset—more useful than gold because of the interest to be earned on them—the dollar was the primary *reserve* currency. Because it was widely used for trading operations as a currency of *contract,* the dollar (along with the pound) was the primary *vehicle* currency. Because it was widely used as the *currency of quotation,* the dollar was the main currency serving as a *unit of account.*

By 1971, however, it was as if mice had suddenly begun to chase cats. The dollar buckled, slid, and groaned beneath the overload of internal and external stresses it had long carried. Government officials in the United States, like those abroad, met the strain only by patchwork expedients. Alone, or after international consultations, they confined their efforts to papering over the most immediately visible crack in the international monetary system. But after a seemingly localized crisis had passed, they took their bearing from the demands of domestic politics. They would not risk reprisals from an electorate by advocating and *persisting* in measures —requiring domestic discipline—to infuse the dollar and the international monetary system with vital new strength.

Worse was to come in the years lying immediately ahead. But even in 1971 the mood of many Americans was one of bewilderment and disenchantment. Bewilderment over the phenomenon of inflation tied at the hipbone to an incipient recession. Bewilderment over the inability of officialdom to "provide for the general welfare" without harmful effects on various sectors of the economy. Disenchantment over the relationship between the United States and its allies. A semiunited Europe and a suddenly powerful Japan were still dependent on the United States for their security. Yet vast shifts in world patterns of economic power deprived many Americans of the sense that their political leaders could protect their money as well as their lives.

It was these contrasts that entered into the question I put to Eccles, "Has anything become clear to you since we were last together?"

His reply extended over hours of talk. He retraced what he believed to be the cause-and-effect links among the events that had unfolded since 1951, en route to the disorders of 1971. In his manner of speaking he was, as usual, full of the fire of flint, and the sparks flew as he carried his argument forward. At one point he paused to suggest that if I were interested in reconstructing the full story of his own responses to those events, I could have the free run of *all* his voluminous records. I accepted the offer, and spent much time in Salt Lake City where his personal files were kept.

The idea of a biography was born that way. Aside from the fact that altogether different things are seen when the perspective shifts from the "I" of an autobiography to the "he" of a biography, the records in Salt Lake City contained a mass of material not previously available two decades earlier in Washington. Further, in some instances they either mutely corrected errors of fact or interpretation in what Eccles had written in 1951, reinforced his version or challenged the versions of "what happened" offered by diarists and some professional economists and historians. In other instances, material which had been left out of account or was touched on only lightly when *Beckoning Frontiers* was being written had grown in importance because of its bearing on later events. Above all, the records indicated that what Eccles tried to do as a "public citizen" after 1951 was as significant as his work in Washington.

The purpose of the biography which took shape under the impact of these considerations is not to canonize Marriner S. Eccles. To place him in the company of saints is either to corrupt the integrity of words, to render him ridiculous or to deny him the right to his own inconvenient humanity. The purpose is in part to tell the story of a Western family, extending over a hundred years of American history. The larger purpose is in a sense addressed to the immediate present. It is to use the outsized figure of Eccles as a lens that can bring into view certain salient lines of force—social, political, and economic—that have shaped our life today. It will be observed in the course of all this how one man tried to move *against* history, in a brave and often frustrated attempt to make events become what he thought they *should* be.

It remains to be explained that, in the pages which follow, all quoted statements not otherwise footnoted are taken from Eccles' files and records presently available in his Salt Lake City office, and destined for ready access to scholars once they are turned over to the University of Utah for safe-keeping.

1. Prologue

THE STRUGGLE TO GOVERN the American nation always draws to itself rival forms of power. It can be a struggle between the power of congealed inertia and the power of causes, between the power of massive organization and the power of strategically placed persons, between the power of ardent ignorance and the power of expert knowledge, between the power of naked force and the power of self-abnegation. The rivalry can also be between the power of empiricists who can count but not think and abstractionists who can think but not count, between the power of despair and the power of hope, between the power in the letter of the law and power in the spirit of equity, between the insistence that all power tends to corrupt and the insistence that the absence of power can corrupt just as thoroughly as absolute power.

Yet, in the four months between Franklin D. Roosevelt's election as president in November 1932 and his inauguration in March 1933, all the recurrent aspects in the struggle to govern the nation were overshadowed by a haunting question. Could America's inherited constitutional order survive the distress of its people, or would the nation go the way of Germany, where Adolf Hitler became the führer of the Reich in January 1933?

While the question remained unanswered, more fear-driven depositors withdrew funds from banks, more banks failed, more script money was issued and more states declared bank holidays.[1] Business bankruptcy cases clogged the courts, hunger riots flared in the cities, unemployed men lengthened the bread lines and robberies filled police blotters. More frenzied proposals for recovery sounded on all sides—ranging from silver or green-back monetary inflationists to Huey Long's "share the wealth" program; from the technocrats, bent on restructuring the management of production, to the Marxists, bent on nationalizing all means of production.

At the same time, more people joined the cult of direct action and physically challenged the validity of the laws and the lawfulness of their enforcing agents. More farmers armed themselves with guns, clubs and lynch ropes to prevent foreclosures on their own or their neighbors' property. More paramilitary units drilled in the open—Minute Men, Silver Shirts, Khaki Shirts, White Shirts—all modeled after Mussolini's Fascist Black Shirts or Hitler's Nazi Brown Shirts.

It seemed possible that Hitler *could* happen here—that a violent man, preaching the higher law of crisis, could seize dictatorial powers and make the American nation the captive of his will—considering that the vital center for constitutional leadership, the American presidency, resembled a ghost ship, with no hand at the wheel to set its course.

Herbert Hoover believed that the results of the 1932 election were a giant error. In the months after his defeat, while he still held the presidency, he wasted his residual authority on an attempt to score points in a useless debating contest with the lame-duck session of the Seventy-second Congress. Meanwhile, the will to believe in the technical magic of President-elect Roosevelt was rapidly being eroded. True, the tenor of his 1932 campaign, coupled with his record as governor of New York, conveyed the impression that he would move in the Progressive tradition of positive government to set right some things that were out of joint in American life.

He would try, for example, to improve labor conditions, would support federal unemployment insurance, back the expansion of publicly owned power plants and advocate the conservation of natural resources, flood control and reforestation. He would favor the regulation of security exchanges, tackle the crop-surplus problem and try to restore agricultural purchasing power. He would move to repeal the Prohibition Amendment, which had placed Americans under a constitutional injunction to be saints by law, at the cost of being hypocrites in practice. All such particular measures carried their worth on their face. None, however, revealed how the president-elect intended to achieve a *general* economic recovery. He was ambiguous. When pressed for clues, Roosevelt smilingly made himself a slave to his interrogators. He said *this* to please one person and an opposite *that* to please the next. His only clearly voiced theory about how a general recovery would be attained had been in his campaign speeches, in which he attacked the Hoover administration for its deficit spending. In Roosevelt's view, the "staggering deficits" incurred by that administration—$5 billion in all—had "weakened public confidence in the government's credit," posed "an inflationary peril" to the savings of the American people and, "like a family that lives beyond its means," threatened "the nation with bankruptcy and a life in the poorhouse." Hence "a reduction in federal spending was the most direct and effective contribution that government could make to business."[2]

II

In the last two weeks of February 1933, the U.S. Senate Finance Committee of the lame-duck second session of the Seventy-second Congress held a hearing on the causes and cures of the depression. The committee chairman, Senator Reed Smoot, was a banker by profession, an apostle of the Mormon Church and a Utah Republican who had represented his state in the Senate since 1902. It was not he, however, who initiated the resolution that gave the hearing its special character and purpose. The initiative was taken by Senator Pat Harrison, a conservative Mississippi Democrat, whose seniority would automatically make him the chairman of the

Finance Committee in March, when the Democrats assumed majority control of the Senate.

In advance of that succession, Harrison meant to douse the inflamed radical proposals for national recovery. This could be done, he thought, if respected captains of American commerce, finance and industry were provided with a Senate forum from which they could broadcast their sensible counsel to the nation.

Of the two hundred men invited to testify before the Senate Committee on the causes and cures of the depression, forty-six did so in person, while an added sixty submitted their views in writing. Of those who appeared in person, twenty-seven—drawn mainly from the Eastern seaboard—were prominently identified with major industrial, financial or commercial operations. Thirteen—again mainly from the same region—represented the "general public," though, with several heretical exceptions, most of these were affiliated with the business leaders. Farm and labor organizations each had three spokesmen.

The renown of the witnesses, and hence their power to attract national press attention, seemed to predetermine the order in which they were called to the stand. Yet the purpose Harrison meant to achieve was subverted soon after the "big names" began to express their views. Each, in better times, had either ably managed a private enterprise or served the nation well in a public post; each, however, was intellectually shipwrecked when he addressed himself to the question of what should be done to promote recovery.[3]

John W. Davis, the 1924 Democratic presidential candidate and an acknowledged leader of the American Bar, said he had nothing to offer, either of fact or of theory, and Jackson Reynolds, of the First National Bank of New York, when asked for his solution, answered, "I have not, and I do not believe anybody else has." Myron C. Taylor, chairman of the United States Steel Corporation, offered a variation on this theme: "I have no remedy in mind," said he, "except that the government should put its own house in order as an example to the community, balance the budget and live within its income." Nicholas Murray Butler, president of Columbia University, echoed Taylor, saying that the road to recovery lay in "government economy and balanced budgets."

More of the same was advanced by David F. Houston, president of the Mutual Life Insurance Company, president of the University of Texas, who had previously been Secretary of Agriculture and Secretary of the Treasury under Woodrow Wilson: "Avoid any unnecessary appropriations," he said. Edward D. Duffield, president of the Prudential Life Insurance Company, agreed—"The thing of primary importance is the balancing of the federal budget"—as did Ernest T. Weir, of Weirton Steel, and General W. W. Atterbury, president of the Pennsylvania Railroad; but Atterbury had something to add as he pronounced a moral sentence for the edification of the gods: "I can see no reason why Government should not conduct its business during these times in exactly the same way as the individual or corporation should. There is no panacea for a resumption of prosperity except the slow, painful one of hitting the bottom, and then slowly building up with a sane and economical foundation on which to build." Atterbury's view, in turn, was fully orchestrated by Bernard Baruch, who brought to his testimony the mystique surrounding both his role as the head of the War Industries Board under Wilson and his reputation as "an advisor to presidents." Said Baruch:

Natural processes are working to cure every evil, but what have we done to aid the cure? . . . We have set every legislative force against the economics of cure. We have used Federal credit in a vain attempt to reconstruct or preserve the ruins of phantom values. . . .

Delay in balancing the budget is trifling with disaster. . . . From the moment when we honestly balance the budget and return to an orthodox Treasury policy, money will flow here from all the world and out of every cautious domestic hoard seeking safety and employment and we shall have reached the end of our downward path. With the monotony and persistence of Old Cato, we should make one single and invariable dictum the theme of every discourse: balance budgets. Stop spending money we haven't got. Sacrifice for frugality and revenue. Cut government spending—cut it as rations are cut in a siege. Tax—tax everybody for everything.

The corporal's guard of farm and labor spokesmen were neither attached to the idea of a balanced federal budget nor haunted, as were most bankers, economists and politicians, by the specter of a German-style inflation, with satchels stuffed with "printing-press dollars" to buy a loaf of bread. If the threat of inflation was real, then retrenchment on governmental expenditures was a rational response. But to raise the fears of inflation when factories were idle, and millions of people both on the farms and in the cities lacked the means to buy the bare necessities of life, was as irrational as the conduct of a man who is starving yet goes on a diet, fearing that he might someday be overweight. What the farm and labor spokesmen proposed as a regimen for recovery amounted, in the main, to a debtor's counterpart to a creditor's dogma—as if a cloud of moths flying out of one mouth flew into another and gave it nourishment.

John A. Simpson, president of the National Farmers Union, argued that since the depression was caused by a shortage in the medium of exchange, the salvation of farmers lay in the remonetization of silver. John L. Lewis, speaking for a nearly moribund United Mine Workers Union, argued for the creation of a national emergency board mandated to "reduce hours of labor, and the number of days in the work week to a point where the industrial machinery of the nationa can substantially take up the slack of unemployment." Sidney Hillman, president of the faltering Amalgamated Clothing Workers Union, called upon Congress to create a labor board empowered to "regulate hours in different industries in a manner that would not only check further layoffs, but would reemploy part of those who are at this time unemployed." The board, by enforcing a work week reduced to thirty hours, "would give employment to tens of thousands who are without work now, and are bound not to have any in the future."

III

Toward the end of the hearings, a man born and bred in the intermountain region of the American West was called to the witness stand. Unlike the captains of commerce, finance and industry who had held the center of attention, nothing about him, not the ring of his name or his physical appearance seized one's attention. At forty-three, Marriner Stoddard Eccles, of Ogden, Utah, was undersized and whippet lean, and his complexion was on the pallid side. The features of his face were American Gothic but for his nose, which was that of Torquemada, and his carefully parted hair was brushed flat and back on his head. His manner, before he began to speak, could be described only as hesitant. It was marked by a reflex upward jerk of his shoulders and a jutting out of his lower jaw and lip, as if to align his head more firmly on his neck and spine.

Except for two members of the Finance Committee—Senator Reed Smoot and Utah's junior senator, William H. King, a Democrat—it is doubtful that any other person in the room had ever heard of Marriner before. It was otherwise on his home ground in Utah and in neighboring Idaho and Wyoming. His family name was widely known among rank-and-file Mormons and non-Mormons alike; the legend that went with the name was known to leaders throughout the intermountain West.

Marriner was the eldest of nine children of Ellen Stoddard, the second wife of David Eccles, a Mormon polygamist, who had twelve children by his first wife. Eccles, the founder of the two families bearing his name, arrived in the United States from his native Scotland in 1863 as a penniless, illiterate youth of fourteen, starting out from the lowest depth of misery. The new enterprises he created in the American West were on such a scale that he was mentioned by the local people in the same breath as E. H. Harriman, of the Union Pacific and Southern Pacific railroads.

After David Eccles' death in 1912, Marriner, at twenty-two, became the legal guardian of the property inherited by his younger brothers and sisters, seven of whom were minors. The way in which Eccles' estate was divided between the two families set the stage for a long, fierce and embittering dual fought by Marriner and his older half-brothers. After he emerged the victor, what he had preserved became the basis on which, throughout the 1920s, he built the superstructure of new wealth—especially in banking, where he far outdistanced his father's achievements.

He was more feared than loved; his economic titles made him a man whom people in the intermountain West addressed in tones of deference. By 1928 he was the president of the Eccles Investment Company; president of the First Security Corporation; president of the First National Bank and the

First Savings Bank of Ogden; president of the Eccles Hotel Company; president of the Sego Milk Company; president of the Stoddard Lumber Company; vice-president and treasurer of the Amalgamated Sugar Company; a director of the Utah Construction Company, a director of the Utah-Idaho Central Railroad, the Lion Coal Company, the Anderson Lumber Company, the Mountain States Implement Company, the Utah Power and Light Company and the Pet Milk Company.

In time of prosperity, the fortunes of thousands of people in Utah and in nearby states were linked to Marriner's role in the management of these enterprises, and after the onset of the Great Depression, the thousands became hundreds of thousands who had a direct stake in what Marriner did. As president of the First Security Corporation, a bank holding company, he had not only safeguarded the constituent banks against the onslaughts of panics but also used the strength of that corporation to prevent the collapse of other major banks in Utah and Idaho and, with them, the collapse of the banking system of the West generally. As vice-president and treasurer of the Amalgamated Sugar Company, he had led a strenuous effort to get all sugar producers—cane and beet, foreign and domestic—to unite behind an "allotment" plan designed to rescue them from the common ruin they faced. As the director of Utah Construction (and president after 1931), he was deeply involved in the affairs of the "six companies" that had the prime contract to build Hoover (Boulder) Dam—one of the few major public-works projects in the early depression years which provided employment to a significant number of workers and was the source of large-scale demands on factory production.

Marriner was only casually acquainted with the two senators from Utah, but what little he knew about Smoot made him bristle at the mention of the man's name. Smoot was of David Eccles' generation and had been his close friend. Any prospect that the senator's friendship would extend to the son was shattered by an encounter between Marriner and Smoot in the summer of 1932. As chairman of the Utah Relief Commission, Marriner had approached the senator to say, in his trip-hammer style, that private or local governmental sources of support for relief work in Utah were exhausted; that the Mormon Church, in common with other religious institutions, could not "take care of its own"; that Church funds depended on the contributing members, and the members were in a desperate condition along with everyone else; that the federal government alone was in a position to provide funds for relief on a scale needed by distressed Utahans, and by people elsewhere. Smoot, however, looked at Marriner "with cold eyes that received light but no images.[4] It was clear that he was either blind to the facts of the case, or was too old and too tired to be stirred by them.

Senator King was different. In Utah, he and his fellow Democrat, Governor George Dern—a director of one of the Eccles' banks, and Roosevelt's postelection nominee as Secretary of War—had backed Roosevelt's bid for the presidency from start to finish. He was to be counted on to support any relief measures the president-elect might propose. Still, though King was the source of the invitation that brought Marriner as witness before the Finance Committee, it was not because of any shared views about the causes and cures of the Depression. Aside from the fact that in Utah the Eccles name was a synonym for "power," the junior senator from the state had no prior knowledge about the witness from Ogden let alone what he meant to say. In setting in motion the invitation that brought Marriner before the Senate Finance Committee, King had merely acted upon the suggestion of his nephew Robert Hinckley, a friend of Marriner for more than two decades; both had served as young Mormon missionaries in Europe.

IV

Prior to 1931, it never would have occurred to Marriner to say that a great society is one in which its men of business think greatly of their functions. He was content to be the son of his father's thoughts—a dedicated adherent to a laissez-faire economic system in which the lion took from the lamb, and the fox from the lion. He lived only for the wealth of his family, cared only for the things that could be measured in dollars and cents, thought only about how to earn more profits for the particular business enterprises in which his family had a large stake. The world of esthetics was for him a dark continent. He had no interest in imaginative literature, the plastic arts or the performing arts. His diversions were few: golf, hunting and fishing. His social concerns were confined to the litanies about "service" sung in his local Rotary club, and the catechisms of "free enterprise" repeated by the Utah Bankers Association.

Marriner's formal schooling had stopped a year short of graduation from high school. In the two decades that followed, he never read a book that might have widened his intellectual horizons. What he read, aside from newspapers, was limited to balance sheets and reports on companies that transacted (or wished to transact) business with those he headed. He was therefore wholly unprepared for the hour in 1931 when he suddenly found that he was encircled by forces threatening ruin to the family enterprises he managed.

Meanwhile, all around him, some of the same men who in prosperity took every offer of advice as a personal insult, in adversity sought counsel from every passerby. No plan was too futile or absurd to be given consideration. Other men, at their wits' ends, could think of nothing else to do but upbraid reason as blind—as though "God had turned away from the wise, and written his decrees, not in the mind of man, but in the entrails of beasts, or left them to be proclaimed by the inspiration and instinct of fools, madmen, and birds."[5]

Marriner Eccles had reason to be more desperate than they. Because he stood at the summit of economic affairs in his region, he had a greater distance to fall. Because he had long looked upon himself as a born protector—and could always justify his imperious manner by pointing to what he had successfully protected—he had more to fear by way of censure. Because he seldom concealed his contempt for the incompetence of people he bested in a business deal, he would be all the more an object of mockery if he failed. Because he was seldom forgiving when things were not done precisely as he had ordered, so he too would not be forgiven if he failed personally.

In his despair, Marriner began for the first time to reflect on the dynamics of the national economy, viewed as a whole. When a flickering insight commended itself to his reason, he tested it against his experiences in business. If it passed the test, he groped for a second insight, and so on for a third and a fourth. In this way, by 1932, he had arrived at what appeared to be a consistent body of ideas that were directly opposite to those current about the causes and cures of the Depression. He had rehearsed and refined his ideas at meetings with young friends in Utah and on local public platforms.

Now, in Washington, with no personal ambition for office to promote, no national reputation for wisdom to defend, no talent and no taste for the small arts of ingratiation, he had an urgent cause to advance, a reasoned argument to unfold, and he would speak to the Finance Committee in his own style—bluntly and with jarring honesty. He would concede nothing to age or celebrity, but would mount a frontal attack on everything that had been said by the spokesmen for finance, commerce and industry who had preceded him on the witness stand.

Unknown to himself at the time, what he had to say would mark his point of entry into the struggle to govern the American nation. But known only to himself at the time was the extent to which his testimony was a kind of posthumous act of patricide—a repudiation of all the economic tenets he had inherited from his father. Why the beliefs that David Eccles had exemplified through his own career had the strength to hold Marriner's thoughts in thrall until he was forty-one years old, lay in the legendary power of that father.

I

FATHER AND SON

2. The Dark Glen

DAVID ECCLES, born in Glasgow, Scotland, in 1849, had good reason to believe that the city derived its name from the Gaelic term for "dark glen" and not, as was more often claimed, from the term for "dear green spot." In the year of his birth, seventy-four years after Adam Smith had published *The Wealth of Nations*—and the same year in which the *Communist Manifesto* was published—the picture Glasgow presented was that of a great and growing gap between the beneficiaries and the victims of Smith's laissez-faire doctrines in practice. The wealth of the leading merchants and manufacturers who lived by those doctrines was sustained by a dense mass of slum dwellers who worked for meager wages in the textile factories, shipyards, iron mills, locomotive and boiler works, sugar refineries and liquor distilleries.

In a corner of Glasgow's slums known as the Kucadens, human misery reached its lowest depths. David Eccles was born there, the second oldest son in what became a family of five boys and two girls. His father, William, was sturdy Scotsman, pious and patient. Though he was blind in both eyes because of cataracts, he accepted the affliction without protest. "If the good Lord has decreed that some men must be blind," he would say, "why should it not be my lot to be one of them?" Years later, toward the end of his life in the United States, an operation restored his sight in one eye, but he refused an operation on the second. Either he saw enough or, as a frugal Scot, did not want to risk the loss of what he had belatedly gained. Content with a one-eyed view of the New World, he sermonized his grandchildren on the virtues of patience, saying, "I knew all along that things would turn out well."

His wife, Sarah, of the Hutchinson clan in Northern Ireland, and four years older than he, was volubly impatient with patience. When there was no food on the family table, she fed herself and others on caustic complaints. When there was some food, she was full of complaints about other deprivations.

If children could be found in Kucadens who spent at least a few days in a grammar school, the Eccles children were not among them. Poverty forced them to scratch for pennies soon after they lost their baby teeth. John, the oldest son, went to work at the age of eight in a coal mine; at nine, in a sugar factory; at eleven, in a brewery. Two years later, he went daily to Greenrock, where he bought boxes and barrels that had seen service as containers for raw sugar shipped from the East Indies to Glasgow's refineries. Of the load he brought back to Kucadens slum, part was chopped into kindling wood for sale to such customers as could be found. The rest was converted by William into wooden utensils such as rolling pins, bowls, and potato mashers. His feet were the motor power for the wood lathe he used, and the touch of his fingers shaped the finished items which the older children hawked in Glasgow's streets.

In the early 1850s, the Eccleses moved from Glasgow to Paisley, where they shared a thatched roof adobe hut with their kinsmen, the Moyeses: Elizabeth Moyes, the widowed head of that family, was Sarah Eccles sister. The family hoped that William could improve the economic lot of the Eccles by making wooden spools for use by weavers in the Paisley mills. But products of a foot-powered lathe could not compete with the spools made by the new steam-powered machines geared for mass production. William was thrown back on his old line of trade—rolling pins and other kitchenware.

It was in Paisley that David Eccles, as a child of eight, was launched on a career as a traveling salesman and entrepreneur.[6] Loaded down with the objects his father made, he went frequently by train to Glasgow in search of a market. He also skimmed about the New Caledonia railroad station as well as the hotels of Glasgow, offering his service as a porter. In his full growth, he was "five feet ten in his stockinged feet," and was endowed with a sinewy, muscular body. But as a child, he was so scrawny and obviously undernourished that some travelers were moved to pity by his appearance, gave him a penny, and carried the bags themselves. When by one means or another he amassed a shilling in capital, he bought trinkets at a Glasgow wholesale outlet, for resale on the street at twice the cost of his investment.

The trips to Glasgow often kept the child away from home for a week at a time. To speed his "formation of capital" during the week, he limited the consumption of his current earnings. He lodged himself in a Salvation Army flophouse; for two pence he got one bowl of soup and a night's access to a reeking straw mattress. His "roommates" were the derelicts, the diseased, the outcasts of the city, but he managed to hang on to his money, his health and his throat. That is how it went from one year to the next until 1863, when he reached the age of fourteen. He was still illiterate. So far, he had done nothing except survive—which itself was no small achievement.

Then came a change. Mormon missionaries, preaching the gospel of "continuous revelation"—by direct communication from God, by visitation from angels, and by impressions upon the mind of man by the Spirit of God—became active in Great Britain and in Northern Europe in the decades after Joseph Smith first published the *Book of Mormon*. The Eccleses, and their kinsmen the Moyeses, accepted that gospel, and in 1863 were among a company of Scottish converts to Mormonism being readied for a migration to Utah. The Church of Jesus Christ of Latter-day Saints, with its talent for organization, had formed a Perpetual Immigration Fund to bear the costs of moving needy converts from Europe to the Promised Land of

Utah. A family so aided would work to repay that Fund the price of the ocean passage, and the monies returned would then be loaned to other immigrant families.

In the lurid anti-Mormon polemical literature of the day, it was commonly charged that Mormon missionaries cared only to convert attractive women. The Eccles family, however, graphically refuted that charge. There was nothing in its profile that could stir the prurient interest of a missionary. The Eccleses consisted of a blind male adult who could work a foot-powered wood lathe, a crabbed female adult, and a brood of seven children—nine people who stood a few rags away from nakedness, and a crust of bread away from starvation. Yet the strength of the early Mormons had its taproots in families drawn from the lowest depths of life in Europe and America into the western sunlight. Families who had been cast out or held in suspicion by the well-bred and the well-born, families who had nothing to their name and were given something—even if it were merely a hope that they might form a kingdom of priest-saints—could face incredible hardship and accept extraordinary self-discipline to get what had been promised or to keep what had been given.

II

The Eccleses, the Moyeses, and others in their party—which included the future parents of David O. McKay, a major figure in twentieth-century Mormon history—sailed from Glasgow for the United States on May 3, 1863, on the wind-propelled ship "Sunnyshower" or "Cynoshire." After the usual miseries of a sea voyage in steerage, with its ceaseless battles against the aggressive rats who attacked the cache of food each family brought along for survival, the vessel anchored at Castle Garden, New York City, on July 1, the day the battle of Gettysburg began.

In the United States—then a nation of twenty million people, divided by a civil war and caught up in the process of urbanization and industrialization—the Mormon Church maintained staging areas across the country for the group movements of converts to Utah. In this way, the party to which the Eccles and Moyes families belonged traveled by rail from New York City to St. Louis, and from there to Omaha, the end of the railroad line at the time. They then crossed the plains by ox carts, reaching Salt Lake City on October 5, four months after they first set foot on American soil.

One member of the Eccles family was lost along the way. Back in St. Louis, John, the oldest son, then aged seventeen, found the buzz of maritime activity on the Mississippi waterfront more to his taste than the prospects of working a farm. So he hired himself out as a deck hand on a river steamer that supplied Union garrisons along the river banks won by General Grant's earlier victories. John's defection, combined with the father's blindness, made David, aged fourteen, the de facto male head of the

Eccles family. This was not unusual in a setting where boys of eleven often served as sharpshooters on the Pony Express, which began to run out of Salt Lake City in 1860.

More dangerous ammunition was about, however, when the Eccleses reached Salt Lake, and the cause was related to the "principle" of polygamy. In the mid-1850s, when that "principle" was openly promulgated by Mormon Church leaders for the first time, the practice was not in violation of any federal law.[7] In 1862, however, when the Mormons in the Territory of Utah drew up a new constitution for a "State of Deseret," elected a legislature and governor, and petitioned Congress for admission to the Union, Congress gave a peculiar reply to a "peculiar" people. It passed the first federal law against polygamy.

The War Department now feared that Mormon loyalty to the Union side was not to be trusted. At this distance in time, the fear seems irrational. The Mormons had been among the earliest abolitionists, and they had petitioned to join the Federal Union during the Civil War. Nonetheless, the War Department sent Colonel Patrick Edward Conner with three hundred California-Nevada volunteers into the suspect Mormon domain. He established his camp on a bench above Salt Lake City, loudly boasting that his cannons were within range of Brigham Young's residence. These flourishes, however, were of less concern to the newly-arrived Eccles family than was the question of where they were to be settled by the leaders of the Mormon ecclesiastical government.

Mormon religious doctrines endowed each member of the Church with the right to divine guidance through direct revelation and inspiration in matters within the realm of their individual lives. The doctrine, however, also asserted that there was but one man on earth at a time who could receive revelation for the guidance of the whole Church. He was the president of the Church and as such held "the keys" of the priesthood. His official word, when speaking in the name of the Lord, was to be received by the faithful as God's Word. With religious sanctions that doctrine reinforced the economic decisions reached by the central planning agency of the Church regarding the material development of the Mormon community as a whole. In their drive for economic self-sufficiency, and guided by revelation, the planners "called" families from one place to break new lands in a second, or to develop new natural resources in a third place. The people affected might protest and scratch their heads in wonderment, but the faithful generally went where they were told to go. The same applied to newly arrived immigrant converts.

Church authorities sent the Eccleses and the Moyeses to the village of Eden near the villages of Liberty and Huntsville[8] in a canyon fifteen miles east of Ogden City. Encircled by mountains with elevations of up to ten thousand feet, the area today is valued for its natural beauty and for its prosperous dairy farms. It appeared differently to the Eccles family in 1863.

A friendly Scotsman named William Fife gave them access to a one-room lean-to structure, which served as their home in their first year. The Mormon church allotted them sixty acres to be farmed when the spring came, though they had no experience in farming. But beyond this—and a wood-turning lathe—they were bereft of worldly goods. The immediate hardships they faced in Eden made their bleak existence in Glasgow and Paisley seem luxurious in retrospect.

To the Eccleses the wilderness was something fearful, something that only the strongest could survive. Even families whose previous station in life was a cut above that of the Eccleses were declassed to a stone age existence in places like the Ogden Canyon. People lived with their animals, provided they were fortunate to own any. The Eccleses, in their first winter in Eden, owned none. To survive, David gathered maple saplings for his father to convert into kitchenware, and then tried to sell the finished products. He would pile the kitchen implements onto a homemade sled, then lead his blind father between the shafts of the sled, bind himself to his father with a rope, and set off through the snow to make the rounds of other inhabitants in the valley. When fortunate, they would barter some of their wares for goods. Yet it often happened that at the end of a bitter cold day there was nothing except hunger and exhaustion.

With the coming of spring in 1864, David regularly trudged on foot between Eden and Ogden in an attempt to sell door-to-door the items his father made. Later in the season, he supplemented the family's cash income by digging potatoes for Ogden Valley farmers at the wage rate of fifty cents for ten hours of work. In this way, by rigorous savings, he bought a team of oxen for family use. More often, however, he was paid in produce, as when he hired himself at harvest time to the owner of a threshing machine. A threshing machine then represented a huge capital investment and a single one was made to serve a wide circle of farms in the valley. The owner of the machine was paid in grain for the work done, and he used part of the grain to pay his own helpers. In the second year after the Eccles came to Eden, the wheat David earned at threshing time was all that stood between his family and starvation.

Part of the grain had been milled in late fall. But the winter of 1864–65 proved exceptionally severe and long, and the store of milled flour in the Eccles lean-to home was used up. Though several bushels of unground wheat remained on hand, there was no miller close by. To reach the nearest one in Ogden meant a fifteen mile trip through a river canyon where the snow was waist-high and the trails were impassable. Yet the bite of family hunger overrode all causes for hesitation. David loaded the unground wheat on a hand sled, pushed his stumbling way through the snow-drifts, and reached Ogden at the end of two days. There he was told that he faced a week's wait before the miller could get to the wheat David had brought with him. The youth pleaded the emergency needs of his family and offered to work with the miller that night. The proposal was finally accepted; the grist was ground out of the grain, the milled wheat was loaded on the hand sled, and early next morning David began the return to Eden.

His homeward bound trip was all uphill. To make matters worse, new snows had fallen. He must again clear a trail for his cargo. When night fell, David, as he had done at the end of the first day down from Ogden, wrapped himself in a blanket and dug deep into the snow for warmth. Lying there, before he was overcome by a perilous sleep, he vowed that if he lived long enough and found the means to do so, he would some day build a railroad through the canyon to Ogden. When he was in his fifties, he would build the envisioned railroad.

The flour David brought back from Ogden eased the family's immediate food crisis. Soon afterward, however, they were staggered by the sudden death of one of their two oxen. The fear that the remaining ox could also succumb to the severe winter induced the family to bring him inside their cabin and to grant him what amounted to royal privileges. As the family's sole source of energy, his survival took precedence over anything else, even the things on which the family slept. When the supply of hay was exhausted, and when all the neighbors had given what they could to fill his belly, the members of the Eccles family emptied their mattresses of their content of dried wild grass and fed it to the ox.

When at last the snows melted and spring was at hand, the Eccles family rejoiced that they had nursed their source of energy through a time of great peril. Green grass sprouted on all sides. Released from his sedentary indoor life, the ox lumbered toward the green grass, filled himself on it, became bloated, lay down on a hillside, lowed for a while, and died. The Eccles family again was left with only the wood lathe. The painful struggle for survival had to start all over again.

3. Genesis of a Gold Spike

IN 1848 WHEN THE MORMONS first reached Utah, their total stock of money did not exceed $3,000. The size of the stock was gradually expanded in the years following, but the currency in circulation fell so far short of need that the Church became an ad hoc central bank. On the basis of existing or anticipated "reserves" represented by the payment of tithes, it issued a tithing script exchangeable for goods and service. It continued to do so, even when the end of the Civil War opened the doors elsewhere to rapid developments along many economic fronts. It was the time of the Great Barbecue, fueled by cheap raw materials, whose sizzling watchword was, "preempt and exploit."

In most other matters, the Eccleses, as wood turners, and their kinsmen and Moyeses, as weavers, were loyal to all the arrangements, decisions and directives they received from Church authorities. Yet after four years in the Ogden Valley, they saw no hope of ever reaching an economic "Kingdom Come" if they depended for their material betterment on a tithing script which chained them to a barter and barnyard economy. They ached for hard cash, and the ache was particularly acute in the case of young David Eccles. At nineteen, he was in need of capital to launch some sort of business whose prospects were more promising than those hinged to the turn of his father's wood lathe. Hard cash, so it was learned from some fellow Mormons, was available in the Oregon woolen mills along the Willamette River. Sheep were grazed in the area, and the cloth woven from their wool was sent to the growing California market. Moreover, many weavers in the Oregon mills were Mormon converts from the Paisley and Glasgow district in Scotland. Their wages—six cents for each yard of cloth they wove—could go as high as $50 a month, an astronomical sum compared to what weavers earned in Scotland.[9]

When news of Oregon money reached the Eccleses and Moyeses in the Ogden Canyon, the two families were lured by the new promised land, but the dangers in the way were considerable. Not until the advent of the western railroads—and the defeat of Chief Sitting Bull and Chief Crazy Horse in October 1876—would it become safe for the lone individual or the single family to travel unescorted into the far West. Before then, most people who migrated westward over the Oregon Trail—or any other trail—did so as units in a caravan led by a wagon master and an escort of armed scouts.

The Eccles and the Moyes families, however, were in no position to pay the fees charged by the wagon masters for a caravan. When they finally decided to head for Oregon, they knew they must rely on themselves. The combined families could not muster more than five effective riflemen—the three grown sons of the Moyes family, John, James and Robert, and the two Eccles sons, David and Stewart. No less worrisome, neither family could afford to buy a standard-type wagon built by experienced carriage makers for use by westward-moving migrants. Each family had a wagon designed and built by the blind William Eccles. Further, they had to be content with two oxen for each family instead of the usual three-yoke team of six oxen. Even so, they had to work long and eat little in order to save $100, the purchase price of a brace of oxen. The younger children might ride the wagons, but for the rest, the Oregon Trail meant a thousand miles on foot, often over very rough terrain.

After leaving Eden in May 1867, the only other living souls the two families saw in the four months on the trail were those they met at Pony Express stations, or at the "home stations" placed twenty miles apart where cattle could be fed and rested. If things went well, the normal rate of advance was two miles an hour, and the distance between "home stations" could be covered by steady travel from the break of dawn to the onset of dusk. Things, however, seldom went well. "Tires" came off the wagon wheels or wore out. Axles and shafts were broken. The cattle sagged to their knees and would not budge because of their sore feet. Trees tied to the wheels to break a sharp-angled descent gave way, and during one such mishap Elizabeth Hutchinson Moyes was hurled from a wagon and broke an arm. Hunger and thirst were ever present. Now the heat broiled; now the cold seemed to congeal the blood. In one place the party passed the freshly dug graves of people slain in an Indian attack a few days earlier. After that there were no more camp fires at night, for fear of attracting Indians.

At another point, when the party reached a mountain plateau, they faced a great fire ahead, apparently ignited by Indians. There was nothing to do but pass through the conflagration. Blazing trees crashed around them. Stepping on the scorching boulders, the frightened cattle bellowed in pain. The shoes of the travelers were burned off their feet, and soles of their bare feet blistered on the seared earth.

All that young David Eccles experienced on the trail, however, was overprinted by the picture of the majestic stands of timber he saw on all sides when the party entered eastern Oregon. Since early infancy, he had lived with wood and wood shavings from his father's lathe. But the Oregon timber was a world apart from barrel staves or maple saplings. To David's imagination, the tips of the towering trees seemed to poke a hole through the soles on the sandals of the Heavenly Choir. Better yet, they existed to be preempted and exploited. He then vowed that he would some day "put in a lumber outfit here," and he would make good on the vow sooner than he thought possible.

The Dalles, Oregon, was as far as the party could go by wagon. The trip down the Columbia River was by steamer. Money to cover a portion of the fare was secured when the ox teams and the wagons were rented to a rancher in the Dalles. To pay for the remaining portion, the able-bodied men in the Eccles and Moyes families got jobs as deck hands on the steamer for the run to Portland and down the Willamette River to Oregon City. There, the young men in the Moyes family, citing their background as weavers in Paisley, found work in the Chikoff Woolen Mills. The Eccleses headed for the timber about a mile outside Oregon City. After building a log hut for shelter, David and his father went to the Jacons Brothers woolen mill, and secured a contract to furnish the mill with firewood at three dollars a cord; the average yield of a single tree, cut into four feet lengths, was about eighteen cords. The contract enabled them to acquire on credit a team of oxen, saws and other equipment. The debts incurred would be liquidated when the mill paid them for the wood.

At the end of a year, William Eccles wearied of the work he blindly did. He went to San Francisco to try his fortunes there, but whatever he hoped to gain by the move eluded him. Besides, as a deeply religious man, he missed the fellowship of the Mormons he had left behind in Utah. So he doubled back to Oregon, assembled all the members of his family except David, took a steamer to the Dalles, picked up the wagon and the yoke of oxen that had been rented to the rancher, and managed somehow to take himself and his family safely back to Eden in Utah.

David, who remained in Oregon, worked for another year, twelve to fifteen hours daily. Building a huge stockpile of cordwood for the woolen mill, he literally chopped, burned and sawed himself out of his contract. Aside from food, his total personal consumption from his current earnings was represented by the costs of a pair of gloves and a pair of overalls. He had also paid off the costs of the team of oxen, tools and wagon he had used in his work. The rest of his earnings, saved for future use as investment capital, amounted to $400 by the time he returned to Utah.

On his return, he moved with his family from Eden to Ogden, the town where the Union Pacific met the Central Pacific in 1869. Its population at the time did not exceed 1,500, but it was thought to be a "coming city" where men of vision could some day own gold spikes like the one that had been driven at Promontory Point to mark the link-up of the two railroads. The blind William Eccles shared this vision. Besides, it made more sense to relocate his wood lathe on the cite of an urban market than for his children to tote his products over the fifteen miles between Eden and Ogden. But, in the pattern of all the earlier moves—from Glasgow to Paisley, from Eden to Oregon, and from Oregon to San Francisco—William Eccles did no better in Ogden than he had done anywhere else. He failed to get his hands on a gold spike.

II

When the Eccleses were settled in Ogden, David entrusted to his mother's care the $400 in capital he had saved in Oregon. He then began to act on a plan which had been germinating in his mind. He meant to get into the lumber business, but, to round out his knowledge of logging, he went to work for Bishop David James, the owner of a sawmill at White Pines in the mountains above Huntsville. His resources were the team of oxen, the wagon, and tools he had brought back from Oregon.

Throughout the West, a person with talent in the lumber business could profit from the factors that made the decade between 1869 and 1879 a time of very rapid national economic growth.[10] First, the outcome of the Civil War—which decided the political question of how the great plains west of the Mississippi River were to be settled and developed—exposed the area to the full force of the Homestead Act that had been enacted in 1862. That act, it is true, never fulfilled the hope that it would be a safety valve for the release of the social and economic pressures causing labor troubles in the East. Few workers knew how to farm homesteads, and even experienced farmers found the going so rough that not more than one out of five home-steaders retained the farm lands they were the first to till. In consequence of the act, however, there was a rapid extension of the area brought under cultivation on the great plains. At the same time, the national population, augmented by waves of immigrants—many brought from Europe by agents of the new western roads for settlement on western homesteads—increased by 30 percent between 1869 and 1879.

The great plains had few stands of timber, and the first settlers often had no better shelter than sod huts. But when those who managed to settle on new soil could afford a wooden frame house, they provided a market for the lumber milled and shipped to them from the mountainous regions lying to their west. Meanwhile, in the decade following 1869 when the coasts were linked by rail, the miles of track operated more than doubled. Newly built western roads accounted for much of that increase, and these in turn pro-vided a market for the heavy timber used in railroad ties and bridges, and for the milled lumber used for sheds and stations, box cars, flat cars, and pas-senger cars.

In the same decade, the advent of cheap transportation went hand-in-hand with the opening of new mines in the west which doubled the output of coal, iron and copper ores, and increased sixfold the output of lead. The mines and the "company towns" built around them comprised yet another market for western timber and milled lumber. The rapid national growth of manufacturing establishment—33 percent more wage earners were engaged in manufacturing in 1879 than in 1869—entailed the construction of factories which drew on western lumber, as did the expanding Pacific coast port cities like San Francisco and Seattle. And since recurrent fires often reduced large sections of wood-built towns to ashes, they had to be rebuilt from the ground up.

David Eccles eventually turned all the needs of this market for timber and milled lumber to his own profit. But his initial point of entry into the lumber business was no larger than a pin hole. Even so, he was a star-crossed entrepreneur. Because of his youth and inexperience, lumberjacks feared he would be unable to pay them for their labor and were reluctant to work for him hauling logs to Bishop James' saw mill. To complicate matters, his oxen slipped off a precipice in the summer of 1870 and were killed. The worst was to come. David could, so he thought, buy another yoke of oxen by drawing on the four hundred dollars he had deposited with his mother in Ogden. Yet it turned out that his mother could no more guard the hoard prudently—the largest lump sum of money the Eccles family had ever had access to—than the ox nursed through the wintertime in Eden could digest the green grass he ate in the springtime.

While David was in the White Pines, his oldest sister Sarah, then aged seventeen, was courted by a glib-tongued Scotsman named Robert Baird. He won her heart and charmed her parents. There was a rush to a wedding, set for a time which, by chance, coincided with the death of the oxen up in White Pines. David came down from the mountains for what he thought would be a simple wedding ceremony, only to learn on arriving in Ogden that every cent he had saved in two years of back-breaking labor and self-denial in the Oregon woods had been spent on the nuptials of his sister.

Later in life, when David had daughters of his own, he came to the wedding of one of them bearing a suitcase containing $10,000 in gold as a gift for the bride and groom. But at the time the $400 was consumed by Sarah's wedding, it seemed to him that the world was made of frenetic fools who mocked the labors of honest men. There was no money left to buy a new yoke of oxen so that he could resume his operations for Bishop James. He was forced to give up the contract and again to start from scratch the process of capital formation. His attention was drawn to Almy, Wyoming, where a coal mine had been opened up by the new Union Pacific Railroad. He found work in that mine, and clamped on himself a strict regimen of self-denial so that he could conserve most of his meager wages.

When he saved enough to reequip himself for logging operations, he secured a contract to provide logs to the firm of Gibson & Valloy, owners of a sawmill at Beaver Canyon near Spencer, Idaho. This was to be the turning point in his career. He was twenty-three at the time, and without schooling except for some wintertime and night-time classes that he had managed to attend at Moench's school in Ogden. He had enrolled in the school under the spur of shame. Offered a job which he was forced to decline as he did not know how to read or write, he determined never again to have to turn down an offer of work for that reason alone.

The hours David spent at the Moench school made him only function-ally literate but aware that his chief intellectual aid was his memory. In the years ahead, he never "kept books" on his business transactions. He simply used a pocket notebook and entries based on a system of arithmetic he devised. Since he never sold anything he once bought, what he devised seems to have been confined to the arithmetic of addition, starting with the contract for Gibson & Valloy.

To meet the terms of the contract, David hired several teams of oxen and a crew of four lumberjacks. He quickly saw that the lumberjacks spent valuable morning hours watering and feeding the oxen before they began their productive labor. He had to pay for this unproductive time and it irked him to do so. Henceforth it was his practice to rise before dawn, do all the preparatory chores himself, and have the oxen in harness by the time the lumberjacks arrived. Though they grumbled, they respected his craftsmanship—even when they were its victim—and they stuck by him, as did his labor force in his subsequent ventures. He always worked side by side with his employees, knew all of them by name, and lived on a scale only a notch above them, "just for disciplinary purposes," he used to say. To those who held more responsible posts, he often gave shares in his firms by taking their notes for the shares and then letting the dividends earned pay off the indebtedness. His son, Marriner Stoddard Eccles, was to benefit in his day from the friendship of these men. Like his father before him, he would take care not to permit any great and visible gaps to develop between his own standard of living and that of his labor force. Also like his father, but on a national scale, he would be among the first men to spot a falloff in the productivity of the American labor force generally, and to warn against the consequences that would follow.

The first logging contract netted David a profit of $1,500. This, the largest sum of money he had ever made up to that time, supplied the means which got him into the sawmill business. First he used the profits to become a partner in the firm of Gibson & Valloy by buying out Gibson. Then, in the next season, he used the profits on the same logging contract to buy out Valloy—after the latter traded a team of horses David had acquired for a team of oxen. To have done this while David was away, and without prior consultation, was offensive enough. But the offense became monumental in David's eyes when he inspected the oxen and concluded that Valloy got the worst of the bargain. He would not have his own economic destiny linked to that of a man who showed such poor judgment in a horse-oxen trade.

From the moment he parted company from Valloy, David neither worked for nor borrowed one cent of money from anyone else. He proudly noted that, unlike many other Western businessmen of the time—and unlike many Western bankers who had to meet the seasonal needs of farmers and ranchers—he never looked to the East for capital. He would generate his own capital for all his ventures, saying that a business, like an individual, could remain free only if it kept out of debt, and that the West itself could remain free only if it kept out of debt to the East. What he failed to see were certain critical realities which his son Marriner would also overlook until his eyes were opened by the shock of the Great Depression of the 1930s: namely, that if everyone kept out of debt, there could be no capitalist system; that the very essence of capitalism implies a debtor-creditor relationship; that to save successfully, someone has to borrow what is saved; that bankers, the archsymbols of capitalism, are the greatest borrowers of all;

that anyone else who had as many debts in relation to their assets as do bankers would be promptly thrown into bankruptcy.

Yet if David Eccles—like his father William—was blind in one eye in his outlook on the economic world as a whole, he was quick to see and to grasp opportunities for the expansion of his *personal* business. Soon after he became the sole owner of the sawmill in Beaver Canyon, Idaho, he started the Eccles Lumber Company in Ogden as a distributing yard for the lumber he milled or bought from other sources. The new venture prospered, not only to his own benefit, but to the benefit of his father, mother, and the other members of his family who looked to him as their main source of support. By 1875, when he was twenty-six, the growth of his business interests were large enough to assure him that he could afford a family of his own making, besides providing for the one into which he was born. It was at this time that he made the first of his two marriages. His first wife, Bertha Marie Jenson, of Danish descent, would bear him six sons and six daughters: David, Leroy, Vida, Royal, Bertha, Joseph, Lila, Laura and Flora (twins), Jack, Vivian and Homer. Because their original home was Ogden, the twelve in all would be identified as the "Ogden Eccleses."

4. Multiplication

IN 1885, TEN YEARS AFTER his first marriage, David Eccles married Ellen Stoddard—herself the child of a polygamous marriage and whose father and mother came from backgrounds similar to the Eccleses'. John, her father, was born into poverty in Edinburgh and migrated with his parents to Utah in 1851, following their conversion to Mormonism. Emma, her mother—the second of John's wives—was born into poverty in Manchester, England. At the age of eight she was put to work in a textile factory where she remained until her parents were converted to Mormonism and moved themselves and their children to Utah in the 1850s.

John Stoddard, who was to die while still in his fifties, was engaged in the lumber business in a modest way in three successive places—in Wellsville, Utah, in Aspen, Wyoming, and in the coal mining district of Scofield, Utah, lying to the south of Salt Lake City. He and David Eccles met in 1883 after David had established three sawmills in the latter district, along with a lumber yard and a general store in Scofield proper. The two men soon discovered the similarities in their Scottish backgrounds, in their business interests in the American West, and in their outlook. Neither man ever read—or could read—a book on political economy. Yet their personal experiences on Western soil, where they began with nothing and survived great hardships to become men of substance, made them ardent advocates of what learned people called "Darwinian Capitalism."

As faithful Mormons, they were their "brother's keeper" to the extent demanded of them by their religious creed. Both men regularly paid their full tithes to the church, and David Eccles would eventually become the largest tithe payer of his day. Both men also viewed capital as "congealed labor," and hence accepted a "moral" obligation to manage capital in ways for more jobs to be created for people willing and able to work. Further, both men recognized the right of their Church to organize and directly own and manage certain cooperative economic ventures whose initial capital needs exceeded the means of any single individual or group of private individuals. But beyond these concessions, both were firmly attached to the free competitive system on grounds which they also called "moral." The system, said they, insured the survival of the morally fit. Through it, the improvident, the weak and the wastrels fell by the wayside, while the prudent, the strong and the thrifty survived and passed on their traits to their children. Thus both men found their best holiday in work. Indeed, the whole of their world, aside from wives, children and Church, consisted of little more than work, and talk and worry about work, and plans for investments which could make money work as hard as they did personally.

Ellen Stoddard had been introduced to this same point of view at a very early age, and would transmit it to her sons, starting with Marriner, the firstborn. Though her birthplace was Wellsville, Utah, she spent many of her formative years in the forest of Aspen, Wyoming, during the period when her father was active there in the lumber business. As a child she was the object of admiring comments because she had advanced as far as "the fourth reader," a noteworthy educational accomplishment considering the sketchy resources for schooling that were at hand. But beyond that? The only link between Aspen and the outer world was a path cut through stands of timber. Here, during the logging months, Ellen and her sister would rise at four in the morning to prepare bread and other food for the lumberjacks in the logging camp. There were two other meals to be prepared during the day, and then to bed, only for the monotonous round to be resumed at four the next morning. To survive the experiences of loneliness in the wilderness, and to surmount all the pressures on the mind which made for idiocy, a child had to be made of very stern stuff. Ellen Stoddard was so made.

When David Eccles eventually met Ellen Stoddard—the place is believed to have been the Eccles general store in Scofield—his investment-prone eyes were drawn to the prospects he saw in the girl as she was blooming into young womanhood. There followed a courtship, a proposal, an acceptance, and a compliance with the provisions of the Mormon code which allowed a couple to be "sealed" in a plural marriage. In January 1885, David and Ellen were "sealed" in the Mormon temple in Logan, Utah, where the wedding ceremony was performed by Marriner W. Merrill, an apostle of the Mormon Church. Ellen was then eighteen years old, David thirty-six.

The marriage came at a time when the spreading railroad boom led to a direct confrontation between the Mormons and United States society as a whole.[11] The federal law enacted in 1862 against polygamy had for some years remained in a quiescent state, an entry "on the books" but of no great moment in the realm of action. Utah itself, save for Colonel Conner's presence during the Civil War, could be overlooked as long as it was viewed as an aberrant theocratic kingdom, living within itself somewhere in the West. But when the railroad forged iron links between it and the United States —and, incidentally, facilitated the movement of federal law-enforcing agents—new efforts were made to bring the territory of Utah into line with the rest of American society.

"Majoritarian" Americans specifically disapproved of plural marriages, of theocratic control of the political life of the Utah territory, and of theocratic influences on the economy. There followed an extravaganza of muckraking journalism and Congressional investigations, all leading to new restrictive legislation which reopened wounds still sensitive thirty-five years after the Mormons had been expelled from Nauvoo, Illinois.

In 1882, Congress enacted the Edmunds Law, presently strengthened by the Edmunds-Tucker Law, under whose terms federal agents mounted sweeping punitive expeditions against suspected polygamists in Utah, Idaho and Arizona. Mormons, in turn, challenged these laws on the grounds that they constituted an infringment of religious liberty as guaranteed by the constitution. But as the legal challenges in the courts moved upward through the federal judiciary en route to the Supreme Court, Mormon husbands and wives were fined and imprisoned, and many Mormon leaders were driven into exile, some finding refuge in Mexico and others in Western Canada. Even monogamist Mormon households—representing an estimated seven-eighths of the total—suffered from the accusations of paid spies and informers.[12]

David Eccles had reason to believe that while the immediate point of the attack was the Mormon religious teaching concerning polygamy, the attackers had a larger object in view: to destroy the tightly knit economic fabric of Mormon life held together by blood ties among leading Mormon families—and, in so doing, to promote the dominance of non-Mormon business interests brought into Utah by the railroads. It was even more obvious to him that the economic development of the region would be paralyzed unless Mormon and non-Mormon businessmen agreed to coexist in peaceful competition.

His views on the matter affected his design for living with his young wife. Ellen continued to dwell with her parents in Scofield or Logan, while David continued to make his main base with his family in Ogden, so that he could better discharge a task he assumed in 1885. Previously, though known to be "Republican" in his sympathies, he had avoided holding public office and shunned an active role in political affairs. The only ecclesiastical office he held in the Mormon Church was as a member of the "Seventy." Now, to help bridge the dangerous divisions between Mormons and non-Mormons, he entered the political arena. In 1885, the year of his second marriage, he was elected to the Ogden City Council, a part-time post he held for two years. He was then elected Mayor of Ogden, another part-time post, which he voluntarily gave up in 1887. In that period, David helped organize the Ogden Chamber of Commerce—the first in Utah to include both Mormons and non-Mormons. He helped organize the Home Fire Insurance Company of Utah, and he also moved from his role as a director of the First National Bank of Ogden into its presidency—an institution originally formed by Mormons to emancipate Mormon businessmen from a preexisting non-Mormon monopoly of Ogden banking facilities.

David Eccles eventually became the president of five more banks —Hyrum State Bank, State Bank of Brigham City, Richmond State Bank, Ogden Savings Bank, and Burely State Bank—in addition to being a director and stockholder in three other banks—Deseret National Bank, Deseret Savings Bank, and Thatcher Brothers Banking Company. Yet he never maintained an office in any bank or looked upon himself as a banker or an active bank manager. In his view, the banks of his day were too often "only a bundle of notes," and he thought it a waste of time to look after them personally. He was a builder who brought his influence to bear on banks by giving his counsel to their active managers.

II

While still serving as Mayor of Ogden in 1887, David began to act on the vow he had taken two decades before when he first viewed the timber stands in eastern Oregon. He built a sawmill in North Powder, Oregon, and another at Hood River on the Columbia River. John Stoddard, his father-in-law, who had a business interest in these ventures, was put in charge of mill operations at the North Powder site, and Ellen was moved there as well. That location at the time was "outside the United States," and provided a haven from the federal marshals who were concentrating their antipolygamy forays in Utah, Idaho and Arizona.

The first two Oregon mills were only a beginning. In 1889, David erected a very large sawmill at Baker City, located on Powder River between Elkhorn Range and the Eagle Spur of the Blue Mountains, whose white peaks form an imposing background. He then incorporated the Oregon Lumber Company, which took over the Fir Mill west of Hood River, and also a pine operation at Pleasant Valley. As president of Oregon Lumber, he supplied most of its capital. Additional capital, however, was provided by W. W. Ritter and Bishop George Romney, both of Salt Lake City. David also advanced funds to a Scotsman from Edinburgh, C. W. Nibley, so that he could buy into the business and become its vice-president and general manager.

The Oregon Lumber Company provided the corporate roof for yet another venture, which David organized and set in motion in 1890. This was the construction of the Sumpter Valley Railroad which eventually extended from Baker City to Austin, Oregon, and then from Austin to Prairie City. The road became the most notable and long-lived of all the narrow-gauge "short lines" in the Pacific Northwest, though its initial equipment was a potpourri of every known make and variety of narrow gauge locomotive cars acquired secondhand from the major railroads. It was originally meant only to haul out logs for the Oregon Lumber Company and other lumber companies in Eastern Oregon. But a boom, which began with the discovery of gold-bearing quartz in the upper reaches of Cracker Valley, led to a rush of people to the area, and a passenger service was promptly inaugurated by the railroad to move people from Baker City to the town of Sumpter.

In this gold-made town, the fictions of Bret Harte became the realities of life. Sumpter was wide open around the clock. The night was the same as the day, and the day was intense. Of the 1,500 people in the town by the middle of the 1890s, half were in business; the other half were transients, newcomers, prospectors, miners, common laborers, curious visitors, and the ragtag and bobtail of humanity who follow whatever leads anywhere. As one wave moved out dead or alive, another moved in, while, all through the changes, the saloons, hotels, restaurants, lodging houses, dance halls, and the Sumpter Valley Railroad reaped a rich harvest.

The Sumpter Valley Railroad not only transported people back and forth in its passenger cars, but it also hauled out gold quartz on its flatcars along with logs. When the old boom was spent, Sumpter itself consumed by fire, the men who had come to town for an evening of hard liquor and soft women moved elsewhere. The Sumpter Valley Railroad, however, continued to haul logs. In place of the gold quartz, it had something new to haul to market: the yield of the livestock industry that had come into being in the valley. Every Saturday, a trainload of livestock was shipped over the road to Baker City where the cattle or sheep would then be transported to standard-gauge cars for shipment to the Portland Union Stockyard, the largest of its kind west of Kansas City or Omaha. Sumpter Valley Railroad survived until after the Second World War, when superhighways and trucks invaded its transportation domain and conquered it.

III

The Oregon Lumber Company transformed its own wood into gold in amounts that would have dazzled ancient alchemists. The profits David Eccles extracted from Oregon wood enabled him to invade other territory. He was among the main sponsors of one of the first major beet sugar factories in the United States, and its success encouraged him to get into the beet sugar business more fully and thus to duplicate his achievement with wood by transforming sugar into gold.

In 1747, Andreas Margraaf, professor of physics in the Berlin Academy of Science, discovered that the sugar in beet juice was the same as that in cane. But the creation of a beet sugar industry dates from the Napoleonic Wars, when France's sugarcane supply from the West Indies was cut off by the blockade of the British fleet. On March 18, 1811, Napoleon ordered his Minister of the Interior to take "all steps" necessary to see that seventy thousand acres of sugar beets be planted as soon as possible, and that sugar beet factories also be erected. In consequence, 334 small sugar beet factories were set up in France between 1812 and 1813, giving the French a clear lead in the development of both the machinery and the chemistry needed to convert the beets into sugar.

In the United States, meanwhile, the farther settlers got away from the various coastal ports where West Indies cane sugar was imported, the more they were dependent on substitute sweetening agents, such as honey. Disputes over places in the West where beehives abounded sometimes led to "honey wars" between rival groups of frontiersmen. Among the Mormons, once they settled in Utah, the search for a local means of making sugar was carried on with great zeal for reasons best stated in an 1850 study by the First Presidency of the Church.

Sugar is not only a beverage, a luxury, but it is, in its nature and substance, one of the component parts of our animal structure; and a free use thereof is calculated to promote health; and could the Saints have a more abundant supply, they would need less meat. Should every person in Deseret [the name the territory gave itself] consume one-third of an ounce of sugar per day through the coming year, it would require about one-hundred and twenty tons, more than has been or will be brought in by our merchants this season; and according to the best estimate we can make, three hundred tons would be consumed in this State the next year, if it could be obtained.

A French convert to Mormonism invested his capital in the first attempt in Utah to manufacture beet sugar. When the venture ended in bankruptcy, the Mormon Church took over the machinery brought from France. If the venture could be made to succeed, Mormon farmers would have a market for their sugar beets, and currency previously sent east in payment for cane sugar would remain in Utah. The Church hoped, moreover, that Scottish converts to Mormonism who had some experience of work in the cane sugar refineries of Glasgow could adapt that experience to the conversion of beets into sugar. Yet the church did no better in managing the factory than the original bankrupt owner had done. The French companies which had sold the machinery kept the facts of beet sugar chemistry and controls to themselves.

The hope for a factory, however, did not die. In 1879 F. H. Dyer, in Alvarado, California, using machinery of his own design, built the first small, but productive, beet sugar factory in the United States.[13] The Mormon Church, in 1889, sponsored a meeting in Salt Lake City where twenty-eight citizens became the incorporators of a projected new sugar beet factory and subscribed $15,000 in capital to it. Church officials then went into the community as a whole in order to raise $400,000 of the remaining capital that was needed. Upon being approached by Heber J. Grant, later president of the Mormon Church, David Eccles contributed $5,000.

A financial panic occurred in 1890—the same year that the Commissioner of the Census publicly announced that the frontier had ceased to exist in the United States—and Church leaders found that they could neither reach their goal of $400,000 in capital for the sugar factory nor honor the pledges they themselves had already made. A proposal to abandon the whole scheme was argued. Church president Wilford Woodruff insisted that the project should be pressed forward despite the panic. He appointed a committee headed by Heber J. Grant to pursue funds for the factory. A minimum of $100,000 was needed. Grant went to San Francisco to try his luck at the Wells Fargo Bank, then being managed by a friend who had once been stationed with their branch in Salt Lake City. He was told that if he could get thirty men in Salt Lake City to give their personal notes for a total of $100,000 a loan in that amount would be made to the Church. David Eccles voluntarily reendorsed all the notes signed by the other guarantors, making the loan possible. In this way, the Lehi sugar factory was built and the Utah-Idaho Sugar Company was launched on its career.

Another kind of panic hit the Mormons in 1890. All appeals to the Supreme Court to void federal laws against polygamy had been exhausted by then, and their constitutionality was upheld. If Utah was to be admitted into the Union as a state—a project that had failed repeatedly ever since the first Mormon petition to the Congress had been made in 1862—the Church must formally renounce its teachings and its practices with respect to polygamy. In an official Manifesto, Wilford Woodruff declared: "My advice to the Latter-day Saints is to refrain from contracting any marriage forbidden by the law of the land." Later, at a meeting in October 1890, where a General Conference of the Church upheld the Manifesto, Woodruff added: "For me to have taken a stand in anything which is not pleasing in the sight of God, or before the heavens, I would rather have gone out and been shot. My life is no better than other men's. I am not ignorant of the feelings that have been engendered through the course I have pursued. But I have done my duty, and the nation of which we form a part must be responsible for that which has been done in relation to this principle."

What was to be done with plural wives? Most Mormon men who had contracted plural marriages under the teachings of the Church—implicitly received as the word of God—would not abandon the women they had made their legal wives and who were the mothers of their children. Yet a polygamous wife, other than the first, now had no standing in law to the right of a widow's inheritance in the event her husband died intestate. Any provisions made for her would henceforth depend on the affection and good will of her husband during his lifetime.

In the midst of this upheaval, Ellen Stoddard Eccles—who by then had been married five years—neared her "lying-in" hour. She left Baker City for a trip to the Logan home where her mother lived. In September 1890 she gave birth to her first son there. He was named Marriner, after Marriner W. Merrill, the apostle of the church who had officiated at the marriage of the parents in the Logan Temple.

5. Young Marriner

ELLEN STODDARD ECCLES remained in her mother's Logan home for three years following Marriner's birth, and there another child, Marie, was born. David Eccles then arranged for their return to Baker City and into a new home, where he subsequently made a practice of joining the family for monthly visits lasting several days. Seven more children were born —Spencer, Jessie, Emma, George, Nora, Ellen, and Willard (born in Logan)—spaced at two-year intervals. The future would show that, next to Marriner, the "ablest" child among these was George, the third oldest son and Marriner's junior by nine years.

In 1896, at the age of six, Marriner was enrolled in a school in Baker City. In that same year he acquired a nickname, "Nickel-face," a byproduct of mis-pronouncing the word "first." On a summertime visit to his grandmother in Logan, his uncle Robert Anderson saw the child holding a beautiful apple, and offered to buy it for a nickel. Young Marriner was cautious. "You give me the nickel face," said he to his uncle. The exchange between the two went the rounds of the family, and the nickname born of it stuck. At a critical moment in later years, Robert Anderson supported his nephew in a business matter where something far more important than an apple was at issue.

Marriner began his business career when he was eight. His father was by then a millionaire. Yet the precedent of David's own childhood as an eight-year-old traveling salesman, merchant and would-be porter made him believe that his sons at that same age should be put to work during the summer months. Work would keep them out of mischief; it would also prevent their acquiring a taste for idleness and high living.

The father's general pedagogic plans seemed to misfire in the case of his sons by Bertha Jensen Eccles in Ogden, but were strictly applied by Ellen Stoddard Eccles to her own sons as they came along. Aside from the fact that child labor was part of her family heritage, the grounds for her attachment to a "work ethic" went beyond the "character-building" virtues she saw in it. When the Mormon Church withdrew its religious sanction from plural marriages, Ellen, as the second wife, linked the future of her relationship with her husband to the promise shown by her sons, starting with Marriner. The daughters didn't count. But Marriner must be shaped from his earliest years "to make good." He must outshine the sons of the Ogden Eccleses. He must not be indulged in anything, not even in harmless liberties. He must be disciplined in the most minute details of self-denial, so that nothing would distract his attention from business.

Marriner's introduction to business entailed an assignment to the Baker City box factory that was a division of the Oregon Lumber Company. His father said to the eight-year-old: "If you will save $100 from your wages, I will sell you a share of my Oregon Lumber Company stock, which is worth much more." Throughout that summer, Marriner worked for five cents an hour, ten hours a day, six days a week. His wages were increased to seven and a half cents the second summer and to ten cents the summer after—each time at a different job. By the end of the third summer, he had saved a hundred dollars. "Son," said his father as he gave Marriner one share of Oregon Lumber stock, "you are now a capitalist because you have saved more money than you have spent. That is how capital is created." The pleasure Marriner derived from his father's words was multiplied many times over by the pleasure he found in his financial acumen. He never ceased being a capitalist after that—though he was to learn that savings alone, unless put to use, could lead to economic stagnation.

Meanwhile, any signs of backsliding from his dedication to work were dealt with in summary fashion by his mother. When he was about twelve, he was put in charge of an old dump cart, pulled by a swayback horse named Old Bleuch. His job was to collect sawdust from the sawmill and dump it into a separate field to be used as additional fuel for a nearby power plant. It was boring work, and Marriner sought diversions. Squirrels abounded in the area, and one day he set a trap on one of his trips from the mill to the dump, finding on his return that he had bagged a squirrel. He continued the process for some days until he had caught several live squirrels. But to enjoy his dominion all by himself struck him as selfish, and he thought that his captives would make an imperial gift to his mother. At the presentation ceremony, however, there was no word of thanks. Ellen pursed her lips, opened the door of the cage and released the squirrels. Her motive was not kindness to animals, but to punish Marriner for allowing himself to be distracted by the antics of squirrels when all his thoughts should have been focused on increasing the number of loads he hauled from the mill to the dump yard.

There was a far more serious breach of discipline. The summer Marriner was nearing fourteen, he and one of his classmates worked together in the lumber yard, stacking boxwood. One day they were seized by the idea that if they put a roof of wood across an aisle formed by the piles of stacked wood, they would have a little house of their own. Having done that, they realized they had a craving for frogs' legs, and there were swarms of frogs in a nearby creek. Each morning when Marriner left for work, he managed to conceal in his lunch pail some flour, salt, pepper and kitchen oil. His co-conspirator brought to work a BB gun and some tapioca. Tapioca fired at the frogs stunned them. The two boys then rushed in, cut the legs off, skinned them, and retreated to the little house they had made. They built a fire inside and Marriner fried the legs to a turn. The slaughter continued for several weeks to the delight of the boy's stomachs and to their pride in their shrewdness.

There came a day, however, when a plume of smoke rising from the boxwood caught the eye of the yard foreman who was highly sensitive to the ever present danger of fire in the area. He rushed to the peril point, discovered the two boys at their meal of frogs' legs, raked them fore and aft for their criminal negligence, and threatened them with exposure to a punishing world. After the foreman's wrath blew itself out, the crime was buried in the secret archives of his memory. No report of the deed was conveyed to David Eccles, or to the latter's proconsul, Ellen. Marriner and his classmate, trembling in every limb from their brush with disaster, were transferred to another job.

There was one occasion, however, when Marriner successfully broke a tabu regulating his conduct, and the way in which he did it was to be duplicated years later at a tense moment in his business career. His repeated requests for a 22-caliber rifle were repeatedly vetoed by his mother. But he circumvented her disapproval when he was assigned, at the age of fifteen, to summertime work in the Baker City commissary of the Oregon Lumber Company. Laborers chewed plug tobacco called Star, Horseshoe or Piper-Heisik, and in each ten cent cut the respective tobacco companies inserted a premium metal tag stamped with an insignia. It therefore became a matter of enlightened self-interest for Marriner to promote the sale of the plugs, and to ask if the buyer was saving the insignias. When the answer was no, the youth asked if he could have the premium tag. When he accumulated the requisite number for a 22-caliber rifle, he cashed them in and received the rifle from the premium company. After that, there was much mourning among the cottontail rabbits in the area.

6. The Call

IN THE YEARS WHEN MARRINER was passing from childhood into his early teens, David Eccles was busy expanding his business interests. In 1898, he organized the Ogden Sugar Company, and in the following year, the Logan Sugar Company. A third plant, built at Le Grande in Oregon, could not support itself and was moved to a new site at Burely, Idaho. Later the three factories were merged into the Amalgamated Sugar Company. A fourth plant at Lewiston, Utah, also became part of Amalgamated. David bought and reorganized the Ogden street railway system, and in 1901 bought the Ogden Hot Springs and the Hot Springs railroad, opening up the health resort.

When the "sugar war" erupted at that time, Henry O. Havemeyer, Claus Spreckles and John Arbuckle headed the embattled factions involving cane and beet sugar producers alike. David Eccles, who was drawn to Havemeyer's side in the clash, often recalled how, when he was a guest in Havemeyer's New York home, Havemeyer entertained him by playing the violin. David admired this accomplishment, since the only other music he knew came from the bagpipe players he engaged. Yet, when it came to business, it was the sugar king who danced to David's tune. As part of the deal, Havemeyer bought 51 percent of the stock of Amalgamated, but paid a price for it that exceeded the cost of the whole investment. David Eccles was retained as president and general manager of the company until the time of his death. Years later, when the government forced a dissolution of the sugar trust, the controlling interest in Amalgamated was brought back to Utah at a price less than Havemeyer had paid. The company was destined, under Marriner's leadership, to become one of the largest, most efficient and profitable beet sugar companies in the nation.

Another enterprise made possible by David Eccles was destined to be converted by Marriner into one of the largest of its kind in the world, namely: the Utah Construction Company, now known as Utah International.

The beginnings were modest. In 1900, the First National Bank of Ogden loaned $50,000 to the Corey Brothers Construction Company of Uinta to help finance a construction contract in Astoria, Oregon. The Coreys afterward came to the bank to say that their company was in need of a further loan, only to be told by bank officials that this was not possible, as the legal limit on loans to any one borrower was 10 percent of the bank's capital and surplus—or the $50,000 already loaned to the company. David

Eccles, as mentioned earlier, did not maintain a desk in the bank. But when he heard about the Coreys' request, he asked to see the construction supervisor on the Astoria project. "What has gone wrong with the job?" David asked W. H. Wattis when they met. "Why do you need more money?" To which Wattis replied: "Nothing is wrong on the construction side of things, but the job is not good enough to support the seven Corey families now living off of it."

David called in the Coreys and named the alternatives. Either they would assign the contract to a new company he meant to organize or he would throw them into bankruptcy. They assigned the contract to the Utah Construction Company. In organizing that company with $100,000 capital, of which $24,000 was paid in, David took 1/3 of the stock in the new enterprise; 1/6 shares of the stock were assigned respectively to Thomas D. Dee, to James Pingree, to W. H. Wattis and his older brother Edmund who worked with him on the job. It was arranged that the Wattis brothers would direct field operations and David Eccles took their notes for the 1/6 share of the stock issued to each. Thomas D. Dee became the first president.

Utah construction experienced incremental growths for a period of four or five years after successfully completing the Astoria project, but the great spurt in its development dates from the contract it secured to build the Western Pacific Railroad from Salt Lake City to the San Francisco Bay. David Eccles won the contract for Utah Construction through his friendship with Henry O. Havemeyer, an intimate of George Gould, son of Jay Gould, the railroad magnate and Wall Street buccaneer.

When the elder Gould died in 1892, he was in virtual control of ten thousand miles of railroad track and was headed for a transcontinental railroad system. George was to fulfill the grandiose aim of his father. To the Missouri Pacific and the Rio Grande roads which the elder Gould had ruled, the son added a railroad network comprised of the Little Rock and Fort Smith; the St. Louis, Iron Mountain and Southern; the International and Great Northern, the Texas and Pacific, and the Manhattan Railway Company. The Western and Pacific link between Salt Lake City and San Francisco would round out the structure of a transcontinental "Gould system." At meetings in New York when the building of this link was under discussion, Havemeyer convinced Gould that David Eccles out in Ogden could assume financial responsibility for the project and that the Wattis brothers—W.H. and E.O.—could handle the execution. Completion of the Western Pacific Railway impressively enhanced both the income and the prestige of Utah Construction, but its great days still lay well in the future.

In 1905, while the Western and Pacific Railway was not yet completed, a party held in the spacious home which David Eccles maintained for his Ogden family was emblematic of how far the Eccleses had come since they left their adobe hut in Paisley for a one-room lean-to in Eden. Upward of two hundred guests were assembled to help celebrate the diamond anniversary of the marriage of his parents. William, his father, was then seventy-nine; Sarah, his mother, was then eighty-three. Both would soon be taken away by death. There was a lavish banquet for the guests, and a gift from David to his parents—an enlarged family photograph framed in gold and studded with rows of imitation diamonds.

II

Schooling, work, very little play, and the role of a surrogate father to his young brothers and sisters during the periods when his father was away from Baker City constituted the round of Marriner's years until he was fifteen. Then he was sent back to Logan, where he was lodged in the home of an aunt so that he could attend Brigham Young College. The living arrangement was continued for a year and a half until Marriner's mother and the other children were moved to Logan in 1907. Ellen had had her fill of life in Baker City, with its long stretches of loneliness and with its taxing demands on her nerves. Each summer, however, there was a trek back to Oregon and a job for Marriner in some aspect of the lumber business, whether in the forests, on the railroad, in the company store, or in the sawmills.

Brigham Young College in Logan, which is no longer in existence, was a "college" in name only. It offered students little more than a high school level of education, though this was a considerable advance over the general pattern of instruction in the area, in which relatively few children went beyond the eighth grade. In Marriner's classroom work, where pupils were assigned desks according to their academic performance, he always won the "first desk" in mathematics, but in other subjects he was generally assigned the "second desk" of honor. At the end of the school term in June 1909, he had completed three and one-half years of high school. That was the limit of his formal education.

His father did not believe in a college education for his sons unless they meant to prepare themselves to enter a profession. If they were to enter the business world, then the earlier the better. "Of all the men working for me," he would say, "only two men had a college education. One was a street car conductor and the other was a motorman on the Ogden Rapid Transit."

Marriner later regretted his lack of a formal higher education. Not the least of his stated reasons was that if he had been trained "to take notes in class," he would have been able to take notes at meetings of corporations —so that he could afterwards write "the minutes" of what had or had not been agreed to. Later on, too, he seemed shy at first encounter with graduates of Ivy League Schools, and shyer still when he first met theoretical economists. He knew what to do in the thick of battle but did not know the technical language of formal economics. On the other hand, some academic economists often seemed to simplify life in order to simplify their measurements of its economic aspects—but did not know what to do when supreme strategic decisions had to be made. But Marriner did not stay shy for very long, no more than all academic economists were quivering Hamlets. One of those who thought he knew exactly what should be done about everything was John Maynard Keynes—whose encounter with Marriner will appear later.

Upon leaving Brigham Young College in June 1909, Marriner spent six months on an assignment which could be construed as a compliment of trust. His father put him in charge of the commissary for a contruction project which was to extend the Sumpter Valley Railroad from Austin, Oregon, over a mountain range to Prairie City, twenty-three miles away. As commissary manager with two assistants, the youth brought up supplies for successive work camps, kept payroll records, and issued pay checks to the engineers, surveyors, timberjacks, graders, and track layers. Most of the timberjacks were Americans, but the graders were mainly Greeks and Japanese, and they could not speak English. To surmount the language barriers, Marriner gave each of these a number which anyone could understand on payday and match with a work record. Indeed, the number itself —representing work—became a form of "currency" backed by the pay due for work done.

One of the timberjacks, a certain Ward Grote, a giant of a man physically, had difficulties of his own understanding the youth who ran the commissary. Grote, reeling from drunkenness, came to the commissary to pick up his check. On receiving it from Marriner, he pulled out a flask of whiskey and extended it to the youth: "Here, kid," said he, "Have a drink." "No, thank you," the youth primly replied. "I said, kid, have a drink!" The youth again refused. Grote, enraged by the rejection of his friendly gesture, drew a six shooter he had concealed on his person and slammed the weapon on the counter table with the muzzle pointed at Marriner. The youth promptly discovered why revolvers were called "persuaders." He grabbed the flask, gulped a swig of liquor, burned his throat, gasped, and fleetingly wondered if death from a bullet in his head would be less agonizing than death by choking. But he regained his breath; by putting his life in hazard when he drank Grote's offering, he may have saved himself from sudden death.

By December, the extension of the Sumpter Valley Railroad, marked by switchbacks and hairpin turns, crossed the last of the three summits at Dixie Mountain. Dixie was 5,280 feet above sea level, but the temperature was forty degrees below zero. The builders decided to stop work before Christmas and to resume in the spring of the next year. Marriner was relieved from his job and returned to Logan for a Christmas-time reunion with his family before leaving for a foreign adventure. Through the intercession of his father, he had received his "call" from the Mormon Church. He was due to leave for a mission to the Glasgow slums at the start of 1910. He was nineteen years old at the time.

III

The Mormons never intended to be merely an American religious sect. Since the "dispensation of the fullness of times" was meant for the salvation of all men, the Church viewed its own role in that dispensation to be general and world-embracing. Hence it was the policy of the Mormons to "call" male members, as early as possible in their religious life, to be missionaries of the faith. Like the apostles of old, they must respond whenever they were called and go wherever they were sent, not with reluctance or anger, but eagerly, gladly, in a spirit of willing obedience. They must go in imitation of Jesus—"without purse or script"—trusting to the Lord to supply all their needs. An exception was made for missionaries sent to large cities. They were provided in advance with a "purse," since without money in their pockets they risked being arrested as vagrants.

Yet more than religious motives often lay behind these "calls." Mormon leaders remembered how their struggle to rise in the world was made all the more difficult because they had little or no formal schooling. Brigham Young, for instance, had only eleven days of formal instruction in his lifetime. Many fathers similarly situated wanted their sons to have generous access to schooling even if it heavily taxed family resources. To them, missionary work abroad was as much a form of "higher education" as it was an instrument for winning converts.

The family of the young missionary, or the youth himself, paid the fare to his destination and bore the costs of his stay abroad. The Church paid the return fare, and it also determined the length of the mission. A youth could come home with head high only if he had been granted an honorable release by Church authorities. He would disgrace himself and his family if he returned on his own say-so, without permission from the Church. It was a "cultural exchange program," tinged with paramilitary discipline.

Marriner's tour of duty in Scotland ran for two years and two months, of which the first and last parts were spent in Glasgow, with an eight-months' period at Dundee. In Glasgow, the green served the cause of free speech, much as Hyde Park does in London. In Dundee, the same cause was served by St. Andrews Square, which is flanked on one side by St. Andrews University and on the other by a branch of the Bank of Scotland. In both places anything could be said, and orators harangued crowds on subjects ranging from astrology to the coming revolution.

In both places, too, Marriner used a labor-saving device to spare his lungs while he sought a crowd. Dressed in his high silk hat and frock coat on Sundays—the garb of a Mormon missionary—he would pick out the largest crowd ringed around a speaker, and would worm his way forward to the speaker's stand. The instant the orator was through declaiming on the human condition, Marriner would shoot up his hand and cry out: "Now wait a minute here!" He would then give his own talk about the meaning of Mormonism and its implications for converts. Hecklers and heckling abounded—a valuable "learning experience" which may account for Marriner's later ability, in different situations, to face up to every kind of hostile cannonade. He was not aware of every having made a single convert, but he was aware that the challenges he faced in his missionary work somehow bolstered his self-confidence. An extract from one of his letters bearing on the point, written in a cheerful spirit, stands for others in the same key:

I am thankful to say that all is well with us in Scotland. There are only two of us here at present, as my companion left for home on Friday, and the other Elder left this morning for a trip to London, as he hasn't been there yet. . . . We had an excellent social for Elder McGhee on Wednesday night. It was a success both socially and financially. There were sixty-five present, two-thirds of them being non-members, but all very good friends and some interested investigators. . . . We hope to get a few converts before long. After our hall meeting, we held two street meetings. I held one all alone. I put my tracts on the ground and laid my silk hat on them and started to preach. (I'm afraid a Mission gives one almost too much nerve.) I succeeded in giving out 196 tracts after I had finished, so that wasn't so bad was it? Some men in the crowd wanted to ask questions, so I stayed and argued for two hours. I then told them it was against instructions to argue on the street, but I would debate with them on any of the principles of the Gospel if they appoint a place, but no one would accept my challenge. About half the crowd took my part. Most of them just wanted to argue. They didn't want truth, so I am not going to waste my time with them again.

When his mother in Logan received letters in this vein she lost no time in sending them to the youth's father in Ogden. Marriner, as he later recalled, lived "in mortal fear" of his father. David Eccles, for his part, seldom complimented the youth, or anyone else for that matter. He believed that if a person did an assigned task well, he was merely obeying God's will, and it would be blasphemous if he praised someone for doing what the Almighty expected of him. Nonetheless, on one occasion David reacted positively to a particular series of letters Marriner sent home. His reply—itself rare—was treasured by the youth as though it were a "laying on of hands." The father, in a letter dictated to and transcribed by a literate associate, had this to say:

My dear son Marriner:

I have been very pleased to read the letters which you have sent to your mother and me. I am gratified to know that you are enjoying your mission and that you are feeling the Spirit of the Lord. I like the tenor and spirit of your letters, and hope you will always continue in the same spirit, both in your field of labor and after you return. . . . I just talked through the phone to your mother a few minutes ago. All is well at home and we are all well here. Business seems prosperous. I am always pleased to hear from you, and I don't want you to think that because I don't write I am not thinking of you, for I am. As you say in one of your letters you are proud of your father and mother. I will say the same in mine: I am proud of my son, and always will be as long as you continue to be an upright and honorable son.

Praying the Lord to bless you and protect you, I remain,

Your loving father.

While Marriner was on his Scottish mission, his mother underwent a serious goiter operation at the Mayo clinic, and afterward received a "convalescence gift" from her husband: a trip with him to Scotland solely to visit their son.

Marriner met his parents in the New Caledonia railroad station in Glasgow. Glancing around, David recalled how as a scrawny child he had scurried around in the station, trying to earn a few pennies as a porter. Later, other places of the bleak past were revisited—the Kucadens slum, the streets where kitchenware and trinkets had been hawked, the flophouses, and the area of the adobe huts in Paisley. In the twenty years of his own life, Marriner had never spent at any one time more than two or three consecutive days in the presence of his father. This was the first and only time when their being together amounted to a "long visit," and it was over all too soon. The impressions retained, however, cut deep. As father and son together toured the desperate scenes of family "genesis," David Eccles' rise out of misery to achieve a place of preeminent economic importance in the intermountain region of the American West seemed overawing. If Marriner had started from the same point, could he have equaled his father's achievements?

IV

In the last two months of Marriner's stay in Glasgow, he came to know May Campbell Young, whom he met in the home of her aunt. The time they spent alone was very limited, but Marriner would remember the tenor of their hours together. The two never talked about religion, and she was not his convert. Instead she would become his wife in 1913.

Of more immediate interest to Marriner were the young men of his own generation who were on overseas Mormon missions. Royal Eccles, his half brother and five years his senior, was then in Europe, having been sent there on a mission following his graduation from the University of Michigan Law School. Two of Marriner's cousins, Elmer and Earl Stoddard, were also in Europe on missionary duty, as was Robert Hinckley, who would later have a fine career in government and as a leader of the American Broadcasting Company. There was also a young man whom Marriner first met at the Brussels Fair, and with whom he would be intimately associated in future years, Lawrence Clayton, grandson of William Clayton, the clerk of the company that made the advance trek with Brigham Young from Nauvoo to Great Salt Lake City. The journals of William Clayton are primary source materials for early Mormon Church history, and the hymn he wrote in a time of great tribulation is a favorite among Mormons to this day. Its first stanza reads:

> Come, come, ye saints, no toil nor labor fear;
>   But with joy wend your way.
> Tho' hard to you this journey may appear,
>   Grace shall be as your day.
>   'Tis better far for us to strive
> Our useless cares from us to drive;
> Do this, and joy your hearts will swell
>   All is well: All is well.

Lawrence Clayton's sister Isabella was believed to have great promise as a concert pianist, and to expose her to the best teachers of the day the Clayton family as a whole had taken up residence in Berlin. Lawrence Clayton was enrolled in a German high school, and from there he was called on a Mormon mission to be performed in Berlin.

At a Rotterdam conference held in 1911 for all Mormon missionaries in Europe, those who had been assigned to Germany were of special interest. German nationals were allowed to proselytize for Mormonism, but foreign missionaries were barred by law from doing so. To elude the police, Americans such as Clayton described themselves as students, and entered fully into the rich university life of Germany. They heard lectures given during the day by famous professors, sang lustily with their German comrades at night, and sometimes addressed meetings in halls built or rented by German Mormons. No hardships were entailed in this kind of underground activity, but there were instances where the German police caught up with the young subversives from the United States.

Lawrence Clayton was arrested in Berlin, jailed for thirty-six hours, and on the personal order of Von Gagow, the Berlin police president, was banished from Germany by the terms of an order that included Clayton's children "down to the third generation." Eight years later, Clayton, who had by then secured a B.A. from Stanford and a law degree from Harvard, was back in Europe, and soon on German soil. This grandson of Brigham Young's aide who had marched across an uncharted American desert to get out of reach of the United States, Clayton was among the first Americans to see combat action in France as an artillery officer. From the Argonne Forest onward, each time he ordered a lanyard pulled, he would cry out: "And now, boys, we'll fire this one for Von Gagow." At last the Hindenberg Line gave way, and Clayton reached the Rhine as the victor in a very personal sort of war.

At the end of Marriner's stay in Scotland, he was to tour Europe with his two cousins, Earl and Elmer Stoddard. Earl, who had also been in Scotland, had gone ahead to study German in Cologne, where Elmer had been stationed as a missionary until he was banished by the German police and headed for a pleasant exile in Vienna. Accordingly, Marriner first toured Germany alone with Earl, and then the two youths joined Elmer in Vienna to make a grand tour of the rest of Europe.

What they saw was a Europe where the sound of sabers rattling seemed to rise only from exchanges of royal visits, and from ceremonial parades. If the prospects of war entered into the conversations of the young Americans, they could cite a dozen logical reasons why there would be no war. To a man, they shared their father's faith in perpetual progress, in the wealth-producing power of laissez-faire economics, in the liberating and purifying powers of an advancing science and technology. All without exception, and with no mental reservations, could loudly sing the hymn of their parents, born in the mid-nineteenth century:

> Come, come, ye saints . . .
> All is well: All is well.

7. *Death in the Family*

SOON AFTER MARRINER had returned to Logan in April 1912 from his Scottish mission, he repacked his bags and was sent on a different mission—this time by father. David Eccles and several of his business associates, such as the Brownings, had undertaken to build a hydroelectric power plant at Blacksmith Fork Canyon, about ten miles south and east of Logan. The actual construction work was to be performed by an engineering firm on a fixed fee basis, but Marriner was to live at the project site so as to manage the funds and keep the costs down. If more money was needed as the work progressed, then, according to his father's instructions, he was to call on all the partners in the venture for added contributions in proportion to their original subscription.

The funds used were carried in the Hyrum State Bank, of which Orval W. Adams was cashier. The bank was a midget, and the deposits to the account of the hydroelectric project were not only the largest ever carried in the bank, but exceeded the total of all other deposits. Marriner became Adams' favorite customer. Twenty-three years later, when Marriner was chairman of the Federal Reserve Board and Adams was a successor-designate to the presidency of the American Bankers Association, he took a far less favorable view of Marriner's operations.

During work on the power project, Marriner, who had joined the ranks of capitalists while still a child, was given his first significant investment. It came about on a Sunday in late November 1912 when his father was in Logan for one of his periodic visits. Marriner told him that the power project needed more money. Accordingly, David Eccles wrote out a check for thirty-five thousand dollars, representing the bulk of his own pro rata share. He also wrote a check for $5,000, representing the remainder of that share, and gave it to Marriner for his own investment in the enterprise. It was the father's way of saying that he approved of the son's performance at the construction site. Unknown to both, the gesture was a deathbed benediction.

Late at night on December 5, 1912, when Marriner was at the camp in Blacksmith Fork, he was awakened from sleep and was numbed by what he was told. His father, at the age of sixty-three, had died of a heart attack hours earlier in Salt Lake City while running to catch the nine o'clock train for Ogden.

The next day, the front page and the greater part of the *Salt Lake Tribune* and the *Deseret News* were devoted to a reconstruction of David Eccles' last hours on earth, to the story of his life, and to expressions of sorrow. His loss to the community was compared to the one suffered when Edward H. Harriman, "The Colossus of Roads," died three years previously. "The Death of David Eccles," declared Joseph F. Smith, president of the Mormon Church, "is a statewide calamity. He was a man who has been able to provide employment to thousands of people in Utah, Idaho, and Oregon." Heber J. Grant, next in the line of succession to the presidency of the Mormons, struck the same note: "No financial loss that could come to this state and its people in the way of building up the country can equal the loss all of us have suffered through David Eccles' passing away."

At the time of his death, David Eccles was closely connected with twenty-seven companies. He was president of eighteen of these and a director of the others. He was the president of the Ogden Rapid Transit Company, Eccles Lumber, Utah Construction, Oregon Lumber, Amalgamated Sugar, Lewiston Sugar, Ogden Savings, Wyoming Coal, Lyon Coal, Union Fuel, Ogden Milling and Elevator, Vineyard Land and Cattle, Anderson and Sons Lumber, Sumpter Valley Railroad. At the same time, he was a director of the Utah-Idaho Sugar Company, Home Fire Insurance, Utah Condensed Milk, Thatcher Brothers Bank in Logan, State Bank in Brigham City, Deseret National and Deseret Savings Bank in Salt Lake City, Consolidated Wagon & Machine, Utah Implement, Utah Lumber, and the Knight Sugar Land and Livestock Company, a Canadian corporation with headquarters in Alberta.

It was noted earlier that the entire cash capital of all the Mormons who arrived in Utah in 1847 did not exceed $3,000. In sharp contrast, David Eccles' estate was appraised for state inheritance tax purposes at more than $7 million. A present-day equivalent would, perhaps, be in excess of $50 million. The Utah inheritance tax was 5 percent, and there was no federal inheritance tax. More important than the size of the estate—and the point here was etched on the thoughts of young Marriner—was the way it had been formed.

The watchwords of David Eccles' career in business had been "thrift" and "hard work." Spurred on by these, he had brought a varied range of productive enterprises into being and managed them in a direct and personal way. He saw no reason why other men could not duplicate his own achievements, provided, of course, they were not subject to government interference. He believed that the free competitive system, if left to its own devices, could by itself combine men, money, methods and materials in ways that would ceaselessly create new wealth, lead to a wide diffusion of purchasing power, and promote a continuous rise in general living standard.

He also believed that the only important role for government to play in the economic process was to balance the budget in all seasons. A balanced budget would promote "confidence." Confidence, in turn, would give people an "incentive" to accumulate savings by curtailing current consumption, so that the capital formed through savings could be reinvested in new instruments of production.

It is true that David Eccles had lived through successive money panics and depressions, some—as those of 1875, 1891–93 and 1907—of marked severity. Yet these disorders, in his view, were only temporary and did not call for any fundamental changes in the established relationships between the economic and political order. Since the disorders were temporary, the distress they caused to private persons could be relieved by the charitable works of private associations after the model of those provided by the Mormon Church, itself a private association. Besides, said Eccles, the system contained natural self-correctives which would automatically come into play at some point after a cycle of bankruptcies and liquidations had run its course. The foremost self-corrective was the American West. In the American West, people who had elsewhere been cut down by the invisible hand of the free competitive enterprise system could start life anew like a New Adam, given a second chance after the Fall. By hard work, by rigid economies, and by the prudent investment of their savings, they could come to enjoy the moral and material benefits of laissez-faire capitalism that had previously eluded them.

II

HALF BROTHERS
BUT NOT FRIENDS

8. The Terms of Battle

WHEN MARRINER RUSHED HOME to Logan from the Blacksmith Fork construction camp, his mother met him at the door and fell into his arms weeping. "Son," she managed to say at last, "I know nothing about your father's affairs. I must rely on you completely to help raise our family." She was forty-six at the time. Marriner was twenty-two. The other eight children were minors; Willard, the youngest, was only four. It never for a moment occurred to Marriner to do anything else but what his mother asked. Shortly afterward he became legal guardian of the property of his sisters and brothers.

David Eccles had died without a will, and the probate of his estate was thus governed by Utah law. Bertha Jensen Eccles, as the first wife, received a one-third share of the estate. Each of her twelve children received prorated shares so that her family in the aggregate had a five-sevenths interest in the properties of the estate. Further, Bertha's two eldest sons, David and Leroy (or "Roy"), incorporated the David Eccles Company as a holding company for that five-sevenths family interest. David, the eldest son, took over the presidency of the holding company as well as the presidency of the Oregon Lumber Company, the Sumpter Valley and Mount Hood Railroads. Leroy became vice-president and general manager of the Amalgamated Sugar Company. The presidency of the Utah Construction Company was assumed by W. H. Wattis.

As the second wife, Ellen Stoddard Eccles received nothing under Utah law, in the absence of a will. During David Eccles' lifetime, however, he had given Ellen a block of stock in the Oregon Lumber Company valued at $100,000, another block of stock in Amalgamated Sugar, also valued at $100,000, plus other stocks valued at $50,000. Each of her nine children received shares equal in value to those granted each of Bertha's twelve children.

Ellen and Marriner came under great pressure from David and Leroy to keep the shares of the second family together with those of the first family by placing them in the David Eccles holding company. Added pressures were exerted by former business associates of the father. They argued that Marriner could not do as effective a job in conserving the inheritance of the second family as could the elder sons of the first family. He was young. He was inexperienced. He had rarely been seen publicly in the company of his father. He had spent most of his life in places remote from his father's Ogden headquarters. He was little known to the officers and directors of the various enterprises in which his father had been the dominating influence. Who would trust him? It was altogether different in the case of David and Leroy. They were already in their mid-thirties and had the advantages of friendships and associations with the other officers and directors of the companies. More to the point, they had served as "agents" of their father in connection with his major business enterprises such as the Oregon Lumber Company and the Amalgamated Sugar Company. Their experiences eclipsed by far anything Marriner had learned while running the commissary in the construction project which extended the Sumpter Valley Railroad, or as the paymaster for the light and power project at Blacksmith Forks Canyon.

Those who pressed this line of argument overlooked an important point—namely, the different ways in which Marriner and his older half brothers had spent their formative years. Marriner, precisely because he had grown up in places remote from his father's close supervision, knew that he must bear full personal responsibility for the results of any decisions he made. On the other hand, the two eldest sons of the Ogden family had done their work under the watchful eye of their father—who could readily correct their errors of judgment.

The only former associate of the senior David Eccles who disagreed with his fellows was Marriner's uncle Robert Anderson, who had given him the nickname of "Nickel-face." He had married Jesse Stoddard, Ellen's sister, and was now manager of the Anderson Lumber Company, in which Eccles had owned 60 percent of the stock. He took Marriner to one side for a confidential piece of advice. "I would not," said he, "go in with the Ogden family. I'm sure you can handle the affairs of your family by yourself, and you can handle them much better than can your half brothers." Marriner remained forever grateful to his uncle for this reassuring word. He was braced from another side by his mother's encouragement. Ellen placed full responsibility in his hands to do what he thought was best for the family.

When the David Eccles estate was eventually probated in 1915, Marriner incorporated the Eccles Investment Company to hold and manage as a single unit the two-sevenths share of his father's estate owned in the aggregate by the nine children of the Logan family. Ellen later added to the Eccles Investment Company her $250,000 in stocks in return for a life annuity. It was originally thought that the company would be dissolved when all the minor children came of age. Instead, it was to remain in being by the consent of its original nine members, and was to have a long and fruitful career.

II

At the time the lines were being drawn for a contest between the two Eccles families, Marriner's private life took a new turn. He had been corresponding with May Campbell Young since returning to the United States from his Scottish mission. What he knew about the girl, except for the time they were together in Glasgow, he learned through letters. What more he learned led to a letter in which he proposed marriage, and to her reply of acceptance.

In June 1913, roughly six months after the death of his father, he went to New York with his mother and his sister Marie to meet May and her mother Sarah on their arrival from Scotland. The marriage took place in Logan a month later.

Marriner and May—or Maisie, as she was called—appeared well matched in the first years of their union. Four children were born, one of whom, a daughter, died of a strep infection at the age of three. The surviving children were two sons, Campbell and John, and a daughter, Eleanore. But the demands of business and, later, of public affairs began to cast their shadows between the two. Indeed, Marriner was forced to repeat an aspect of his father's life. As his father had bypassed youth to overcome poverty, Marriner too missed many developmental experiences in his struggle to manage and conserve inherited wealth. Maisie was not like his mother, tough-fibered, reconciled to being alone while their husbands were doing "very important work" away from home. She was in need of attention, and Marriner either was too busy to give it to her or, as a product of a male-oriented Mormon culture, did not stop to think what she might need beyond creature comforts. In a legal sense the pair were husband and wife for three and one-half decades, but in reality the marriage succumbed to a lingering death until it was terminated by divorce in 1948.

III

In managing his family's affairs, Marriner first moved into the banking business and, without conscious intention at the time, set in place the initial building blocks for what is now the First Security Corporation. In 1913 he was made vice-president and a director of Thatcher Brothers Bank of Logan. He induced the bank to create its first executive committee and embarked on the steady purchase for his family of the stock in the enterprise. He also acquired for his family a substantial interest in the Hyrum State Bank of which he became the president in 1913, as well as an interest in the Richmond State Bank, of which he was made a director. Although these were relatively small institutions, they not only forced Marriner to seek more knowledge about the enterprises with which the banks transacted business, but also provided valuable training for the tests he was destined to face.

Though Marriner had worked for the Oregon Lumber Company since childhood, he knew little about the inner life of the company, and even less about the affairs of Amalgamated Sugar. After he became a director of both as a representative of his family's stock holdings, he soon learned enough to grow restive, irritable and irritating to others. Now, as was to be his lifelong habit whenever he grew restless, he discharged his inner tensions by brusque talk, unbuffered by tact. At successive board meetings, he insisted on the need to change many current policies and practices.

Leaving the merits of his criticisms aside, the emotional force behind his words may have been fueled by a subterranean competition between the two families of David Eccles that was now out in the open—a competition where each family was bent on proving that *its* mother was the favorite wife. In any case, Marriner's older half brothers and their confederates among company directors of David Eccles' generation were not inclined to indulge the young critic in their midst. They contended that he was a brash upstart who had come out of nowhere to challenge the judgment of his experienced elders and betters.

The only area where Marriner was free to maneuver entailed the affairs of smaller enterprises in which the "Ogden Eccleses" represented by the David Eccles Company, and the "Logan Eccleses" represented by the Eccles Investment Company, were the dominant interests. He began to negotiate successive tradeoffs in real estate holdings and in the stocks of these smaller companies, with the object of having one captain on the bridge instead of two. In attaining his end, he not only added to the profits of the Eccles Investment Company but, without conscious design, eventually created the means by which Eccles Investment would expand its banking interests.

One of the tradeoffs gave the Eccles Investment a 10 percent interest in Utah Condensed Milk—a company started in Utah in 1903 by H. B. Rackliffe of the Main Condensed Milk Company. Local farmers had joined Rackliffe in launching the enterprise, in serving as its officers and directors, besides supplying milk to the Utah plant. David Eccles had been a shareholder in the company since its inception. His 540 shares (par value $10), amounting to 10 percent of the total stock outstanding at the time of his death, had passed into his estate and into Eccles Investment Company. Offices of Utah Condensed Milk were located in Richmond, though sales were handled by George Lockhart in Salt Lake City. In early December 1919 the company's president, Saul Hendricks—a farmer representing other farmer interests—called on Marriner in his Logan Office for something more than gossip. He disclosed that George Lockhart had been negotiating the sale of the company to a Chicago organization. Local Utah farmers—mainly in Cache Valley—who owned shares in the enterprise favored the sale and were signing options to sell their stock to the Chicagoans at $30 a share. Hendricks wanted to know if the Eccles Investment Company would also sign an option to sell its 540 shares to the Chicagoans at the price indicated, for a total of $16,200.

Marriner knew nothing whatever about the milk business, but he reasoned that if a Chicago concern was impressed by the Utah Condensed Milk Company, it might be something in which *he* should invest. The question he put to Hendricks was: would the farmers be willing to sell their stock to the Eccles Investment Company instead of to the Chicagoans? By the time Hendricks returned with an affirmative answer, Marriner had studied the financial condition of Utah Condensed Milk and concluded that it warranted the price the Chicagoans were willing to pay. He acquired control of that stock before the Chicagoans could.

Some thirty thousand shares of stock were outstanding at the time. At $30 a share, this made the stock worth $900,000—a sizable sum in that day for a small local company whose total output was less than half a million cases of condensed milk a year. Moreover, 33 percent of the total stock outstanding was owned by Annie B. Rackliffe, the widow of the original founder of Utah Condensed Milk. Mrs. Rackliffe was living in Los Angeles, as was her brother-in-law who managed her interests. It was clear to Marriner that he must contact the man at once, but before leaving for Los Angeles he brought his friend Roy Bullen into the picture. At the time, Bullen managed the Vitamin Company which bought wheat and ground it into whole wheat flour. Marriner had an option agreement drawn up, and Bullen was to try to get all the Utah stockholders in the company to sign it. The terms provided that Marriner and Roy would pay the same price the Chicagoans were offering for the stock. Everyone would be in on the ground floor, and there would be no commission.

With this in motion, Marriner went to Los Angeles, checked in at the Alexandria Hotel, and asked Mrs. Rackliffe's brother-in-law to come over for a visit. What happened next is best told in Marriner's own words:[1]

When he came into my hotel room, I found that the gentleman was old enough to be my grandfather. That to one side, it quickly became evident that he had not as yet been approached by the Chicago interests. We discussed the milk business in general, which was something of a strain since all I knew about it was what I had read in the financial statement of the milk company. Finally, I asked him if at $30 a share, which amounted to $300,000 for his holdings, he would consider giving me an option on his stock for at least fifteen days so that I could determine whether I could gain control of the company. He said he would like to think the matter over and would see me the next morning. I insisted that the deal would have to be closed that night; that he knew the price being offered him was more than the stock was worth; that it was not for trading purposes; and that, moreover, I expected to leave town the next day.

He said he would need a lawyer to draw up the contract; whereupon, as an impetuous young man who presumed to talk about the milk business on the basis of a balance sheet, I told him that a lawyer was not necessary. What we wanted to do was very simple, and we could certainly state it in clear English. The man must have had some painful dealings with lawyers in the earlier years of his life, because he assented to this. I took a sheet of hotel stationery and wrote our one-page contract in duplicate. We signed it, and I left for Utah the next morning. The contract was perfectly good in every respect. I then rushed back to Logan where I found that Roy Bullen was being equally successful in getting local stockholders to sign the stock option agreements. In three days we had enough signatures in hand to buy control of the milk company.

Those who sold the stock earned a handsome profit on the sale, but agreed to take their payments and profits over a period of five years in order to avoid an excess profits tax. The Eccles Investment Company was thus spared the need to pay out lump sums of money from its own comparatively slender resources. The successive stock payments were eventually made largely out of the milk company dividends. The name was changed to the

Sego Milk Products Company. Marriner became president and Roy Bullen vice-president and general manager; Lockhart kept his stock and remained vice-president and sales manager.

At first, the enterprise seemed headed for disaster. As part of the abrupt general collapse of prices in 1920—which ushered in the now "forgotten depression" of that year—the market for condensed milk dropped from $6.50 a case to $5 a case. In the absence of chain stores in those days, milk was sold through jobbers who had to be protected against a decline in the value of the stocks on hand. If the market went off, they would get a rebate from the condensed milk company. In this way the Sego company in the first ninety days of its operations lost $107,000, representing rebates which Lockhart had paid to the jobbers. Marriner, shaken by the report of this loss, asked to see the records of the original purchases. He discovered many instances where rebate payments had been made to the jobbers in excess of the milk they actually bought within the period of protection. In terse communications to the presidents of the jobbing firms, he advised them of the overpayments and recovered $50,000 in rebates.

Another reform was faintly reminiscent of the way David Eccles, early in his career, had put an end to the featherbedding practices of his lumberjacks. In this instance, Marriner learned that the company measured the milk it purchased by putting a ruler into the container cans. The cans, however, were not round as they had been when new. They had been punched, kicked and dented, and had less capacity than the ruler indicated. The company was thus paying for more bulk milk than it got and was also paying for butterfat it did not get. To make certain that the company paid the farmers for what they actually delivered in the cans, no more and no less, Marriner and Roy Bullen put scales in the Utah plant for the first time. They also introduced homogenizers which tested the butter content in the milk cans so that adjustments could be made to meet Bureau of Standards regulations.

There were other changes. Henceforth, the farmers and not the company, as before, delivered the milk to the condensing plants or bore the hauling costs. Factories which operated at a loss at Smithfield and Franklin were closed down, and $100,000 was spent in modernizing and expanding the Richmond plant. Offices of the company were moved from Richmond to Logan. The company financed farmers so that they could acquire an improved breed of milk cows. In addition, John T. Caine II was engaged to edit a new publication called *Milk Pail,* designed to educate farmers in the developing arts and sciences of the dairy industry.

Through these detailed measures, Marriner and Roy Bullen brought the Sego Milk Company through the 1920 depression, and by the start of 1921 had made it a very profitable venture. The stage was thus set for the eventual sale of Sego to the Pet Milk Company at a one million dollar profit to the Eccles Investment Company—a profit which put it in a position to expand its banking interests in new directions.

IV

As of 1919, despite the tradeoffs of stocks, the David Eccles Company and the Eccles Investment Company, representing respectively the first and second families, still held their largest stock interests in the same enterprises such as the Amalgamated Sugar Company, Oregon Lumber Company, Utah Construction, and various sizable banks. Marriner was by now twenty-nine years old, and though he was a director in the enterprises just mentioned, he had little say on how they were being run. He could only protest the decisions that were being made, and in this he was viewed as a "damned nuisance" by his half brothers David and Leroy, who were the presidents of the larger enterprises, and as a "crab" by the other directors.

But in 1919, at about the time when Marriner acquired a controlling interest in the Utah Condensed Milk Company, events led to dissension within the ranks of the David Eccles Company. In particular, it was clear by the end of 1919 that the affairs of Oregon Lumber and Amalgamated Sugar were both in disarray.

The wartime Lever Act, among other things, prohibited sugar companies from making more than a "normal profit." Amalgamated's profits were thus confined to only $1.5 million—though distributors of sugar made large profits at the expense of consumers, who got no benefits whatever from the Lever Act. Meanwhile, Leroy Eccles, as vice-president and general manager of Amalgamated, had entangled the firm in a web of costly ventures, such as the construction of a new sugar factory in an agricultural area whose low yield of sugar beets was a wholly inadequate source of supply for that factory. To make matters worse, contracts with sugar beet farmers negotiated in early 1918 were based on very inflated prices for refined sugar. Marriner protested these flawed managerial decisions. When his proposed changes were rejected out of hand, he resigned as a director of Amalgamated and awaited the inevitable. At harvest time in the fall of 1918, the price of refined sugar dropped drastically to four cents a pound. Amalgamated, forced to honor its contracts, negotiated with farmers when prices of refined sugar were inflated, lost $5 million—a figure equal to the $4 million it had borrowed from two banks in Chicago and two in New York plus the $1 million it had borrowed in the form of commercial paper to finance its operations. Still worse, because of the combined effects of the Lever Act and Amalgamated's costly expansion program, the company lacked the reserves to absorb the loss, let alone pay its various creditors. Leroy was asked to resign his position and was also eased out of his position with the David Eccles Company.

The other directors, hit hard in their pocketbooks, asked Marriner to return to Amalgamated's board. He agreed on condition that Heber J. Grant, representing the Mormon Church's substantial stock holdings in the enterprise, personally asked him to return. The condition was met. Marriner resumed a directorship, and at the same time was made one of a three-member Creditors' Committee. In that role, he negotiated an extension of the loans due the New York and Chicago banks, secured by a trust agreement covering all the property of the company. Further, by assessing the stock at $1 million he paid off the commercial paper owned by forty to fifty banks, and later floated a bond issue that repaid the New York and Chicago banks. The whirl of synchronized activity brought Amalgamated back to financial health, and Marriner turned to another matter.

Back in 1912, at the time of David Eccles Senior's death, the Oregon Lumber Company was in glowing financial health. It owed no debts, held cash and bonds totaling $750,000, had grown from an original $100,000 in capital to $1,000,000 with another million in surplus. It was known as "Old Faithful" because of the regularity with which it paid handsome dividends to its stockholders. The demands for lumber during the First World War should have kept the company far above water, just as the demands for sugar should have been of some benefit to Amalgamated. Yet under David Junior's leadership, Oregon Lumber emerged from the war years too feeble to cope with the problems inherent in a transition to a peacetime economy. It stopped paying dividends, was saddled by debts, and began to issue commercial paper in order to gather enough funds to pay its current operating expenses.

Forty-four percent of the stock was owned by the David Eccles Company, representing the first family. The Eccles Investment Company, of which Marriner was the head, owned 28 percent. The remaining 28 percent was owned principally by the former business associates of Marriner's father. When Marriner saw that his minority holding left him powerless to change the policies of Oregon Lumber, only one course of action seemed open to him. He called at the Ogden office of his half brother to present him with a buy-or-sell offer. He would give David the option of buying the Eccles Investment Company stock holdings in the lumber company at a stated price. Alternatively, but at the same price, he could sell to Eccles Investment the Oregon Lumber stock holdings of the David Eccles Company.

The reply sharply exposed the long-standing tensions between the two families. David would enter into no such agreement. He might buy the stock if the price Marriner stated was cheap enough. But he didn't have to buy or sell. More to the point, he was sick and tired of Marriner's interference. Much more in this vein was capped by a summary order for Marriner to get out of the office before being bodily thrown out.

Bitterly resentful, Marriner left, but kept to himself the ugly encounter with his half brother. His next move was to head quietly for the Portland office of the Oregon Lumber Company. When he arrived, Charles Early, who had a threefold relationship with the company (as a director, vice-president, and general manager) was away on business in the East with David Eccles. Marriner confronted Jed Ballantyne, the keeper of the company records, and demanded that he produce the balance sheets of the company for a detailed examination of its entries. What this brought to light was a number of milking operations by which the resources of Oregon Lumber were being used for private ventures. In one case the company had advanced $75,000 to Leroy for his copper mine venture at Mackay. In another, the payroll of Oregon Lumber had provided a $150,000 advance to David Eccles and Charles Early to use for a mine they owned jointly in Sumpter Valley.

Marriner called together the older men who had been the associates of his father in the Oregon Lumber Company and revealed what he had found hidden in the company's balance sheet. The men were C. W. Nibley, Matt Browning, W. W. Ritter, H. H. Romney, Robert Anderson and a representative of the estate of Thomas D. Dee. When Marriner explained the reasons why the company had failed to pay dividends, the group passed a resolution demanding immediate repayment to the company of the advances made to Leroy and David Eccles and to Charles Early; and they armed Marriner with their proxies for his next encounter with David.

Gathering those proxies was like Marriner's collecting premium horseshoes on the plug tobacco when he was set on owning a .22 caliber rifle. He now paid a return visit to his half brother. He recalled their previous meeting, saying that the brutal reception he got was different from the one he expected. This time, however, he had come to serve an ultimatum, not to receive one. He was giving David one week in which to buy out the interests Marriner represented. Alternatively, David and his managers would have to resign their positions with the lumber company and its subsidiary railroads, to be replaced by men approved by the stockholders whose proxies Marriner held.

David badly wanted to keep his position as president, but he could not raise the cash needed to buy out the stockholders. Besides, he faced a rebellion closer to home: His sisters and one of his younger brothers wanted to remove him as president of the David Eccles Company, just as they had removed Leroy from it and from the management of the Amalgamated. Other members of the family had begun to separate themselves from that company by exchanging their stock for certain of its assets.

By the end of the week, David submitted the following proposal to Marriner's camp. In exchange for their stock in Oregon Lumber and its two subsidiary railroads, he would turn over to the voting trust the bank stocks owned by the David Eccles Company, along with some of its minority holdings in certain manufacturing and retail lumber concerns. This would come to 60 percent of the value of the lumber company stocks he had to buy, with the remaining 40 percent to be paid in cash over a two-year period. Meanwhile, he would place in escrow all the shares of Oregon Lumber Company stock received from the voting trust. The proposal was accepted, and the members of the trust subsequently decided among themselves how to divide the property. Some preferred cash and eventually got it. Marriner took the Eccles Investment Company stock in the First National Bank of

Ogden, in the Ogden Savings Bank, in Anderson Lumber Company and in Stoddard Lumber.

There were auxiliary consequences. The aging former associates of the senior David Eccles in the Oregon Lumber Company who had initially been hostile to Marriner became his active backers in those enterprises in which they shared a common stock interest. Second, in the course of the general reshuffle, David Junior was removed from the board of directors of the Utah Construction Company, and the sixty-two-year-old W. H. Wattis, who had been the president of the enterprise since the death of David Senior, invited Marriner to join the board. Marriner accepted the invitation, but not to be just another name on a letterhead. After attending several board meetings, Marriner proposed two amendments to the way things were managed: board meetings should be held at regular intervals and not at random; and the directors should receive, on a regular basis, statements concerning company operations, for how else could they know what decisions were being made and with what effect?

In a blazing response, Wattis said that the proposals were an unwarranted criticism of his own conduct, that Marriner was a heartless ingrate, self-centered, arrogant, grasping. Marriner was not cowed. The pressures of his eight-year fight to conserve the interests of his family had thickened his skin. He retorted that he had not "bulled" his way to a place on the board of the Utah Construction Company; he was there by Wattis' invitation. He did not have to stay on the board, but as long as he stayed, he expected to fulfill his responsibilities as a director. If he was denied a voice in making decisions, he was prepared to resign.

Wattis spoke for the declining age of the amateur, and Marriner for the rising age of the expert, but the immediate outcome of the clash between the two generations was decided by the graying directors who witnessed it. One by one, they supported Marriner's proposals. Faced by this unexpected insurrection, Wattis had no choice but to agree that meetings would be held regularly, that statements would be regularly submitted to the directors for their examination, and that the directors would have a voice in the formulation of company policies. Marriner, in turn, agreed to remain on the board. His relationship with W. H. Wattis in the years ahead would be marked by friction, but the tensions between the two men were resolved in a poignant exchange of respectful salutes in the last days of Wattis' life, coincident with the formation of the syndicate of "Six Companies," headed by Utah Construction, which was to build Boulder Dam.

The Ogden Eccleses would in time virtually disintegrate as a family, while the Logan Eccleses, with Marriner in command, were held together over the passing decades despite many internal strains. Marriner was never reconciled with his two older half brothers, and eventually lost track of them. But he developed friendly relations with his half sisters and their husbands. Lila, who married Dean Brimhall, a noted conservationist, was his special favorite. A woman of vivacity, intelligence, and bubbling humor, she became the head of the drama department at the University of Utah and a beloved figure in the civic life of Salt Lake City. She would describe herself as a member of the "poor branch" of the Eccles family, though she managed to conserve enough of her share of the inheritance to live in modest comfort. Marriner one day volunteered to manage her investment portfolio so as to increase her income, but Lila refused the offer with thanks. "I didn't want him to have fresh evidence," she explained laconically, "about how poorly my own brothers managed the affairs of our family before some of us got out from under their rule."[2]

It is not improbable that Marriner's later role as a national and international leader of the planned parenthood movement may have had as one of its remote subjective roots his low opinion of most of the twenty-one children sired by his own father. The memory of the squalid struggle between the two families lay behind the strong resistance Marriner later offered to nepotism in the Eccles family empire he built. He would insist that management should be entrusted to men of proven competence, whether or not they had any blood ties to his family. To entrust economic tools to men solely because they had inherited substantial stock holdings could, in his view, result in heavy losses for thousands of powerless individual investors.

Marriner's eventual break with economic orthodoxy in the governance of the nation as a whole was prefigured in his long contest with the Utah hierarchs of his father's generation regarding the management of private enterprises. Until the sting of costly losses won them over to his side, he had regularly clashed with them because they seemed not to recognize where their own true interests lay. His major business decisions were made in the light of four questions which he regularly put to himself: What am I looking at? How do I know what I think I know about it? Am I sure? If I am sure, what am I going to do about it? Years later, in the trauma of the Great Depression, he was to ask these same questions about the national economy. The answers he then formulated would propel him toward lines of action which riled the high priests of national economic orthodoxy.

9. *Shooting Star*

PRIOR TO 1920, MARRINER had involved the Eccles Investment Company in the banking business, but only on a relatively small scale. It had acquired holdings in the Thatcher Brothers Banking Company of Logan, and in the Hyrum and Richmond Banks. In 1917, Eccles Investment on its own opened a bank in Blackfoot City, Idaho, followed three years later by its formation of the Federal State Bank of Preston, also in Idaho. However, in 1920, when the affairs of the Oregon Lumber Company precipitated an exchange of stocks between the David Eccles Company and the Eccles Investment Company, the latter obtained effective control of both the Ogden Savings Bank and the Ogden First National Bank. Combined, they were the largest bank in the city, and ranked third or fourth in the whole of Utah. Marriner, at the age of thirty, assumed the presidency of the combined institutions.

He had no desire to move from Logan to Ogden in order to take personal charge of the banks. He was reluctant to uproot his three children who by then were attending school. He was also resistant to moving into a community where the Ogden Eccleses were established, and where his presence might force other people "to take sides." Like his father before him, he had no taste for the role of an "active bank manager." He already had his hands full attending to the complex responsibilities of the Eccles Investment Company, the Sego Milk Products Company, the Amalgamated Sugar Company, the Utah Construction Company and a miscellany of other business enterprises in which the investment company had interests. Accordingly, he induced Orval W. Adams, who was cashier of the Thatcher Brothers Bank at Logan (salary, $3,000 a year), to come to Ogden for work as the executive vice president of the Ogden First National and Ogden Savings Bank at $7,000 a year.

All banks in Utah and Idaho were in serious trouble, as was the case elsewhere in the nation's agricultural regions. Each country village and town—as a matter of local pride and economic promise—had wanted its own bank without regard to real need. As banks proliferated, they spurred the proliferation of submarginal enterprises. This was especially true after the outbreak of the First World War when the demand and associated high prices for agricultural products caused a farming boom. Lands were brought under cultivation that could not be profitably farmed when demand and prices declined. Yet most of the expansion between 1914–18 was financed by local bankers who seemed to have no misgivings about extensions of credit on the basis of inflated prices. In 1920, although Idaho's population was not much more than 400,000, it had 224 banks—86 national banks and 138 state banks—some established in villages having less than one hundred people.

In the two years after the Armistice, the War Finance Corporation under the direction of Eugene Meyer had insured the financial risks entailed in moving American crops to European markets whose trading patterns and currency had been disrupted by the war. In 1920, however, President Wilson's Secretary of the Treasury David Houston ordered the corporation to cease operations—in defiance of Meyer's warnings about what the consequences would be. At harvest time in 1920, farmers who had borrowed from the banks when agricultural prices were high at the start of the planting season could not repay their bank loans when a glut of products—and the sudden absence of an overseas market—drove prices down precipitously. There was a chain reaction. When farmers could not repay their loans to "country banks," the latter could not meet their obligations to "city" or to Eastern banks from whom they had borrowed funds.

The Ogden banks that came under the control of Eccles Investment had very little liquidity because of the nature of the loans that had been made. Orval W. Adams was well suited for the role of a clean-up man. As his later extended career in banking showed, his talents were more those of a loan *collector* than of a loan *officer*. He studied all loans due the Ogden First National Bank; instead of granting the usual extensions, he pressured borrowers to repay the loans on their due dates. The requests were icily put. Marriner himself had a one-eyed view of the interplay between money and banking and the general economy. He knew that many people were wounded beyond recovery by Adams' methods. That was too bad, but what happened to them was *their* concern. *His* concern was to increase the liquidity of the Ogden First National Bank, and this was done.

The Utah National Bank, of which the sixty-five-year-old Matt Browning was president, was located across the street from the Ogden First National and the Ogden Savings Bank. In the fall of 1922, Browning called on Marriner to say, with characteristic realism, that since the two were associates in other ventures, such as Utah Construction and Amalgamated Sugar, there was no point in their being competitors in the banking business. Besides, he was not satisfied with the way his own bank was being run. He proposed a merger between the Utah National and the Eccles banks. "If we are going to be partners," said he, "we will have to trust each other. You suggest a fair basis for the merger, and I'll buy the shares of any stockholder in my bank who doesn't want to join in." It was understood that if the merger went through, Browning would become chairman of the board; Marriner would be president, and Orval Adams executive vice-president. Further, Marriner was to move from Logan to Ogden so as to be closer to the affairs of the new bank. Browning did not think it proper for the president to live in a town some fifty miles away from the bank.

Marriner agreed that the proposed merger made sense. He then got the reports of the Salt Lake Clearing House examiner, studied them in detail, and formulated a plan of action with the help of Roy Thatcher, his attorney, and Orval Adams. Among other things, the charter, capital, and surplus of the Ogden First National would be used as the cornerstone for the new bank. Something would be left in each bank to take care of the commercial paper, but the merger would be made on the basis of the comparative value of assets, and those values would be computed leaving out of account estimates of good will. The details of the proposed merger, as quietly formulated, met with Matt Browning's approval, but still had to be presented to the directors of the Utah National Bank.

Just at this time, Marriner's brother George, aged twenty-two, returned to Ogden. In the immediately preceding years, when George had been a student at Columbia University's business school, he had been "called" to go abroad on a Mormon mission. If his father had been alive, George might not have attended a university at all and would certainly have responded to the "call." But the Church no longer commanded the automatic obedience of the Eccles family. George asked for a postponement of the call until he received his university degree. The request was granted, but the postponement became permanent. After graduating from Columbia in February 1922, he spent some time as an apprentice in the credit department of the Irving Trust Bank in New York, and then returned to Utah for such work in the family enterprises as Marriner might assign to him.

Marriner had previously entrusted his brother Spencer with tasks related to assorted family interests in the Cache Valley. But he settled on George, who was younger than Spencer, as the brother whose talents were best suited to the demands of the banking business. In the years ahead, unfolding events more than confirmed the merit of that decision. George had an incisive mind, strong nerves, and a bold will. He was adept at making quick managerial decisions, and his physique—he was bigger, stronger, and ruddier than Marriner—made him a "natural born salesman." He and Marriner would have their sharp disagreements as time went by—partly from differences in their formative experiences, partly from their temperamental differences, and partly from the one trait they shared: a competitive drive "to be first." Each, however, needed the reinforcing talents of the other, and despite their mutual frictions they would make an exceptionally effective team in managing the family's banking interests.

When George returned to Ogden to start his business career, Marriner had him determine the extent of the economies that would result from a merger of the Eccles and Browning banks. The detailed report which George quickly produced armed the older brother for an encounter with the directors of Utah National. While Marriner and Matt Browning had secured permission from the Comptroller of the Currency in Washington to merge the two banks, they withheld knowledge of what was afoot from the directors of Utah National. The latter were understandably unstrung when Marriner, at Browning's invitation, came to a meeting where he revealed the terms of the proposed merger. Their response was a cry of indignation. Marriner, by now, was impervious to protests by businessmen who saw themselves threatened by his invasions of their nests. He explained how the merger could be achieved, the economies and other benefits that would ensue, and how the merged banks would result in an institution taking its place among the largest of its kind in Utah. At the end of a stormy session that only partly cleared the air, the merger was approved.

As the new president of the combined banks, Marriner moved from Logan to Ogden, taking with him the offices of the Eccles Investment Company. Like his father, he never maintained a desk in any bank where Eccles Investment had a dominant interest. He meant to adhere to his negative rule in Ogden, but was forced to change his mind when Orval W. Adams, as executive vice-president of the merged banks, accepted an offer to become senior vice-president of the Utah State National Bank in Salt Lake City—an institution controlled by the Mormon Church. Because of the religious tie, the Utah State National Bank should have been specially favored by guidance from "continuous revelation," but its affairs were in disarray, and Adams had the hard-nosed qualities needed to straighten them out.

Adams was reluctant to risk the move from Ogden to Salt Lake City. The move meant a doubling of his salary, but he revealed to Marriner that he had no great confidence in himself. What inducements would be offered for him to remain in Ogden? "None," said Marriner. "I don't want to go into competition with the Mormon Church. You have a great opportunity in Salt Lake City. Grab it. You are equal to it." The two young men thus came to a parting of their careers and of their ways. They remained personal friends in the years ahead, but would engage in repeated public clashes over issues of national economic policy.

Because of Adams' departure, Marriner spent half of each working day in the bank. As a backup measure, he saw to it that George was made a vice-president. The more George added experience to his native talents, the more he assumed the responsibilities which Adams had previously discharged. Promoted to "senior vice-president," he managed things so effectively that Marriner progressively cut back on the hours he personally spent in the bank.

In addition to his brother George, Marriner brought a number of other young men into key positions in the bank; one of these was Lawrence Clayton. By firing more than "one for von Gagow," Clayton had attained the rank of colonel during the First World War. On being demobilized in 1919, he returned to Salt Lake City, where he formed a partnership with Joseph Quinney, his former roommate at the Harvard Law School. One of Marriner's sisters pined for Clayton, but he married someone else at about the time Quinney married Marriner's sister Jesse. The newly wedded Clayton could not live on the slender fees he earned in the infant law firm. He confided to Marriner his immediate need for more income, and was invited to join the staff of the Ogden bank on a trial basis to see if the business was to his taste. It proved to be so; he was made assistant cashier, and later a vice-president. Over and above their good business relationship, he would become one of Marriner's most valued friends.

Joseph Quinney would be intimately linked with the future of the entire family and for reasons which went beyond the ties of marriage, or his role as the head of the law firm which handled many of the legal matters related to the family's economic interests. The family as it matured was increasingly in need of a Hague Arbitration Tribunal of its own. Quinney, a calm, objective-minded man, filled that need. When the call went out, "Better get Joe Quinney," it was another way of saying that family frictions had the makings of an explosion which Quinney alone could defuse.

In 1924 there was a change in the business leadership of the Browning family when Matt Browning died, and his son Marriner took his place. In August of that same year—a time of economic stringency—the Bank of Montpelier in Idaho closed, followed in February 1925 by the First National Bank of Montpelier. The Idaho community was thus left without local banking services, and a group of local businessmen formed a committee under the chairmanship of Dr. G. F. Ashley "to get a bank." They went to Ogden for discussions with Marriner Eccles and Marriner Browning. On August 1, 1925, the Eccles-Browning Bank opened in Montpelier. Soon afterward, the Eccles Investment Company purchased the First National Bank of Rock Springs, thereby increasing to seven the number of banks that were part of the Eccles-Browning group.

Each of the seven banks was operated autonomously. Since each had its own board and officers who functioned independent of the others, their individual demands on Marriner's attention clashed with the demands of his other business interests. Marriner weighed three possibilities. He could take the Eccles family entirely out of banking. He could reduce the scope of its bank holdings. He could enlarge them so as to warrant the costs of forming an efficient overhead staff organization to provide services for all the banks which each performed separately—auditing, advertising, purchasing, credit inspections, and so on. Between fifteen and twenty banks, it was estimated, would be needed to justify such an overhead staff.

Marriner might well have decided on the first or the second of the possibilities, for it had never been his conscious intention to enter banking on a grand scale. He had become involved in it by accident. His status in a hierarchical community never depended solely on his identity as a leading banker. He had other sources of personal power—which may explain why he eventually took a clinically detached view of banks and bankers.

In any case, Marriner tended to be bored by the routine of banking, with its chatter about loans, liquidity, collateral, liens, escrows, collections, payments of principal and interest, extensions, defaults, foreclosures, and its daily worries about the accuracy of records, the honesty of employees, bank examiners who never saw the living realities behind the ciphers on bank records. He always recognized that the flow of money and credit through the banking system, like the metabolic rate in the circulation of blood in the human body, meant the difference between life and death in the economy of a community. Yet, in the manner of his father, Marriner was primarily an organizer of resources rather than an operating banker, less interested in "a bundle of notes" than he was in bringing things to birth where nothing had existed before.

A turn in the affairs of the Sego Milk Products Company resolved Marriner's uncertainty about his future in the banking business. The many changes that he and Roy Bullen had made in the company's operations since 1920 resulted in a vigorous growth in sales and profits, so that four years later Sego's accumulated earnings, after taxes and depreciation, were roughly $1.2 million. In the late fall of 1924 Marriner was approached by representatives of the Pet Milk Company, of St. Louis. Pet Milk advertised in national magazines at the usual national rates, but when it tried to penetrate the market west of the Rockies, it ran up against an aggressively managed Sego Milk Products Company. Nothing Pet Milk did to get over that barrier—and thus to justify the costs of its advertising—worked, and, as a last resort, its managers asked Marriner if he would consider selling Sego Milk. After months of negotiations, the terms of the sale made in February 1925—$1 million in cash and approximately $250,000 in Pet Milk stock —gave Sego stockholders a handsome profit, since the actual purchase occurred only after Sego distributed in dividends all the earnings it had accumulated in the previous five years. As a consequence of the transaction, Marriner became a director of Pet Milk.

The portion of the sale that accrued directly to Eccles Investment made for a nest egg of idle money, which induced Marriner Eccles and Marriner Browning to expand the number of their banks so as to warrant the formation of an overhead supervisory staff. In the spring of 1926 they acquired control of the Blackfoot City Bank in Idaho. But where were they to find other banks for sale?

Salt Lake City was ruled out: the cost of acquiring a bank there was prohibitive. Marriner sought the advice of his friend Gilbert Wright, manager of the Consolidated Wagon & Machine Company office in Idaho Falls, who suggested they approach the manager of the Anderson Brothers Bank, Elbert G. Bennett.

Bennett, then forty-two, was two years older than Marriner. By 1926 he had already had a varied career in small-town banking: in the construction of canals, power lines, hotels, other businesses and in wartime service for the navy. During the postwar years when the War Finance Corporation (WFC) rendered aid to agriculture and the livestock industry, Bennett energetically directed WFC operations in Idaho. After the WFC was liquidated, with no loss to the government, Bennett was given an interest in the Anderson Bank in Idaho Falls to save it. He not only excelled in the technical aspects of bank management; he was a master of both public psychology and state politics.

Marriner and his brother George met with Bennett to disclose their plan of action: Eccles Investment and the Browning Company would advance funds to Bennett for use in buying available banks, but under a name other than Eccles-Browning. If Bennett took charge of the purchase operation, moved from Idaho Falls to Ogden and agreed to serve as vice-president and general manager of the network, he would be given a 25 per cent interest in the Anderson Bank. After some consideration, Bennett accepted the offer and, in 1926, moved to Ogden.

By 1928 Bennett had acquired seven more banks for the Eccles-Browning system. When these were added to those already in operation, they made for the largest banking organization in the Intermountain West.* More banks would soon be acquired; but the seventeen that were now under Eccles-Browning control set the stage for a scene that occurred on June 15, 1928, in an obscure office building in Dover, Delaware. Here a group of Utah-Idaho residents, and another group of Delaware citizens, acting as proxies, went through the motions of a stockholders' meeting conforming to the science-fiction legal procedures for the organization of corporations "foreign" to Delaware. The result was the formal incorporation of the First Security Corporation.† All the stockholders in the banks—newly acquired or previously owned—were permitted to exchange their stock for shares in the corporation, the terms being exactly the same as those that applied to the Eccles and Browning holdings.

Though the holding-company device had been used in several other industries, First Security's organization by this method was the first time the arrangement was used in banking. A primary reason for employing the form was the existing legal prohibitions against branch banking. Since Marriner in future years was to fight *for* branch banking—and for a *unified* banking system—the historical roots of the resistance to branch banking merit a word here.[3]

Branch banking had made an early appearance in the economic life of the American Republic. But, starting in the age of Jackson, a series of bank failures and the fear of economic domination by huge financial combinations generated political opposition to banking in general and to the largest banks, which had branches, in particular. The Panic of 1837 further intensified that opposition and led to legislation known as the free banking acts, enabling any group of individuals who met certain qualifications to open a unit bank. The qualifications set were minimal, and single-office banks swept the coun-

---

*These twenty-eight banks served two communities in Wyoming, eight in Utah and fourteen in Idaho. Of the total number, eighteen had populations of 1,500 to 3,500 and four of 8,000 to 10,000—Logan, Idaho Falls, Nampa and Rock Springs. The remaining four were Pocatello, 16,000; Boise, 22,000; Ogden, 40,000; and Salt Lake City, 140,000.

†The constituent banks were: Hyrum State, Ogden First National, Ogden First Savings, Richmond State and Thatcher Brothers banks in Utah; the Anderson Brothers, Ashton, Blackfoot, Gooding First National, Jerome First National, Montpelier, Nampa, Pocatello, Preston Federal State and Shoshone First National banks in Idaho; and the Rock Springs and South Superior state banks in Wyoming. Also included was the Investors Savings and Loan Company of Pocatello.

try. A National Bank Act was passed in 1863, with the object of meeting Civil War needs for a national and uniform system of currency and banking. The act did not expressly prohibit branch banking, but the ambiguous language used in the legislation was construed by comptrollers of the Currency of the time to mean that national chartered banks were barred from having branches. The interpretation, which passed into precedent, made the unit bank the dominant institutional form for American banking—and thus bequeathed to the future a banking system whose fatal weakness would become clear with the onset of the Great Depression.

The prohibition inspired a form of combination and control known as chain banking. Though one bank could not own stock in another, small institutions could be controlled directly or indirectly by one or more individuals who were free, under existing law, to buy the controlling stock in these institutions. Though the Eccles-Browning system, at its inception, also had features of chain banking, First Security differed in vital respects from the earlier arrangement. For one thing, it was not itself a bank and hence was not subject to regulations that prohibited a national bank from purchasing stock in any other bank, national or state. Further, the new corporation was not a collection of isolated individual banks. Though each bank had its own charter, president and directors, the new corporation was centrally managed as a system. In this way, First Security offered its constituent "country banks" access to capital and specialized skills previously available only to large metropolitan banks.

Communities affected by the formation of First Security reacted positively toward this pioneering venture into group banking.[4] A regional banking periodical, the *North Pacific Banker,* saw in the new organization "one more transition within this region from the 'pioneer' to the 'modern,' with effects that would be felt throughout the financial, agricultural and industrial fabric of the states of Idaho, Utah and Wyoming." The Pocatello *Tribune* stated the case in personal terms: "The name of Eccles and Browning to the people of Utah and Idaho is in itself a guarantee of organization. It is like the word 'Sterling' upon silver, or 'gilt-edged' with reference to securities." The organization of First Security soon attracted favorable national attention as well: C. W. Collins, the former deputy comptroller of the Currency, saw in it a welcome initiative, ushering in sweeping changes in American banking.

The new movement toward branch banking has come to be known as "group banking." Its mechanism is rather simple. It is not based upon any acts of the banks themselves, but rather on the right of a shareholder of the bank to sell his stock and the right of a corporation to buy it. . . . The first definite group of banks, formed over a year ago, centered in Ogden, Utah. The sponsors of this particular group were not conscious of the fact that they were pioneering what now appears to be a great branch banking movement. They simply took hold of a local situation and through the use of local capital and local enterprise established a group system of banks extending over the boundary lines of two other states.[5]

Immediately after its formation, First Security began to purchase other banks to add to its original seventeen. On November 8, 1928, a few days after Herbert Hoover was elected president of the United States in a landslide, First Security acquired the Pacific National Bank in Boise, Idaho; fifteen days later, it added the First National of Mountain Home; and before the year was out, it acquired the First National Bank of Hailey. By the end of 1928, the Consolidated Statement of Banks showed that the deposits listed by the Eccles-Browning affiliated banks in 1927 was almost doubled in one year by First Security; resources stood at almost $40 million, and net earnings were $427,922, of which First Security's share was $374,616.

Despite the agricultural depression, the directors of First Security thought that the earnings of the corporation were sufficient to warrant further expansion. Various acquisitions were made in 1929, and the most important of these brought First Security into Salt Lake City. National Copper, besides being among the largest banks in that city, had also controlled three smaller banks—the Magna, Garfield and Bingham banks, all located in mining districts near Salt Lake where they served as conduits for National Copper's business with large mining concerns. In addition, the owners of National Copper operated the Bankers Trust Company in Salt Lake.

Louis Cates, a director of National Copper, in a confidential meeting with Marriner Eccles, revealed that he and a majority of the other directors were displeased with the way the Armstrong family managed their bank. Would First Security care to get a foothold in Salt Lake City by acquiring National Copper? Marriner expressed a lively interest but explained that First Security could pay only with stock for an acquisition as large as that. Cates presently gave Marriner a go-ahead signal, and the offer was accepted. Negotiations were completed on March 31, 1929 (three weeks after Hoover's inauguration). Cates agreed to serve as president of the bank; but it was Marriner's kinsman Howard Stoddard, aged twenty-seven, and Stewart Cosgriff, a nephew of the owner of the competitor Continental Bank, who would actually run it. Marriner had a keen eye for spotting young managerial talent: Stoddard later became the head of one of the largest banks in Michigan, and Cosgriff the head of one of the largest in Colorado.[6]

During these same weeks, First Security also acquired a bank in Rupert, Idaho. Two more small Idaho banks, the Payette State and the First National in Emmett, would be acquired the following year. But by the end of 1929, the First Security Corporation embraced twenty-eight member banks.*

---

*Serving on the corporation's board were three Eccles brothers—Marriner, George and Spencer; two of the Brownings—Marriner and Jonathan; E. G. Bennett; seven other Utah residents and three other Idaho residents. Marriner was elected president, Marriner Browning vice-president, Bennett managing vice-president and George Eccles secretary-treasurer.

The fact that banks ranging from National Copper to those in Idaho hamlets sought to join the First Security system says something about the high regard other bankers had for First Security's organizational structure, management and centralized methods of operation. No one at the time seemed aware of the gathering storm that would soon put those strengths to the test.

10. The Anatomy of Innocence

I

WITH THE INAUGURATION of Herbert Hoover, Americans seemed to believe that a new era had dawned and that economic progress henceforth would be automatic. Marriner had no reason to dissent from that view. In 1929, at the age of thirty-eight, he could see how his own rise in the business world reaffirmed the truths of precepts he had received from his father. All the truisms concerning work, thrift, production, self-reliance and the wealth-producing potentialities in an economic system functioning along laissez-faire lines had paid off handsomely in the second generation as in the first. Back in 1925, when elected president of the Utah Bankers Association, he had paid formal tribute to that legacy in his presidential address:

Progress is a growing participation of more and more people and more of the good things of life. In spite of our follies and failures, we are slowly but surely getting ahead. Our problems are problems of life and growth, not of death and decay.

As in the recent war, civilization may slip back, but these tragic lapses represent an investment in experience. In spite of the World War, today it is reasonable and normal to think of human history as a forward movement from darkness to light, from slavery to freedom, from poverty to comfort, from aloofness among men and nations to a condition of friendly contact and cooperation.

The recent election of Von Hindenburg gives assurance that there is little danger of a revolution in Germany, the Communist Party having cast less than two million votes out of a total of thirty million.

Here in the United States, to eliminate the disastrous effects of the war . . . it will take time assisted by hard work, patience, confidence on the part of all as well as goodwill and friendship between nations. Greater economy should be practiced in governments, and military expenditures must be greatly reduced.

In the same spirit, when Marriner addressed the Ogden Rotary Club in 1928, he sounded a paen to the Federal Reserve System and the banking system in general:

The best tribute to the efficiency of the Federal Reserve System is that no panic has developed since its inception.

Bigger and better banks are predicted as one of the most important consequences of the Federal Reserve System. . . . I could go on indefinitely enumerating many of the revolutionary changes which have taken place and are taking place in the field of banking, but I believe I have said enough to give you a bird's eye view of the development of this most important business, which today is the foundation on which is being built the great structure of modern civilization.

Along with other businessmen, Marriner believed that America had outstripped the conditions that made for depressions and panics such as plagued generations past. As a Republican and a staunch supporter of Hoover, he could point to a cluster of details all showing that the American dream was now on a sound statistical basis. The consumer-price level had been gradually declining throughout most of the 1920s, and the money supply had increased about 40 per cent over the eight-year period ending in 1929. Federal income exceeded expenditures sufficiently to reduce the outstanding government debt by approximately $7 billion. There was practically no unemployment despite the fact that five million new workers had entered the labor force. The increase in labor productivity was substantially greater than was previously regarded as normal. Corporation taxes were low, the maximum rate being 13.5 per cent, and corporate profits increased in those years by over 75 per cent. Taxes on individual incomes were also relatively low. There was little or no government interference with the free-enterprise system.

Private initiative was given every encouragement, and Marriner Eccles made the most of it. In a contest in which he and his older half-brothers had been tested by the doctrine of survival of the fittest, it was Marriner who had survived. In a contest with aging company directors who had been his father's associates, he had transformed them from impatient adversaries into staunch supporters. He had taken a local milk company and infused it with such strength that one of the nation's leading dairy producers had to come to terms with it. He had spun a web of country and city banks and formed a holding company. As the rewards of hard work piled up, he had no reason to doubt that his good fortune would extend into the future.

II

In his private business affairs, Marriner never took the shadow of economic health for the substance, the name for the object, the promise for the possession. Impatient with unreality, he was an apostle of the bitter truth. Why, then, did none of the economic disorders he had lived through—in 1919–21, 1924 and 1927—raise any questions in his mind about laissez-faire capitalism? When he could spot a dent in a milk can and put a price tag on what the dent implied by way of lost profits, why was he indifferent to the inner life of the American economic system as a whole? Above all, why did it take him until 1931—two years after the onset of the depression—to recognize that something was fundamentally wrong with the national economy?

Several possible answers come to mind. In the first place, the depressions and recessions Marriner had directly experienced prior to the Great Crash were fairly short-lived,[7] while the only one that cut deep—the 1919–21 depression—could be explained as a "necessary postwar adjustment." Since none of these economic disorders was either acute or protracted, he could share, without nagging doubts, the widely held view that recurrent fluctuations in the economy simply reflected the turns and returns in the "business cycle."

Second, Marriner's personal success in banking worked to narrow the moral he drew when he saw how the depressions and recessions of the 1920s closed many banks in Utah and Idaho. It was *not* that the local and national banking structure was inherently unstable. It was *not* that this instability could be remedied only through organic legislative reforms. The moral he drew was that a natural law of selection was having a more salutary, long-range effect on the banking system than any reforms that could be achieved through legislative means; it was eliminating banks that never should have been created at all and was displacing them with "bigger and stronger banks."

Again, Marriner did not look to professional economists for the meaning of events unfolding in the public economic realm. Economic data at best—even under today's elaborate statistical techniques and computerized reporting systems—are seldom precise, comprehensive and "up to the minute." In the 1920s the situation was worse. Even the most eminent academic economists lacked reliable and current estimates about such matters as unemployment, national income, private investment expenditures, expenditures by state and local governments and about the quantitative effects of these factors on the national economy. When they made projections about national economic conditions, they tended to rely, often falsely, on analogies to events in the known economic past.

This is not to say that no advances were made in the 1920s on the frontiers of economic knowledge. Many advances were made on aspects of monetary theory and business cycles, on the theory and realities of real wages and with respect to specific reformist proposals bearing on labor policy and social insurance, tariffs, social security, corporate financing, the regulation of utilities and so on. Moreover, the 1920s was a time when tax cuts had stimulated the economy, and when the idea began to take hold that public-works projects—financed by governmental borrowing—could and should be used as a counter-cyclical stabilizing factor. Still, with one eccentric exception to be noted in a moment, no economist then had synthesized these particular experiences into a comprehensive theory of how the national economy could be kept in a course of orderly growth, free from the pendulum swings of boom and bust.

The exception was *not* John Maynard Keynes in England. Keynes owed his early celebrity to his trenchant critique of the economic consequences of the Versailles Treaty. When he turned his attention to questions of monetary and fiscal policy, the ideas he formulated in the 1920s about the relationship between level of public investment on the one side and of unemployment on the other were, as he said, addressed to conditions special to Great Britain. They were not, as he also pointed out at the time, generally applicable to a country such as the United States, and he did not change his mind about that until the early 1930s, when the Great Depression in the United States was at its depths. The exception alluded to was the strangely mated team of William Trufant Foster, a former president of Reed College, and Wadill Catchings, a former iron manufacturer who had become a partner in Goldman, Sachs.

In 1928 the two men co-authored a book entitled *The Road to Plenty*, which focused on a century-old fundamental tenet of classical economic thought known as Say's law of markets.[8] According to that law, the financing of production would by itself automatically create enough purchasing power in the economy to move all the goods produced. It followed, therefore, that the needs of production should be attended to first, and demand would then take care of itself.

Foster and Catchings argued that adherents to Say's law overlooked two facts of life in the business world: First, as industry increases its output, it does not, "for any length of time, proportionately increase its payments to the people." Hence the flow of money to the consumer could not keep pace with the flow of consumer goods; even Henry Ford, despite the vaunted high wages offered by his factory, did not pay workers on his assembly lines enough money to buy all the automobiles they produced. Second, Say's law overlooked the "dilemma of thrift." Though corporations and individuals alike had to save, every dollar saved was a dollar subtracted from the flow of money to the potential consumer. This led to a decrease in effective consumer demand and from there to a depression—unless government moved to offset the deficiencies in demand caused by oversaving.

What, then, accounted for the prosperity of the late 1920s? According to Foster and Catchings, the volume of money had expanded sufficiently for public works "to make up the deficit in consumer buying due to savings." In the future, however, private and public outlays could not be left to chance. Government, as a matter of deliberate policy, must put more money into the consumer's hand when business falls off, and less money at times of inflation. "When business begins to look rotten, more public spending." The authors agreed that their proposal would increase the national debt, but this would be true only in times of depression. Besides, said they, a debt increase was not a national calamity: "It means scarcely more than that the people of the United States collectively owe themselves more money," while the nation gains in real wealth and spares itself "the greatest waste of all . . . the waste of idle plants and idle workers." The most attractive feature of their policy, said Foster and Catchings, was that it involved no fundamental changes in the established order. Instead, "it leaves the whole domain of commerce and finance exactly where they are to-day."

A few liberals shared Henry A. Wallace's hope that hundreds of thousands of people might read *The Road to Plenty*, but Franklin D. Roosevelt, another good liberal, disagreed. In his copy of the book, he had scrawled a summary judgment of the text: "Too good to be true—You can't get something for nothing."[9] Professional economists responded with zest to the challenging offer by Foster and Catchings of large cash prizes to anyone who could point out errors in their line of reasoning. What bothered professional economists most of all was the cavalier way in the which authors had treated Say's law.

When the Great Crash was followed by the onset of the Great Depression, President Hoover first assured the nation that the depression was an illusion that Americans had a patriotic duty to ignore. A year later, following the economic collapse in Europe, he spoke of the depression as though it were a foreign plot. This is not to say that he was personally idle or indifferent to the course of events. Through telephone calls, letters, White House meetings and speeches, he tried to wheedle and prod *other* public and private people throughout the nation to take economic initiative to simulate recovery. He did not believe that the central government had any responsibilities in the economic realm which were special to its own nature as government. Its responsibilities were in no way different in degree or in kind from those of other elements in the nation at large—state and local government, businesses, banks, trade associations and individual entrepreneurs. The central government, and the presidency in particular, could only help *other* hands to organize national and local drives for relief programs. Hoover seemed not to see that the magnitude of the crisis was beyond the reach of those other people, no matter how well intentioned they were. At the same time, his doctrinaire constraints on what the government and the president should and could do directly under the cover of law led some people to say of him that the Constitution provided for every accidental contingency in the Executive except a vacancy in the mind of the chief executive.

President Hoover's approach to the Great Depression has been the subject of a sympathetic commentary by Professor Herbert Stein.[10] It is an approach, says Stein, that becomes understandable when viewed in the light of the relatively small size of the federal budget in the 1920s. Total federal expenditures were then but a fraction of the gross national product; the percentage of federal purchases of goods and services was an even smaller fraction of the total national purchase, and the federal percentage of total national construction was microscopic. The federal government at that time was not a machine that constantly generated new programs or expanded old ones—one that lent itself to an emergency increase of expenditures merely by advancing the date when plans already in the governmental fiscal pipeline would go into effect. A major change on either the revenue or the expenditure side of small budgets would have been required to make a significant dent in the national economy. Hence it was not unnatural for a man in Hoover's position to conclude that the best economic results would be achieved by his stimulating expenditures by state and local governments and by private business, rather than by his trying to manipulate the expenditures of the federal government.

Like most other American businessmen of the day, Marriner Eccles was either unaware of what leading economists were saying or, like the economists themselves, had no unified vision of the national economy. It was only in 1931, realizing his own "economic illiteracy," that he carefully read William Trufant Foster's post-1929 writings about the causes of the Great Depression and how to get out of it. But he did not stop there. He proceeded step by step to reinterpret underconsumption in the light of his own experiences as a banker and businessman, and his analysis of the Great Depression and his recommendations for recovery would eventually far surpass Foster's in concreteness, trenchancy, and fundamental challenge to the reasoning of major leaders of business opinion.

11. The End of Innocence

IN THE MONTHS immediately following the Great Crash, Marriner Eccles heard and echoed the views sounded by men he respected. The economic crisis, they said, was only temporary. No redemptive intervention by the federal government was needed. The depression was simply following the course of natural economic laws.

The economy was in its lean years. The lean years inevitably followed the fat years because Americans had been spendthrifts in the twenties. In time, however, the economy would right itself through the action of men who had been prudent and thrifty all along. At a propitious moment, they would reinvest their savings in new production—the American West being the traditional place for such reinvestment—and the actions that had pulled the country out of previous depressions would automatically operate to that same end once again.

Thrift, savings, reinvestment, new production, and the American West comprised the terms of a syllogism that dominated Marriner's expectations for recovery in the first year of the Great Depression. His reliance on that line of thought was reinforced by a development in the affairs of the Utah Construction Company—in which Marriner made the pivotal decision for the company to play a major role in the construction of the Boulder Dam, on the Colorado River. In December 1928, following the presidential election, a lame-duck Congress approved the dam project; and six months later, when the economy appeared to be at the height of a boom, President Hoover issued a proclamation authorizing construction. Bids were to be received by the Bureau of Reclamation in 1930.

Utah Construction then had to its credit the building of many dams in the West, including those at American Falls, Deadwood, Guernsy and Hetch-Hetchy. Moreover, much of its success in these ventures was credited to two members of its technical staff, known to be among the nation's foremost practical engineers. One was Hank Lawler, the other "Chief" Barlow, formerly the head engineer of the Southern Pacific Railroad and a man long interested in the Boulder project. He never failed to call the attention of visitors to a diorama he displayed in his office: a model of Boulder Dam, scaled in every detail to the Bureau of Reclamation plans.

Both the quality and the success of the engineering staff of Utah Construction were well known to a group of contractors—Henry Kaiser, W. A. Bechtel, Steve Bechtel, Allan MacDonald and Felix Khan, of San Francisco; Charles Shea and Philip Hart, of Portland; and Harry Morrison, of

Boise. All of them had been hurt by the sharp nationwide decline in the volume of business available to the construction industry following the Great Crash on the Stock Exchange. By the summer of 1930, Boulder Dam was one of the few major construction prospects in sight on the national horizon. Close to the time when construction bids were due, those contractors decided to form a syndicate that would bid for the contract on a partnership basis. They asked Utah Construction not only to join but also to head the syndicate.

W. H. Wattis was still president of Utah Construction. By the summer of 1930, however, he was in the grip of terminal cancer and was confined to the two rooms he occupied in the Southern Pacific Hospital in San Francisco. His brother Ed Wattis and Les Corey wanted Marriner, as a director of Utah Construction representing a large stock holding, to try to persuade "W.H." to make a decision in favor of the project. With the two men standing by, Marriner placed a long-distance call to Wattis, in which he stressed the importance of the project to the immediate and future needs of Utah Construction. Wattis replied that he did not want to get involved with men he did not know. One word led to another, and soon the conversation became tense. At last Wattis said, "Well, if you feel as strongly as you do about the Boulder project, come to San Francisco to see me in the hospital."

So Marriner did. Wattis gradually accepted his argument and agreed that Utah should head the syndicate—soon to be call the Six Companies. When Marriner informed the representatives of the interested firms, he got them to elect "W.H" president of the Six Companies, and his brother Ed as one of its eleven directors.

The first five meetings of the directors were held in the antechamber next to Wattis' hospital room. While the directors wanted the Six Companies to form a partnership, Marriner insisted on the formation of a corporation whose sole purpose would be to bid on and to build the Boulder Dam. His view eventually prevailed. He also insisted that before any bid was submitted, $7.5 million in capital should be paid in full to the corporation to cover the costs of a bid bond and performance bond. Further, each participating company would get one director for every $500,000 it paid in. Marriner's view prevailed only in connection with this last point. Not more than $5 million was actually paid in, with another $2.5 million subscribed (though never called). Utah alone paid in $1 million, giving it a one-fifth participating interest in the project. The sum represented a loan Marriner negotiated with the Crocker First National Bank in San Francisco, subject to repayment in seven years, with the Crocker Bank to lend Utah an additional $500,000 in case of need.

At every turn in these preliminary arrangements, Marriner kept Will Wattis fully informed of the decisions in prospect and secured his consent to them—as though he would live to see their consequences. As Wattis lay on his deathbed, with all ambition and vanity gone, he could think only of the future of the company that had been as much a part of his life as the air he breathed. Now, unknown to Marriner, he called to his bedside his daughters, Mrs. Mary Brown and Mrs. Stella Bowman, and extracted a promise from them.

Under normal circumstances, he said, it would be reasonable to expect that upon his death he would be succeeded in the presidency of Utah Construction by his older brother, Ed. Circumstances, however, were not normal. At an unsettled time in the general economy, the company was entering into an untried relationship with five other firms. The only person equal to the task of leading Utah Construction in the period ahead was Marriner Eccles. "I want you girls to promise me," Wattis continued, "that after I'm gone, you will do everything you can to put Marriner into the presidency of Utah. I can't tell this to Ed, but Ed can't handle the job. He's too old. Marriner can." These were among his last words.

When Wattis died in August 1931, Hank Lawler took his place as one of Utah's two directors on the board of the Six Companies—whose presidency was assumed by W. A. Bechtel. At the same time, Wattis' daughters told Marriner of their father's last request and of their intention to respect it. Marriner replied that he would accept the presidency of Utah Construction on condition that a new post of chairman of the board be created—for Ed Wattis to fill. Matters were so arranged. Twenty years later, in 1951, it would be Ed's grandson Edmund W. Littlefield who would work in tandem with Marriner to bring about Utah Construction's spectacular growth —under the new name of "Utah International."

The Six Companies were awarded the prime contract to construct Boulder Dam.[11]*

Henry Kaiser's new position as public and political relations officer not only made him a public figure for the first time—with consequences reaching far into the future—but also brought about a fundamental change of style in the way heavy construction companies presented themselves to the public. Previously, contractors tended to believe that the noise of their rivets, trip hammers and concrete mixers would bespeak their virtues. Kaiser, a fertile-minded publicist, generated a steady flow of news stories, information kits, progress reports and special "briefings" which built a national and international reputation for the Six Companies. He was also the driving force behind a seemingly small matter with a large pay-off. At an early meeting among the directors of the Six Companies, Kaiser predicted that high government officials, along with important opinion makers, were bound to visit the Boulder camp site while construction was underway —considering that this was *the* great project in the otherwise moribund

---

*The responsibilities were distributed as follows: Frank Crow, who was finishing a new dam in Idaho for Utah Construction and Morrison-Knudsen, was superintendent in charge of construction; Charles Shea, president of Shea Construction, together with Hank Lawler, vice-president of Utah, were on-the-scene advisors and consultants to Crow; Steve Bechtel, the son of W. A. Bechtel, handled all purchasing out of San Francisco; and Henry Kaiser would be in charge of public and political relations.

building industry. It would be well, therefore, to build a guesthouse where the VIPs could stay. Most of the directors balked at the proposal. Nothing of the sort had been provided on the sites of other construction projects. Visitors could "rough it" along with everyone else. Besides, why waste precious money on frills? Kaiser, however, persisted and finally won his point. A guesthouse costing $25,000 was built at the camp site when very little else was there. It was attractively furnished, could accommodate five or six overnight guests at a time and was staffed with several servants. At Kaiser's insistence, it also had an excellent cook. As he predicted, the facility was extensively used by assorted domestic and foreign dignitaries and thus immeasurably enhanced the glamorous reputation of the Six Companies.

Actual construction began in March 1931, and the first stage was a vast project in itself. It called for the completion of four huge diversion tunnels, 4,800 feet long and 56 feet in diameter, the creation of a dry bed on which to construct the dam, the erection of a modern city to house six hundred workers and the construction of fifty-three miles of railway and forty miles of improved highway. Here, it seemed, was the supreme emblem of the hallowed belief that a new cycle of investment in the development of the American West would lead the nation back to economic health.

II

The national economic crisis did not ease; it grew worse. "On a morning toward the first of 1931," Marriner Eccles later recalled, "the scales suddenly dropped away from my eyes." He went on to explain:

I saw for the first time that though I'd been active in the world of finance and production for seventeen years and knew its techniques, I knew less than nothing about its economic and social effects. The discovery of my ignorance, however, did not by itself lead anywhere. Friends whose estates I managed, my family, whose interests I represented, and the community at large, in whose economic life I played a sensitive role, all expected me to find a way out of the economic trap we were all in. Yet all I could find within myself was despair. Having been reared by my father to accept the responsibilities of wealth and having been placed by circumstances at the helm of many enterprises, there were times when I felt the whole depression was a personal affront. Wherein had I been at fault? Night after night following my head-splitting awakening, I would return home exhausted by the pretensions of knowledge I was forced to wear in a daytime masquerade. I would slump forward on a table and pray that the answers I was groping for would somehow be revealed. As an individual I felt myself helpless to do anything.[12]

What was to be done in a situation in which the dollar was so sound when measured by its power to buy goods and services that when prices fell and unemployment increased, it somehow got sounder? What was to be done by the Eccles banks when loans on homes, farms, livestock and securities or to business and industrial enterprises could not be repaid because values had drastically declined? What was to be done when pressures on the banks to "get liquid" so as to meet depositor claims led to a situation where the liquidation of debts made it impossible to pay off debts?

Such questions were intimately connected with the danger of bank runs. If a weak bank was closed by a run, sound banks were imperiled by the sudden wave of fear rolling over the community. Marriner first saw this happen with the Ogden State Bank, one of Utah's oldest and most esteemed banks. Under the adept management of the Bigelow family it had served the community well for over forty years and was held in confidence by all who did business with it. Yet, in mid-1931, Archie Bigelow, the president of the bank, brought an alarming piece of news to Marriner and Bennett. Because of deflation, his bank was suffering heavy losses on its loans. Its capital and surplus were impaired, and its deposits were daily being drained off. It was Bigelow's belief that his bank could be saved if it was merged with the Eccles-Browning banks in Ogden. But the Bigelow bank was so submerged by its afflictions that it would pull down any other bank linked to it.

On a weekend in the summer of 1931, Marriner and Bennett learned that the Ogden State Bank would not open its doors on the coming Monday. The fact was not generally known. What would the effect be on the Eccles-Browning banks in the city if the Ogden doors remained shut? How would the community react toward *them*? After all, they were managed by men much younger than Bigelow, with none of his experience—besides being relatively new to Ogden. Since the Ogden banks were the central institutions in the First Security network, it was imperative to break the anticipated run in Ogden as quickly as possible.

On Sunday, Marriner secured a list of Ogden State's important commercial accounts. He called together the officers and directors of his two Ogden banks and informed them of what was in prospect, observing that the firms on the list of commercial accounts in the Ogden State Bank would be without banking facilities on Monday morning when that institution failed to open its doors. The directors of his banks were to pick out the firms with which they had close personal or business dealings and, on Monday morning, call to invite the heads of those firms to deposit their funds on hand with the Eccles banks. They were also to say that if it was a loan or currency that was needed, the Eccles banks would be glad to meet those needs. The object was not only to gain an inflow of deposits but also to brace the confidence of the employees of those firms. The employees would be paid in checks drawn on the Eccles banks, and the combined incoming traffic would help reverse the current of the outgoing traffic that was to be expected on Monday.

The officers and directors threw themselves into their assignment. But while this plan to stabilize locally held, Marriner knew that a concealed run on the commercial and savings bank accounts could start at points other than Ogden. Like other city banks, the Eccles banks in Ogden held the balances of many outside corporations, as well as of independent country banks in the area. Once the officials of these outside concerns heard of the run on the Eccles banks in Ogden, they could be expected to take precautionary measures to avoid getting caught short. They would either ask for a direct transfer of funds or make drafts or checks on the Eccles banks and deposit them with other banks. Marriner had seen this happen repeatedly; large corporations withdrew funds from the hinterland, concentrated them in New York and other large cities and, in this way, hastened the collapse of countless country banks. He thought he might have a fighting chance to save his own banks if all outside accounts were warned in advance of an imminent run, and if they heard the news directly from the bank officers and not from press reports or some other sources.

That Sunday night, Marriner and Bennett drafted a telegram for delivery first thing Monday morning to each outside account. It read:

The Ogden State Bank will not open its doors this Monday morning. This will cause some demands for withdrawal of funds on our own bank. We have anticipated this for some time and are fully prepared to meet any and all demands which are made upon us. We felt it desirable that you should get this information first hand.

The tactic had its hoped-for effect. There was not a single transfer of funds from among the accounts that received a copy of the telegram. But even before this became clear, Marriner and Bennett knew that their efforts to shore up confidence in the commercial accounts of the First National Bank could be undercut by the fact that this bank shared the same premises with his First Savings Bank. If a panic led to a run on the savings bank, it would do the same to the national bank. With that in mind, all employees of the national and savings banks were contacted that Sunday and ordered to be at work the next morning at eight o'clock.

At that time, Marriner told the employees what they would have to face in a few hours. "If you want to keep this bank open," said he, "you must do your part. Go about your business as though nothing unusual was happening. Smile, talk about the weather, be pleasant, show no signs of panic. The main burden is going to fall on you boys in the savings department. Instead of the three windows we normally use, we are going to use all four of them today. They must be manned at all times. If any teller's or clerk's window in this bank closes even for a short time, that will stir up more panic. We'll have sandwiches brought in; no one can go out to lunch. We can't break this run today. The best we can do is to slow it down. You are going to pay them. But you are going to pay them very slowly. It's the only chance we have to deal with the panic. You know a lot of depositors by sight, and in the past you did not have to look up their signatures. But today when they come here with their deposit books to close out their accounts, you are going to look up every signature card. And take your time about it. Another thing. When you pay out, don't use any big bills. Pay out in fives and tens, and count slowly. Our object is to pay out a minimum to-day."

The tellers and clerks ably played their part of the act despite the crowd that surged through the doors of the bank the moment they were opened. Yet at two o'clock that afternoon, Marriner, his brother George, and Bennett discussed the problem they would have to face when the regular three o'clock closing hour was reached. The crowd in the bank was tense. Some people had been waiting for hours to draw out their money. Their gestures and words spoke of their obsessive fear that when they reached the teller's cage, they would be told that no more money was left. If the bank tried to close its doors at three, no one could predict the consequences. The bank must remain open as long as people were in line who wanted their money.

A call had been put through to the Federal Reserve Bank in Salt Lake City to send currency to the Eccles banks in Ogden as well as to all others in the First Security Corporation. The guards who emerged from the armored cars strode through the rush of people inside the bank, and as they swung their sacks of currency around, all reverently made way before them. Another figure who emerged from the armored car was Morgan Craft, deputy manager of the Federal Reserve Bank of Salt Lake City. When he entered the bank building, Marriner grabbed his arm and led him through the crowd to a black and gold marble counter in the officers' section of the savings bank. Marriner himself now mounted the counter, raised his hand and called for attention, as he had done as a Mormon missionary in Scotland.

"Just a minute!"

There was silence.

"Just a minute!" Marriner repeated, "I want to make an announcement. It appears we are having some difficulty handling our depositors with the speed to which you are accustomed. Many of you have been standing in line for a considerable time. I notice a lot of pushing and shoving and irritation. I just wanted to tell you that instead of closing at the usual hour of three o'clock, we have decided to stay open just as long as there is anyone who wants to withdraw his deposit or to make one. You people who have just come in can return later this afternoon or evening if you wish. There is absolutely no justification for the excitement or the apparent panicky attitude I sense among some depositors. As all of you have seen, we have just brought up from Salt Lake City a large amount of currency that will take care of all your requirements. There is plenty more where that came from. And if you don't believe me, I have here Mr. Morgan Craft, one of the officers of the Federal Reserve Bank, who has just come up in the armored car from Salt Lake City. Mr. Craft, say a few words to the folks."

Marriner pulled him up to the top of the counter. Craft said more than a few words. "I just want to verify what Mr. Eccles has told you," said he. "I want to assure you that we have brought up a lot of currency and there is plenty more where that came from." This was perfectly true. But Craft didn't say whether the currency belonged to the Eccles banks, or whether they would be able to get it at all. Nevertheless, the mood of the day was so uncertain that men were heartened by words just as meaningless as by those which had earlier alarmed them. Faces relaxed, the snarl in voices vanished, some people stepped out of line and left the bank, and the word passed from lip to lip to the crowd lined up on the sidewalk outside: "They're going to stay open. They're going to stay open."

Yet the danger was far from over. Because of what happened to the Ogden State Bank, another bank in the city, the Commercial Security Bank headed by Harold Hemingway, was also caught in a deadly run. It suddenly occurred to Marriner that if his own bank remained open past three o'clock, while Hemingway closed his at the usual hour, the contrast would inexorably lead to the unjust implication that the Commercial Security Bank was unsound. On Tuesday, the run on Hemingway's bank would be all the more severe; he would in all probability be forced to close his doors, and this in turn would intensify the run on the Eccles banks—which could not be stemmed.

Marriner and Hemingway were brisk competitors, but now, if they didn't hang together, they would certainly hang separately. So Marriner telephoned Hemingway to say that his own banks would stay open as long past three o'clock as was necessary. He urged Hemingway in his own interest to do the same, but the latter replied that he couldn't keep open since he had very little currency left. Fortunately, because of the work of the officers of the Eccles banks in bringing in new accounts, by three o'clock in the afternoon almost as much money had flowed into the commercial bank as had been paid out by the savings bank. This fact, coupled with the money from Salt Lake City and the deliberate slowdown by the tellers, enabled the Eccles banks to loan $40,000 to Hemingway so that he could remain open beyond the usual three o'clock closing time.

The first day's storm had been weathered, but Marriner knew that no rainbow was as yet splashed across the sky. At the end of the day, he called together the personnel of the banks for another conference. "Now listen," said he, "A lot of people who've been at work will only hear about this run for the first time when they get home tonight. Tomorrow there will be the makings of another crush, and we are going to meet it by doing the opposite of what we did today. Instead of opening at ten, we are going to open at eight. Nobody is going to have to wait outside of the banks to start any sort of line. When people come in here, pay them very fast. Don't dawdle over signatures. Pay out the accounts in big bills. Above all, don't let any line form. It will mean a continuation of the panic."

It was to be a homely application of how the theory of a compensatory economy worked in practice. On Tuesday, the amount paid out exceeded that of the first day, but the important objective had been attained. No lines formed to inspire belief that the bank was in trouble. Customers came into the doorway of the bank, looked around the lobby and, seeing that things presented a picture of calm, walked away. And that was the end of the run. Marriner thanked God for the strong nerves he had inherited from his father and mother.

III

In the fall and winter of 1931–32 it seemed that the frenetic tensions which had been decimating banks everywhere were at last being eased. The marketing of crops enabled some farmers to meet at least part of their loans. President Hoover departed from his doctrinal principle that the central government *as* government had no direct responsibility for the state of the economy and hence should not directly intervene in its affairs. At the urging of Eugene Meyer, then head of the Federal Reserve Board, Hoover supported Meyer's bill which the Congress enacted, leading to the creation of the Reconstruction Finance Corporation (RFC). Hoover's departure from "principle" was not an act of waywardness. It was his response to the true distribution of power in the American economic community. As long as only the private creditor institutions of the South and West were being crushed by depression, their cry for help fell on deaf legislative ears. Eastern banking institutions felt safe while they could call in obligations owed them in the South and West. But when those were no longer collectable, and the Eastern creditors themselves were exposed to the depression, they demanded something like the RFC and they got it in late 1931.

Eugene Meyer himself, who for a while combined his work as the head of the Federal Reserve Board with the work of making the RFC operational, could scarcely conceal his disgust with the very people he hastened to rescue. "There is not a single railroad president," said he, "that I would hire as a $50-a-week clerk." As for the bank presidents who appealed to the RFC for help, very few of them, in his opinion, "were qualified to run anything more substantial than a sideshow at a carnival."[13] Donald Richberg, who was to have a brief moment of celebrity during the early New Deal, was even more caustic. He observed that "trying to save the country by saving the banks was like trying to revive a dying tree by applying fertilizer to its branches instead of to its roots."[14]

Marriner Eccles in Utah was not critical of help from any quarter. He was grateful for having survived what he thought was the worst phase of the depression. He was grateful also for learning in February 1932, on the site of Hoover (Boulder) Dam, that the engineers and builders were making swift progress, and at a cost far below original estimates. Utah Construction could not only repay its $1 million loan from the Crocker Bank but could also make a handsome profit on its share of the work being done. The prospect came as a welcomed relief from the oppressive banking atmosphere in which Marriner had been living.

On the homeward-bound train, somewhere between Las Vegas and Ogden, he was handed a telegram: "COME IMMEDIATELY TO THE FEDERAL RESERVE BANK IN SALT LAKE CITY." Marriner had only one clean shirt left in his traveling bag, but instead of going on to Ogden he got off the train at Salt Lake City. He found that every bank president in the city was present in the Federal Reserve Bank, and the reason made his head spin. The Deseret

Savings Bank in Salt Lake City was in very serious trouble. Its capital, surplus, and reserves were completely wiped out; its deposits were critically impaired. It now exercised its right to require sixty-day notices for withdrawal by its depositors, a right that was rarely invoked; banks customarily paid out savings funds on demand. The Savings Bank could not stay open unless a substantial sum of money was raised by its stockholders. Under existing conditions, to do that would have needed God's power to make a crab walk straight.

An even greater danger lay in the fact that the Deseret National Bank and the Deseret Savings Bank shared the same premises. The National Bank, founded by Brigham Young, was the oldest national bank in Utah. The joint premises and the prominence of the interlocked directors underlay the popular belief that the two were really a single bank owned by the Mormon Church. When the savings bank required sixty-day withdrawal notice it was rumored—without foundation—that the national bank was in trouble. Increasing numbers of depositors lined up at the teller windows in the national bank and withdrew their funds. The national bank was solvent, but it could not require a sixty-day notice to hold back a flash flood of withdrawals.

Worse, a failure of the Deseret National Bank would not be limited to itself. All of the Intermountain banking system would be disrupted, since the national bank carried the reserves of more country banks than did any other institution in the region. With their reserves tied up, the country banks would be forced to close. Because of the Deseret National Bank's history, its collapse would certainly extend the range of disaster. If a bank brought to birth by the heroic Brigham Young and thought to be owned by the Mormon Church failed, what confidence would the public have in banks founded and directed by ordinary mortals?

Within Salt Lake City, itself, a collapse of the Deseret banks would immediately affect two banks that were part of the First Security Corporation: the National Copper Bank and the First Security Trust Company. The spirit of panic would leap to them in a matter of minutes.

At the meeting in the Federal Reserve Bank, Marriner was among those who urged that the Mormon Church should take over the Deseret banks in order to prevent their collapse. Church representatives said no to this. Marriner then suggested that the banks should be absorbed by the Walker Brothers Bank, the largest in Salt Lake City. Again the reaction was no. After meetings extending over several days, it was clear that no one would do anything. The Salt Lake bankers either were paralyzed by fear, or thought they had a better chance to save their own institutions if they did nothing to save the imperiled one. Marriner had no desire for the First Security Corporation to take over the Deseret banks. Yet once again, as in previous cases, a poverty of alternatives made a bold course imperative. If he did not take over the Deseret banks, it would be impossible to protect his own banks in Salt Lake City, and all the other First Security banks in the

Intermountain region. He telephoned Bennett in Ogden and Roy O. Thatcher, the attorney for the First Security Corporation, to come to Salt Lake City, prepared for a long siege.

They agreed that the First Security Corporation must intervene directly in the Deseret banks and take them over. The Deseret Savings Bank would doom any institution linked to it, but the Deseret National Bank was solvent. Marriner and his associates decided that they must cut the link between two banks—they should concentrate on rescuing the national bank while letting the savings bank close. The Deseret National Bank would be moved over the weekend into the quarters of the National Copper Bank and consolidated with it. The charter of the Deseret National Bank would be used to effect the consolidation, and the merged banks would then operate under a new name: The First National Bank of Salt Lake City.

While the directors of the Deseret banks debated this proposal, the auditing staff of the First Security Corporation began work on the merger. The plan would have collapsed if Roy O. Thatcher and First Security's auditors were not previously experienced with mergers and reorganizations. But the veteran skill with which they went about their work freed Marriner to handle the negotiations with the directors of the Deseret National Bank, while Bennett prepared the critically important press releases and communications.

On Friday afternoon, however, there was a sudden hitch. The directors of the Deseret banks informed Marriner of their intention to close their savings bank, but to keep the national bank open in the same quarters. The decision, though brave in spirit, was as illogical as an attempt to tattoo a soap bubble. The next morning, Saturday, the national bank was hit by a fierce run, and on the afternoon of the same day, the directors agreed to the terms Marriner had proposed for the merger. Among other things, the terms included the acquisition by the First Security Corporation of the Deseret Bank Building and land for $500,000.

Three steps of a legal nature had to be taken, and the first was completed after a round of long-distance telephone calls to Washington where the Comptroller of the Currency approved the consolidation of the two national banks. The next two steps, however, were sticky. The law required a four-weeks' notice to stockholders of both banks, calling them to vote on the proposal. It required the approval of two-thirds of the stockholders present at such a meeting. However, the law on the books bore no relationship to the practices in action. Marriner and his associates had to carry out their plan within the thirty-six hours between Saturday afternoon and Monday morning—and the stockholders of the Deseret National Bank were scattered.

In the hours of grace that remained, while a desperate effort was made to secure written pledges from the stockholders of the Deseret National Bank, other logistical matters were attended to. Armored cars were readied to move the money, security and books of the Deseret National Bank to the

National Copper Bank. The Salt Lake City police department was alerted to provide guards and escorts. The staffs of the two national banks were subject to a crash training program for the struggle that would start Monday morning. A teller from the Deseret National Bank would stand side by side with one from the Copper National Bank, so that the customers of the former institution would feel at home in a new setting. Above all, the critically important news story was prepared by Bennett for readers at the Monday morning breakfast table. The story was not to be released to the newspapers until word had been received that the necessary two-thirds of the stockholders of the Deseret National Bank approved the merger.

Bennett posted himself in the offices of the *Salt Lake Tribune,* the largest newspaper in the Intermountain region, and whose presses normally begin to roll at ten o'clock in the evening. The press run was delayed until Bennett received word from Marriner that written approval for the merger had been secured. The editors and reporters of the *Tribune,* on their part, fully understood that the fate of Intermountain banks would largely depend on how they handled the story about the Deseret Bank. The headline which they prepared was designed to have an instant calming effect. It read: "FIRST SECURITY CORPORATION TAKES OVER DESERET NATIONAL BANK AND MERGES IT WITH ITS AFFILIATE THE NATIONAL COPPER BANK." The story underneath, in the same key, implied that the First Security Corporation, with its many arms throughout the intermountain region, was so strong that it could take over the oldest and most conservative bank in the territory, as a matter of ordinary business routine. The First Security neither feared nor could be affected by a bank panic.

Even as this tranquilizer was rolling off the presses, the funds, securities, and books of the Deseret National Bank were moved to the National Copper Bank. The auditing staffs of the First Security Corporation had to merge the books of the two institutions between midnight on Sunday and the next morning when the newly merged banks were due to open. The deadline was met with two hours to spare. At seven o'clock that Monday morning, when Marriner was at a desk in the National Copper Bank, the chief auditor of the First Security Corporation brought him a consolidated balance sheet. It reinforced Marriner's certainty that there would be no run on the merged banks. He returned to his hotel for the first decent sleep in a week.

All other banks in town experienced a run. The one at the Zions Savings Bank, owned by the Mormon Church, lasted for three days. There was no run, however, either at the newly merged banks, or at any other banks in the First Security Corporation network.

When it was clear by the late afternoon of that Monday that the First Security Corporation had surmounted a fatal threat, Marriner left Salt Lake City for Ogden. He had saved the shirts of many people as a result of his week's effort, and was at last free to change his own. Later, the nature of the merger and the way the event itself was announced to the public had effects throughout the Intermountain region which exceeded his highest hopes. Because the First Security Corporation appeared to have been immune to the financial panic in Salt Lake City, there was a surge of public confidence in all the banks owned by the corporation. This experience, and the lessons Marriner and his associates had learned in the crucibles of Ogden and Salt Lake City, enabled them to ride out explosive situations elsewhere.

A representative case occurred in Boise, Idaho, which had three banks. One of these, the Boise City National Bank, locally owned with no affiliates, was closed by a run on August 1, 1932. The remaining two banks were the First Security Bank which was part of the First Security Corporation's network, and the Idaho First National, the mother institution for a family of nine affiliated banks in Idaho, all owned by a corporation of which Crawford Moore was the head.

On Saturday, August 27, Moore informed Lynn Driscoll, president of the First Security Bank in Boise, that he meant to close all the banks in his chain. Driscoll at once contacted E. G. Bennett in Ogden, who in turn prevailed on Moore to withhold any irrevocable action until he came to Salt Lake City to see "if something could be worked out" with the Federal Reserve Bank and the local office of the RFC. Nothing was settled by that visit, but when Moore got back to Boise on Tuesday night, it was arranged that he and Senator William E. Borah of Idaho would talk by telephone the next morning with the whole of the RFC board in Washington. It was also arranged that the results of the telephone conversation on Wednesday morning would be immediately conveyed to Driscoll.

It was later learned that Moore agreed to keep his banks open on condition that the RFC do for him what it had done for the Charles Dawes bank in Chicago—namely, to advance whatever funds were needed to meet depositor demands. The RFC refused to go along with the proposal, and Moore abruptly closed every one of his Idaho banks without informing Driscoll beforehand of his action. In fact, Driscoll first heard of the news when someone interrupted a meeting he was having with the governor of Idaho to say that the closing of the Moore banks was being broadcast on radio. This left the First Security Bank the only bank remaining open in Boise, while the other banks of the First Security Corporation were the only ones still open in three smaller Idaho towns where Moore had also closed his banks.

Driscoll rushed out of the governor's office to await the inevitable onslaught of fear-crazed people bent on withdrawing their deposits from the First Security Bank. Several days previously, he had taken the precaution of getting $500,000 in currency from the Federal Reserve Bank in Salt Lake City. This was on hand. But he had also ordered an additional $500,000 in currency which was scheduled to arrive that Wednesday morning. When he reached the First Security Bank, he sighed with relief on being greeted by two "guards" who had made the trip from Salt Lake City, ostensibly to protect the currency in transit.

"We are here," said they.

"I see that," said Driscoll. "Where's the money?"

"It is supposed to be here," the guards said.

It turned out that the additional $500,000 in currency had not been put on the train in Boise. It was still in the Railway Express Office back in Salt Lake City. Driscoll at once telephoned the Federal Reserve Bank there and demanded that a plane be chartered to bring the currency up immediately. This being agreed to, he promptly issued a statement to the Boise public: "We can stand a run of any duration. We have wired for a great additional supply of currency to add to the emergency supply already on hand." At the same time he called Harry Hopfgarten, a local sign painter, and dictated the text of a sign he was to produce as quickly as possible on the largest canvas on hand. Before the paint was dry, the huge banner Hopfgarten completed was unfurled from the second story windows of the First Security Bank:

> FOR THE BENEFIT OF OUR PATRONS THIS
> BANK WILL BE OPEN UNTIL LATE TONIGHT.
> IF YOU WANT YOUR MONEY, COME AND GET IT.
> J. L. Driscoll, President, First Security Bank.

The banner both taunted and reassured. It seemed to say that regardless of how much money was withdrawn by depositors, the bank was in a position to pay out funds in an unruffled way as if it had been empowered by the United States Constitution "to coin money and regulate the value thereof." The audacious gesture, which had behind it the prestige the First Security Corporation won during bank runs in other cities, helped lower but did not break the fever of fear. There was more to be done before the temperature of depositors returned to normal. Driscoll assumed that much of the money withdrawn from the bank would go into Postal Savings, and the assumption was confirmed by a telephone call to his friend Harry Yost, Boise's postmaster. Yost, on his own, volunteered a suggestion which was gratefully accepted and acted upon. Every half hour, he brought in Postal Savings currency through the back door of the bank and deposited it in the postmaster's account, thereby supplying more money for the bank's use.

Meanwhile, at the height of the run, Senator Borah fought his way through the mob in the bank to reach Driscoll's office where he offered to give a speech of reassurance to the depositors. It was Driscoll's private view that a senatorial pronouncement would heighten the panic rather than decrease it, but he cited other grounds for politely turning down the offer of an oration by Borah.

A different order of individual reactions later became the source of legends repeatedly told to the sound of laughter in a time of tranquillity, but deadly serious at the moment of occurrence. One customer, for example, after advancing to the teller, declared: "If you've got my money, I guess I really don't want it. But if you haven't got it, then, by God, I want it now and in full!" In another instance a wealthy widow withdrew $75,000 in one bundle during the afternoon, could not sleep during the night for fear robbers would take it, and brought the bundle back early the next morning still unopened. There were also local variants of the mindless decisions Marriner had witnessed during the bank runs in Ogden and Salt Lake City. At the height of the commotion in Boise, some depositors who withdrew their savings promptly converted the currency into cashier's checks in the innocent belief that the checks would be honored at their face value even if the bank closed.

The run lasted two days, but by the late afternoon of the first day, Wednesday, August 31, Driscoll could see that the bank was going to weather the hurricane. The chartered plane flying from Salt Lake City with $500,000 in currency had safely landed in Boise, and the First Security Bank was out of danger. That night, Driscoll, in a gesture of confidence, had the employees of the bank serve sandwiches and coffee to depositors who were still waiting in line to withdraw money. By the end of Thursday, many people sheepishly stood in line to redeposit the savings they had withdrawn the previous day. There were no runs on First Security banks in other Idaho towns where Crawford Moore had closed his banks.

IV

No bank of the First Security Corporation ever closed during the Great Depression, and no depositor in them lost one cent on his deposits. Yet to "keep liquid" Marriner and his associates were compelled to adopt harsh and distasteful credit and collection policies. "Living with yourself under the circumstances," Marriner later recalled, "was a daily ordeal. I cursed the accidents of fortune that had put me into the banking business in the first place."[15]

His conscience was scarred by the cold-blooded policies he pressed home in order to keep the banks of the First Security Corporation open. His conscience was no less scarred by the answer he gave at the end of a pathetic telephone conversation with his half brother David. After their contest came to an end in the early 1920s, Marriner had no further contact with him until a day in the summer of 1932 when his half brother, then living in Portland, Oregon, called him. David had lost all the property he had ever owned, was heavily in debt, and his credit was exhausted. The furniture in his home was the only possessions he had left, and he was about to lose that. Could Marriner help him out? "I would if I could," was the reply, "but I can't."

The effects of the depression on First Security are made vivid by a comparison of the statements issued between 1930 and 1933. The total earnings for subsidiary companies had dropped from $715,032 in 1930, to only $33,583 in 1933, less than 4 per cent of what they had been three years previously. In 1931, six banks in the First Security System were reported to be losing money.[16] Of the twenty-six banks in the system, fifteen were running at a loss by 1933. And Marriner's headaches were not confined to the banking business. They extended to the affairs of the Amalgamated Sugar Company where an internal struggle, which had been underway since 1929, was aggravated by both disasters of nature and equally disastrous conditions in world markets.

Between 1920 and 1929, control of Amalgamated's management passed from Horace Havemeyer to Henry H. Rolapp. From there it passed into the hands of Marriner's half brother, Joseph M. Eccles, representing the David Eccles Company—the largest holder of common stock in the enterprise. In 1929, however, the David Eccles Company, along with the Mormon Church—the second largest single stockholder—sold their stock to the American Beet Sugar Company. That, in turn, gave S. W. Sinsheimer, the new president of American Beet, control of Amalgamated.

As part of the latter shift, it was agreed that minority interests would get one share of American Beet common for every eight shares of Amalgamated common which they turned in. But after securing American Beet common for the Eccles Investment Company, Marriner sold the American Beet common and used the proceeds to buy Amalgamated preferred stock. It was an 8 per cent preferred that had not paid any dividends for twelve years. Amalgamated preferred stockholders had the right to elect five directors to Amalgamated Sugar's board, and the common stockholders ten. Marriner became one of the five elected by the preferred stockholders to the board of the Amalgamated Sugar Company. He was thus in a position to watch and eventually to capitalize on a growing estrangement between S. W. Sinsheimer and H. A. Benning—a man who played a major role in the subsequent development of Amalgamated Sugar. Benning had been a district manager of Amalgamated Sugar Company in the early 1920s, but left to join the Holly Sugar Corporation when Sinsheimer became its president. When Sinsheimer left Holly in early 1929 to assume the presidency of American Beet, he induced Benning to go along on the promise that he would be made vice-president and general manager of American Beet. Benning was given the title, but his managerial activities were confined to the production end of the business. Sinsheimer, who had moved the headquarters of Amalgamated from Ogden to his own Denver base of operations, could not, or would not, honor all the terms of his promises to Benning. Board meetings were marked by acrimonious exchanges between the two men.

Marriner formed a high regard for Benning's executive abilities, and was convinced that they merited a wider scope for action than the narrow one allowed him by Sinsheimer. Benning welcomed Marriner's help in getting other directors representing preferred stockholders to support a move to separate Amalgamated's management from that of American Beet. The separation was successfully completed in mid-June 1932, and the general office was returned from Denver to Ogden. American Beet continued to control the common stock, but Amalgamated became an autonomous operating unit with Benning as vice-president and general manager, and with Marriner as vice-president and treasurer. When Sinsheimer died in 1933, Amalgamated's common stock held by American Beet was acquired by the American

Crystal Sugar Company, but in 1936, Marriner and Benning brought it back in full to Amalgamated's own control.

Cutting across the struggle for the control of Amalgamated were the consequences of a drastic drop in the price of sugar. The world price of raw sugar fell to less than one cent a pound in May 1932, and the United States price reached a low of less than three cents a pound at about the same time. Cuba, the main supplier of cane sugar, had long received special protection in the American market, while the sugar produced in Puerto Rico, Hawaii and the Philippines was admitted duty-free. But the cataclysmic fall in sugar prices—Amalgamated lost in excess of $500,000 in 1932—fueled a move on the part of domestic producers of cane and beet sugar alike to raise tariff barriers against Cuban sugar. The immediate consequences were a new paralysis of Cuba's one-crop economy, an outcry from American investors in Cuban sugar production, a crippling of Cuban trade with the United States, and a loud protest from American manufacturers whose products entered into that trade. As in the case of American banks, every interest in the sugar industry, in its fight for life, pursued self-protective policies which served only to increase the common peril.

To break the pattern of the war of each against all, Marriner led an attempt to bring together all elements of the sugar industry—domestic and foreign producers of cane sugar, and domestic producers of beet sugar—in the hope of reaching an agreement on a sugar policy that would serve three concurrent purposes: to maintain a healthy domestic industry of limited size, to promote America's general export trade, and to assure adequate sugar supplies (whether from foreign or domestic sources) to consumers at reasonable and stable prices. His first attempts in this direction—hinged to an agreement on an "allotment plan"—foundered when various elements in the industry insisted on using every weapon at hand in the hope of gaining an advantage over a rival element. It would not be until 1934, when Congress passed the Jones-Costigan Sugar Act, that the "allotment plan" Marriner advocated became official United States sugar policy.

12. Self Cross-Examination

I

IN THE MIDST OF CRISES, Marriner subjected himself to a searching cross-examination. What could be said about the conduct of bankers like himself in times of panic and depression? In their efforts to "keep liquid" under the pressures of deflation, weren't they driving prices down further, by forcing the liquidation of loans and securities to meet depositor demands? Didn't that in turn make it increasingly hard for debtors to pay back what they had borrowed from the banks? By their policies of credit stringency in time of drastic deflation, weren't they garroting an economy that was already gasping for breath? Wouldn't a rational credit policy be the reverse of the one which he and other bankers followed? Wouldn't it call for monetary ease in time of deflation, and a tightening of credit in boom times? But how could individual bankers act on what reason said should be done when the economy was contracting?

In answer to his own questions, Marriner concluded that "bankers, as individuals, were powerless to reverse the policy of credit stringency. Each did what he thought he must do if he wanted to keep his own bank open. Each, however, in seeking individual safety, contributed to the collective ruin."

What policies could bankers pursue in the public interest without risk of self-destruction? In his search for an answer, Marriner no longer accepted on faith what established business and financial leaders in the East, along with their "kept" journalists and economists, had to say about how the nation had got into the Great Depression and how it could get out of it. Now, at last, the skepticism and the analytical powers he had previously confined to things in the private economic realm were brought to bear on the condition of the public economic realm. His new skepticism was prefigured in a speech he gave on March 26, 1931, to the Bank Management Conference in Salt Lake City, where his words and tone were in striking contrast to the note of automatic progress he had struck six years previously in his presidential address to the Utah Bankers Association. He now said:

The solution of the depression is not an easy one and will not correct itself as some people like to believe. If it were simply a condition of psychology which existed only in the minds of people and due only to a state of nerves, or if all that was needed was the optimism which has been pumped into the air in vast quantities by political and business leaders for more than a year, then our problem would be much simpler. But industrial depressions cannot be cured by any such shallow remedy. The causes lie too deep and are too complex and widespread to be removed easily. Before we can begin to think in terms of permanent cure and before we can be assured that whatever we accomplish is more than temporary, it will be necessary for us to face more frankly than we have some fundamental economic facts upon which our modern business structure is based.

He still had a considerable distance to go before he reached a coherent view about the causes of the depression and its cures. But, driven by his skepticism on the one side and by the spreading contagion of economic disaster on the other, he proceeded step by step, in the months ahead, to an internally consistent body of ideas concerning the plight of the national economy.

First, he dismissed as false all that he heard said—as if in a posthumous echo of his father's voice—about how self-corrective forces would appear in the economy when values had been deflated, and the debt structure had been scaled down to meet existing price levels. He also dismissed as false the collateral saying that when that condition was reached, the men who still had money and credit would make new investments on the "Western" or on the "technological" frontier. Marriner observed that the Western frontier had largely ceased to exist. Its development in the first instance—by men like his father—was based on ready access to free and cheap land, to an abundance of cheap raw materials, and to cheap immigrant labor. None of those elements was present in the thirties. As for investment on the technological frontier, Marriner observed that developments in this field tend to coincide with times of high prosperity when the mass of people have the purchasing power for more than subsistence requirements, and can increase their effective demands for a higher standard of living. But in the 1930s, when millions of people lacked the purchasing power to meet their barest needs, were there any rational grounds on which one could anticipate new investments on the technological frontier? Marriner could see none. What he saw instead were unemployed men arriving on the site of Boulder Dam, where they offered to work for only food and lodging, without asking for the going wage of fifty cents an hour.

In the case of existing domestic producers, for example, he could see no need for new productive facilities when the yield of existing mines, factories and farms could not be absorbed—since potential consumers lacked the money to buy the things produced by the existing economic plant. Further, given the rate at which debts were being liquidated in the early 1930s, the parallel reduction in creditor claims would result in a further decline in prices. Marriner observed that if all debts could be scaled down overnight in line with economic necessities, as was possible in a country like the Soviet Union, then the problem of maintaining employment in the face of a drastic liquidation of debts and a reduction of prices would be much simpler. But under capitalism, to bring debts in line with economic necessities would require the further liquidation of banks, of insurance companies, and of all credit institutions—leading in turn to an increase in the hoarding of money, a decrease in the speed with which it turned over, and an endless deflation.

Marriner also attacked head-on the widely held view among business and financial leaders that depressions were due to God-made economic laws, and that for human beings to interfere with those laws amounted to blasphemy. That is what his father had believed. Yet in a critical reappraisal of his father's career, and his own as well, Marriner concluded that economics expressed itself in multiple ways, each of which posed its own questions of choice. At the core, however, it consisted of the production and distribution of the wealth created when labor, capital, and managerial talents were applied to raw materials. It was all man-made.

I saw at this time [so Marriner later recalled] that men with great economic power had an undue influence in making the rules of the economic game, in shaping the actions of government that enforce those rules, and in conditioning public attitudes towards those rules. I did not want to politicize every aspect of economics. I wanted the widest latitude left to the individual to make his own economic decisions, whether they might be wise or foolish. But I no longer believed that the rules of the market place were Holy Writ. The rules were made by men who had special interests of their own to serve or protect. If this was true, then my own reason said that *all* the people, and not just a favored few, had an equal right to share in the *political* process by which economic rules are not only made but changed.

At this point in his self-examination Marriner seized upon the current writings of William T. Foster of the old team of Foster and Catching. As an economic heretic of the twenties, Foster was far quicker in gaining his feet after the Great Crash than were the grand figures of academic economics—Taussig, Ely, Mitchell, Commons, Seligman. For if the crash and depression could have been predicted in terms of what Foster had to say about the gap between production and consumption, then presumably his theory about consumption also pointed to the way out of the depression.

Foster expressed his views in little more than skeleton form. But among the points he made, two were of seminal importance. First, he argued that the breakdown in the economy was not due—as was widely believed—to America's riotous spending instead of saving in the twenties. "Far from having been profligate," said he, "the nation wasted its substance in riotous saving." Industry stops making goods and hiring labor "solely because it cannot sell the goods." Second, he argued that the only sound way speedily to stop the depression was to increase total pay rolls and thereby increase effective purchasing power, which would not revive of its own accord. It was folly to wait until the "lazy fairies" of private enterprise put the necessary currency and credit in circulation. When private enterprise failed, public enterprise was the only remaining resource. "We can," said Foster, "restore consumer purchasing power by collective action, and in no other way. Collective action means, necessarily, action by the Federal Government." It should deliberately increase the national debt, "as far as is necessary to restore employment and production," by spending freely for all forms of public works, and by tax reductions that could release more money for spending.[17]

These two theoretical points squared sufficiently with Marriner's own practical experiences that he not only enlisted himself on the side of the "underconsumptionists" but also brought to their support a formidable mass of personal information. He observed that while there had been a 10 per cent decline in prices between 1921 and 1929, the inflation in the stock market was financed mainly out of the surplus funds that corporations and wealthy individuals accumulated in the twenties. The latter supplied most of the credit that enabled the public to purchase on a low-margin basis the inflated stocks many of these same corporations and wealthy individuals were offering for sale. But he had more impressive proofs to offer of the nation's thriftiness in the twenties:

We replaced by a very large margin every physical loss we had suffered in the war. We more than balanced a four billion dollar annual budget. We paid off seven billion dollars in government debts. We made four major reductions in income tax on the eve of elections. We extended ten billion dollars of credit to foreign countries in the form of surplus production shipped abroad. We added approximately one hundred billion dollars in physical properties to our national wealth—this, in the form of millions of new homes and apartment houses, thousands of new office buildings, hotels, and other commercial structures. We laid down a cross-country network of new roads to serve the automobile industry that had more than doubled its output. We vastly expanded our entire public-utility industry. We greatly increased our oil-production and distribution system to supply the growth of the automobile industry. In addition, our religious, education and social institutions as well as our cities and state governments greatly improved or expanded their facilities. This vast effort was not the work of a profligate economy. It was the result of an economy that in the aggregate was, if anything, too thrifty.[18]

In a young and expanding economy, it was quite proper to withhold larger portions of currently produced wealth—by restricting immediate consumption—to provide the means for future progress. That is what his father had done in his day. But a point had been reached at which further advances in the national income and in the standard of living, even the maintenance of the existing standard, depended on finding an adequate outlet for the nation's savings. Savings invested in new enterprises are beneficial not only to investors but also to the entire economy; savings that accumulate as idle funds interrupt the flow of national income and result in a depression.

Mass production, he said, must go hand in hand with mass consumption. Mass consumption, in turn, implies a distribution of wealth—not of existing wealth, but of currently produced wealth—to provide men with buying power equal to the amount of goods and services offered by the nation's economic machinery. But, in place of the desired distribution, a giant suction pump had, by 1929–30, drawn into a few hands an increasing portion of currently produced wealth. This served them as capital accumulations. By taking purchasing power out of the hands of the mass consumers, the savers denied to themselves the kind of effective demand for their products that would justify a reinvestment of their capital accumulations in new plants. Consequently, as in a poker game when the chips become concentrated in fewer and fewer hands, other players could stay in the game only by borrowing. When their credit ran out, the game stopped.

That, said Marriner, is what happened in the twenties. The high levels of employment were sustained by a 50 per cent increase of private debt outside the banking system. The funds involved came from the large growth of business savings, as well as the savings of individuals, principally in the upper income groups, where taxes were relatively low. The exceptional expansion of private debt outside the banking system at high interest rates largely took the form of mortgage debt on housing, office and hotel structures, consumer installment debt, brokers' loans and foreign debt. The stimulant to spending by this kind of debt creation was short-lived. It could not be counted on to sustain high levels of employment for long periods. If current income from the national product had been distributed more evenly—if there had been less saving by business and the rich and more income in the lower groups—the economy would have been far more stable. If, for example, the $6 billion that corporations and wealthy individuals had loaned for stock-market speculation had been distributed to the public in the form of lower prices or higher wages, the economic collapse that began at the end of 1929 might well have been prevented.

When no more poker chips were available for loan on credit, debtors were forced to curtail their consumption in order to apply the margin saved to the reduction of outstanding debts. But, with the reduction of demand and the onset of underconsumption, prices fell—which increased unemployment, further decreased the consumption of goods, further increased unemployment, led to another fall in prices, wiped out earnings, forced rigid economies in the wages, salaries and work time of those employed—leading to a situation in which one third of the entire working population was unemployed and the national product was reduced by 50 per cent. Yet the aggregate debt burden when measured not in dollars but in current values and income, representing the ability to pay, was greater than ever before. Fixed charges, such as taxes, railroads and other utility rates, insurance and interest charges, clung close to the 1929 level and required such a portion of the national income to meet them that the amount left for the consumption of goods was not sufficient to support the population.

This, then, was Marriner's diagnosis of the economic pathology that brought on the Great Depression. In what direction did the cure lie?

The leaders of the business community believed in a solution that had the charm of esthetic simplicity: "Balance the federal budget by cutting expenditures, restore confidence and all will be well." If the government ran into debt and its credit was imperiled, it would "shake the confidence of businessmen," and they would hesitate to make the new investments needed to restore the national economy. On the other hand, if the government continued to spend money at the pace then current, it could cover the costs only by borrowing money or by increasing taxes. Either would shake confidence. An increase in taxation in an economy already strained would kill off any inducement to businessmen to take the risk of investing new money in productive enterprises.

The argument had the ring of a maxim, but did it really make sense? Marriner concluded that it did not. "Confidence," he said, "is not a cause. It is an effect. The 'lack of confidence' was nothing more than an investor's sensible conclusion that new plant facilities were not needed at that time —that the existing plant was overbuilt when judged by the low level of effective consumer demands for the output of that plant." So, too, in the case of the arguments about the need to balance the federal budget. "An unbalanced budget," Marriner said, "reflected a deep-seated unbalance in the economy. If the economy were balanced first, then the task of balancing the government's books would be simplified."

Marriner formulated a tenet that became central to his approach to fiscal policy in the years ahead—and to which he consistently adhered:

A policy of adequate government outlays at a time when private enterprise is curtailing its expenditures does not reflect a preference for an unbalanced budget. It merely reflects a desire and the need to put idle men, money, and material to work. *As they are put to work, and as private enterprise is stimulated to absorb the unemployed, the budget can and should be brought into balance, to offset the danger of a boom on the upswing, just as an unbalanced budget could help counteract a depression on a downswing. Timing and method are the essence of the problem in either case.*

He had in mind minimal government expenditure that could generate as rapidly as possible a maximum amount of private expenditure. It was wrong, he said, to conceive of the federal government as though it were an individual, a family, a corporation, a city or a state—each of which "could end in the poorhouse" if its outlays exceeded its income for any length of time. The federal government was in a fundamentally different position from any of these. It alone had the lawful power to make and change the rules of the economic game as national needs required. It alone had the power to issue money and regulate credit, and thus to influence the price structure. Through its taxing power, it alone had the means to control the accumulation and distribution of wealth nationally. It alone had the power to mobilize the resources of the whole nation for the benefit of all the people in it.

Marriner went on to observe that during World War I, when there was no depression, there was a deficit of $9 billion in the federal budget for 1918 and $13 billion in 1919. Why, he asked, was there no outcry then about the need to balance the budget? Why was there no unemployment at the time? Was it consistent for political and financial leadership to demand a balanced budget in the depths of the depression—to balance it by inaugurating a general sales tax that would further diminish the buying power of the people? Was it necessary to conserve government credit to a point where millions of Americans would be reduced to a starvation level of existence? Was the "lack of confidence" in any way due to an unbalanced budget?

Assuming it was not, what, then, would create the kind of economic situation to yield profits that could be taxed to balance the budget? One answer, spoken in a loud voice at the time, called for monetary inflation to help raise the price level. It was specifically demanded that the price of silver be set in relationship to gold under a system of bimetallism and that the dollar be devalued in terms of gold by increasing the price of gold. These measures, it was argued, would raise prices, enable debtors to pay off what they owed, invite new investments, increase employment and so on in a chain reaction of blessings.

But would all this follow?

Marriner answered that they would not. "Monetary inflation," he said, "would have little effect upon the purchasing power of the nation, which alone could increase demand and raise prices. It would not create jobs or put money in the hands of those who didn't have them. Foreigners who sold their gold or silver to America would acquire more dollars with which to buy American goods, but the amount of gold and silver foreigners sold to America even at increased prices would have only a negligible effect on the American economy." True, the sale of gold would increase bank reserves and therefore strengthen the basis for bank, as well as federal reserve, credit. "But this would not revive the economy, since the gold currently held by the Federal Reserve was already in excess of what was needed to meet the banking system's demands for credit."

Marriner capped his analysis by affirming that the only way to get the nation out of the depression was through governmental action that could quickly place purchasing power in the hands of the people who needed it. This proposition did not stand alone but was related to a larger credo he had begun to formulate.

The main concern of the American economy, he said, was to assure maximum employment to all its members. "Under capitalism, private enterprise must be the main means to that end. Government can and should insist on minimum standards of decency in the mode and conditions of life for its people. Within the limits of the nation's resources, it can and should insist on a minimum income for its families; a minimum age for schooling and employment; a maximum age for retirement; decent and safe working conditions; increasing benefits for labor as productivity increased; adequate protection and security for the aged and unemployed; and adequate educational, health and recreational facilities." These standards of honesty and decency could and should be set by the government. "But in the final analysis they must, under capitalism, be enforced and supported by the productivity of the business community itself."

Government, under capitalism, could not and should not do more than care for those individuals left unprovided for, owing to a failure in the private-enterprise system. "It should undertake this task in a way that would not displace or compete with private activities. But it can put idle men, idle funds, idle productive facilities, and unused material resources to work in socially useful ways." It could provide roads, bridges, public housing, educational facilities, hospitals and many other necessities of modern civilization that private enterprise could not be expected to provide. "These tasks of construction should be pursued in increased or lesser degree according to the greater or lesser degree to which private activity absorbed the unemployed and used available money, credit and material resources in pursuit of its own ends." Government efforts of the kind indicated were warranted not only for social and cultural reasons but also for hard-headed economic reasons. "The efforts comprised the only way for maintaining an equilibrium between the goods and services we are able to produce, and the effective demand for those goods as presented by mass purchasing power. The federal government alone has the taxing power and the borrowing power to redirect unused savings back into channels where they will fan out and provide the mass purchasing power on which an economy in our advanced technological state depends for its health."

II

Marriner was now forty-two years old. In the preceding two decades, the organizing principle of his life had been the pursuit of money for himself and the increase of wealth for the members of his family whose economic affairs he managed. By very rough expedients, he had succeeded, during the first years of the Great Depression, in surmounting the immediate dangers to his family holdings and to the twenty-six banks comprising the First Security Corporation. But he saw with increasing clarity that no matter what he personally did to defend his private world, he was virtually helpless to improve conditions in the economic world around him. As of this time forward, therefore, he was consumed by the idea of balance in the national economy. On all occasions—in encounters with individuals, at luncheons, at board meetings, in public forums—he appeared as a reborn missionary with a cause and a gospel to preach.

He argued again and again that too few people could gain security through individual effort alone; that the average person's security was no greater than the stability of the economy in which he was a participant; that the contemporary problem was one of producing a steady distribution of the goods and services that an advancing technology and a skilled labor force knew how to turn out. Further, unless the income from the national product was currently spent on consumer goods or on new investment of a private or public character, a deflation was likely to set in; while millions of people and tens of thousands of businesses in the country received income and decided how to use it, there was no assurance that they would make a sufficient total expenditure to disburse the total income received; the job of warding off the foregoing kind of trouble was nobody's individual responsibility but everybody's collective responsibility, acting through the organs of the national government.

It was false to pose the great social and political issues of the day in terms of whether or not there would be any government planning or intervention in the economic order. The American economy had reached a stage of development where some kind of government planning and intervention was a prerequisite to survival. The great social and political issue of the day subdivided into two parts: one general, the other specific. How could the political powers of a free society and the economic powers of the private enterprise system be brought into a working relationship so that the needs of the society as a whole would be served, without the imposition of crippling controls over the initiatives of risk-taking entrepreneurs? How could the government foster an economic climate conducive to orderly economic growth in the society as a whole—and to social justice for the individual in it—a climate in which the productivity of the private-enterprise system could continue to be the principal guarantor of maximum employment and an equitable income for the nation's labor force?

The tenor of his many public utterances about these matters is suggested from the following extract of the address he gave in June 1932 before the Utah State Bankers Convention.

Our difficulties are not material; they are due, in my opinion, to the failure of financial and political leadership in the world, and particularly in America. They are due to a failure to be able to use the superabundance of wealth which we have been able to produce. We have failed, in the development of our political and financial system, to keep pace with our economic and scientific development . . .

The theory of hard work and thrift as a means of pulling us out of the depression is unsound economically. True hard work means more production, but thrift and economy means less consumption. Now reconcile those two forces, will you?

There is only one agency in my opinion that can turn the cycle upward and that is the government. The government, if it is worthy of the support, the loyalty, and the patriotism of its citizens, must so regulate, through its power of taxation, through its power over control of money and credit, and hence its volume and use, the economic structure as to give men who are able, worthy and willing to work the opportunity to work, and to guarantee to them sustenance for their families and protection against want and destitution.

Many bankers in his audience were made uneasy by Marriner's blunt statement that only the resources of the federal government were equal to the emergencies of the hour—all the more uneasy because they were in no moral or economic position to throw him out of their midst. They knew, as did other bankers throughout the intermountain region, that though Marriner talked like a dangerous radical and had boldly rejected the economic tenets taught by all their fathers, his banking organization had successfully weathered successive crises precipitated in many instances by the failures of banks headed by orthodox believers.

Some of the bankers nodded their heads in sage agreement when one among them said, "Marriner Eccles is like a poker player. He plays tight and talks loose." Others shook their heads sadly and repeated what a president of a Western railroad said to a friend: "Poor Eccles, he must have had such a terrible time with his banks that he is losing his mind." There were similar reactions from within the First Security Corporation itself, the most surprising of these from E. G. Bennett.

The support he had given Marriner in the intricate maneuvers required to surmount threats to the life of their banking corporation was of inestimable value. Bennett had first hand experience with the deep-seated afflictions in the economy. Yet, speaking on behalf of other directors in the corporation, he said to Eccles: "All of us know you are overwrought by the general economic situation. But you should know that some of the members of the board of directors are deeply disturbed by the views you are expressing. They think you are hurting business, and suggest that in the future, you should be much more careful in what you say. You should avoid giving the impression that you think all is not well in the economy, because it might create a lack of confidence in our banking organization."

"Listen!" Marriner said in a blaze of anger. "The people are not so dumb that they don't know something is radically wrong with our economy. They know our economy is deathly sick, and they expect the leaders of banks to have some idea about how to cure the sickness. If the directors of our organization feel that I'm a liability—if the price of being president of this company means that I will have to think and talk as other bankers are doing, rather than openly voice my own views—then the board of directors better vote themselves a new president." Not long afterward, the nation at large voted itself a new president in the person of Franklin D. Roosevelt.

III

Meanwhile, a group of young men in Ogden had concluded that the popular explanations of both the causes and the cures of the depression were bogus. Members of this group included Robert Hinckley, Abe Glassman, Darill Greenwell and Dean Brimhall (whose wife, Lila, was Marriner Eccles' favorite half sister). They looked to each other for a clearer understanding and, to this end, formed a bimonthly discussion group called the Friedenkers. The name may have been suggested by Hinckley's recollection of a group he had encountered years earlier when serving as a young Mormon missionary in Germany. The Friedenkers stood for a nondoctrinaire approach to the search for truth. They dropped their name, however, after some town wags altered it to the Free-Drinkers. Marriner was invited several times to join in their discussions. They were impressed by his arguments about the causes and cures for the depression, and began to make his case their own. Several members, led by Hinckley, urged him to amplify his voice beyond the confines of Utah and try to get it heard in Washington. Hinckley talked with his uncle, Senator William H. King, and King invited Marriner to be a witness at the Senate Finance Committee hearing set for the last week of February 1933.

Among other things, Hinckley was a regent of the University of Utah and a moving force behind a Chatauqua-type lecture series the university sponsored. Whenever a lecturer was to speak on an economic topic, Hinckley would ask Marriner to come to Salt Lake City for the event. He did so in early February 1933, when one of the lecturers was Stuart Chase, whose felicitous writing style and willingness to examine vaguely charted continents of thought made him a journalist of increasing influence. In 1932 Chase brought together in book form the series of articles he had written for the *New Republic* about the plight of the nation, and his title—*A New Deal*—was to be kidnapped by Franklin D. Roosevelt. Roosevelt, however, being a budget balancer, did *not* kidnap one of Chase's contentions: "Prosperity," he had written, "can never be restored by spending less but only by spending more." Indeed a "rigid programme of economy might so far shatter purchasing power and provoke unemployment that the dole, naked and wholesale, would be the only substitute for revolution."

On the day Chase was scheduled to lecture at the university, it had been arranged that he would also speak to a large group of businessmen at a luncheon meeting to be held in the Hotel Utah. Marriner was among those present. He was poking abstractly at the remains of his dessert when Hinckley announced that Chase had been stalled by a snow storm and would be late. Since the luncheon was due to be over at the announced hour, he would introduce Chase in advance of his arrival and thereby save him a margin of time for the address. There followed a five-minute introduction, at the end of which Hinckley confessed that he had nothing more to say. But, he added, all was not lost: "I know that my good friend Marriner Eccles, who is in the audience, holds some very strong views about the current economic picture and is not shy about expressing them. I am going to ask him to take over until Stuart Chase arrives."

The sparse applause of the uneasy audience was coupled with its audible sigh of resignation. Marriner had no recourse but to rise and talk. His theme was the one he had been repeating over and over again to any person who would stand still long enough to listen. At the end of twenty minutes, though he had just gained the momentum of a good running start, he could tell from a stir at the door that Chase was on the scene. Contrary to his habit when he had something on his mind to say, Marriner stopped in mid-passage and sat down. Chase spoke only briefly, adding that anyone present who wished to hear the full stretch of his views could come to the university for the evening address.

Marriner did not have to wait that long. Hinckley invited him and several other men to join the hungry guest in the hotel restaurant. The party was no sooner seated than Marriner began to cross-examine Chase about the "brain trusters" who were gathering round president-elect Roosevelt. He was particularly interested in Rexford Tugwell, Raymond Molely and Adolph Berle. Perhaps to turn the flank on the cross-examination, Chase said to Marriner, "All right, now, supposing you had a job in Washington, what would you do specifically to achieve recovery? You tell me while I eat."

Marriner proceeded to deliver the full text of the speech he had aborted earlier. As he talked on for the benefit of this visitor from the outside world, Chase, who had written much in years past about Wall Street figures and whose view of them was jaundiced, underwent a change of face. He looked intently at Marriner with authentic surprise: He was hearing things one would least expect from a man who had been introduced to him as a leading banker and businessman. Much less was this to be expected in such a conformist state as Utah, which had nurtured Reed Smoot and kept him in the Senate for thirty years, where he bore himself as the iron high priest of an iron faith in economic orthodoxy. When Marriner was through, Chase remarked that Marriner had carried his economic analysis and action program well beyond the point Chase himself had reached in his writings and speeches. Turning directly to Marriner, he asked, "Why don't you get yourself a larger audience?"

Hinckley mentioned Marriner's date to testify before the Senate Finance Committee. "Well, in that event, " said Chase, "why don't you go up to New York and see Rex Tugwell and have a talk with him about the things you've been telling me? I'll write him a letter to say that you will be calling on him." After a moment of reflective silence, Marriner agreed to make the trip to New York, the shaky financial center of the nation, following the trip to Washington, the center of political paralysis.

III

THE STRUGGLE TO GOVERN

13. Witness for the Future

MARRINER ECCLES, A WESTERNER with no national reputation, was well down on the list of the witnesses who testified in the last two weeks of February 1933 before the Senate Finance Committee. He was prepared to repeat his basic arguments about why a program of deficit financing was an indispensable prerequisite to recovery in a time of serious depression, while a balanced budget or a budgetary surplus was mandatory as an inflation control in boom times. It was one thing, however, to talk that way on his home ground and quite another to repeat it in the financial, intellectual and communication centers of the East, where the Baruchs, Taylors, Atterburys, Houstons, Butlers and Weirs—"with the monotony and persistence of Old Cato"—clamored for a balanced budget, as did the president-elect. Still, as Marriner later observed: "I find pleasure in recalling that if I was a 'traitor to my own class,' I earned the distinction long before Franklin D. Roosevelt was called one."

In his testimony, Marriner went beyond a theoretical analysis of the causes and cures of the depression. He crossed the perilous gray area between theory and practice, and laid out a five-point program for immediate remedial measures, as well as the terms for a long-range program for economic stability.[1] The details of his proposed action programs were parallel with those of certain programs favored by other men around the nation who later played a role of their own on the Washington stage. So far, however, he did not know who they were or where they were to be found; they had not appeared before the committee. Mutual discoveries came later. The main points and the supporting arguments for the first-aid program he advanced were as follows:

Make available as a gift to the states on a per-capita basis at least $500 million to be used during the balance of the year 1933 in assisting adequately to take care of the destitute and unemployed, pending a revival in business.

"We shall either adopt a plan which will meet the problem of unemployment under capitalism," Marriner said, "or a plan will be adopted for us which will operate without capitalism. Private charity is exhausted. Practically all our political subdivisions have reached the end of their tax and borrowing powers. The federal government alone is in a position to act in the present emergency. The minimum of $500 million in federal funds to be pro-rated among the states should be a direct gift, not a loan, and it should be in such amounts that the relief organizations in each state can meet the urgent needs of the unemployed in a more adequate manner than is now the case."

Marriner's suggested figure for emergency federal relief funds was microscopic compared with the need. Yet it met instant objections from members of the committee and particularly from two Democratic senators —David I. Walsh, of Massachusetts, and Thomas P. Gore, of Oklahoma—who were identified with the "liberal" wing of their party. Neither man could understand why the separate states—and especially a wealthy state like New York—could not do what the federal government was being urged to do. In reply to their protests, Marriner delivered a short lecture in civics. "The individual state," he said, "is not sovereign. It has no money-creating powers. It cannot call men to war and provide billions for that purpose. It cannot end a nation-wide depression by using public credit on a national scale. The federal government alone can do this. And the longer it waits before it does it, the greater will be its difficulties when it gets around to doing it."

Increase the amount of government funds $2.5 billion, and more if necessary, for self-liquidating government projects and loans to cities, counties and states for public works on a liberal basis at low rates of interest.

In support of this second proposal, Marriner observed that during the four years of the depression everyone, in an effort to protect himself, did what proved to be wrong for the economy as a whole. "The production of wealth and the consumer's ability to pay," he said, "begins with the payroll and the individual producer of raw material, the agriculturalist. Today we are losing close to $3 billion per month of national income because of unemployment, and this, in turn, makes it impossible for people to purchase the goods necessary to sustain production." No program of governmental economy and of budget balancing was as important as the need to stop the loss of wealth and the human suffering that loss entailed. He recognized that $1.5 billion in federal funds had been granted the RFC for use on self-liquidating public-works projects. It was imperative, however, that the amount be increased by an added billion dollars, and that a separate agency be created to take over all public-works projects from the RFC in order to get money as rapidly as possible into the hands of the consumer. "Emergency speed," he said, "is mandatory," and he proposed ways to cut through "legal obstacles and the red tape of administration."

As an alternative to the self-liquidating public-works problem—an alternative that would more quickly put money back into the hands of consumers—Marriner urged the committee to weigh the merits of his modifications of a plan recently advanced in *Harper's Magazine* by J. W. Daiger, namely that the federal government should pay to the depositors of the nationally chartered banks that had failed the amount of their deposits that were tied up. Those deposits totaled approximately $5 billion. Half of this would probably be recovered or had already been returned to the depositors through the receivers of the closed banks, through advances from other banks or, lately, through the RFC. A bond issue of approximately $2.5 billion would be needed to cover the net loss represented by funds that could not be recovered, but, as Daiger said, this was a "political price" that was worth paying in order to restore credit and confidence in the banking system as a whole.

Marriner's plan, if adopted, would quickly get large sums of money into circulation and into those communities hardest hit by bank crashes. It would re-establish confidence in banks as institutions, lure money out of hoarding, tend to raise prices and spur the necessary flow of money and credit in the economy. The future effect would be greatly to increase the value of the assets taken over from the closed banks, to facilitate their liquidation and thus to reduce the losses incurred in the liquidation process.

The refunding operation should be confined to losses incurred by bank failures during the depression, from 1930 or until the necessary liquidation became effective. Marriner did not want the operation extended backward in time to cover the losses incurred through the failure in the 1920s of many shoe-string banks. Second, he urged that a bank-deposit-guarantee law be incorporated in the refunding measure. Such a law should cover *all* banks, since those that were excluded because of their inability to meet certain banking requirements would have to close. The fact of their exclusion would by itself announce their instability, and depositors in such an institution would swiftly mount a "run" and doom it. But if *all* banks were covered, it would prevent the impression that the banks needing such insurance as the law would provide were only the weak ones.

Each bank should be assessed a necessary percentage of its deposits to provide and maintain an adequate fund to meet losses to depositors. In order not to put a premium on bad banking practices, rules and regulations required for the continuation of the benefits of the fund should be gradually promulgated and enforced over the next few years as business recovers, so that in time a strong banking structure would be developed as a bulwark in future depressions. If banks failed to meet their requirements of eligibility after six months' notice, they would be suspended, which would mean their liquidation; the fund would be drawn on to prevent any loss to depositors. It is not difficult to see in much of the foregoing the outlines of the Federal Deposit Insurance Corporation that was to be established in 1934.

Among Marriner's first-aid measures, one in particular reflected his intimate knowledge of how the woes of the sugar-beet and other farmers in the Intermountain region had spread to the general economy far beyond the limits of the farms.

Adopt the domestic allotment plan so as to regulate production and raise prices in agriculture.

Marriner candidly admitted that the allotment plan—which was meant to bring into balance the costs of the things the farmer sold and bought—was not a perfect solution to that problem. But it appeared to him to be the most practical among various schemes being discussed at the time: "I believe that some form of the allotment plan is necessary as a permanent measure as long as tariff policy is in effect in this country. The allotment plan is no more artificial than the tariff, the money system, and all the regulatory operations in the government. Our whole economic system, in the same sense, is artificial and must out of necessity continue so unless we revert to a primitive society."

Parity between the farmer's role as a producer and that as a consumer, however, was not to be viewed as self-contained. Marriner tied it to another measure:

Refinance farm mortgages on a long-term basis at low interest rates.

Many foreclosures on farm mortgages in default had been prevented by the armed resistance of the farmer's neighbors and friends or by the legislative enactments of farm-debt moratoriums in most of the agricultural states. This gave only temporary relief to the farmer and none to the holder of his mortgage, who was often as hard pressed as the farmer in default. Marriner proposed to meet the two sides of the problem by granting authority to the Federal Land Banks to take over farm mortgages in the amount of $5 billion if that sum was necessary. This would help stop foreclosures, permit the refinancing of the farm debt at greatly reduced annual interest and principal payments on the indebtedness, re-establish farm values and aid in restoring the credit of farmers for essential current requirements.

The benefits were not to run only in one direction. The total farm-mortgages debt of the United States at the time was between $8 billion and $9 billion. Of the total, about $1.5 billion was held by the Federal Land Banks, $500 million by joint-stock land banks and $1.7 billion by the insurance companies. The balance of roughly $4.7 billion was held by private mortgage companies, banks and individuals. It was clear from these figures that any step taken to check the further foreclosure of farm-mortgage indebtedness would be of direct help to farmers and also indirectly benefit their creditors—the banks, insurance companies and purveyors of supplies—as well as the counties and states to which they owed huge sums of taxes on which they had defaulted.

Marriner's proposal was received with indifference by the Senate Finance Committee. But when the Roosevelt administration took office in March 1933, it set up a Farm Credit Administration, backed by governmental financial resources to finance and refinance agricultural needs that were not covered by private credit. This included the refunding of all defaulted farm mortgages, livestock loans and the financing of current agricultural production and farm cooperatives.

The fifth of Marriner's first-aid measures was rooted in his conviction that there was a direct connection between the ramshackle structure for financing World War I debts and reparations and the onset of an acute economic crisis in Europe, which compounded the economic crisis in the United States.

The failure in May 1931 of the Kreditanstalt, Austria's largest private bank, was followed by the closing of banks in Germany on July 14 and 15, as well as bank closings in other countries and the freezing of British short-term assets in Germany. A one-year intergovernmental-debt moratorium, and a "standstill agreement" among commercial banks not to press for repayment of short-term international credits, both proposed by President Hoover, were agreed to in July 1931. But this gave the countries involved only temporary relief, as did strict control of foreign exchanges by Germany and borrowing by Britain and France in the United States. At the same time, the failure of world-famous financial institutions and the widespread closing of banks in a great country could not but render depositors throughout the world uneasy and enhance the desire of bankers everywhere to strengthen their position—without regard to the aggregate effect on their own economies or those of their neighbors.

The chain reaction of foreign difficulties growing out of the way in which war debts and reparations were financed reached a shattering climax on September 21, 1931, when Great Britain abandoned the gold standard after a run on sterling precipitated by France and the Netherlands. In the belief that the United States would also abandon the gold standard, central banks and private persons in a number of foreign countries—most notably France, Belgium, Switzerland, Sweden and the Netherlands—converted substantial amounts of their dollar assets in the New York money market to gold. In the period between September 16 and October 28, this conversion amounted to $725 million, much of which was exported from the United States. The consequent decline in the gold stocks of the Federal Reserve increased the pressures on the reserves of American banks and hence the preexisting monetary stringency.

With all these unsettling factors in mind, Marriner had a special piece of advice to give the committee:

Bring about a permanent settlement of the interallied debts on a sound economic basis, the cancellation of the debts being preferred.

The words were no sooner out of his mouth than Senator Shortridge, of California, leaped up as though he had heard a proposal to fry a missionary and eat him on the steps of the local Methodist church. "What!" he boomed. "Cancel these debts?" And having found his voice, he kept on booming his opposition.

Marriner responded that debts between nations could ultimately be paid only in goods, gold, services or a combination of these. Divorced from all else, foreign debtors might accumulate large dollar accounts to their credit and then, in a panic, convert the dollars to gold, with a shattering effect on the American structure for money and credit. Conversely, foreign debtors were unstrung by the pressures to pay their wartime and other obligations to America, all of which went hand in hand with this nation's restrictive tariff policies. Those who could not sell a sufficient amount of their goods to meet their dollar needs could repay their obligations only by shipments of gold. But the loss of gold in foreign lands forced many of them to go off the gold standard and to depreciate their currencies so that they could produce goods at costs that would offset the effect of the high tariffs. "We thus," Marriner said, "have had a major hand in making the very boomerang that hit us in the pocketbook, if not the head. We must either choose between accepting sufficient foreign goods to pay the foreign debts owed this country or we must cancel the debts. This is not a moral problem, but a mathematical one."

Turning to the long-range economic problems facing the nation, Marriner then proceeded to lay out lines of action necessary to build a strong foundation of institutions and laws in support of orderly economic growth:

There must be a unification of our banking system under the supervision of the Federal Reserve System in order to more effectively control our entire money and credit system. High income and inheritance taxes are essential in order to control capital accumulations and to maintain a better balance than the one existing between consumer purchasing power and capital expansion. In other words, productive capacity should not outrun effective consumer demand, and the tax system is the balance wheel for this undertaking. Moreover, there should be national child labor, minimum wage, unemployment insurance and old-age pension laws. Any of these laws when left to the states merely create confusion and would not meet the situation nationally unless similar and uniform laws are passed by all states at the same time—which is improbable. As a further measure for economic balance, all new capital issues offered to the public, all foreign financing should receive the approval of an agency of the government; this control should extend to all means of transportation and communication so as to insure their operation in the public interest. A national planning board, similar to the industries board during the war, is necessary to the proper co-ordination of public and private activities of the economic world.

By the time Marriner had finished testifying, he had established himself before the Senate Finance Committee as a man endowed with a probing mind and a forceful tongue. With one notable exception, however, none of the committee members on either side of the party line voiced agreement with the major points in Marriner's proposals for recovery. The exception was Wisconsin's Senator Robert M. La Follette, Jr., the son of "Fighting Bob."

It was two years before Marriner gained any personal satisfaction from his session before that committee. In 1935 he was the subject of a long article in *Fortune* by Archibald MacLeish, who mentioned various aspects of the program Marriner had presented in Washington in February 1933, and then added: "Anyone who will translate the latter suggestions into their present (New Deal) alphabetical symbols and compare the earlier general statements of economics with the economics of the present administration will be forced to conclude that M. S. Eccles, of Ogden, Utah, was not only a Mormon but a prophet."

14. Confusion of Tongues

I

BEFORE LEAVING WASHINGTON by train for his New York appointment with Rexford Tugwell, Marriner placed an urgent telephone call to E. G. Bennett in Ogden. Despite the indecision enveloping the question of whether a national bank holiday should be declared, Marriner was convinced that such action on a national scale was inevitable. Bennett, therefore, was to intercede with the governors of Utah and Idaho and have them promptly declare, by executive order, a bank holiday in their respective states, and Bennett got them to do just that.

It was noon when Tugwell appeared in his Columbia University office to meet with the visitor from Ogden. The telegram previously sent by Stuart Chase won a friendly reception for Marriner and an invitation to lunch in a drugstore booth. The setting of food, pills and nostrums was whimsically appropriate for the talk the two men had about the nation's ills.

Tugwell, the son of a prosperous farmer, was then in his early forties, like Marriner. As a member of the student generation at the Wharton School of Finance and Commerce, which produced leaders of the new school of "institutional economists," he believed that the logic of scientific management required the extension of planning from the single factory to the industry and then to the entire economy. The depression had intensified his interest in planning. A national council with advisory powers could not, in his view, do the necessary planning job, since people might try to distinguish between partial and total planning. The logic of all planning amounted, in the end, "to the abolition of business." Profits would have to be limited and their uses regulated, prices controlled, speculative gains eliminated. There would have to be constitutional changes, too, "the laying of rough, unholy hands on many a sacred precedent," doubtless calling for "an enlarged and nationalized police power for enforcement." The dual conflict deepest in our modern institutions would be abated, he said, when industry was government and government industry. It was, he added, "one of the basic reasons why the prospect of a planned economy is congenial to every other hope and belief I have."[2]

Much of the foregoing had been spelled out by Tugwell in his articles, books and public addresses. Sitting opposite Marriner now, he restated it in conversational form. He agreed with his visitor that getting purchasing power into the hands of consumers was a first priority for economic recovery. But, unlike Marriner, he did not believe that the instruments of money, credit and fiscal policy, properly framed and synchronized by government, could revive and save the system of private enterprise. That system, in his view, was beyond redemption.

During lunch, Marriner gave Tugwell a copy of the statement he had made before the Senate Finance Committee. His host read the text and expressed surprise that a banker could urge a program of logical radicalism. "Other than the compliment implied in this reaction," Marriner later recalled, "I thought my meeting with Tugwell, while pleasant and very interesting, would have no sequel. I was mistaken in this belief. I was to hear from him again six months later when, after a synthetic spurt in recovery under President Roosevelt, the cycle of deflation began all over again, and there was no Herbert Hoover near at hand who could be blamed for it."

After leaving Tugwell, Marriner called on George Dern, the former governor of Utah, who was to be the Secretary of War in the new administration. Dern was then at the Commodore Hotel, readying himself for the inauguration. Since Dern was a director of the two Salt Lake City banks that were part of the First Security Corporation (and Marriner was the chairman of Dern's State Committee on Unemployment Relief), the two men could speak freely to each other about creditors and debtors, producers and consumers, and the need not only to check *deflation* but also to promote *reflationary* measures as well. The management of the nation's economy was not to be Dern's affair—though, under his direction later, the War Department proposed many of the projects on which Works Projects Administration funds were spent. Dern expressed interest in Marriner's statement before the Finance Committee and said that he would bring a copy of the text to the attention of interested parties in Washington. With this final piece of missionary work done, Marriner sped back to Utah to deal with the consequences of the bank holiday.

The story of how the institutions of the Federal Reserve System were brought to a point on March 4, 1933, where they joined the commercial banks in the most absolute restriction of payments to depositors ever experienced in American history has been told many times from different perspectives. However, since there would be a direct connection between the moral Marriner Eccles drew from the final collapse, and the reformist work he undertook during his Washington career (and pushed for in the years beyond), it is necessary to focus on certain features in the picture of confusion and indecision visible at the height of the 1933 banking crises.

II

Every major American monetary crisis prior to 1933 was overcome by the leadership of one or more men in or out of government. Between 1914 and 1929, such a man held a strategic post within the Federal Reserve System: He was Benjamin Strong, governor of the New York Federal Reserve Bank and a "banker's banker." While other governors of Federal Reserve banks tended to confine themselves to local and regional matters, the power of the New York financial community gave a national and international reach to Strong's operations. When he acted on behalf of the New York Federal Reserve Bank, he dealt not with the Federal Reserve Board in Washington but directly with the president of the United States and the Secretary of the Treasury. Similarly, it was Strong who spoke for the Federal Reserve System in matters of interest to the European banks in an era when their great central banks were each personified in and dominated by a single individual: Montague Norman meant the Bank of England; Emile Moreau, the Bank of France; Hjalmar Schact, the German Reichsbank. When those men came to the United States with serious business to discuss, they seldom called on the Federal Reserve Board in Washington but put their case to Benjamin Strong, because they knew he had the courage and personal force to make his views prevail among the governors of the 11 other Federal Reserve banks in the nation.

Strong died in October 1928. George L. Harrison, his successor as governor of the New York Federal Reserve Board, seemed well-equipped for his post. He had served between 1914 and 1920 as that board's first legal counsel, and in the next eight years, he had been one of Strong's deputies in New York. He meant to be a leader in the mold of his predecessor and was initially sustained by the aura of Strong's legacy. When the aura faded by the end of 1930, Harrison was thrown back on his natural character as a very competent lawyer, a efficient administrator and a negotiator bent on harmonizing all opposing views about an issue in dispute. Unlike Strong, he had neither the standing in the Federal Reserve System nor the personal prestige outside it to get his policy views accepted in the face of either opposition or inertia. His proposals were repeatedly voted down by governors of the other Federal Reserve banks.

At the same time, the Federal Reserve Board—in a delayed reaction to Strong's bypassing the board and dealing directly with the White House or the Treasury Department—was determined that the New York Federal Reserve Bank should no longer lay down the law for the whole of the Reserve System. However, it was not in a position to make its will prevail. The fault here did not lie with Eugene Meyer, who became governor of the board under emergency conditions in 1930. Meyer was no innocent in the world of high finance, any more than he was made of thistle down. He was a determined man, a master of capital, a brilliantly imaginative banker, and he thought in international terms. Yet the board he had inherited was weak, divided and gave the appearance of serving more as a place of dignified retirement for its aging members than of being the command post for the management of an infinitely complex financial crisis. Its members had no standing in the eyes of the governors of the Federal Reserve banks, who had grown accustomed, in the 1920s, to view the board as a supervisory and review body and not a regulatory agency with a title of right to initiate policies and to secure compliance with them.

The events which led to the final banking collapse were long in coming, but the climactic episodes date from Thursday morning, March 2, 1933, when George L. Harrison, in New York, sent a jarring message to Eugene Meyer and to Secretary of the Treasury Ogden Mills. The foreign and domestic drain of gold, he said, had reduced the New York Federal Reserve Bank's percentage of the gold reserve below the legal limit. Hence he would "no longer take the responsibility" for running the New York Federal Reserve Bank "with deficient reserves in the absence of legal sanctions provided for by the Federal Reserve Act."[3] The Federal Reserve Board, acting in concert with Secretary Mills, replied that it was reluctantly ordering a thirty-day suspension of the gold-reserve requirements set by law. Harrison countered with a message that the suspension would solve nothing, since the New York Federal Reserve Bank would still have to pay out gold and currency to hoarders. The best course, he said, would be to declare a national bank holiday, which "would permit the country to calm down and which would allow time for the enactment of remedial legislation."

But who would take the initiative in declaring such a holiday? It could not come from Mills or Meyer. It could come only from President Hoover—who appeared incapable of any kind of incisive action. Meyer tried but failed to get through to Hoover. He joined Mills in suggesting that Harrison ask Herbert Lehman—who had succeeded Roosevelt as governor of New York—to declare a bank holiday in that state. Now it was Harrison who balked. Even if Lehman agreed to the request, the New York Federal Reserve Bank would still have to pay out gold to foreigners. Besides, to halt all banking operations in New York, the nation's financial center, would make it impossible for the banking system to function in the rest of the United States.

Another set of actors now added their voices to the confusion. Representatives of the Clearing House banks of New York called on Governor Lehman to voice their strong opposition to a bank holiday. Such a holiday, they said, "would hurt their prestige." They would "rather stay open and take their beating." As part of a move to get the Clearing House banks to change their minds and the nature of their pressure on Lehman, Mills telephoned Winthrop Aldrich, president of the Chase National Bank of New York. "It is imperative that you come to Washington," Mills said, "and if you have in your organization a good man, bring him, too—even if he knows nothing about banking but has a lively imagination." Aldrich replied that he had been in Washington the previous day and was reluctant to return. Besides, he was about to leave for a vacation in Bermuda. Mills response was: "If you go to Bermuda, don't get a round-trip ticket—because when you are ready to return, there'll be nothing worth returning to." Aldrich arrived in Washington that afternoon.

The next day, Friday, March 3, the arrival of President-elect Roosevelt in Washington inspired a request that Mills put to Senator James Byrnes, Democrat of South Carolina, a Roosevelt intimate and a member of both the Senate Banking and Currency Committee and the Senate Appropriations Committee. Acting as Mills's messenger, Byrnes asked Roosevelt if he would join President Hoover in a statement to the general effect that there was no reason for the panic spreading among the people; that the country was basically sound; that if the people would have confidence in government, a solution for the banking troubles could be found. Roosevelt promptly and categorically refused. Mr. Hoover, he said, had made so many statements about prosperity's being just around the corner that he had lost the confidence of the people. "If President Hoover doesn't know what to do, I do, and I will do it just as soon as I take the presidential oath of office."[4]

The directors of the New York Federal Reserve Bank adopted a resolution requesting the Federal Reserve Board in Washington to urge President Hoover to proclaim a nationwide bank holiday on Saturday, March 4, but to no avail. When Harrison realized that no bank holiday would be declared by the outgoing president, he joined a conference at Governor Lehman's home in New York City, attended by the New York state superintendent of banks and by spokesmen for the New York Clearing House banks. Harrison reversed his own earlier opposition and affirmed his support for a state holiday. Spokesmen for the Clearing House banks agreed to co-operate if Lehman declared a bank holiday in New York, but they wanted it to be understood that they neither sought nor directly requested the action. Lehman declared the holiday effective March 4, Inauguration Day. Similar actions were taken by the governors of Illinois, Massachusetts, New Jersey and Pennsylvania. On March 4, the Federal Reserve Banks remained closed, as did the leading exchanges.

III

In Washington, many persons in the crowd who had gathered to pay homage to the new leader—and to be the first in line for whatever jobs were available—found that they could not cash checks to pay for food, hotel bills or transportation home.

The new leader did not approach the inaugural stand on a white horse but in a wheelchair. What would happen to American democracy if it turned out that Roosevelt possessed the qualities of an Adolf Hitler or even of a Huey Long. The people did not have to wait long for him to reveal his political character in clear and irrevocable ways. In less than two thousand words of his inaugural address, he made it clear that he was going to press for "action now" on a wide front. The most famous phrase of that speech was "the only thing we have to fear is fear itself." But there were other memorable words that were to gain weight as they crossed the bridge spanning the distance between rhetoric and action in the marketplace:

Our greatest primary task is to put people to work. . . .

In every dark hour of our national life, a leadership of frankness and vigor has met with that understanding and support of the people themselves which is essential to victory. . . .

We do not distrust the future of essential democracy. The people of the United States have not failed. . . .

In the event that the national emergency is still critical . . . I shall ask the Congress for the one remaining instrument to meet the crisis—broad Executive power to wage a war against the emergency, as broad as the power that would be given to me if we were in fact invaded by a foreign foe. . . .

Our Constitution is so simple and practical that it is possible always to meet extraordinary needs by changes in emphasis and arrangement without loss of essential form. . . .

In Ogden, Utah, seated by the radio, Marriner Eccles cheered the spirit that vibrated in Roosevelt's words. He soon had more specific things to cheer. After midnight on March 6, President Roosevelt issued an executive order that proclaimed a nationwide banking holiday, closed all banks and suspended gold redemption and gold shipments abroad. Three days later a special session of Congress received from Roosevelt the text of an Emergency Banking Act, which legitimized the powers he had previously asserted. On that same day, March 9, the act was approved by the Senate with only seven dissenting votes; the House approved it by acclamation after only thirty minutes of debate, and at eight o'clock that night, President Roosevelt signed the measure. Among other things, the Emergency Banking Act provided that banks would reopen only under license by the Treasury; those deemed sound would be opened immediately; those about which there were any questions would be operated by conservators until it was determined that they were completely solvent; hopelessly insolvent banks would be kept closed and liquidated.

In addition to the emergency banking legislation, Marriner also hailed most of the early measures of the New Deal, such as the Emergency Farm Mortgage Act and the Home Owners Loan Act. In his view, however, these worthy emergency actions did not get at the root causes of the economic collapse; they dealt only with the effects. They helped check any further decline in the economy, but they did not of themselves generate an increase in effective purchasing power which could stimulate production and hence create jobs for the unemployed.

As Marriner watched from afar what Roosevelt proposed to do about consumer purchasing power, he was jarred when he read the budget-balancing arguments central to the message Roosevelt sent to Congress on March 10 in support of his proposed Economy Act of 1933. "Too often in recent history," said Roosevelt, "liberal governments have been wrecked on the rocks of loose fiscal policy." He then estimated that the budget deficit for the four fiscal years 1931–34 would probably amount in the aggregate to $5 billion. "With the utmost seriousness," Roosevelt continued, "I point out to Congress the profound effect of this fact upon our national economy. It has contributed to the recent collapse of our banking structure. It has accentuated the stagnation of the economic life of our people. Our Government's house is not in order and for many reasons no effective action has been taken to restore it to order." On this basis, he asked Congress for emergency powers to cut expenditures, especially government payrolls and veterans' benefits for non-service-connected disabilities. "If this were done," he said, "there is a reasonable prospect that within a year the income of the Government will be sufficient to cover the expenditures of the Government."

It was later argued that Roosevelt's desire for a balanced budget, while real enough, was not so high in his scale of values that he was prepared to sacrifice much for it. His immediate concern was to satisfy the public's desire for what it understood to be sound fiscal policy, in contrast to the profligate spending to which the Great Crash was popularly ascribed. Hence, for psychological reasons, he must at once place himself at the head of the economizing, budget-balancing forces. By thus casting a golden glow of fiscal integrity over the whole of the New Deal, he would be better placed to resort to deficit financing as circumstances required.*

It was indeed a "brilliant strategy"—if the basis for judgment is confined to the way orthodox bankers reacted when Congress at an early hour passed the Economy Act of 1933. Thus the National City Bank *Monthly Letter* said that the monetary expansion that would have to accompany the reopening of the banks made a balanced budget doubly imperative in order to avoid inflation. "For this reason," it said, "the grant to the President upon his own demand, of authority to enforce economies necessary to balance the Federal budget, comes at a time when it is of incalculable value. Complementing the banking program, it has renewed confidence in the integrity of the dollar."

Marriner Eccles reached an altogether different conclusion. In his reading, America's economic affairs—if guided by the concepts in Roosevelt's budget-balancing message of March 10—were destined to get worse. He spelled out his views in a circular letter he wrote for distribution among his business associates, copies of which he sent to Rexford Tugwell and Senator Robert La Follette "Referring to the manner in which our new administration is handling the present financial crisis," he wrote, "it seems to me that if the proposed budget-balancing policy is carried out, it can only result in further drastic deflation, a further decrease in buying power and a great increase in unemployment." In the absence of an increase in purchasing power, he continued, employers clearly would not hire men to produce goods and services that couldn't be sold. And no restoration of confidence would take place simply on the basis of a promise to balance the budget. "Unemployed men can be put to work and idle factories can be fully utilized only through government deficit spending on a vast scale, and financing largely by the banks."

*Herbert Stein, in his *Fiscal Revolution in America,* maintains that "however muddled" Roosevelt's early fiscal maneuvers may have seemed and actually were at the time, "in retrospect they look like a brilliant strategy to make possible inflationary, or as we might now say, expansionary action."

In reply to Marriner's letter, Senator La Follette indicated that he was in full agreement and added:

I am devoting such energy and using such contacts as I have in an effort to convince the administration of the absolute necessity of an adequate program and of its being launched as speedily as possible. Time is the most important factor in the situation just now. Whether they realize it or not, the economy bill has launched an engine of deflation which in my humble judgement will create a crisis in the near future unless a program is launched to counteract it.

Senator La Follette was one of a number of people around Roosevelt in the early days of the New Deal who favored a big public-works program, which then meant something like $4 billion or $5 billion. Other people who favored such a program included Senator Robert Wagner, Secretary of Labor Frances Perkins, Secretary of the Interior Harold Ickes, Rexford Tugwell and Hugh Johnson. In general, however, their support of a spending program did not rest either on the idea that temporary spending would prime the pump for sustained prosperity, or on a "multiplier" idea that public spending would generate private spending, which would also create jobs. They simply wanted to increase employment for government contractors, suppliers and hence for workers.

Roosevelt initially resisted all arguments in support of a big public-works program, and his reasons went beyond his real or simulated addiction to a balanced budget. For one thing, he doubted that there were any considerable number of good or useful public-works projects on which the government could wisely spend its money. For another, he did not believe that spending could stimulate the economy to a point where prosperity would be sustained without a continuation of spending. Roosevelt also doubted that public-works spending would provide jobs beyond the number actually employed at the construction site, plus possibly those employed in producing the materials for the project. He was skeptical of an argument about jobs that would be created as a result of the consumption expenditures of the construction workers.

Only the faint echoes of the public-works debate within the administration reached Marriner Eccles in Utah. Roosevelt's budget-balancing policy, however, came through loud and clear, and Marriner railed against that policy with increasing passion. The reasons stemmed from his direct and painful personal encounters with the needs of people in distress. He was the chairman of the Utah Committee on Relief, of which his friend Robert Hinckley was the fulltime manager. In recalling what they faced, Marriner later wrote:

We had strained local private giving to the limit. We could only give inadequate care to the most destitute cases. We could not put people to work, and I failed to see where a balanced budget would change a desperate case for the better. The Mormon church, to its credit, diligently tried to "take care of its own." But within an economy that was prostrate, no organization could be expected to do anything of the kind. . . . Church investments, like investments held by private persons, were un-productive. In fact the Church-owned Utah-Idaho Sugar Company was forced to sell its Canadian factory in order to meet long-overdue payments for sugar beets and to gain working capital in order to keep the company going.[5]

In the first months of the New Deal, the federal government's relief work adhered to the structure inherited from the last days of the Hoover administration, when the RFC was authorized to make available for relief purposes, upon application of the states, a total of $200 million—at 3 per cent interest. The sum, viewed as a loan, was to be deducted from federal road funds when they were later appropriated by Congress and allocated to the states. Moreover, the federal government was responsible only for the bookkeeping and not for the actual application of the funds. For bookkeeping purposes, an Emergency Relief and Construction agency was created within the host body of the RFC. The funds were administered by local private charitable organizations—in deference to the belief that federal relief must be disguised in all possible ways and private enterprise must always provide the cure for any and every ill.

In Utah the funds were administered by the Utah Committee on Relief. Marriner and Hinckley concluded that Utah's share of the $200 million would be only a dew drop compared to need and that the loan would never be repaid to the RFC or taken into account or deducted from the road funds. Hence they should personally try to get all the funds the RFC was willing to grant.*

As I witnessed the course events were taking [Marriner later wrote], I made life uncomfortable for all who came near me. Unlike Hamlet, I did not curse my fate that I was born to set the world aright. I had asked my questions for three years, reached what I thought were true answers and, never being given to modesty, I felt that these answers could set the world aright if only men in high places would listen to them. In this feeling, of course, I was not different from tens of thousands of other Americans who felt their advice was being ignored. From various places in Utah and Idaho where my business affairs took me, my eye raked the nation's capital and I judged every move there for its bearing on the general plan for recovery I had urged in my testimony before the Senate Finance Committee. Any peep from Washington bounced back as a roar from my mountainside.

On March 30, Marriner wrote a long memorandum to Secretary of War Dern, in which he bitterly criticized Roosevelt's budget-balancing biases and restated the reasons why a broad-gauged government lending and spend-

*The initiatives they took met with a critical reaction from Wilson McCarthy, a director of the RFC, a Utahan, an associate in the First Security Corporation and a close friend of both Marriner's and Hinckley's. In the course of an official tour of Western states, McCarthy stopped in Salt Lake City to meet with the Utah State Relief Committee. He said that he was personally embarrassed by the figures, which showed, on a per-capita basis, that his home state used more RFC money than did any other state in the Union. Marriner was neither embarrassed nor apologetic; all that Utah got, he said, was shamefully inadequate.

ing program was essential. Dern informed Marriner that he had discussed the latter's thesis at a Cabinet meeting and had made a special point of calling it to the attention of Secretary of the Treasury Will Woodin. Dern did not think the administration would endorse the policies Marriner advocated.

Administration leaders in those early weeks were aware of the pressing need to restore national purchasing power. The main problem was the question of means, and the decision reached was signaled by President Roosevelt in his press conference on April 19, where he indicated his intention to raise commodity prices through a devaluation of dollars in terms of gold. The theory here was clear enough. If the gold content of a dollar paid for a bale of cotton was decreased, then after devaluation a buyer would have to pay more dollars for the same bale. This price increase would in theory increase the earnings of the cotton producer, and he in turn, having more purchasing power in his hands, would increase his demand for goods—i.e., when less gold was required for purchases expressed in dollars, more purchases would be made by sources having gold, and this would inevitably raise commodity prices and hence purchasing power.

The foremost exponent of devaluation was Professor George Warren, of Cornell University, an intimate of Henry Morgenthau, Jr.'s. Yet, as Professor John Morton Blum has rightly observed in *The Morgenthau Diaries*[6], Warren's theory would not have been embraced by Morgenthau and then by Roosevelt "had there not been a wide spread enthusiasm for inflation and, specifically, for raising the price of gold. Not laymen and politicians only, but many businessmen and professional economists believed in 1933 that depressions were simply the result of a collapse in prices. Given the insistence of Warren's theory that prices varied directly with the price of gold, the conclusion was inevitably suggested that recovery would follow an increase in the price of gold." It was a conclusion shared, for example, by the Committee for the Nation to Rebuild Prices and Purchasing Power, whose leaders included such influential figures as J. H. Rand, Jr., of Remington, Rand; General Robert E. Wood, of Sears, Roebuck; and Frank A. Vanderlip, president of the National City Bank.

Not until ten months after the April 19 press conference was a full and formal devaluation of the dollar enacted by law. But at the time of the conference, Roosevelt was under fierce political pressures to endorse many inflational nostrums. In fact, by the terms of the "Thomas Amendment," Congress had just voted him discretionary powers to issue paper money and provide for the unlimited coinage of silver. Since the same amendment included an authority to devalue the dollar by increasing the price of gold, Roosevelt may have embraced this provision as being the least objectionable course of action and a means of forestalling any resort to the preceding two.

The range of political choices facing the president at the time were not of concern to Marriner. In his testimony before the Senate Finance Committee, he had argued against the devaluation of the dollar as a means for raising commodity prices. Devaluation by itself, he said, was besides the immediate point. Prices could be raised—without any change in the price of gold—if the government created effective consumer demand by increasing purchasing power through a spending program based on deficit financing. His criticism of the devaluation program was later reinforced by references to the monetary measures enacted by Congress in the first days of the New Deal. By those measures, the very few Americans who held any gold were required to turn it back to the banks in exchange for dollars. The millions of destitute and unemployed, however, had neither gold nor dollars. How, then, could an increase in the price of gold that might be exchanged for more dollars lead to more purchasing power, more effective consumer demand and hence to price increases? In Marriner's view, "the results would be nil." The view was to be confirmed by events.

When Marriner read of the devaluation policy and the economy message of March 10, he dashed off an angry letter to Dern, hoping that its point would reach Roosevelt directly:

It seems to me that the government is attacking our economic problems in the usual orthodox manner and I see little fundamental change in the methods they are pursuing and those pursued by the Republican Administration. New York, as usual, seems to be in the saddle, dominating fiscal and monetary policy.

The next day, April 20, Marriner received a telegram from Senator John C. Townsend, Jr., a member of the Senate Banking and Currency Committee. Would he state his views on the question of whether or not Roosevelt's proposal to devalue the dollar would actually help reinflate a depressed economy? Marriner immediately wired back:

Any form of inflation to be effective must involve getting money to the source of consumption. Recommend this be done by five billion dollar government bond issue to be purchased by the Federal Reserve Banks and credit passed to the Treasury Department and not offered to public. Otherwise no inflation would result as no new money would be created. Money thus created to be distributed five hundred million for unemployment relief and all kinds of self-liquidating projects and public works. Also favor refinancing home and farm mortgages at low rate on long-term basis. The above action I believe would effectively bring about controlled inflation.

The continuing ambiguity of Roosevelt's approach to the problems of economic recovery were brought home to Marriner in different ways: In early May, at FDR's request, Congress had appropriated $500 million for direct relief to be allocated to the states by a newly created Federal Emergency Relief Administration. Unlike its predecessor agency—the RFC's Emergency Relief and Construction Agency—the FERA was empowered to make outright grants, rather than loans, at 3 per cent interest. (The change corresponded with a proposal Marriner himself had urged in his testimony before the Senate Finance Committee.) The FERA also differed from its predecessor agency in that it would have at its head a man who seemed to come out of nowhere but whose actions, as Marriner judged them from afar, seemed to flow from a spirit congenial with his own. The man was

Harry L. Hopkins, a trained social worker, who had served under Governor Roosevelt in New York as the head of the state's Temporary Emergency Relief Administration.

On May 22, after seventy-nine of Roosevelt's "first hundred days" had passed, Hopkins was brought down from New York to run the FERA in Washington. The next day, the *Washington Post,* under the headline "MONEY FLIES," stated, "The half billion dollars for direct relief of States won't last a month if Harry L. Hopkins, the new relief administrator, maintains a pace he set yesterday in distributing more than $5,000,000 during his first two hours in office."*

As an onlooker, Marriner approved of this, but he was puzzled by an intervening development. On May 17 Roosevelt submitted to Congress a proposed National Industrial Recovery Act. Title I of NIRA (or NRA, as it swiftly came to be known) had as its object the raising of wages and prices through "planned" production. Businessmen were to agree among themselves—free from the constraints of antitrust laws—on minimum prices and maximum levels of production. In this way, there would be an end to "unfair competition, "chiseling" and "overproduction." As part of the same plan, labor was to agree to a reduction of weekly hours of work in return for an increase in hourly wages. Not only would more work opportunities open up for the unemployed; other benefits would accrue.

In a psychopolitical sense, this aspect of the NRA was legitimized by incorporating into its structure several precedents dating from the War Industries Board under Bernard Baruch. It appeared to combine volunteer cooperative action with government regulation. Second, its price and wage agreements were expressed in "codes" framed on a case-by-case basis for each industry. But how could one increase wage rates more than prices without a depressing effect on profits? The answer called for an increase in the level of spending on public works. Such an increase would lead to a greater *aggregate* volume of industrial production and thereby permit the payment of higher wages without decreasing the *total* profits in the national economy. The line of reasoning here was sealed in Title II of the NRA. It called for an expenditure of $3.3 billion on public works—a figure, reportedly, that was a compromise between the $5 billion program being advocated by some of the president's advisers, and the $900 million program Roosevelt believed was the limit of good and useful public works. FDR went out of his way to clothe the measure in the trappings of "sound" finance. "In carrying out this program," he sternly declared, "it is imperative that the credit of the United States Government be protected and preserved." He therefore proposed that new taxes be raised to pay interest and

---

*In his haste, Hopkins was contemptuous of bureaucratic procedure. When inspectors from the Bureau of the Budget came round asking to see the organizational chart, they were told there wasn't any, as Hopkins would not permit one to be made. "I don't want anybody around here to waste any time drawing boxes," he said. "You'll always find that the person who drew the chart has his own name in the middle box."

amortization on the cost of the program, saying that "careful estimates" indicated that at least $200 million of additional revenue would be required for that purpose.

While Marriner welcomed the external physical facts of the announced program, he could not follow the logic of a fiscal policy whose claim to soundness entailed a tax increase to make deficit financing possible—all in the name of a balanced budget. But a befuddled Congress accepted the soundness of the method and, on June 13, approved the whole of NRA. Meanwhile, though Title I and Title II were conceptually linked on paper, they were not similarly linked in Roosevelt's thinking. Thus, instead of a single administrator he appointed two: General Hugh Johnson was placed in charge of the codes, and Secretary of the Interior Harold Ickes was entrusted with the public-works spending program.

It has been argued that the whole course of the recovery program might have been different had Roosevelt made the appointments the other way around! Ickes, a Chicago reformer and Bull Moose Progressive Republican who had backed Theodore Roosevelt in 1912, was a very careful, deliberate administrator, who took pains to examine personally every detail of every project and the disposition of every nickel that it cost, whether it be a village post office or a Triborough Bridge. He brought to each problem the approach of a hard-headed businessman as well as that of a conscientious public servant. He was concerned about the return on the taxpayer's investment and thought primarily of the finished job. This was hardly to his discredit. Yet, the Ickes approach had the vice of slowing down to a trickle the number of public-works projects that were launched, when what was called for was a tidal wave of projects in a race against time itself.

In this, as in other matters, Marriner did not know the variable factors Roosevelt was weighing. If he was disturbed by the slow progress of the public-works program, he was appalled by the logic behind the NRA codes. In the climate of the hour, it was a risky business openly to attack the structure of the codes. After years of immobility, *something* at last was being done, and to object to that something on the ground that it was wrong-headed was tantamount to being unpatriotic. Nonetheless, Marriner risked being misunderstood. In successive local forums, he frontally attacked the assumptions underlying the NRA.

The NRA has been launched on the premise that the nation is suffering from overproduction. This is false. What appears to be overproduction is, at bottom, a nation-wide case of underconsumption due to the absence among tens of millions of Americans of the effective purchasing power that would enable them to buy the things they desperately need. We are told, furthermore, that the NRA is not monopolistic—that it is merely designed to end cutthroat competition and put people to work. I don't question the integrity or the good will of those who take that position. I do, however, question their judgment. The NRA's assumption that prices can be raised by restricting production is another name for monopoly practices. We should call things by their right name.[7]

Though production statistics shot upward between July, when the NRA was formally established, and September, when the codes went into effect on a broad scale, Marriner repeatedly called attention to the widely ignored reason for the spurt. Within the business community, the reason sounded in the phrase "beat the code." Between July and September, businessmen rushed to take advantage of existing low wages and prices. So they produced goods at a furious pace for resale at higher prices in the fall, when authorized curtailments of production would go into effect. The anticipated happy windfall of profits, however, failed to materialize. The September wind proved a carrier of ruin.

The codes, by increasing wages along with prices, were of temporary help to workers who already had jobs, but they made matters worse for the unemployed, since prices were jacked up while their pocketbooks remained flat. Paul H. Douglas, Mary Runsey and other members of the Consumers' Advisory Board of the NRA, valiantly tried to close the gap between consumer income and prices. "My training as an economist," Douglas later wrote, "gave me no enthusiasm for trying to restore prosperity by restricting production. Convinced that we should build up total demand whether of consumption or investment, and not allow the weight of the depression to fall upon those least able to bear it, I helped file dissents to all the codes."[8] The dissents were to no immediate avail. They were ignored, brushed aside or snapped like matchwood by monopoly forces to which the NRA, by law, gave a free hand under the cover of Hugh Johnson's dazzling theatrics —parades, placards, trombones and drums.

Labor could get higher wages and no jobs. Businessmen could get higher prices and no markets for their swollen inventories. The NRA, in common with much else that had been done in the name of the New Deal up to that time, failed as a reflationary measure. It did not generate the consumer purchasing power necessary to spark and sustain an increase in production. The consequences became clear soon after the codes went into effect. The public's confidence in the banking system that Roosevelt had restored by his emergency banking measures began to wane, and new bank failures were reported on all sides.

In a time of retrospect, Marriner remarked that many students have overlooked how close the nation came in the fall of 1933 to suffering a second collapse. But he also added that during the 1937–38 recession, when he was President Roosevelt's guest at Hyde Park, Mrs. Eleanor Roosevelt recalled the events of that fall with a clarity that irritated her husband. Marriner's conversation with Roosevelt about how the economy could be revived carried past the cocktail hour and through dinner, with the president at his jovial best. Mrs. Roosevelt joined in the discussion. In Marriner's words:

"I suppose [said Mrs. Roosevelt] people will call this the Second Roosevelt Depression."

The President sat upright in his chair. "No, dear," he corrected her, "the First Roosevelt Depression."

"It's the Second one," Mrs. Roosevelt insisted. With an edge in his voice, the President replied. "The First!"

"But, Franklin," Mrs. Roosevelt said, "aren't you forgetting the depression in the fall of 1933 after you tried to balance the budget and the NRA codes went into effect?"

I had meant to remain an armed neutral in this husband-and-wife exchange between the President of the United States and the First Lady of the land. The President, however, looked in my direction as if to rally my loyal support for his stand. I regretted that I could not give him what he expected. My memory told me that Mrs. Roosevelt was right and he was wrong on this issue of historical fact, and I managed to say just that.[9]

IV

On October 10, 1933, Marriner received an unexpected letter from Rexford Tugwell, written on Department of Agriculture stationery. In the six months that had intervened since their introductory meeting in New York, contact between them had been confined to copies of statements Marriner had made and sent to Tugwell, followed by pro-forma notes of acknowledgment. Now Tugwell wrote to ask whether Marriner was planning another trip to the East and, if so, whether he could include a stop in Washington. "I am anxious to exchange views with you," said Tugwell, "about a number of things which are rather pressing problems at the present time." Marriner replied that he was going to New York at the end of October for the Amalgamated Sugar Company and could afterward come to Washington.

Marriner's reply had barely been mailed when there was a telephone call from Washington—not for himself, but for his associate, Elbert G. Bennett. Jesse Jones, the new head of the Reconstruction Finance Corporation, was searching for a practical banker who could serve as the Republican member on a three-man board of directors for the newly created Federal Deposit Insurance Corporation. The other directors, both Democrats, had already been selected. One of these, the chairman designate of the FDIC, was without experience in banking and owed his appointment solely to his friendship with Secretary of the Treasury Will Woodin. The other was the Comptroller of the Currency. Though the law automatically made him a director of the FDIC, he was a lawyer, not a banker, by profession. Besides, he had been appointed comptroller as part of a political pay-off for electioneering services rendered in the Democratic cause. By law, the third director had to be a Republican.

Under the terms of the law creating the FDIC, deposit insurance was automatically extended to national and state banks that were members of the Federal Reserve System, but not to non-member banks. To qualify for FDIC coverage, they must be checked and examined before the end of

1933. Those that failed to qualify would probably close down. Jones said there was an urgent need to examine and qualify for FDIC coverage approximately eight thousand state banks not members of the Federal Reserve System. The task seemed impossible to complete within the time limit set by law. But Wilson McCarthy, an RFC director, had told Jones that there was one man in the country—E. G. Bennett—who had the skill to achieve the impossible. Could Bennett come to Washington as the Republican director of the FDIC?

Bennett replied that he would have to talk the matter over with his "associates" in the First Security Corporation. There was in fact only one associate—Marriner Eccles—whose views were decisive in all matters pertaining to First Security. Since Marriner had repeatedly advocated a bank-deposit-insurance scheme along FDIC lines, he could not refuse the government the service of a man deemed necessary to make the FDIC operational. He knew that the banks in the First Security network could again be in danger if neighboring banks were closed. He arranged a leave of absence for Bennett and divided his work among other officers of First Security, with new responsibilities devolving on Marriner's brother George.

15. Meetings

I

IN NEW YORK CITY, at the end of October 1933, Marriner moved through a financial world still frozen with fear. He brought to his negotiations with the New York bankers the moral authority of a man who had guided the banks of the First Security Corporation safely past massive threats to their life. He made the case for the kind of financing he wanted for Amalgamated, signed the necessary documents and informed his Utah associates of the terms. Then he boarded the train for Washington and his meeting with Rexford Tugwell.

In Washington he was caught up in a round of conferences lasting three days, beginning with his call at Tugwell's offices in the Department of Agriculture. Tugwell introduced him to Mordecai Ezekial, who had been in the department for many years. A moment later, Tugwell and Ezekial said in unison, "You should meet Henry Wallace," and a moment after that, the three men were across the hall and in Wallace's office. There the interruptions of ringing telephones, buzzers and the traffic of assistants whispering into the ear of the Secretary of Agriculture made conversation impossible. Marriner asked Tugwell, Ezekial and Wallace to join him for dinner at the Shoreham Hotel, where he was staying. That was agreed to for the following night. The next morning Tugwell telephoned to ask if he could bring Harry L. Hopkins and Jerome Frank to the dinner so that Marriner could meet them. For his own part, Marriner brought two more men into the group: Secretary of War George Dern and E. G. Bennett.

At that time, all bona fide New Dealers in Washington—whether registered Democrats, one-time Progressive Republicans or Republicans who had voted Democratic in 1932—looked to the person of President Roosevelt as their party *pro tem*. All saw in him the instrument through which they could personally contribute to the nation's economic recovery. They were not, however, all of one mind about what should actually be done. Some New Dealers, for example, believed that all the leading economic institutions of the nation must be fundamentally reformed before there could be any recovery. Some, to the contrary, believed that recovery must come first and reforms second. Others believed that the free-enterprise system was beyond redemption and had to give way to direct governmental planning of the entire economy—for which the NRA was an initial step. Still others, such as the former law students of Felix Frankfurter at Harvard, believed that the free-enterprise system was salvageable provided some of its central institutions were restructured and placed under the discipline of new laws.

There were also the divisions along the lines of the 1912 pseudo-debate between the adherents to Woodrow Wilson's "New Freedom" and the adherents to Theodore Roosevelt's "New Nationalism." The first believed that since "bigness in business is always badness," the nation's large industrial combinations should be broken up into smaller competing units. The second believed that since industrial bigness was inevitable, "it should be made subject to government regulation in the public interest."

Some of these differences could be noted in the men who met with Marriner in the Shoreham Hotel, but all agreed that an assault on the concentration of wealth and economic power, though necessary, could not by itself produce recovery. Whether they favored a program of regulated bigness or enforced littleness, a program of national planning or one of competition, all shared an uneasy sense that something had gone wrong with the expansionist aims of various New Deal policies and programs. In their respective governmental posts, all were daily reminded that a balanced budget would not lift tens of millions of Americans over the hump of mass misery. Each of these men, therefore, became an advocate of public spending as a pragmatic solution to the specific problems they immediately faced.

But there was another factor to be weighed. Assuming a program of spending to meet immediate emergency needs, could the larger objective of a general economic recovery be achieved by a program of deliberately planned deficits? Tugwell's asking Marriner to the capital was, in part, an invitation for him to speak to that question. What the men at the dinner wanted—and what Marriner eagerly supplied—was an internally consistent argument showing how a policy of planned deficit financing could serve the humanitarian objectives with which they were most directly concerned; and second, how the increased production and employment that would follow from a policy where the government spent more and taxed less could end the depression, and how the budget could eventually be balanced by less spending and more taxation in boom times.

Marriner's thesis concerning the dynamics of a compensatory economy later came to be known as Keynesian economics, a phrase suggesting that John Maynard Keynes was the fount of New Deal economics. The truth is something else: Marriner had not yet read a word of Keynes, and in the years ahead, he would not read more than fragmentary extracts from Keynes' writings. Further, while Keynes and the New Deal were moving along parallel lines, Keynes had not yet fully formulated a theory of fiscal policy with which American professional economists would agree or disagree. As for his "journalistic" writings on economics, they were not generally known to the original members of the New Deal's Brain Trust, perhaps because, except for Tugwell, they were not economists.

Elsewhere in the nation, some professional economists were reaching, by a route of their own, conclusions similar to Marriner's. This was particularly true among a circle of economists at the University of Chicago. By

January 1933, eleven of that university's economists and political scientists —including Jacob Viner, Paul Douglas, H. C. Simons and H. A. Millis —had issued a public statement in which they recommended a deliberate policy of deficit spending. "The federal debt," they said, "should be permitted to increase in times of depression and be rapidly retired in prosperous times."

The statement was either unnoticed or dismissed by the New York–based original members of the Brain Trust. Marriner himself might have been denied the close hearing he got at the Shoreham meeting if it had not been for his eccentric identity as a millionaire banker and industrialist whose economic concepts ran contrary to the budget-balancing dogmas not only of the Eastern financial community but also of some of Roosevelt's influential advisers in the administration. It clearly served the interest of the New Deal spenders to have on their side a man like Marriner Eccles, who was a not a professor, a social worker, a professional do-gooder, a socialist or even a registered Democrat but a man with flawless credentials as a cost-conscious, hard-nosed businessman. He knew what it was like to meet a payroll on which thousands of people depended for a livelihood. He knew what it was like to manage the life's savings of tens of thousands of hard-working people. This man was well armored to articulate the concepts of a compensatory economy, and it would be hard for anyone to denounce him on the grounds that he was an impractical dreamer or "an agent of the Kremlin."

At the end of the evening at the Shoreham, one of the men present, apparently speaking for the rest, said, "All right, Eccles, you've made your case. We are convinced that you are right and we should follow the line of policy you've laid out. But our problem is this. How are we going to get around Lew Douglas over in the Bureau of the Budget and Will Woodin over in the Treasury, who are holding Roosevelt fast to a budget-balancing policy?" A second voice suggested the possibility of "working" on Undersecretary of the Treasury Dean Acheson. "Dean is open to reason, and it's imperative that we have the Treasury's support if a program of planned deficits is to get anywhere with the president."

George Dern, who "outranked" Acheson in Washington protocol, said that he would try to bring Acheson to Marriner's suite for dinner the next night. Tugwell volunteered to be present. When Dern, dressed in a tuxedo, duly showed up with Acheson, he explained that he could not stay beyond a friendly drink, since he was due to dine with Army Chief of Staff Douglas MacArthur.

In the serious business of the evening, Marriner, energetically backstopped by Tugwell, rehearsed all his arguments in support of government-planned deficit financing. Acheson, an attentive listener, also asked rapier-sharp questions that got to the heart of an issue. "I believe," Marriner later remarked, "that if Dean Acheson had not been asked to resign from the

Treasury Department soon afterward because of his justifiable opposition to the gold-price policy, he most likely would have supported the unorthodox fiscal policy I was urging with Tugwell's support."[10]

The following day, Tugwell took Marriner to meet Ickes, who, as always, was half buried under a mountain of documents and had time to surface for only a short conference. A longer one was not needed. He expressed general agreement with what Marriner had to say, shook hands, returned to the documents and that was that.

"And now," said Tugwell to Marriner when they were out of Ickes' office, "I'd like to arrange an appointment for you with President Roosevelt so that you can tell him, as you've told us, what you think should be done to stimulate recovery." Marriner begged off. He would of course be honored to meet the president, but he realised that Roosevelt was pressed for time. Besides, it would be best for men such as Tugwell, Hopkins, Wallace and Ickes to make the case for planned deficit spending. As members of the official family, they had a better chance than a stranger to influence Roosevelt.

Tugwell dropped his suggestion but now revealed the purpose behind their brief call on Ickes. It was part of an effort, begun the day Marriner arrived in Washington, to draw him into the administration. Ickes was responsible for administering the terms of newly enacted public-housing legislation, and Tugwell hoped that Marriner could consider a presidential appointment to head the public housing program contemplated by the new legislation. Marriner, while flattered, listed the reasons why he could not accept the job. He was a banker and a businessman; he knew nothing whatever about public housing. As a Westerner, he knew nothing about the slum-clearance problems of great cities, the primary concern of the newly created Public Housing Authority. He would fail in the job and embarrass not only himself but also the administration.

"Well," said Tugwell, "suppose you got a wire from the president once you were back in Utah? What if he should ask you to take the housing post?"

Marriner replied that he would have to refuse the offer. Aside from the fact that he had no personal aspirations for a presidential appointment, he must remain in Utah—with Bennett on leave in Washington, working on FDIC matters—to look after the affairs of the First Security Corporation, the Utah Construction Company and the Amalgamated Sugar Company. To save Marriner the embarrassment of refusing a presidential summons, Tugwell did not press him. Marriner returned to Utah and once again immersed himself in his private affairs and in the problems of state relief.

II

It was on November 1, the day Marriner had begun his round of conferences in Washington, that Harry Hopkins won President Roosevelt's consent to a direct work relief program.[11] Hopkins estimated that four million people could be put to work within thirty days on assorted projects —schools, playgrounds, airports, roads and sewage systems to be built or improved. In FDR's calculation, four million people meant roughly $400 million, which he thought could be provided from the Public Works Fund. The news had to be broken gently to Ickes, who administered the fund and was not extravagant in his admiration for Hopkins personally or for his methods. The decision led to the creation of the Civil Works Administration. Unlike the FERA, which was mostly a state and local program loosely supervised and in part financed by the federal government but administered locally, the CWA was to be completely operated and 90 percent financed by the federal government. More important, in contrast to the dole-like FERA, the CWA was to provide work for individuals as near as possible to their previous employment and to pay the prevailing wage in each category and region with a minimum of thirty cents an hour. The CWA also abolished the "means test" whereby a man who sought government relief was denied it if any member of his family was already employed.

In mid-November, at about the time the CWA program was moving into high gear, there was a change in the leadership of the Treasury Department. Will Woodin, battling a fatal illness, relinquished his post. Dean Acheson, the acting Secretary, had previously submitted an undated letter of resignation, and his resignation was now accepted. With these two men gone, Roosevelt offered Henry Morgenthau, Jr., formerly the head of the Farm Credit Administration, a recess appointment as acting Secretary of the Treasury. "You made good for me at Albany," FDR remarked, "and you are one of the two or three people who have made an outstanding success in Washington, so let's you and I go on to bigger things. . . . We will have lots of fun doing it together." Morgenthau later confessed to his diary that he was "so dumbfounded" that he "broke out in perspiration." But he "managed to get something out about how much he appreciated the opportunity."[12] The fateful decision was sealed in a handshake.

About a month later, Marriner received a telegram signed by Tom K. Smith, a new assistant to Morgenthau. Could he come to Washington in order to discuss certain monetary matters with the acting Secretary of the Treasury? Marriner had never met Smith or Morgenthau, so he called Bennett in Washington to ask if he knew what was in the wind. Bennett did not, but he knew Smith, a St. Louis banker, and would sound him out. The next day, Bennett called to say that Smith had no idea what the Secretary had in mind beyond what the telegram stated. Marriner was reluctant to return East. On Bennett's advice, however, he wired Morgenthau to say he could come at the start of the new year. He left Ogden on the night of January 1, 1934.

Marriner's name had been brought to Morgenthau's attention by the New Dealers he had met in November. With Woodin gone, they wished to surround the new head with people who recognized the need for large-scale deficit financing, who could impress their views on the Treasury Department and on the president. In this they would be only partly successful. They could not control Morgenthau.

Morgenthau had many personal quirks, but the name given him—"Henry the Morgue"—should not obscure the fact that he was intensely loyal to FDR and supported most of the works of the New Deal, especially those of a humanitarian nature. Yet the point of departure and return for all his economic views was his contention that "loose fiscal policy"—meaning big expenditures and big deficits—retarded recovery by "weakening business confidence." FDR himself, moreover, was intermittently of the same mind, as was revealed in the ambivalence of his presidential acts. Emergency needs, along with reformist political and economic motives, forced him to press policy lines that wore a seemingly antibusiness face. In a different direction, because he also wished to strengthen business confidence as a stimulant to recovery, he persistently tried to curtail expenditures and to appear as a dedicated budget balancer. The future would show that New Dealers such as Marriner Eccles who advocated deficit spending as an instrument for recovery would not decisively win "the struggle for the soul of FDR" until the moral drawn from the 1937–38 recession was sealed in Roosevelt's Budget Message of January 1939.

When Marriner left Ogden for his scheduled meeting with Morgenthau, hostility to the New Deal was already running strong in business circles. Though he still had no clue as to what was in Morgenthau's mind, he knew what he would say if the subject to be discussed concerned the anti-New Deal rancors that were on the rise among businessmen, namely, that part of the hostility stemmed from Roosevelt's attempt to balance the budget, by advocating higher taxes to pay for relief expenditures. He would go on to suggest that the administration could remove a salient political cause for that hostility if it pursued a logical economic approach to the problems of recovery. Specifically, since a deficit achieved by tax reduction in time of depression could be as reflationary as one achieved by extraordinary outlays, a logical way to generate recovery and economic expansion was through a tax *reduction,* as well as through increased expenditures.

Yet, when Marriner called at the Treasury Department and was escorted by Tom Smith to his first meeting with Morgenthau, he found himself denied a chance to unfold his views in an orderly way on any subject. "The more we talked," Marriner later said, "the less I understood why I had been asked to cross the continent for a meeting with the Secretary of the Treasury. Morgenthau was edgy and his thoughts seemed to wander. The reasons why escaped me at the time."[13]

In the brief period between Morgenthau's appointment as acting Secretary and his becoming Secretary, he had no opportunity to get a feel for the levers of power in the Treasury Department. He knew that he owed his rise in the administration mainly to the long-standing personal friendship between the Roosevelt and Morgenthau families, and he was determined faithfully to serve FDR to the best of his abilities. But when he was suddenly catapulted from the Farm Credit Administration to head the Treasury, he found himself on a high wire in a high wind where any misstep could lead to a fatal fall. Moreover, he saw to his dismay that one of his first steps had whirled a congressional storm. He had been instrumental in securing the nomination of Earl Bailey, a New York banker, to the post of Undersecretary of the Treasury—only to discover that the nominee's record made him painfully vulnerable to congressional attacks, with an implied peril to Morgenthau's own confirmation as Secretary. In fact, when it became clear that the Senate would not confirm Bailey, his name was withdrawn. The post of Undersecretary of the Treasury eventually went to Thomas Jefferson Coolidge, a Boston banker whose economic views—as Marriner came to know and judge them—"were to the right of President McKinley." George L. Harrison, the head of the New York Reserve Bank, was reportedly the invisible hand responsible for placing Coolidge in the number 2 post in the Treasury Department.

A nervous and distracted Morgenthau cut short his meeting with Marriner by suggesting that he write a report about what he thought should be done in the field of money and banking. In Marriner's view, the report could just as well have been written in Utah as in Washington, and he wondered if he was being treated to a brush-off. His sense that this was the case was reinforced when Morgenthau, in parting, told Tom Smith to take Marriner to see Herman Oliphant, who had just been brought over from the Farm Credit Administration to serve as the new general counsel of the Treasury Department.

Marriner and Oliphant were destined to clash head on over many points of fiscal and monetary policy, but the clashes left untouched the respect Marriner had for the man. "Oliphant," he said, "was one of those gifted and dedicated public servants whose names seldom appear in headlines, and who work outside the glare of spotlights. Yet if it were not for their attention to the thousand details which make the wheels of government go round, the political executives in the public spotlight would flounder helplessly."[14] When the two men first met, Oliphant, staggering under a load of work, could spare but a few minutes for an exchange of views. He asked Smith to take Marriner to see professors George Warren and Lindsey Rogers, who were tucked away in a corner of the new Commerce Building.

Marriner had met Warren once in Ogden and, as noted, was no enthusiast for his plan to increase commodity prices by increasing the price of gold relative to the dollar. This, however, was his introductory encounter with Rogers. Contrary to his expectation, he found that he had an ally in the man. When the three-cornered conversation was launched in earnest, Rogers sided with Marriner's criticism of Warren's views. But when the argument broke off at the end of three hours, the positions taken remained unchanged. Warren conceded nothing to the contention that the best way to raise commodity prices was to increase both the volume of money in circulation and its velocity, or rate of turnover.*

After the encounter with Warren, Marriner spent several days in Washington without hearing a further word concerning his aborted discussion with Morgenthau. He had never before been kept waiting outside the doors of the powerful. He was galled by the experience, especially because on his home ground he was available to all who wished to see him. At last he telephoned Tom Smith to say that he had not come to Washington to seek a job or to beg a favor; he had come in response to an invitation and at no small inconvenience to himself. The way things had turned out, however, he had been made to look ridiculous in his own eyes. He was leaving Washington for New York, where he had some business to transact, and from there would return home. In short order, Smith was back on the telephone with a message from the Secretary of the Treasury. Could Marriner come to Morgenthau's home on Saturday afternoon so they could talk without interruption?

"At the start of that meeting," Marriner later recalled, "Morgenthau began by asking me if I objected to personal questions. When I said that I had no objections to any questions, personal or impersonal, he cross-examined me at length about my business connections, my financial condition, the condition of my various enterprises, whether any of them had gone bankrupt, the debts, if any, they owed, and so on. I wondered why he didn't get all this information from Secretary of War George Dern, who was a director of the First Security Bank in Salt Lake City. It occurred to me only later on that Morgenthau's troubles over the Bailey appointment intensified his natural wariness, and made him distrust any information he got second hand."[15]

Morgenthau at last ran out of questions and took Marriner into his confidence. He had spent the last few weeks examining the human resources of the Treasury Department and discovered that they amounted to "an empty shelf." The department's responsibilities had been vastly expanded because of the legislation enacted since President Roosevelt's inauguration, but he lacked a staff competent to perform the Treasury's new tasks. He was in urgent need of help. "You've been recommended as someone who

*With Morgenthau's backing, Warren had already won Roosevelt's support for a plan to go beyond the devaluation of the dollar that had occurred in the previous April and, by law, to formalize the change in the value of the dollar relative to the price of gold. Indeed, on January 14, 1934, FDR sent to Congress the text of a measure that conformed to the lines of Warren's theory. Called the Gold Reserve Act, the measure was passed and signed sixteen days later. Under its terms, there was to be a fixed buying and selling price of $25 an ounce for gold, thereby devaluing the gold dollar to 59.06 percent of its former weight. Moreover, title to all coin and bullion was to be vested in the United States government; all gold coins were to be withdrawn from circulation and melted into bullion; further gold coinage was to be discontinued; the Secretary of the Treasury was to control all dealings in gold; and the president was authorized to fix the weight of the gold dollars at any level between 50 and 60 percent of its prior legal weight.

could give me the help I need," Morgenthau said. "Would you be willing to go to work in the Treasury Department?"

Morgenthau did not say what job he had in mind. He seemed to imply that Marriner should move from Utah to Washington and then find a place in the Treasury Department where he could fit in. Marriner was struck by the vagueness of Morgenthau's proposal. Even if it had been put in more specific terms, however, he was not prepared to respond immediately. He explained that he had previously declined an invitation from Tugwell to head the Public Housing Authority under Ickes, and was not at liberty to consider an appointment to any other governmental post. If he came to Washington, Bennett would have to return to Utah to manage the affairs of the First Security Corporation, and it was not clear when he would be finished with his FDIC work. On the other hand, even if Bennett went back to Utah, Marriner's moving to Washington would mean increased responsibilities for his younger brothers and associates in the Eccles family business enterprises. Were they equal to the added responsibility? Would they be willing to assume them? He would need time to weigh these matters before responding to Morgenthau's proposal.

Later that same day, Marriner met with Bennett, and the two men, veterans of many battles together, talked frankly. Bennett contended that his own presence in Washington should not deter Marriner from accepting a post in the Treasury Department; he was nearing the end of his work with the FDIC. Besides, he was not a New Dealer and had no interest in a government career. Not only was he willing, he was anxious to return to his regular work with the First Security Corporation. After being persuaded that Bennett meant what he said, Marriner placed telephone calls to his brothers in Utah and to Marriner Browning. His brothers replied that Marriner should be free to accept any offer from Morgenthau that held interest for him. He had safeguarded the interests of the family when all the children except one were still minors. He had expanded those interests and had then conserved them during the successive crises of recent years. He had more than earned the right to follow his own inclinations if they led to a period of government service. The years his brothers had spent under his tutelage made them fully capable and willing to assume extra duties while he was away. Marriner Browning, for his part, joined in encouraging Marriner to accept Morgenthau's invitation. It was time, said he, that "someone west of the Mississippi River had a strong voice in the Treasury Department."

This encouraging reaction from Utah did not settle a question Marriner alone could answer. Did he really want to get involved in the work of official Washington? His business affairs took him to New York on the Monday after his conversation with Morgenthau, and when he was alone, he was of two minds about the question and debated both sides with himself.

What he had built—whether in banking, in the construction industry, or in the sugar industry—was a superstructure rising from foundations which David Eccles had laid. A career at the seat of the national government, however, was something different. It was one thing for his father to have been a city councilman and mayor in a small out-of-the-way place like Ogden during the 1880s. It was another thing for the son to assume a high position in the Treasury Department, where decisions were made that could affect the destiny of the nation in a time of worldwide upheaval. In that kind of position, there could be no comparison between father and son, nor any whispered word that the son merely carried forward what the father had begun. The son would stand or fall on his own merits.

On returning to Washington from New York, Marriner again saw Morgenthau to inform him of what he was prepared to do. He did not want to disrupt the schooling of his three children by moving the entire family from Ogden to Washington. But he was personally prepared to establish himself in Washington on February 1, 1934, and to remain there until June 1935. The time schedule would permit his children to finish a school year in Ogden, following which they would move with their mother to the capital, where they would be able to finish a full academic year in Washington's schools. However, said Marriner, he would make no move at all until he knew the nature of the specific post Morgenthau had in mind for him. He had no desire to play the part of a solvent Micawber, "waiting for something to turn up."

When the issue was put this way, Morgenthau said that he wanted to designate Marriner as his special assistant to deal with monetary and credit problems. If this was agreeable, the appointment would be made and publicly announced at once. It was agreeable, and the "official" appointment took the form of a letter from Morgenthau to Marriner. The brief text read:

You are hereby appointed Assistant to the Secretary of the Treasury, at a salary of $10,000 per annum, effective January 29, 1934, payable from the appropriation, "Expenses, National Banking Emergency Act, March 9, 1933, Comptroller of Currency."

Out of this strained beginning, the two men were destined to have a long and ever-changing relationship with each other. It was to be a thing full of accords and cross-tensions, of felicity and hard infighting—all of which left their imprints on the economic and political life of the nation during the length of Roosevelt's presidency, and afterwards as well.

Marriner returned to Utah to set his affairs in order in anticipation of serving no more than sixteen months in Washington. The circumstances of his appointment did not require any severance of his business connections. But for the contemplated length of his absence, he assigned various stop-gap roles to his brothers Spencer and Willard, to H. A. Benning in the Amalgamated Sugar Company, to L. S. Corey in the Utah Construction Company, to Wesley Anderson and Lyman Hyde in the lumber business, and of course to his brother George and to E. G. Bennett and Marriner Browning in the banking business. The sixteen months, however, were to stretch out into the seventeen and one-half consecutive years Marriner was to spend in the public service. In that long interval, many things changed in Utah.

16. The Assistant

IN REPORTING FOR DUTY at the Treasury Department, Marriner was installed for a while in the vacant office of the Undersecretary of the Treasury. He was excited by the vistas to be seen from his office window—the White House across the street to the west, the nearby new building of the Department of Commerce, the Washington Monument a block away on the Mall to the south, Capitol Hill a mile to the east on Pennsylvania Avenue. Yet almost at once, the aura of things that excited him cast the shadows of troubles to come in his family life. The first sign of the matter is reflected in a letter of February 18, 1934, Marriner wrote to his son Campbell in Salt Lake City. May, Marriner's wife, was in Washington at the time, and the letter to Campbell began with a reference to her.

Mother is looking and feeling better than she has done for some time. If you and the other members of the family were here, I am sure she would be quite happy and contented. But she does get so lonesome and homesick, as I am so busy I don't get to see much more of her here than I did at home. . . .

The Shoreham Hotel where we are living, is about a fifteen-minute ride in a taxi from my office. I take a taxi to work every morning at 9:00 o'clock and return every evening about 7:00 or later. You can see from this that I could certainly use my car. Maybe this summer, if Mother should decide to move here as soon as school is out, I will give you the job of my chauffeur. I am hoping we will have a lot of fun taking side-trips out of Washington in the car. There are so many, many interesting places to go. . . . I miss a great deal the week-end visits I enjoyed so much having with you at home.[16]

Campbell revered his father. He was used to seeing him as a dominant figure on the Utah scene; but he would soon see him emerge as the source of front page news on the national scene. His father no longer belonged to him alone. And though Marriner's affectionate letters conveyed his continuing interest in the youth's development and problems, Campbell would be wounded by his father's public career.

Marriner's public career began with the New Deal. It needs to be said, however, that the New Deal did not invent itself on the spur of the moment. Many of the emergency reforms it enacted when the iron of history was red hot had been formulated by cloistered scholars prior to the Great Depression or during its first years. Strangely, the New Deal was not forearmed to cope with a challenge central to its other efforts to revive the economy. It had no clearly defined ideas about how the components of economic management—fiscal, banking, money, credit, and the work of regulatory agencies such as the Federal Reserve Board and the Comptroller of the Currency—should each be related to the other as parts of a single whole. What actually happened seems to have depended on the last person who tugged at Roosevelt's sleeve, and the results were a monument to confusion.

This negative condition served in its own way to underline Marriner Eccles' eventual importance on the Washington scene. Marriner was not vested with plenipotentiary powers; his stock of ideas, deduced from his experiences, were still rough-hewn when he joined the struggle to govern the nation. They needed the refinements that presently came with the help of gifted young economists such as Winfield W. Riefler and Lauchlin Currie, whom he met in the government. He still had much to learn about how to convert ideas into policies, programs, legislative enactments. He had even more to learn about the immense difficulties that beset any effort to move the engine of an administration forward in the face not merely of resisting external forces, but of those within an administration—starting with its presidential commander-in-chief. Some of the things he tried to change in the name of rational economic management still remained the same four decades later.

Yet Marriner achieved no small thing. He brought to Washington and tried to imprint on the New Deal (and on its Fair Deal successor) a body of coherent ideas about how to promote and maintain the conditions for orderly economic growth.

Among other things, he noted that bookkeeping transactions constitute nine-tenths of the "money" used by the American people. The tangible tenth—gold, silver, paper, nickel and copper—was used for pocket money or in the case of international payments under the gold standard to balance accounts. Control of credit was, therefore, the ultimate measure of monetary power. Velocity was more important than the volume of money in circulation; centralized credit management was more important than any amount of currency tinkering; and the taxing and regulatory powers of public bodies were fully as important as the money control power. To assume that a single instrument could keep the capitalist system on an even keel was to assume the impossible. The government could hope to spare the nation a destructive inflation and a destructive deflation only if it aligned all the components of economic management in ways by which they would both strengthen and draw strength from each other.

III

At first, Marriner had no power of command on the Washington scene. He merely "represented" Morgenthau in matters where the Treasury had dealings with other governmental agencies such as the Reconstruction Finance Corporation, the Federal Farm Mortgage Corporation, the Home

Owner's Loan Corporation, and the Interdepartment Committee for the Coordination of Commercial policies. Within the Treasury Department, however, he represented *himself,* starting with the construction he placed on an event that ran its course shortly before he assumed his governmental duties. The Treasury had offered $1 billion in securities for purchase by banks and other investors in order to finance the deficits indicated in President Roosevelt's budget of January 1934. The offer was not only quickly snapped up but was oversubscribed several times over.

To Marriner, the event clearly supported his contention that a balanced budget was not by itself either an absolute determinant of "confidence" in the public credit or the sole precondition for private investment. When the First National Bank of Chicago—one of the strongest and most ably led banks in the nation—wanted to move from its defensive policy of high liquidity to an aggressive loan policy, it had to coax major Chicago-based enterprises to borrow funds for use in corporate reorganizations. Marriner observed that, despite the polemical opposition to governmental deficits, investors with substantial sums of idle funds were willing to finance the deficit, as doing so would earn them a profit when no other outlets for such funds were in sight.

Secretary Morgenthau, however, did not see things in that light, nor did Lewis Douglas, whose Budget Bureau was located within the Treasury and was viewed as an instrument of the Treasury—and not, as it became after 1939, part of the Office of the President and an instrument of White House control. Morgenthau and Douglas continued to insist that there was a direct connection between a balanced budget, confidence in the public credit, and the kind of "business confidence" that could generate the private investments upon which recovery depended.

This is not to say that the two men were identical in every detail of this outlook. Morgenthau, though firmly attached to the principle of "fiscal integrity," was also firmly attached to the "humanitarian" or "social justice" objectives of the New Deal. He tried as best he could to ease the cross-tensions between these dual loyalties by justifying deficit spending only insofar as it was necessary to provide relief to people in distress. He was opposed to deficits that would be deliberately incurred for the purpose of general economic recovery. Budget Director Lewis Douglas thought in absolutist terms. In contrast to Morgenthau, he was not tied by long-standing bonds of friendship to Roosevelt personally and had no need to soften his absolutism if it should imperil his personal relationship with the President.

Marriner, in his early encounters with the man, concluded that Rexford Tugwell had understated the case back in November 1933, during the dinner meeting in the Shoreham Hotel when he described Douglas as being "awful." Douglas, who came from Arizona where his father had made a fortune in connection with the Phelps-Dodge copper interests, was ready to stand or fall on the dogma that an unbalanced budget—even when tens of millions of people were unemployed—was unthinkable. He ceaselessly painted for President Roosevelt a lurid picture of how the charge of "fiscal irresponsibility" would lead inexorably to the loss of support for the New Deal legislative program, as well as votes in the 1934 Congressional election. Roosevelt partly shared Douglas' convictions. Marriner shared none of them. He reasoned that, despite the depression, the private conomic system still contained latent sources of wealth-producing strength, but they could not activate themselves as if by spontaneous combustion. If idle funds in private hands were to be converted into new private investments, the federal government must provide the incentives for such a conversion through devices that would induce investors to help themselves.

Marriner noted that, during the most acute phase of the depression, 275 major corporations substantially reduced their debts and increased their liquidity even though they suffered heavy operating losses. In the three years between 1929 and 1932, they increased their cash holdings of the nation's supply of deposit currency from 7.6 percent of the total to 11.8 percent. Further, a substantial part of the new money that was being created through government financing under New Deal programs was flowing into those same corporations and was not being redistributed by them either in the form of investments or dividends. In New York and Chicago, individual and corporate demand deposits in 1934 were substantially higher than in 1929 at the peak of the boom. (They would be 42 percent higher in 1936.) If these idle funds did not flow back into the spending stream, the government would be forced to create more money for use by consumers through deficit spending. But how could private investors be induced to put their idle funds to work? It was by way of these thoughts that Marriner was led into the field of housing, where he would become one of the "Founding Fathers" of the Federal Housing Administration—known to present-day home owners simply as FHA.

IV

The onset of the depression found most savings and loan associations, the principal source of home mortgage money, in relatively sound condition. After more than a year of pressure, however, mortgage delinquencies increased, and withdrawals became widespread. Many members of the Congress were directors of local savings and loan associations and in July 1932 they moved to aid the associations and to bolster a collapsing mortgage market. The aid took the form of the Federal Home Loan Bank Act of 1932, which brought into being a central reserve credit agency similar to the Federal Reserve's function in the Federal Reserve System. The act created a Federal Home Loan Bank System of eleven regionally located banks whose capital was to be raised by subscription of its member associations. Each regional bank was governed by its board of directors but answerable to a Federal Home Loan Bank Board in Washington. The regional banks were originally financed in part by stock purchased by the U.S. Treasury, but there was a gross misfit between the small size of the aid the banks could render and the massive size of the need. So the collapse of the mortgage market continued.

Later in June 1933, at the request of President Roosevelt, Congress approved the Home Owners Loan Act. The HOLC was of enormous benefit to home owners and to creditors alike. Yet the barriers it raised against mass foreclosures did not at the same time generate economic recovery. A home owner whose mortgage was refunded and whose back interest and taxes were paid by the HOLC gained not an added penny with which to buy the goods he wanted. Moreover, the act applied only to mortgages in default. It provided no help to home owners who tried by all means to keep up their mortgage payments so that the mortgages would not be foreclosed. That group, along with those whose homes had been foreclosed, could be helped in the long run only by a general economic revival.

President Roosevelt knew that almost a third of the unemployed were to be found in the building trades, and housing was by far the most important element in that trade. A program of new home construction, launched on an adequate scale, would not only gradually provide employment for building trade workers but would accelerate the forward movement of the economy as a whole. Its benefits would extend to everyone, from the manufacturers of lace curtains to the manufacturers of lumber, bricks, furniture, cement, and electrical appliances. Transportation of supplies would stimulate railroad activity, while the needs generated for steel rails and rolling stock would have spin-off effects on steel mills. All this was known to President Roosevelt, but his decision to initiate a housing program was reached in a round-about way. In the four and one-half months following the establishment of the CWA under Harry L. Hopkins, it employed 4.3 million people and completed 180,000 projects. But it also spent $1.3 billion, and not the $400 million originally contemplated.[17] The whole of the CWA program thus came under public attack on the grounds that it was "state socialism," "gross waste," and a "feedbag for outright corruption." Within the administration, Lewis Douglas repeatedly warned Roosevelt that unless the program was quickly terminated it would bankrupt the country—since CWA workers who settled in government-made jobs at wages roughly equal to what private industry paid would never leave the relief rolls and seek employment in the private sector. His influence on Roosevelt was decisive.[18]

FDR had previously created the National Emergency Council under the chairmanship of Frank Walker to supervise all the New Deal agencies that had sprung into being. Now, in January 1934, he called a White House meeting of the council to consider when and how his decision to terminate the CWA could be carried out. Other matters also surfaced in the course of the discussion. At one point, John H. Fahey, chairman of the Federal Home Loan Bank Board, asked for an additional $2 billion for use in HOLC operations. Though Fahey had ably reorganized the Home Loan Bank System following the inept management of its first administrator, Roosevelt reportedly responded to the request by throwing up his hands in horror. He asked the men grouped around his desk if there was no way to get the government out of the lending business. Someone suggested that the question could be answered in part at least by a new housing program. After much talk, Roosevelt appointed Frank Walker as Chairman of the President's Emergency Committee on Housing, with orders to explore both the implications of a housing program and the preconditions for launching it. Other committee members included Harry Hopkins, Henry Wallace, Frances Perkins, Rexford Tugwell, John Fahey, and W. Averell Harriman. Harriman, "a tame millionaire," was not yet a member of the Roosevelt administration. He had been brought into the group because of his national standing as a businessman and his known personal friendship with the president. When the terms of the new housing program were finally agreed to, he was expected to "sell" the program to the president, to the Treasury, and to the business community at large. The economic adviser and secretary for the group was Winfield Riefler, whom Walker had recruited from the Federal Reserve Board's technical staff after conducting a wide canvas among universities and government agencies for their ablest economists.

The creation of the Emergency Committee on Housing predated the time when Marriner joined the Treasury staff, and he first heard of its existence when Riefler, at Morgenthau's suggestion, called to bring him abreast of how things stood. The situation, said Riefler, resembled a saw that scarred the bark of a log without finding its cutting groove. Various members of the Emergency Committee had advanced some general ideas about a "new style" housing program. But no one had yet presented a concrete plan that could be translated into legislative and administrative terms. When Marriner responded to this report with a flash flood of suggestions, Riefler challenged some, agreed with others, built on still others.

Back in Utah, Marriner had known many "operating executives" within his own companies who were masters of the details which made a particular business go round. He leaned heavily on them for their special technical competence. Among these, however, few if any had a spacious outlook on the business of the nation as a whole. The difference in Washington—and part of the excitement of the place—was exemplified in a public servant such as Riefler. Here was a soft-spoken, broad-gauged, hard-headed conversational partner. Here was a man who did not need Marriner to spell out for him the ABC's of a public case or controversy. He could start with the XYZ's, and turn an Eccles' monologue into a clarifying dialogue.

After many hours of talk—when engrossed in an idea, both men forgot the clock—Riefler put a proposal to Marriner. Why not become associated with Walker's committee as the Treasury's representative? Morgenthau subsequently approved the proposal without knowing that (under the terms of a gestating Eccles-Riefler plan) the Treasury Department would indirectly assume the function of a mortgage guarantor.

In March 1934, on the eve of the scheduled termination of CWA, Marriner attended his first meeting of Walker's group. All the major figures of the New Deal or their chief deputies were present, and the meeting itself was held against the background of national protests—and in some places of riots—against the impending end of CWA. Yet the tenor of the discussions within the Walker group served only to confirm what Riefler had previously reported. Everyone agreed on the need to stimulate new construction, eager to help promote that objective, but the concrete ways and means had yet to be devised. At this and at a subsequent meeting, Marriner as a newcomer listened more than he talked. He was struck by the tendency among members of the Walker group to bring a social service worker's perceptions to bear on the problems they faced. "Housing," to them, seemed to mean "public housing" along the lines of the government-financed slum program of Harold Ickes' Public Works Administration. Private home construction, privately financed in communities across the nation, held a lesser place in their thoughts. So far as Marriner could tell, none linked a housing program to the need to give mobility to idle funds in private hands, awaiting profitable investment opportunities beyond the purchase of government securities.

Marriner had previously concluded that the paramount objective of government deficit financing in a depression was to generate maximum private spending through minimum public spending. A large scale *public* housing program, though warranted on other grounds, would miss that objective. It would entail public ownership and government financing, increase the public debt, be strongly opposed by real estate interests as well as by financial institutions, be slow in getting underway, and apply only to larger cities. Marriner wanted the housing program to be private in character, financed by creditor institutions of the community where individuals lived. Every kind of credit agency in the country with idle money on its hands should have a right to participate in financing the program he had in mind. In particular, if banks with excess reserves made loans for home construction, the effect would be to create the basis for new money, and thus to replenish the money supply that had been greatly contracted in the drastic post-1929 deflation. But how could the people in control of idle funds be induced to put them to use in the modernization and construction of homes? How could banks be induced to make loans for that purpose?

After the first and second meetings of the Walker group, Marriner and Riefler privately continued their intense discussions. At the third meeting, Marriner cleared his throat to make a "procedural" suggestion. Everyone, he said, was agreed on the need for action, but he doubted if a specific housing plan could be shaped by a large group that met only at irregular intervals. Why not have a subcommittee draft a legislative measure containing the terms of the desired program? Once the draft was produced, the full committee could endorse, modify or reject it. The suggestion was adopted. "It should cause no surprise," Marriner dryly remarked later on, "that as the source of the suggestion, I was appointed to head the subcommittee.

Apparently, I was beginning to learn the ways of bureaucracy—where nine points of the law starts with the title of right to produce 'the first draft' of what is to be done.''[19]

Riefler was made secretary of the subcommittee under Marriner's chairmanship, backstopped by a top-flight three-man technical staff consisting of Albert Deane, assistant to the president of General Motors and an expert on consumer credit; J. M. Daiger, a housing expert; and Frank Watson, a young lawyer recruited from the RFC. Frank Walker imposed only one condition on the work to be done. To avoid the further mushroom growth of new emergency agencies, any proposed housing legislation should be drafted as an amendment to the law previously creating the Home Loan Bank Board. In that way, John Fahey, the head of the board, would be in a position to administer the whole of the government's housing mortgage program.

The proposal made sense—on paper. Marriner and his staff worked closely with Fahey until it became clear that Fahey was opposed to the whole of the evolving program. The reason why was of a piece with an old Washington story. Though the Home Loan Bank Board was meant to exercise a supervisory and regulatory control over the federal savings and loan associations, it was an all-too willing "captive protector" of the private interests it was meant to regulate in the national interest. In Fahey's intransigent view, the building and loan associations would be at a disadvantage if local banks and other creditor agencies were granted a right—as Marriner insisted—to participate in the financing of private housing in their respective communities. What happened to the economy as a whole seemed not to rank high in Fahey's priorities. His immediate concern was to serve the interests of the building and loan associations by keeping possible competitors out of the home mortgage field. Marriner explained the situation to Frank Walker and the latter agreed that the legislation be drafted in ways whereby the administration of the proposed housing program would be entrusted to a wholly new agency. And so it was.

The draft act consisted of three parts or in legislative language: "Titles." Title I dealt with the emergency modernization of home and business construction. It was a child of the marriage between Albert Deane's knowledge of consumer credit as applied to the sale of automobiles and a plan Marriner devised to finance credit in connection with housing. In general, a home owner or businessman who wished to modernize his property would be granted a credit of up to $2,000—without collateral—solely on the basis of his character and job prospects as judged by the local lending institution.

Marriner was aware that, even before the depression, few banks dealt in what is now called "retail credit," of which consumer loans are a part. Most banks, other than those which made farm mortgage loans, confined themselves to "wholesale credit"—meaning loans to assorted business enterprises. In the context of the depression, banks would be even more reluctant to risk consumer loans for the modernization program he had in mind unless the federal government shared the risk with them. Thus, in collaboration with Albert Deane, he devised a credit scheme where the federal government, in case of need, would underwrite 20 percent of the total loans made by any qualified lending institution. In the national aggregate, the government could absorb losses amounting to a $200 million subsidy for the modernization program but would draw an estimated $1 billion of stagnating private funds into the spending stream.

Title II, the heart of the draft bill, contemplated a revolution in the nature of home mortgages, so as to stimulate small home construction for owner occupancy, as well as large-scale rental housing by corporations. It should first be said that until 1916, national banks did not have the right to make real estate loans, and the same prohibition governed many state banks as well. Even after 1916, many commercial banks refused to make real estate loans on the grounds that they were "illiquid." Those that were willing to make such loans believed it was "bad business" to lend more than 50 percent of the appraised value of a home. Building and loan associations loaned up to 80 percent or more of the appraised value, but at interest rates ranging between 8 and 12 percent of the loan.

The conventional wisdom about the elements of a "sound mortgage loan" was sealed in state laws. Almost everywhere in the nation, states restricted banks and insurance companies to a maximum loan of 50 percent of the appraised value of a home, and limited to five years the life of a loan made by a national bank, and to ten years by insurance companies. What this meant to the head of a family was vividly recalled by Mayor Richard J. Daley in 1958 when a delegation of prominent Chicagoans solicited his political support for legislation that would permit branch banking in Illinois:

I know [he said to the delegation] that banks probably fulfull some useful function, but I also know that when my wife and I wanted to have a home for our kids, we went to one of the Chicago banks and asked if we could borrow some money for a home. The banker turned to me and said, "No, we won't loan you money for that purpose." So I went to a savings and loan institution and got the money I needed. If these two types of institutions are now on different sides of the branch banking issue, I feel no loyalty to the banks.[20]

Few people could make a down payment of 50 percent on a new home. Most of them took out second and third mortgages payable in installments at high rates of interest and with due dates extending beyond the life of the first mortgage. When first mortgages went into default during the depression years, second and third mortgages were wiped out.

To reverse the whole of this negative picture, Marriner advanced an idea that was endorsed by other members of his subcommittee. He had in view an arrangment where a high percentage of the appraised value of a home would be covered by a *single* mortgage, coupled with a reduction in interest rates, and an extension of maturity date so that the mortgage could be amortized through monthly payments in small and equal amounts. The members of the subcommittee recognized, as did Marriner, that the change being contemplated was so radical a departure from all past rules that private interests would never support or participate in the housing program on the proposed new basis unless they could rely on some sort of government protection against loss. Halfway protection would be useless. On the other hand, an unbuffered government guarantee would invite the objection that it increased the government debt. Such a guarantee might develop into direct government lending to individual borrowers on the order of the HOLC's refunding of defaulted mortgages. And the Walker committee on emergency housing had been created by Roosevelt to get the government out of that kind of lending.

The nature of the guarantee that was wanted—now the FHA's celebrated insurance principle—was largely the invention of Winfield Riefler. Riefler would have the FHA insure a mortgage up to 80 percent of the appraised value of a new home and lot whose total appraised value was not more than $16,000 on a single family unit. Interest rates could not exceed 5 percent, plus an insurance fee of 1 percent, making a total of 6 percent on the unpaid balance of the mortgage. The insurance fee would go into a fund for use in taking up defaulted mortgages if a lender foreclosed upon the property and delivered title to the FHA. If the fund, plus the proceeds from the resale of foreclosed properties, was not enough to cover the costs of all defaulted mortgages, then the FHA could issue 2.5 percent bonds to the lender, guaranteed by the government and payable three years after the mortgage matured. The insurance funds would be privately created. The government would merely guarantee that losses would be made up through the use of public credit. The same terms applied to large-scale rental by corporations as well as to small-home construction for owner occupancy except that the builder had to secure FHA approval for his rental schedules and dividend payments.

The third part of the draft FHA Act—or Title III—was largely the invention of a man whom Marriner added to the original membership of his task force, Charles A. Miller, a former president of the American Bar Association and a notable savings and mortgage banker. Title III authorized the creation of National Mortgage Associations which could buy up mortgages, large and small, and issue bonds against them in denominations that could be purchased by investors anywhere. It was hoped that through the medium of the associations fluidity would be given to the whole mortgage market and that mortgage investment funds could flow from areas where they were in excess to areas where they were in short supply.

The extent to which Marriner was engrossed in the this task appears in a revealing letter he wrote to his son Campbell on April 5, 1934:

I would have sent you a wire of congratulations on your Twentieth Birthday, which occurred last Monday, but for the life of me I couldn't remember your Salt Lake address. I then put off writing you a letter expecting to get to it each day since then, but I have been so swamped I simply have not had time to dictate a single letter. It is now 7:30 in the evening and I have not yet left the office, but I made up my mind that I would write to you before another day went by if it were the last thing I did. It hasn't been that I have forgotten you nor your birthday—I have thought of both a good deal as you mean such a very great deal to me, and your birthday reminds me of how old I am getting to have a 20-year old son and also how happy and proud I am to be the Dad of such a fine looking and splendid young man. I am sorry I couldn't be home personally to congratulate you and wish you all happiness and success on your birthday, but as that was impossible I know you will accept the will for the deed and let this letter, together with the $20 check enclosed ($1.00 for each birthday), act as my proxy. I hope you will use the check to buy something of a personal nature for yourself which you otherwise would not buy.

I hope Mother will decide to come back here in a couple of weeks as it is very doubtful that I will be able to get home now before June. However, tell Mother that I will write her in a day or two. . . . With reference to magazine articles about me which you mention in your letter, there was one in *Sphere,* I think the March issue. I also understand there is something in the last issue of *Fortune,* but I have not seen it.

I have been working on a very interesting job, because I feel that if it can be put over, it will have a wonderful constructive effect on our whole economy—that is, the Federal modernization, repair and housing program. . . . This, together with the routine Treasury work which I must take care of, has been fully occupying my time. All of my work is still very interesting and I am gaining a great deal of experience and making numerous new acquaintances.

The terms of the housing bill, into which Marriner had invested his highest hopes, were in due course submitted to and approved by the full membership of Frank Walker's Emergency Committee on Housing. President Roosevelt had yet to see it. So arrangements were made for the committee to meet with him in the White House. It is not clear whether this was the first time Marriner was personally introduced to FDR, but it was the first time he argued a case with Roosevelt as the presiding judge. It was also the first time his own views about the substantive merits of an economic proposal collided with FDR's higher political logic, and came off second best.

At the White House meeting, all the agreements previously reached by Marriner's subcommittee and by Walker's full committee were placed in hazard by a shift in the strategy of John Fahey, acting as the "in-house" spokesman for the building and loan associations. Having previously failed to abort the movement to present the Congress with some sort of housing bill, Fahey now insisted that if the draft measure that had been prepared went to the Congress with White House backing, it should be provided with an insurance scheme on the order of the FDIC's. Banks whose deposits were insured by the FDIC, said he, could get public savings funds at very low rates of interest and could lend them profitably on the proposed FHA mortgages. Since building and loan companies were not covered by the FDIC, they would have to pay high rates of interest for savings and, hence, would be compelled to lend their funds at rates higher than those permitted by the draft terms of the FHA act. This would unfairly throw the mortgage business to the banks—unless a government-created insurance program, equivalent to the FDIC, provided coverage for the deposits of the building and loan companies.

Marriner strongly objected to Fahey's proposal, saying that it had no bearing on a program designed to get the maximum number of creditor institutions to channel idle private capital into home construction. Besides, the building and loan associations had been and were being bailed out of their troubles by the Home Loan Bank Board. If "fairness" was the issue, was it fair for them to block the participation of banks and insurance companies in a home construction program unless they got—in addition to all the other help provided by government agencies—an FDIC-type insurance scheme for themselves?

Roosevelt listened intently to the sharp exchange of views and then rendered his verdict. He was far more sensitive than Marriner to the presence in Congress of a significant number of representatives and senators who were officers of building and loan associations in their home communities. A controversy with them could imperil the whole housing program, and that was something Roosevelt wanted to avoid. So he sided with Fahey and directed Marriner to work with him in devising an insurance plan that would satisfy the interests connected with the building and loan companies. Marriner had no choice but to comply.

Two episodes soon opened his eyes to what FDR knew all along about the political fist of these companies. First, the general counsel of the Home Loan Bank Board, who participated in Marriner's negotiations with Fahey, presently resigned his governmental post and revealed his true identity when he became general counsel for the Building and Loan League. Second, Morton Bodfish, the skilled lobbyist of the League, was brought by Fahey to the meetings of government officials Marriner called in his Treasury office to devise the insurance plan that would be the "ransom price" Roosevelt thought was politically necessary if the whole of the housing program was to be saved.

Marriner was opposed from the start to Bodfish's presence, but initially tolerated it out of deference to Fahey. Bodfish not only made himself at home; he proceeded to raise the ransom price to a point where Winfield Riefler, otherwise a model of patience and forbearance, walked out of the negotiations in disgust. Marriner managed to contain his own temper until Bodfish had carried his demands to their utmost stretch. But then, with the snap of a spring that had been coiled tight against itself, he told Fahey not to come to future meetings with the lobbyist in tow. Fahey agreed, and once Bodfish was excluded, Riefler returned to the group.

In time, the discussions led to the terms of Title IV of the FHA, creating the Federal Savings and Loan Insurance Corporation (FSLIC) under the Home Loan Bank Board. Each savings and loan association belonging to the FSLIC was to pay an annual premium, originally established as one quarter of 1 percent of share accounts and creditor liabilities. In return, the FSLIC was to insure all share accounts up to $10,000 in the event of default of the organization and proclamation of such default by a competent authority. What happened to these provisions will be noticed presently.

The revolutionary concept of mortgage financing at the heart of the FHA measure, should have made the largest headlines. Ironically, however, Marriner and his associates were forced to mute that aspect of the unveiled FHA bill and to place their stress on how the bill would spur new construction. They could not openly justify the proposed reform on what was in fact its strongest ground—namely, that it would end the mortgage loan practices of creditor agencies which had ruined the agencies, themselves, had ruined debtors, and had dried up opportunities for building and thus employment of construction workers. To dwell publicly on those practices of the past would be to enlarge the circle of hostility to the FHA beyond the hostility of the building and loan associations. Most banks and many insurance companies were opposed to the mortgage market reforms set forth in the FHA. Though the draft bill limited bank holdings of insured mortgages to 60 percent of their time funds, bankers as a group shared the common view that the commercial banking system should not be encouraged to engage in any kind of long-term mortgage financing. The larger banks were particularly hostile to the FHA, influenced by the oppositon of the larger insurance companies.

At the Senate and then the House Banking and Currency Committee hearings on the FHA bill, extending from mid-May to the first week in June 1934, Title I—which dealt with the emergency modernization program—had fairly clear sailing. Titles II and III, however, which were to stimulate new housing construction, ran into heavy weather. Worse, though Title IV had been written into the act at FDR's express direction in order to appease the building and loan associations, John Fahey and Morton Bodfish were prepared to kill the whole housing bill, even at the price of losing the insurance benefits contained in Title IV. Their chosen field of battle was the House of Representatives.

On the Senate side of Capitol Hill, the FHA measure was considered by a subcommittee of the Banking and Currency Committee whose dominant figures were senators Alben W. Barkley and Robert E. Wagner. Marriner's appearance before them to testify on behalf of the FHA measure was the first time he addressed a committee of the Congress as an official representative of the administration. The atmosphere was jovial, and the tone was set by Senator Barkley. After Marriner had stated his name, residence and occupation, the colloquy began like this:

Senator Barkley: Are you a real "mariner" from Utah?

Mr. Eccles: Yes, sir; I am from Utah. I do not know that I am a real "mariner;" I'm from Utah, however.

Senator Barkley: You are so close to the Great Salt Lake that I did not know but what you are a real mariner.

Mr. Eccles: Well, if this drought continues we might have to become pedestrians instead of mariners.

If Marriner believed that sweetness and light would prevail whenever he came before congressional committees, rude jolts would soon educate him. For the moment he was pleased to see that Barkley and Wagner brushed off the forces hostile to the FHA proposal and that the bill they shaped for submission to the Senate followed the lines of the White House version. The picture was reversed by the House Banking and Currency Committee. The bill it reported out to the House as a whole was deprived of the vital parts of the White House draft—cut out to suit the interests represented by Morton Bodfish.

Marriner now had his first lesson on how an "absolute minority of one," plus another "to second the motion," can affect the legislative process. Representative Fred J. Sisson of New York, a member of the House Banking and Currency Committee, had strongly favored the original version of the housing measure and would not give up the fight for it. He had an ally in Representative John J. O'Conner of New York, a powerful member of the Rules Committee, who was then in the New Deal camp (though he would later defect from it and be "purged" by Roosevelt). The two men submitted several amendments from the floor of the House to restore the vital parts of the housing bill. When a round of test votes showed they had enough strength in the House to prevail, the floor managers for the interests Bodfish represented ordered a strategic retreat by having the bill sent back to the House Committee for further "deliberations."

When agents of the Senate and House banking and currency committees met in a conference committee, Marriner learned yet another lesson about the legislative process: despite preceding months of effort, deadlines set by the hands on a clock can affect, for good or ill, the fate of measures. In this instance, Congress was due to adjourn on June 30 so that members facing fall elections could go home and mount their campaigns. By June 30, Congress had completed all work on the agenda of the administration's "must" legislation, except for the final vote on the housing measure. So the clock was stopped while the Senate and House conferees thrashed out their differences. The imperatives of time, the firm stand of the Senate conferees, and the carrot and stick flourishes of White House representatives became the forceps that brought the bill out of the conference committee with the main provisions of the White House version intact. Both chambers then approved of the measure by decisive votes, though as usual many members seemed wordlessly to say: "I don't know what's in this bill, but let's vote for it and find out." President Roosevelt quickly signed the enabling act, and the FHA came to legal birth as an independent agency.

All along the way, from conception of the act to its birth, Marriner had been introduced to the realities of the legislative process of which he had only faintly been aware back in Utah. Now, however, he had to digest yet another reality. In Utah he could pick the operating executives of his companies on the basis of their technical competence without regard to their prior celebrity. Indeed, most of the men he chose for key executive positions were, at the time of their selection, young and virtually unknown beyond a small circle of associates. But in Washington he learned that his basis for choosing an operating executive of a private enterprise did not encompass all the considerations a president weighed in selecting a person to adminster a public enterprise.

Marriner's candidate to administer the whole of the new-born FHA was Albert Deane. He noted for Roosevelt's benefit that Deane had helped draft the legislation, had a clear grasp of its aims, and had had extensive experience in the wide world of consumer credit. Roosevelt, however, wanted some "window dressing" for the innovative housing program; Deane could not provide it; he was not sufficiently well known to the general public. "Mr. President," argued Marriner, "Deane will become very well known the moment you appoint him the FHA administrator." Roosevelt was not persuaded.

Meanwhile, on orders from FDR, Frank Walker sent J. M. Daiger to New York to search for someone in the banking community who met the specifications for window dressing. Daiger did better than that. He found a very able man who held a high post in a New York bank but was willing to leave it in order to administer the whole FHA program. The sequel, as Marriner later recalled it, was that

while the search for an administrator of the FHA was going on, President Roosevelt left for a 10,000 mile cruise on the *U.S.S. Houston* through the Caribbean and the Panama Canal to Cocos Island and Hawaii, and back to Portland, Oregon. It's not clear whether he personally settled the FHA matter before he set sail, or whether it was settled by someone else. But I've been told that while the President was at sea, his secretary, Marvin McIntyre, telephoned James A. Moffett in New York. Moffett, who was in charge of foreign operations for a large oil company, no doubt knew all there was to know about the way leases are secured in Middle East oil fields. But this had no relationship to the mortgage financing of a new bungalow in Broken Bow, Nebraska. When Moffett was informed that the President wanted him to administer the whole of the new housing program, he candidly confessed that he had never heard of the FHA before that moment. But he was told to come to Washington anyway.[21]

Moffett did come, was appointed Federal Housing Administrator and was confirmed as the head of an agency that was to help take the government out of the lending business. From all accounts, he had an unblemished moral character. Unfortunately he was in the dark about what the FHA legislation was meant to achieve. Worse, the deputy administrator he chose for Titles II and III—to get new home construction underway on the basis of private capital—was a retired New York commercial banker who was not qualified by experience or outlook for the responsibilities that devolved upon him. Like most bankers, he was opposed in principle and in detail to the revolution in mortgage financing contained in the FHA legislation. When a battering ram was needed to break the financial community's wall of opposition to the program, the most that was forthcoming from the banker in question were some flicks with a feather duster.

Partly because of the this deputy's inadequacy to his task, the FHA's new home construction program failed to fulfill the hopes that rode on it. It failed for other reasons as well. It was no easy thing to formulate and win assent to workable nationwide rules for appraising homes. The task was time-consuming, though in Marriner's view it was needlessly prolonged. Second, the rules formulated were so restrictive that virtually the only people who qualified for an FHA-insured mortgage were those who did not need the benefits. In consequence, the FHA act stimulated only a trickle of new home constuction. Private funds remained idle, the government was forced to increase its lending operations and the public debt grew.

Nonetheless, an impressive result was achieved under Title I of the FHA legislation providing for home modernization. Backed by other members of his task force, Marriner managed to get Albert Deane appointed as deputy administrator directly in charge of that program. If he was not sufficiently well known to serve as "window dressing," he knew in precise detail what he was supposed to do and how to do it. Thus, though the government was empowered to absorb up to 20 percent of the aggregate losses on home improvement loans, in actual practice it absorbed only 5 percent. Translated into dollars and cents, this meant that at a cost to the government of $50 million, in contrast to an anticipated cost of $200 million, the modernization program generated $1 billion of useful private expenditures. Moreover, although the life of the modernization program was meant to cease once the $200 million subsidy was exhausted, its achievements induced the Congress later on to increase by another $1 billion this specific governmental stimulus to private spending. While the new grant was made under the condition that the aggregate losses the government could absorb was cut in half—by decreasing the guarantee from 20 to 10 percent—the volume of home improvement loans increased instead of diminishing. Untold millions of home owners have since continued to benefit from such loans, and countless banks have found in them a steady source of profit. Still it is improbable that more than a handful of home owners and banks knew who the architects of these loans were, and how the Home Loan Bank Board and the Building and Loan League, in pursuit of their own narrow interests, had been prepared to keep the system for such loans from being born (see Appendix A).

V

The extent of the economic recovery attained in 1934 drove a wedge into the New Deal ranks. In February of that year Rexford Tugwell said: "This battle for the New Deal is not yet over; indeed, I suspect it has just begun." But a few weeks later, Raymond Moley announced: "The New Deal is practically complete." Tugwell stood with most of the young lawyers and economists in the administration and the progressives in Congress, all sharing a mistrust of business and a conviction that the economic house must be swiftly set in order before the popular demand for change evaporated. With Moley were ranged the advocates in the administration of business-government "cooperation," the conservative Democrats in the Congress, and all who felt that the pressing need was to restore business "confidence" and who wished, in the distinction of the day, to subordinate "reform" to "recovery."

The NRA, like the AAA, was the emblem of the New Dealers who shared Tugwell's hope that, through "planning," America's enormous energies could be disciplined and channeled into one national effort to establish a secure base for economic well-being. By September 1934, however, the NRA was in grave trouble, and from the signals being transmitted by Roosevelt, it was clear that it was done for—even before the Supreme Court administered the coup de grâce. Tugwell and his supporters were deeply disturbed by those signals. Marriner Eccles welcomed them.

He had been opposed from the start to every aspect of the NRA—its assumptions, structure, and effects. Not that he was opposed to framing government policy with an eye to the national economy as an integrated whole. Far from it. He was opposed to the kind of *direct* planning and administration embodied in the NRA. From the perspective of his experience in banking crises, he believed that the federal government could *indirectly* influence the life of the entire national economy through a reformed Federal Reserve System, a unified banking system, fiscal policies, and changes in the practices of the various regulatory agencies whose decisions affected the flow of money and credit. He had been thinking and talking about all of this since 1931. He had underlined it in the course of his testimony before the Senate Finance Committee in February 1933. Events would presently enable him to come directly to grips with what he thought should be done to "modernize" the Federal Reserve System.

17. *The Law of Surprise*

I

IN JUNE 1934, MARRINER'S WIFE Maisie and the three Eccles children moved from Ogden into a seven-room apartment in the Shoreham Hotel in Washington. In the fall, Campbell enrolled in the Wharton School of Finance; the two younger children, John and Eleanore, entered the Friends' School in Washington. The design for Washington living was meant to last only a year. By the terms of his agreement with Morgenthau, Marriner still planned to return to Utah the following June. The first law of life, however, is the law of surprise.

Not long after Marriner was joined in Washington by his family, Eugene Black resigned as governor of the Federal Reserve Board and returned to his post as governor of the Federal Reserve Bank in Atlanta, claiming that he could not afford to stay in Washington at a 60 percent reduction in his Atlanta salary. Until his successor was chosen, the board was presided over by its vice-governor, J. J. Thomas, a man whose exemplary personal virtues did not, regrettably, compensate for his sketchy knowledge of central banking. Other Federal Reserve Board members included Adolph Miller, Charles S. Hamlin, George R. James and Matt Szymczak (see Appendix B).

In the summer months immediately following Black's resignation, the names of his possible successors as head of the board rose, fell, and rose again on the stock exchange of Washington gossip. If Marriner's name figured in this kind of speculation, he was not himself aware of it. But on a blistering day at the end of August, he was seated next to Henry Morgenthau at a White House conference soon after Roosevelt's return from his cruise aboard the *U.S.S. Houston* when Morgenthau suddenly whispered into his ear: "Marriner, I've been talking to the president about your filling Eugene Black's place." There was no whispered reply, nor were any questions asked when the meeting ended.

Several days later, Morgenthau put the case directly to Marriner. What did he think of the prospect mentioned at the White House conference? Marriner parried the question by asking one of his own. Was he in fact being seriously considered by Roosevelt for an appointment as governor of the Federal Reserve Board? The answer—yes—was confirmed in September when Marriner went with Morgenthau to another White House meeting. Here, amid discussions about other matters, he learned from Roosevelt directly that he was being thought of as a possible successor to Eugene Black. The president wanted to know if Marriner was interested.

Marriner wasted no words. "I would not," he said bluntly, "touch the position of governor with a ten-foot pole unless fundamental changes were made in the Federal Reserve System." He explained how decentralized private interests, acting through each of the Federal Reserve banks, had become the true if concealed "governors" of the Federal Reserve System, while the Federal Reserve Board in Washington—which was supposed to be the central authority guarding the public interest with respect to monetary and credit policies—had been reduced to impotence. Any man who accepted the governorship of the Federal Reserve Board would therefore be hobbled from the outset by the divorce between his official responsibilities and his lack of effective power to discharge them. "*But,* Mr. President," he added, "if *you* will help bring about by *law* the necessary legal changes in the Federal Reserve System, then I would welcome any consideration you might give to my personal fitness to serve as governor of the Federal Reserve Board."

The unconventional reaction aroused FDR's interest. What specific changes, he asked, should be made in the Federal Reserve System? Marriner replied that, with many changes in mind, he would need a "little time" to formulate them in concrete detail. It was not until November 4, the day after the 1934 congressional elections were held, that he again met with the president. The election itself was the first real test of New Deal strength with the voter. The Democrats won an overwhelming victory, and the Republicans found themselves feebler as a minority in the new seventy-fourth Congress than they had been at any time since before the Civil War. Some New Dealers were euphoric over the possibilities lying ahead. "Boys," said Harry Hopkins to his inner circle of aides, "this is our hour. We've got to get everything we want—a works program, social security, wages and hours, everything—now or never. Get your minds to work on developing a complete ticket to provide security for all the folks of this country up and down and across the board."[22] The reform of the Federal Reserve System was not on Hopkins' list for a "complete ticket." Yet it was central to the financing of everything which he and other like-minded New Dealers hoped to achieve.

II

Marriner brought to his November 4 meeting with President Roosevelt—the first private one he had had—a memorandum he prepared with the help of Lauchlin Currie. A Canadian by birth and an economist by training, Currie had come in 1934 from his post on the Harvard faculty to the Treasury Department, where he joined the "Freshman Brain Trust." Marriner found that he and Currie had similar views, and welcomed his refinements on points of detail. Currie, in addition to Winfield Riefler and a later associate, Bertram Knapp, was to be among Marriner's most intimate collaborators in countless future economic battles.

The full text of the memorandum Marriner brought with him was titled

"Desirable Changes in the Administration of the Federal Reserve System." It will suffice here to summarize the history of the Federal Reserve and Marriner's main points.

Since the creation of the Federal Reserve System, each Federal Reserve Bank was under the majority control of private bankers. Executive authority in each bank had gravitated to the governor of the bank, an ad hoc officer of the bank, not mentioned in the Federal Reserve Act of 1913 but elected by the private bankers who formed the majority of the bank directors. The private banking community was granted an additional voice in the Reserve System through the Federal Advisory Council, comprising twelve bankers, one from each Reserve District and representing nearly always the larger metropolitan banks within their respective districts. The twelve met with the Federal Reserve Board to *advise* on business conditions. But the occasional publications of the council, representing the private-banker viewpoint, were often presented to a confused public as though they were the views of the board itself. This was the critical point: whereas the United States public debt was less than $1 billion when the Reserve System was created, it was roughly $27 billion by the end of the First World War, a fact that had important consequences for the Federal Reserve System. It gradually became clear to the autonomous Federal Reserve Banks, to the Federal Reserve Board in Washington, and particularly to Benjamin Strong, the governor of the New York Reserve Bank, that when they bought and sold government securities connected with the $27 billion public debt, they were not engaged in a self-limiting activity. They directly influenced not only market conditions but the reserves of member banks. The reserves, in turn, influenced the volume of deposits, the deposits determined the volume of loanable funds that could be made available to the commercial banks, and the volume of loanable funds influenced the minutest operations of the economy. These chain reactions, once set in motion, were national in their consequences.

In the face of these realities, Federal Reserve bankers concluded that the principle of regional autonomy would have to be modified so that purchases and sales of government securities could be nationally coordinated through some sort of "open-market" investment committee. There followed a decade-long evolutionary process without foundations in law, but whose institutional aspects were simply improvisations that went unchallenged.

Several aspects of that evolutionary story must be noted here. For one thing, through twists and turns, control over open market decisions remained in the hands of the bank governors, who owed their own offices to an election by private bankers. It was not until the Banking Act of 1933 was passed that open-market operations were expressly recognized and defined by law. The act authorized the creation of an Open Market Committee consisting of one member from each Federal Reserve district, designated annually by the board of directors of each Reserve bank—meaning, by the private bankers who were in the majority on each board. The committee was to meet in Washington periodically to perform the functions authorized by law.

The new law did not touch the fundamental weakness that characterized the previous history of open-market operations. While no Reserve bank could engage in open-market sales or purchases unless it conformed to Federal Reserve Board regulations, the 1933 act preserved its right to *refuse* to participate in the sales and purchases the Open Market Committee recommended. The arrangement made for administrative chaos. The Federal Reserve Board, which was ultimately held responsible for policy, could not initiate open-market operations; it could only ratify or veto the policies initiated by the Open Market Committee. That committee could initiate policy but could not execute it. The board of directors of the individual Reserve banks, who took no part in forming policy, had the power to obstruct it. A more effective way to fragment responsibility, and to encourage inertia and indecision, could hardly have been devised. Yet, it seemed to suit the New York Federal Reserve Bank; the arrangement enabled various private interests in that financial district to exercise enormous influence over the national economy.

This was the background situation when Marriner met President Roosevelt on November 4. Of the eight points in his memorandum, the first stressed the relationship between monetary management and business activity. ("Fluctuations in production, employment and the national income are determined by changes in the available supply of cash and deposit currency, and by the rate and character of monetary expenditures, etc.") The second and third points commented on the immediate possibilities of monetary control and on such future control. ("The most important role . . . at the moment is assuring that adequate support is available whenever needed for the emergency financing involved in the recovery program; the object for the future was to assure that a recovery does not result in an undesirable inflation," followed in turn, "by a depression.") The fourth, fifth and seventh points indicated some of the desirable changes in the administration of the Federal Reserve System, with special emphasis on the need to strengthen the authority of the Federal Reserve Board. ("Complete control over the timing, character and volume of open market purchases and sales of bills and securities by the Reserve banks should be conferred upon the Federal Reserve Board." Since "banker interest, as represented by the individual Reserve Bank Governors, has prevailed over the public interest, as represented by the Board," the public interest must be reasserted by giving the Federal Reserve Board the right to approve or disapprove of the choice of governors of the individual Federal Reserve banks made by their boards of directors.")

The sixth point of the memorandum, which dealt directly with open market operations, was the heart of the whole matter. Marriner contended that if past practices were not changed, the future consequences of open market operations would be as melancholy as those visible during the depths of the depression. His language here deserves to be quoted directly:

Far and away, the most important instrument of reserve policy is the power to buy and sell securities in the open market. In this way reserves, on which deposits are based, may be given to or taken from member banks. It is not too much to say that who possesses this power controls the banking system and, in large measure, the supply of money. . . .

At present the Federal Open Market Committee is composed of the twelve Governors and, hence, is dominated by the same men who were responsible for the policy followed during the Depression. The Governors, by the nature of their appointments, duties and associations, cannot help but be profoundly influenced by a narrow banking rather than by a broad social point of view.

There is no reason to suppose that this administrative organization which functioned so badly in the past, will function any better in the future. The diffusion of power and responsibility, the root cause of the trouble, remains. Over 100 individuals are responsible, in varying degrees, for the formulation of policy. Obviously, the more people there are who share the responsibility, the less keenly any one of them will feel any personal responsibility for the policies adopted. It is, therefore, almost inevitable that such a loosely knit and cumbersome body as the Federal Reserve Administration should be characterized by inertia and indecisive action generally. Moreover, a complete stalemate resulting from a disagreement of the Reserve banks and the Board is always possible. To correct this condition, reform must be in the direction of concentrating authority and responsibility for control into the hands of a small policy formulation body.

The final point of the memorandum established a link between the reforms proposed through the text, and their effect in neutralizing the traditional opposition to all moves in the direction of central banking:

The adoption of these suggestions would introduce certain attributes of a real central bank capable of energetic and positive action without calling for a drastic revision of the whole Federal Reserve Act. Private ownership and local autonomy are preserved, but on really important questions of policy, authority and responsibility are concentrated in the Board. Thus, effective control is obtained, while the intense opposition and criticism that greets every central bank proposal is largely avoided.

There were other issues, not mentioned in the memorandum, which came up at the meeting on November 4. Marriner conceded that banks were uneasy over their increasing dependence on government obligations to prop up their income. But, he said, this did not mean that the budget balancers were right when they stressed the need to reduce deficit spending in order to bolster business confidence. The banks themselves had the means to reduce the grounds for their unease. If they put to use in the form of real estate loans and other long-term investments the savings and excess funds they had on hand, bank activity would be greatly stimulated—and the government could rapidly withdraw from the lending field.

To that end, however, it was imperative to broaden the types of paper eligible for discount at the Federal Reserve Banks. Marriner noted, for

Roosevelt's benefit, that the provisions of the Federal Reserve Act which restricted the discount privilege to short-term commercial loans and investments shackled Reserve System operations and the life of the entire banking system. In October 1934, for instance, the paper eligible for rediscounting privileges within the meaning of the Federal Reserve Act came to little more than $2 billion nationally, and, even so, the total was substantially reduced by the exacting hand of the "eligibility" provisos. Banks could not live on the interest from so small a volume of loans and any attempt to do so would obviously sharply curtail the scope of banking. The more business the banks refused—and their decisions would be influenced by the extent to which their loans were eligible for discount as well as the rediscount rate—the more a dominant role in the credit field would go by default to other agencies, including the government.

However, Marriner saw a solution to the sticky problem of "eligibility." In place of a stress on the word "liquidity," he would stress "sound assets"; he would "bestow liquidity" on all "sound assets" and these would be an "eligible" basis for borrowing at the Reserve banks in time of need. In that way, banks could concentrate on efforts to keep their assets sound and to pay less attention to the calendar date when a note was to mature. Reliance on that latter kind of "soundness" had not protected the banking system from the disaster of 1929–32. On the contrary, it was a contributing cause of that disaster. If a single bank wished to protect itself against good loans going bad in a depression, its portfolio would have to consist of super-liquid, open-market paper. It could then pay off all its deposits at a moment's notice—even though the national income was cut in half. But it could not adequately perform its duty to serve the community as a middleman-investor of a substantial portion of the community savings.

In the course of Marriner's two-hour elaboration of the memorandum and the legislative program it would entail, Roosevelt's attention never wavered, though he could on other occasions be evasive. Now and then, he fired an electric question, as when Marriner suggested that branch banking should be included in the proposed legislative program. Branch banking, with its connotation of "bigness," ran contrary to Roosevelt's bias for an economy based on small local units of power. Now and then, he would race ahead of Marriner's line of exposition, and project forward the trend of what was being said. But above all, as a finely tuned political instrument, Roosevelt clearly understood the nature of the political in-fighting Marriner's proposals were bound to invite.

At last, in a characteristic gesture signaling a decision, Roosevelt slapped his powerful hands down on top of his desk. "Marriner," said he, "that's quite an action program you want. It will be a knock-down and drag-out fight to get it through. But we might as well undertake it now as at any other time. It seems to be necessary." He had something more to add. "It's being gossiped around that I am considering appointing you the new governor of the Federal Reserve Board. It's only fair that you should know that formidable opposition has developed as a result. However, I don't give a damn. That opposition is coming from the boys who I am not following.''

"Well, Mr. President," said Marriner in reply, "if you don't give a damn, I don't see why I should.''[23]

It was a case where ignorance was not only bliss but was the source of something fruitful. "If I had then known how strong the opposition would be," Marriner later observed, "I doubt whether I would have had the courage to accept the appointment and the revolutionary work it entailed. But at the time, Roosevelt's pledge of support was all I needed to hear."

The impending appointment entailed a change in Marriner's relationship with the First Security Corporation and its banks. When he first came to Washington as a "special assistant" to Secretary of the Treasury Morgenthau, he was not legally required to alter the nature of his relationships with any of his companies. An appointment to head the Federal Reserve Board was different. To conform with the law, Marriner resigned as president of the First Security Corporation and of the First Security Bank of Utah, and disposed of his personal stock in them. His brother George, then thirty-four, assumed the presidency of the First Security Bank of Utah; E. G. Bennett took over the presidency of both the First Security Corporation and of the First Security Bank of Idaho. Marriner relinquished the presidency of the Utah Construction Company but was designated "chairman of the board on leave." He remained the vice-president and treasurer of the Amalgamated Sugar Company and, under an interpretation of the law, also retained the presidency of the Eccles Investment Company. Throughout his seventeen and one-half years of public service in Washington, he would never once take a "vacation." He rationed his "accumulated leave" so that he could return to Ogden for quarterly meetings of the various enterprises in which he could legally participate free from any conflict of interests.

On November 10, Roosevelt announced Marriner's appointment as governor of the Federal Reserve Board—making him the first Westerner ever to hold the post. A White House statement accompanying the announcement contained a sketch of his banking and business connections. Written as though it was a stockholder's report, it listed the capital value of each Eccles enterprise, the volume of business it did each year, and how each had "successfully weathered the years of the depression." The form of the announcement was unique among those which accompany presidential appointments. But its obvious intent was to offset the charge then current that all New Deal officials were crackpots and visionaries, unqualified to hold office or to have an opinion about public policy because they had "never met a payroll." The announcement was also designed to reassure millions of plain people around the country who had known the pain of bank crashes. Here was a Westerner who had headed a far-flung banking organization that had come through the worst depression years without the loss of one cent to its depositors.

Marriner had nothing to do with the preparation of the White House summary of his life and was amused when he saw it in print. He adhered to the innocent view that the legislative program he had in mind and hoped to initiate as the new head of the Federal Reserve Board deserved to be and would be judged on its own merits—without regard to his past career in Utah or personal fate in Washington.

In Utah, press reaction to Marriner's appointment was mainly in the "local boy makes good" vein. National press reaction was mixed. The *New York Evening Post* welcomed his appointment: "Marriner S. Eccles is a unique figure in American Finance—a banker whose views on monetary policy are even more liberal than those already embraced by the New Deal." The *NewYork Evening Journal* and the *Wall Street Journal* were sharply critical of the appointment, as was the *Washington Post*. In an editorial comment on the appointment, the *NewYork Times* recalled the "bombastic utterances" of Mr. Eccles when he appeared before the Senate Finance Committee in 1933.[24] The only hope it saw for the future was that his "inflamed views" would undergo a "cooling process" as he encountered the responsibilities of governor of the Federal Reserve Board. These comments could be brushed off. What could not be ignored, however, were the consequences of a presidential oversight involving the person of Senator Carter Glass of Virginia.

18. Ruffled Feathers

FOR THE GREATER PART of his life, Senator Carter Glass of Virginia was honored on all sides as a man of high intelligence, courage, fluency and integrity. In the course of his distinguished career, he had been chairman of the House Banking and Currency Committee, "father" of the Federal Reserve System, and a Secretary of the Treasury in the second Wilson administration. Special respect was paid to him, in the Senate, when he spoke of banking matters.

In March 1933, when the Democrats organized the Senate, Glass had a seniority claim to the chairmanship of either the Banking and Currency Committee or the Appropriations Committee. But if he became chairman of Banking and Currency, the Appropriations post could go to the next in the line of seniority. This was Senator Kenneth D. McKeller of Tennessee, a product of the Memphis machine of "Boss Crump," a vendettist by temperament and a spoilsman by habit. Leaders of the incoming Roosevelt administration were appalled by the prospect of having McKeller as chairman of the Appropriations Committee. To block him, they prevailed on Glass to assume that chairmanship. The chairmanship of the Banking and Currency Committee went *in name only* to Senator Duncan Fletcher of Florida, who was then getting on in years and was content to crown his Senate career by holding merely the title of chairman. Actual power was vested in Glass. He was made chairman of a subcommittee of the full Banking and Currency Committee—which was to have the right to deal with all vital matters bearing on banking and currency and the formulation of policies in that field.

On the face of things, the subcommittee was a "varsity team" of legislators. Besides Glass, it included Senator Robert J. Bulkley of Ohio, who had been on the House Banking and Currency Committee in 1913 and had worked with Glass in framing the original Federal Reserve Act. Another member was Senator William Gibbs McAdoo of California who, like Glass, had once served as Secretary of the Treasury in a Wilson cabinet. The remaining members were Senators James P. Byrnes of South Carolina, John H. Bankhead of Alabama, Peter Norbeck of South Dakota, John G. Townsend, Jr., of Delaware, and James Couzens of Michigan. These were willful men, in complete self-possession. Glass, however, was dominant among them and generally managed to wheel the subcommittee members into a position of support for his views—or his personal pique.

In every governmental post he held, whether in the House of Representatives, the Treasury or the Senate, Glass had presided over the operations of the Federal Reserve System. After Eugene Black resigned as governor of the Federal Reserve Board, Glass expected either personally to pick the next governor or be consulted by Roosevelt before one was chosen. This was not done. Marriner's appointment was announced without discussion with Glass. It never occurred to Marriner to suggest that the senator be consulted. He was still a tenderfoot in the political jungle of Washington and assumed that Roosevelt, the master political craftsman, had secured Glass's "proxy" before announcing the appointment.

It is not clear why Roosevelt failed to consult Glass, but that failure colored the senator's views toward the reforms Marriner advocated in the Federal Reserve System. Moreover, since the Senate hearings on the confirmation of Marriner ran concurrently with the hearings on the proposed Banking Act, the two matters were fused in Glass's tactics. To avenge himself on the president, he tried to defeat the confirmation of Marriner Eccles as Governor of the Federal Reserve Board, as a means for defeating the key reforms contained in the provisions of the Banking Act.

Glass was encouraged in this course by men who had other motives of their own. For example, George L. Harrison, governor of the Federal Reserve Bank of New York, correctly understood that if the changes Marriner proposed became law, they would end the New York Reserve Bank's longstanding power to dominate the nation's supply of money and credit. To preserve the status quo, he made common cause with Glass, opposing portions of the proposed law. His intimate personal relationship with Glass was reinforced by his friendship with Admiral and Mrs. Cary Grayson; the admiral, who had been President Wilson's physician, was Glass's crony. Harrison plucked the mystic chords of memory to recall how things were in the Golden Age when President Wilson was in the White House, Glass was his Secretary of the Treasury—and Franklin D. Roosevelt was but a stripling undersecretary of the Navy.

In one respect, Marriner was "unmuzzled" the moment he was appointed governor. As an assistant to the Secretary of the Treasury, he had found colleagues in the department such as Lauchlin Currie, who shared his views about the importance of deficit spending. They observed that all government schemes for placing money directly in the hands of potential consumers were small-scale affairs. The moderate business recovery between 1933 and 1934 could be directly traced to the government's total deficit spending of $3.3 billion for relief purposes. The total, however, was less than 7 percent of the depressed national income at the time, and less than 4 percent of the nation's normal income. The aggregate effect of small yearly increments of deficit spending would serve only to increase the public debt without stimulating the massive outpouring of private expenditures needed for recovery. Public spending must be on a scale that could increase consumer income and expenditures, thereby triggering the full utilization of the capital goods industry.

These views, however, were not publicly associated with the Treasury

Department. Within the department, Budget Director Lewis Douglas banned all talk about large-scale deficit financing. When he resigned from the administration in August 1934 over the budget balancing issue, the ban did not depart with him. It was reimposed by the Undersecretary of the Treasury, Thomas Jefferson Coolidge, who owed his post largely to the intercession of his friend George L. Harrison. A safe and orthodox man, Coolidge let it be known that he would regard it as a hostile act if anyone within the Treasury talked loudly about how large-scale deficit financing could help promote recovery.

In addition to those two men, Henry Morgenthau served in his own way to muffle Treasury voices. Morgenthau meant to make of his own person the communication channel through which all Treasury opinion would reach Roosevelt's ears. From the standpoint of "tidy" administration, he was no doubt right in insisting that none of his subordinates should engage in back-door dealings with the White House. But since he leaned heavily on Coolidge's advice, the views he passed on to Roosevelt fostered the impression that there were no sharp divisions of opinion within the Treasury on the issue of deficit spending—that the department's political executives and technical experts were as one in calling for a balanced budget. With dissenting voices in the Treasury reduced to silence in public, and with Morgenthau repeating the catchphrases of economic orthodoxy, the burden of publicly arguing the case for large scale spending programs went by default to two men—Harry Hopkins and Harold Ickes—whose work relief projects exposed them to the charge that they were "playing politics with human misery."

It was Marriner Eccles' view that Hopkins and Ickes did indeed "play politics"—a *proper* politics—with human misery. "They worked every day," he said, "in a sea of misery. Better than most people, they knew that if the regular political organs of government did not offer some relief from the distress in which millions of people were held captive, the government as we had known it would be torn from within by a cataclysmic social upheaval." Yet the truths they spoke, instead of being judged on their own merits, were prejudged and discounted in many quarters as being merely "vote-catching devices." The case for deficit spending might have been better received if it had been put forward by the Treasury Department as an *economic* argument in the interest of the *nation's* general welfare.

Soon after Marriner was appointed Governor of the Federal Reserve Board, Roosevelt invited his chief lieutenants to throw their ideas into a common hopper from which he could draw material for his next State of the Union address. It was common knowledge within the administration that the president was prepared to ask Congress for approximately $4.5 billion to launch some sort of work relief program, but the form of that program was still in doubt.

Now able to speak freely, Marriner presented to the White House some ideas based on his experiences in the construction industry. He sent FDR a memorandum in which he argued that, while speed had been essential in providing emergency work for the unemployed, even at slapdash jobs, the time had come for the government to undertake on a *contract* basis billions of dollars of essential, nonprofit public works projects. The proposed contract basis assumed competition and a small but necessary profit to the contracting agency, so that private capital would come out of hiding. The paramount object of the recommended new approach would not be to stimulate the growth of *private* capital goods facilities. It would be to stimulate *public* capital goods facilities which would use private capital goods that were already in being, and whose facilities in the absence of effective consumer demand were excessive. As anticipated, FDR's State of the Union message of January 1935 proposed that the Congress enact a relief program with an initial appropriation of about $4.5 billion. The relief program itself, however, bore no resemblance to the one Marriner had advocated; it took the form of the Works Progress Administration (WPA).

In subsequent private arguments with President Roosevelt and Harry Hopkins, Marriner repeatedly cited the defects of WPA as a *form* of relief expenditure. In the first place its outlays fell far short of real needs. At no time was WPA able to care for more than three million people, though it functioned during periods when tens of millions were unemployed. With limited relief funds and with a vast relief load, workers on WPA projects rarely received more than two or three days of work during a week—or a cash income of between forty to seventy dollars a month—which barely maintained families at subsistence levels. Second, he thought it was dehumanizing to subject everyone who got WPA help to a means test—a test which amounted to a public announcement that any man on the WPA rolls was a failure and a pauper who had exhausted his insurance, savings, credit; who could not be helped by friends and relatives. Third, the American tradition of efficiency in production was violated by the restriction placed on the kind of tools WPA workers could use. Allocation of WPA funds depended on the ability of local communities or states to provide equipment and materials, while WPA funds proper were mainly earmarked for the labor costs of community projects. Since equipment and material were expensive, the poorest communities naturally tended to choose not the most desirable projects, which would have entailed the purchase of costly machines and material, but projects that could use the most hand labor and the simplest tools.

Still, this was for the future to show; Marriner had a more immediate concern. It was clear that in the event Congress approved the president's request for public works, the Federal Reserve System would be the conduit through which the banking system would have to absorb the securities and provide the credit for financing the program. But under the existing Reserve setup, a group of private individuals in control of the Reserve banks had the latent power to block the flow of funds for the program or to block Federal reserve operations toward a resumption of large-scale spending. Hence the urgency to overhaul the Federal Reserve System. The initial moves could not be delayed until after Marriner's confirmation as governor. Marriner began to press for action the day after he moved into his new office in the Treasury Department. The five months that were to pass between his recess appointment and his confirmation by the Senate were among the most strained in his life—doubly strained, because of the link between his appointment and the battle over the new banking bill. Nothing he had ever previously known in business approached the intensity of the in-fighting he had to surmount. But then he had never had a business ally with President Roosevelt's genius for rallying men with a single phrase or gesture.

"On an uncommonly warm day in April 1935," Marriner later recalled, "I was to report to the President on the status of the banking bill. The droop of my shoulders as I approached him on the south portico of the Executive Mansion where we were to have lunch, must have signalled in advance the dreary, discouraging tenor of my report. But before I could voice my woes, Roosevelt changed the mood of our meeting by the manner of his greeting. 'You know, Marriner,' said he, 'when I appointed you a member of the Federal Reserve Board, it never occurred to me that a Mormon had to be confirmed.' With this, he exploded with laughter. The weight of the world was lifted from my shoulders and I was again eager to resume a battle that had been going so badly."[25]

The battle was overprinted by legislative contests over two other significant measures—the Social Security Act and the National Labor Relations Act—that were before the seventy-fourth Congress. The subject of these two measures had direct and immediate personal implications and most Americans were aware of their importance. The Banking Act, however, dealt with matters seemingly impersonal, and "technical." It required a tutored observer to grasp the extent to which the terms of the Act could have a pervasive and fundamental effect on the everyday life of the American economy. Walter Lippmann, for example, commented that "in the whole long list of bills still before the Congress, the one that has by far the greatest possibility for good or evil, the one that may affect most powerfully the economic and political fortunes of the whole nation, is the banking bill. . . . Compared with this bill, every other bill now before the Congress is relatively unimportant." H. Parker Willis, a Columbia University Professor, agreed, but saw only evil in the bill. He called it "the worst and most dangerous measure that has made its appearance for a long time—perhaps at any time in American history." Irving Fisher, Yale's eminent professor of economics, saw the matter in a different light. The banking bill, said he, "will represent a great step forward, probably the greatest in the president's administration."[26]

19. Fire Fight

TWO INSTITUTIONAL MATTERS in need of immediate attention prepared the stage for the larger battle over the banking bill of 1935. One involved the Committee on Legislative Program for the Federal Reserve System. The committee, as its name suggested, was responsible for framing and initiating new legislation bearing on the work of the Federal Reserve System. Yet all the committee members—except for a single spokesman for the Federal Reserve Board—represented the private-banking viewpoint. The chairman of the committee was not the representative of the board. He was George Harrison, governor of the New York Federal Reserve Bank. He was not a public official with prescribed statutory powers and duties, but was chosen by and beholden to the directors of a Reserve Bank—an odd arrangement which had met with the mindless approval of the Federal Reserve Board.

Several days after Marriner's appointment as governor was announced, but before he was sworn in, George Harrison dropped by his office in the Treasury Department ostensibly to offer congratulations. When Harrison turned to leave, he paused to say, as if in a casual afterthought, "By the way, you know there is a legislative committee for the Federal Reserve System. Mr. Thomas, a vice-governor of the Federal Reserve Board, has been serving as the board representative on the committee. Now that you are about to be sworn in as governor, I assume you will want to take Thomas' place."

Marriner wasted no words. "I've been advised," said he, "of the existence of the legislative committee. But I don't intend to be a member of it. I have other plans. One of my first acts after I'm sworn in as governor will be to move the abolition of your committee. I will do this because the Federal Reserve Board—which reports directly to Congress and whose members are appointed to represent the public interest—also have a direct responsibility for the legislative program for the Federal Reserve System. Moreover, I have accepted the post of governor mainly to carry out an important legislative program which you, in all probability, are going to oppose. It would therefore be doubly incompatible—from the point of view of the board's responsibilities and my own intentions—to have a legislative committee controlled in any way by the officers and directors of the Federal Reserve Banks."

"Of course," said a flustered Harrison, "you have the right to do what you think you ought to do. Our committee has tried its very best to . . ." He finished the sentence and left the office, and the war between the two men was on.

The field of combat was widened on November 19, 1934—three days after Marriner was sworn in—when he met for the first time with the Federal Advisory Council. As representatives of the private banking system, the twelve bankers who made up the council were obliged by statute to "confer and advise directly" with the Federal Reserve Board, but they construed the statute differently in late September 1934 when the congressional elections were underway. The advisory council issued a public statement in which they demanded a prompt balancing of the federal budget. The Federal Reserve Board did not sign the statement, nor had it been asked to review it. The council acted unilaterally for partisan electioneering purposes. Council members failed to explain publicly that they represented only private banking interest, and were not authorized to speak for the Federal Reserve Board, which gave the impression that the statement was issued under the imprimatur of the Federal Reserve Board and that the board was strongly opposed to the deficit financing of the Roosevelt administration.

At Marriner's first meeting with the council, he remarked that he did not intend for the moment to argue the case for or against a balanced budget. What did interest him—and what needed prompt correction—was the way the council, as in the case of its September statement, had turned its role as an *adviser* to the Reserve Board into an instrument for partisan political polemics. The record of the meeting reads as an extension of Marriner's clash years previously with his half brother David:[27]

Mr. Eccles: You gentlemen of the Council have created the general impression that your opinions are those of the Federal Reserve System. Yet you know that is not the case. There is no established procedure for an exchange of views. You come to us without even an agenda of the things to be discussed. You call in staff members at your pleasure, get whatever information you want from them, and then issue a public statement condemning this or that government policy. It is only after the statement appears in the press that the Federal Reserve Board learns of your condemnation.

You have clearly deviated from your statutory role as advisers to the Federal Reserve Board and are, instead, engaged in the work of political propaganda. Since the Board is anxious that you *do* fulfill your statutory role as our advisers, we have a program to suggest as an alternative to one you've been following. Here it is:

We suggest that the Council issue no public statements without first submitting their recommendations and advice to the Federal Reserve Board and staff. If the Council then wishes to issue a public statement or submit recommendations of its own to the Congress, it should advise the Board to that effect. This will give the Board a chance to prepare a statement of its own in the event it objects to the Council's position, and the two statements will be released, simultaneously. On the other hand, if the Board is of the opinion that the Council's statement should not be released, the Council will be notified of that fact. It will also be provided with an opportunity to hear the reasons behind the Board's decision, and to present counter arguments of its own. If after a free and full discussion the Council is not persuaded to accept the Board's point of view, the Board will release its own objections to the position taken by the Council.

A Council member: Mr. Eccles, am I to understand that you are trying to tell us how to run our affairs? If so, you should know that the law creating the Council made us an independent agency. We are not required to submit anything to the Federal Reserve Board for approval. We have a legal right to saying anything we want, whenever we want, in whatever way we want.

Mr. Eccles: I am not questioning your legal rights. I am questioning your judgement about the way to manage matters in the public interest. But if you are going to argue legal points, remember that the Federal Reserve Board also has a few legal rights of its own. Among others, it has a legal right to ignore you, and to deny you access to its staff. So, in legal terms, we reach a stand-off, and while we each assert our independence, the whole purpose for which the Council was established is defeated. It was the intention of the Congress that the Council should be *helpful* to the Federal Reserve Board—helpful by *advising and consulting directly* with it. What I've suggested is simply a system by which advice and consultation can proceed in an orderly way.

Several Council members: We are an independent agency.

Mr. Eccles: Very well, gentlemen. But remember the Federal Reserve Board is also an independent agency, and as Governor of the Federal Reserve Board, I assert that independence right now. I don't want to discuss this matter any further with you. I suggest this meeting should adjourn until tomorrow to give you a chance to consider, without the Board's presence, what your decision should be.

The meeting adjourned in an explosive atmosphere. When the Council rejoined the Federal Reserve Board twenty-four hours later, they brought with them a draft of the terms that were to govern any future statements they would release. The terms differed in but a few verbal respects from those Marriner had proposed, and implied that the council was maintaining its independence from the board. Marriner didn't care who scored the most vanity points in the controversy as long as the council agreed to obey the law which required them to act as an *advisory* and not as a propaganda body. He accepted the verbal changes.

On November 23, four days after the end of his dispute with the Federal Advisory Council, Marriner, revealed to the Federal Reserve Board that he had agreed to undertake the duties of governor on the basis of Roosevelt's pledge to support legislative changes in the Federal Reserve System. He would therefore appreciate the board's providing him with the means to give specific shape to the proposed program. This entailed two interrelated moves. Since the existing legislative committee under the chairmanship of Harrison was a barrier to new legislation, its existence should be terminated as soon as it submitted its usual annual report. Without waiting for the demise of that body, a new legislative committee should promptly be formed from the professional staff of the board to work with Marriner on a legislative program. The board endorsed both proposals. Members of the new legislative committee, besides Marriner, were E. A. Goldenweiser, director of the board's Division of Research and Statistics; Chester Morril, secretary of the Board; Walter Wyatt, general counsel of the board; and Lauchlin Currie, whom Marriner brought over from the Treasury Department and, with the board's approval, appointed assistant director of research and statistics.

It was understood that the draft of the new Banking Act, as prepared by the legislative committee, would be reviewed by the Federal Reserve Board. Subject to the board's approval, the draft would then be submitted to a subcommittee on banking legislation (chaired by Treasury Secretary Morgenthau) of the administration's Interdepartmental Loan Committee.* If the draft measure cleared all these hurdles, it would then go to President Roosevelt and, subject to his approval, would be submitted to Congress soon after it convened in January 1935.

Marriner brought Lawrence Clayton from the First Security Corporation in Utah to serve as a personal aide. Here was an old friend who could be relied upon to be an unfailing source of selfless and sensible advice. In the final stages of the fight over the Banking Act of 1935, Marriner secured another adviser, Elliot Thurston, a former newspaperman, who carried in his head a pilot's chart of all the Washington's hidden reefs on which the best of purposes can be shipwrecked. His warnings and guidance were of inestimable value to Marriner in the years ahead.

During this time, Marriner gave no thought to Senator Carter Glass or what he might be hearing from pilgrims to the Senator's home in Lynchburg, Virginia. On December 17, however, he wrote Glass a belated note:

Ever since my present appointment, I have been hoping that I would have an opportunity of making your acquaintance. I recognize the leading role which you played in bringing the Federal Reserve System into being, and the active part and great interest which you have taken in its operation since that time. I have great respect for you and I want to express to you my admiration for the valuable and untiring work which you have rendered. I hope you will permit me to call upon you either at your office or your residence in the near future, sometime at your convenience.

The reply came a day later. It was an invitation to call on Glass when he returned to Washington after the first of the year. "Needless to say," the senator added, "I am obliged to you for your most courteous personal allusions to me and to my persistent efforts to maintain the independence of the Federal Reserve Banking System. I sincerely trust that we shall be able to cooperate in that direction." When the two men first met, Marriner referred to the prospective new banking measure, but he could not discuss its details, as the measure was under review by the interdepartmental subcommittee on banking legislation. The act would affect other agencies, besides the Federal Reserve, represented on that subcommittee. With each having a voice in the measure, no one could predict its final form. Marriner promised Glass that, as soon as the draft bill was cleared within the administration, he would describe its terms with the senator personally before discussing it with anyone else.

He was not being evasive when he told Glass he could not predict the

---

*Other members were T. J. Coolidge, Undersecretary of the Treasury; Herman Oliphant, general counsel of the Treasury; Jesse Jones, head of the RFC; Leo T. Crowley, head of the FDIC; and J. F. T. O'Connor, Comptroller of the Currency.

final form of the measure to be sent to Congress, but he could not reveal to Glass the main ground for his uncertainty. At the start of the drafting process, Roosevelt, as a legislative strategist, laid down a far-seeing order of battle where Marriner's proposed reforms for the Federal Reserve System—or Title II of the Banking Act—were tied for defensive purposes to two other parts which the banking community urgently wanted. Title I, for example, proposed to change the FDIC law so that after July 1, 1935, the rate and nature of FDIC assessments would be liberalized to the advantage of the bankers. Similarly, Title III proposed to give bankers relief from the harsh prospects many of them faced on July 1, 1935, when, under the terms of the 1933 Banking Act, any bank official in the Reserve System who had not repaid the loans he had previously received from his institution would lose his job. As the due date of July 1935 approached, it was apparent that many bankers had not yet paid back their loans, nor was there any immediate prospect that they could do so. Title III, therefore, among its other desirable provisions, held out the prospect that bankers would be granted a period of grace beyond July 1935.

Roosevelt's strategy of tying the reforms of the Federal Reserve System, which the bankers didn't want, to changes they very much wanted, was energetically fought by Leo T. Crowley, the then head of the FDIC, and by J. F. T. O'Connor, at that time Comptroller of the Currency. Their respective areas of responsibility could not be isolated from the character of the banking system as a whole. Yet both men insisted that single bills should be presented, each containing the particular amendments affecting their agencies. In that way, the changes proposed in the Federal Reserve System would draw all the point-blank fire of the banking community.

After much in-fighting, it was agreed that Henry Morgenthau's office—Morgenthau being chairman of the Interdepartmental Loan Committee—would serve as a neutral meeting ground for the separate efforts of Crowley, O'Connor and Eccles. Each of the three would send his own measure to the Treasury Department, where the parts of the banking bill as a whole would be spliced together and approved by the Interdepartmental Loan Committee. Morgenthau had known of Marriner's proposed reforms from the day of his appointment as governor of the Board, and favored their aims in principle. He also went along with Roosevelt's strategy of linking the Crowley, O'Connor and Eccles proposals together in a single omnibus bill. But the interagency conflicts about this continued down to the moment when the text of the bill was introduced in the House on February 5 by Congressman Henry B. Steagall, chairman of the House Banking and Currency Committee, and on the following day in the Senate by Senator Duncan Fletcher, chairman of the Senate Banking and Currency Committee.

Glass was outraged when the Banking Act of 1935 was sent to Congress without his having seen an advance copy of it. He had every reason to feel that some sort of trickery was afoot, since Marriner had not honored the promise made to him. However, the Federal Reserve portions of the bill were not completed and approved by the Interdepartmental Loan Committee until a day before the measure as a whole was sent to the House and Senate. More to the point, it was delivered to Capitol Hill before Marriner himself had received a copy of the full text. On discovering how things stood, Marriner promptly called Glass to explain what had happened and to say that he had no idea the bill would be sent to the Capitol so soon. Glass would not be mollified. He had been deeply offended and intimated that Marriner was lying to him. This was another mischance that taxed the relationship between the two men.

In advance of the hearings, Walter Wyatt, the general counsel for the Federal Reserve Board, joined Marriner in preparing for distribution among friendly representatives and senators a detailed memorandum packed with ammunition for the battle ahead. As part of the same preparation, Marriner addressed the mid-winter convention of the Ohio Bankers on February 12, a few days after the banking bill had been sent to the House and Senate. His explanations of the reasons for the proposed changes were printed in the *Congressional Record* and were widely distributed afterward. A presentation he also made to the executive council of the American Bankers Association in Pass Christian, Mississippi, had a promising sequel. The executive council approved the formation of a five-man committee to be located in Washington, where it would act as liaison between the banking community and administration leaders in the House and Senate while the banking bill was being considered. Included on this committee were Ronald Ransom of Atlanta, the then chairman of the American Bankers Association's committee of federal legislation; Rudolph S. Hecht, president of the ABA; Robert V. Fleming of the Riggs National Bank in Washington and first vice-president of the ABA; Tom K. Smith of the Boatman's National Bank in St. Louis and second vice-president of the ABA; and Winthrop W. Aldrich of the Chase National Bank in New York.

The five-man committee took strong exception to the draft formula for the composition of the Open Market Committee, but went a long way toward endorsing the other changes proposed in the Reserve System. Marriner was further encouraged when their recommendations were approved by a subsequent meeting of the ABA executive council held in Augusta, Georgia. It seemed for a while that a policy of concessions as a price for reducing banker opposition would pay off. But the five-man committee and the executive council of the ABA were generals without troops; they could not carry the majority of the nation's bankers with them. The generals themselves split into two camps when Aldrich placed himself in the forefront of the banker attack on Title II during the Senate hearings. Marriner was dumbfounded by such contradictions, but on reflection he realized that the performance conformed to a pattern. Although he had been able to convince bankers individually of the need for changes in the Reserve System, when they returned to their native camps, they generally resumed the beliefs of their provincial thinking.

All the while, Roosevelt was moving with muffled oars out of the public eyesight and earshot to muster support for the banking bill. His strategy for flanking Title II with Titles I and III was only a starter. When Congress convened in January, he quietly engineered the addition to the full Senate Banking Committee of three new members who were known to be strong supporters of the administration. He also braced the nerve of Senator Fletcher for the inevitable confrontation with Senator Glass. In a letter sent to Fletcher at the time the banking bill was introduced into the Senate, FDR encouraged Fletcher to use "all his power" in steering the legislation through the Senate.

Between February 21 and April 8, twenty-three witnesses offered testimony on the banking bill at the hearings of the House Banking and Currency Committee. The chairman of the committee, Congressman Steagall, and Congressman Alan Goldsborough, the second-ranking member, were friendly toward the bill. And so were most of the witnesses they brought before the committee. Marriner remained in close touch with Steagall and Goldsborough during the House hearings, and had his eyes opened to the meaning of authentic legislative talent. A small army of experts in the executive had already refined details of the bill, but Steagall and Goldsborough drew on their own knowledge to pinpoint aspects of the measure which still needed amendment. With virtually no exceptions, Marriner found their proposed amendments highly desirable, and he readily associated himself with them.

Marriner testified for several days before the House. Arthur Kroch, the influential columnist and Washington Bureau chief of the *New York Times* had been among the early critics of Marriner's appointment as governor of the Federal Reserve Board, but he radically reversed his judgment after watching Marriner in action at the House hearing. "His appearance," Kroch wrote, "established him as a man of intelligence, ability and poise. He had good reasons for everything he proposed. Rarely did questioning from the most hostile source put him in anything resembling trouble."[28]

This was true enough, but "trouble" was being planned elsewhere to unfold at the hearing of the Senate Subcommittee on Banking and Currency. The tactics which Harrison and the other directors of the New York Federal Reserve Bank were to follow in fighting the bill started not with an attack on the substance of the bill but on the way the measure came to birth. "I am," said Harrison to the other directors, "more concerned about the star chamber procedure in devising the bill than about its particular provisions, because it is indicative of a purpose to make the System a tool of the Administration." Harrison meant to avoid a personal confrontation with Eccles and the administration, and on the advice of T. J. Coolidge, his trusted friend in the Treasury Department, it was decided to "try to postpone action" on the bill rather than to attempt to modify it or "fight it openly." The advisability of Harrison's personally testifying before the Senate subcommittee had been discussed with Glass but decided against, since his testimony would be criticized for "too much concern with the Open

Market Committee." He would, however, line up witnesses for Glass "from districts outside New York."[29]

Marriner may have exaggerated the subservience of the New York Federal Reserve Bank to Wall Street interests. As objective-minded an observer as Allan Sproul, who was associated with the New York Federal Bank in 1935 and who became its distinguished governor and close friend of Marriner, believed that his friend did, in fact, exaggerate. But this does not say that Marriner's views were unwarranted. The members of the Federal Advisory Council who testified at some point during the congressional hearings came out strongly against the bill. When bankers were found who, as individuals, openly favored the proposed reforms of the Federal Reserve System—A. P. Giannini of California's Bank of America is an example —they were generally based in the far West or South.

Senator Glass knew that, in an overwhelmingly Democratic Congress, the most promising strategy for defeating the bill lay in disassociating it from the administration. On April 14, five days before the House Committee reported out the bill, he informed the *New York Times* that he was "authorized to deny" that the banking measure was an administration measure. Hence, "the Congressional Committees are authorized to handle the bill as they see fit." The story gained credence when Glass's charges became the subject of questions put to Roosevelt at a press conference, whereupon FDR quickly changed the subject as if to say that he had no great interest in the measure. The truth was something else. On March 25, Roosevelt sent House committee chairman Steagall a memorandum marked "Private and Confidential." "I hope that you can get the Banking Bill out and passed as soon as possible. I am leaving for Jacksonville, Florida, in such a hurry that I did not have a chance to talk to you." On returning, Roosevelt sent a letter by special messenger to Senator Duncan Fletcher, chairman of the full Senate Committee on Banking and Currency, with instructions that the letter "be placed right in his hand." The reason for the precaution lay in the key sentences: "Can't you keep the Banking Bill in the whole Committee and not refer it to Carter's subcommittee? This would be a great help!" The proposed bypass of Glass was not politically possible. But the day after Glass had released to the press his charge that the president was not backing the bill, Senator Fletcher paid a hurried visit to the White House. "The President favored having the bill considered as drafted by the Federal Reserve officials, and not in two sections," the Senator told newsmen later. "Title II is the gist of the whole bill and the proposition ought to be considered as a unit. The President is of this way of thinking, too."

The day Fletcher's statement was published, Senator Glass took his turn calling on the president. Later he lamely told reporters, "I have to believe . . . that leaders of the House have induced the President to change his mind and to think that it would be a better procedure, so far as the House is concerned, to proceed with the bill as a whole."[30] Still, the president refused to make a public statement in support of the bill, confining his efforts to quiet and confidential political maneuvers. He did not want to spend his political capital on an open fight for the measure until it was abolutely necessary for him to do so. He needed that capital for other measures before the Congress such as the National Labor Relations Act, the Social Security Act, and for the Emergency Relief Bill which Glass was holding up in the Appropriations Committee.

On April 15, the Senate Subcommittee on Banking and Currency began hearings on President Roosevelt's nomination of Marriner Eccles as governor of the Federal Reserve Board. Pigeon-holed in Glass's subcommittee for more than three months, it might have remained there indefinitely if it were not for the clear sign that the House Banking and Currency Committee was about to report out a banking bill—whose Title II gave specific and strengthened expression to Marriner's reformist aims. Since it had come to be known as the "Eccles bill," the House committee's approval of the measure would be discredited if the Senate subcommittee rejected Marriner's nomination as governor of the board. If the nomination were rejected *before* the Senate subcommittee began its hearings on the bill proper, it would simplify the task of rejecting the whole of Title II, with which Marriner was linked.

That something of the sort had long been in Glass's mind appears in a guarded letter he wrote in January 1935 to former Senator Reed Smoot of Utah. He had been informed, Glass said, that Eccles had not severed his banking connections. If so, his nomination as governor of the Federal Reserve could be rejected on that ground alone. Could Smoot advise him about the facts of the case? "The information," Glass assured him, "would be kept confidential."[31] Later, in a letter to Professor H. Parker Willis, Glass was more direct in stating his plans. "I have not yet gotten rid of the Five Billion Dollar [Relief] Appropriation Bill," he wrote Willis on April 3, "and as soon as that is out of the way, I must go to work on the Eccles Banking Bill and do my best to wreck it. I have some hope also of wrecking Eccles."[32]

At one point in the intervening months, Marriner received a long distance telephone call from E. G. Bennett in Utah. "Marriner," said Bennett, "I'm merely acting as a messenger on this call. But I think you should know of some advice I've received from some very influential bankers. They say that if you consent to having Title II taken out of the banking bill, you will be quickly confirmed as Governor of the Federal Reserve Board, because the bankers will withdraw their opposition."

"You can tell your banker friends to go to Hell," Marriner hotly replied, "The Governorship doesn't mean that much to me. But the changes in the Federal Reserve System must be made with or without me."

On April 15, having called his subcommittee together to consider Marriner's nomination, Glass accounted for the long delay by explaining that he and four other members of the subcommittee were also on the Senate Appropriations Committee—engrossed by work on the relief bill. Glass said to Marriner directly, "We have been unable to consider the matter before this time, much to my regret and very likely to that of the other members of the subcommittee as well as yourself." The explanation rang less than true. The April 15 session, lasting only an hour, produced no more than fifteen pages of testimony on Marriner's banking connections, the substance of which was confined to Glass's efforts to broadcast certain accusations passed on to him by the Democratic national committeeman from Utah, a man who had once applied for a loan at an Eccles bank but was turned down on grounds of personal character. (Some time after the subcommittee hearing, he was brought to trial before a criminal court in Washington, D.C., and found guilty of rape.)

A subsequent session of Glass's subcommittee lasted only ten minutes and was called merely to add two letters to the record. Thus, after a delay of more than three months before Glass could find time in a "busy" schedule to consider Marriner's nomination, the formal proceedings were over in seventy minutes. Glass apparently believed that the confirmation hearings could better serve his own purposes if there was no inquiry into Marriner's views—if, instead, a brief recital of his business connections was followed by his swift decapitation, thus suggesting to the public that the subcommittee had heard enough to warrant the execution. Things almost worked out that way. At voting time, three subcommittee members were known to favor confirmation, with two known to be opposed. The decision depended on senators Couzens of Michigan and McAdoo of California. George Creel, a friend of the Californian, brought word to Marriner that McAdoo would vote to confirm, but McAdoo was absent at voting time and gave his proxy beforehand to Glass. The result was a 3-3 deadlock, with the deciding vote going to Couzens, a Republican. He was an intimate of the Republican leader of the Senate, Charles L. McNary of Oregon, who knew of the Eccles family and its Oregon lumbering operations. When Couzens, by chance, asked McNary what he knew about Marriner's "views," he was assured that Marriner was neither the dangerous radical nor the knave he was made out to be. Couzens, therefore, voted aye, and the tally in the subcommittee (though unrecorded) stood at 4-3 in favor of confirmation.

When the full Senate Banking and Currency Committee met to consider Marriner's appointment, Glass was conspicuously absent, and the vote was unanimously in favor of confirmation. On April 25, when the Senate as a whole considered the matter, Glass stood alone in voting no. He now repeatedly lectured his Senate colleagues on the errors of their ways. He complained "that as so frequently happens now, my sound opinions do not count for much." He complained bitterly that the Senate had surrendered its constitutional right to share the presidential power of appointment.

When Glass failed to scuttle Title II by the indirect means of vetoing Marriner's confirmation, he was forced to turn his attention to a direct attack on the legislation. Of the sixty witnesses he called to testify on the banking bill, the majority—representing the backstage work of **George L.**

Harrison—confined their attention to Title II, and the majority were against it. In addition to professors Edwin W. Kemmer of Princeton, Henry Parker Willis of Columbia, and Oliver M. W. Sprague of Harvard, an impressive corps of great and near-great names in the world of finance voiced their opposition to Title II.*

Glass spaced the witnesses to fit his design for killing off Title II by delaying tactics. On the House side of Capitol Hill, Marriner had been accorded the courtesy of appearing as the first witness before its Banking and Currency Committee so as to present the administration's case for the bill viewed as a whole. Nothing of the sort was true in the case of Glass's subcommittee. The first witness called was Leo T. Crowley, head of the FDIC, whose agency was affected by Title I. If Glass meant to follow the logical order of the parts of the banking bill, the second witness should have been Marriner Eccles. Instead, J. F. T. O'Connor, Comptroller of the Currency, was called, whose agency was affected by Title III of the banking bill. The purpose of the sequence became clear when both men, in their opening remarks, directly or indirectly stated their opposition to the union of the three titles in a single bill. Like Glass, they were eager to give bankers all they needed and wanted in Titles I and III, while sacrificing Title II.

The next witness called was James P. Warburg, Vice Chairman of the Bank of Manhattan, who had resigned an administration post during the gold controversy in November 1933, and had subsequently attacked Roosevelt's monetary policies at every opportunity. "I am hearing Mr. Warburg this morning (April 27)," Glass blandly explained, "because he finds it necessary to go to Europe on Friday. I had not contemplated calling him until the officials of the Federal Reserve Board had first been heard; but owing to his arrangements, it is desirable to hear him this morning."

It was all the more desirable—from Glass' point of view—considering what he knew beforehand about Warburg's views. "I believe," said Warburg in his opening remarks, "that it is the function of political government, in the field of economics, to do just one thing, and that is to insure free and fair competition. . . . If you want me to express an opinion on open market operations, I will tell you that I do not believe in them at all." The coupling of all three titles in the same bill, said he, was like a dinner invitation that included "an offer to buy dinner, buy a drink, and cut your throat." Title II, the throat-cutter in the simile, was a case of "Curried Keynes, for it is in fact

*They included Winthrop W. Aldrich, president of the Chase National Bank of New York; James H. Perkins, chairman of the National City Bank of New York and a member of the Federal Advisory Council; Joseph H. Frost, also of the Federal Advisory Council; Frank A Vanderlip, former president of the National City Bank of New York (who had led the banker opposition to the Reserve Act of 1913 and to Glass personally on that occasion); John B. Byrne, chairman of the special committee of the executive committee of the Connecticut Bankers Association; Elwyn Evans, representing the clearing house banks of Wilmington, Delaware; Henry Ridgely, president of the Farmer Banks of the State of Delaware; William L. Sweet, chairman of a special committee on banking legislation of the United States Chamber of Commerce; H. Grady Langford, president of the Georgia Bankers Association, and many others.

a large half-cooked lump of J. Maynard Keynes . . . liberally seasoned with a sauce prepared by Professor Lauchlin Currie." In Warburg's view, the proposed changes in the organic structure of the Federal Reserve Board and the Federal Open Market Committee would give the government "political control" over the people's money, and would be tantamount to the nationalization of the banking system. They were plainly "not designed to accelerate recovery." Indeed, said Warburg, "since there is no present emergency which makes necessary the adoption of the drastic and funda-mental changes advocated by Governor Eccles, I urge this committee to consider whether it would not be far wiser to appoint a commission to study the entire banking and currency problem thoroughly and at leisure before any basic legislation is attempted."

Other witnesses who appeared before the subcommittee also referred to the danger of "political control"—present but somehow elusive, now a mere condition of the atmosphere, now concrete. Some believed that monetary controls were needed but should be left with the private banks who, so it was thought, "owned" the Federal Reserve System. Others maintained that no control of any kind was necessary, that through the free play of natural economic forces the monetary system would function for the general wel-fare. The discordant voices, however, were agreed on two points. First, the president of the United States would become a dictator if the Congress approved the changes in the Federal Reserve System as proposed in Title II of the Banking Bill. Second, all agreed that Title II should be separated from the rest of the bill, and that a commission should be appointed to study it in detail. These views were spread on the record of the hearing by men who did not have to catch boats for Europe but were called to the witness stand by Senator Glass between April 19 and May 20—before Marriner was given a chance to speak.

Since Glass was intent on delaying as long as possible the hour when Marriner would be called to appear before his subcommittee, Marriner used other forums to reply to the charges leveled against the bill. What he had to say at the annual convention of the Pennsylvania Bankers Association in Scranton on May 5 can be read as an introduction to the testimony he finally gave before the Senate Subcommittee on Banking and Currency:

Your function [as bankers] is a private business function; but the regulation of changes in the total volume of money is a public function.

You are told that since the Reserve banks deal with your money you should have some say in its investments. But this argument will not stand examination. When the Reserve banks buy securities they do not do so with existing money; they create new money for the purpose, and this increases your reserves and reserve funds. When they sell securities, you lose deposits and reserve funds. The Reserve banks, in other words, are not agencies for the investment of member-bank funds; they actually create and destroy money. Neither are open-market operations a regional or local matter. Their effect cannot be confined to a single district, but is nationwide and affects all classes.

Some people who do not approve of the government's spending program feel that if the banking system were under banker control, it might be made so difficult for the government to borrow that it would have to cease spending and balance the budget at once. That, I assure you, is the most dangerous and irresponsible argument that any group of bankers could present. Congress, which has the power to appropriate money, has also the power to find means to raise it. Make no mistake about that. If you disapprove of the government's policy, you must resort to the ballot to make your opposition effective. To attempt to hinder the government in carrying out the mandates of Congress and in raising the funds necessary for the purpose is to invite disaster for the banking system.

On May 10, nearly a month after the Senate hearings began, Marriner was finally called to appear. On the previous day, the House of Representatives had turned back a last-minute attempt to divorce Title II from Titles I and III of the act, and, by a vote of 271-100, approved of the measure. Since the House refused to act as the devil's hangman, Senator Glass must attempt the role himself. In his testimony Marriner observed that

the most widespread criticism [of the] bill has come from those who see in it an attempt to subordinate the Federal Reserve System and, through it, the country's banking system, to political control. On this subject, there appears to be much misinterpretation of what the present bill provides, coupled with a lack of clear understanding of existing law and the proper relationship between the Reserve System and the government. This bill aims to clarify the powers and responsibility of the Reserve Board in matters of public concern. There is nothing in this bill that would increase the powers of a political administration over the Reserve Board. That matters of national credit and monetary policy should be under public control has been recognized since the System was first proposed.

He expressed his view that not all economic ills could be cured by monetary action alone. It had been claimed that the proponents of the bill, and Marriner in particular, held such a belief.

Speaking for myself alone, I am keenly aware of the limitations of the influence of monetary measures on economic conditions. I realize that without a properly managed plan of government expenditures and without a system of taxation conducive to a more equitable distribution of income, monetary control is not capable of preventing booms and depressions. The volume and cost of money are important, however, and are the peculiar responsibility of the Federal Reserve System. That is the reason why our immediate concern in this legislation is to make the machinery of regulating the volume of money as efficient as possible so that the system may exert its influence toward the achievement of the desired objective.

He then paid his respects to the argument that action on Title II of the banking bill should be delayed until a committee of experts studied the whole question. He observed that committees of experts had been at work on Federal Reserve operations for twenty years, that their conclusions were available in House and Senate committee reports, and that specific proposals in the banking bill before the Congress were drawn from those studies and from the experiences of the depression. But differences of opinion over the proposals contained in Title II of the banking bill were not the kind that could be resolved by more study. They represented fundamental differences of approach to economic problems. They called for a decision by the Congress of the United States.

Though the House of Representatives had made its decision on May 9, when it passed the "Eccles Banking Bill," in the Senate the bill resembled a downed kite. The string that could make it airborne remained in Glass's hands, but the senator was not running with it. He busied himself with another matter—a grand tour of commencement exercises of leading universities where he was awarded honorary degrees. When Marriner ran down the list of bankers who were trustees of the Universities that chose to honor Glass at this particular time, he noted that virtually all of them were opposed to Title II of the Banking Act of 1935. "The bankers," so Marriner dryly observed, "are trying to kill the bill by degrees."

20. A Bill Is Born

MARRINER SELDOM RESTED during the war he waged on behalf of the banking bill. He did not seek personal publicity, but he had become national news. He was the subject of laudatory "cover stories" by the *Saturday Evening Post,* and the *Literary Digest. Time* magazine also made him the subject of a highly complimentary feature story, saying, among other things: "Many people in Washington are convinced that Marriner Eccles is all that stands between the nation and disaster."[33]

His effects on two newspapers central to the life of official Washington—the *Washington Post* and the *New York Times*—could be gauged by the shift in their editorial reactions to Title II of the banking bill. The *Post,* published by Eugene Meyer, a former governor of the Federal Reserve Board, had been mildly opposed to Title II when the bill was unveiled in January 1935. But by May, when the House hearings were concluded, the *Post* had become an eloquent partisan for Marriner's point of view. So, too, in the case of the *Times,* which had initially been critical of Marriner's appointment as governor of the Federal Reserve Board, and took an equally dim view of the banking bill when it was first introduced. But by the time Marriner had completed his testimony, the *Times* abjured its earlier views and strongly backed him and his bill.

"Mr. Eccles," an editorial in that newspaper read, "established himself in this trial by fire as a man of the first capacity." He proved "in a difficult atmosphere that he had a sequential set of economic ideas and reasons, backed by experience and history, for all of them." As the sessions proceeded, "he grew surer of his mastery of his own view, he dropped his guard and, in words of one syllable, discussed a variety of monetary subjects." The editorial added that "at times the committee discussed points with Mr. Eccles as college seniors might argue with a young but highly respected economics instructor, coming away from class with more than they gave and appreciating the intellectual courage of their preceptor."[34]

Writing in *Collier's* magazine, George Creel put his impressions into an article entitled "A Banker Who Can Talk." He described Marriner as a "small, spare man, somewhat undertakerish at first sight, with his pallor, jet black hair and eyes." But at second sight, "the whole of him glowed with a certain incandescence." When he talks, the effect is "electric," for he "not only has ideas—trail blazing ideas"—but he has also a "gift of intense, incisive speech," that gives "every idea the drive of a bullet." Raymond Clapper, in the *Review of Reviews,* was equally intrigued by Marriner, whom he described as "the strangest character in that strange wonderland of Washington." Here, said Clapper, was a "brilliant master of capital, sitting at the head of the country's national banking structure and advocating 'revolutionary ideas' about fiscal policy, money and credit that brings shudders to most of his fellow capitalists.

Marriner did not confine his teaching to journalists alone. He went out of his way to explain himself to any banker or groups of bankers who would meet with him. Herbert Corey, writing in the *Financial Observer,* gave an eyewitness account of one of these encounters:

It was at a luncheon meeting with Marriner Eccles and the bankers present were full of millions. They sat high on their seats, were large faced and heavy browed, and they produced a mass impression of suppressed fury. Eccles, in the presence of the great, was as free of awe, humility and self-consciousness as a wet dog is of discretion. The bankers did not even like his looks. They were shocked to find a slender, friendly, interested little man in a position of great power. A large man with jowls would have pleased them better.

Some of the bankers were intentionally rude to Eccles. They evidently proposed to put him in his place with a thump. Most men in Eccles' position would have been either hurt or angered. Eccles was so much interested in the ideas he wished to put over, and in the questions he wanted to ask that he did not even notice they were trying to take him for a ride. At first, he aroused my protective instinct. He made me think of a nice, gentle little boy surrounded by high school bullies, and I was sorry for him. Before he got through, I was sorry for the bankers. He knew everything about banking—by periods, details, totals, panics, causes and effects.[35]

Yet it was by means of these grinding encounters that Marriner made headway in converting to his view some individual bankers who were relatively free of Wall Street domination. The converts were still a minority in a surrounding sea of hostile bankers. Nonetheless, Marriner reenacted the process whereby he had won to his side, step by step, the hostile directors of the business enterprises his father had built.

In the last days of June 1935, the bankers who had been eulogizing Glass's statesmanship at convocation ceremonies looked at the calendar and read it with alarm. They had thus far failed to detach Title II from the rest of the banking bill. It was clear that the version of the title which the House had already approved and the version likely to emerge from the Senate were so far apart that there would be a long delay in the conference committee before any kind of compromise could be reached. The delay could extend beyond July 1, when many bankers would either lose their jobs or FDIC insurance for their banks if the relief they needed in Titles I and III was not law on that day.

Within the administration, Jesse Jones, the head of the FRC, joined Leo Crowley and J. F. T. O'Connor in pressuring Marriner to withdraw the controversial title from the banking measure. Marriner stood firm. The bankers offered a last-minute "compromise": the whole of the Banking Act should be held over for the next session of the Congress, but in the meantime the bankers would be relieved for an indefinite period from the punitive aspects of existing banking laws. Marriner objected; to accept the compromise would be to place the bankers beyond any need to come to terms with the reforms promised in Title II, and the advocates of reform in the Federal Reserve System would find themselves without leverage.

The bankers and their Senate friends brought heavy pressure on Chairman Steagall of the House Banking and Currency Committee to accept the compromise. Marriner tried to warn him away from the trap, but Steagall was "not taking any phone calls." Congressman Alan Goldsborough, however, was accessible. He joined Marriner in drafting a countercompromise: Congress, by joint resolution, should extend for sixty days the date on which the punitive provisions of existing banking laws would go into effect, unless changed by Titles I and III. At the end of the sixty days, the supporters of Title II would still be in a position to force definitive action on the whole of the banking bill before Congress adjourned. With this in hand, Marriner called at the White House on the morning of June 28 for a bedside conference with Roosevelt. He explained the extraordinary legislative situation that has developed, showed FDR the text of the countercompromise, and asked him for help in stiffening Steagall's back. The president phoned Steagall, urging him to stand aloof from the banker-inspired Senate compromise. He should resist any attempt to split the banking bill into three parts but should offer the counterproposal Goldsborough and Eccles had formulated. Steagall agreed to do what the president asked of him. The Senate was forced to bow to the will of the House. On June 29, resolutions which conformed to the terms of the Goldsborough-Eccles proposal were approved by both chambers of the Congress.

The pressure was now on Senator Glass and his Senate subcommittee. On July 2, it reported out a version of Title II. Amendments on the floor of the Senate made marginal improvements, but the text as finally approved by the Senate enfeebled the aggressive version of Title II which had passed the House back in May. Seeing it in that light, the House voted on July 29 to reject the work of the Senate. The cockpit of battle then became the conference committee, where Congressmen Steagall, Goldsborough and Hollister represented the House, while Senators Glass, Fletcher, Bulkley, McAdoo, Townsend and Norbeck represented the Senate.

By custom, the negotiations of conference committees are joined in by representatives of the agencies due to administer the particular bill under consideration. At Glass's invitation, Judge L. E. Birdzell of the FDIC joined the "mark-up" work on Title I, while Lloyd Awalt, Deputy Comptroller of the Currency, was present for work on Title III. To help with Title II, Steagall asked for Walter Wyatt, general counsel of the Federal Reserve Board. Glass, however, flatly refused to call Wyatt, claiming that Wyatt was "personally obnoxious" to him. The two men had been friends for many years, but Glass's unexpected hostility stemmed from the hearings on Marriner's appointment as governor of the Federal Reserve Board. When the senator argued at the time that Marriner was not qualified to serve as governor because of his links with the Eccles Investment Company, Wyatt responded with a legal opinion showing that nothing of the sort was true. Glass was enraged by the legal opinion and would never forgive Wyatt for his "treacherous" stand on the letter of the law.

In place of Wyatt, Glass permitted Lloyd Awalt to work on Title II during the mark-up sessions of the conference committee. Awalt was on friendly terms with both Marriner and Wyatt, and tried to keep them abreast of unfolding developments. But his personal interests were naturally focused on the portions of the bill which dealt expressly with his own FDIC agency, and Title II was not among those parts. In the absence of someone like Wyatt, Goldsborough not only assumed full personal responsibility for the fate of Title II, but drew even closer to Marriner in what was already an intimate collaboration. Goldsborough was armed with a document resembling the double entries in a bookkeeper's ledger. In one column were listed all the provisions of the House bill, each weighted for its relative importance. In a symmetrical column were similar analyses for each provision of the Senate bill. In this way the five most important provisions of the House bill were identified. Goldsborough was to do everything within his power to win approval for them; all the other points could be used for bargaining purposes.*

The conference report was presented to the Senate and House on August 19, and both chambers accepted it the same day. Three days later, Roosevelt signed the bill. As when the original Federal Reserve Act was signed by President Wilson in 1913, the several pens President Roosevelt used for the ceremony were given as mementos to the men who had played a major part in getting the new legislation enacted. When FDR gave one of these pens to Senator Glass, someone present commented in a stage whisper: "He should have given him an eraser instead."

Marriner certainly did not get all he wanted in the final bill, and in several vitally important respects was forced to bow before the senator's imperious will. What he achieved was a more effective central banking

---

*Once Goldsborough had assumed full responsibility for the fate of Title II, he met with Marriner at the end of each conference session to discuss the next day's strategy. At the end of one such session the whole of the legislative enterprise seemed headed for the rocks. Goldsborough informed Marriner that Glass refused to go on with the work in hand. "The old man," Goldsborough explained, "said I insulted him and that he will not meet again until I make a public apology. That's the end of the banking act. I'll be damned if I apologize."

"Now wait a minute," an alarmed Marriner replied. "We both care more for this legislation than we do for our personal pride. What difference does it make if you give in to Glass's demands? If it will satisfy him, then apologize. You've done a masterful job up to now and final success is within reach of your fingertips. It would be foolish to let the old man's pique deny you what you've worked so hard to attain." Goldsborough agreed to make the public apology Glass demanded. When he took the floor of the House the next day, few people within earshot knew what lay behind his words. What Goldsborough had to say was one of the most backhanded apologies in the history of debate in the House. Later, when Marriner anxiously asked Goldsborough if he had made the apology, he boomed out: "Hell, no! But the old man accepted it." The conference committee resumed its work.

control mechanism than had previously existed—one that firmly established the authority of the Federal Reserve Board as the central source of direction for the Reserve System as a whole, as against the previous dominance of the New York Federal Reserve Bank. It will appear in due course that without the new mechanism, the financing of the Second World War would have been enormously more complicated than it proved to be. But what Marriner was forced to concede to Glass exacted an increasingly heavy price as the years went by—to Marriner's continuous protests and efforts to get the excised clauses back into the act.

Many changes in the Federal Reserve System stemmed from the Banking Act in 1935, but foremost among these was the reshaping of the Federal Open Market Committee—a change representing a compromise between the Glass and Eccles positions. The House version, which reflected Marriner's preferences, called for an Open Market Committee comprised solely of members or governors of the Federal Reserve Board. The governors of the Federal Reserve banks, for their part, would annually elect five of their number to serve in an *advisory* capacity to the committee. The board would be required by law to *consult* with that advisory group before making any changes in open-market policy, discount rates or reserves removed from member banks. But when the consultative process had run its course, the board would have the ultimate power to prescribe open-market policy for the Federal Reserve System, and the policy would be binding on all Federal Reserve banks.

As approved, however, the Banking Act of 1935 provided that the old Federal Open Market Committee, comprised of the twelve governors of the Reserve banks, would be replaced on March 1, 1936, by a new-style Federal Open Market Committee comprised of the seven members of the Federal Reserve Board, plus five representatives of the twelve Federal Reserve banks. The latter five (together with one alternate for each) were to be selected annually by the boards of directors of the Federal Reserve banks under the following grouping: one from Boston and New York; one from Philadelphia and Cleveland; one from Richmond, Atlanta and Dallas; one from Chicago and St. Louis; and one from Minneapolis, Kansas City and San Francisco. Meetings of the Open Market Committee were to be held in Washington at least four times a year at the request either of the chairman of the board of governors or of any three committee members. Further, the law for the first time required the Open Market Committee to maintain an accurate record of its transactions, to record the votes cast on every open-market policy question, with the Federal Reserve Board submitting to the Congress annually a full report of all such decisions.

Marriner greatly preferred the membership structure of the Open Market Committee contained in the House version of the bill to the one that emerged from the conference committee. In the years ahead, he would not only be increasingly critical of the one provided for in the Banking Act of 1935, but he would agitate to have it changed along lines congruous with the

House formula. For the moment, however, he saw a net gain in the fact that the new law established the principle that open market operations would henceforth be initiated in Washington by a responsible public body, and not by one located elsewhere and dominated by private interests. "On this general point," he said later, "Glass and I saw eye to eye though we disagreed sharply on the composition of the instrument that was to advance it. I believe that Glass never fully grasped the importance of open-market operations, since they were of little significance when he framed the original Federal Reserve Act."[36]

The new law recognized, as Marriner had argued, that executive authority in the Federal Reserve Banks had moved from the hands of the chairman (where the 1913 Federal Reserve Act meant it to be lodged) into the hands of the governors of these banks. The 1935 law, therefore, provided a legal foundation for this pragmatic reality. The governor and the deputy governor now became the chief executive officers in the Reserve banks, and as of March 1, 1936, would discharge their responsibilities under the new titles of president and first vice-president respectively. Moreover, while the Federal Reserve Board previously had no power over their appointment —except to approve of their salaries—under the new law these officers would be appointed by the board of directors of each Federal Reserve Bank for terms of five years, subject to the approval of the board of governors of the Federal Reserve System.

Under the old law, the Federal Reserve Board could increase or decrease the reserve balances of member banks during a declared emergency, provided five members of the board and the president of the United States approved. Under the new law, the board by an affirmative vote of four members, and without the prior declaration of an emergency or the approval of the president, could change requirements for both demand and time deposits of member banks. Marriner had argued against any limitations on the *extent* to which reserve requirements could be changed. Glass, however, objected and his will prevailed. The reserves any bank was required to keep could not be decreased on the initiative of the board below the level specified by law, or increased to more than twice that prescribed level. The new authority granted the board, however, flowed from a recognition that the board was competent to determine the need for changes in reserve requirements without first securing the president's political consent.

The House version of the bill reflected Marriner's desire to shift attention away from "liquidity" and center it on "sound assets," which qualified as "eligible" paper for the purpose of bank loans. Though Senator Glass objected to the substitution of the term "sound assets" for "eligible paper," the bill as finally approved nevertheless was a step in the right direction. It granted permanent authority to any Federal Reserve Bank, under the regulations of the board of governors of the Federal Reserve System, to make advances on any "satisfactory" as well as on eligible paper to any member banks. Of a piece with this, provisions governing the real estate loans of national banks were changed in line with Marriner's expressed desire to permit banks to make longer-term loans and thus put a greater portion of their savings to work. The old law restricted real estate loans to the area in which the national bank was located and restricted the kind of real estate loans the Reserve Banks could acquire for discount purposes. These restrictions were removed or liberalized.

One more change merits notice. Effective February 1, 1936, the renamed board of governors of the Federal Reserve System was reduced from eight to seven members appointed by the president and confirmed by the Senate. While Marriner had argued for a five-member board, the House bill left the number unchanged at eight, with six appointive members, and with the Secretary of the Treasury and the Comptroller of the Currency serving ex officio. In the final version of the bill, however, the ex-officio memberships were abolished, largely because Glass could not control the full consequences of what he set in motion. He contended that the political independence of the board would be increased if the Secretary of the Treasury was not a member, but it was not his intention to remove the Comptroller of the Currency from the picture. When Morgenthau heard that his ex-officio membership was to end while the Comptroller's was to continue, he was deeply offended—especially because the Comptroller was merely a Treasury Department bureau chief, subordinate to Morgenthau. Calm was restored when the Comptroller as well as the Secretary of the Treasury was denied the right to be an ex-officio member of the board of governors. "This was one case," Marriner laconically observed, "where Morgenthau's bruise-prone sensibilities contributed to a desirable public result."

The 1913 Reserve Act provided that, when appointments to the board were made, the president should give fair representation to all the major economic interests and geographical divisions in the country. The House version of the 1935 Banking Act altered this in line with Marriner's view that persons appointed to the board "should be well qualified by education, experience or both, to participate in the formation of national economic and monetary policies." Decoded, this meant that they should be appointed not as "window dressing" but for their competence to manage very sensitive levels of power in the national economy. The proposed change did not survive the conference committee, and the 1913 selection principle was retained in the 1935 act.

Marriner wished to give a "new look" to the human face of the Federal Reserve Board. Elsewhere in government, many of the aged men who held key posts in regulatory agencies, where long tenure was the rule, had been insulated from the new needs and currents of thought created by the facts of the depression. The Federal Reserve Board was an example of this. Four of the six active members were nearing or in their seventies. The vice-governor, John Jacob Thomas, was seventy; Adolph C. Miller, a Wilson appointee, was seventy; and Charles S. Hamlin, another Wilson appointee, was seventy-four. Marriner wanted the Banking Act to revise the compulsory retirement age for board members to seventy. If a whole group exited from the board for reasons of age, mandated by law, no public humiliation would be attached to any one person. Since Miller and Hamlin in particular were among Roosevelt's oldest and most intimate friends, the compulsory retirement rule would spare the president the pain of having to explain why they would not be appointed to the reorganized Board of Governors. However, the retirement provision was not adopted with consequent complications for restructuring of the Federal Reserve Board.

In mid-1935, the New Deal was almost thirty months old, and its stamp was on a great mass of legislation. Yet none of the new laws explicitly stated that the federal government must use its powers in timely ways to forestall the wild swings of boom and depression in the economy. Marriner had long believed that the government did have that duty, and so did a growing number of New Dealers. But he wanted it formally expressed in law, and he saw a chance to do this by writing into Title II a new goal for the Federal Reserve Board. The 1913 goal had called on the board to accommodate the monetary and credit needs of commerce, agriculture and industry. Marriner thought this was so vague as to be meaningless. With the strong support of Steagall, he inserted into the House version a new mandate: the Federal Reserve Board was required "to exercise such powers as it possesses in such a manner as to promote conditions conducive to business stability and to mitigate by its influence unstabilizing fluctuations in the general level of productions, trade, prices and employment so far as may be possible within the scope of monetary action and credit administration." The purpose here, as Marriner explained at the time, was to inform the nation what to expect of monetary management, and yet to leave the Federal Reserve Board discretion as to the choice of means. It would provide the public and its congressional representatives with a standard for assessing the merits of the monetary policies being pursued. It would enjoin the Federal Reserve Board itself to exercise its monetary controls in the interests of the nation as a whole.

Glass refused to accept the phrasing of the new mandate. He claimed that it did violence to Jeffersonian democracy, since the effect would be to give the central government "too much power." The restated mandate died in the conference committee, and the vague 1913 mandate it was meant to replace was incorporated in the Banking Act of 1935. Though the consequences of that death were not immediately visible, they eventually came into view after the Congress passed the Employment Act of 1946. That act did not include *stability* as one of its goals, and, by its accent on full employment, became in its own way a built-in source of inflationary pressures on the economy. At the same time, because the mandate of the Federal Reserve System neither specifically stated any of the objectives of national economic policy, nor defined what could be expected of monetary policy alone, the management of the economy was shot through with the confusion which follows when power is divorced from responsibility.

Marriner later repeatedly urged the Congress to make consistent the legislative mandate expressed in the Federal Reserve Act and the Employment Act of 1946. He would have these two fundamental statutes use identical language in stating the nation's economic goals of a low level of unemployment, adequate rates of economic growth, and reasonable price stability—and that these same goals should be extended to all federal agencies administering economic programs.

21. Teething

IN THE SEVEN MONTHS between November 1934, when he was appointed to head the Federal Reserve Board, and August 1935, when the Banking Act was signed, Marriner lived and breathed that battle to the exclusion of everything else. In Washington, as in Utah, he was at his office early in the morning, and he was among the last to leave the Federal Reserve headquarters in the evening, well past the hour when most people had finished supper. Like his father, he found his best holiday in work, and more work. His "recreation," insofar as he had any, was confined to golf at the all-male Burning Tree Country Club, of which he was a member, or to the Chevy Chase Country Club, which was "family-oriented." But even as he was standing before a tee, he would pause amid his club-wagging and speak to his partners about the latest crisis in the battle for the Banking Act of 1935.

His wife and children were "somewhere" in the background of his thoughts; he was always ready to provide for their comforts. But he had little time to spend with them alone or to minister to their emotional needs although they were uprooted from their secure places in Ogden and deposited on the impersonal, ambition-swept terrain of Washington. The "powerful" of Washington invited Marriner and Maisie to dinners, or welcomed dinner invitations from them. But after the meal, when the wives retired to talk among themselves and the men retreated to cigars and brandy, the talk invariably turned to the struggle to govern. Maisie may have hoped that her husband, who had become a national figure overnight, would have more time for intimate family matters, once the issue of the Banking Act of 1935 was settled. But this was not to be. The end of any one battle would prove, again and again, to be only the prelude to a new struggle which consumed Marriner's attention and energies. Marriner himself thought that once President Roosevelt had signed the Banking Act of 1935, no impediments would stand in the way of a swift reorganization of the Federal Reserve Board and System to conform to the changes authorized by the act. He was soon disabused of this notion, first by Senator Glass, and then by FDR, each for different reasons. Seven more months of strain would elapse before the machinery for the authorized changes was set in place.

Prior to the signing of the Banking Act of 1935, some members of the Washington press corps had riled Glass by dwelling on his failure as chairman of the Senate Appropriations Committee to achieve his manifest aim of eviscerating the 1935 Work Relief Bill. Now, in their post-mortems on who got what in the Banking Act of 1935, they riled him even more. They noted that while Glass claimed a sweeping personal victory in the legislative fight over the banking measure, there was a misfit between the claim and the realities of the case. "The truth is," wrote Raymond Clapper, a leading columnist of the day, "that the bits of fluff at the corners of Marriner Eccles' smiling but silent mouth, look very much like canary feathers."[37]

The senator believed, quite without foundation, that Marriner was the source of the scoffing press comments. In a series of Senate speeches he denounced Marriner as a man whose public ambitions were a mortal danger to the Republic, and whose private business dealings were a long train of abuses.

Marriner at first discounted Glass's new round of philippics, and in any case he had other things on his mind. On August 23, the day after the Banking Act was signed, he met with FDR in the White House to discuss the contents of a memorandum he brought with him. At the outset he observed that the Banking Act had changed the Federal Reserve Board from a "largely" passive agency for the accommodation of commerce and business into an active agency where the board was brought into line with "modern economic thought," and a "more rational relationship to the country's entire economic life." It was wrong to assume, however, that the act automatically set right all things out of joint in the nation's banking system as a whole. The stability of the system and its effective power to serve the national economy were threatened by many unresolved issues in need of immediate study by the new board of governors.

Not only did the enumerated issues comprise Marriner's personal cause in the years ahead, but virtually all of them remain of critical importance —and unresolved—to this day. They included "the reforms necessary to bring about a unified banking system under federal control, unified banking supervision and administration in Washington, the problems of branch, group and chain banking, and a practical solution to the question of the proper relationship between commercial banking and investment banking." To neglect these matters would be to hobble the capacity of the Federal Reserve to contribute, through its own mechanical operations, to the health of the national economy.

For these reasons, Marriner urged that new members be appointed to the Reserve Board in the light of more exacting standards than those carried over from the 1913 Federal Reserve Act. He would have the president take his guidance from the higher criteria for board members contained in the House version of the 1935 Banking Act—namely, that all persons appointed to the board of governors "should have a grasp of national economic issues," and "should be qualified by experience, education, or both, to assist in formulating monetary policies and the continued study of banking problems."

At that meeting, Roosevelt did not agree to the removal of *all* incumbent board members. He agreed, however, that the proposed standard be followed in choosing *new* board members. He also endorsed a related suggestion. Marriner was due to leave Washington with Lawrence Clayton and several other intimates for a few days of relaxation at a hunting lodge in the West. He thought that on the way he could stop in key cities for meetings with bankers, where he could both explain the meaning of the Banking Act and gather the names of men qualified to serve on the new board of governors. Roosevelt encouraged him to do just that, and their meeting ended with an exchange of congratulatory comments.

When Marriner left Washington at the end of August, Senator Glass's new attacks had been underway for several days, but he ignored the reports of them. On his westward-bound trip he first heard of a theory making the rounds of banking circles: the senator's new blasts were meant to warn Roosevelt that, if he named Eccles chairman of the new Federal Reserve Board—to take office in February 1936—there would be a bitter Senate confirmation fight that could stretch well into the 1936 presidential election year. With his own reelection needs in mind, therefore, Roosevelt would dump Eccles in favor of a noncontroversial figure.

Marriner did not want to keep running to Roosevelt for reassurance. Yet his efforts to interest qualified men whom he might want to recommend to the president as possible appointees were cramped by the rumors that he was to be dumped. Thoughts of this kind cast a shadow over his brief vacation at the hunting lodge, and the shadow trailed him until the second week of September when he reached Ogden. On the advice of E. G. Bennett, he called long distance to Marvin McIntyre, one of Roosevelt's secretaries, and briefly sketched the problem he encountered. He received a quick invitation to fly to Hyde Park for a luncheon with FDR. Bennett was due to be in the East on business of his own, and it was agreed that he too should come to Hyde Park, where he would stand by in McIntyre's office.

At lunch, Marriner alluded to the banker-favored theory that he was to be cast aside to appease Glass, and added that it was not his own purpose to try to force the president's hand. When he accepted the appointment in November 1934 as governor of the Federal Reserve Board, he recognized that there was no explicit understanding that he would be named to head any new board formed in line with the proposed changes in the Reserve System. He also recognized that he had angered many people during the fight for the Banking Act, and might now be a political liability to the Roosevelt administration. But if FDR did mean to appoint him, a timely announcement to that effect would strengthen his hand for the immediate tasks to be discharged.

Roosevelt replied that he would immediately make public his intention to appoint Marriner as chairman. Marriner and Marvin McIntyre were to draft a statement for release to the press that day. This was done, with Bennett joining in the composition of two simple declarative sentences on which Marriner's governmental life seemed to depend. As released to the press, they read:

In The President's conference today with Governor Eccles, plans for the operation of the new banking laws as it affects the Federal Reserve System were discussed. The President further stated he will nominate Eccles for membership on the new Board of Governors to be appointed for a term commencing February 1, 1936, and will designate him as Chairman.

The announcement did not mark the end of all storms. But as the chairman-designate, Marriner could now speak more effectively about the meaning of the Banking Act of 1935, and could search with greater assurance for possible new members of the board of governors.

The mid-September meeting at Hyde Park fell on the eve of Roosevelt's scheduled departure by train for a Western trip, during which he stopped at Boulder Dam for a dedication ceremony. Marriner, who had created the corporate organization for that vast project, boarded the presidential train at Ogden with the plan to introduce the president to the directors of the Six Companies at the dam. Ushered into the president's car, he was invited to stay for supper. After answering Roosevelt's questions about the Boulder project, Marriner steered the table talk around to the composition of the new Federal Reserve Board.

He had given much thought to the forbidding figure of Senator Glass and how he had threatened the president's power of appointment. To avoid what had happened in his own case, was there any way to "consult" Glass before appointments were made to the board, and yet secure the kind of governors qualified to make the new Federal Reserve machinery work? Marriner had a plan. "Mr. President," he said, "I believe that every effort should be made to avoid the bitter and costly controversy that developed in connection with my own appointment. The confirmation of the new board will be simplified if Senator Glass is consulted on its composition beforehand. We can do this without risk . . .''

"What's your idea?''

"I suggest," Marriner replied, "that at an appropriate time you call Senator Glass in and say to him: 'Here is a list of prospective appointees as governors of the new Reserve Board compiled from suggestions sent to me from many quarters. Now, I'll pick the first four men I want to appoint from this list, and you can pick three men from the balance. Our combined choices—four for me and three for you—will make the nominations I'll send down to the Senate for confirmation.''

"You are giving Glass a free choice?" the president asked.

"Only *seemingly* so," Marriner said. "I'll bet you a dollar he will pick from the list three men we want him to pick.''

Roosevelt's interest quickened.

"Now, here is Ronald Ransom," Marriner continued. "He was the head of the legislative committee of the American Bankers Association. We didn't agree on many things before the banking bill was passed, but he is intelligent, independent, and courageous. I know he will have the strong support of the ABA to be the new member from the Atlanta Federal Reserve District. Also from the Atlanta district, there is John Parsons, president of the First National Bank of Birmingham. He is an exceptionally able man and would make an excellent addition to the board. Either of these two would be first-rate choices for their district. But they should not be among the four men *you* pick. Let *Glass* pick either one, and I am sure that is exactly what he will do."

"What's the trick?" Roosevelt asked.

"Between now and the day you make your offer to Glass," Marriner explained, "I will quietly arrange for Glass to be visited by delegations of people I know he likes and respects. They will urge him to do everything within his power to make sure that either Ransom or **Parsons** will be appointed a governor of the Federal Reserve Board from the Atlanta District. Exactly the same procedure will be followed in the case of the other two men he will 'pick.' Glass will feel that he's taught you not to trifle with him."

Roosevelt seemed to hug himself with delight. "What a perfectly charming idea!" he exclaimed. With the president's approval, Marriner was to work on the project as soon as possible.

At the end of the dinner, Roosevelt had a suggestion to make about a different matter. He remarked that Harry Hopkins and Harold Ickes were back in a train compartment working on a draft of the speech he was to give at Boulder Dam. "Why don't you drop in on them, see how they are getting along, what they are writing, and whether you have an idea or two to add?" Marriner needed no urging. He quickly made his way to their compartment, where the two men welcomed him as a comrade in arms. Together they put some key passages into a speech which, if delivered by the president free from Henry Morgenthau's veto, would express some of their own thoughts about "spending."

Previously the president had tended to consider only the number of men to be put to work *directly* through public expenditures. He had long resisted the argument that public spending could also lead to indirect employment. His most recent expression of resistance was his message vetoing the soldier bonus bill in the summer of 1935. Under Morgenthau's influence, he had specifically denied the propriety or efficacy of "mere spending of money to hasten recovery." The "sounder principle" was to prevent the loss of homes and farms, to save industry from bankruptcy, and to provide relief for people faced with starvation. Two weeks later, on the train to Boulder Dam, the team of Hopkins, Ickes and Eccles wrote into the draft text of Roosevelt's speech a passage in support of what the president had rejected in his veto message—namely, the case for the *indirect* benefits of public spending. The passage survived FDR's blue pencil. On September 30, he made their words his own, saying in his dedicatory remarks:

In a little over two years, this great national work has accomplished much. We have helped mankind by the works themselves and, at the same time, we have created the necessary purchasing power to throw in the clutch to start the wheels of what we call private industry. Such expenditures on all of these works, great and small, flow out to many beneficiaries; they revive other and more remote industries and businesses. Money is put in circulation. Credit is expanded and the financial and industrial mechanism of America is stimulated to more and more activity.

This did not mean that Roosevelt was irrevocably committed to the indirect benefits of spending or to its corollary—deliberately planned government deficits as a means for recovery. He had a speech to give on a dramatic occasion, which influenced the text. Since he did not as yet have his own general theory of fiscal policy, other situations would influence other speeches differently, and he would continue in the months ahead to steer a zig-zag course.

III

Rudolph Hecht, the outgoing president of the American Bankers Association, invited Marriner to address the ABA convention in New Orleans on November 14. The lines for the 1936 presidential contest were already being drawn, and all signs pointed to Governor Alfred Landon of Kansas as the Republican nominee and to the New Deal spending program as a key issue of the campaign. Starting in March 1935 the stock market had begun a sustained climb, causing many business leaders to voice fears about "inflation." Some did this through force of their painful memories of 1929. Others did so as part of a political onslaught against the administration. If the nation was to be spared a collapse of the 1929 variety, then the spending program would have to end, and the first step toward ending it was to remove from public office all of those who were responsible for the offensive program. Marriner had been one of its most vocal advocates—besides harping on its inadequacy—and he wanted to make his case directly before the people who had bitterly attacked the policy of planned deficits.

The mood of the convention was surly, a hangover from banker hostility to the New Deal measures enacted in the immediately preceding months.* Most objectionable of all was the Revenue Act of 1935, growing out of Roosevelt's tax message of June 12, by which, for the first time, the New Deal reached directly into the pockets of the wealthy—through higher tax rates on large individual incomes, higher tax rates on large corporations, and federal inheritance tax superimposed on existing federal and state taxes on estates.

In New Orleans, banker hostility erupted when it was time to elect the second vice-president of the ABA, who, by the usual route of succession,

---

*Along with the Banking Act of 1935, the measures included the National Labor Relations Act, the Social Security Act, the creation of the Works Progress Administration, the start of Rural Electrification Administration, and the Public Utility Holding Act, which authorized the Securities and Exchange Commission to regulate the financial practices of interstate holding company systems controlling gas and utilities.

would become the ABA's president within two years. The nominating committee put forward the name of E. G. Bennett. His candidacy was violently attacked, not by the Big Bankers or the branch bankers, but by the Main Street or unit bankers. Their own choice for the second vice-presidency was Orval W. Adams, who, it will be recalled, had once worked in the Eccles-Browning bank in Ogden. Bennett was said to be "Eccles' stooge," and through him Eccles "meant to socialize the banks that had eluded his grip" when framing the Banking Act of 1935. The leaders of the opposition conveniently ignored the plain fact that few bankers in the nation had Bennett's qualifications to speak for small as well as big bankers. A whipping boy must be found for a pounding whose real object was Marriner. The attack became so frenzied that Bennett withdrew his name from consideration. Adams was elected and proceeded to celebrate his election in an inflammatory speech, saying:

Since the federal government cannot spend without using the bankable funds of the nation, it is up to us to declare an embargo. We must decline to make further purchases. We must declare that we will not finance further spending by the government until a genuine, honest, sincere effort is made by the federal government to restore a balanced budget. The bankers of America should resume negotiations with the federal government only under a rigid economy, a balanced budget, and a sane tax program.

In this atmosphere, Marriner defiantly held the fort in defense of the Roosevelt administration. He first dealt with the fears concerning inflation. Classical inflation, said he, implies a condition where an excess of dollars competes for limited goods and services on the existing market. At the moment, however, no such thing was true. The labor supply was many millions in excess of any effective consumer purchasing power. Marriner then dealt in blunt words with Orval W. Adams' summons to bankers to boycott the government as a means of ending the government spending program.

The bankers above all have been the beneficiaries of the government intervention. The government alone could and did replenish the supply of deposits when individual borrowers were lacking and when banks had no other profitable outlet for their funds than the investment in government securities. Banks bought government securities, not because of compulsion, but because they had no other avenue of profitable investment.

Those who talk about boycotting government bonds suggest to me a drowning man to whom a life line is thrown out but who objects that it is an interference with his individual right and liberty to drown.

The achievement of a stable, orderly economic progress, free from violent extremes, and conducive to maximum productivity and distribution, involves neither a regimented nor a restricted economic order. It calls for government intervention only to the extent that the exercise of governmental authority affecting monetary and budgetary factors may be a stabilizing and corrective influence in an individualistic, capitalistic system when it, left entirely to itself, generates distortions, lack of balance, and cyclic extremes. The government must unbalance its budget during deflation and create surpluses in periods of great business activity.

Still it would take much more than this or any other speech to silence the critics of the administration. As a year-end spurt in the stock market intensified the fears of inflation, Charles R. Gay, president of the New York Stock Exchange, placed at the door of the Federal Reserve all responsibility for controlling the stock boom. When Marriner, in an embattled mood, returned to Washington from New Orleans, he thought it important to try to set straight the truths of the case. Backed by the Reserve Board, he issued a statement on November 22 in which he again defined inflation; distinguished between it and a stock-market boom; noted that the rise in security prices was being financed by cash instead of bank credit; and also noted that the Reserve Board had only limited power to deal with stock market fluctuations.

The effect of the statement was a press uproar. Marriner was dismayed to read that what he said was "reminiscent of former days when spokesmen for previous administrations came to the support of the stock market on some of its most disastrous days." He was identified with "President Coolidge's unfortunate remark that the volume of broker's loans for stock market purposes appeared to be not too high." He was reminded that "this was the first time a high government official had given his blessings to the stock market." And more of the same. Years earlier, when the boy Marriner was caught frying frogs' legs over a fire inside the "house" he had built between flammable rows of wood in his father's lumber yard, he feared the worst if the misdeed was reported to his father. Now, at forty-five, he had unwittingly lit a fire in the tinderbox of preelection-year politics. How would the president of the United States, far more powerful than David Eccles, react to the press versions of the event?

Roosevelt, who had often mocked the cozy assurances of his White House predecessors regarding stock market activity, could not overlook "a bullish statement" ascribed to the head of the Federal Reserve Board when security prices were rising, and when Wall Street was in an enthusiastic mood. The president knew it was false to compare stock market conditions in late 1935, with those on the eve of the 1929 Crash. But as a political leader about to enter an election year, when all things touched by his administration were due to be attacked, he did not wish needlessly to expose himself to the fire of his adversaries. On December 3, 1935, he sent Marriner the following note from Warm Springs:

I have read your press statement of November 22nd and I think it is entirely sound. We must remember, however, that there is real danger in any statement relating, even remotely, to actual stock market operations. This is where Coolidge, Mellon and Hoover got into such trouble.

A word to the wise!

The cautionary word *from* the wise was heeded by Marriner in the future.

IV

In mid-December 1935, after a nationwide search, Marriner gave President Roosevelt the names of twenty-four men who merited consideration for appointments to the new board of governors. The next step—in line with the plan FDR had approved on the train ride en route to Boulder Dam—called for a meeting between the president and Senator Glass. On the occasion of the meeting, Glass objected to the proposed split, whereby he would pick three members and the president four. He insisted on personally picking all seven governors of the new board. It was only after much grumbling that he agreed to choosing three men from the names on the list he was given at that time. Marriner's invisible hand now set in motion the delegations which called on Glass, urging him to work for the appointment to the Reserve Board of particular individuals whose names were on the list of qualified candidates.

Yet a new difficulty suddenly cropped up unlike any Marriner had known in private business when he had to hire or fire a company executive. The difficulty involved Roosevelt personally, and for reasons that were not to the president's discredit. He was angered when "old men" on the Supreme Court or in other agencies of government blocked the surge of New Deal policies, and he had stressed the need to fix sixty years as the maximum age for appointments to the federal judiciary. Yet when the old men in governmental posts were his personal friends, he tried to evade as long as possible the ordeal of dislodging them. "What am I to do about my old friends on the board such as Charles Hamlin and Adolph Miller?" the president despairingly asked Marriner at a White House meeting in early January 1936. "And what about J. J. Thomas? Only last year, I reappointed him to a twelve-year term. If I fail to name him to the new board, won't people have a right to ask: 'If Thomas is wrong for the new setup, wasn't he also wrong for the old one?' "

There was, said Marriner in reply, a humane solution to the problem. The three men could still do valuable work, but in roles other than as board members. Hamlin could be made a special counsel to the board, with an office in the Reserve Building. He needed a job, would do well in the one suggested, and would certainly accept the post if it were offered to him. Adolph Miller, on the other hand, didn't need the salary he drew as a board member. But he had devoted more than two decades of his life to the Federal Reserve System, and was in love with it. He had worked hard in planning the new Federal Reserve Building, and should be asked to continue to serve as chairman of the building committee until the structure was completed and ready for occupancy. After that, he could be given an office in the building where he would be readily available to offer advice on Federal

Reserve matters. As for J. J. Thomas, he could be made the chairman of the board of directors of the Kansas City Federal Reserve Bank, his original territory. Under the new banking bill, the post carried no remuneration but it was within the power of the new Federal Reserve Board to make an exception so that Thomas could be paid a salary for a three-year term.

When Roosevelt tentatively agreed to the proposed solution and passed the details on to Glass, the senator specifically objected to the removal of Adolph Miller from the board. "I strongly urge," he wrote Roosevelt, "the retention of Dr. Miller for the present until the newer members have become acquainted with the philosophy and practices of the Federal Reserve System. I know there are some objections to this, but still think the desirability of this course outweighs the objections," In the same letter, Glass urged the president to appoint Joseph A. Broderick, John K. McKee and Ronald Ransom to the new board of governors. Marriner won his "dollar bet" with Roosevelt. The three men Glass favored topped Marriner's own list of possible appointees.

Glass's intervention on behalf of Miller reinforced Roosevelt's preexisting tendency to exempt his old friend from retirement for reasons of age. When this became clear, Marriner sent Roosevelt a terse memorandum. The text read:

To scrap the impersonal reason of age on the question of the reappointment and to name Dr. Miller would be a terrible blow to Mr. Hamlin in particular. Both were appointed to the original Board more than 20 years ago—Hamlin as the first Governor. He has been faithful, cooperative, a hard worker, of real ability and courage. He is admired by everyone on the staff. He has been loyal to the Administration and a true supporter of its principles. To throw overboard the faithful and beloved Hamlin, who is a poor man incidentally, and to rename Dr. Miller would be an injustice Mr. Hamlin would never get over. Nor would those on the staff and the System generally be able to look upon it as other than a rank injustice.

Roosevelt finally agreed to the principle of equal retirement for reasons of age, but a different cause for anxiety remained. Though the new board members were due to take office on February 1, 1936, the days dropped away with no official word from Roosevelt concerning his choices for the board. By the third week of January, Marriner was perturbed. He wanted an irrevocable decision, but Roosevelt seemed instead to be playing hide and seek. At last Marriner called Marvin McIntyre to say that the deadline was at hand for unveiling the new board of governors, and that they must be confirmed by the time the new law went into effect. "I must see the president," Marriner exclaimed, "and prod him into action." He was told that the only free slot on FDR's schedule was the following Saturday afternoon at two-thirty. Marriner was to come to the executive mansion at that time, and two hours would be set aside for him so that the protracted business of the new appointments could finally be wrapped up.

That Saturday, at the precise moment indicated, Marriner called at the White House and was told to go upstairs to join the president. Stepping out of the elevator on the first floor, he heard the sound of music, and saw the president seated before a radio in a large hall. Grouped near him were his mother and his secretaries Missy Le Hand and Grace Tully. Roosevelt looked up, beckoned Marriner forward, pointed to the seat he was to take, then put his finger to his lips.

I had come to him [Marriner later recalled] brimming over with banking matters. But it turned out instead that I was his very unwilling guest at the opera. The radio was tuned to the Metropolitan's performance of one of Wagner's works. Had I been the "Bishop of Berlin" in my young missionary days, like my good friend Lawrence Clayton, I might have acquired a taste for Wagner. But I had spent those days in Glasgow. Moreover, my indifference to Wagner turned into deep resentment that his music got in the way of an immediate consideration of matters vital to American banking. Once or twice I was about to say audibly that I had not been advised that my business appointment at the White House had been changed into an invitation to the opera. But I had no chance to speak up. Roosevelt, having gestured to me to sit down and be quiet, listened intently to the music and seemed unaware that anyone else was in the room. As the minutes dropped away, I could only mutter to myself: "Well, there goes more of the time he had set aside to save the Reserve System."[38]

When the first act was over and the voice of Milton Cross announced that the soloists were taking curtain calls, Roosevelt applauded with gusto. At last, so Marriner thought, he would get down to cases. There *was* talk, but not about appointments to the Federal Reserve Board. Roosevelt used the whole of the intermission to explain in minute detail, and with smiles cast in his mother's direction, that, as a boy, he spent almost every summer in Europe with his parents. They were, said he, great devotees of the opera, took him along, and forced him against his will to sit quietly through a performance. In this way, season after season, he had come to know something about opera. Since he had also learned German, the language gave him an added key to Wagnerian performances. That is how he acquired his great love of Wagner, and that was why he was sitting before the radio that Saturday afternoon listening to Wagner's music.

Marriner later wrote:

My impulse was to tell him that he was neither my father nor my mother, though he made me sit quietly through the performance; that this was Washington, D.C., in the year 1936, and not Baden-Baden in the year 1890; that I didn't know a word of German and, for that matter, didn't know the words of any song except the Mormon hymn "Come, come, ye saints"; that my taste in music never advanced beyond the bagpipes that used to be played in my father's home, though my father liked to hear "Sugar King" Havermeyer play the violin; that regardless of how much I was exposed to Wagner, thanks to the President's kind efforts, I doubted whether the treatment would take. Or, to sum up, with the utmost respect and affection, I'd be damned glad if he'd made up his mind whom he wanted to appoint to the Board of Governors. But the impulse never translated itself into a spoken word. And so the opera continued through two more acts.[39]

After what seemed like an eternity to Marriner, the president at last said with a sigh: "Well, I guess we had better get to work." Marriner also sighed, but with relief, and followed the president into his study. There was one young member of the old board whom Marriner wanted to see reappointed, M. S. Szymczak of Chicago. Roosevelt readily assented to the choice. Then Marriner, referring to a call he had received a few days previously from Vice-President John Nance Garner, said: "The vice-president wants me to support a man named Ralph W. Morrison for a place on the new board. I've looked into Morrison's record, and he is in no way qualified to serve on the board. Yet I thought you should know of the vice-president's interest."

"You are absolutely right in not wanting Morrison!" Roosevelt said emphatically. "Don't pay any attention to what Garner wants you to do! I know Morrison, and he's no choice of mine!"

The second act of this particular drama occurred a week after the Wagnerian broadcast. Lingering problems concerning appointments to the board again brought Marriner to the White House. The moment he entered the president's Oval office, Roosevelt greeted him by saying sheepishly: "Marriner, do you know what happened a while ago? The vice-president came in here speaking on behalf of Morrison. And do you know what he said to me? He said: 'I've never asked a personal favor of you, but I'm going to ask my first one right now. I want you to appoint Morrison to the new board of governors, as a personal favor to me!' " Roosevelt was not through with his report. "You know," he said, "*that* was not the first favor he's ever asked. He's asked plenty of them before, and he's been given plenty of them. But Marriner, what would you do if you were in my position and the vice-president asked you for a personal favor?"

"I'd do exactly what you are going to do," Marriner said.

"What's that?"

"I'd appoint Morrison as a governor."

Roosevelt smiled gratefully, and said nothing more. Ralph W. Morrison was ultimately appointed, though the same newspapers that were later to build up Garner as a savior of the Republic because of his opposition to Roosevelt, flayed FDR for having made this "purely political appointment to pay back a campaign contribution." Within two months after Morrison was confirmed, he suddenly left the United States and went to Mexico. He seemed bent on escaping the truth and consequences of the rumors that his business affairs were in disarray, financially and legally.

At this same session between Marriner and FDR, Glass came to the White House for a final conference of his own on the composition of the new board. He had appeared without any scheduled appointment, and Roosevelt was taken by surprise when he was told by an aide that Glass was drumming a table-top in the waiting room. It was easy to imagine Glass's reaction if he found Marriner with the president. "I'd better not keep him waiting," said Roosevelt hastily. "Marriner, you slip into that room over there and talk to Grace Tully and Missy Le Hand while I attend to the senator." Marriner later summarized the episode:

The President's secretaries kept toys on hand to amuse his grandchildren when they visited the White House. I began to fumble with those toys, while next door in the Oval room, a climax was being reached to a national contest begun in November 1934. I suddenly thought: My God! this is really ludicrous. After all the bitter accusations, the man in that room who has fought me at every step—and whom I fought with equal passion—is finally agreeing to what I want, not knowing that I am but a few feet away. It's all the more ludicrous that I should be forced to hide from him, and to spend this moment of decision playing with toys. The theatrics of the matter came to an end when a buzzer rang, and, as prearranged, I rejoined the President. "Marriner," said Roosevelt as he pointed to the main door of his own office and then to the one from which I had just emerged, "you're just like a jack-in-the-box. You come in here and you pop out there!" The remark was an apt summary of fifteen months of effort.[40]

Soon afterward, Roosevelt sent Marriner's name to the Senate, along with five other names on which he and Glass had agreed: John K. McKee, Ronald Ransom, Joseph A. Broderick, M. S. Szymczak, and Ralph W. Morrison. Despite the lingering fears of a last-minute blocking action led by Glass, the six nominees were confirmed by the Senate without hearings or a record vote. The seventh member of the board, who was to represent agricultural interest, was not chosen at the time because of an unresolved controversy. On Marriner's advice, the president deferred action until a man was found who could meet the standards set and followed in all cases except the one involving Morrison. The delay proved fortunate. Within a few months, Chester Davis, who had been the head of the Agricultural Adjustment Administration, became available. His appointment to the Federal Reserve was well received in all quarters, and rightly so.

In the last days of its life, the outgoing board let the contract for the construction of the new Federal Reserve Board Building. Marriner had initiated the move for a new building not long after he was first appointed to head the board in November 1934. At that time, the board itself was housed in the Treasury Department, while its technical staff was housed separately in two other office buildings in downtown Washington. This scatter-pattern arrangement, besides being a formula for administrative inefficiency, was itself a commentary on the declassed status of the Reserve Board before Marriner assumed its leadership. He had at once insisted on bringing all elements of the Reserve Board together under one roof in a new home of its own. He also insisted that the costs of constructing such a home did not entail the need for a congressional appropriation. It was within the legal power of the board to cover the construction costs by drawing on the profits the Reserve System earned through its transactions in government securities. This point being agreed to, Marriner won the assent of the board on other points.

A committee of acknowledged leaders in the fine arts should be formed who would then ask a carefully selected group of architects to submit designs for the proposed new structure. The architects, in turn, would each be paid a fee for the designs they submitted, but the judges of the designs would not know the names of their respective sources. In the end, there was a virtually unanimous agreement that the sketch submitted by a Philadelphia architect, Paul Cret, should be adopted. So it was, and the merit of the decision was to be underlined later on when the design for the Federal Reserve Board Building was the gold medal winner at an international competition among architects held in Rio de Janiero.*

A new building-to-be, a new banking law, and a new board—all combined to suggest the dawn of a new day in the affairs of the Federal Reserve System. But would the dawn prove false? The question lay behind a ritualistic act Marriner performed on February 6, 1936, as if to propitiate a jealous God. In a rare instance where he deliberately deformed the truth of what he actually thought, he wrote the following letter to Senator Glass:

In view of the public response generally and the many letters and telegrams received from prominent men in all parts of the country, reflecting a favorable opinion of the new Board of Governors of the Federal Reserve System, I cannot refrain from writing you this note to express appreciation of all that you have done in helping to bring about this gratifying result, which is so eminently satisfactory not only from the standpoint of the banking and business community, but from that of the Administration as well.

I should like very much to have an opportunity to discuss with you and have the benefit of your advice with reference to one or two matters of immediate importance to the Board and to the System.

Years later, Marriner wondered aloud about the root sources of the tension between himself and Glass. Was it at least partly due to the fact that he and the senator had many things in common? Both were self-assured men. Both were convinced of their personal integrity. Both were incapable of suppressing their convictions. Both tenaciously pursued the objectives they set for themselves. At almost identical periods in their lives, they had both engaged in a fight to wrest from private bankers the powers they held over the nation's monetary mechanism, and to return those powers to Washington. Each found deep personal satisfaction in service to and close association with a particular president. Each liked to create institutional mechanisms. Ironically, aside from differences in age, the two men were said to bear a striking physical resemblance to each other.

---

*At Marriner's insistence, Federal Reserve Board members were to keep away from the construction site. He did not want them to impose their personal preferences on the layouts of their individual offices, to the confusion of the architect and contractors. He applied that self-denying ordinance to himself as well. The result would be one of Washington's most aesthetically harmonious public structures—coveted by the Joint Chiefs of Staff during the Second World War.

IV

IN DUBIOUS BATTLE

22. Prologue to Future Troubles

I

To MARRINER there was an obvious corollary to his proposition that government spending, borrowing and taxation exert a powerful influence on the volume of money and on its use by the public. It was that neither the Treasury Department nor the Federal Reserve System could be self-centered when each discharged its own special responsibilities in the common task of maintaining economic stability. The Reserve System, in its management of money and credit, must take into account the Treasury's fiscal and debt management policies; and the Treasury, which borrows, taxes and spends, must be assured that the Reserve System within the limits of its powers will promote monetary and credit conditions favorable to the Treasury's purposes. Since these two arms of government resembled mountain climbers tied together by a single rope, sustained consultation and cooperation were indispensable to their own and the nation's general welfare.

As head of the Federal Reserve Board, however, it was easier for Marriner to state the case for cooperation than to secure it as a matter of routine in his encounters with Secretary of the Treasury Henry Morgenthau. What he personally owed to the Secretary of the Treasury should not be overlooked. It was Morgenthau, for all his fretful traits, who had launched Marriner on his government career. It was Morgenthau who put Marriner in a position where he could first make "a name for himself" in Washington in connection with the federal housing legislation. It was Morgenthau who took the lead in suggesting to Roosevelt that Marriner be appointed the head of the Federal Reserve Board.

Yet for all this, the subsequent relationship between the two men was a deeply troubled one extending over the remainder of the New Deal years, throughout the war years, and up to the hour after Roosevelt's death when Morgenthau resigned from the government. In the whole of that period, attempts to synchronize Treasury-Reserve movements repeatedly foundered either on the rock of honest differences of opinion or because of their respective institutional prides and prejudices. In the conflicts over what should be done and who should do it, neither Morgenthau nor Marriner was immune from a tendency to personalize the issue. Morgenthau, as his diary entries make clear, ascribed Marriner's position in successive controversies to an insatiable drive to gain personal power for himself.[1] Marriner, for his part, was inclined to view his difficulies with the Treasury Department as being due mainly to the quirks of Morgenthau's personality. It was only after Morgenthau passed from the scene that Marriner began to see the *institutional* sources of the difficulties in clearer perspective—since the troubles he had with Morgenthau cropped up in an even more inflamed form when Fred Vinson and then John Snyder followed Morgenthau as head of the Treasury.

Against the background of that relationship, mention must be made of an undistributed profits tax which came to a misshapen birth in 1936. The tax died in 1939, and its life was too short to have any lasting impact on the national economy. It is from the circumstances surrounding the origin of the tax, however, that one can date the first open breach between the Treasury and the Reserve Board.

II

In early 1936, two events unhinged President Roosevelt's political aim of giving business "a breathing spell" from new taxation, and of entering the presidential election with a budget seeming "in balance" except for relief expenditures. First, on January 6, a majority of the Supreme Court in the case of *United States* v. *Butler* declared the Agricultural Adjustment Administration's processing tax unconstitutional. The decision, at a stroke, denied the Treasury an estimated $500 million in revenue it expected to collect through the processing tax and, at the same time, confronted the administration with a painful question. If AAA payments to farmers were to be continued, how were they to be financed?

Though Roosevelt was to add the *Butler* decision to his indictment of the Supreme Court, few people at the center of events in his administration, aside from Secretary of Agriculture Wallace, shed any real tears when the processing tax was declared unconstitutional. Marriner Eccles, for one, shed no tears at all. He was among the members of the administration who helped block an effort to rewrite the tax in the hope that it could survive a challenge in the courts. In his view, the tax was a regressive revenue measure which retarded recovery by reducing consumer income, and was bad on that ground alone. On much the same ground, Marriner argued against a proposal for a new sales tax or for an increase in the tax on personal income. But if these sources of revenue were ruled out, how was the budget to be brought "into balance"—for Roosevelt's polemical purposes in the 1936 presidential contest?

Three weeks after the administration was hurt by the Supreme Court's ruling in the *Butler* case, Congress enacted a new version of the soldier bonus bill and then overrode the president's new veto of the measure. The $2 billion in soldier bonuses which now had to be paid out would have to be borrowed at a carrying charge of $120 million annually. The sum, added to the loss of $500 million in revenue from the AAA processing tax, meant that Roosevelt must now find $620 million in new taxes if he was to keep the budget "in balance," continue AAA contract payments to farmers and care for the unemployed.

This was the fiscal-political situation when Morgenthau, urged on by Herman Oliphant, reverted to a proposal he had floated more than a year earlier for a tax on undistributed corporate earnings. Precedents for such a tax, going back to the Civil War, had cropped up periodically in subsequent revenue measures, the last being in the early 1920s. Morgenthau viewed the undistributed earnings tax mainly as a device to increase revenue by combating an estimated $1.3 billion in tax avoidance on an estimated $4.5 billion in corporate profits. Oliphant, the foremost proponent of the tax within the Treasury, was initially more concerned with its possible bearing on recovery. To this extent he had an ally in Marriner Eccles, who had long favored such a tax so as to force back into the consumer spending stream the undistributed profits which were accumulating in large corporations, the main beneficiaries of the New Deal's recovery programs.

Marriner's approach to an undistributed profit tax was thus in line with his general views about the mechanics of a compensatory economy. His formula for such a tax, however, was not the one favored by the Treasury, which—for its immediate interest in "revenue plus reform"—proposed to abolish the regular corporate income tax, and to put in its place a graduated tax on the undistributed income of *all* corporations, without regard to the size of the enterprise. It was the Treasury's formula that served as the basis for the revenue message Roosevelt sent to the Congress on March 3, 1936. The proposed graduated tax upon undistributed income, said the president, would not only yield the $620 million in needed revenue, but "would accomplish an important tax reform, remove major inequalities in our tax system, and stop 'leaks' in the present surtaxes."

Secretary Morgenthau had been exhausted by the double strain of the monetary negotiations he had been conducting with China, France and England, and by the last stages of the debate over the soldier's bonus. He contracted an acute respiratory infection and, to regain his health, left Washington with his wife for a stay of several weeks in Sea Island, Georgia. Since these weeks coincided with the period when the House Ways and Means Committee under the chairmanship of Rep. Robert L. Doughton took up Roosevelt's proposed undistributed profits tax, the star witnesses scheduled for the Doughton committee were Herman Oliphant, the Treasury's general counsel, and George Haas, the veteran head of the Treasury's Research Division.

On the eve of the hearing, Marriner came to Oliphant to say that even if the Treasury's version of the undistributed profits tax was confined merely to raising $620 million in revenue, it would fail to attain that objective. Second, the draft bill was vulnerable to sharp and valid objections on many counts, but these could be met through certain amendments which Marriner sketched in. Oliphant, however, was unmoved. In his testimony before the House Ways and Means Committee, he stood firm on the Treasury's version of the tax set forth in the presidential message of March 3.

In April, the Democratic Majority on the House Ways and Means

Committee reported out a bill which contained an undistributed profits tax "for revenue," a continued capital-stock tax at half the existing rate, a related temporary excess profits tax, and several other features. The Republicans on the committee, in the preamble to their minority report, called for a "stop to the waste of public monies." They then listed fourteen objections to the "New Deal experiment" in corporate taxation, asserted the bill had Communist approval and, for extra measure, added that the bill would be a "Chinese puzzle to the most able board of directors, the most learned lawyers, and the most skilled accountants."

The bill was approved by the House with little argument nevertheless. Three quarters of the members were absent during most of the period when the measure was debated, and among those on hand it is doubtful if more than a handful understood the complex 236-page text. The only record vote in the House occurred on April 29, when a roll call on the final passage showed a split almost entirely along party lines, with 267 "ayes" and 93 "nays."

By the time the legislative fight shifted to the Senate Finance Committee under the chairmanship of Senator Pat Harrison, Morgenthau was back in Washington. As a witness before that committee, he came under the heavy fire of critical senators, including those in the New Deal camp. The latter in particular pointed to the gross errors in the Treasury's estimates of the revenues the tax would produce. They also detailed the ways in which the House schedule for the tax would enable corporate giants to avoid paying *any* taxes for a year, though the tax would handicap a man starting a new business, and would also prevent small and medium-sized corporations from building up adequate reserves.

Marriner Eccles had been an attentive bystander during the hearings before the Senate Finance Committee. He agreed that the House version of the tax invited the attacks of its critics, but thought the attacks might be met by amendments along the lines he had previously suggested to Oliphant. Still, he knew that the Treasury Department viewed the whole realm of fiscal policy to be its exclusive responsibility, and that if he encroached on any corner of it as chairman of the Federal Reserve Board, he would rouse the wrath of Treasury officialdom. He again tried to get Oliphant to consider the salvaging amendments, but when they were rejected a second time, Marriner risked the storm he knew was bound to come. He secured appointments with President Roosevelt on May 7 and again on May 11, when the Senate hearings on the tax measure were in their final hours. On both occasions he presented FDR with lengthy memoranda containing his critique of the House version of the undistributed profits tax, suggesting changes that could make the proposed tax "really effective" in promoting the "desirable monetary goal" of "forcing corporations to pass along cash as rapidly as it is received."

A few days after Marriner put the suggested changes to Roosevelt, a majority report of the Senate Finance Committee categorically rejected the work of the House Ways and Means Committee. Some of the reasons given for the rejection were fatuous, but others were solidly based. FDR, in a reflex response to the report, not only sent Marriner's version of the undistributed profits tax on its way to the Senate Finance Committee, but gave it the imprimatur of the *administration* bill in place of the Treasury version.

A donnybrook followed, rocking official Washington. Within the Senate Finance Committee, the forces led by senators Byrd and George attacked the new version as violently as they had the old. Within the House, Representative Doughton, chairman of the House Ways and Means Committee, was enraged because the president's change poured salt in the wounds inflicted on Doughton by the majority report of the Senate Finance Committee. Within the Executive, Secretary Morgenthau was personally insulted because Marriner had both trespassed on the fiscal preserve of the Treasury and had won the president's support for "the Eccles bill" in place of the one developed in the Treasury. Morgenthau was made no cheerier when a comment in the *New York Herald Tribune* aimed at Eccles included a sideswipe which hit him directly:

This was the first time the head of the nation's banking system assumed the responsibilities of the Secretary of the Treasury. When the Secretaryship of the Treasury is permitted to go to seed as it has under Mr. Morgenthau, and when the head of the banking system is a man who loses no opportunity to appropriate any financial prerogatives that are not nailed down, the inevitable result is what we are now witnessing.[2]

Meanwhile, at Union Station, reservations were piling up for berths on trains that would take senators and representatives to the 1936 presidential nomination conventions of the Democratic and Republican parties. Congress could keep its appointment with party politics only if the work of the Senate Finance Committee was quickly ratified—provided the committee itself could agree internally on a tax bill. Senator Pat Harrison, the committee chairman, tried to strong-arm a decision by threatening to carry the tax fight to the floor of the Senate if there was no agreement within his committee, thus delaying adjournment.

The response was a "compromise" tailored to the wishes of senators Harry F. Byrd and Walter George and approved by a crushing majority of 18-1 in the committee. Since this represented an "agreement," Harrison was bound not to make a floor fight. The points of the "compromise," in Marriner's view, not only failed to meet the president's immediate objectives but were a backward step in the progress of tax policy. In a note hand-delivered to the president on the morning of May 27, he showed how the terms of the Senate "compromise" would penalize small corporations, make the cost of the corporate form of enterprise virtually prohibitive for small businessmen, constitute a departure from the principle of taxing according to ability to pay, permit wealthy stockholders to continue to evade their fair share of taxation, favor rather than check the growth of economic bigness, and be ineffective in forcing more purchasing power into circulation.

Prodded by the note, the president called a meeting at the White House that night, attended by the Democratic members of the Senate Finance Committee. Senator Harrison sent word that he was ill, but Senator Joseph Robinson, the Senate majority leader, was on hand, and he did all within his power to bind the conferees to accept the "Eccles plan" as the basis for a new attempt to write a tax measure. At the end of the acrimonious meeting, however, the only agreement reached was on a procedural point. The Finance Committee would again consider the "Eccles plan."

At its meeting the next day, the committee stood fast in support of its original regressive tax measure. Three days later the Senate, by a vote of 38 to 24, approved the Finance Committee's radical rewriting of the House bill. Very little could be salvaged in the conference committee since both the House and the Senate versions of the measure were deeply flawed. The final bill was better than nothing, but not by very much. It was a far cry from what Marriner had advocated. But he would be blamed for having fathered the tax, and he would be the subject of angry mutterings within the Treasury Department for his "usurpation" of the Treasury's jurisdictional authority in fiscal matters. Later, anti-administration forces would blame him and the tax for having brought on the 1937–38 recession.

23. Middle of the Journey: Assessments

WHEN THE LINES WERE DRAWN for the 1936 war for presidential succession, some managers of Roosevelt's reelection bid wanted Marriner to play an active role in the contest. They argued that, since the government's spending and lending program would be a key issue, and since Marriner was prominently identified with the rationale for that program, he was the right person to defend it against the anticipated Republican attacks. Marriner thought it would be highly improper for the chairman of the Federal Reserve Board to engage in electioneering. To do so, said he, would compromise the institutional role of the board of governors as an independent government agency, with a nonpartisan membership chosen for the nonpartisan task of helping to restore and maintain national economic stability—responsible to the Congress. Roosevelt agreed.

The one public speech Marriner made in 1936 not directly related to legislation before the Congress was on May 8, well before the presidential nominating conventions gave the nation a choice between President Roosevelt and his Republican adversary, Governor Alfred M. Landon. The faculty and alumni of the University of Pennsylvania's Wharton School of Finance and Industry sponsored a conference in New York on "Debt, Taxation and Inflation," and Marriner was invited to speak on the "Theory and Progress of the Recovery Program." Since his own "theory" has already been spelled out at length in these pages, it need not be repeated here. Two aspects of his speech are, however, of special interest. First, he brought together a mother lode of figures on the economy which were to help explain, later on, Roosevelt's landslide reelection in November. Second, in advance of that landslide, Marriner pointed to the long road still lying ahead before it could be said that a general economic recovery had in fact been achieved, and that all the necessary reforms in the nation's major economic institutions had in fact been made.

In the picture he drew of the nation's economic ledger, Marriner first focused on the debit entries. Between March 1, 1933, and March 31, 1936, the federal debt rose from $20.9 billion to 31.4 billion. But when this gross figure was adjusted to take into account recoverable assets in the hands of government lending agencies such as the Reconstruction Finance Corporation, the net increase in the national debt was only $5.9 billion. This was less than a month's national income in 1928–29, while the total carrying charge on the debt amounted to little over 1 percent of the current national income in 1936.

On the credit side of the ledger, Marriner noted the rise in national income and production, the restoration of the supply of money, increasing tax revenues, and the rise in building activity. As of March 31, 1936, the national income was approximately $60 billion, an increase of $20 billion over March 1933. Stocks on the New York Exchange increased in value by $35 billion, while listed bonds increased in value by around $10 billion. The deposits of all commercial banks rose by more than $10 billion, so that the contraction in the money supply which occurred in the deflation was largely offset—partly by an inflow of gold from abroad, but mainly because government borrowing in connection with relief and recovery expenditures increased bank holdings of government securities.

Notwithstanding the increase in the public debt, some issues of government bonds which sold as low as 83 in March 1933, when the debt was $20.9 billion, were selling at 104 at the end of March 1936. Tax collections ran about $2 billion a year higher than in the depths of the depression, and the output of industry was 65 percent higher. The corporations of the country, whose combined operations in 1932 showed a loss of $3.7 billion as evidenced in their tax returns to the Treasury, were showing profits comparable to predepression levels—which accounted, in turn, for the buoyancy of the New York stock market. Long-term interest rates were brought down to encourage and make profitable the use of capital for new enterprise, and to adjust, through refunding, a substantial portion of the existing debt structure on a supportable basis. A rise in rents, an increase in real estate values, coupled with favorable long-term interest rates, made it profitable to increase building construction again.

But did this mean that all was well? Should the government stop its program to revive effective consumer purchasing power? Should it shift directly to a policy of a balanced budget? It was Marriner's hope that a budget balanced through increased taxes or decreased expenditures, or both, could be attained within a reasonable period once the national income was restored. In fact, a balanced budget was an "absolutely indispensable element" for economic stability in boom times. But it was dead wrong to assume, he said, that the time to balance the budget was *now*. The volume of unemployed continued to be "very heavy."

He observed that, even prior to the depression, between 2 and 2.5 million people had been unemployed. Between 3.5 and 4 million *more* new workers came of employment age in the three years since March 1933. At the same time, new labor-saving machinery, which increased the output per worker, acted as a constraint on new employment opportunities. But above all, millions of workers who, though listed as employed, had formerly worked only one or two days a week had increased their work week to four or five days. In consequence, the increase in *man hours worked* was much greater than the increase in the *number of men working*. On these grounds, said Marriner, "the present phase of the recovery movement, and the way it is managed, is of critical importance."

Despite the many encouraging signs he had enumerated, a leading question continued to haunt the present and future condition of the economy. "Will the disbursements of private business and individuals increase sufficiently to warrant a lessening of the government's contribution to the growth in the national income?" The answer to the question continued to hang in inference. But Marriner concluded his remarks with a ringing statement of what he felt the ruling policy should be:

The Federal Government cannot and should not decrease its expenditures on recovery faster than private industry is able profitably to take over the load. To do so would reduce consumer buying power and thus retard, if not reverse, the progress of recovery. The flow of money must be maintained and increase in an expanding economy. If private capital fails to maintain and expand the flow, and widespread unemployment exists or develops, government must act as a compensatory factor.

Marriner did not at the time allude to a development that was causing no small unease throughout the Federal Reserve System. It was that since late 1935, the excess volume of bank reserves already on hand were being swelled by a heavy influx of gold to America, stimulated by the Treasury gold-buying price, the dollar shortage, and unstable political and economic conditions in Europe. The influx of gold could become the basis of a potential expansion of bank credit of such proportions that the Federal Reserve would lose all control or influence over the supply and cost of money; but opinion was divided over what should be done to reduce the excess reserves. Some people advocated selling a portion of the Federal Reserve holdings of government securities. Others advocated an increase in the reserve requirements of member banks.

When the issue landed on the agenda of the Federal Open Market Committee on December 17–18, 1935, no immediate decision was reached, but the Board of Governors subsequently followed the lead of Marriner Eccles. In a statement it issued after that meeting of the committee, the board stressed two points. First, while the volume of excess reserves was far beyond existing or prospective needs of business, there was as yet no evidence of overexpansion either of business activity or of credit. Second, the problem created by excess reserves would continue to be studied with a view to appropriate action at such time as might be in the public interest.

Follow-up studies by the board indicated a wide geographic distribution of the excess reserves among banks. Even if reserve requirements were increased by as much as 50 percent, the remaining excess in most banks would still be beyond the needs of business and would provide a more than adequate basis for legitimate credit expansion. On the other hand, the longer action was delayed, the more the interest rate would drop under the pressure of excess reserves. More banks would then try to overcome that decline by increasing the volume of loans and investments. It would thus be more difficult to deal with any inflationary consequences that might develop —since any later order for a substantial increase in required reserves would lead to a painful liquidation of holdings.

Timing was central to any decision made in line with the studies.

Specifically, it was believed that an immediate increase in reserve requirements would decrease the volume of money available for the purchase of government bonds, thereby complicating a financing operation the Treasury had set for June 15, 1936. After consulting with Morgenthau in April, 1936, Marriner decided not to do anything about reserves until July 1, when the Treasury would have completed the indicated financing. By then, the continuing inflow of gold from an increasingly disturbed Europe brought the excess bank reserves to a record level of $3 billion. It was at last clear that the Board of Governors must increase the required bank reserves by an amount that could bring the remaining reserves under the direct influence of open-market operations.

The Banking Act of 1935 empowered the board to change reserve requirements without prior presidential approval. Yet it was Marriner's view that the nation, now caught up in election-year fever, would hold Roosevelt personally responsible for whatever the board did on its own initiative. Accordingly, as the liaison officer between the board and the president, Marriner called at the White House on July 9, 1936, to explain to FDR why the board meant to order a 50 percent increase in the required reserves. He also gave Roosevelt a memorandum which spelled out the reactions he could expect when the board's decision was made public:

Action may be misinterpreted as putting the brakes on recovery just as the capital market is reviving and new investment and construction are getting well under way.

Banking opinion is divided with an apparent preponderance now opposed to action. Those who had been most sympathetic toward administration policy, including the Morgan partners, have been against action—so is David Stern.

The Lemke-Coughlin group might be expected to attack the action as restrictive, deflationary, and typical of the "money-changers."

The action contemplated will not satisfy those groups which have been clamoring for action in the hope that it would stiffen interest rates. If there was any serious danger of such a result, I should oppose action.

I would not favor action under any circumstances unless assured of authority through the Open Market Executive Committee to counteract any recession of a point or more in the price of government [securities].

With Roosevelt's back-stage assent, the board on July 15 ordered a 50 percent increase in the reserve requirements of member banks, effective August 15, 1936. The anticipated outcries against the order were topped by a protest from a source not anticipated in Marriner's memorandum to FDR. Secretary Morgenthau had not been alerted to the board's decision before it was made public. He already resented Marriner's invasion of the Treasury's fiscal domain in connection with the undistributed profits tax; now, with a new insult added to the previous injury, he telephoned Marriner to criticize him for his high-handed "unilateralism" and other assorted wrongs.

Marriner insisted that the failure to give Morgenthau prior notice of the board's order was not part of a melodramatic plot to usurp power at the Treasury's expense. The reasons behind the communication breakdown were as prosaic as oatmeal. In the first place, Morgenthau was out of town and inaccessible when the order was to be released. Secondly, it was Marriner's understanding that at the time of his April conference with Morgenthau it had been agreed that the order to increase reserve requirements would go forward in July after the Treasury had completed the financing operation during June. Then, too, instead of high-handed "unilateralism," the board's impending decision had been discussed with President Roosevelt on July 9 and was approved by him.

Morgenthau realized that the time was as good as any for a change in reserve requirements, but refused to accept Marriner's version of what had happened. "I certainly put the fear of God into him," so Morgenthau confided to his diary after the denunciatory telephone conversation, "and doubt if he will pull off another fast one. I can't make Eccles out unless he wants to be important and show his independence."[3]

The marketplace effect of the order in no way reversed the board's easy-money and credit policies. The $1.79 billion in excess reserves that was actually siphoned off merely eliminated what was superfluous to the needs of the economy. Reserves were still so large and well spaced that all but a few member banks met the August 15 order either by using their balances with the Reserve banks or by drawing on their excess balances with correspondent banks. Subsequently, Marriner and Morgenthau held a series of meetings to iron out the emergent pattern of conflicts stemming from the Treasury's and Reserve Board's institutional roles, from the Reserve Board's need for vital information the Treasury kept to itself, and from a bulging package of other causes. After an accord was reached on something Morgenthau had proposed and which Marriner found "one hundred percent satisfactory," Morgenthau pleasantly said: "Well, now, that's fine Marriner. Now we are partners." The remark would not qualify for a place in any book of prophecy.[4]

II

Leaders of the Roosevelt administration, beginning with the president, differently construed the meaning of his sweeping victory in the 1936 presidential contest. Partisans of a spending program, for example, thought that the triumph had defused "planned deficits" or "balanced budgets" as a political issue. They noted how Roosevelt increasingly gave his fiscal policy more credit as a source of general recovery, not just as a source of specific benefits to needy people. He had increasingly stressed the indirect benefits of his spending program, showing by homespun examples how the dollars spent on work relief and other emergency programs stimulated a circular flow of income and expenditures.

Marriner Eccles could have found in such speeches, and in the president's decisive political victory, a vindication of his own views. But he had other things on his mind. He saw in the triumphant outcome of the election—and the concurrent heavy influx of gold from Europe—a chance to win Roosevelt's support for a unified banking system. So, on November 12, 1936, he went with high hopes—and a memorandum in his briefcase—to a White House lunch with the president. In his memorandum, he approached his objective by indirection:

One of the greatest accomplishments of the Administration was the rehabilitation of banking and the concentration in Washington, instead of in New York, of such controls as exist over money and credit. There was no opportunity, however, in the period of emergency for a more fundamental reconstruction which is imperative for the future of sound banking. The opportunity now exists for the Administration to supplement its distinguished work by such a broad revision based upon experience both here and in other countries and upon the pressing needs of the hour arising from drastically changed economic conditions. I assume that the Administration desires to take full advantage of this opportunity which may never arise again and be so propitious. . . .

There is no field in which this Administration could make a more constructive contribution than in banking reform, and broadly, changes which need to be instituted at this time would undoubtedly stand as a landmark no less notable than the enactment of the Federal Reserve System under Woodrow Wilson's leadership.

After this prologue, Marriner turned to his direct line of argument. Unbeknown to himself at the time, he would be compelled again and again to return to it, just as successive heads of the Federal Reserve Board down to the present day would echo what he formally put to FDR in November 1936.

He observed that as long as the Federal Reserve Board was vested by law with primary responsibility for monetary and credit management, it should also have the means to carry out its legal mandate. Instead, the board was under the constraints of a national banking structure based on organized anarchy. "We have in this country," he said, "forty-eight separate banking systems—forty-eight state authorities to charter banks which create money, conduct examinations and prescribe regulations." The state systems are infinitely complex, and many of them were "notoriously lax." It was still possible for persons who had no competence to open so-called banks which were in reality "nothing more than pawn shops." It was in these state-chartered banks, not members of the Federal Reserve System, that the greatest bank failures had occurred in the late twenties and through the depression. It was these "mushroom miscalled banks which caused the greatest losses and misery among their depositors and brought a large share of discredit down upon the heads of bankers generally."

The Reserve System could not meet its responsibilities with respect to the maintenance of economic stability when federal law allowed state banks to get FDIC insurance without requiring them to join the Reserve System; and yet the law imposed burdens on members of the Federal Reserve System—most notably in the matter of control over reserves—of which the nonmembers were free. Clearly, Marriner said, the Reserve System "cannot function efficiently or effectively in the national interest as long as half of the banks are in it and the other half out. Currency management, which is inevitable in a world off the gold standard, becomes almost a mockery under a divided banking system, one half of which is free to combat and to negate management in the national interest. The whole of the dual system makes for a competition in laxity.''

Within the federal government itself, existing conflicts of authority made for ''inefficiency, confusion, harassment of the banks themselves, and for division of responsibilities which are inimical to the kind of banking management that was indispensably necessary in the national interest.'' Here Marriner brought into evidence the three following examples. First, the power of the federal government to conduct bank examinations and to issue regulations was divided among the FDIC, the Comptroller of the Currency, and the Federal Reserve Board—''yet each of these had a different interest to be served by the examinations it conducted and the regulations it issued.'' Second, since the Comptroller of the Currency had plenary power to charter a national bank, the Federal Reserve System was automatically compelled to accept that bank as a member. It had ''no voice in ascertaining whether that bank is necessary, whether it is properly managed, or whether it complies with what should be sound fundamentals of banking practice.'' Third, the FDIC had the right to insure banks which could then apply for membership in the Federal Reserve System. The system had no voice in determining whether such a bank was an institution it could properly embrace, yet ''to refuse it membership is tantamount to repudiating it as a proper subject to be insured by the government.''

What was to be done about all such problems?

Specifically, if state banks chose to be members of the FDIC and to enjoy the benefits of that government insurance agency, then they should be obliged to join the Federal Reserve System—where they would be subject, as are national banks, to credit restrictions involving reserve requirements. It was also reasonable to consolidate bank examination and regulatory functions under the the single roof of the Reserve System, since these functions have a direct bearing on the system's overriding concern—the maintenance of economic stability.

If the system, said Marriner, is committed to monetary ease in time of depression, then bank examination policies should support that objective. If the system is committed to credit stringency in order to curb inflation, that objective should also be served by bank examination policies. But did the record of experiences under the existing regulatory setup show any such alignments? On the contrary, it showed, said Marriner, ''that the Comptroller's office has repeatedly pursued a policy of restraint when correct central bank policy called for an easing of restraints, and conversely, has eased restraints when correct central bank policy called for a tightening of what would be acceptable in the credit structure of banks.'' The Reserve Board would work closely with the FDIC and the Treasury in drafting legislation to remedy the way things stood, but, unfortunately, cooperation with the Comptroller was "out of the question." Marriner concluded the memorandum with a peroration combining politics and an appeal to the verdict of history:

If the revisions suggested constituted a reform such as would be disturbing to the country, or designed to create serious political difficulties, or would tend to interrupt the recovery program, I would not venture to urge it at this time. However, I believe that the program outlined would be welcomed enthusiastically by the most competent banking and business opinion throughout the nation as a contribution toward consolidating and perpetuating the recovery movement. And if carried through as I believe it can be, I am convinced that such a program will go down in history as among the outstanding achievements of this Administration.

Though Roosevelt read the memorandum in Marriner's presence and listened carefully to its elaboration, his response was simply that he "would think the matter over." He was about to leave for an extended South American cruise, and would not be back in Washington until mid-December.

III

In the weeks while Roosevelt was away, Marriner, addressing several banking associations, tried to build some bridges between the banking community and the administration—all in the hope that the bridges would support a political move toward the unification of the nation's banking system. But his conciliatory remarks to bankers, who were staggered by the results of the election, met with little enthusiasm; his appeal to them to join in a common effort to support the indivisible relationship between human rights and property rights was no more welcome than a hawker of tambourines at a funeral.

A more immediate matter soon engrossed his attention—a new intensification of the old problem of excess reserves. In November 1936, total bank deposits and currency, the most liquid resources at the disposal of the public, exceeded their 1929 level. At the same time, because of mounting war threats in Europe, more and more Europeans liquidated investments in their own countries, bought dollars, and invested them in American stocks and bonds. As the gold equivalent of these dollar purchases flowed into the United States, the Treasury, after taking possession of the gold, deposited corresponding gold certificates in the Federal Reserve System. These foreign funds—"hot money" in Roosevelt's phrase—continued inexorably to swell the already high level of excess reserves.

The presence of excess reserves did not by itself lead to a more active use of the existing money supply, but it was estimated that if the excess was used as fully as in the past, it would form the basis for an expansion of $15–20 billion in deposits. Even if reserve requirements were increased to the full amount permitted by law, the remaining excess would still form the basis for a potential credit expansion of more than $7 billion without further action by the Federal Reserve Banks. It was against this background that several decisions were made whose effects—or lack of effects—on the recession of 1937–38 remain to the present day a subject of debate among professional economists and economic historians.

The Treasury and the Reserve System were equally concerned over a potential runaway expansion of credit because of the unchecked growth of excess reserves. Within and between both institutions, however, opinions were divided on how to meet the danger. Proposals agreed to one day became unstuck the next, were revived or modified a day later. So it went until early December, when the Treasury staff hit upon a relatively simple plan to divorce the management of the domestic monetary system from the effects consequent upon the settlement of international balances. The staff proposed that as the Treasury's Stabilization Fund accumulated gold by converting foreign exchange to bullion, it would use dollars to buy gold from the fund, but would not follow the usual procedure of depositing counterpart gold certificates with the Federal Reserve banks. The gold instead would be segregated or "sterilized" in a special account in the Treasury's General Fund, and this would prevent the incoming gold from entering bank reserves and expanding the credit base.

When Morgenthau first revealed this plan to Marriner on December 8, Marriner's reactions were strongly positive. To control excess reserves by sterilizing gold, he said, was far better than the alternative of continually increasing reserve requirements—a practice that could drive member banks out of the Federal Reserve System. Two days later Marriner had second thoughts about the institutional aspects of the matter, and believed these were in need of clarification. In a personal note to Morgenthau on December 10, he stated that he would endorse the Treasury's plan, provided the mechanics of the sterilization process would not interfere with the board's responsibility under the law to regulate the flow of money and credit. To have the Treasury and the Reserve Board each give orders concerning gold and gold reserves—with their immense effect on money and credit—would only widen an existing gap between power and responsibility, the Reserve System having no control over the state nonmember banks that were amassing excess reserves.

In a present-day perspective, the memorandum reads as an impersonal comment on orderly public administration. Morgenthau, however, read it against the immediate background of his clashes with Marriner on other matters. When he met with his Treasury staff, he described Marriner's note as being "peremptory" and "impertinent." His irritation increased the next day when Marriner, acting on behalf of the board, ordered a suspension of an existing arrangement where the Reserve System helped support government bond prices by absorbing half of the Treasury's purchases in the open market. A technical reason prompted the suspension. The acquisition of securities by the Reserve System added to excess reserves and hence further complicated the problem of dealing with them. Morgenthau, however, again imagined a personal motive behind the action. He told his staff that he was being subjected to some sort of "squeeze"; that Eccles was trying to "trade" in terms that were an assertion by Eccles of a prerogative he had no right to claim.[5]

When news of this outburst reached Marriner on December 15 he wrote Morgenthau what he hoped would be a conciliatory letter which would put his case in an institutional context.

I don't suppose it is necessary for me to say so, but I want to assure you that I am in no way influenced by questions of prerogative. . . . What I feel is important above all else . . . is to make sure that everything is done to preserve the spirit of complete cooperation which has been brought about between the Treasury and the Federal Reserve Board. I have no anxieties on that score so long as you and I are here, but I am thinking ahead to the time when one or both of us may not be here, and if some of the questions involved in this important and complicated matter are left up in the air, with uncertainty as to obligations under the law and how far and for how long either the System or the Treasury is to deal with this problem, there is real danger, it seems to me, of confusion and impairment of the one thing which both of us wish to see preserved. . . . Now, Henry, if I have in any way incurred your displeasure it would certainly cause me the deepest regret. . . . I want you to know that whatever your decision may be in this matter, you will continue to have my wholehearted cooperation.

There was another letter Marriner gave Morgenthau at this time, a formal communication from the Board of Governors to the Secretary of the Treasury. Marriner conveyed the view, held by a majority of the board, that it was still unnecessary to start the sterilization of gold but that, if such a policy was put into effect, it should be continuous and automatic. To permit the policy to be turned off and on episodically at the Treasury's discretion would have a number of disruptive effects. It would obscure lines of responsibility for monetary management, insure recurrent crises in the matter of excess bank reserves, and frustrate the Reserve Board's own attempt to maintain an orderly flow of money and credit.

The second letter provoked Morgenthau anew, and there followed another bruising encounter between the two men, more angry charges, more explanations and, after tempers had cooled, another exchange of expressions of mutual willingness to ascribe honorable motives to the other party. Marriner finally offered to return to the Federal Reserve and explain that the purpose of the Treasury was not to exercise control over excess reserves as such. It was to build up a fund to insulate reserves from the effect of future inflows and outflows of gold, and thereby give the board of governors authentic control over domestic credit. Now that Marriner had a clear understanding of what was at issue, he hoped that the matter was also clear in Morgenthau's mind.

By December 17 Roosevelt was back in Washington from his South American cruise, and Eccles and Morgenthau called on him jointly to settle matters still in dispute. The president closely questioned Marriner about the implications of gold sterilization in the event of war in Europe, and Marriner's responses took Morgenthau by surprise. He spoke forcefully about the advantages of allowing the Treasury to sterilize gold right now. If this were done, "the gold would be available for export to countries which, in time of war, would sequester the American securities owned by their nationals, sell them on the American market, and take home the gold thus obtained." While mechanisms were available to the board of governors which would accomplish the same purposes as sterilization, he personally preferred the Treasury's proposal—but had been duty-bound to convey to Morgenthau the apprehensions voiced by a majority of the board. He favored the Treasury's proposal because it would enable the board to conserve its own brakes instead of using them up. Since the Treasury now intended to "cooperate" with the Federal Reserve, the sterilization policy would be flexible enough to be stopped at any time, and the procedure could be reversed whenever there was an outflow of funds.

At the end of the discussion, Roosevelt authorized Morgenthau to prepare for his signature the orders necessary to begin the sterilization program. Union and harmony had again been attained in the relationship between the heads of the Treasury and Federal Reserve, but, once again, discord would follow.

IV

At the December 17 meeting in the White House, the President did not mention the subject of bank unification, and the circumstances were not opportune for Marriner to do so. He continued to hope that his proposed reforms of the dual banking system might show up in the text of any one of the three major addresses FDR would presently give. But this was not to be.

In retrospect, when Marriner tried to account for Roosevelt's inertia with respect to bank unification, he arrived at the following hypothesis. The dual banking system—some banks belonging to the Federal Reserve System and some to the state banking system alone—was held in nostalgic affection by FDR. To him, the state nonmember banks were small, democratically controlled institutions, responsive to local needs, with officers who had the welfare of the home folks at heart. On the other hand, he thought of the Federal Reserve as representing the banking giants and, in a way, conceived of the Banking Act of 1935 as a curb on them. In Roosevelt's view, therefore, to unify the banking system implied either or both of two consequences inimical to his values. One would be the end of the state banking system. The other would be the end of small state banks, since, by being forced to join the Reserve System, they would be vulnerable to destruction by the banking giants.

Marriner thought it not uncharitable to describe Roosevelt's reasoning as "naive." In the first place, three-fourths of the Reserve System members were small banks, both state and national. Secondly, Marriner's call for unification did not entail an end of the state banking system. He merely wished to eliminate the jurisdictional conflicts among three federal banking agencies so that the regulatory, supervisory examinations and investment policies for the banking system could be coordinated in support of overall monetary and credit policies. Each state would still have the right to charter and examine banks or, as it saw fit, to permit or forbid branch banking. Bank unification simply meant that banks would no longer have the option of joining the FDIC without joining the Federal Reserve. If they enjoyed the benefits of the FDIC, they would be required to assume the responsibilities of membership in the Reserve System.

In the years ahead, Marriner repeatedly returned to the subject of bank unification and repeatedly tried to win Roosevelt's support for the politics of the matter. Yet every seeming gain he made in bringing Roosevelt closer to an understanding of what was at issue was later lost again. The process of impressing on FDR the importance of reformist actions in this field had to begin all over again, one step at a time.

24. Silver Cloud, Dark Lining

I

IN THE LAST DAYS OF 1936, President Roosevelt buckled down to work on the final version of three major and interrelated utterances—the State of the Union message, the inaugural address, and the budget message. The economic picture he faced at the time was so ambiguous that any man could find in it what he was looking for. Some statistical measurements could be cited to support the contention that there was no need for further large-scale governmental stimulants to recovery. Recovery, and a balanced budget with it, would be attained through the momentum of things currently in motion. For example, the aggregate impact of approximately $14 billion in government spending and relief since 1933—coupled with the free spending of approximately $1.7 billion in soldier bonus payments in the last half of 1936—had already spurred a marked expansion of commercial installment credit for the purchase of automobiles, refrigerators and other durable goods. Production was drawing close to 1929 levels. Agricultural commodities brought higher prices, partly because of a drought, but mainly because more families had the means to buy more food. The long arm of the rearmament program underway in Europe reached across the Atlantic for American raw material to increase their prices. Tax revenues promised to continue their rapid rise along with a rise in national income.

However, the unionization drive in the mass-production industries by the newborn Congress of Industrial Organization (CIO) had been marked by a wave of sit-down strikes. More strikes loomed on the horizon, while the fear of consequent shortages and higher prices led to the speculative accumulation of inventories in many sectors of commerce and industry. Throughout the economy, unemployment remained at a high level—around 15 percent of the labor force in the winter of 1936–37. Roosevelt himself would presently observe in his inaugural address that one third of the nation was "ill-housed, ill-clad, ill-nourished." But if so, should the administration pursue a policy of extensive expenditures until *full* employment had been achieved? Roosevelt thought not. He leaned toward a restrictive budget policy which would still leave a large amount of unemployment to be handled by "structural" devices designed to reduce the size of the labor force —this, by retaining more young people in school, retiring the majority of workers at sixty-five and reducing the work week. Roosevelt could not endlessly debate the true nature of the economic picture. His old theory that deficits were defensible only in a depression—and his new conviction that the depression would end before full employment was regained—made him welcome the near approach of a balanced budget. Thus, in December 1936, he took some moderate steps to slow down the rate of authorized spending under the budget for fiscal 1937—which still had more than a half year to run. He also contemplated substantial cuts in spending as part of his design for a balanced budget to be achieved in fiscal 1938.

When Roosevelt revealed his intentions to Marriner during their White House meeting on December 17, 1936, Marriner promptly dissented from them, and subsequently sent FDR a memorandum formally stating the grounds for his objections. The president, impressed and disturbed, forwarded the memorandum to Secretary of the Treasury Morgenthau and asked for his reactions. An entry in Morgenthau's diary accurately summarizes the substance of what Marriner had to say:

Eccles' December memorandum on the budget advanced in his own words and in his own spirit, the ideas which had been given their classic statement by John Maynard Keynes. An attempt to balance the budget, Eccles argued, would put the country into an economic tailspin. The popular analogy between the debt of an individual and the debt of a nation was utterly false. The crucial consideration was not the size of the deficit but the level of national income. It would be unsafe to slash federal expenditures until the expansion of private enterprise took up the whole slack of employment. Meanwhile, deficit expenditures were a necessary compensatory form of investment which gave life to an economy operating below capacity. Ultimately they would lead to restored business activity and increased national income. An attempt to balance the budget for the fiscal year 1938, Eccles maintained, would be dangerously premature, would lead to a new wave of deflation and reverse the processes of recovery thus far set in motion. This would spell doom for the Democratic party, perhaps even pave the way for totalitarianism.[6]

Morgenthau urged the president to reject the whole of this thesis, which Roosevelt presently did, but not because of any theory of fiscal policy put to him by the Secretary of the Treasury. Revised budget estimates sent him by budget director Daniel Bell showed that, with only a little restraint on expenditures, recovery forces on the move in the economy as a whole would "naturally" bring the 1938 fiscal budget into balance. The president, surprised and delighted, teased Bell for holding out on him, while Morgenthau's reaction was euphoric. "I think," he said to his Treasury staff on December 29, "that all of us have every reason to face the new year with the greatest complacence and comfort."

The arithmetic underlying the prospect that the $2.2 billion deficit estimated for fiscal 1937 could be displaced by a balanced budget for fiscal 1938 went like this. First, Treasury collections on individual and corporate income and in excise taxes would be increased by $1.4 billion. Another $450 million would be collected from the newly imposed Social Security taxes. While this would still leave a deficit of $800 million, the greater part of that figure was represented by the $564 million final payment due to be made in 1937 on the soldier's bonus. Since no such payment would have to be repeated in fiscal 1938, the budget could be balanced at that time if other expenditures were reduced by only $250 million, or 3 percent of the total.

Given the trend of recovery, this seemed a reasonable prospect, and a welcome one. It meant that relief could be painlessly reduced, and that a balanced budget for fiscal 1938 could comfortably provide for the regular expenditures of government, including those for the new Social Security program.

Marriner's arithmetic was different, but, having lost the argument to Morgenthau and Bell, there was nothing he could do until more was revealed about the variables in their calculations. Roosevelt's budget for fiscal 1938, which was sent to Congress in January 1937, was incomplete as usual. It contained no estimates or requests for relief expenditures, which would come later. The president stressed two points. If work relief expenditures were held below $1.5 billion for fiscal 1938, the budget would be in balance for that year. Secondly, he was confident that the relief figure would not have to be exceeded provided business did its part in providing employment.

II

Meanwhile, the fears of a runaway expansion of bank credit continued to be fed by the ongoing influx of gold from Europe and the consequent increase in excess reserves. At a meeting of the Federal Open Market Committee on January 26, 1937, the Reserve Bank presidents on the committee agreed that the money market, as judged by the low level of short-term interest rates in relation to long term rates were "abnormally and dangerously easy."* Later in the day, when the discussions within the committee spilled over into a separate meeting held by the Board of Governors, the board decided to order a 33⅓ percent increase in the required reserve. Morgenthau then complained that the decision would leave less than $600 million in excess reserves. Marriner observed that the amount would still be more than the Reserve System had had in predepression years, but the Secretary and his advisers feared that the contemplated increase would increase the costs of Treasury financing by making money tighter. The increase in reserve requirements, they said, should be limited to only 16⅔ percent. In a compromise with the Treasury's views, when the Board on January 30, 1937, publicly announced a 33⅓ percent increase in the required reserve, it was added that the increase would be spaced out. One half of the increase, or 16⅓ percent, would take effect on March 1, and the remaining half would take effect on May 1.

In the Open Market Committee discussions preceding the Federal Reserve Board's January 30 announcement, opinions were divided on the ex-

---

*This was also the view of Dr. E. A. Goldenweiser, research director for the Federal Reserve Board and chief economist for the Federal Open Market Committee. John H. Williams, the vice-president of the New York Federal Reserve Bank and an associate economist of the committee, directly and emphatically argued for an increase in reserve requirements. "The business and economic situation in the United States," he said, "had in certain respects moved well beyond the normal state" of affairs. It was imperative, therefore, to "reconsider attitudes formed during the depression" about matters such as excess reserves.

tent to which the committee should intervene to support the government bond market if it should sharply decline under the impact of an ordered increase in reserve requirements. Some Reserve Board members, along with George Harrison and other Reserve bank presidents on the committee, claimed that any vigorous intervention would be inconsistent with a decision to increase reserve requirements. Having used the same argument himself on an earlier occasion, Marriner recognized its force. But he now contended that the committee should do whatever was necessary to stabilize the situation. It was true, said he, that the banking system as a whole had a great excess of reserves. It was to be expected, however, that *individual* banks would not be in a position to meet the new increase in reserve requirements except by selling some of their government securities. It was also to be expected that banks in a position to buy the securities offered for sale would defer doing so. They would assume that the longer they waited, the more prices would drop. Vigorous intervention by the Open Market Committee would therefore be necessary to undercut that assumption. Marriner's view prevailed, as did his related proposal. To check any possible disturbances following upon the March 1 increase in reserve requirements, the New York Federal Reserve Bank, acting as the agent for the Open Market Committee, was to buy government securities to a total of $500 million in order to steady their market.

When the first increase in reserve requirements went into effect, some banks, as Marriner had anticipated, began to unload their government securities. But the New York Federal Reserve Bank did not follow the instructions previously given it by the Open Market Committee and did not vigorously intervene to stabilize the situation. Instead, at the direction of George L. Harrison, who had his own notions regarding what the right response should be, the New York Reserve Bank bought only small amounts of the unloaded securities. The government security market sagged to an alarming extent, but not when compared to the price level of government bonds prior to the New Deal recovery program.

Marriner, who had been away from Washington during the opening days of the sag, rushed back to the capital to do what he could to reverse the picture. On Saturday morning he telephoned Morgenthau and found him highly agitated because of the fall in government bond prices. Morgenthau contended that the increase in reserves had broken the market, and insisted that the Federal Reserve Board should promptly cancel its order for the part of the increase set for May 1. Further talk between the two men was suspended until they met in Morgenthau's home that night for another high-tension encounter.

Morgenthau warned that if the board failed to cancel the May 1 increase, he would release substantial sums of sterilized gold and thereby create new reserves for use in bolstering the government bond market. Marriner, speaking just as emphatically, replied that it continued to be his own view that the policy of the Board of Governors and of the Open Market

Committee should be to maintain easy money conditions. The remedy to Morgenthau's justified concern about the prices of government securities was not to cancel the next scheduled increase in reserves. It was to have the New York Federal Reserve Bank obey the instructions calling for a vigorous intervention in the government security market. With tempers high, Marriner won Morgenthau's assent to only one point. Before anything was done, they should discuss the whole problem with President Roosevelt.

At a meeting with the president on Sunday afternoon, Marriner reviewed the inept way the New York Reserve Bank had conducted open-market operations after the March 1 increase in reserves went into effect. He then dwelt on the adverse consequences that would follow if the Treasury released sterilized gold as the immediate answer to the drop in prices for government securities. First, any such action would show that the administration could not stick to a steady course of action. It would show that the Federal Reserve Board had surrendered to the Secretary of the Treasury its legal responsibilities for monetary and credit policies. It would show that the Banking Act of 1935 was a failure, since the reorganized Open Market Committee—the heart of the act—proved a broken reed. Marriner recalled that the structure of the committee, with the representation it gave to presidents of the Federal Reserve banks, was not the one he had advocated. Yet he thought that the committee, despite its flawed composition, should have a chance to show its potential for constructive action. He then asked FDR for a week's grace in which to stabilize the government security market. If he failed, he would himself urge the drastic remedies proposed by Morgenthau. The requested margin of time was granted.

At an emergency meeting of the Open Market Committee which Marriner convened on March 8, the minutes quote him as saying to Morgenthau that "it was imperative that assurances be given that the budget would be balanced in 1938; that any expenditures that would increase indebtedness should be covered by taxation; that steps should be taken to reduce the outstanding debt as fast as commercial credit expands, and that the government deal effectively with labor and armament problems which result in abnormal price increases." If all these things were done, "there was no question that the price of government securities would increase instead of decline."

The phrase "armament problems" is an obvious reference to the purchase of American raw materials by European powers in connection with their rearmament programs. The phrase "labor problems" can also be readily decoded. At the time, the new wave of sit-down strikes roused in some circles new fears that a social revolution was at hand. More to the point, Marriner had watched with alarm the way in which new home construction was being priced out of the market. Though estimates made at the end of 1936 indicated that between 400,000 and 450,000 new home units would be built in 1937, by March of 1937 it was clear to Marriner that the increased costs of materials and of wages in the building trades had become so strong a deterrent to new home construction that the administration would be fortunate if the 1936 construction figure of 270,000 units were reached, let alone exceeded.

At the emergency meeting of the Open Market Committee on March 8, Marriner posed the key question. Should the scheduled May 1 rise in reserves be rescinded, or should the schedule still stand but with the rise in reserves offset by purchases in the open market? George L. Harrison and most of the Reserve bank presidents on the committee wanted to go ahead with the scheduled rise. The system's policy, said they, was to reduce excess reserves, and the flurries in the government bond market was an insufficient reason to alter the policy. The most that should be done, in their view, was to promote an orderly market "but without pegging and without preventing a decline in the price of government securities which was on the whole desirable."

Marriner Eccles, almost alone among the members of the Open Market Committee, took an opposite view. He favored large-scale purchases of government securities, while adhering at the same time to the final rise in reserve requirements. His position was summarized in a memorandum prepared at the time by John H. Williams.[7] "There is no inconsistency," Williams quoted Eccles as saying, "in decreasing excess reserves by a large amount, through the relatively clumsy instrument of increasing reserve requirements, and then effecting a partial increase by the elastic and adjustable instrument of open market operations, in order to facilitate an orderly process of transition."

A majority of the Open Market Committee reluctantly approved of this course of action, "partly out of deference to Eccles," and partly because Secretary of the Treasury Morgenthau flatly blamed the whole setback in the bond market on the increase in reserve requirements. In any case, Marriner now took the lead in formulating new instructions which could not be misconstrued or evaded by the New York Federal Reserve Bank. The bank, acting as an agent for the Open Market Committee, now bought securities in amounts that should have been purchased right from the start. The drop in government bond prices was immediately stopped. At no time after the second increase in reserve requirements went into effect on May 1 were the Reserve System's excess reserves less than $500 million over and above legal requirements—a figure, to repeat, that exceeded the size of the excess reserves sustaining the boom of the twenties.

The final increase in reserve requirements coincided with the peak in the economic expansion, in May 1937, which had been underway since 1933, and which was followed by a contraction. On this account, it would be claimed that the recession of 1937–38 was primarily due to the cumulative effects of the August 1936 increase in reserve requirements and the increases of March 1 and May 1, 1937. It would also be claimed that the recession was due to the effects of the 1936 undistributed profits tax. The claims will be examined presently. First, though, it is in point to note how

Marriner Eccles appraised the state of the economy in the days right after the government bond market was steadied.

III

On March 9, 1937, President Roosevelt had observed in the course of a radio address: "Today we are only part way through the [recovery] program, and recovery is speeding up to a point where the dangers of 1929 are again becoming possible, not this week or month perhaps, but within a year or two." This was said in the context of another presidential concern. The president wished to justify his proposal to reorganize the Supreme Court, and his references to "the dangers of 1929" were another way of saying that the nation was in need of a Supreme Court which would not obstruct possible emergency measures necessary to maintain economic stability. Roosevelt was due to leave Washington three days later for a stay in Warm Springs. But before his departure he asked Marriner to come to the White House for lunch, and for a detailed review of the true conditions of the economy. The mood of the lunch—a mixture of apprehension and hope —mirrored the continuing ambiguity in the economic picture. Revenue collections for the first quarter of the year were falling behind the estimates contained in the budget message of January 1937—though the cause here, as Roosevelt would later explain, was "due in large part to the obstruction of collections by numerous lawsuits against the government." If these obstacles were removed, and if the anticipated springtime spurt in economic activity materialized, it was reasonable to expect that the budget would show a cash balance for the last half of 1937. In any case, so the president seemed to believe, the private economic engine appeared to have gained sufficient momentum to move forward under its own power; the trend of the recovery movement was secure, and no further positive stimulant was required by the government.

But there was another perspective on the economy, and it was the one which Marriner Eccles compressed into a memorandum he gave the president and developed orally in their luncheon conversation on March 11. The memorandum read in part:

The problem now is to maintain the orderly character of the movement that prevailed throughout 1934–36. The problem threatens to be as difficult of solution as any we have faced. The danger spots are still localized and it would be most undesirable for the monetary authorities to adopt drastic measures, which, if successful, would result in keeping 9,000,000 unemployed. What is needed is a further increase in production and employment, while at the same time preventing inflationary developments from gathering headway in particular industries. This objective can be achieved only by the proper use and co-ordination of all the major activities of the Government affecting business conditions. Unless this is done there is grave danger that the recovery movement will get out of hand, excessive rises in prices encouraging inventory speculation will occur, excessive growth in profits and a boom in the stock market will arise, and the cost of living will mount rapidly. If such conditions are permitted to develop another drastic slump will be inevitable. . . .

Why the situation is more dangerous than that confronting us in any past revival is attributable to the enormous backlog of demand for the production of durable goods accumulated in the past seven years. At the present time capital facilities in many important lines and skilled labor in others will be deficient to handle the production of durable goods necessary to meet normal growth requirements plus accumulated deficiencies. In many fields, on the other hand, the available supply of labor and plant facilities is sufficient to handle a greatly increased volume of production. . . . The grave danger is that strategically situated industries and skilled trades will capitalize on the scarcity factor to secure excessive wage and price advantages. There is already abundant evidence that this is happening. This means redistribution of real income at the expense of agriculture, unorganized workers, and fixed income groups.

There was no single instrument available to cope with the situation, the memorandum continued. What was required at the outset was a clear indication that the administration would not allow the prospects for stability to be jeopardized by excessive and unjustifiable price advances, excessive profits, and unreasonable labor demands. It would use all the power of government then available and would request additional powers if needed to control this unhealthy development.

After the meeting, as Marriner walked out of the president's oval office, waiting members of the White House press corps put a familiar question to him. What had he and the president talked about? Marriner answered that he was not at liberty to go into details, but that there had been a discussion in general terms about problems such as commodity price increases and labor conditions. The words were guarded but, as reported in the press, they did not stand alone. Joined to an earlier misreading of what lay behind the recent increase in reserve requirements, they caused a buzz of talk in financial circles to the effect that Marriner had prevailed on Roosevelt to support a tight money policy in order to curb the growing price inflation.

In the next four days, the buzz became a roar. Marriner did not think he could safely ignore it. He was not in touch with Roosevelt at Warm Springs. The position ascribed to him was so contrary to the one he and Roosevelt had agreed to that he proceeded to issue a clarifying statement without first consulting the president.

I have been and still am an advocate of an easy-money policy and expect to continue to be an advocate of such a policy so long as there are large numbers of people who are unable to find employment in private industry, which means that the full productive capacity of the nation is not being utilized. Under such conditions, to restrict the available supply of capital and thus to make it difficult, if not impossible, to employ these people would be not only anti-social but uneconomic.

I do not believe that sharp price rises in certain basic commodities should be controlled at this stage of the recovery by a restrictive monetary policy which would tend to freeze and might bring about an actual reduction in the total volume of employment and production. The price rises to which I refer are the result primarily of non-monetary factors including foreign armament demands, strikes and monopolistic practices by certain groups in both industry and organized labor. These conditions have in turn led to speculative security and commodity buying which serves to accelerate the price advances.

The remedy for a price inflation when the country has unused manpower, natural resources, and capital is through more, not less, production; through an orderly, balanced use of these three fundamental factors and not by creating a needless, artificial shortage of any one of them.

In publicly taking a slap at the economically disruptive practices of labor as well as industry, Marriner might well have brought his career in government to an end, since organized labor had made major contributions to Roosevelt's victories at the polls. Yet Roosevelt himself, provoked by the rash of strikes, was on the point of colliding with his labor supporters. In a radio speech where he expressed his irritation with labor as well as with capital, he drew on Shakespeare's *Romeo and Juliet* to say: "A plague on both your houses." John L. Lewis, the head of the CIO, whose unionizing efforts had led to the new wave of strikes, would answer Roosevelt in kind, saying: "It ill behooves one who has supped at labor's table and who has been sheltered in labor's house, to curse with equal fervor and fine impartiality both labor and its adversaries when they become locked in deadly embrace."

Soon afterward, the inflated price bubble burst, and a contraction in production got underway. The figures for new home construction in the spring of 1937 confirmed Marriner's earlier fears that it might prove impossible in the months ahead to duplicate the volume of new home units built in 1936, let alone double it. Armed with the figures, Marriner tried, unsuccessfully, to win Roosevelt's support for a line of action that would stimulate new home construction. But Roosevelt placed his main reliance for a construction revival on a limited amount of publicly financed housing (and a related slum-clearance program) as set forth in the Wagner-Steagall housing bill before the Congress. In Marriner's view, the federal expenditures contemplated by the bill—$500 million, spaced over a three-year period—were a drop in the bucket compared to the need. But he was sharply critical of the bill on a more important count. The proposed program ignored a basic point he had been stressing ever since he had fathered the FHA act, namely, that only through expenditures of private funds on *various* forms of housing could the economy as a whole as well as the construction industry make any recovery.*

Marriner urged senators Wagner and La Follette, and congressmen Steagall and Goldsborough, to incorporate the amendments into the draft

---

*In support of this view, he had allies in Isador Lubin, the commissioner of labor statistics; J. M. Daiger, who had become the financial adviser to the FHA; and Charles E. Merriam, who spoke for members of the National Resources Council. Taken together, however, they could muster little additional support for their stand as long as the general economic picture in the early spring and summer of 1937 still seemed sunny.

public-housing measure. All four men agreed to do this, but Steagall added a caveat. He asked for proof that Roosevelt personally wanted the amendments included in the bill. Marriner informed the president of the request, adding a word of explanation. "Those of us who have considered this matter since the recent White House conference," he wrote FDR on August 10, "are satisfied that far more rental-housing construction will take place through private channels under these amendments than the maximum of public housing financed under the Wagner-Steagall bill. But the amendments are needed in order to get this additional private construction, because at the present time, an effective financial mechanism for handling rental-housing projects does not exist."

When Roosevelt gave Steagall the requested reassurances, the amendments in question were introduced as a rider to the Wagner-Steagall bill. The Congress, however, was rushing to adjourn, and a majority of the Senate members found it convenient to speed their way homeward by ruling the amendments out of order on the grounds that they were not germane to a public-housing measure. No such scrupulous respect for the fine points of procedure had been shown in limitless numbers of other instances, where riders were attached to measures which would have required a crowbar to align their disparate subject matter. In any case, once the procedural point was decided, the Congress adjourned. The country at large, however, did not breathe more easily. The time of the adjournment coincided with an accelerated contraction in the economy that was more severe and precipitous than the one which began in 1929.

25. Clarity of Crisis

PROFESSIONAL ECONOMISTS have extensively studied and debated the causes of the 1937–38 recession, and the points at issue remained unresolved as late as December 1971 when a panel discussed the matter at the annual meeting of the American Economic Association. The nuances of the debate fall outside the scope of these pages. It is enough for present purposes to note the views of Milton Friedman and Anna Jacobson Schwartz as stated in their influential book, *A Monetary History of the United States 1867–1960*. They contend that the 1937–38 recession and the severity of the decline were largely due to the decreases in the stock of the money supply, following the Federal Reserve Board's August 1936 and March–May 1937 increases in reserve requirements.[8]

Marriner Eccles saw the case from a different perspective. He always recognized the importance to the economy of the stock of the money supply *and* of its velocity, and he never entrusted the well-being of the economy solely to fiscal policy. But he flatly denied that the increase in reserve requirements tightened money rates, stopped the flow of credit in the economy and thereby brought on the recession. There were some fractional increases in the rates on Treasury bills, notes, and on long-term government bonds. But the levels reached were not high, nor long sustained. The degrees of change were not large when compared with changes in previous periods, nor did they materially affect the interest-rate structure in the economy as a whole. Further, the increase in reserve requirements was not immediately followed by a contraction in private credit or by a slackening in industrial production. The sharp downturn in production began to develop only in late August 1937, or more than three months after the final increase in reserve requirements went into effect. Private credit did not begin to contract until the end of 1937, sometime after the recession was underway. In Marriner's view, then, all these negatives added up to a conclusion that the private-credit contraction was an *effect* of the recession, and not, as Friedman and Schwartz contend, a *cause* of it.[9]

His personal interpretation of what brought on the recession began with the contrasts he saw for the years 1936 and 1937. He observed that in 1936, when the government was expending substantial funds on the recovery program, and private business was also increasing its activity, a soldier's bonus of $1.7 billion was paid. This increased the 1936 cash deficit of the Treasury to more than $4 billion, or the government's net contribution (after taxes) to consumer disposable income. Meanwhile, the heavy influx of gold from Europe, the increased demands for American raw materials by European powers that were rearming, war fears in Europe, labor unrest at home—and the conviction that the government would continue to pour out money and ease credit—combined to fuel a major inventory boom. The drive was on everywhere to convert money into things in the belief that the costs of goods would go higher. Many business interests, fearing difficulties in getting deliveries, placed orders for future as well as for current needs. The effect drove prices higher, and speculation in inventories grew to more than $4 billion in 1937.

In 1937, however, while the business world was still taking its bearing from the events just described, the government in two ways *reduced* consumer disposable income by almost $4 billion—in contrast to the $4 billion *increase* in 1936. First, the new Social Security law that went into effect in 1937 brought in $2 billion in social security taxes. No part of this was paid out in benefits, and the tax denied potential buying power to the very people most likely to spend the money if it had not been taxed away from them. Second, no soldier's bonus of $1.7 billion was paid in 1937 as in 1936. The combined effect of the funds collected with no offsetting disbursement resulted in a $66 million federal cash surplus for the first nine months of 1937 in contrast with the $4 billion deficit of the previous year. The consumer disposable income in 1937 thus contracted by an amount roughly equal to the $4 billion in accumulated inventories. In the end, the piper had to be paid. In the absence of purchasing power, upon which the speculative growth in inventories had been based, the inventories were dumped on the market in a drastic deflation, and the conventional pattern of a recession was reenacted.

II

The contraction started at the end of August, and daily grew worse. Yet President Roosevelt for the next six weeks stressed the importance of cutting federal expenditures so as to present Congress with a balanced budget for fiscal 1939. On October 11, the contraction hit the stock market, followed by a relentless wave of selling until October 19—"Black Tuesday"—when the market disintegrated. Seventeen million shares changed hands in a day. Prices collapsed in the absence of known units of value. Telegrams poured into the White House urging the president to close the Exchange by edict. The smell of the Crash of 1929 was in the air.

Few businessmen had previously weighed the implications of events in the building industry—or the growth of inventories on a wave of speculative forward buying—or the unwarranted price increases in commodities such as steel and copper. Few had reflected on the implications of another fact: for the first time since 1930, the government's fiscal operations had deducted as much from the nation's buying power as it had contributed. Most businessmen (save for those who would form the nucleus of what eventually became the Committee for Economic Development) ascribed the slump to the administration's wrong tax policies—witness the undistributed profits tax; to wrong monetary policies—witness the increases in reserve requirements; to wrong fiscal policies—witness the program of deficit financing.

A mood close to panic seized some highly placed figures in the Roosevelt administration. A devil of the piece must be found, and Marriner was chosen. "The sour looks cast in my direction," he later recalled, "spoke wordlessly to this effect:

Eccles sold us a wrong bill of goods, and we bought it at a high price. He argued for an undistributed profits tax. We got it. He stressed the need to increase reserve requirements. They were increased. He argued for a program for planned deficit financing. We got such a program. But now we've landed in a God-awful mess. We've learned the hard way that the nation can't lift its economy by its bootstraps. A capital goods expansion is the only road to recovery. Since that expansion depends on business confidence, which in turn depends on a balanced budget, we'd better try to balance the budget as quickly as possible. That's the only way to check the recession.

Marriner could say that the undistributed profits tax as enacted was neither the tax he wanted nor had any bearing on the recession. He could say that the increase in reserve requirements had neither contracted credit nor produced an appreciable change in the cost of money. He could also say that the recession—like the Great Depression in 1930—began at a time when the budget *was* in balance. Yet in the mood of the hour, he seemed to lose the few friends he had and to influence fewer people. Among the professional economists in the administration, his unshaken allies were limited to men such as Lauchlin Currie, Winfield Riefler, Leon Henderson and Isador Lubin, who had always favored transforming deficit spending from a temporary expedient into a standard tool for governmental use in combating deflation.

At that very moment, however, new allies were being trained on the elite campuses of the nation.

John Maynard Keynes' *General Theory of Employment, Interest and Money,* published in 1936, had cast in the code language of his profession a comprehensive economic analysis which embraced within itself the precepts of a compensatory economy such as Marriner had been advocating since 1931. Previously, in the United States, intellect-proud graduate students and young instructors of economics had apparently paid little attention to Marriner's published statements prior and subsequent to his appointment to head the Federal Reserve Board. He was not one of *their* kind. He was a banker and businessman, had no academic degrees, had not completed even a high school education.

It was different with John Maynard Keynes. Here was an elegant product of Bloomsbury, a Cambridge don, a man who knew his way around the "corridors of power" in his native Great Britain. *He* was worth studying. So, under the spur of the 1937–38 recession, a group of young graduate students and instructors at Harvard, Tufts, and the Massachusetts Institute of Technology publicly proclaimed their support for the policy implications in the *General Theory*. They also won over to their side senior professors such as Alvin Hansen of Harvard. What was begun in this elitist way spread to other major universities, whose graduates would soon draw one another into governmental posts where they would influence official thought.[10]

In the long view of history, it can be argued that Marriner Eccles was a John the Baptist of the new dispensation. In the short view, however, the question whether he would stay on as chairman of the Federal Reserve Board depended on the thoughts of one man, the president of the United States. In late October 1937, Marriner went to Hyde Park to discuss the economic situation with Roosevelt.

III

A shaken president greeted Marriner, not with sour looks, but with a request for candor. The response was in kind. Marriner gave FDR a coldly objective memorandum. The economy, he said, was tending toward a "really serious depression," while the chances of a "natural upturn were remote." Deflationary forces were everywhere at work, and it was "difficult to find any place apart from governmental action where an impetus of sufficient magnitude would arise to turn the tide." A sustained upturn could get underway only through an increase in consumer demand, through increased consumer borrowing, increased capital expenditures or increased governmental expenditures. The exact opposite, however, was the current condition. Consumer debt was being liquidated, and the deflationary effects would be felt in the months ahead. Inventories were still generally high in relation to current sales trends, but their reduction would also be deflationary. As inventories declined and bank loans were paid off, deposits would also decline and the money supply would contract, while the proposed repeal of the undistributed profits tax would encourage the deflationary hoarding of funds by corporations.

With excess productive capacity increasing daily and profits dwindling, capital expenditures would continue to decline and would not increase until after a considerable expansion of consumer demand had taken place. The high cost of labor was forcing prices up, particularly in the building trades. People would not build homes, and railroads would not lay tracks or construct new facilities. Small business needed tax relief. At the same time, the federal government, in contrast to 1933–36, was making negligible contributions to the expansion of consumer buying power.

As a first step to check deflation, Marriner urged an expanded program of residential construction to be spurred by a simple amendment granting the Federal Housing Administration authority to reduce down payments and interest taxes on residential construction covered by FHA mortgages.

David Eccles,
Marriner's father.

Ellen Stoddard Eccles,
Marriner's mother.

The family of David and Ellen Eccles. Front row (left to right): George, David, Ellen, Willard, Nora; back row (left to right): Emma, Jessie, Marriner, Ellen (in front of Marriner), Marie, Spencer.

Marriner, at about five years of age.

Marriner (left) and his friend Norman Salisbury, living in a box car on the Sumpter Valley Railroad around 1908, while working on a new track over Blueberry Mountain, Oregon.

Marriner, on mission for the Church of Jesus Christ of Latter-day Saints in Scotland, 1910.

President Roosevelt signing the Banking Act of 1935. Standing (left to right): Senator Carter Glass, J. F. T. Connor, Senator Duncan Fletcher, Henry Morgenthau, Jesse Jones, Representative Henry B. Steagall, Marriner Eccles, Leo Crowley (FDIC).

Marriner (left) greeting Franklin D. Roosevelt and his son James upon arrival at the New Federal Reserve Building for the dedication ceremonies, 1937.

The Federal Reserve Building, shortly after completion, 1937.

All Others, Cash!

Cartoon by Talburt, *Washington Daily News,*
January 24, 1939.

THE SOUR NOTE.

Cartoon by C. K. Berryman.

THE JEALOUS SUITOR!

Cartoon by C. K. Berryman, *Washington Evening Star*, January 5, 1941.

Cartoon by C. K. Berryman, *Washington Evening Star,* September 30, 1941.

Cartoon by C. K. Berryman, *Washington Evening Star,* 1948.

Marriner in his office in the Federal Reserve Building.

Marriner (right) receiving an honorary doctorate from the University of Utah, June 9, 1943. Left: B. Roland Lewis; center: Walter Lippmann, who spoke at the ceremonies.

Marriner (left) as governor of the Federal Reserve Board, with Senator Robert E. Wagner, 1944.

Marriner (right) as governor, with Senator Robert A. Taft.

Marriner leaving the Federal Reserve Building for the last time, 1951.

Marriner, 1965.

President Lyndon B. Johnson in Marriner's apartment (Marriner at left) in Hotel Utah, Salt Lake City, 1964, before the president spoke at the Mormon Tabernacle.

Marriner, accompanied by his wife Sallie, receiving the International Achievement Award of the World Trade Club of San Francisco from C. R. Redlich, president, May 23, 1972.

Roosevelt expressed interest in the idea, without saying he would personally push for the amendment when he called Congress into special session to deal with the developing recession; but he would bring together all government agencies concerned with housing so that a joint housing program could be worked out for submission to the special session.

"If you do that," Marriner cut in to say, "you can count me out."

"Why?"

"Because the agency heads won't agree. You have only to recall that John H. Fahey, chairman of the Home Loan Bank, has opposed any liberalization of the FHA program since its inception."

"Well," said Roosevelt, "what do you recommend?"

"Appoint a small committee whose members would be drawn from circles *outside* the government, and whose support for the housing program would carry weight in the nation as a whole." The President agreed.*

Morgenthau, meanwhile, continued to resist any increase in expenditures. He stuck by his plan—born in a different economic context a month earlier—to speak with the full authority of the administration on behalf of a balanced budget before the American Academy of Political Science, on November 10 in New York City's Astor Hotel. It was understood that Roosevelt would blue-pencil the speech before it was actually made. At a stormy Cabinet meeting on November 3, Roosevelt acidly protested that the men around him were full of talk about what was wrong with the nation's economy but none told him what to do. Morgenthau, Postmaster-General James Farley and Secretary of Agriculture Wallace, insisted that the complaint was groundless. There *was* something the president could do. He could "reassure" business.

"What business wants to know," said Morgenthau, "is whether we are headed toward state socialism or are we going to continue on a capitalistic basis."

"I have told them that again and again," Roosevelt answered. "You want me to turn on the old record."

"All right, Mr. President, tell them for the fifteenth time. That's what they want to know."

"All right, I will turn on the old record."[11]

After the Cabinet meeting, Morgenthau resumed work on the budget-balancing speech he meant to give. He had completed the draft when Marriner Eccles, at the request of FDR, came to the Treasury to offer his interpretation of the developing recession. Morgenthau showed him the draft of the speech, and Marriner called it deflationary. Frugality would

---

*He subsequently appointed a non-government housing committee consisting of S. Sloan Colt, president of the Bankers Trust Company, New York; Edward F. McGrady, director of labor relations, Radio Corporation of America; Gerard Swope, president of the General Electric Company; Henry C. Turner, president of the Turner Construction Company of New York; and Robert F. Wood, president of Sears, Roebuck & Company.

have been good a month ago, but not now. The Secretary of the Treasury disagreed. Marriner did not know whether the text he had seen would actually get past the president.

On the morning of November 8, the nongovernmental committee on housing, which Roosevelt had previously appointed, met with Marriner at the Federal Reserve Board to discuss a plan he had formulated with the help of Isador Lubin, J. M. Daiger, and Abner H. Ferguson, general counsel of the FHA. At the core of the plan were the housing amendments offered as riders on the Wagner-Steagall bill back in August, which the Senate had ruled out of order.

At noon on that day, Secretary Morgenthau, with his budget-balancing speech on his mind, and perhaps in his pocket, went to the White House for a luncheon with the president. Most of their conversation was about a different matter, which weighed heavily on FDR. He talked at length about the gains fascism was making in the world, about its threat within the United States, about how important it was for the United States to avoid an industrial slump since such a slump would give the totalitarian powers a chance to gloat over the failure of the world's strongest democracy. In a diary entry made after the luncheon, Morgenthau judged Roosevelt "to be deeply troubled—a President fighting like a cornered lion who did not want to be tamed, yet did not know where to put his strength to bring about recovery."[12]

That same day, Marriner temporarily left the members of the nongovernmental housing committee to go to a White House meeting where the causes and cures of the recession were thrashed out in detail. The focus for the things said was a now famous memorandum prepared by Lubin, Henderson and Currie, indicating—as Marriner had argued—that reduced government spending had helped trigger the recession. Roosevelt seemed impressed by the data marshaled to support that argument, and Marriner hoped that the adherents to the concepts of a compensatory economy had at long last won the battle for "the soul of FDR." If so, then Morgenthau would not publicly beat the drums for a balanced budget when he addressed the American Academy of Political Science.

His beliefs were reinforced two days later, on November 10, when he brought his housing committee to the White House to review with Roosevelt the details of the plan agreed to by the group. The president approved the proposed amendments of the FHA, but seemed to convey through an *obiter dictum* his awareness that, while the contemplated housing program was an important down payment toward economic recovery, it could not by itself reverse the economic decline. To reverse it entailed a resumption and not a curb on large-scale government spending.

The hopeful impressions which Marriner gained at the afternoon meeting at the White House were shattered that night when Secretary Morgenthau made his speech in New York. The text covered many matters, but its nuclear paragraph stated that for the four years ending June 30, 1937, the war against the depression had necessitated emergency federal expenditures totaling $14 billion in excess of receipts. Now, "that policy has succeeded," and the emergency "no longer exists." He was "aware that some persons" contended that "another great spending program" was "desirable to ward off the risk of another business depression." But his was a different view.

I have reached the firm conviction that the domestic problems which face us today are essentially different from those which faced us four years ago. Many measures are required for their solution. One of these measures but only one, in the present juncture is a determined movement toward a balanced budget. . . . We want to see private business expand. We believe that much of the remaining unemployment will disappear as private capital funds are increasingly employed. . . . We believe that one of the most important ways of achieving these ends at this time is to continue progress toward a balance of the Federal Budget.

Marriner was shocked when he read that paragraph. If the call for a balanced budget was endorsed by FDR, how could it be squared with the opposite view Roosevelt seemed to endorse on the afternoon of November 8, and especially two days later? "The contradictions between the afternoon and evening position on November 10," Marriner later observed, "made me wonder whether the New Deal was just a political slogan, or if Roosevelt really knew what the New Deal implied from the standpoint of a recovery program. This is a harsh and ungenerous comment, yet it is what I thought at the time. On reconsidering the event, it now seems clear that the President assented to two contradictory policy approaches within the space of a few hours—because of his own deep uncertainty about where he wanted to move."

IV

Soon after the special session of Congress convened, Roosevelt asked Marriner to prepare the draft of a message incorporating the proposed housing amendments, along with the reasons why they should be speedily approved. The draft was sent on to the Congress on November 27 and was well received. Even the *New York Herald Tribune* described the proposed measure as "the soundest piece of economic legislation to come out of the White House." Not the least of the factors working in its favor was the goodwill generated by the minimal costs to the government of earlier FHA operations. Hearings before the House Committee on Banking and Currency, with Congressman Steagall in the chair, began on November 30 and were concluded in eight days. Senate hearings began on December 1 and were also concluded in eight days under the direction of Senator Robert J. Bulkley, chairman of the subcommittee. But a last-minute turn of events in the Senate subcommittee—the kind that is generally excluded from the things civic books teach the young—jeopardized the move to stimulate new construction.

Senator Bulkley had unveiled a "pro-labor" amendment requiring that any mortgage contract issued pursuant to Title II of the FHA should contain a "prevailing wage" clause, as in legislation governing *public* contracts or *publicly financed* construction. Adoption of the Bulkley amendment would make the senator a one-day hero in the eyes of organized labor. But the next day private lenders would refuse to make FHA insured loans: not because they were anti-labor, but because any loan made could suddenly be voided on a showing that builders, contractors and subcontractors had not paid the prevailing wage rate to their labor force. Even if it were possible to determine what the rate was in every community in the nation, Congress might as well repeal the whole of the FHA act, if its continued operation depended on the enforcement of Senator Bulkley's "pro-labor" amendment.

When Marriner put the case in such terms to Robert Wagner, chairman of the full Senate Banking and Currency Committee, the latter agreed that the Bulkley amendment should not have a place in the Senate version of the bill. But as labor's foremost spokesman in the Senate, Wagner could not vote against the amendment if it was proposed on the floor of the Senate. He called an executive session of the full Senate committee, candidly stated his plight, and prevailed on Senator Bulkley to withdraw the amendment. He also secured what he thought was a pledge from all the other committee members, Republicans and Democrats alike, not to introduce the amendment on the floor of the Senate. The committee bill reported to the Senate omitted the "prevailing wage" clause, and there was no minority report.

The show of unanimity inspired the hope that the Senate would pass the housing measure by Christmas. Speed was imperative. Between September 15 and December 15, approximately 1,800,000 people lost their jobs, and the Works Progress Administration expected another 1,000,000 to be out of work by mid-January. But the rate of speed was suddenly arrested in a strange trap. Senator Henry Cabot Lodge, without forewarning, rose on the floor of the Senate to inject the "prevailing wage" issue into the debate. A member of the Senate Banking and Currency Committee, he was reportedly present at the executive session when Senator Wagner secured pledges no one would introduce the prevailing-wage amendment. A pro-labor move here would be a disaster to Labor itself, since all FHA operations would come to a halt, and tens of thousands of additional workers would be thrown out of jobs.

No one in the Senate seemed to know how to cope with Lodge's strange move except to get the housing bill off the floor at once to prevent further discussion. This was managed after some arm-twisting by majority leader Alben Barkley. He twisted out enough votes to send the bill back to the committee so that it could "consider" the prevailing-wage amendment. There matters stood until after the Christmas holidays. By that time, a matching complication had surfaced in the House. A New York City congressman, who trumpeted his love for labor, publicly announced that he would introduce the prevailing-wage amendment when the housing bill reached the floor of the House. J. M. Daiger, who monitored the legislative course of the bill for the administration, tried but failed to change the man's mind. In need of weightier arguments, he reached builders and contractors in the congressman's district, and asked that they send a delegation to Washington. Daiger brought the delegation to the congressman's office about a half hour before the housing bill was to be presented to the House, and made a final plea. When he came out, members of the delegation crowded around him asking, "What does the congressman say?"

"He says," a crestfallen Daiger replied, "that he's going ahead with his amendment."

A burly contractor shouldered his way forward, saying, "I'm going to see him." What happened next has not been reported. But the congressman failed to appear in the House of Representatives at the time the housing bill reached the floor. It was explained that he had "unfortunately been stricken with a sudden illness."

By an overwhelming vote, Congress ultimately passed the housing bill after the Christmas recess, and without the prevailing wage proviso. As the *only* measure adopted by the special session, it managed to stimulate an appreciable volume of new housing, but much more was needed to reverse the deflationary trends that were perceptible in the economy generally.

While the Congress was wrapping up the new housing, Marriner was called before the Senate Committee on Unemployment Relief under the chairmanship of Senator James F. Byrnes. He had previously been informed that he might at some future point be asked to testify. But only on January 3, a day before the hearing was due to start, did Senator Byrnes phone Marriner to say he was to be the opening witness. The sudden change in scheduling was not explained; Marriner said he would need more than a day's notice to prepare his testimony. "If you are not ready at all times to discuss the causes for the slump and its cures," the senator sharply replied, "you shouldn't be the head of the Federal Reserve Board."

"You are absolutely right," Marriner said. "But there is one difficulty I face. If I speak off the cuff before your group, I might make statements that would offend the Treasury Department and officials elsewhere who are pressing for a balanced budget as a cure-all for the recession."

"Come anyway," said Byrnes.

"I will," Marriner replied, "but only on one condition. You must make it perfectly clear at the outset of the hearing that I am not a voluntary witness—that you dragged me before your group."

The bargain struck over the telephone was kept the next day when the hearing began.*

---

*The record of Senator Byrnes' opening remarks reads: "I want to say to the members of the Committee that I had asked Governor Eccles of the Federal Reserve Board to appear on Friday of this week, and only yesterday afternoon requested him to appear today. Mr. Eccles did not want to come at any time. I did not have to resort to sending him a subpoena to bring him here, but at one time I thought I would have to do it. He is not only reluctant, but is a very recalcitrant witness. Nevertheless, he is here."

Marriner, speaking extemporaneously, again described how a compensatory economy could and should work, and how the orderly mechanics of the process had been thrown out of gear by the combined factors that brought on the recession of 1937–38. There was a tense moment when Senator James J. Davis of Pennsylvania, who had been Secretary of Labor during the terms of the last three Republican presidents, challenged Marriner's statement that excessively high labor costs in the building industry had contributed to the recession. This, to Davis, was not a comment about the facts of productivity, but a piece of anti-labor bombast.

"How," he caustically asked Marriner, "do you determine that the building labor [sic] is asking too high hourly rates and pay?"

"Because," said Marriner, "no one will buy their services. That is the best evidence of that."

There was a pause while Davis regrouped his forces.

Marriner, meanwhile, moved on to another matter, knowing that he would ruffle more than a few feathers. He frontally challenged Secretary Morgenthau's insistence on a balanced budget as a precondition for recovery. The record here reads:

Mr. Eccles: You can only balance the budget out of increased national income. I am as favorable as anybody could be to the objective of a balanced budget, and over a year ago I was advocating the need of approaching a balanced budget. However, I think that at this time to try to balance the budget either by substantial reduction in expenditures, or by increasing taxes, would be deflationary; and that it is not so much what the total debt of the Government is, as it is the timing of the increase of the debt. In other words, assume that in 1936 there had been no debt at all, and, therefore, it would have been said that the Government could well afford to spend five or ten billion dollars. Nevertheless, the spending at that time would have been very bad because of inflationary developments then under way.

In the early months of 1938, when a gentleman's agreement was reached between unions and contractors regarding voluntary cuts in construction costs, the result was an increase in new construction. But the task of checking the deflationary tide called for a resumption of government spending as well as an expansion of private spending. Morgenthau's drive to balance the budget, despite its admirable motives, had made matters worse, not better. Equally disturbing was the continuous hesitation on Roosevelt's part, as if he feared making a break with a discredited fiscal policy.

Marriner was in no mood to wait. In early March 1938, his impatience spilled over into a memorandum he sent the president. At the outset of the text, he referred to the statement he had given Roosevelt at the Hyde Park meeting in late October 1937, where he warned against a "really serious depression" while the chances of a "natural upturn" were remote. "Events since then," he continued," have confirmed that warning." Marriner then reviewed the many deflationary forces that were ravaging the economy, and capped the review with an impassioned appeal:

We appear to be launched on a severe depression of considerable duration. If this is allowed to happen, the New Deal and all it stands for is in danger of being discredited. Alibis will not be accepted. The only final test of success is success. Big Business is utilizing the opportunity to drive for repeal and inaction. . . . The conciliatory attitude adopted by the Administration has borne no fruits either in dollar terms or in goodwill. By the nature of the case, leadership can come neither from business nor from the Congress. It is the responsibility of the Administration.

The greatest threat to democracy today lies in the growing conviction that it cannot work. . . . I urge you to provide the democratic leadership that will make our system function. Only in that way can the growing threat of Fascism be overcome.

Congress should be provided with a reflation program *now*. To permit it to adjourn without adopting vigorous remedial measures is to waste precious time and to court the danger of a 1931–32 winter. The stresses and strains, frictions and conflict that would result from another year of deepening depression would make our system even more difficult to work in the future.

You have always been stronger on the offensive than on the defensive. The recent policy of comparative inaction has, to be frank, been harmful to the morale of your adherents, both within and outside the Administration. It has given a new lease of life to the reactionaries. They see both you and the New Deal discredited.

Marriner then outlined a range of action programs. He proposed, among other things, "a bargain year" for low-cost housing units by the granting of a cash subsidy of 10 percent on all new homes built at an appraised value of $6,000 or less, and on new apartments appraised at $10,000 or less. "The proposed subsidy," said Marriner, would be "simple, speedy, effective, popular, socially and economically beneficial, and would entail little, if any net cost to the government." On the assumption, for example, that a maximum of 400,000 low-cost housing units were built during the remainder of 1938 at an average cost of $4,500, the government would pay out only $180 million to stimulate $1.8 billion in new construction. Much more than $180 million would be saved, because increased private employment in building and allied industries would permit reduced WPA expenditures.

A second proposal—with a prophetic thrust in it—stemmed from Marriner's observation that the nation's railroad system was rapidly decaying because it lacked modern equipment and was saddled with heavy fixed charges carried over from a bygone era. To improve the railroads, and at the same time to stimulate new production in the general economy, the Reconstruction Finance Corporation should create a subsidiary Federal Railroad Corporation to finance the construction of new railroad rolling stock for rental to the railroads at prices geared to railroad earnings. Since the corporation's investments in new rolling stock would be met by these rental fees, large immediate expenditures would be stimulated with little charge to the federal budget. The corporation would eventually own the bulk of the rolling stock, but individual roads would be gainers by being able to reduce their fixed charges as they retired their old equipment.

One more suggestion is worth noticing. As a stimulant to consumer purchasing power, Marriner proposed that payments on old-age insurance accounts, due to start in 1941, should start instead in 1939. At the same time, he said, "the field of *public health* is rapidly coming to the fore and has not yet been exploited. If legislation were enacted at this session for increased grant-in-aid for general medical care and for hospitals, a National Health Program could be put under way in 1939," which would be of major benefit to the physical health of the nation, while the outlays for the program would be of major benefit to its economic health.

There was no White House response to the memorandum. By the last days of March 1938, however, a few business leaders had begun to intimate that they were not averse to planned government deficits. Without saying so openly, they seemed to have gained some insight into the relationship between their own prosperity and the rate of government spending, since the national income was dropping at the rate of $800 million a month. At this time, too, the financial community which had bitterly attacked on high "moral" grounds all reform measures such as the Securities Exchange Act of 1934, the Banking Act of 1935—as well as deficit financing of any kind —was put on the defensive by the wayward conduct of one of its highly visible magnates. Richard Whitney, head of a blue-chip brokerage house, president of the New York Stock Exchange, and a field marshal of the financial forces opposed to reform, was brought to trial in a criminal court after his firm went bankrupt under morally doubtful conditions. He was found guilty on various counts in the indictment and was sent to prison.

Marriner had a strong ally in Harry L. Hopkins in pressing the case for a resumption of deficit spending over the opposition of Secretary Morgenthau and others with the administration such as Vice-President Garner, Secretary of State Hull, RFC Chairman Jesse Jones, and Postmaster-General James Farley. At the end of March, Hopkins was in Florida recuperating from a critical operation, when a sharp drop in the stock market caused him to believe that the political timing was right to urge the president to resume deficit spending. En route from Florida to Warm Springs, Hopkins stopped in Atlanta and called to his side Leon Henderson, Aubrey W. Williams and Beardsley Ruml. Together they prepared a memorandum which again stated the case for planned deficit spending, and which Hopkins used in his Warm Springs discussions with Roosevelt. By April 2, when the presidential train with Hopkins aboard headed back for Washington, the whole concept of budget balancing had been scrapped. Morgenthau, and then the nation, would soon be informed of that fact.

During the prior period of presidential indecision, congressional hoppers were filled with draft bills calling for new forms of monetary and banking magic to cure the recession. It was Roosevelt's practice to send Marriner written comments in which he derisively dismissed these magic formulas, but in late March 1938, while still at Warm Springs, he received a telegram from state senator Nelson W. Cheney of New York which he could not airily toss aside. The senator complained that small country banks, "trying to loan to your average or needy citizen," were being harassed by examiners who "threw these small loans out of the window," because the customers could not issue "wonderful statements" regarding their financial position. "Why," he asked "cannot the authorities be reasonable and let the small banks help our people?"

In forwarding the telegram to Marriner, Roosevelt asked him to draft a reply to it. The draft was ready on April 6, when Roosevelt was back in Washington from Warm Springs and a convert to deficit spending. In a memorandum attached to the reply, Marriner noted how Cheney's plea forcefully illustrated a point he had personally stressed during many talks with the president in the last two years—namely, "that there should be a unification of the banking system and consolidation of federal supervisory functions." He added: "The real remedy, in my opinion, for the basic trouble about which the senator complains, is to put examination functions under the same tent and to see that examination policy takes account of changing economic conditions." In a strategically placed next sentence, Marriner suggested that Roosevelt, who was then at work on a congressional message detailing the steps necessary to check the recession, should include in the text a proposal for the unification and liberalization of bank-examination policies. Roosevelt agreed and asked for some draft paragraphs, which were eventually used in his April 14 message to the Congress. For the moment, Marriner had the sense that he was about to emerge personally from a long tunnel of frustration.

Morgenthau had been at Sea Island, and it was not until the night of April 10, four days before the congressional message was to be delivered, that he saw Roosevelt at the White House—where he shared the president's company with Harry Hopkins and James Roosevelt, FDR's oldest son. He had come to the meeting armed with a memorandum containing an outline for a proposed recovery program that would spur private investment through government lending instead of spending. But before he could clear his throat, he learned to his dismay that Roosevelt had come to a quite different conclusion. As John Morton Blum tells the story, the encounter in the White House went something like this:

"We have been travelling fast this week and have covered a lot of ground," the President said, "and you will have to hurry to catch up."

"Mr. President," Morgenthau said, "maybe I never can catch up."

Roosevelt smiled. "Oh, yes you can—in a couple of hours."

With that he presented his ideas. Morgenthau's heart sank. It was clear that Hopkins had "sold" the President on spending. Ickes was to be put back into the business of lending money to states and municipalities. The United States Housing Authority was to have its loan authorizations doubled. The Federal Housing Administration was to build $500 million worth of houses. A transcontinental highway was to be started. And so on . . .

When he finished, the President asked, "you are in agreement with this?"

"What you have outlined not only frightens me, but will frighten the country," Morgenthau replied. "How much is it going to cost?"

"Oh," Roosevelt said, "we have all of that . . . we have all that."

Morgenthau asked to see a list of proposed expenditures, but none was forthcoming. "Please Mr. President," he said on departing, "don't decide on this until you sleep on it."[13]

For the next two days, as Roosevelt revealed his plans to congressional leaders, Morgenthau brooded. On the morning of April 13, after a sleepless night, he telephoned Roosevelt to ask for "his day in court" before the president sent his message to the Congress twenty-hours later. Professor Blum reports their meeting in the White House as follows:

"Mr. President," Morgenthau said, "I am going to say something which is one of the most difficult things I have ever had to do, but if you insist on going through with this spending program I am seriously thinking of resigning. . . . After all, nobody in the Treasury has had time to study this program, and we have not been consulted as to whether it can or cannot be financed; furthermore, whether it will achieve the results you desire."

The President then, as Morgenthau recalled it, became excited. If the Secretary resigned it would mean the destruction of the Democratic party, the creation of a third party and the loss of the Administration program in Congress. Morgenthau, moreover, would go down in history as having quit under fire. . . .

They parted without resolving their difficulties. Roosevelt simply would not listen to the talk of resignation, and Morgenthau for the moment saw no alternative.

As he later recalled, he spent the next few hours in a gloomy daze of indecision. But gradually the relative values of the situation began to sort themselves out, and his position began to clarify itself. He and the President had differed over an issue concerning which, it was fair to say, there were, at the very least, two sides. It was also a technical rather than a moral issue; a difference about means, not ends. And it was but one of the many issues involved in the Roosevelt Administration.

Morgenthau might disagree with Franklin Roosevelt about spending, but they were in agreement on most other broad questions. . . . So Morgenthau stayed on.[14]

The program Roosevelt sent to Congress the next day called for a resumption of large-scale government spending—for WPA, for Farm Security, for the National Youth Administration, for the Civilian Conservation Corps, for slum clearance, for federal highways, for federal buildings, for flood control. Also, to provide additional bank reserves, it was announced that the Treasury would desterilize about $1.4 billion in gold, while the Federal Reserve would make available an added $1 billion in credit by reducing reserves requirements. These lines of attack on the recession not only would help the American people "but would give democracy courage the world over."

It seemed to need the clarity of crisis provided by the 1937–38 recession to reveal to the president, at least, that recovery could not proceed on its own without the intervention of heavy public spending. Marriner could see in the event a governmental counterpart to his earlier experiences in business, when it required the contagion of troubles afflicting the companies his father built to open the eyes of their directors to certain truths he had stressed all along.

V

After the April 14 presidential message, Roosevelt, at Marriner's suggestion, asked Secretary Morgenthau to bring together representatives of the FDIC, the Comptroller of the Currency, and the Federal Reserve so that they could "coordinate and liberalize their bank examination policies." The meeting was held, but the result was a behind-the-scenes fire fight where the Treasury Department, the FDIC, the Comptroller's Office and the state bank examiners formed a solid front in opposition to the Federal Reserve's proposals. The fight continued for several weeks, with no breakthrough in sight.

Marriner reached for such outside allies as could be found "The need to do so," he later admitted, "was distasteful, and I would not have found fault with Roosevelt if he viewed what I did as a disloyal act. But I was so intent on doing anything I could lawfully do to help check the recession, as to be indifferent to any personal and political niceties standing in the way."

The assistance he looked for was forthcoming, by chance, from a Republican leader, Senator Arthur Vandenberg of Michigan. The senator had for some time been discomfited by his location within range of Father Coughlin's radio at the Shrine of the Little Flower in Michigan. So, without making any explicit references to the source of his discomfiture, Vandenberg on May 31 wrote Marriner to say:

Every depression produces an inevitable crop of agitators out in the country who have no trouble in whipping up a substantial attack upon the American monetary system. Our present experience is no exception to the rule. My part of the country is once more full of earnest souls who familiarly insist that we should rid ourselves of the Federal Reserve System and—of course—substitute greenbacks for bonds.

I have my own answers for them. . . . I am not suggesting that you should take cognizance of all this agitation or that you should join issue with any of these agitators. But I should like to see the Federal Reserve System provide—abstractly—what it conceives to be the authentic answer to these attacks upon its own foundations and its own existence. Of course I am assuming that you can produce an answer.

Marriner asked for time "to work out a simple statement which would be useful" in exploding the propaganda of all those "who are hounded by the money cranks." Two weeks later, on June 14, he mailed the senator an eleven-page, single-spaced document devoted to an analysis of the existing money mechanisms of the country. At the same time he fit into text a pointed aside where he dealt with the effect bank examinations had on the flow of credit. In this way, seemingly because Vandenberg's request alone demanded it, he could publicly criticize the Treasury and note also how the

Comptroller's restrictive rules for bank examinations dammed up the necessary flow of credit into productive business channels.

Marriner's letter represented one of the few times that an official in the inner citadel of the New Deal did not blame the banks for all the nation's economic ills but pointed to the administration's own policies as a source of at least some of them. Senator Vandenberg, who was then being freely mentioned as a possible candidate for the 1940 Republican presidential nomination, knew when he had a "good thing." He promptly inserted Marriner's statement into the *Congressional Record* for June 16 and, by warm praise, alerted the press to its existence. The press ignored the portions of Marriner's letter devoted to a full description of the nation's money mechanism, but broadcast the passages devoted to examination procedures. The captions over news stories, picked at random, tell of the open fire fight that replaced the one behind closed doors:

EASING OF BANK LAW URGED BY ECCLES TO RELEASE CREDIT: WRITES VANDENBERG BILLIONS ARE DAMMING UP

GLASS OPPOSES EASING CREDIT

SHOWDOWN SET ON RULES FOR BANK CONTROL

BANK RESTRICTIONS ARE TOO SEVERE ECCLES ARGUES: FAVORS RELAXING RULES DURING DEPRESSIONS AND TIGHTENING THEM IN BOOM TIMES

CRITICS ANSWER ECCLES ON BANK EXAMINATIONS; OTHER AGENCY OFFICIALS SAY LIBERALIZATION PLAN NOW READY GOES AS FAR AS IS CONDUCIVE TO SAFETY

MORGENTHAU, ECCLES IN BANK CONTROL FIGHT, ROOSEVELT REPORT TO BRING SHOWDOWN. HOPED FOR COOPERATION SEEN ENDED BY RESERVE BOARD CHAIRMAN'S NEW PLEA FOR LIBERALIZATION

TREASURY GIVES ECCLES 48 HOURS TO O.K. BANK PLAN. RECOMMENDATIONS TO WHITE HOUSE MAY OMIT APPROVAL OF RESERVE HEAD

FDR MAY HAVE TO SETTLE ROW OVER BANKING POLICY

AGREE ON A POLICY TO EASE BANK LOANS. EACH SIDE GIVES GROUND

LIBERALIZED BANK RULES MAY FREE 3 BILLIONS CREDIT. TREASURY ADOPTS CHANGES DESIGNED TO ASSIST SMALL BUSINESS

The controversy, which raged in print for six days before it subsided, was enlivened from one hour to the next by Treasury Department bulletins which set deadlines for an agreement on the issue in dispute. Morgenthau let it be known that unless Marriner gave ground to the stand of the Treasury, FDIC and the Comptroller of the Currency, he would issue his report to the president without further ado. "The Comptroller of the Currency and the

Secretary of the Treasury," he told the press on June 20, "have just one thing in mind and that is protection of the depositor." By implication, Marriner's advocacy of liberalized bank-examination policies was an invitation to profligacy. "Eccles," said Senator Glass, "proposes to let the banks do as they damn please with their depositor's money."

In the end, the new procedures adopted for bank examinations corresponded to Marriner's long-standing view that the "slow" classification of bank loans should be scrapped; that bank investments should be considered in the light of their inherent worth; that the rules should strike a balance between the need for caution in judging a bank's soundness and the need for resiliency in the granting of loans. In this way, banks would be encouraged to shift their own emphasis from liquidity and quick maturity to "soundness." With the shift, member banks of the Reserve System could purchase sound investment securities issued by established commercial or industrial enterprises that could demonstrate their ability to service the securities.

Though these simple changes comprised a fundamental—and historic—reform in examination procedures, their practical effect depended on how they were applied. Sympathetic administration of the changes could not be expected when there were sharp differences in interpreting an agreement fashioned in the first instance out of widely diverse views. Moreover, even if all federal supervisory bodies actually coordinated their examination policies—and this was more than could be expected—it would represent only one aspect of bank unification. Larger problems would still remain.

26. *Frustrations*

I

ALONG WITH OTHER FIGURES in the administration, Marriner knew that any proposals for new legislation must await the outcome of the 1938 congressional elections. Roosevelt, meanwhile, had something else to think about, besides helping hard-pressed New Deal Democrats in their contests for House and Senate seats. On September 12, 1938, he was with Harry L. Hopkins in the presidential railroad car at a siding in Rochester, Minnesota, when the two men heard a short-wave broadcast of Adolf Hitler's speech at Nuremberg. It was a venomous speech, prefiguring the Nazi takeover of Czechoslovakia despite the assurances given at the Munich conference.

Roosevelt, who could understand German, not only grasped the hate in Hitler's message, but saw in it a portent of a new world war. In a reflex reaction, he sent Hopkins to the Pacific coast for a secret survey of the aircraft industry's capacity to expand the production of military aircraft. "The President," Hopkins later wrote in a reference to his secret mission, "was sure that we were going to get into the war and he believed that air power would win it."[15] None of this was known to Marriner, but by the end of October 1938 he sensed that Roosevelt was about to shift the focus of his concern from domestic to foreign affairs. If so, proposals for major domestic reforms would probably seem less urgent to him than measures bearing on American power and diplomacy in the world arena.

The probability that the president would be personally disinclined to drive for major domestic reforms was underlined by the 1938 congressional election results. Though the administration's antirecession moves in the immediately preceding months eventually revived the faltering economy, the evidence of the revival came too late to help administration-backed candidates in "swing districts" and states. The Democratic party retained control of Congress, but the fabulous majorities the Democrats won in 1936 were reduced from 244 to 93 in the House, and from 58 to 46 in the Senate. On paper, these were still formidable margins. But a coalition of conservative Republicans and Southern Democrats was forming with sufficient strength to serve notice on Roosevelt that Capitol Hill was capable of revolt. The mere existence of the coalition made Roosevelt wary of giving it battle over domestic issues, considering his need to husband his political strength for use in an attempt to get increased military appropriations to meet the threat of war abroad.

Against this background, Roosevelt on November 18 appointed an advisory committee with Secretary of the Treasury Morgenthau as chairman, to canvass fiscal and monetary problems relating to production and national incomes—a roundabout way of saying that the committee was to help shape the budget for the next fiscal year. The other members were Marriner, Daniel W. Bell, acting director of the Budget, and Fredrick A. Delano, chairman of the Advisory Committee on National Resources. They were to formulate budget-related proposals on matters such as taxes, capital expenditures by private sources, a public-works program that could contract or expand according to need, the debt structure of all levels of government, and the modest armament program then underway. After a brief meeting with this new type of committee, Roosevelt left Washington for his Thanksgiving holiday at Warm Springs. Marriner was to join him there on November 26.

Three days before his own departure for Warm Springs, Marriner wrote another of his many memoranda on the need to unify the nation's banking system. In addition to all the earlier arguments, it made several new points. A unified banking system was needed, for example, to support any policy proposals that might be forthcoming from the newly appointed Fiscal and Monetary Committee. It was needed to help cushion the impact on the United States of a war in Europe. The politics of the matter called for a new approach, dictated by the results of the 1938 congressional elections. Above all, the memorandum appears to have been written in a take-it-or-leave-it mood, starting with the opening paragraphs addressed directly to the president:

In March, 1933, you declared a National Emergency. It should be terminated before your term expires. Yet it cannot be safely terminated. The Administration's courageous and effective actions in dealing with the most acute banking collapse in history have evoked universal commendation. The restoration of confidence in the banks and the subsequent recovery, however, have tended to obscure the fact that our banking system remains fundamentally unsound. It has been dealt with on an emergency basis. It needs now to be dealt with on a broader, more permanent basis of reconstruction so that it can function effectively as an integral part of the Government's mechanism for coping not only with potential emergencies of inflation or deflation but also with an emergency that might be created by the international situation. The effective organization of the banking system is a basic and essential part of any comprehensive program of preparedness. The system is not so organized. . . . It is a mockery which makes for "competition in laxity" which has long been a blot on American banking. . . .

The banking system is in no position today to withstand another severe inflationary or deflationary crisis, and the Federal authorities are without adequate means of exerting a control over the vast and volatile credit reservoirs, swollen by the fortuitous inflows of foreign capital and gold, nor has the banking system any adequate means of protecting the domestic economy from these foreign movements. . . .

In coming to the politics of any drive for bank unification, Marriner referred to Roosevelt's previous reluctance to associate himself with bank unification except for the recent changes in examination procedures. He therefore proposed that the initiative in the matter should be placed squarely on the shoulders of the Congress as its responsibility. To this end, it would be desirable if Roosevelt inserted several paragraphs in his State of the Union message indicating the general need for further constructive banking legislation so that the banking system could deal more effectively with the current economic picture and with "future developments." If this were done, then the Federal Reserve Board in its 1938 annual report to the Congress should "make a reasonably complete statement of the existing conditions and express a willingness to appear before Congress, if called, to advise on appropriate legislation.

"As chairman of The Board of Governors," said Marriner, concluding his memorandum, "I find myself in the situation where I would be open to the charge of failing in my public duty, and I feel I would be equally remiss in my obligation to the President, if I were to let the impression stand that I felt that the banking situation was safe, and that no steps needed to be taken to safeguard it against the dangers ahead." His term as chairman would expire in February 1940, and he had no choice but to bring to the president's attention well in advance of that hour the need for remedial action before banking problems became acute.

Unless the changes he had proposed in the nation's banking structure were actually made, he would leave the administration once his current term as chairman expired. He "would not wish to continue in the Chairmanship of a System which in the minds of the public and of Congress is charged with great responsibility for exercising controls over domestic credit and monetary conditions when, in fact, as it exists today, the System's powers and authority are largely limited to the performance of mechanical functions." True, his "reappointment a year from February might be out of the question for other reasons." Yet in his view of the case, he "should not put the President in the position of considering for reappointment an official who had so far failed in the discharge of the responsibilities of his office."

Later, in Warm Springs, when the memorandum was discussed at length, Roosevelt—as on previous occasions—neither approved or disapproved of the proposed unification plan. But to brace Marriner's morale, he agreed that the Federal Reserve Board, in its annual report for 1938, should call congressional attention to the defects in the banking structure and, by implication, invite a congressional remedy. The decision on this point was reflected in the text of the annual report. But the intended effect was partly frustrated beforehand when the *Wall Street Journal* on December 2, 1938, carried a long story that looked suspiciously like a "plant." Its heading read:

ECCLES BANK LAW CHANGES BROADEN CONTROL OF CREDIT TENTATIVE AMEND-
MENTS SUBMITTED TO TREASURY DEPARTMENT FOR COMMITTEE STUDY.

The story itself gave the impression that the administration was about to send to Congress a new banking measure tailored to Marriner's wishes. So now, contrary to the plan agreed to at Warm Springs whereby the Congress would be held responsible for initiating necessary banking legislation, the story pinned the responsibility on the administration, and particularly on Marriner. The source of the "plant" was the Comptroller's Office, whose leaders were prepared to go to any length to cling to the powers they might otherwise have to give up if banking unification materialized.

Bankers rushed to the defense of the Comptroller's Office. Their rallying cry—"Independence for the Comptroller"—reflected their view that it was in their interests to keep government banking agencies weak and divided. Roosevelt himself was affected by the uproar caused by the story in the *Wall Street Journal*. He now leaned toward a measure whose terms, drafted by Treasury officials, fit the Comptroller's interest in self-preservation as well as the bureaucratic interests of the FDIC. Marriner entrusted his reaction to a note he sent the president on December 22:

In accordance with the memorandum I discussed with you at Warm Springs with regard to procedure for dealing with the banking situation, I am enclosing a paragraph that you might use as the basis for a reference to this important subject in your message to Congress. . . . I would very much like to see you put squarely up to Congress the responsibility for acting or failing to act, not only in improving the present unsatisfactory setup with respect to Federal banking supervision, but in providing authority to deal with such emergencies as may arise in the future which we are in no position now to cope with adequately.

The paragraph Marriner enclosed coupled a presidential announcement of the end of the bank holiday with a request that Congress give further study to the structure of the nation's banking system. The paragraph was not used in the State of the Union message, but Marriner's move was not altogether barren of results. It kept the president from endorsing a Treasury measure that was just another patch on a rickety banking system and in no way dealt with its fundamental weaknesses. Marriner was still left with the question of how he could prod the Congress into taking the necessary action.

II

Another matter cut across Marriner's line of vision. In the immediate aftermath of the 1938 congressional election, when the administration's new spending program was at last checking the recession and reviving the economy, the coalition of conservative Republicans and Southern Democrats launched an assault on the concept of planned government deficits. Their opening salvo was fired by Senator Harry F. Byrd of Virginia on December 10, 1938. In an address in Boston to the Massachusetts Taxpayers Federation, broadcast over a national radio hookup, Senator Byrd demanded an end to "nine years of fiscal insanity." He said he was convinced the Roosevelt administration could not be looked to for leadership in any program of economic recovery, since its spending program had been a "tragic failure." He went on to single out Marriner Eccles for a special muzzle blast. According to the senator, "the economic philosophy of Eccles" indicated "to what depths of false reasoning we have sunk in the crackpot legislative ideas of those holding important public positions." The remainder of Senator Byrd's address dealt with the saving power of a balanced budget.

Marriner, by now, had become inured to personal poundings in the press and in the Congress. But he was determined not to allow Senator Byrd's broadcast to go unchallenged. He must mount a counterattack because of what he knew as a member of the Fiscal and Monetary Committee that was helping to shape the new budget. It seemed increasingly likely that, for the first time in the history of the Roosevelt administration, the budget to be submitted for fiscal 1939 would signal the administration's formal embrace of the concepts and implications of a "compensatory economy."

As part of the planned counterattack, Marriner drafted a letter of reply to Byrd, but before mailing it he showed the text to Roosevelt. He explained to FDR that his aim was to make the front pages. "With malice aforethought" he was deliberately inviting a fight, and was fully prepared to face any and all personal consequences. Roosevelt was delighted with the plan and the letter, but he became apprehensive when a week passed by and the text was still not released to the press. He called Marriner on the phone and without preliminaries asked: "What's happened to that letter? You're not backing down are you?"

Marriner had forgotten that December 23, 1938, would be the twenty-fifth anniversary of the signing of the Federal Reserve Act by President Wilson, and that the Board of Governors meant to mark the occasion with a brief ceremony. When the new Federal Reserve Building was constructed, a bas-relief in bronze of President Wilson was placed on the east wall of the lobby fronting Constitution Avenue. A corresponding space on the west wall was due to be filled at an appropriate time by a bronze bas-relief of Senator Carter Glass, as the chief Congressional champion of the Federal Reserve Act. The bas-relief was recently completed, and though it was unusual to erect a memorial to a living person, the board felt that in view of the historic occasion—and Senator Glass's advanced age—it would be appropriate to mark the twenty-fifth anniversary by placing the bas-relief of the senator on the place waiting for it.

"So, Mr. President," Marriner said as he came to the main point of his long explanation. "I felt it would cause some embarrassment to attack the junior United States senator from Virginia while immortalizing the senior one. It seemed best to get history out of the way first, and then attend to current affairs." Roosevelt roared with laughter when the delay was explained in these terms, and he approved of the proposed sequence of events. Two days after the plaque to Senator Glass was unveiled, Marriner unveiled his letter to Senator Byrd. It read in part:

You appear to believe that a large part of Government's expenditure is "waste."

You are fearful about the Government's credit and alarmed about the "burden" put upon the country by the public debt. There is not space within a letter adequately to discuss these matters, but in view of your program and since you saw fit to make a personal attack upon me, I feel that it is in order to raise a number of questions with respect to each of the foregoing considerations.

As to the "burden of debt": the pertinent facts are the volume of total debt in the country, the interest on that debt, and the income out of which interest may be paid. You failed to mention any of these pertinent facts. Are you aware of studies . . . indicating that the total of all domestic debts, both public and private, is no greater today than it was in 1929? That being so, does it not give a one-sided and alarming picture to concentrate attention solely upon the increase in the public debt without regard to the contraction of private debt since 1929? Is it of no significance that, owing to the decline in the rates of interest, the total interest payments today is far less than in 1929?

As for your concern about the burden of taxation, have you not overlooked the fact that as national income increases, tax revenues increase, even without a rise in tax rates? . . . Tax receipts of the Federal Government increased from $2,080,000,000 for the fiscal year ending June 30, 1933, to $6,242,000,000 for the fiscal year ending June 30, 1938. The country paid about $4 billion more in taxes but it had $30 billion more of income a year out of which to make these payments. Would you have the public believe that the country was better off in 1932 with lower taxes and a lower public debt than it was in 1937 with higher taxes and a higher public debt?

Marriner then turned to the question of what was to be entered on the credit side of the ledger as an offset to the increase of the public debt. Byrd had evidently contended that nothing was to be entered; that the government's expenditures for which the debt was incurred represented "waste." With this in mind, Marriner continued:

Do you think, as your speech seemed to indicate . . . that government debt is evil, whereas private debt is not? One would gather from your attitude that if a private builder, for example, borrows money to build houses you would commend him for "raising capital for private enterprise," whereas if a public housing authority borrows money for the same purpose, you would denounce it for "incurring debt."

You stated that you are concerned about "the character of the individual citizen" and "the dignity and the rights of the individual." So am I. I believe, however, that the most basic right of all is the right to live, and next to that, the right to work. I do not think empty stomachs build character, nor do I think the substitution of idleness and a dole for useful work relief will improve either the dignity or the character of the people affected. We cannot expect to preserve our free institutions in this country if we condemn a substantial proportion of our people to prolonged idleness on a bare subsistence level of existence. Further than the right to eat and the right to a position, I think the individual, whether rich or poor, has a right to a decent place to live. I think he has a right to security in old age and to protection against temporary unemployment. I think he has a right to adequate medical attention and to equal educational opportunities with the rest of his countrymen. The government expenditures which you condemn have in large part been the means of translating these basic rights into realities. . . .

I, for one, am not prepared to believe that this nation is doomed to stagnation, to a low level of national income, to a wholly unsatisfactory standard of living instead of the high standards, the achievement of which depends only upon our correct understanding of the operations of our economic system. I am convinced that your program is not only a defeatist one, a program of retrogression and not of progress, but that it would jeopardize the salvation of our democracy, which I know you are as sincerely desirous of preserving as I am.

The press uproar following the release of the letter was welcome music to Marriner. The text was featured on front pages and, as expected, was fiercely attacked on editorial pages. Soon Marriner had a more substantial basis for pleasure. Despite last minute hauling and pulling, President Roosevelt's State of the Union and budget messages of early January 1939, for the first time since the New Deal came to power, explicitly stated that the administration meant to balance the budget, not by decreasing expenditures nor by increasing taxes on consumption, but by increasing receipts rising from an increase in national income. The messages further declared frankly that federal deficits could be expected until such time as the budget could be balanced out of a national income of around $80 billion.

Following the delivery of the two messages, Marriner, in the mood of a vindicated yet embattled prophet—but with Henry Morgenthau still in mind—wrote to the president on January 11 to say:

I am firmly convinced that the position taken in your annual message to the Congress as well as in the budget message is the only sound one that can be taken at this time which will give assurance of a continuing recovery. I feel that it is of the greatest importance that your position, which I would describe as a compensatory fiscal policy, should be aggressively presented to the country. Needless to say, I am eager to do my utmost to this end. However, my role seems to be more or less cut out, as a result of my reply to Senator Byrd, his intention to reply on the Senate floor, and another open letter from me in reply thereto, possibly with a simultaneous broadcast. . . .

It is imperative that others holding important positions in the Government, particularly in the Cabinet, should participate in a program of presenting your case to the country. Most important of all, such a presentation should authoritatively be made by the Treasury, which, I understand has accepted the objective of an $80-billion national income as the means of balancing the budget.

If the Secretary of the Treasury were to make a public address very shortly explaining the soundness of this case, it would pave the way for others to follow this up. . . .

But until the Secretary of the Treasury makes a speech, it would seem to me inappropriate for the rest of us to attempt to lead out in this field which is so predominantly the Treasury's responsibility. Once he has presented the case officially for the Administration, it will be much easier for the rest of us to follow up, acting under his leadership and avoiding the appearance of dissension within the ranks or encroachment upon the Treasury's domain.

On January 16, Senatory Byrd, as expected, returned to the attack by sending Marriner an open letter drawing its ideas and phrases from *Poor Richard's Almanac, Bartlett's Quotations,* and *McGuffey's Reader* and including a history of the English people since Magna Carta. Marriner's plan for a counterattack—with Secretary of the Treasury Morgenthau as the lead-off man, followed by Hopkins, Ickes and Wallace—did not materialize. The 1940 presidential nominating conventions were in view, and many leaders in the Administration became extremely cautious about what they said and did. At a moment when Roosevelt at last embraced the tenets of a compensatory economy, some men who had long urged him to do so left him in an exposed position while they courted people they thought could serve their personal ambitions—in the event that FDR should not seek a third term.

Marriner's associates on the Board of Governors strongly opposed his further involvement in a public debate with Senator Byrd. They feared he would drag the whole Reserve System into a partisan political fight, thereby destroying its role as an independent agency. Marriner was not deterred. He joined the issue with Senator Byrd, not to defend the political fortunes of the president, but to defend his *own* economic ideas, the same ideas that brought him to Washington in 1934 and had kept him there. He would, however, make it clear that he was voicing his own views and not those of the board, and so he did, when the National Broadcasting System invited Senator Byrd and Marriner to engage in a radio debate.

The senator spoke first, on January 16—the evening of the day on which he sent Marriner the letter mentioned earlier. Like his letter, Byrd's radio address made a difficult target to shoot at. He denounced the government's spending programs, denounced Marriner's ideas, called attention to "the staggering burden of debt" that would be passed on to future generations, and declared that "waste and extravagance" should be cut out of government spending. Marriner's radio reply came on January 23, and it developed the theme of his earlier letter:

Why not worry also about the burden of all of the private debts on our children and their children? These debts will also be passed on to future generations, who will have to pay the cost of servicing or paying those debts just as in the case of government debts. We should know that all debts, both public and private, are passed along from one generation to the next, just as all assets, both public and private, are handed down from one generation to the next. It may be that Senator Byrd would be less worried if there were no debts, but in that case there would be no banks, insurance companies, or other financial institutions. . . .

The whole problem of internal debt, public and private, must be considered in relationship to the total real wealth of the nation. Our total debts are great or small, depending upon total national income. . . . Now make no mistake, I am not advocating ever-increasing debt, but I am merely pointing out that we should see the problem of debt in true perspective.

Marriner had not yet left the radio studio at the end of the broadcast when a call came to him from the White House. Steve Early, Roosevelt's press secretary, was at the other end. "Marriner," he said, "I want you to know how much 'the Boss' appreciated your speech. Here you are, with much less reason to stand up for him than many others, yet you were the only one who did it."

The next morning there was another phone call from the White House. It was Roosevelt at the other end this time.

"Hello," he said, "How are you this morning, Marriner?"

"Fine, Mr. President."

"Well, I just called to *condemn* and to *commend* you. I want to condemn you because you kept me up late last night. I usually go to bed at ten. But you kept me up until ten thirty listening to your speech. But now I want to commend you. I think your address was excellent. You made the problem so simple that even I was able to understand it."

One radio speech, however, did not still the rising clamor for a balanced budget. Marriner himself reached a point where he grew weary of talking to no seeming effect. So it was on March 23, 1939, when he appeared before a special congressional committee formed to investigate the administration's "silver policies." As a witness at the morning session, he met successive attacks on the concept of a compensatory economy expressed in the new budget, but his words seemed to fall on deaf ears. At the noontime recess, Marriner reassessed the defensive role into which he had been pushed at the hearing and decided there was no gain in it. He should instead invite the Congress to take full responsibility for the nation's fiscal policy. He skipped his lunch and used the time saved to draft a statement which he read to the committee when it reconvened for the afternoon session:

A school of thought believes that business confidence cannot be restored until a balanced budget is assured through reduction of government expenditures, that continued deficits are holding back private investment, that government employment is demoralizing and destructive to the moral fibre of our people, that the public expenditures are wasteful and are piling up a burden of debt which our children and grandchildren will have to pay for. Senator Byrd has stated that he believes that for every dollar the government borrows and spends private enterprise is deterred from spending two. . . . This appears to be the prevailing point of view among business men and the public generally, as reflected by a recent Gallup poll, by innumerable resolutions of trade associations, by bankers' groups, and—as I can testify from personal experience—by the overwhelming majority of newspaper editorials. . . .

The majority of the business leaders on whom would fall the task of producing the activity necessary to recovery are convinced that the government's expenditures compete with and discourage private investment in existing and new enterprise.

A majority in both houses of Congress have indicated that they also hold this view. While I am convinced that such a policy of retrenchment under present conditions would have disastrous results, we live in a democracy and, therefore, I believe that the viewpoint of the majority should promptly be made effective.

The country is entitled to a clear-cut and prompt determination of policy on this vital issue. It is Congress that determines the rates and nature of our taxes; it is Congress also that determines the amount of government money to be used for different purposes. If balancing the budget will bring about recovery, then Congress can promptly do so by reducing expenditures to the level of receipts. . . .

In order to effect sufficient economy and reduce taxes, Congress would have to reduce substantially practically all of the large items in the budget. Not much economy could be effected in the regular establishments of the government, which in the aggregate absorb only about one tenth of the national budget. Such items as work-relief projects, CCC camps, roads and public works of all kinds, veteran's benefits, all farm-benefit payments, and national defense, some or all of these would have to be drastically curtailed.

This would not be my program, but if, as would appear, it is the program of the majority, they should assume full responsibility for it and put it into effect without delay and without compromises for the benefit of any special groups.

The congressional reaction to the invitation was a long sputter. Some budget balancers quickly protested that they had never insisted that the budget be balanced immediately. Some accused Marriner of "political trickery" and "low political cunnings." Others, for want of anything better to say, dismissed the invitation on the ground that it was "naive." Still others, in an attempt to brazen it through, challenged the administration to join the Congress in instituting drastic economies. And so it went, in a continuous confusion of tongues.

III

On another front—the need to unify the banking system—months had passed by, with no congressional reactions to the portions of the 1938 annual report of the Federal Reserve Board which called attention to the creaky structure of the nation's banking system. The Congress, however, did have before it President Roosevelt's bill for the reorganization of the executive branch of the government. As approved by the Congress in May 1939, the bill, among other things, created an Office of the President (for the first time in American history), authorized the creation of a White House staff with a number of special assistants to the president, and shifted the location of the Bureau of the Budget from its position of subservience in and to the Treasury, to a new home and role as part of the Office of the President. The bill also gave the president the authority to venture a limited reorganization of the Comptroller's Office.

In Marriner's view, the latter detail was no more than a cosmetic project. It was not the equivalent of the thoroughgoing job of bank reform he had been advocating. Moreover, the further steps the Congress appeared posed to take all pointed in the wrong direction. This was particularly true of the great interest the Congress then showed in the so-called "Brown bill," introduced by Rep. Clarence Brown, an Ohio Republican; by its terms, the bank examinations of both the Comptroller's office and of the Federal Reserve Board would be transferred to the Federal Deposit Insurance Corporation. The proposal made little sense: to vest all bank examinations in an agency whose main interest was the protection of its insurance funds completely ignored the interplay between examination and investment policies, and between the objectives of credit policy and the money supply. Secondly, the FDIC, as an insuring agency, was in no position to formulate and execute monetary and credit policies. It was not the purpose of the sponsors of the "Brown bill," however, to improve the nation's banking machinery. The purpose was to stage a congressional hearing where they could broadcast their animosities toward the administration—all in prologue to the 1940 presidential contest.

The case here was so viewed by President Roosevelt, and he was receptive to a suggestion Marriner put to him on May 15 at a White House meeting. The best way to block the Brown bill, said Marriner, would be to get the Senate to adopt a resolution introduced by Senator Robert Wagner, the new chairman of the Banking and Currency Committee. The resolution called upon the committee to conduct a study to determine "a national monetary and banking policy by which the monetary and banking authorities of the Federal Government shall be guided and governed, and to determine the character of governmental machinery best calculated to carry out such a policy." The terms were sufficiently broad to permit the committee to deal with the whole range of closely related monetary, credit, and banking problems.

Marriner informed the president that he had talked at length with Senator Wagner, and the latter was pushing hard to get the resolution approved. Moreover, the senator clearly understood the priorities for reorganizing the banking agencies of the federal government. The fundamental objectives of monetary policy should *first* be decided by the Congress: the location of executive agencies—along with the powers to be vested in them or removed from their control in order to carry out the stated objectives of monetary policy—should be decided *afterward*. To reshuffle existing agencies first, and only then to state monetary policy, was patently illogical. Finally, Senator Wagner would allow no one to use his committee to work off personal political grudges. He was interested in a constructive study, and not in an inquisition.

"I am convinced," Marriner said to the president, "that this course is eminently desirable from the administration's standpoint. It would forestall the possibility that in the 1940 presidential contest, the administration would be assailed on a charge that it failed to deal with pressing banking, credit and monetary problems. It would instead complete the administration's achievement in reopening and rehabilitating the banking system following the banking holiday of 1933—which is still officially in effect."

At the end of the round of talk, Roosevelt summoned one of his secretaries. He seemed to sense that his two and one-half years of indecision concerning the matter at issue gave Marriner sufficient cause to be skeptical about the sequel to this new discussion. He dictated a memorandum to Senator Wagner in which he urged the adoption of the resolution by the Banking and Currency Committee, and pledged his own support for it. Marriner left the White House in a buoyant mood. He hoped that what he had set in motion would eventually result in a fundamental reorganization of the nation's banking system—and this, in his view, could be more important than the reforms in the Federal Reserve System stemming from the Banking Act of 1935.

In due course, Wagner shepherded his resolution through Banking and Currency. The Senate empowered the committee to pursue for an indefinite period—whether the Congress was in session or in recess—a study of national monetary and banking policies which were to guide the government's monetary and banking authorities, and determine the nature of the governmental apparatus required to carry out such policies. But of the $100,000 Senator Wagner had asked to finance such a study, the Senate approved only $25,000. Actual work began in January 1940, four months after the outbreak of war in Europe.

Questionnaires were sent to the American Bankers Association, the presidents of the Reserve banks, and to all the government banking agencies in Washington. At intermittent moments, it seemed that the replies to the questionnaires would be converted by the committee into a clear set of proposals for submission to the Congress. Yet for all practical purposes, the Nazi attack on the Netherlands in May 1940 had as one of its casualties in the United States the death of all interest in bank reform. The members of Wagner's committee turned their attention to more pressing matters. President Roosevelt turned his attention to a bid for a third term.

V

THE ECONOMICS
OF WAR

27. The Gathering Storm

BACK IN SEPTEMBER 1939, a few days before the Nazi march on Poland, Marriner was involved in a ludicrous incident which foreshadowed some of his recurring experiences during the defense preparedness and war years. Roosevelt asked him for lunch to talk about how the American domestic economy would be effected if there was war in Europe. As far as the government security market was concerned, Marriner came to the meeting with a reassuring word. The Federal Reserve System had been prepared for months to check any violent market swings in case Europe went to war.

However, Marriner had some other worrisome matters on his mind —such as the grave inflationary threat posed anew by the continuing flight to America of foreign capital in the form of gold. During the year ending in August 1939, an influx of $3.4 billion in gold was added to the excess already on hand. The result could be a vast credit expansion by the banking system and a cheapening of money at the very time when defense and war demands could produce a scarcity of goods and services. The Reserve Board had formulated certain proposals to deal with such dangers, and it was Marriner's intention to discuss them with the president. What happened instead at the White House luncheon was later recalled by Marriner as follows:[1]

On arriving at the White House for my luncheon engagement, I was told by General "Pa" Watson, secretary and military aide to the President, that Roosevelt was running behind in his scheduled appointments. Senator McAdoo, who had been defeated the year before by Sheridan Downey in California's Democratic primary, was with him at the moment.

Watson unsuccessfully tried to end the talk inside the President's office; it was after a delay of more than twenty minutes in all that Roosevelt buzzed Watson, indicating that I was to be brought in. On entering his office, I saw McAdoo standing over the President's desk as he talked earnestly about California politics. Roosevelt interrupted him long enough to ask if McAdoo knew me. The Senator snorted a greeting and kept right on talking.

At this, the President tapped the side of his desk and said: "Bring up a chair, Marriner." Then he added pointedly to McAdoo: "Marriner and I are about to have lunch."

"Oh, that's all right, it's perfectly all right," said McAdoo airily. "You two boys go right ahead—I'll talk while you eat."

A warming oven was rolled in next to the President's desk. He pushed back the cover and pulled out a plate. It was scorching hot. He juggled it in an uncertain way as he held it out to me. I should have had enough sense to relieve him of it instantly.

But even in the presence of the President of the United States, banker instinct told me to reach for a napkin first to insulate my hand when I took the plate. A second later, when the food was before me on the table, I apologized to the President for my banker-caution. He continued to shake his finger for awhile. McAdoo, in no way thrown off balance, continued to stand over us, talking of things close to his heart. For the added ten minutes he remained there, neither Roosevelt nor I said a word. By this time, my whole insides were aflame with irritation over the Senator's intrusion. But finally he turned to go.

"Now, remember, Franklin," he said to the President as he wagged his finger at him, "I want to leave one last thought with you. When it comes to appointing any of those federal judges in California, I wish you would take the matter up with me instead of with that son-of-a-bitch Downey. You know you can rely on me to steer you correctly."

When McAdoo was out of the room all thought of him seemed also to have left Roosevelt's mind. He turned to me and, as though I had just come in, said cheerfully: "Well, Marriner, and how are you today?"

The example of the President's patience and courtesy in the face of McAdoo's great provocation to anger made me lie outrageously.

"Well, I'm fine, Mr. President. Just fine."

A minute later the President motioned to a waiter to remove the food before us, but it seemed to be a double signal understood in another quarter. In scampered Fala, the President's Scotty. Roosevelt opened a desk drawer, took out a ball, and threw it across the room. Fala raced after it, brought it back, and the game was continued in this way for four or five minutes.

I simulated interest and felt like a hypocrite every time I voiced a word of praise for the beast's tricks. Fala was a fine dog and justly beloved by his master. Still, when minutes alone with the President represented the margin between alternative national policies, any intrusions on those minutes, so far as I was concerned, were offensive, and especially after the McAdoo episode.

At last the President said to Fala: "That's enough now. I've got to get back to work."

This was a signal for me to start talking. I began to present an action program to cushion the impact on our economy of an outbreak of war in Europe and the inflow of gold from abroad. After three or four minutes of this I lost my audience. Roosevelt was looking around the room to locate Fala. When he found him, there was a Presidential bellow: "Well I'll be Goddamned! Marriner, do you see what I see?"

I did. Fala was off in a corner of the room purging himself on the rug.

Roosevelt quickly pressed a button. A guard entered the room and was ordered to rub the dog's nose in the mess under the general supervision of the President of the United States. The procedure from start to end, plus a post-mortem discussion took five or ten minutes more. And finally, when this non-historic event in White House annals had run its course, Roosevelt said to me: "And now, Marriner, we can talk about *our business.*" Which, of course, was no longer possible. General Watson appeared in the doorway to announce the next visitor. Between McAdoo and Fala, the hour set aside for a luncheon discussion with the President had expired.

The blocks between the White House and the Federal Reserve Building on that day were blanketed with a layer of volcanic ash as I made my way back to my office. Arriving there, I was met by my two associates Elliot Thurston and Lawrence Clayton, who were anxiously awaiting the report of my lunch with the President.

"Well?" they asked eagerly.

"I was with him for an hour."

"And—?"

"And nothing! Not a damned thing that was worth while!"

I then told how a policy decision had been delayed while McAdoo said his piece about California judges and Fala went through his act. It was not until Thurston and Clayton met my faithful report with unbecoming laughter that I mustered a sickly smile of my own.

So, too, during the defense preparedness and war years, a few minutes with Roosevelt was a prize sought by all. To gain it and exploit it took careful planning and timing. Yet when an appointment was finally set, a host of distractions often blurred what was discussed or eroded the outlines of what was decided. Like others, Marriner was often riled when his views regarding events on his sector of the defense and war front did not reach the president's ears. It was not from a lack of zeal but from a full flood of it that he and other administrators snapped at one another and harassed the president when they saw things go badly. It was only in a hindsight view of the war as a whole that they could see an impressive fact that had been obscured in the thick of battle—namely, that more mistakes were *not* made.

II

Early in January 1940, Marriner was back at the White House for another lunch with the president. By this time, the economy had recovered almost to the point where it had been before the 1937–38 recession. Substantial profits to business as a whole seemed to be developing irrespective of the volume of operations. Yet despite the relatively good showing of industry in the last quarter of 1939, unemployment never fell below eight million, or one-sixth of the total available labor force. While approximately ten million additional workers had found jobs in private industry since 1933, the high level of continued unemployment was due to the entry into the labor market of an estimated half million new workers each year. Since industry had accommodated itself to the depression, as indicated by the size of its earnings, there was a strong disposition in many places to freeze the army of unemployed at eight or ten million. This was to be done by reducing public employment in pace with increases in private employment. But with the steady influx of new labor on the market, a decrease of public employment by half a million whenever private employment absorbed an equal amount would make no net reduction in the total number of unemployed.

The substance of Marriner's discussion with the president during their lunch in January 1940 was the need for continued appropriations for public works. There was an unexpected turn in the discussion. Marriner later recalled:

I was about to leave Roosevelt's office when he said to me: "By the way, Marriner, how would you like to stay here a while longer? The boys from the Bureau of the

Budget are bringing over a draft copy of my budget message, which will be sent to the Congress next week. I'd like you to stay—if you can spare the time—and give me any suggestions you care to make."

He did not need to twist my arm.

"However," Roosevelt continued, "don't ever tell Henry Morgenthau that you sat in on this meeting. As you know, the budget is a very sore spot with Henry and he will be deeply offended if he learned that you had judged its contents beforehand. As it is, he cries on my shoulder all the time."

I assured the President that I knew from experience how important it was to adhere to the letter of his advice. In a moment, the budget message was brought into the room, along with Harold D. Smith, the Director of the Bureau of the Budget, Jack Blansford, the Deputy Director, and Lauchlin Currie, one of the President's new assistants in the recently created Office of the President. There was a bit of horseplay when Roosevelt ceremoniously introduced me to "Dr. Currie" as though I had never before seen him in my life.

In this particular connection, I should explain that some months before, Roosevelt called me on the phone to say: "Marriner, I guess you are going to give me hell." Without knowing what he had in mind, I replied: "Mr. President, I don't know what good it would do me to give you hell, even if I wanted to."

"Well, I'm going to steal Lauch Currie from you, I need him here as one of my assistants." He quickly baited the hook. "I'm sure you will realize," he continued, "that it isn't such a bad thing after all as far as the Board and you are concerned. You, of course, immediately see the advantage of having a friend in court who can represent and speak for *your* point of view." Needless to say, Currie changed jobs without further argument.

Following a reading of the budget message, the President turned to me for comment. I told him that, apart from some minor suggestions, there was but one observation I felt was important. I noted that $500,000,000 had been cut from the previous year's relief appropriation; I felt this was a great mistake in view of the fact that there were still over eight million unemployed and that not more than three million of these had ever been cared for by the government even before relief appropriations were cut.

To this the President replied: "You are absolutely right. But with the war in Europe likely to spread, we simply must increase last year's military budget from $1 billion to $1.5 billion in the coming year. But with the total budget being what it is, the relief budget is the only place from which I can transfer the additional funds needed for the military. Congress simply will not support an increase in the total budget so as to increase our military preparedness. There is no real pressure in the country for such expenditures. Later on, however, Congress will support further relief appropriations as pressures develop on all sides. In this roundabout way, I hope ultimately to take care of the unemployed. But even so, Marriner, despite the immediate decreases in relief appropriations, it is going to extremely difficult to get the Congress to pass the military budget.

When this was said, I argued that the President should try to get the increase he wanted in the military budget without cutting the relief budget. If he presented all factors to Congress, and if the state of our affairs called for an increase in military appropriations, I felt certain that the Congress would authorize it. But Roosevelt remained unconvinced that Congress would act as I thought it would. Events were to prove that I was wrong, and Roosevelt was absolutely right.[2]

Subsequently, Marriner carefully tracked congressional reactions to the new budget. As of May 10, 1940, when the Nazis launched their attack on the Netherlands, the military budget had not even been reported out of the committees of either the House or the Senate. The committees, instead, had been busy making substantial cuts, amounting in the aggregate to more than $100 million. The picture changed only when the Nazis broke through the Maginot line. Within forty-eight hours, Congress not only approved the military budget but authorized $2 billion more in case it was needed by the president.

The day after the Nazis entered Paris, Marriner went to the White House to convey to Roosevelt a report on how the impact of the event on the government bond market had been cushioned by the operations of the Federal Reserve's Open Market Committee. As he walked to the president's desk to shake his hands in greeting, he saw that FDR looked dark. The exchange that followed, as later recalled by Marriner, went like this:

"How are you today, Mr. President," I asked.

"I'm damned mad."

"I hope you are not mad at me."

"No," said the President. "But do you know who just left this office? It was the French Ambassador. I called him over here to try to find out what the French Army and Navy and his government were going to do now that the Nazis were in Paris. And what do you think he told me? He stood there in front of me and beat his breast. 'Mr. President,' he said, 'France will live on and on and on!' I asked him again what the French government, Navy, and Army were going to do and again he beat his breast. 'France will live on and on and on!' Do you know what I said to that?"

"No, sir, I don't."

"I said: 'Jee-sus Christ!' "

"But that isn't all that happened today," Roosevelt continued. "When I woke up this morning, the first thing I saw was a headline in the *New York Times* to the effect that our Navy was going to spend two billion dollars on a shipbuilding program. Here I am, the Commander in Chief of the Navy having to read about that for the first time in the press. Do you know what I said to that?"

"No, Mr. President."

"I said: 'Jesus Chr-rist!' "

Having unburdened himself in this way, the President's anger subsided and he became reflective.

"The Treasury," he said, "is so large and far-flung and ingrained in its practices that I find it is almost impossible to get the action and results I want—even with Henry there. But the Treasury is not to be compared with the State Department. You should go through the experience of trying to get any changes in the thinking, policy, and action of the career diplomats and then you'd know what a real problem was. But the Treasury and the State Department put together are nothing as compared with the Na-a-vy. The admirals are really something to cope with—and I should know. To change anything in the Na-a-vy is like punching a feather bed. You punch it with your right and you punch it with your left until you are finally exhausted, and then you find the damn bed just as it was before you started punching."[3]

Marriner thought that the Treasury still took the palm for obstinacy. But for the moment, he tried to cheer Roosevelt by handing him a report which showed how well the market for government securities had withstood the shock in the war news. At no time was there any disorder in the market that needed large-scale intervention by the Open Market Committee. "I think," Marriner wrote in his report, "that the remarkable stability of the market has been due to the Reserve System's assurances that it stood ready to exert its influence towards steadying the market—and also to the fact that the volume of excess reserves of the banking system is so vast that the market can be depended upon to absorb virtually any conceivable amount of government securities that may be necessary to offer in the future." He hoped the president would be reassured that the market would and could readily support "any additional financing as may be necessary because of increased defense needs in the United States."

Marriner's own cheeriness, however, turned sour when he read in the newspapers for May 28 that an agreement had been reached between administration and congressional leaders to raise the debt limit by $3 billion and to impose additional taxes of about $700 million to pay interest and amortization charges on this amount. In his view, the details of this agreement seemed to reflect slap-dash decision making. He was convinced that financial preparedness for a defense program on the dramatically expanded scale to be foreseen made it essential to plan a comprehensive revision of the whole tax structure adapted to the total economic situation.

With this in mind, Marriner secured an appointment with FDR for the next day. His position was that if there was any way that the Federal Reserve Board and the System could help lighten the president's load, they were ready to do so. Their expert staff was underemployed. Other agencies of the government such as the Treasury Department and the Reconstruction Finance Corporation were already buckling under the new loads of defense-related work and were expanding their organizations accordingly. The Federal Reserve System could assume some of the new work load without expanding; for example, by lending to small businessmen who wished to tool up for defense production.

"Would it not be advisable," Marriner asked, "to revive the administration's interagency fiscal and monetary committee in the interest of proper coordination?" No meeting of the committee had been called by its chairman, Secretary Morgenthau, since the outbreak of the European war in September 1939. The Federal Reserve Board thus found itself "in the unhappy position of reading in the papers that action is proposed, vitally affecting it, on which it has not been consulted." He was not, said Marriner, being "a carping critic." He meant only to make the point that responsible officials are so overworked that they could not keep up with normal responsibilities and have time to deal with new ones. He went on to stress the vital importance of the whole field of credit and proper credit management in any defense program.

Fifth columns, said he, are all too often bred out of economic distress at home, and while pressing for the utmost in defense measures, the morale of the domestic front is of primary importance. Properly coordinated fiscal-monetary action would look to preparation against future inflationary dangers, to avoidance of idle manpower and idle money. Francis Bacon pointed an analogy between money and manure. "To be useful it cannot be piled up but must be scattered around the fields." The desirability of coordinating the credit-banking mechanism, tying it in with the rest of the defense program, is apparent. The Board and staff, as well as the system, would welcome any opportunity to be of help to the Administration.

Roosevelt was not of a mind to focus on the long-range implications of the methods used to finance the defense effort. But he did ask Marriner to find and formulate answers to three general questions. "What about gold? About idle money? About price stability?"

Marriner's memorandum of reply, presented to Roosevelt in mid-June, started by dismissing any parochial approach. "The answer to these three questions," he said, "should be framed in the light of their bearing on the real objective of our Government policy—namely, the full utilization of our human and material resources" so as to assure our people secure employment and an income adequate to maintaining an American standard of living. "Ways of handling gold, of utilizing idle money, and of establishing a dollar of constant purchasing power are important only as pieces of machinery to facilitate the achievement of this objective." Marriner then defined the central problem as he saw it:

The crisis in which American democracy has been for the past ten years has assumed a different aspect as the result of Hitler's successes in Europe. Until recently our real enemy—unemployment—was viewed as a domestic problem and we as a people were content to fight this enemy in a half-hearted and tradition-bound manner. Now our potential enemy is a totalitarian world—and we as a people are prepared to fight this enemy in a whole-hearted way with every means at our command. For the moment, this simplifies our problem. We have popular support for vigorous programs of defense and armament which as an immediate consequence is certain to help alleviate, even though it may not forever cure the disease of unemployment.

In going full steam ahead on this program, however, we must so plan our efforts as not only to achieve the maximum results in a minimum of time, but also to make the best use of the fact that traditional economic bogeys, such as an unbalanced budget and Government controls and participation in economic activity, have for the time being lost their terror to the people. We must so plan our efforts as to achieve adequate national defense without unduly distorting our economy and to be prepared, when the time comes to relax our efforts for defense, to do so without relapsing into a state of underactivity and large-scale unemployment. . . . Our problem is to achieve the results that we desire within the framework of our institutions. We must devise means for directing voluntary efforts into the necessary channels and limiting the intrusion of the state, through controls and participation activity, to the minimum necessary for successfully carrying out our program. Less than that would sacrifice the success of the undertaking; more than that would involve unnecessary loss of freedom.

Marriner then indicated how the Federal Reserve Board would search for answers to the three questions Roosevelt posed. The board and its staff, for example, would survey the fields in which industrial expansion must be made, review the availability of the labor force for this expansion, analyze actual and potential supplies of material, attempt to formulate the policies that would produce the results immediately desired and, at the same time, lay the basis for achieving long-term objectives. This would entail a review of public projects of all kinds, labor policies, and tax and fiscal policies.

We also propose [Marriner continued] to study the dangers of price maladjustments which may frustrate the efforts to achieve defense and fuller employment and to maintain employment at a high level. . . . Action now to assure adequate supplies of materials and thereby to keep prices within bounds would help to prevent the necessity later on for direct price fixing and restrictive credit policies. As part of the whole program for maintaining stable economic conditions, improvements in our banking system will be proposed. The question of how to control the reserves created by the gold inflow is an essential part of this problem.

The board and its staff also meant to study the American international trade position in a world where the United States would "have to compete with totalitarian states." Individual Americans, so Marriner observed, "who could hold their own in competition with individual foreigners, cannot successfully compete with state-controlled foreign monopolies." Here Marriner drew the moral of the story he had in mind all along. "I realize that other governmental agencies are working on many of the problems I've outlined. I suggest that close cooperation between them and mutual assistance to avoid unnecessary duplication is essential. Machinery for assuring cooperation and coordination of effort should be adopted."

It was a cry in the wilderness.

The need for cooperation and coordination was underlined by an intramural battle that began in the fall of 1940 just when the presidential election was being heated up. The Federal Reserve Board and its Open Market Committee had been struggling with the limited tools at hand to control the rising volume of money created by new bank credit, but the efforts were sharply opposed not only by private bankers but by the Treasury and other banking agencies of the government. At the height of this clash, the Federal Advisory Council to the Federal Reserve Board, in an assertion of its independence, unanimously endorsed a statement that roundly condemned administration and Reserve policies. Publication of the council's attack would have drawn public notice to the breach in the Reserve System, but because of the agreement reached back in November 1934, when Marriner first became the head of the Federal Reserve Board, the Board of Governors had a chance to review the statement before it was released to the press.

After weeks of argument between the board and the council, a substitute statement was drafted that was unanimously approved by the council, the Reserve Board, and the presidents of the twelve Reserve banks. The unanimity achieved was without precedent in the history of the Reserve System. In fact, Marriner was surprised at how far the council and the Reserve banks had been willing to go—abandoning points in their previous stand and embracing the board's stand—on a plan of action that would tend to reduce potential inflationary dangers.

Long before the report was made public, Marriner showed the text to Roosevelt, explaining that it was a substitute for the blast the Federal Advisory Council had meant to issue. It was in no way critical of the administration; it was designed to assure the public that the Reserve System was on the alert to inflationary dangers but needed congressional authority to deal with them before they became real. The council would never have agreed with the proposals in the special report if the board itself had been ignorant of the underlying causes of inflationary monetary conditions that might develop if the huge increases in excess reserves and deposits on hand were further flooded by the president's use of his power to devalue gold and silver, issue greenbacks, and utilize silver seigniorage. The board wanted the president to surrender these latent powers in order to improve his strategic position with respect to the Congress in the event he asked for a stronger central-banking mechanism.

When the special report was made public, some critics said it was "a typical banker's ploy to get higher interest rates." Others said it was a slap at the president since it proposed to curb his powers to issue greenbacks or devalue the dollar. Within the administration, Leo T. Crowley, as head of the FDIC, opposed it because it would have put all state banks under the reserve powers of the Federal Reserve System. Jesse Jones, representing the Federal Loan Administration, opposed it on the ground that there was "no sign of inflation," nor did he "see why we should expect any such tendency." He added: "I am trying to get the banks to lend more. I want to see as much bank credit available as possible." Of special interest was the reaction of Henry Morgenthau. Marriner's version of the matter was this:

Henry Morgenthau had read a copy of the report in advance of its release. He held it for ten days, declined to assume any responsibility for it, but made no objection when it was sent to Congress. This last was surprising. Uncontrolled excess reserves offered the Treasury an easy way to dispose of government bond issues. As long as bonds were sold, Treasury officials showed little concern over the inflationary consequences arising from the means used, though the inflation that followed forced them to sell more bonds to finance the government and in the end made everything more costly during the war years.

There was a strange and uneasy silence in the Treasury Department for eight days after the report was made public. Rumors that the Treasury and the Reserve Board were engaged in another of their vendettas were temporarily checked by Steve Early. But then on January 9, 1941, in the course of a press conference, Morgenthau broke the truce and the sniping was on.

A few days before, the price of government bonds had dropped on the market, and accordingly Morgenthau was asked whether he attributed the decline to the issuance of the report. To this he replied: "I do entirely. It is a fact, not an opinion. Notice the date when he [Eccles] gave out his plan and notice what happened. From the day the statement came out, money started to go up. The decline was absolutely not warranted. There is no reason I know of for interest rates to harden at this time unless some such proposal as that of the Federal Reserve Board should be put into effect."

A correspondent present mentioned talk to the effect that the Federal Reserve plan was "an attempt to take control of the money market from the government and give it to the New York Bankers."

Instead of quashing this implication, Morgenthau gave it further currency by answering: "It raises an interesting thought."[4]

Until that press conference, Marriner and other members of the Federal Reserve Board thought they had well served the public interest. With Morgenthau's comments on the special report, however, Marriner and the board felt that they had been capriciously slapped across the face. The further effect on Marriner personally was to make him all the more determined to try to bring into being a new institutional structure—not dependent on Morgenthau—which could give coherence to the administration's economic policies in support of the defense effort. The economic policies Marriner wished to see adopted in connection with the defense effort were the exact reverse of those he had favored in order to reflate the economy. But, inside government and external to it, he bucked up against a widespread holdover of depression psychology. When money and not goods had been in short supply, Americans never seemed to have enough to buy the things they wanted or needed. The attitudes so formed carried forward into the years of the defense effort. Americans found it hard to believe that, in this new context, goods and not money would be in short supply.

President Roosevelt's own insight into this aspect of the nation's psychology was among the strands of his thoughts that led to Lend-Lease. At least that is how he explained the matter to Marriner during a White House dinner on December 18, 1940—a day after the press conference where he announced the Lend-Lease plan. During dinner, Roosevelt leaned over in Marriner's direction and said: "How did you like the idea of Lend-Lease in the papers this morning?"

"I am sorry to say," Marriner replied, "that I only had time to read the headlines and didn't study it. But I'd certainly like to hear about it."

"Well," said the president, "I had a little free time to think when I was on my cruise to the West Indies. And this idea just occurred to me while sunning myself. I knew the British were at the bottom of the barrel for cash. They had to get some direct help from us, or the Nazis would win the war. I also knew that with the isolationist sentiment in the country, the desire to keep neutral would lead to opposition blasts if I proposed a direct loan to a country that had not paid back what it borrowed from us during the last war.

"But I think people can better understand what happens in international trade. You sell goods to the world and you must take goods back in payment. Well, everyone knows we have a lot of surplus goods which we don't need and can't use, but most people feel there is a shortage of dollars. If we made a dollar loan to the British, it would seem to our people that we were giving the British money, of which we were short, instead of goods, which were in surplus. But it's different if we lend them goods which we don't want and get goods of theirs sometime in the future. Of course, even if we give them goods, they must be paid for in dollars. But by presenting this problem as an exchange of goods which they now greatly need, for goods to be returned to us at some future date, it takes it out of the field of an international dollar loan and places it in the field of lending and leasing things with your neighbor.''

Roosevelt's grasp of national psychology in winning support for Lend-Lease was not by itself a method for managing the economic aspects of the defense effort. Marriner daily lived with this problem, and thought long and hard about how best to solve it. On December 21, 1940, three days after the previously mentioned dinner in the White House, he sent another of his many memoranda to the president. He proposed the creation of an ''Advisory committee to the President on Economic Policy'' to coordinate the policies of the various monetary and fiscal agencies of the government and to work out plans for dealing with monetary, fiscal and price problems related to the defense program and to the ultimate transition to a peacetime economy.

The chairman of the committee would be vice-president-elect Henry Wallace. Members serving under him might be comprised of the Secretary of the Treasury, the Federal Loan Administration, the chairman of the Federal Reserve Board, and the member of the Defense Commission in charge of prices. One of the administrative assistants to the president (the choice of Lauchlin Currie was implied) could act as the committee's secretary, thus providing a direct personal link to Roosevelt. The director of the Bureau of the Budget, by sitting in as an observer, could provide an auxiliary link to the president. To justify the recommendation, Marriner wrote:

Some progress has been made in coordinating the *physical* side of the defense program. No progress, however, has been made in coordinating its financial counterpart. . . . As the defense program gains momentum there is increasing danger and likelihood of conflicting or duplicating policies being adopted. There are almost bound to arise individual disagreements as to whether or to what extent recourse should be had to the use of monetary controls, fiscal controls, direct credit or rationing controls. Some difference, of course, will always exist. Many others, however, could be resolved around a table. As a means of relieving pressure on the President and in the interests of developing consistent and comprehensive progress, there is urgent need of an administrative device to insure that conflicting or duplicating policies be avoided, that the areas of controversy that must be settled by the President be reduced and that alternative courses of action to be placed before the President be clearly and sharply defined. A frequent cause of disagreements in policy matters is traceable to differences in the factual and analytical studies on which policies are based. The suggested committee would facilitate an interchange of views and a narrowing of differences at the technical level.

Marriner went on to suggest that the designation of the vice-president as *chairman* of the proposed committee would have numerous advantages. Since the vice-president was also president of the Senate, he could "provide a communication link between the executive and legislative branches of the government," and could thus "lessen misunderstanding" between them. The chairmanship would also provide the most satisfactory way of keeping the vice-president in touch with the policies of the administration and the range of considerations that entered into their making.

The proposed "Advisory Committee to the President on Economic Policy" prefigured what would eventually materialize in transfigured form after World War II as the Council of Economic Advisors to the President. Roosevelt, however, let the idea fall through a crack in the White House floor. He apparently was reluctant to put Vice-president Wallace in a position where he would take precedence over Secretary of the Treasury Henry Morgenthau in shaping the administration's overarching financial programs in support of the defense effort—the very condition which Marriner would have welcomed. Eventually, when the Board of Economic Warfare was created—to deal with the *daily administration of foreign economic matters*—Wallace was appointed as its administrative head. This is not what Marriner had in mind, and the consequences of Roosevelt's action came to a head several years later in a squalid row that shook his administration.

III

Now and again in the months before Pearl Harbor, Marriner's views about particular matters did prevail with Roosevelt, as in the issue over consumer credit when Marriner was supported by Leon Henderson, head of the Office of Price Administration. At the end of July 1941, two months after Roosevelt had declared a national emergency, Marriner and Henderson jointly emphasized to FDR the imperative need to institute controls over installment credit used to finance purchases by consumers of durable goods which absorbed resources needed for national defense. Aside from facilitating the transfer of productive resources to defense industries, the object of the control would be to create a backlog for consumer durable goods in the postdefense period, and to restrain the development of a consumer debt structure that would repress effective demand for goods and services in that postdefense period.

It was appropriate that such credit be controlled through the Federal Reserve Board, since it was the government agency with primary responsibility for determining and administering national credit policies—and particularly, as they involved the transfer of credit between the payments by or to banking institutions. Consumer contracts made in violation of any regulations prescribed by the board would be worthless as a basis for an extension of bank credit to sellers of durable goods. Roosevelt agreed, and on August

1 he signed an executive order for the regulation of consumer credit which Marriner had prepared. "This is done," said the president in a note to Marriner, "with the understanding we reached in our conversation that you would consult with Henry Morgenthau before taking any action under the Order which might affect the fiscal activities of the Treasury."

The executive order coincided with the publication of a lead article Marriner wrote, entitled "Price Fixing Is Not Enough," for the August 1941 issue of *Fortune* magazine. A full-dress statement of the "integrated policies" he thought should govern the financial aspects of the defense effort, it can be read as a matching piece to his testimony before the Senate Finance Committee in February 1933 on the causes for the depression and the means for recovery. Second, it is a witness to the fact that Marriner was consistent in his views about how a compensatory economy should function—not only to overcome depression and deflation, but to cope with the dangers of overexpansion and inflation. It foreshadows one of the main battles in which he would be engaged throughout the war years, and in the decades thereafter.

Marriner observed that, for a decade "we have been striving to stimulate consumer demand and purchasing power sufficiently to match our productive capacity." If the nation nonetheless remained in a state of semidepression throughout the decade, it was because "we were not willing to have the government supplement private expenditures with a sufficient amount of activity and expenditures to employ our idle manpower and resources." Prophecies of inflation were heard throughout the decade, but inflation did not materialize "because we were never able to take up our industrial slack." All this, however, was now drastically changed because of huge defense expenditures and their consequences—a rapid movement toward the full use of the nation's physical plant, though not yet of the total available manpower. On the same ground, public monetary, credit and fiscal policies must also undergo a fundamental change. Savings must henceforth be encouraged, not discouraged. Consumer spending must be curbed whenever it threatened to encroach on defense needs or to distort prices. Instead of stimulating consumption by deficit financing, the new need was to reduce the deficit as far as possible, and to approach a balanced budget as the country reached a condition of full utilization of its productive capacity. Instead of a tax structure designed to encourage consumption, the new structure should "recapture for the government a large part of the outlays for defense." Interest-rate policy should be directed toward encouraging savings and investment in government securities for the financing of defense—not to stimulate private credit expansion.

It is perfectly apparent that in that sector of the economy where the government is a huge purchaser—the portion that might be called the military sector—we must have immediate and *direct* controls. Priorities, rationing and specific price fixing are going to be the order of the day here. In the case of aluminum and machine tools, for instance, allocation is made not by a bidding up of prices to determine what buyer shall receive what, but by government edict. You may offer right now any price you want for a machine tool but it will not help your chances of getting it. It would be silly to leave distribution of any vital war material to the mercies of "the market."

But what of the more general problem of inflation? What of the bidding up in prices of consumer goods when the public receives increased purchasing power and comes up against a diminishing or static supply? Marriner recognized the need in some cases for direct "rifle" rather than "shotgun" controls. Yet, said he, "when you fix a price, you are just at the beginning of our troubles. You have taken away from the market its normal functions of distribution and there will be more buyers at the fixed price than goods to go around." To avoid a resort to totalitarian methods until they are absolutely necessary, "we should apply to the civilian sector of the economy the traditional *functional* methods of price control"—namely, the curbing of consumer demand through taxation and other means. This did not mean taxing all people equally. Taxation should begin with the more fortunate groups who can get along with fewer automobiles and other goods needed for defense but not essential for civilian well-being, rather than starting at the bottom and working up. Marriner explained:

The tax system should be designed to recapture for the government a large part of the defense expenditures and, so far as possible, to reduce consumer demand for goods where the supply is inadequate. . . . During the emergency we shall have to rely heavily upon the excess-profits tax and the tax on corporate incomes. This is true because, generally speaking, business units are the greatest beneficiaries, directly and indirectly, from defense expenditures.

Still, while taxation was the most important weapon for combating inflationary price rises by drawing off purchasing power, there was also the need to dampen buying power by drawing off funds into government savings bonds and other U.S. securities.

The sale of government securities to the public rather than commercial banks, will have the same effect on buying power as taxation in absorbing funds that otherwise might go to the market place. Furthermore, purchases of such securities have the advantage of storing up buying power—in effect of deferring demand—until such time as our productive machinery can revert from defense to civilian production. The transition to a more normal peacetime basis can be more readily effected without a postdefense slump if such a storehouse of buying power is created during this period. . . . It is important that the volume of funds obtained through taxation and borrowing from the public be sufficient to cover all of the government's outlays during the defense period without resort to borrowing from commercial banks. For the sale of government securities to the banking system creates new deposits, that is, new money, and the volume of deposits has already reached formidable proportions. Demand deposits and currency outstanding now aggregate about $45.5 billion as compared to about $18.5 billion in 1918 during our participation in World War I, or about 40 percent as much as we have today. And it should be recalled that the World War I price level was far higher than it is at present, thus requiring much more money to do the same volume of business. The volume of funds already created is more than ample for all present and prospective requirements. It is not necessary or desirable to add new deposits by selling government securities to the commercial banks.

After setting forth the measures which would serve as the basis for a broad, integrated fiscal and credit policy, Marriner asked, How much further must we go in the way of direct controls? "As is so often true in matters of public policy, the whole of the case turned on trade-offs among alternatives." Drastic, unpalatable as high taxes and other functional mechanisms may be, they were infinitely preferable to the virtual dictatorship of prices, the enforced savings, the ration cards, complicated priorities, and all the other compulsions and interferences necessitated by more direct measures. These were going to be difficult to administer in the military sector of the economy where they were essential to rearmament, without extending them to all consumer goods. In any event, every effort must be made to prevent inflationary price developments, which had caused economic havoc in every war and are potentially as destructive as war itself. Marriner concluded:

When we talk of saving our system, we mean to save a going concern. We propose to save it not only from the threat of foreign domination but also from the danger of internal disintegration through shortsighted policies and half-hearted protective measures. If we will do whatever is needful, even though we may have to abandon for the time being some of our cherished economic freedom, we shall bequeath to posterity a country that is strong and sound, an economic system that has vindicated itself.

But a weak fiscal policy, plus laggard buying of government securities by nonbank investors and Treasury policies that induced excess buying by banks of government securities, produced a situation in which direct controls were rushed to the fore to save an economy torn by too much money and too few goods. It is true that the American performance was better in the Second World War than in the First, but only because of the rationing system and direct control that were used to curb serious inflation. It took the precipitate removal of rationing and price controls at the end of the war to reveal the deep layers of economic instability that wrong policies in the realm of war finance helped produce.

28. Double Vision

EARLY IN 1942, MARRINER ECCLES and the United States chiefs of staff squared off for a brief clash known to insiders as "the Second Battle of the Alamo." No headlines were made, and the cause for the clash was not dramatic. The event, however, was emblematic of a recurrent problem Marriner faced during the war years but never solved. Was it possible to get policy makers to bring a double vision to bear on issues of wartime finance—to see both the pragmatics of immediate needs and the long-range effects of the choice they made among alternative lines of action?

The genesis of "the Second Battle of the Alamo" dated from December 1941, when Prime Minister Churchill and the British chiefs of staff reached Washington for the ARCADIA conference with President Roosevelt and the American chiefs of staff. Some discussions were to be held in the White House, but another place had to be found where the combined British and American chiefs could proceed on their own to formulate a joint strategy, now that the United States was at war not only with Japan but with Germany and Italy as well. It occurred to Roosevelt that their workshop could be the great boardroom and its adjacent offices in the Federal Reserve Building.

American chiefs of staff had long been familiar with the insides of the Treasury Building and with the offices of the Bureau of the Budget. These were the places where they talked about money for the armed forces. But, prior to ARCADIA, it is doubtful if they were familar with more than the external facade of the Federal Reserve Building—though eminent foreign visitors to Washington often examined the whole of the edifice closely. For example, R. F. Harrod, the noted English economist and biographer of John Maynard Keynes, saw it as a "structure of beauty and dignity, albeit on a modest scale, perhaps the most successful of the splended piles" lining Constitutional Avenue. To Harrod, "every detail was perfect." He was especially struck by the great boardroom, "where the furnishings were luxurious but restrained" while round the walls of the room, "charts showed forth the current economic picture of the United States in frames designed by the architect as part of the structure."[5]

It was in this boardroom that the American chiefs gave to their British counterparts a sheet of paper whose two sentences fixed the basic strategy of the war: "Notwithstanding the entry of Japan into the war, the American view remains that Germany is the prime enemy and her defeat is the key to victory. Once Germany is defeated, the collapse of Italy and the defeat of

Japan must follow."[6] By the end of the ARCADIA conference—twelve meetings in all were held in the boardroom—the American chiefs reached another conclusion. All aspects of the Federal Reserve Building were very much to their taste. They wished to commandeer the place for "the duration." What about the Federal Reserve Board and its personnel? No problem. To the military, the seemingly placid detachment from events which permeated the air in the glistening marble corridors of the Reserve Building "obviously" meant that the Reserve Board was not directly engaged in important war work, or that whatever work it did could just as well be done somewhere else. The seed of this idea quietly germinated for some weeks after ARCADIA, then bloomed in a plan which the American chiefs endorsed. To facilitate a military takeover of the entire Reserve Building, the Reserve Board, its staff, files, charts, and paper clips should be packed up and resettled somewhere in Maryland.

When Marriner got wind of the plan, he promptly let the military know what he thought of it. It made no sense. He also brought the matter to Roosevelt's attention before the chiefs of staff got to him with a plea of "absolute necessity." When he met with the president, his remarks about the chiefs of staff reminded FDR anew of the rising strains between the Federal Reserve Board and the Treasury Department.

The military bid to commandeer the Reserve Building, said Marriner, could only be ascribed to their ignorance of how the Federal Reserve Board worked in ordinary times, and how its operations now had special wartime features—support for war loan drives, support for the government bond market, regulation of installment consumer credit, Federal Reserve Bank insurance of commercial banks against losses when they made war production V-loans to qualified private enterprises. Marriner agreed that the daily decisions the board made about such matters lacked drama and seemed far removed from battlefield clashes. Yet its decisions noiselessly triggered other decisions in the national economy which led directly to the full inventory of concrete things the chiefs of staff needed for the war effort. Would the items on the inventory be more readily available to the chiefs of staff if the Reserve Board and its technical staff were evicted from their regular home and resettled in Maryland?

The eviction would not only physically disrupt the communication lines between the board and the nation's infinitely complex financial machinery but, more immediately, would further complicate the board's relationship with the Treasury Department. As the president knew, the fiscal policy the board favored to finance the war called for higher taxes and less borrowing. The board had nonetheless entered into an agreement with the Treasury to help it borrow rising sums of money at low interest rates set by the Treasury. To this end, it stood ready to support government securities at fixed prices and bought them if they tended to fall below the pattern set.

It was the conviction of the board that the Treasury had pegged too low the short-term interest rate on government securities, and that the result added to existing inflationary pressures. The Treasury, however, was unrelenting in its insistence that the Federal Reserve should toe the mark that had been set. It sent the board a weekly chart showing the agreed-upon pattern of rates and those which actually prevailed in the market. More than that, even on an hour-by-hour basis, when trading in the government security market was a little weak and interest rates rose close to the pegged pattern, Treasury officials would call Federal Reserve Board members into an emergency meeting to remind them of their commitment and to find out what had gone wrong. These "emergency" calls were onerous, but meetings in response to them could be quickly arranged because Federal Reserve and Treasury personnel worked in buildings that were relatively close to each other. Broken connections, delays, and a possible nervous breakdown in the Treasury would be inevitable if the Federal Reserve Board and its staff were packed off to Maryland.

Then there were important psychological factors to be considered. If the Federal Reserve Board was uprooted from its regular home, the event in effect would say that the administration viewed the Federal Reserve System as an inconsequential institution of wartime government. Did the president want that impression to spread across the nation?

As things stood, said Marriner, the imperatives of war had already curbed the legal independence of the Federal Reserve, and had made it a junior partner subordinate to the Treasury. The board's advice carried no more weight with the Treasury than the advice of commercial bankers, insurance company executives, and bond dealers. Its suggestions were often left unanswered for weeks, and then were usually rejected without serious explanation. If the nation gained the impression that the Reserve Board was of no significance—that it would henceforth be denied even its limited power on other fronts to resist inflationary pressures—what confidence would Americans in the mass have in the long-range value of the dollars they were being urged to invest in war bonds? It was one thing, said Marriner, to provide various allied military missions with quarters in some of the rooms of the Federal Reserve Building. This could be done without needless complications. But it was quite another thing to evict the Board from its own home so that the military could take over the whole of the place.

The argument gained its object. President Roosevelt ruled that the Federal Reserve Board should stay put in the Federal Reserve Building. Marriner thus emerged the victor in his brief clash with the chiefs of staff. He did not emerge the victor in the larger running battle, in which the pattern of war finance was the decisive issue and the Treasury his principal adversary. Nor was he victor in a related battle, in which he tried to secure in advance the institutional means to deal with the postwar inflation he saw coming. His immediate adversary here was Roosevelt's escape and evasion tactics.

29. Disorder

I

THE WINTER AND SPRING OF DISASTER on the fighting front following Pearl Harbor had its counterpart in the chaos on the domestic front. Nineteen forty-two was a congressional election year, and while that was not a consideration which ranked high on the priorities list in the White House, it was a matter of life or death on Capitol Hill. Senators and representatives who faced hard fights for reelection knew that they must keep their records clean insofar as the war was concerned by voting loyally for all the vast appropriations that were required, and they did so; but they balked over controversial political issues embodied in measures which entailed interference with the civilian economy.

Various parts of the economic community—businessmen, laborers and farmers—felt the heady wine of "prosperity" for the first time in thirteen years. Each of these was prepared to have prohibitive rules clamped down on another group, but not on itself. Roosevelt, meanwhile, could not be brought around to focus sharply on the question of controls on the civilian economy. He welcomed the reassurance of those who said that everything could be settled on a purely voluntary basis. As a result, a spector of inflation—held at bay until 1941 because productive facilities had not previously absorbed all of the slack of the depression years—was plainly beginning to stalk the land. This was something that Roosevelt could clearly recognize with his keen memories of the First World War and its distressing aftermath.[7]

Many people in Washington pressured Roosevelt for action. Yet there is reason to believe that it was a series of conferences held between Marriner, Budget Director Harold D. Smith and Leon Henderson that brought matters to a head. With Smith acting as the gadfly, on March 7, 1942, Roosevelt was at last induced to order staff work on the problem of inflation. He directed Vice-president Henry Wallace, Morgenthau, Henderson, Secretary of Agriculture Claude Wickard and Marriner to draft an integrated anti-inflation program. Morgenthau knew the cast of thought likely to govern the committee's work, and held aloof from the joint effort. Other members, however, met episodically during the month, and the program they drafted with the technical help of professors Alvin V. Hansen and Gerard Colm was reported to the president on April 18. Morgenthau's name was not on the report. He opposed the lowering of income-tax exemptions and a wage freeze, both of which were essential to any inflationary-control program. The remainder of the committee informed the president that, after examining the possibilities of a partial program to check inflation under an all-out war effort, they had reached the conclusion "that partial programs will not work and that only a simultaneous attack on prices, rents, wages, profits, and mass purchasing power will suffice. Every element is essential to the effectiveness of every other element. Any lesser program must fail."

The committee made specific recommendations with respect to all of those elements but its main emphasis was on the control of mass purchasing power. "Price and wage stabilization were doomed to fail unless the explosive pressure of excess purchasing power was reduced through appropriate tax and savings measures." In the committee's view, the Treasury's voluntary-savings plan was hopelessly inadequate. Less than 10 percent of all savings bonds had been bought by individuals in the lower-income bracket. Over 90 percent of the bonds sold merely represented the normal savings of middle- and higher-income groups. Thus a voluntary savings program would not sufficiently curtail the consumption of the lower-income groups. To do the job, the committee strongly recommended the adoption of some type of compulsory universal savings, and also suggested that the Congress be asked to reduce exemptions under the individual income tax. The proposed reduction, based on the then cost of living, would not add a great burden on the person who was brought under the income tax for the first time.

When the committee's proposals were formulated, but before they were sent to FDR on April 18, Marriner left Washington to attend to his private affairs in Utah. While he was there, he learned that Roosevelt meant to send to Congress the full package of what the committee recommended. A few days later, however, he heard that FDR was having second thoughts. Marriner didn't know if the wavering was due to Morgenthau's influence or if the latter merely reflected the president's own views. Morgenthau was ready to see controls clamped on every other kind of price, but balked at clamping a ceiling on wages. "Labor," he said, "is not a commodity." Viewed in humanistic terms, he was absolutely right. But in economic terms? His stand ignored the fact that wages and salaries came to more than two-thirds the overall costs of production. Hence any program to control a price inflation was bound to fail if it left uncontrolled the cost or price of labor.

When Marriner heard that Roosevelt was wavering, he telegraphed him from Utah on April 25 to say:

After ten days spent in this rapidly growing defense area talking to numerous people, I am more than ever convinced that the public desire and are prepared for a drastic anti-inflationary program of enforced savings, withholding income taxes, ceilings on wages and salaries, lower income exemptions, and higher income and excess-profit taxes, as well as freezing all prices and rents. The standard of living must be greatly reduced through curtailing mass purchasing power by the methods indicated if war production is to succeed without bringing on inflation.

Pleas of a similar nature doubtless reached the president from many other sources, and, as a result, Roosevelt seemed to move off dead center. In a message to the Congress on April 27, he directed attention to the imminence of inflation and called for action in seven areas. Those he enumerated—taxes, prices, wages, credit and installment buying, bond purchases by private persons, price stability for farm products—were drawn from the committee document. Before each of the seven points, he used the words: "To keep the cost of living from spiralling upwards, we must . . . " Yet, despite the repetitive use of the phrase, Roosevelt did not really face up to the terms for an integrated anti-inflationary program. His generalizations lacked substantive grip. In essence, he called on the Congress to build a strong basement for prices, but did not specify how the roof was to be built. Congressmen fearful of their constituents' wrath in the November election were able to evade the issue of controlling inflation until Roosevelt presented it to them in precise and unmistakable terms four months after his April 25 message.

II

For its bearing on the future, it is worthwhile to interject here a word about Marriner's relationship with the young disciples of John Maynard Keynes in wartime Washington. It was not Marriner's practice to read monographs on economics written by university professors "in the chair," and he had not read Keynes' *General Theory* when it was published in 1936. To judge from his records, the extent of his knowledge about what the book contained—along with its flaws—was confined to a ten-page analysis of the text which Lauchlin Currie had prepared for members of the Federal Reserve Board. One might have supposed that Keynes himself, who valued greatly his "influence on American thought and policy," would have taken the initiative at an early date in establishing some sort of direct contact, at least by letter (after his disabling heart attack) with a strategically placed figure such as Marriner Eccles. Yet there was no letter and no face-to-face meeting between the two men until the summer of 1943, when Keynes was on his first wartime mission to Washington, empowered to discuss matters of concern to the British treasury. His main business was with Secretary Morgenthau, Harry Dexter White, who headed the international division within the Treasury, and E. M. Bernstein, White's gifted aide. However, Keynes had long been associated with E. A. Goldenweiser, the chief economist for the Federal Reserve Board, in efforts to rescue and to find teaching posts for academicians who were refugees from Fascism and Nazism. It was through Goldenweiser that Marriner was introduced to Keynes, for what initially amounted to no more than a brief exchange of small talk.

If the introductory meeting with Keynes himself was quickly over, Marriner had plenty of Keynesian intellectual company, first among the corporal's guard of academically trained disciples who arrived in Washington at the end of the 1930s, followed by the battalions who arrived after Pearl Harbor to work in wartime agencies. All knew how to manage a compensatory economy appropriate to the restrictive accents of "secular stagnation" in the depression years, to cope with underconsumption, and to achieve full employment. Yet these matters, which had engrossed the thoughts of the young Keynesians when they were graduate students and economic instructors, were not the components of the wartime economic problem. By 1939, the conceptual battle with respect to their peacetime concerns had been fought and won in Washington *without* their help or the help of their senior professors. After that, the defense program had ended "secular stagnation" and had brought about full employment.

The first of the new problems to be faced—and the point here must be repeated again—was the one Marriner had been foremost in spelling out in detail. It was the need to shift from the reflationary accents of a compensatory economy appropriate to the depression years, to the restrictive accents appropriate to the defense and war years: to control inflation by inducing saving instead of spending, and by tax increases where the government would recapture the highest proportion of the new income generated by its own defense expenditures. Some of the young Keynesians such as Walter S. Salant and Gerard Colm were quick to recognize the imperatives of the new realities to be faced. Others were slower in doing so, perhaps because they continued to see things from the perspective of depression experiences, when doing too much hardly seemed possible and when the questions of how much to do and what *instruments* to use were not critical.[8] Most of the young economists eventually came to share Marriner's stress on fiscal restraints, but they did not as yet occupy governmental posts where they could take their case to the Congress over the head of a resisting Treasury Department. That was Marriner's role.

There were more pronounced differences over the nature of the economic challenges facing the nation in the immediate postwar years. Would the challenge be on the side of inflation or on the side of depression? Some of the most talented young Keynesians, Paul Samuelson[9] and Robert Nathan among them, predicted that the immediate postwar years would be marked by a cataclysmic return to depression-time conditions of massive unemployment. Marriner Eccles, at an early hour, saw the future in a different light. He recognized that particular businesses would face acute problems in making the transition from wartime to peacetime production, and would need special help if they were to stay alive. But every time he glanced at Federal Reserve charts on "liquid assets" in the nation, their upward moving curves persuaded him anew that the immediate postwar years would be marked by a "classical" inflation where "too much money chased too few goods."

Another problem to be faced was also future-oriented. How was one to moderate fluctuations in the postwar economy in order to prevent them from developing into upward and downward spirals? In their approach to this issue, the young economists saw the need to refine their "received" Keynesianism in points of detail and nuance. Marriner Eccles agreed. But his own responsibilities as chairman of the Federal Reserve Board brought home to him the strict limits on the ability of the board to manage the nation's monetary and credit policies in ways that could moderate postwar economic fluctuations—because of the nation's dual banking system. The situation, as he saw it, did not call for theoretical studies to be completed in an indeterminate future. It called for the institutional remedy of bank unification he had urged since 1934. He wanted that remedy adopted *during* the war so that it would be available for use in dealing with the inflationary pressures that would be released with the coming of peace. Whether or not the young Keynesians privately agreed with the importance he placed on the institutional remedy of bank unification, it is hard to find evidence that they overtly supported him. In this matter, as in many others, Marriner appears to have stood virtually alone, and no doubt was considered as a "crank" or "monomaniac" in doing so.

One more detail. In June 1942, the name of John Maynard Keynes appeared in the Birthday Honors List with the award of a peerage. He was to be Lord Keynes of Triton. When Marriner Eccles in Washington read this piece of news out of London, he wrote a letter on June 11, 1942, marked "Personal and confidential," and addressed to an unlikely recipient—his old adversary, Senator Harry F. Byrd. It was an extraordinary letter, combining an elegiac mood with foresight and a rapier thrust:

Such vast events have washed over our little debate about debts and deficit spending—how puny they seem now—that what we have said then will deserve the obscurity which I have no doubt it will achieve. Then, too, it has been my good fortune since then to get to know you, not as well as I would like, but well enough to have a personal regard for you that our very different views on public fiscal policy cannot obscure.

So it is in no mean spirit that I want to make sure you do not overlook the fact that John Meynard Keynes was the sole peer on the King's annual list of birthday honors, being elevated from a commoner to a Baron, a recognition of his many years of service to the Crown, including the very great contribution he has made to the intelligent and orderly financing of the British war effort as a chief adviser to the British Treasury and, incidentally, as a director of the Bank of England to whose Court he was elected some time ago. However much you belabor me for my views, I feel that Keynes deserves to be exempted.

On reading of this latest honor bestowed upon him, I could not but recall your letter of January 14, 1939, in the course of which you leveled some telling blows at the idea that underspending and oversaving were the chief cause of the last depression, and added, "That is also the doctrine and dogma of that erratic English economist, Dr. J. M. Keynes, who, though a prophet without honor in his own country, seems to have sold his seductive schemes of spending and borrowing to those vested with power and responsibility in this country. England rejected his fantastic fallacies of spending, borrowing and lending. . . ."

Until comparatively recently, I had never met Keynes, nor had I ever, so far as I can recall, read or studied any of his works. We came out at about the same place in economic thought and policy by very different roads, and we have had the common experience of being highly unpopular in orthodox circles.

When the war is over the debate no doubt will be resumed as to whether we can afford full production and full employment in peace as we do in war—whether we can manage it, as I believe we can, without continued deficits and growth of the public debt, though not without heavy taxation and government expenditures. That is the most difficult task the democracies will have to perform. I suppose you and I will be friendly enemies again on opposite sides of that debate, and the temporary and comfortable cloak of orthodoxy which covers me now because I advocate savings in times like these will be snatched off and I shall be revealed in my true and awful colors, allied again with this now honored prophet. I do not expect you to spare me, but you might spare him. Time has a curious habit of justifying this man Keynes.

It was conceivable that "time might also have a curious habit of justifying this man," Marriner Eccles.

III

When Congress continued to evade the issue of inflation, members of the administration debated the question whether Roosevelt should make another attempt to prod the Congress into action or should try to stabilize prices by means of an executive order issued under his emergency presidential powers. It appeared for a while that Roosevelt would take the route of an executive order, but the final decision was a compromise. He sent Congress a demand for action by October 1, 1942, and coupled it with a clear warning that if Congress did not act, he would. Congress eventually responded with the Stabilization Act, which Roosevelt signed on October 2. Among other things, the act established an Office of Economic Stabilization, and Justice Byrnes stepped down from the Supreme Court to become director of that office. The broad powers granted him to stabilize farm and wage prices represented a major step forward in shaping grappling-hooks with which prices were bound to the earth. But the grant of powers left open a wide area of disagreement on how they should be used, especially in connection with wage stabilization. The bulges and strains in the economy continued to disfigure the national scene.

To assist Byrnes in his work, an advisory committee had been formed consisting of eight members, with two each representing labor, agriculture, business and the general public. In November 1942, Marriner came before this committee to point out weak areas in the wartime economic structure and to urge the adoption of far more drastic measures to curtail civilian spending power than those in force at the time. He noted that, as of November 1942, expendable income had grown to where it exceeded by $40 billion the value of the goods available for sale. In view of American habits of saving and spending, the pressure of the excess purchasing power on hand meant that the nation's cost of living could rise by at least a third.

America's failure to meet the problem of inflation could be gauged through force of contrast with British and Canadian wartime experiences. Whereas Canada financed about half of its expenditures by taxation and half by borrowing, one-quarter of the American financing was by taxation, and three-quarters was by borrowing. Further, whereas two-thirds of the sums borrowed in Britain and Canada came from the general public, and one-third from the inflationary process of borrowing from the banks, the American case was exactly the reverse.

We all recognize [said Marriner] the limitation on what price control and rationing can do by themselves. The strongest administrative machinery would crumble under the pressure of the excessive purchasing power now flowing into the hands of the American public. A hard-boiled fiscal policy is our only hope of reducing the pressure enough to permit rationing to function.

On the fiscal front, Marriner urged the committee to support lines of policy where the ratio of taxation to borrowing, as well as the ratio between nonbank and bank borrowing, should be on the order of the British and Canadian case. While decreasing purchasing power in this way, there was the offsetting need to increase the supply of goods. Here, too, much could be learned from the British experience. In Great Britain the average working week was about 54 hours for nonagricultural workers. In the United States it was only 43 hours. The work week should thus be increased to 48 hours. "Organized labor," Marriner said to the committee, "won the 40 hour week after many years of painful effort and struggle. It should be made unmistakably clear that the government does not propose to abolish but merely to suspend the legislation guaranteeing this achievement."

Marriner also argued that advertising should be cut down in order to release resources for essential use. "When it was the government's desire to curb civilian demand," said he, "it was contradictory for advertising of all kinds to continue to whet the public's appetite to buy. The government not only permitted this to go on, it actually encouraged the misuse of resources because advertising was virtually paid for out of the public treasury—since tax laws allowed generous deductions for advertising expenses."

When Marriner had finished his statement, Byrnes commended it as being "courageous and interesting." He then went around the table and called on each of the eight board members to criticize or to associate himself with it. Not a person present spoke up for the program. Marriner admitted that it was strong medicine to swallow. That, however, did not mean he should keep silent. He publicly repeated his arguments before the Senate Banking and Currency Committee on February 17, 1943, stating bluntly that the government "was doing a very bad" job of war finance compared with Great Britain and Canada. If inflation was to be controlled, higher taxes and less borrowing from the banks were the indicated means. He repeated the argument in a nationwide broadcast on April 14, when the Treasury's second war-loan drive was underway to raise $13 billion through the sale of war bonds.

The question [said Marriner] is not whether the goal of this campaign shall be reached, but how it is reached. The government can always raise the money it needs. What is of vital importance to every man, woman, and child in this country is that the money needed to wage this war is raised in a way that will not result in a disastrous rise in the cost of living. This means it must be financed out of savings and not by additional bank money.

The heavy oversubscription of the second war loan was viewed by many people as decisive proof that there was no further need for stiffer taxes. Marriner fastened on the fact that the Treasury offering was absorbed ultimately by banks, not individuals, with inflationary consequences. He also noted that the second war loan drained off only a fraction of the $55 billion purchasing power on hand in excess of available consumer goods. Later, as a witness before the House Banking and Currency Committee on May 13, 1943, he argued for the separation of individual and bank borrowing when the special drives for bond sales were mounted. The effort, he said, should be centered on getting individuals to buy. If this were done, then an estimated $15 to $20 billion more bonds might be purchased by individuals in the new loan drives. Even so, since this would still leave around $25 billion in excess purchasing, more taxes and still more taxes were the only solution to the curbing of inflation. In flatly denying that the success of the Treasury bond drive in any way reduced the need for a comprehensive tax program, Marriner compounded the preexisting strains between himself and Morgenthau. In a time of retrospect he wrote:

I regret to say that each of us who served in Washington during 1940–45 fought a civil war within an international war. Apart from encounters with other agencies of government and congressional committees, my principal disagreements—as during the preceding New Deal years—were with Treasury Secretary Henry Morgenthau. It is important to add at once that Morgenthau's great role in aiding our allies in the period before Lend-Lease was enacted has been too little noticed. At a time when most liberals had yet to disentangle themselves from a sentimental isolationism or pacifism, the Treasury Department, under pressure from Henry Morgenthau, used every lawful avenue to get England and France the supplies they urgently needed. For this, Morgenthau deserves many monuments of gratitude.

Morgenthau and I both wanted to secure for the American military and for our allies all the resources and manpower that were needed to win the war as quickly as possible, and to secure also the means to pay for the costs of victory. Yet we disagreed profoundly and regularly on the methods by which these objectives should be reached. Unfortunately, as our tempers were rubbed raw by abrasive events, the nature of our disagreements was often distorted so that they appeared to be disagreements over objectives. And this, in turn, in the tense and nervous war atmosphere, invited charges and countercharges, suspicions and quarrels which I, and, I am certain, Morgenthau, later regretted.[10]

Still, the natures of the institutions the two men headed make it doubtful whether clashes could have been avoided, regardless of who was Secretary of the Treasury or who was chairman of the Board of Governors. In the shadows that conceal the precise boundaries of the Treasury Department and Federal Reserve, split-fence cases are bound to arise.

30. *Time Bomb in a Technical Point*

ON THE BATTLEFIELDS OF WARTIME WASHINGTON, a dry "technical point"—the interest rates set for government securities issued to finance the war—was the main cause for a running conflict between the Treasury and the Federal Reserve. The public at large either was not aware of the conflict, did not understand the issue in dispute, or dismissed it as just "another one of those bureaucratic squabbles." But when the passing years revealed what the days hid, the "technical point" turned out to be as dry as gunpowder, and its explosion compounded the inflation that hit the economy in the postwar years.

The Reserve System, in wartime, recognized the imperative need actively to support the government's security market. In the absence of that support, the Treasury would face an impossible task in managing the heavy deficit financing and huge refunding operations required by the war effort. It could not tell from day to day the terms on which it could sell or refund securities, and would be entirely at the mercy of uncontrolled and demoralizing market forces. All this was understood. It was beyond dispute that the Federal Reserve must insure a stable market for the government securities the Treasury issued. The Reserve System argued that the interest rates on two pivotal securities—ninety-day bills and one-year certificates—and on long-term marketable bonds were set too low. The rates should be designed to induce banks and other investors not only to *buy* ninety-day bills and one-year certificates but to *retain* them. If investors did not retain what they bought, what they sloughed off would have to be bought by the Open Market Committee of the Reserve System. The effect would add to the excess reserves in the banking system, and, inexorably, to add still more force to existing inflationary pressures.

The Treasury was unmoved by this argument. It stood pat on its institutional interest in managing the government debt at the lowest possible rate. Nor did it alter its stand even if the early warnings of what would happen in connection with the ninety-day bills in particular materialized with a vengeance. The Reserve System eventually came to hold practically all bills outstanding, though their volume rose from $1.3 billion in 1941 to $17 billion in 1945—a fifteenfold increase. The bills ceased to be a market instrument that could be controlled, but automatically created excessively easy money conditions—not with the consent of the Federal Reserve but by the Treasury fiat.

Meanwhile, banks and large nonbank investors were fully aware of the

Treasury's program, which required the Federal Reserve to support government securities at a fixed pattern of rates; and they proceeded to exploit the situation to their own advantage. The mechanical details of the matter need not delay us here. It is enough to say that they played the "pattern of rates" in a game of "free riding" which earned them fabulous profits at no risk to themselves.

As part of that game, the banks in particular circumvented the object of a rule governing the various victory-loan drives. The object was to restrict the amount of bonds that banks could buy directly—since bank purchases would add to their excess reserves—and to maximize purchases by nonbank investors. To get around the rule without openly breaking it, the banks loaned billions of dollars to their customers to buy new securities, and especially bonds. They then turned around and bought back six times as many securities from nonbank investors as the banking system sold to the Federal Reserve. This created a like amount of deposits in the banks, led to a multiple expansion of money and credit and, from there, to still more inflationary pressures.

The patriotic zeal Treasury officials showed in their immensely complicated task of wartime financing was never at issue. Starting with Morgenthau personally, the zeal was all-consuming, tireless, selfless, a model of honesty down to the last penny. Moreover, each of the eight war-loan drives was a smashing success—in the sense that each attained the sales goal in view. What was at issue was the realities of wartime finance which lay behind the picture of personal dedication among Treasury officials and the dollar goals they reached. The realities were found in an analysis Marriner made of the changes that occurred among the holders of securities sold in all eight war-loan drives to different groups of investors.

His analysis revealed the following. While all nonbank investors during the loan drives bought a total of $147 billion of government securities, the actual increase in their holdings was only $93 billion—representing savings bonds, savings notes, and other securities bought during or between drives. The commercial banks, on the other hand, which were permitted to subscribe for only $10 billion during the first two war-loan drives, increased their holdings by $57 billion in the period, while the holdings of the Federal Reserve banks increased by $18 billion. It was clear that various nonbank investors, instead of retaining the securities they had bought during the war-loan campaign, sold a striking proportion of the total back to the banks.

The Federal Reserve proposed a number of remedies to end the speculative and demoralizing effects of "free riding" and to limit the amount of indirect purchases banks could make of government securities issued in connection with the war loan drives. The following three proposed remedies were of prime importance.

First, no bank-eligible securities should be offered during the loan drives. This would have largely, if not entirely, prevented "playing the pattern of rates" and "free riding," since the market for resale of securities at premiums would have been much more limited.

Second, from the standpoint of the public interest, the advantage of such an issue was that it could not be shifted. The disadvantage from the standpoint of those who wanted large sales during drives was the claim that these issues would be more difficult to sell. Yet the issues that were easy to sell—the marketable securities that could be resold to banks—were precisely those that defeated the main purpose of the war-loan drives.

Third, the Federal Reserve recognized that banks would have to buy some additional securities. It therefore proposed that bank-eligible securities should be offered to banks between war-loan drives, with the subscriptions limited to the amounts the Treasury actually needed.

None of these three proposals was adopted. But suppose they had been? Would the Treasury have been able to raise all the money needed to finance the war by borrowing? Would the proposals at the same time have effectively reduced bank purchases of securities? These questions continue to be debated by students of public finance. Some contend that if more restrictions had been placed on purchases, the effect would have reduced the sales of securities to nonbank investors, and that the Treasury in the end would have been forced to turn to the banks for the vast sums of money that were needed. Marriner rejected this contention.

During the war [he said] nonbank investors had limited opportunities for the favorable investment of their money except in government securities. Nonmarketable, redeemable issues, if offered, would have provided protection against price fluctuations at a time when there was no definite assurance that marketable issues would be permanently protected against price declines. Those issues, therefore, would have been popular. Besides, it is demoralizing to finance the government by depending upon the opportunity for speculative gain in violation of stated rules. There was no reason whatever to question the Treasury's ability to sell securities in the amounts needed. The insurance on this point lay in the fact that the Reserve System had a tremendous capacity to purchase securities—this, in the event of a failure of even a vigorous effort to sell securities to nonbank investors on terms which would discourage resales to the banks.[11]

II

The heat generated by differences of opinion about such judgmental matters spread to other relationships between the managers of the Federal Reserve System and Secretary Morgenthau. One of the more unhappy personal clashes among them occurred on May 14, 1943, over a seemingly impersonal question, namely: how best to manage the sale of war bonds.

The early war savings organization which functioned on a state basis directly under the Treasury raised less than one-fifth of the funds borrowed by the government. To raise the remaining four-fifths, a Victory Fund Committee was formed in the spring of 1942, based on Federal Reserve districts. Reserve bank presidents served in their respective districts by appointment of the Secretary of the Treasury, and Marriner was the liaison officer between them and Morgenthau personally. Later, in December 1942 and April 1943, the state and Federal Reserve sales organizations were temporarily merged on a Federal Reserve district basis under the War Finance Committee. To set the terms for a permanent organization, Morgenthau invited the presidents of the Reserve banks and Marriner to meet with him at the Treasury on Friday morning, May 14, 1943. On May 3, Roosevelt put a question to Marriner in a delicately phrased note. Could he make available for a two-week period, starting May 8, the part of the Federal Reserve Building containing the Board of Governors' room, an adjacent conference room, and four nearby offices? "The purpose," said the president, "is so secret that I cannot mention it yet. However, I assure you it has a most important bearing on the war effort." If the answer was yes, then a designated officer would contact him "in order to work out the necessary details." The answer was yes.

The facilities were needed for the Anglo-American TRIDENT conference which got underway on May 11, when Winston Churchill and his party of one hundred reached Washington. In the next two weeks, the combined chiefs of staff met daily in the Federal Reserve Building, and the core agreement they reached was ratified by Roosevelt and Churchill. The main strength of the allies would be committed to the opening of a "second front" in Western Europe, starting with a landing in Normandy on or about May 1, 1944.

Marriner stood outside the circle of men who knew the details of the secret decisions being reached during the TRIDENT conference. But he assumed that a sharp expansion of the war was being planned, and that this in turn would impose new demands on the financial management of the war effort. Against this background, on May 13, a day before the Reserve Bank presidents were to meet with Morgenthau, Marriner was a witness before the House Banking and Currency Committee. At one point in his testimony, he hurled a harpoon at the Treasury Department, which was congratulating itself at the time because its recently concluded bond drive offering of $13 billion was heavily oversubscribed. Marriner noted that far too large a portion of the offering had been bought by banks instead of nonbank investors. To Morgenthau, who had strained every nerve to make the bond drive a success, Marriner's criticism—echoed by other major figures in the Reserve System—seemed mean-spirited and belittling. Morgenthau's personal reaction came at an unexpected moment during the May 14 meeting in the Treasury.

At the outset of that meeting, Morgenthau seemed to have his emotions under control. He gave Marriner and the Reserve Bank presidents copies of a proposed Treasury plan for a war-loan organization, saying it was being offered merely for discussion purposes. Some differences of opinion were to be expected, but he thought they could be ironed out. It was presently agreed that the meeting should adjourn so as to give the Reserve Bank presidents a chance to report back that afternoon.

When they were alone, the Reserve Bank presidents and Marriner accepted the Treasury proposal, subject to a few changes related to the choice of personnel. The presidents wanted the right to initiate the appointment of the sales managers and other executive personnel who were to serve under them. This was to be done after consultation with and approval by the Secretary of the Treasury, in contrast to the Treasury version where the personnel in question were to be picked by the Secretary *after* consultation with Reserve Bank presidents. No burning issue was at stake here. It seemed tidier from an administrative standpoint for the presidents to nominate subordinates for whose work they would be responsible.

The changes in Morgenthau's draft plan were presented to the Secretary and his staff when the two groups reconvened in the afternoon. The Secretary now proposed, and it was readily agreed, that matters would be expedited if he retired with his staff to consider the redraft. There was a wait of about fifteen minutes. When Morgenthau rejoined the bank presidents, his first words were a thunderclap. His remarks, as they appear below, are based on notes taken at the meeting by a Reserve Board stenographer and later transmitted to war mobilizer James Byrnes.

Morgenthau began by recalling an event that happened a decade earlier. Soon after becoming Secretary of the Treasury, he said, he had been invited to the home of George L. Harrison, president of the Federal Reserve Bank of New York. There Harrison and Owen D. Young stood over him and said: "You will do what we want you to do, or we will not support your government bond market." The impression this left on him was one he would never forget, and it was followed by many other incidents where the Federal Reserve officials "pointed a gun at his head," to make him do what the System wanted done. However, as long as he was Secretary of the Treasury, he was not going to turn government financing over to the Federal Reserve. And that is what was behind the form of the war savings organization advocated by the Reserve Bank presidents. It was an attempt to take control away from him. He would resign as Secretary of the Treasury if Roosevelt sided with the bank presidents in the matter at issue. All through the bond drives, "Reserve bank presidents had tried to wrest control from the Treasury and take credit for the job, and this was not done from any patriotic motive." He had been "shamed and humiliated by them" on his recent cross-country trip. He continued:

You think I am incompetent to handle my job and that it should be turned over to you. You think I haven't learned anything in the years of experience I have had as Secretary. I worked with Governor Roosevelt for a period of time. I organized the Farm Credit System and did a difficult job in that field. And yet you don't think I know anything. I can do this job. If you want to accept me on my own terms, I would like to have you. But I am not going to bargain with you. I don't have to. You need me, but I don't need you. I am not going to turn this job over to you and have nothing to do but sit back and do what you say. Before that, I would resign.

I am not seeking the favor of any bank or other financial institution, and when I leave the Treasury I am not going to work for a bank as some of you are. I am at peace with the world. There have been no disputes in my Department such as in others. I am on good terms with bankers, the various state organizations, with the Congress, and have willing and patriotic volunteer workers who are anxious to help out. I am not going to put the President in the position in which he has been placed by an ultimatum of John Lewis. I told General Marshall that he could go ahead without any worry about the financial ends; that he would not have to make any decision on purely financial grounds. I can do this job with you on my terms, or without you. I am not going to turn it over to you when I have the responsibility to the President for it. That is the way I feel about it. You can take it or leave it.

After an embarrassed silence, Marriner managed a reply. He was shocked, said he, by Secretary Morgenthau's words, and he could not understand what prompted them. The Reserve System was not trying to usurp the powers of the Treasury. At the Secretary's invitation, the bank presidents had examined his plan. They believed he wanted them to suggest such changes as might strengthen the bond-drive organization, and their amendments were aimed solely at that objective. In fact, there was no great difference between Morgenthau's plan and the proposed revisions.

Several of the Reserve Bank presidents now joined in to protest the grounds for the Secretary's attack on them. They had cooperated with him to the limit of their ability, and his charges were unfounded. Furthermore, since he had no confidence in them, why should he still want them to head his district organizations even on his own terms? Morgenthau presently left the room, and the suppressed fury of the Reserve Bank presidents found free rein.

On that day and for several succeeding days, the bank presidents insisted they would personally cease to participate in the war-financing effort, or would no longer assume the heavy burdens they had thus far carried in order to insure the success of the loan drives. Their sentiments, moreover, were shared by the entire Federal Reserve Board. Tempers were so inflamed that Marriner had reason to fear the Reserve Bank presidents would publicly denounce Morgenthau and then walk out of their jobs. So much internecine fighting of a similar kind had occurred elsewhere in the government that it seemed inhumane to saddle President Roosevelt with an added squabble whose mainsprings were taut nerves, physical weariness, and wounded pride. Still, a blow-up over a minor point of organization could do more damage to public confidence in the government than a disagreement over a high issue of state which warranted an open airing of rival convictions.

In the search for help in heading off more troubles, Marriner turned to James Byrnes, brought him abreast of what had transpired on May 14, showed him a transcript of what Morgenthau had said, and voiced his personal concern over a possible walkout of Reserve Bank presidents unless something was done to heal their breach with Morgenthau. Was the matter of sufficient importance to be brought to Roosevelt's attention? "Yes," said Byrnes, "it was." Marriner saw the president on May 24, when the TRIDENT conference was in its last hours. As usual, that harassed man took the necessary steps to heal the bruises suffered on all sides.

III

In 1941, Marriner's wife, Maisie, had left Washington for Utah, ostensibly to look after her mother, who had suffered a paralytic stroke. She had always been heavily burdened by the sense that she could not "keep up" with her husband—that she could not bridge the distance between the boundaries of her own interests and the summit Marriner had scaled as a public figure of the first rank in the nation's capitol. Two years had passed by since Maisie had returned to Utah, and it was clear that she would try to avoid rejoining her husband in Washington.

At first when Marriner was left on his own in Washington, he either thought the separation was only temporary or was so absorbed in the controversies bearing on the financial aspects of the defense program and then the war effort as to be unmindful of what the absence of his wife implied. Even when he came to sense the danger to the continuity of his marriage, he could justify staying on in Washington as long as he believed he had a fighting chance to duplicate in a wartime context what he had achieved during the New Deal period—to make his own ideas about wartime finance prevail in shaping public policy.

But now, in the early summer of 1943, the security checks on Marriner's movements during TRIDENT, the Anglo-American military leaders moving to and from their secret sessions in the Federal Reserve Building, and the unhappy relations between Federal Reserve and Treasury forced Marriner to confront an irrepressible question. Was need for his presence in Washington so compelling as to warrant risking the further disintegration of his marriage? Even within the realm of his own special responsibilities as head of the Federal Reserve Board, was he really contributing anything significant to the war effort?

He had registered his objections to the hardening pattern of war finance shaped by the Treasury. In marathon talks with Treasury officials, he had argued that the pattern not only intensified immediate inflationary pressures but stockpiled multipliers of inflation that would afflict the nation's postwar economy. Yet nothing he said won these officials over to his view; he appeared to be beating his forehead against a stone wall.

In prewar years, when fundamental policy issues were at stake, Marriner could find "permissible" ways open in which to contest his differences with the Treasury. But the wartime demands for "unity" in the administration put the public airing of differences under a tabu. This was all the more true after a public conflict between Vice-president Wallace and Commerce Secretary Jones forced President Roosevelt on July 15, 1943, to dissolve the Wallace-headed Board of Economic Warfare. On that same day, a sorely vexed president sent to all heads of federal departments and agencies one of the most caustic directives of his administration. After referring to a directive sent them in August of the previous year, Roosevelt went on to say:

Notwithstanding my earlier positive instructions, disagreements between agencies have been publicly aired on several occasions. I realize the nervous strain under which government officials are working in war time, but I cannot overlook any further violations of my instructions. By this letter I do not place any restrictions upon your furnishing statements in response to Congressional inquiries. But if when you have a disagreement with another agency as to fact or policy, instead of submitting it to me or submitting it to the Director of War Mobilization for settlement under the terms of the Order creating that office, you feel you should submit it to the Press, I ask that when you release the statement for publication, you send to me a letter of resignation. If any subordinate of yours violates my instructions in this regard, I shall expect you to ask for his immediate resignation.

When the president and war mobilizer Byrnes lacked enough hours in the day to cope with urgent questions bearing on battlefield developments, how could they find time to focus on recurrent arguments about the adverse *long-range* effects of the Treasury-dominated pattern of war finance? The right to appeal to them in such matters would tend, in practice, to be very self-limiting. And this reality would make the Treasury itself all the more confident that it could press its policies without taking into account contrary views, or even acknowledging the suggestions of the Federal Reserve Board.

That Marriner was not suffering from paranoia on the latter count appears by indirection in the testimony of John Maynard Keynes. "Thus far during the war," he wrote in October 1943, "I have altogether spent five months in close negotiations with the United States Treasury and on no single occasion have they answered any communication of mine in writing, or confirmed in writing anything which has passed in conversation. In this, my experience is not unusual"[12]

With public argument ruled out, and with the Treasury unresponsive to private argument from members of the administration, Marriner's own work by the end of the summer of 1943 had settled into an administrative routine in support of what the Treasury wanted done. Aside from continuing to press for additional taxes and for a compulsory savings program, what else could he do?

Had he outlived his usefulness in Washington? To resign as chairman of the Federal Reserve Board would seem both an act of desertion from a wartime post and a slap at a president to whom he was bound by the strongest ties of loyalty and personal affection. If he was to leave Washington and return to Utah, the right time would be in February 1944, when he would have completed his appointed term as chairman of the board. Until then, however, there was something he could do which went beyond his daily administrative routine: he could begin to think systematically about the economic problems the nation was bound to face when the war was over.

He was, of course, not alone in doing so. When the Pabst Brewing

Company organized an essay contest on the topic of postwar employment, it was inundated by 36,000 entries, including contributions from leading economists. The Legislative Reference Services' annotated bibliography on important books and articles on the same subject written between 1943 and 1945 covers fifty-six closely printed pages. Within the government, postwar planning had been an undercover matter until American armed forces began to win victories in the Pacific, Tunisia, Sicily and Italy. It was then that government postwar planning surfaced for public discussion—as did the existence of the Committee for Economic Development, formed initially with the support of the Department of Commerce.* Before the Congress effectively silenced the National Resources Planning board by denying it further appropriations, the Board produced a 400,000-word report on *Security, Work and Relief Policies.* The report favored redistributive tax policies, continuing programs of public works, broadened social security, and assaults upon monopolies, and a new Bill of Rights.

Marriner kept abreast of all such developments, along with the evolving concepts of what would emerge at the Bretton Woods conference as the International Monetary Fund, and the World Bank. But he appeared to have little company when he focused his own thoughts on an old piece of unfinished business—the need to unify the nation's banking system. That need had grown daily all the more acute, in his view, partly because of the vast wartime growth in the size of the public debt, but mainly because the banks had come to hold the greater part of that debt. If the government were to have a fighting chance after the war to defuse inflationary potentialities, it must provide itself in advance with the instruments of control that went with a unified banking system.

In the hope of reviving a public discussion of this issue, Marriner accepted an invitation to address the annual convention of the National Association of State Bank supervisors held in Cincinnati in September 1943. The topic assigned to him by the association's president took the form of a question. "In the wartime and postwar era, how far, and by what means, is it desirable or possible to preserve the dual banking system?" In his opening remarks, Marriner recognized the "venerable" history of the dual banking issue and the related issues of branch and unit banks, and prophesied that "we, or our successors, will still be debating them far into the postwar period." He then proceeded to connect the need for banking reform with the fundamental duties of government—to foster conditions conducive to a maximum of sustained private production and employment," to provide opportunities for employment in ways "that will stimulate and not impede private enterprise" when "deflationary or inflationary developments endanger economic activity."

---

*Among others, postwar planning projects were undertaken by the Department of Agriculture, the War Production Board, the Public Works Administration, the Maritime Commission, the Defense Plan Corporation, the Bureau of the Budget, the Rural Electrification Administration, the National Housing Agency, the Treasury Department, and the State Department.

Looking to the future [said Marriner] the federal government is destined to play a crucial role in the maintenance of economic stability. It is difficult to see how its basic functional powers can be effectively employed to this end so long as the nation's banking machinery is a hodge-podge of some fifty-two different jurisdictions, laws, and supervisory agencies, so long as approximately half of the banks of the country are subject to uniform central banking policy and half are not, so long as these multiple agencies, state and federal, with their differing philosophies, divided and conflicting policies, dominate the banking picture.

Nowhere did Marriner advocate the outright abolition of the dual banking system. Yet toward the end of his remarks he meant to amuse himself and his audience by citing a "long line of eminent authorities who could hardly be charged with indifferences to states' rights"—a list running from Thomas Jefferson to Senator Carter Glass—who urged that the dual banking system be ended. The bank supervisors found nothing funny in his attempted humor. They broadcast the news through the organs of their association that he personally wanted to demolish the structure of state-chartered banks upon which they depended for their livelihood.

Despite the uproar, Marriner did not intend to drop the subject of bank reform he had raised. But there was a question to be asked. When his prewar attempts to interest President Roosevelt in the matter came to nothing, could he be more successful now? Could he get Roosevelt to see how the intersection between wartime developments and the preexisting mixture of banking jurisdictions would make it all the more difficult for the Federal Reserve to help promote postwar economic stability through monetary and credit policies? Merely to define the problem anew for Roosevelt entailed a struggle with the more immediate and urgent battlefield claims on the president's attention. Marriner seized a chance to raise the subject of bank unification in late 1943, shortly after Roosevelt returned to Washington from his conference in Teheran with Churchill and Stalin. In the period the president set aside to touch base with domestic matters, he asked Marriner to come to the White House for a talk about the affairs of the Federal Reserve Board.

In the course of his review, Marriner observed that a particular picture he had drawn several times in the early phase of the war years was all the more true now. The Board of Governors was underemployed. It was now engaged mainly in the mechanical work of supporting the Treasury's policy, and this fact was uppermost in his mind as he neared the end of his appointed term as chairman of the Federal Reserve Board. He cherished his association with the president over the past decade, but was more than ready to step aside if Roosevelt had someone else in mind for the chairmanship. There was only one thing that would justify his interest in being reappointed to the board when his term expired in 1944. He would stay on if he could count on the president's support in bringing about bank unification.

The pressure of people lined up to see the president cut short any further discussion of the matter, but it was understood that Roosevelt would withold any action on Marriner's reappointment to the Board of Governors until the two men had conferred again. Soon after, however, without any intervening conference, Marriner received a brief note from FDR on January 7, 1944, saying.

The time has come, the walrus said, to speak of many things—among others, that your renomination goes to the Senate for confirmation for another term, whether you like it or not! Enuf said!

Marriner also drew on Lewis Carroll when he framed his reply:

Your thoughtful personal note of January 7 in regard to my appointment leaves me somewhat in the predicament of the snark-hunting banker, endeavoring to say what my tongue can no longer express. But if I may paraphrase the oysters, however, may I say, "But wait a bit, until we have a chat?"

Gratified and honored as I am by your felicitous note, the question inevitably arises in my own mind as to whether I may not have served out my usefulness under the present set-up of the Federal Reserve in relationship to the economic, monetary and credit responsibilities of the Government. I am reluctant to ask for any of your overcrowded time, but I would greatly appreciate having an opportunity to talk with you about this matter.

In a subsequent meeting with Roosevelt, Marriner again stressed his reluctance to accept reappointment to the Federal Reserve Board. He was not insisting, said he, on an immediate overhaul of the nation's rickety banking structure, but, as a first step, he urged an end to the existing division of responsibility for bank supervision between three federal agencies which constantly frustrated the Reserve System's attempts to give coherence to the nation's monetary and credit policies. He would, said Marriner, "happily retire from the governmental scene if his presence as the head of the Federal Reserve Board was the main stumbling block to unification of at least bank supervision at the federal level. The president could achieve that unification by means of an executive order issued under the authority of the First War Powers Act. In all the government's wartime operations, the banking field was conspicuous for being the only area not touched by a use of executive orders authorized by that act. Anyway, said Marriner, the prospect of continuing in the public service was still linked in his mind to the prospects of presidential support for bank unification, starting with the unification of bank supervisory functions performed by federal agencies.

Roosevelt gave the desired formal pledge of support, and also arranged for Marriner to work with Budget Director Harold D. Smith in drafting alternative kinds of executive orders that could achieve the ends he had in view. With all this in motion, Marriner accepted a reappointment to the Board of Governors and, following Senate confirmation, was designated by the president to serve as chairman. The board membership was for a fourteen-year term, this being the only vacancy available at the time. The chairmanship was for the four-year statutory term expiring in February

1948. The difference between these two points were to be of critical importance later on when Marriner served under the Truman presidency.

When the draft executive orders were ready, Marriner turned them over to James Byrnes and to Judge Samuel I. Rosenman, who had been asked by the president to handle legal problems arising in connection with the reorganization of various war agencies. A draft of a press statement, attached to the orders justified the new arrangements on three counts. First, the Congress had vested in the Federal Reserve Board primary responsibility for the administration of national monetary and credit policies. Second, these policies could not be successfully carried out when the subordinate but important related functions of bank examination and supervision were lodged in two other federal agencies. Third, the executive orders were designed to end the divorce between power and responsibility, and to center them instead in one place.

In his response to all this, Roosevelt either reflected a simple and honest failure to grasp the main aim of the proposed unification, or it was part of his calculated design to appear as a man who had been previously confused about the true nature of that aim and now saw the light. Thus his note of February 9, 1944, to Marriner:

Jimmy Byrnes has shown me your letter and the proposed statement and I am a bit worried because there is really nothing to show the overlapping of examinations of banks. . . . It raises a question in my mind as to whether anything should be done at this time unless it would result in a great saving of manpower and also duplication or triplication of examinations. As it stands, I cannot discover any great savings except possibly a little in overhead in Government agencies.

In answer to the president's letter eight days later, Marriner voiced both surprise and regret that Roosevelt had misunderstood the real purpose behind the proposed unification scheme—which was not to save money and manpower but to give the Federal Reserve System the effective means to discharge the responsibilities vested in it by the Congress. Marriner's sense that he had been mousetrapped into accepting reappointment as chairman of the Federal Reserve Board was conveyed in the carefully chosen words with which he concluded the note:

As you will recall, I strongly urged the need for consolidation of the Federal banking agencies, regardless of whether it was under the Federal Reserve or some other setup, and said that I would gladly step out of the picture if it would help bring about this result. My term was expiring, it was an appropriate time to withdraw, and it seemed best for me to do so in view of the way I felt. You generously said, however, that you wished me to stay, that you agreed there was need for improvement, and that you would do something about the situation.

A conversation Marriner had with Byrnes at this time restored the problem of bank unification to its domestic political context. Recent voting patterns in the House and Senate indicated that, on significant domestic issues, the president could no longer control his own Democratic party.

"Bank unification." said Byrnes, as he drew the moral of the political story, was a "controversial subject." It was bound to stir up a storm of opposition from the bankers, the Comptroller and the Treasury. With a war on, and with a fast-approaching presidential election, "nothing should be done that would needlessly rock the boat."

Byrnes did not flatly reject the idea of unification but suggested that the executive orders be redrafted so that their form would be less likely to arouse bitter opposition in the Congress and in the nation. This was done, but, when Roosevelt saw the redraft, he raised the question of whether he actually had the authority under the War Powers Act to issue an executive order such as the one before him. Marriner tried to lay that doubt to rest by forwarding an opinion from the general counsel to the Federal Reserve Board, showing that bank unification could so be achieved. The days became weeks, the weeks months, and there was no reply from the White House.

Marriner continued to respect the ban against public controversy within the administration. But the extent to which bank unification was fused in his mind with the inevitable postwar struggle to avoid either a costly inflation or deflation appears in the body of testimony he gave before successive congressional committees in the spring of 1944. A representative example was his testimony on March 24 before the Senate Banking and Currency Committee. In urging that the existing price control legislation be extended for a sufficient time after the war to allow industry to get back to producing goods that could meet peacetime production, he observed:

No one can say with certainty what economic conditions will confront us when the war ends or whether the predominant forces will be inflationary. We know, however, that the inflationary *potential* will be enormous. We know that there will be a vast backlog of accumulated wants, and an unprecedented amount of purchasing power in the hands of the public, which has resulted largely from our heavy reliance upon borrowing in the financing of our war expenditures. . . . Inflation seldom gets out of hand during wartime, but the danger carries over after peace comes and a war-weary people, tired of wartime controls and restraints are eager to throw them off. . . . That is just the time when it may be fatal to relax prematurely the controls of war-engendered inflationary forces. . . .

Marriner then reminded the committee of the special reasons why the Federal Reserve System was interested in an extension of the existing price control legislation. The remainder was the heart of his polemic:

The less we raise in taxes and public borrowing, the more the banks have to be relied upon to supply the funds to fight this war. And the more the banks buy, the greater the pressure of dollars on the economy. . . . But as the tide of money raises, it becomes increasingly important to maintain the restraints that hold it in check.

If we fail to sustain public faith in the dollar, the liquidation of securities which would result would inevitably force the Federal Reserve System to absorb the bonds thus liquidated. This, in turn, would amount to pumping that much more money into the economy, with increasingly perilous results. This must not happen, but it could happen if we allowed the faith of our people to be undermined by a failure to hold this line against inflation.

The need to maintain private banking and credit on a sound basis, removed from the perils of inflation or deflation, brought Marriner to a point where he again stressed the need for a unified governmental approach to matters bearing on bank supervision and examination. The Congress listened to him with deaf ears, and other matters absorbed the attention of the White House. They included the widening scope of the American military effort in the Pacific, the accelerating pace of preparations for the D-Day landing in Normandy, the liberation of Rome on June 4, the Normandy landing two days later, the preparation for the 1944 presidential nominating conventions, and the prologue to the United Nations monetary and financial conference at Bretton Woods.

As far as the Roosevelt presidency was concerned, Marriner's strategies to win FDR's support for bank unification came to an end after one more direct exchange of notes. On June 29, 1944, when Marriner was preparing to leave for Bretton Woods as a member of the United States delegation, he wrote the president to say that, despite earlier doubts voiced by James Byrnes, a streamlining of federal banking agencies seemed politically feasible after all. In evidence, he enclosed an extract from a report which Senator Walter F. George had just submitted to the Senate on behalf of the Special Committee on Postwar Economic Policy and Planning. The text called for a careful study of "all government bureaus and departments with a view to the elimination of those which do not perform a real and vital function, and of the overlapping functions of others." It also urged that steps be taken to coordinate and unify the activities of all the departments to be certain that they did not pull in different directions. In Marriner's view, the language of the report plainly fit the picture of three federal agencies engaged in bank supervision—the Comptroller, the FDIC, and the Federal Reserve Board—overlapping and working at cross purposes. Yet when he returned from the Bretton Woods conference, there was a note on his desk, dated July 7, from the president.

Although I appreciate the force of the point made in the recent report of Senator George's Postwar Committee with respect to the desirability of eliminating overlapping functions of Government, I do not think this is a good time to be thinking of "streamlining" the Federal banking agencies. Let's put it on the shelf for the rest of this year, at least.

The cause of bank unification did not remain "on the shelf " merely for the rest of the year. Despite recurrent attempts made by people other than Marriner, it remained on the shelf for almost three decades until the mid 1970s, when Dr. Arthur Burns, as head of the Federal Reserve Board, resumed the half-forgotten battle Marriner had begun to wage in 1934.

31. Engine of Inflation

I

THE PROTRACTED ANGLO-AMERICAN EXCHANGES which preceded Bretton Woods were conducted by John Maynard Keynes for the British Treasury and by Harry Dexter White for the U.S. Treasury.[13] What they had to say to each other bore directly on the responsibilities of the Federal Reserve Board. Yet no official communications were passed on to the board for its consideration until April 1943, when the plans being formulated by the British and American treasuries were first made public.

In the early phase of the Anglo-American discussions, White proposed the formation of an international bank with functions like those of a central bank. Besides providing the regular services of a central bank, its purpose would be to eliminate worldwide financial dangers and to reduce the likelihood of worldwide economic depressions. Marriner, who had far more direct experience than White or Keynes with the central bank operations, was painfully aware of the difficulties encountered in making such an institution an instrument of rational economic control even for a single, stable, economically mature nation. He therefore doubted whether one could successfully establish an international central bank amid the turmoil likely to prevail among most nations in the immediate postwar period.

Even when White's initial idea evolved into something different—the International Bank for Reconstruction and Development—Marriner was skeptical. He noted that most of the initial capital and loanable funds would be drawn from American sources, but that the governance of the proposed bank pointed to the dilution of any fixed center of responsibility for the way the funds were used. He believed, subject to correction later on, that the purposes of the projected international bank could be better served through bilateral loans made by the United States and a second nation.[14]

The Stabilization Fund—Keynes' chief interest, before White tied it to the concept of an international bank—was a different matter. Marriner strongly favored such a fund, calling it "absolutely essential" to all nations in the postwar period. If the mutually destructive policies of economic autarky pressed by nations after the First World War was not to be repeated, debtor nations that would emerge from the war, as well as the single giant creditor—the United States—must be able to conduct trade while reconstruction was going forward. World currency arrangements must be amended so as to combine short-term stability in the value of each nation's currency with long-term flexibility. This in turn implied two things: freedom to alter currency ratios without the danger of prompt retaliation from other nations, and freedom to plan for full employment at home without fear that gold losses would enforce a domestic deflationary policy.

In late April of 1944, the terms of the agreements reached between representatives of the British and American treasuries were set forth in a "joint statement of principles of an International Monetary Fund." The Bretton Woods conference, held in the first days of July, was largely designed to familiarize other prospective member nations with the operational concepts behind the fund, and behind a contemplated Bank for Reconstruction and Development. It was further designed, as President Roosevelt observed in his letter of instruction to Secretary Morgenthau, chairman of the U. S. delegation, to show "the world that international postwar cooperation is possible." It now labors the obvious to say that far more than a Bretton Woods conference was needed to lay the foundations for a stable world economic order.

II

After Bretton Woods, when Marriner refocused his attention on the future of the American domestic economy, all things within his line of vision indicated that inflation and not deflation would be the immediate postwar problem facing the United States. Part of the evidence was based on a contrast between the economic picture at the end of the First World War and the one in late 1944.

In 1920, for example, currency and demand deposits were less than $25 billion; at the end of 1944 whey were in excess of $110 billion. In 1920, government securities held mainly by individuals and corporations were less than $20 billion; at the end of 1944 they were in excess of $80 billion. Total liquid assets in the hands of individuals and business in 1920 were approximately $45 billion; at the end of 1944, the total approached $200 billion. Government debt, which was approximately $25 billion at the peak of the First World War, was nearly ten times as large in 1944 and was still growing. Yet the relatively small volume of liquid funds after the First World War led to one of the worst credit inflations in American history, followed by the economic collapse of the 1930s.

After the November elections, which returned Roosevelt to the White House for a fourth term, Marriner secured an appointment with the president so that he could spell out the implications of the foregoing realities. He meant to stress the imperative need to maintain intact the wartime harness of controls until industry had resumed civilian production on a scale large enough to meet effective demands. In the absence of such controls, the consumer would try to convert his saved dollars into goods, though he would thereby bid up the prices of the very things he wanted to buy. Marriner had not seen FDR face to face for some time prior to his postelection meeting in the White House. He was now shocked by Roosevelt's appearance, and saddened by his manner.

He was [Marriner later recalled] haggard and drawn. His eyes lacked their playful sparkle. He did not speak with his usual ease, and he seemed to have some difficulty in speaking without slurring his enunciation. More often than not, his mind seemed to wander off into a secret hideout, as if to escape from the pounding of the arguments it heard. After that November meeting, I thought it would be cruel to harass Roosevelt with my problems. I had never been restful to him in previous years. I had continually ragged and nagged and poked him to do what I thought should be done. I believe I held the President's respect for this tenacity of purpose, but it was not the sort of relationship that could bring comfort to an exhausted man. He was known to have remarkable recuperative powers, and I hoped against hope that they would come to his aid once again as they had in times past. Meanwhile, I thought that the very least I could do to help him in the circumstances, was to take my arguments and goads to other quarters.[15]

One of those other quarters was Fred M. Vinson, then Economic Stabilizer. In February 1945, Marriner called his attention to the way the continued acceleration in the rate of wartime expenditures increased the volume of money and other liquid assets in the hands of the public, and the way these factors had combined to inflate capital values. Subsequently he came before Vinson's Stabilization Board to contend that a penalty rate on capital gains, corresponding to the highest surtax rate, was the most effective and simple overall instrument to take the speculative fever out of the market for real estate, stocks, commodities, and other capital assets. By removing the cause for the fever, people would not "run from the dollar," and the danger of speculative investments in goods would be largely if not entirely met. There were even more compelling reasons for imposing the tax in question, and Marriner spelled them out for the benefit of the Stabilization Board:

The so-called GI Bill of Rights is one of many assurances to returning veterans that they will be helped in buying a home, a farm. What becomes of such assurances if the prices of homes and farms are driven to prohibitively high levels because of a failure to close this gap in the tax laws? How can anyone defend a situation in which the bigger the speculator, the greater the advantage to him in escaping from high surtaxes through the loophole of the capital gains tax? What becomes of pledges to take the profiteering out of war when this invitation to make fortunes out of war conditions is held out to big speculators, businesses, as well as individuals? How can we hold the line on the labor front if we fail to put a stop to this flagrant war profiteering?

The Stabilization Board had nothing to say and did nothing in response to Marriner's fervent plea.

III

Roosevelt's death on the eve of victory in Europe was likened by many editorial writers to the death of Moses, short of an entry into the Promised Land. Marriner did not "editorialize" his emotions. In this instance, as in so many others, he found it hard to voice his deepest personal devotion. Yet he silently mourned the loss of a leader with whom he had been intimately linked for eleven stormy years. In all those years, he usually agreed with Roosevelt's social objectives but often disagreed with the president's choice of means for achieving them. Varied, too, had been his influence on the decisions Roosevelt made. In some matters, his influence was decisive; in others, only slight; and in still others, nonexistent. But he never had reason to doubt that he was one of Roosevelt's partners in a great, exciting adventure.

Toward the end of May 1945, about six weeks after Roosevelt's death, when the immediate pressure on his successor had eased somewhat, Marriner called on President Harry S. Truman, whom he had known since the latter's days in the Senate. He recalled that, in February 1944, the Senate had confirmed his appointment to the Board of Governors for a fourteen-year term and that thereafter he again had been designated by President Roosevelt as chairman of the board to serve a statutory four-year term, expiring in February 1948. His chairmanship still had nearly three years to run. But, Marriner said, he was prepared to resign on notice so that President Truman could designate someone of his own choice. Truman replied that he had no one else in mind as a replacement, that he fully approved of Marriner's work and expected him to remain at his post and help in any way he could.

IV

With the end of the war in Europe, there remained three fronts on which the nation must expend its efforts. The first of these, the unfinished war against Japan, called for sizable expenditures. But it did not, in Marriner's view, call for the huge level of expenditures made prior to Germany's defeat. It seemed to him that now the rate and scope of military spending could be cut back sharply, with the object of strengthening two other fronts—the domestic economy and the peace front in Europe. Thus if military expenditures could be curtailed and if the economy were allowed a partial conversion to peacetime production, some of the pressures in existing inflationary forces could be eased. Thus, too, if military funds were diverted to European relief and the reconstruction of Europe's productive facilities, it might be possible to nip in the bud what was already the obvious aim of the communists to exploit the social and economic disorders in postwar Europe.

Marriner first voiced these views at meetings with generals Brehon Somervell and Lucius Clay, the key figures on the supply side of the army. He voiced them again to President Truman on May 29; to Harold Smith (director of the Bureau of the Budget) the next day, and to Harry L. Hopkins a day after that. But the full-dress presentation—and its rebuttal —occurred at one of those social affairs in Washington where things said in a private context can be as important if not more important than official and public utterances. The particular affair was held on an evening in June in the home of Senator Brian McMahon. The guests, in addition to Marriner, included a number of congressional leaders and the then undersecretary of war, Robert P. Patterson. At one point in the afterdinner conversation, Senator Scott Lucas asked Marriner to appraise the inflationary prospects facing the nation.

Marriner replied that, while it would be presumptuous on his part to tell the military how to wage the war against Japan, he thought he could properly make some observations about the relationship between current military expenditures and the problem of inflation. In support of his now familiar thesis that the rate of military expenditures should be sharply cut, he noted that, with Germany out of the war and with Japan alone in the field, the United States could wage a war of attrition against Japan instead of redeploying American forces in Europe for an amphibious attack on Japanese territory. The Japanese navy had been driven from the seas, and her aircraft from the skies, and the Japanese home islands were under blockade. Even in time of peace, Japan had to import much of her foodstuff and major industrial ran materials such as iron ore, coal, oil, and copper. The problem was infinitely more difficult, now that the home islands were being subjected to a devastating bombardment. How could Japan escape an inevitable surrender in a war of attrition?

Marriner could see no reason why, with all enemy fleets sunk or captured, the U.S. navy proceeded to order the construction of ships that would not be ready from one to three years. He could see no reason why the induction of men into the armed forces continued at a rate that brought the size of the American military establishment to its peak after VE day. The manpower could better have been used in civilian production so as to meet the problems of inflation at home and reconstruction in Europe. In sum, since the problem of winning the peace in Europe depended in large degree on what could be done to maintain economic conditions at home that would serve both America's and Europe's wants, the most prudent course would be to make an immediate cutback in military spending.

There was silence when Marriner finished his argument, and all eyes turned to Undersecretary Patterson. His reply was short and sharp. "The public," he said, "are demanding an all-out war and an immediate and all-out peace. There is no way to slow down. We must continue to make a maximum effort until the war ends, because in addition to an all-out war and an all-out peace, the public wants a complete demobilization, not a partial one such as you are suggesting."

Marriner could argue that this kind of absolutism did not come cheap —that its costs would bear hard on the economy and on the fight for peace. But as he later admitted: "There was no disputing the fact that Patterson accurately summed up what the American people wanted."

v

In the period after VJ day, as during the war years, every economic group in the nation was avid for the benefits of inflation, provided someone else paid the costs. Farmers wanted a floor for their prices but not a ceiling.

Real estate interests and building-materials people wanted easy credit so that they could dispose of their houses and sell their materials at inflated prices, while strongly resisting an excess-profits tax that would help the government recapture some of the profits made. Labor always wanted price controls, but vigorously resisted wage controls. Bankers wanted higher interest rates but did not want federal banking agencies to control the expansion of credit.

None of the things were done that could have helped promote a postwar adjustment with a minimum of inflation. Controls over manpower were precipitously dropped, and the Office of Price Administration removed ration restrictions on gasoline, fuel oil, processed food and heating stoves—all within three days after Japan surrendered. Three days after *that,* President Truman, by executive order, instructed federal agencies "to move as rapidly as possible without endangering the stability of the economy toward the removal of price, wage, production and other controls and toward the restoration of collective bargaining and a free market." The dismantling was carried out with zest. The harness of controls was swiftly lifted from strategic and other metals, building and industrial construction, motor vehicles and railroads, exports and so on. By the end of 1945, only sugar continued under rationing and price control.

Direct controls, however, dealt only with the effects of inflation and as such were, or should have been, subordinate to fiscal and monetary policy which struck at causes. For this reason, the circumstances surrounding the abrupt removal of the excess-profits tax in the late fall of 1945 served only to worsen the mistake of the premature removal of direct controls. During the war years, the excess profits tax had reduced the desire of business for price increases, and of labor for wage increases. The income it produced for the government helped hold down the deficit, and hence the need to borrow.

When the issue of whether or not to maintain the excess-profits tax was still open to debate within the administration, Marriner vehemently argued that all the reasons that had justified the tax in the war years applied with equal or even greater force in the postwar years, and especially in the reconversion period right after VJ day. The budget was still heavily unbalanced. Each dollar of government expenditures not raised by taxes had to be borrowed. To the extent that banks furnished the funds, new money supplies would be added to the vast accretions of liquid funds which the system of war financing had already placed in the hands of the public. Profits made immediately after the end of the war could rightly be viewed as having been a direct result of war expenditures, and thus were as much "war profits" as if they had occurred during the shooting. There was a clear obligation to protect government credit and the billions upon billions invested in government bonds and other savings. This could be done only by moving as soon as possible after the war to bring about a balanced budget and to prevent any further expansion of bank credit.

In all the years from the early New Deal to the end of the Second World

War Henry Morgenthau had been Marriner's main adversary in the running disputes over economic policy. When Morgenthau resigned as Secretary of the Treasury soon after VJ day, it was hoped that Marriner's relationship with the Treasury would turn for the better. The hope was short-lived. The new Secretary, Fred M. Vinson, seemed in his institutional outlook to be an identical twin of the departed one, as was brought home to Marriner after he wrote Vinson on October 20, 1945, and strongly stated the case against the repeal of the tax at that time.

First, with but few exceptions, business and industrial firms who would be required to pay the excess-profits tax had never been so well off. They possessed unprecedented accumulations of cash or its equivalent and could look forward to glittering profits as they met the unprecedented backlog of demands from domestic and foreign sources. Second, the contention that business needed a special tax incentive to produce and employ people in the immediate postwar period did violence to basic economic realities. The war showed that if business had orders, it would produce and provide employment despite high taxes. Given the intensity of demand for goods of every kind, capacity production would follow even if there were an excess-profits tax.

As for new enterprises, their main problem lay not in taxes but in the securing of labor and material so as to get operations underway in competition with established industry. Marriner also rejected the contention that repeal of the excess-profits tax would help provide employment and prevent deflation. He could foresee certain deflationary aspects in long-range economic forecasting, but in his view it made no sense to characterize the immediate outlook in 1945–46 as predominantly deflationary. He concluded:

The underlying need at this stage is not to arrest a deflationary spiral and to put funds into the hands of people who will spend them or to offer special tax inducements to business to produce. The basic underlying need is to restore as rapidly as possible a budgetary situation which will maintain faith in the currency and preserve the buying power of the billions invested in government securities and other savings.

The plea was ignored. On the advice of Secretary Vinson and others, President Truman in November 1945 asked the Congress to repeal the excess-profits tax. *That* request met with a quick response, and the consequence was the onset of the postwar wage-price spiral. When corporations were to be granted an extraordinary measure of relief from a burden that was not onerous, why should labor continue to bind itself to "no-strike pledges" or to the "little steel" formula carried over from the war? The labor market was relatively tight, and labor's take-home pay was reduced when many industries eliminated overtime work. So labor withdrew its no-strike pledge and demanded substantial wage increases. Continued production should have been among the main weapons used in the fight against inflation, but labor's way of trying to improve its own position in the light of the profits made by management was by ordering massive work stoppages in key industries. The effect was to give the winter of 1945–46 the aspect of one long strike.

As the wage-price spiral got underway, Marriner Eccles often wondered why Americans still clung to their war-bond savings even though a continuing inflation reduced their value. He could only attribute the behavior to the force of memories carried over from the depression years. People with savings in those years had learned the enormous value of the dollar, just as people who were in debt learned how painful it was to pay off debts. So they clung to war-bond savings after the Second World War, though inflation silently devoured their purchasing power even as these securities were kept in a snug box in a carefully guarded safety vault.

In late December 1945, when the next budget message was being drafted, Marriner wrote budget director Harold D. Smith to say that it had become the custom "during recent years" to include in the message some general statements concerning the trends of federal tax policy. As chairman of the Federal Reserve Board, he had a direct interest in the matter because "I believe that our own powers and responsibilities, taken alone, will be wholly inadequate to prevent inflationary developments that are in prospect." In Marriner's view, it was of the greatest importance to avoid any immediate commitments regarding further tax reductions for 1946. Since one of the most critical problems facing the administration was the need to strengthen and extend price control, both through direct Office of Price Administration measures and through absorption of excess buying power, "the administration's case for price control would be greatly weakened if recommendations for tax reductions were advanced at the same time as the fight was being made for extending OPA."

"To forestall an expected Congressional drive for tax reduction," Marriner continued, it was imperative for the administration "to take a firm stand in the budget message." This was "no time to reduce excise or any other taxes which curb buying power." In fact, excise taxes should not come off "until buying power is no longer vastly in excess of the supply of goods." This was all the more true if labor was to get general increases. "To cut down or cut out excise taxes on top of that, would amount to an unwarranted and inflationary subsidy." Developments since VJ day ran "contrary to the deflationary forecasts and anticipations of extensive unemployment which were so widely accepted." Current trends indicated that inflationary pressures were not only strong but could "possibly gain in strength." Hence the prospect for a further weakening or even a discontinuation of price controls and for further tax reductions "would be most unfortunate" and "entirely incompatible with a hold-the-line policy in other areas." Marriner concluded his note to Smith with a short lesson about the dynamics of a compensatory economy:

As one who has advocated low taxes and an adequate level of Federal expenditures during the depression years, I urge that the same logic be applied to the present situation. Then the economy was excessively deflated, now the opposite conditions prevail. Then a deficit was inevitable and needed. Now every effort should be made to approach a budgetary balance as soon as possible. If we do not exert our efforts in this direction now, it will be difficult indeed to persuade the bondholder that we shall ever intend to do so.

Quite likely the problem some years hence will again become one of preventing deflation, but that is not the present situation. The present need is for giving assurance to consumers and bondholders that prices will not increase and that the purchasing power of their savings and incomes will be protected. A forceful statement along these lines in the budget message would contribute greatly to dispelling the growing belief that rising prices are inevitable.

This plea, like the others, was without effect. A sorely beset President Truman tried in the winter of 1945–46 to restore the industrial peace that had been shattered in the first instance by a request for the repeal of the excess-profits tax. Among other things, he appointed fact-finding boards to hear major disputes and to make recommendations for settling them, but the recommendations had no force of law, and could be ignored by the parties to a dispute. Effective wage controls were virtually eliminated in February 1946, when the settlement of major strikes led to a general pattern of 18 percent wage increases. After that, the desultory life of the National Wage Stabilization Board was terminated by an executive order.

With the excess-profits tax repealed, with wages uncontrolled, with an end to rationing, allocations, and building permits, the Office of Price Administration faced an impossible job of maintaining a price-stabilization program. The administrator could fix prices, but goods were not available at the prices fixed, and the policing and enforcing job had the texture of a rope of sand. Anything and everything could be bought on the gray and black markets. It was a period of fabulous, illegal profits with associated tax evasions. Ironically, the strongest support for the tattered semblance of price control came from the black marketeers, just as the bootleggers were the strongest supporters of prohibition. The taint of the black market was widespread, smearing not only the vendor but the otherwise law-abiding citizen who "wanted something special."

32. The British Loan

ON THE MORNING OF SEPTEMBER 13, 1945, a confident John Maynard Keynes mounted the steps of the Federal Reserve Building for the opening round of the negotiations bearing on the British request for a loan of $6 billion. He knew that behind the words "Federal Reserve" deeply cut in the marble over the main doorway was an invisible $20 billion in gold owned by the United States. He would ask for what amounted to a 30 percent draft on those billions, not as an act of charity and not in repayment for wartime sacrifices. He would ask for them because, so he would argue, support for Great Britain would assist world stability and peace. With that support, she could begin the slow work of expanding her exports and of liquidating her massive foreign debts. Without that support, her rations would be drastically cut, her factories would stand idle for lack of material, and she could not participate in the newly created International Monetary Fund. Her inability in such matters would have dire effects on other nations belonging to the "pound sterling" monetary network, leading to mutually destructive trade wars.

On the same grounds, Marriner Eccles would be foremost among Washington officials to convey to the Congress the reasons why Britain had a title of right to American help—in America's *own* interests. Indeed, as Keynes' biographer R. F. Harrod has written, "The British case was so clearly engraved upon the mind of Mr. Marriner Eccles, that when he had to give evidence to the Senate [Banking and Currency] Committee on the British loan, he could enter into all sorts of details of the British case, without any references to notes, just as if he was testifying about his own private affairs."[16] Still, if the British case was overwhelming, the atmosphere in Washington and in the nation at large was not what it had been during the war, or what it would be in 1947 when General George C. Marshall proposed his European Recovery Plan. In the fall of 1945, though ominous rumblings from Russia could be heard, the strength of communist forces inside eastern European countries was not fully appreciated. Spokesmen for economic aid to Great Britain thus lacked the support which a fear of Russia later gave to American programs of assistance.

In the Congress and in the American nation, there was a will to alleviate acute distress and the danger of starvation among nations overseas. But as R. F. Harrod assessed the mood of the time, "they were not prepared to enter deeply into the financial problems of the Allies, to sustain their balances of trade, to support their welfare programs." The very respect Great

Britain enjoyed because of her wartime performance was, paradoxically, an argument for *not* rendering her any special assistance. After all, during six years of war she had shown herself a Great Power, with great economic reserves. She "would not quail before the minor problem of rebuilding her homes and her trade, with no bombs flying to distract her energies."[17]

In the great boardroom of the Federal Reserve Building, where the negotiations over the British loan began, Keynes held the floor for three consecutive days as he comprehensively reviewed Great Britain's economic position. His original request for $6 billion was eventually reduced at the insistence of Secretary Vinson to the figure of $3.7 billion, since, said he, the Congress would reject out of hand any substantially higher sum. Moreover, the $3.7 billion was not to be a gift, nor a loan without cost. It was to be an interest-bearing loan. The real value of the loan, however, was approximately $4.7 billion. This was because the British were to be given the full stock of American surplus property—shoes, clothing, food, and so on —previously stockpiled on British soil for use in the war.

Once the dollar figure of $3.7 billion was set, the terms of the loan were thrashed out in a remarkable encounter between John Maynard Keynes and Marriner Stoddard Eccles. Here was Keynes, whose remote ancestors were among the Norman conquerors of England, himself a member of the House of Lords, a product of Bloomsbury and Cambridge, a don, the most renowned academic economist in the world, a patron of the arts, and husband to a beloved former ballerina. And Marriner Eccles? He was only two generations removed from illiterate forebears who had lived in the depths of misery in a Glasgow slum, who had reached the United States only with the help of the Mormon Perpetual Immigration Fund, and who had risked extinction before they took root on American soil. As for Marriner personally, he had no formal education beyond the third year of high school, had no eye or ear for "the arts," suffered a blighted marriage, had no credentials as an academic econmist, and had never "read Keynes." Yet he had emerged as a master of "capital" and had arrived *before* Keynes at "Keynsian" insights into the workings of the economic order in industrial societies. Now these two men from different worlds, each a representative of his own country, were also emblematic of the shift in the power relationships between England and the United States. No transcript exists of what they had to say to each other. But the substance of their encounter, as Marriner later recalled it, went something like this:[18]

Keynes: What terms are you going to make on the loan?
Eccles: Being a banker, I want it to have the *form* of a banker's loan, with a schedule of payments on the principal and interest that the British will be able to honor. The terms are these . . .
Keynes (bristling): You are being entirely too tough, setting such terms.
Eccles: Do you want the loan?
Keynes: Yes.

Eccles: Listen. If my own convictions could decide the matter, I'd give you the money as an outright gift. It would be a trifle compared to what Great Britain did for all of us during the war. But I have no such personal power of decision. The only way to get the loan is to have the Senate and the House authorize it by a majority vote, and there is a great deal of opposition in the Congress to the whole of this business. I want the loan to come before the Congress in an armored form where it will survive the detailed attacks of all the lawyers and small town financiers who hold seats in both chambers.

Keynes: I have my problems at home with the Treasury, the Cabinet and the Parliament.

Eccles: I know something about such problems. We are both in the same boat. We will both have to speak within the limits of what the politics of the case allows us, though the result falls short of what we both agree should happen ideally.

The two men agreed to exchange copies of what they would eventually say publicly in defending the terms of the loan before political bodies —Keynes, in a speech before the House of Lords, and Eccles, in testifying before the Senate Banking and Currency Committee.

Though Marriner spoke of a "banker's loan," the *form* agreed to at the end of three months of negotiations contained elements of a major gift. For one thing, aside from turning over to the British the stockpiles of American supplies previously mentioned, all British obligations to the United States under the Lend-Lease agreements were canceled. For another thing, no interest would be charged on the loan itself for a period of six years, after which the charge would be 2 percent. A valuable waiver clause went with this provision. No interest would be payable on the loan or carried forward in any year in which British exports, visible and invisible, did not suffice to buy imports from abroad at the prewar levels.

When Keynes returned to London on December 17, he was asked by a reporter if the rumor was true that he had made Britain the forty-ninth state of the United States. "No such luck," he replied.

By the time he was back on his home soil, the debate in the House of Commons on the terms of the proposed loan had already been held; the Commons voted to approve the terms of the loan. The preceding debate, however, had brought out the strong current of anti-Americanism that was running in Great Britain and the pervasive ignorance about the true state of Britain's critical economic plight. Strong prejudices against the proposed settlement were voiced by Socialist backbenchers, who claimed that the terms of the loan smelled too much of laissez-faire. Equally strong prejudices were voiced by Conservative backbenchers, who saw in certain aspects of the loan a threat to their cherished system of imperial preferences in the conduct of international trade.

Much the same kind of ignorance and misunderstanding prevailed in the House of Lords before Keynes rose to address it on December 18. Though a majority of the Lords voted to support the terms of the loan, Keynes came away from the event deeply depressed at the state of opinion in Britain. The debate cast doubt on England's future capacity to grapple effectively with the infinitely complex economic problems she faced.

On December 21, Keynes sent Marriner a copy of his speech in the House of Lords as it appeared in the record of the debate. "I hope," he wrote in a covering note, "I was able to clear away at least a part of the misunderstandings in this country. Nevertheless, I fear that a large measure of disappointment remains. May I add a word of thanks to you for all the help you gave in getting the thing straight." Woven into the texture of Keynes' remarks in the Lords were lines of argument Marriner himself had used when he tried to persuade Keynes to accept the terms of the loan. The implied compliment was reciprocated months later, on March 8, 1946, when Marriner appeared before the Senate Banking and Currency Committee to testify in support of the loan. In what he had to say, he drew on points which Keynes had earlier stressed.

Marriner's testimony was designed to answer some questions which he posed at the outset. First, why did the British need American help? "They need," he said, "a blood transfusion to help them regain their international economic health. The proposed credit is not and, therefore, should not be judged as a commercial loan. It is more like a draft on a blood bank." The British were in a dangerously anemic condition because, in their wartime extremity, they had thrown all their resources into the battle without considering where they would be left after victory. Marriner then cited the arithmetic of the British case, adding a prophetic aside: "We shall have to share with the world some of our scarce resources. This fact has been recognized in our food program. We shall need to recognize it as it affects other necessities if we are to help bring about economic and political stability in the world."

What would the United States get in return for the loan?

Marriner answered that, although the contemplated loan to Great Britain provided for repayment of the principal and for a moderate rate of interest, the United States expected from it far more than a mere financial return. "The basic justification for the British loan," he said, "is that it would enable Britain to join us in making a living reality out of our blueprint for world recovery and reconstruction"—as embodied in the Bretton Woods agreements, and in the proposals for an International Trade Organization. Here Marriner spoke with passion:

We live today in a sick world. We have yet to attain the objectives of the Atlantic Charter, freedom from want and freedom from fear. These objectives will never be attained, and our ideals of peace and democracy cannot long survive if we merely indulge in pious hopes and do nothing to prevent the world from degenerating into further economic chaos in the aftermath of the most devastating of all wars.

You will have noted that I advocate this loan on its own merits and primarily as a contribution to world stability. I do not believe in foreign lending for the sake of creating employment here and exporting unemployment to foreign shores. We get employment, yes, while the money is being spent, but the fruits of that employment are lost to us permanently if we persist in refusing to take goods and services from foreign countries to enable them to service and repay their debts. If we desire to maintain a thriving export business and receive service on our investments abroad, we must make the exchange of goods and services a two-way street. In the end, responsibility for making it possible for our debtors to pay is ours, and ours alone. The decision is in your hands. It is a fateful one.

In the sharp questioning that followed, senators Alben Barkley and J. William Fulbright reinforced Marriner's case by the clarifying questions they posed for him to answer. The opposition amounted to a mixture of Senator Robert Taft's studied ambiguities, Senator Homer Capehart's natural muddle, and Senator Eugene Millikan's scorn. A lawyer by profession, Millikan pressed the kind of attack Marriner had foretold in his conversations with Keynes. Indeed, the senator from Colorado spoke for anti-British sentiment rising on the American side of the Atlantic in counterpoint to the rising anti-Americanism on the British side. A representative extract from the hearing reads:

Senator Millikan: We have heard now that we were all to sit around and devise rules for the game, design the playing cards and lay out everything for this game. Now it appears that we have to furnish the chips and back everybody that plays the game.

Mr. Eccles: I think that is correct. . . . We have been doing exactly that during the war. We have been furnishing the chips for the game of war. I see no reason why we should hesitate to furnish some chips for the game of peace. I don't see anything so terrible about that. It was in our own interest to furnish the chips for the game of war, and now it is in our own interest to furnish some of the chips for the game of peace. What is so different about that?

Senator Millikan: [Let me] remind the Governor that the embezzler usually increases his theft on the theory that one more play at the races or with the chips will put him in a position to restore what he has stolen. Then he goes on and on and finally he says, "They can only put me in jail once and I might just as well steal another $50,000." Now, isn't that the philosophy at the bottom of this business? That because it costs so much every day to fight the war, what does another four or five billion dollars amount to?

Mr. Eccles: This is not philosophy at all. It is anything but that. I think this is a question of values. It is not my idea that the Government should either loan or should spend one dollar, certainly at this stage of inflationary development, that is not fully compensated for with other considerations. . . .

Senator Millikan: I would like to have your observations on the weight that we should give to the fact that the British defaulted on their World War I loan.

Mr. Eccles: I wouldn't give it any consideration, absolutely none. I think we were largely responsible in a way for that default. Britain didn't have the dollars to pay us, but she wanted to pay us in goods. But at a time when the depression was on in the United States, and we didn't have the ingenuity within our own country to keep our own factories and labor busy producing goods for ourselves—do you think we should have been willing to add the surplus British goods in our market so that they could get dollars to make payments? . . .

Senator Millikan: Then the people should understand that in making this loan, if it gets tough for Great Britain to pay it, she may unilaterally decide not to pay it.

Mr. Eccles: That's not the right way to state the case. The right way is to say that she won't repay the loan if it gets tough for *us* to accept her goods and services.

Senator Millikan: That is a very enlightening statement.

After three more months of enlightening statements, Congress approved the loan on terms corresponding to those Marriner had helped negotiate.

33. *Federal Reserve vs. the Treasury*

AMONG ITS OTHER CONSEQUENCES, the Second World War "won" one side of the argument for a compensatory economy—the side, born of the Great Depression, that prescribed ways to reflate a drastically deflated economy. The economics of the war offered convincing testimony on two points in particular. First, large-scale public spending could propel the economy forward beyond all previously imagined bounds. Second, though budget balancers in the 1930s warned against national bankruptcy when annual deficits never exceeded $4 billion, the testimony of the war showed that America could carry a vastly enlarged public debt—$250 billion on VJ day—provided its gross national product was much larger. Americans who lived these new realities in the 1941–45 years of unprecedented effort and record production had good reason to look back on the days of massive unemployment with a kind of posthumous shame.

But what about the future? What about the *underside* of the argument for a compensatory economy? Would the public support fiscal, monetary and credit restraints to forestall a runaway inflation? The question, if asked on VJ day, would have seemed unreal to most Americans and to most professional economists among them. Their common expectation was that the "reconversion" period immediately ahead would be dominated not by the challenge of inflation but by a fall in employment, incomes and prices.

That, however, is not how Marriner Eccles viewed the years ahead. He anticipated some transitional unemployment. But even in advance of VJ day he had warned that immense forces for inflation, generated by the wartime fiscal and debt-management policies, were held in check only by the harness of wartime controls. If the harness were prematurely lifted, massive liquid savings would be set free to chase after scarce goods and services, leading to a vicious inflationary spiral that would feed on itself. The more his urgent warning was ignored, the more his impatience drew closer to desperation. The more also Marriner was impelled to mount—without concern for personal consequences—a frontal assault on what he regarded as the citadels of willful blindness.

His initial point of attack after VJ day was centered on the "technical point" that had engendered wartime controversy between the Treasury and the Federal Reserve. Backed by the Board of Governors and by the heads of the Reserve banks, Marriner now argued that the Federal Reserve should be allowed to adopt monetary and credit policies suited to postwar economic conditions, rather than mechanically execute the Treasury's debt management policies framed solely with an eye to the carrying costs of the public debt. The rate of Treasury short-term securities, he said, should be permitted on terms fixed by the Treasury. The problem the board faced, so the Annual Report stated, could be met in one of three ways subject to congressional approval. The board could limit bank holdings of government bonds; it could increase the regular reserve requirements provided the limits were raised beyond existing law; it could segregate short-term government securities or cash under a special reserve requirement similar to the Special Fund the Treasury had formed in 1936 to "sterilize gold."

There was no response from Capitol Hill; there was no response from the White House, where President Truman was besieged by the problems of power and diplomacy in the world arena; there was no response from the Treasury Department where Secretary Fred Vinson, who had Truman's ear, was dead set against changing the wartime pattern of Reserve System subordination to the Treasury. The picture did not change in July 1946, when Vinson became Chief Justice of the United States, and John Snyder took over as Secretary of the Treasury.

In introducing John Snyder it is necessary to touch on several aspects of his previous career, because of a possible internal connection between them and the role the Giannini banking interests in California may have played in the final phase of Marriner Eccles' career in Washington. To start with, when the defense program got underway in 1940, John Snyder, then head of the Reconstruction Finance Corporation office in St. Louis, was brought to Washington to serve as executive vice-president of the newly formed Defense Plant Corporation, an FRC subsidiary. Here he became an intimate of Samuel Husbands, who wore two hats as an RFC director and as president of the Defense Plant Corporation. In 1943, Snyder left Washington to become vice-president of the First National Bank of St. Louis, but when his close friend Harry S. Truman succeeded to the White House in April 1945, he returned to the national capitol as the newly appointed head of the FRC. After that, he twice inherited posts left behind by the upward-bound Fred Vinson, succeeding him first as director of War Mobilization and Conversion and then as Secretary of the Treasury. Meanwhile, Husbands accepted a major executive post at a large salary with the Transamerica bank-holding company of A. P. Giannini. At about the same time, Samuel Stewart, who had been general counsel to the Truman committee, became general counsel to the Bank of America, one of the cornerstones of the Transamerica structure.

Marriner was on friendly personal terms with the Gianninis. He valued their support in the fight for the Banking Act of 1935, respected their talents as bankers and warmly acknowledged their role in helping Western banks generally overcome their dependence on and subordination to the dictates of

Wall Street. Since Marriner had organized the first bank-holding company in the United States and had long advocated branch banking, he had no reason to object to the nature of Transamerica as a bank-holding company. He recognized that its creation, like that of the Eccles-Browning First Security Corporation, concentrated banking resources, fostered better management, meant greater diversification of bank investments and loans, reduced operating costs, provided bank credit mobility between communities and so on. But as long as Marriner was in government, he drew a sharp line between his official responsibilities and his personal sentiments or economic interests. This was true with respect to the First Security Corporation. It was also true with respect to the Gianninis.

One morning, as Marriner scanned the mail on the desk at his Federal Reserve office, he read a letter from A. P. Giannini offering him the presidency of the First National Bank of Portland, another cornerstone institution of the Transamerica Corporation. More than that—if Marriner accepted the offered post and served one year in it, he would then be made the head of the Bank of America. On the evening of that same day, when Marriner returned home, he telephoned A. P. Giannini in San Francisco and wasted no breath on thanks. "Listen," he rasped, "I am chairman of the Federal Reserve Board. Remember that. Don't even write me another line about an offer of any bank presidency anywhere." No such line was forthcoming.[19]

There was, however, more to the story. The mere receipt of the unsolicited offer, coupled with the Eccles' family interest in a bank-holding company, complicated Marriner's role in the protracted, costly and ultimately fruitless controversy known as "the Transamerica case." The Treasury Department had initiated the controversy, but once the Federal Reserve Board was drawn into it, Marriner could not remain aloof from what went on. As chairman of the Reserve Board, he was the official channel of communication between the board and the heads of other governmental departments and agencies that had interests of their own in the matter. Yet the massive records of what transpired show that once the Federal Reserve Board was "seized" of the Transamerica issue, Marriner regularly disqualified himself when the board cast votes on aspects of the case—a case that ran concurrently with an intensification of the conflict between the Federal Reserve and the Treasury over debt management policies.

III

A full history of the Transamerica case would cover at least three decades, starting in the 1920s and extending to the mid-1950s, when William McChesney Martin was chairman of the Federal Reserve Board. It will suffice here merely to touch on that history prior to John Snyder's appointment as Secretary of the Treasury.

In the late 1930s, as an offshoot of the Roosevelt administration's attempt to mount a general attack on all forms of collectivism in business, Secretary of the Treasury Henry Morgenthau focused on bank-holding companies and especially on the Transamerica Corporation of A. P. Giannini. He subsequently asked four agencies—the Federal Reserve, the Federal Deposit Insurance Corporation, the Comptroller of the Currency, and the RFC—to review their own position toward the matter. All without exception opposed the dissolution of existing bank-holding companies yet wanted to limit their expansion. But they could not agree on which government agency should regulate them. A governmental stalemate followed, during which Transamerica busily acquired additional banks, not only in California but in the neighboring states of Oregon, Arizona, Nevada, and Washington. In February, 1943, three government agencies—the Federal Reserve Board, the Comptroller of the Currency, and the FDIC—jointly notified Transamerica that they would decline permission for it to acquire directly or indirectly any additional banking offices. The same government agencies then deputized Marriner Eccles to call on Transamerica officers and explain the implications of that notice. In doing so, Marriner secured a "stand-still pledge" from A. P. Giannini. Transamerica did not stand still for very long, and acquired additional banks, with the intention of converting them into branches either of the Bank of America or the First National Bank of Portland.

In 1944, when the Treasury Department asked the Federal Reserve Board to "police" Transamerica's activities, J. P. Dreibelbis, the then general counsel of the board, indicated in a legal brief that, under the Clayton Act, the board had the legal right to move against monopolies or monopoly practices related to banking. The case, however, was put on the back burner for the remainder of the war. But in October 1945 the Federal Reserve Board, spurred by the continued expansion of Transamerica, asked Attorney General Thomas C. Clark to explore the prospects for antitrust actions against that holding company. In a letter of reply, Clark summarized the results of a Justice Department investigation. "There was," said he, "no persuasive evidence that the Transamerica Corporation was a complete monopoly." And there was no persuasive evidence that Transamerica had abused its dominant position in the commercial banking field, either through "illegal trade practices as those terms are defined in court decisions interpreting the Sherman Act, or that it abused its dominant position once it was achieved." In the absence of a complete monopoly, evidence of one or both of the forementioned types of abuse was essential to make an actionable case under the Sherman Act.

A round of meetings followed where representatives of the Justice Department, the Federal Reserve Board, the Comptroller's Office, and the FDIC agreed on three points. First, though it seemed unlikely that a Sherman Act antitrust suit against Transamerica could succeed in court, it was in the public interest to try by *legislative* means to check the further expansion of the Transamerica group. Second, while the proposed legislation could not change preexisting things, it could stop the expansion of a bank-holding company. Third, to the latter end, the Federal Reserve Board should be armed with the necessary legal means. Accordingly, the board initiated the preparation of a bank-holding company bill with the object of having it introduced into the Congress in 1947.

IV

It was amid the events so far related that John Snyder became Secretary of the Treasury. Tensions rising from policy differences between the Federal Reserve Board and the Treasury did not take any immediate turn for the worse. But neither was there any let-up in the inflationary expansion of bank credit, stemming from the Treasury's continued insistence that the Reserve System support the market for government securities at fixed prices. In the economy itself, price increases in the fifteen months between August 1945 and November 1946 in many cases exceeded the aggregate increases in the five years between 1940 and VJ day.

Meanwhile, the 1946 congressional election—known as the "housewives' pork-chop election" because of the high price of meat at the grocery store—gave the Republicans majority control of both chambers of Congress for the first time since 1930. After the election, the Federal Reserve Board, in its 1946 annual report to Congress, again called attention to the Federal Reserve System's inadequate powers to cope with inflation. But, in contrast to its 1945 report, the board did not propose a specific plan of action. It had learned in advance that it could get neither administration support nor congressional consideration for adequate legislation from the incoming eightieth Congress.

In the fall of 1947 inflationary pressures were so acute, and the public clamor for relief so intense, that President Truman called a special session of Congress in November. The Reserve Board prepared a specific plan to restrain the expansion of bank credit and of consumer credit as well. The plan as applied to bank credit was based on the idea for a special reserve set-up first mentioned in the 1945 annual report. The terms proposed would apply to all banks receiving demand and time deposits, insured and uninsured banks, member and nonmember banks of the Federal Reserve alike. But they would not apply to banks doing a savings business exclusively. All banks covered by the proposed plan would be required (in addition to their regular reserves) to hold a special reserve consisting of United States obligation such as Treasury bills, certificates and notes or, at the option of the bank, cash or its equivalent. The power to impose and to vary the special reserve requirements—subject to a maximum amount fixed by statute —would be vested in the Federal Open Market committee and would be limited by law to a three-year period.

Marriner and the other members of the Federal Reserve Board believed that the plan would give the Reserve System a working tool to support government securities and, at the same time, restrain bank credit. By partially separating government financing from private financing, the low rates on the former would not determine the rates on the latter. Restraint on private lending could be imposed by substantial increases in the discount rate of the Federal Reserve banks. Nor would the plan deny income to the banks, as would be the case if further increases in reserve requirements were authorized. Banks would get some returns on short-term securities which the Reserve System would lock up.

Some banking leaders were opposed to the special-reserve on grounds that it was impractical, socialistic, drastic and, in any event, not strong enough to achieve its expressed objective. Others considered the plan unnecessary, since the banks themselves, as a matter of ordinary business prudence, had a vital interest in preventing excessive credit expansion. Marriner noted that "ordinary prudence" had no real meaning as long as banks could readily meet unlimited private credit demands when those demands were vigorously sustained by the very inflation they contributed to. Banks could not refuse safe credit demands of individuals whose requests for loans, taken separately, were based on legitimate credit needs. The rub was that, in freely accommodating legitimate credit demands, the banking system expanded bank deposits and added to the money supply.

Despite these objections, Marriner believed that he could count on the administration's support. He had been approached by President Truman's general counsel, Clark Clifford, who was drafting a ten-point inflation-control program the president was to present to the special session of the eightieth Congress. The first two items on the draft program called for restraints on both bank and consumer credit, and Clifford asked Marriner for suggestions from the Federal Reserve Board.

On behalf of the board, Marriner sent him the special-reserve plan, as well as another plan designed to restrain consumer credit. Clifford, in response, asked the board to prepare a short statement covering its legislative recommendation, for incorporation in the president's message to Congress. Secretary of the Treasury Snyder, meanwhile, had been sent successive drafts of the material the board had prepared, including the final draft, which Clifford had approved. The explanatory statement read in part:

Under prevailing conditions of employment and production, with the continued shortage of labor and materials, an increase in the aggregate outstanding volume of credit extended to individuals or to business would increase demand for goods and services without increasing total production. For this reason, I recommend two measures at this time which would help to restrain extension of credit beyond what is necessary to maintain the highest possible production. . . .

As a more basic means of restricting excessive growth of bank credit, I recommend that Congress give to the Open Market Committee of the Federal Reserve System a temporary authority under which all banks engaged in receiving and paying out demand deposits may be required to hold in addition to present required reserves, some specific proportion of their deposits in the form of cash and balances with the Federal Reserve banks or other banks or in Treasury bills, certificates, or notes. At present the banking system has access, without effective limitation, to reserves upon which a multiple expansion of bank credit can be built. The proposed measure would serve to retard expansion of bank credit beyond the requirements of full and sustained production.

The president's message, as delivered, stated the need to curb the creation of inflationary bank credit but, surprisingly, failed to mention the special-reserve plan. Marriner learned that the Secretary of the Treasury had deleted the reference to it.

Later, in a meeting with Snyder and John Steelman, Truman's special assistant, Marriner observed that if the administration balked at supporting the board's proposal to restrain bank credit in line with the president's message, it should present an alternative plan. Snyder replied that since the flow of money and credit was a primary concern of the board, Marriner could speak for the board's position—and not for the administration—when Congress considered the president's inflation-control program. Snyder also added that, while he would not personally support the board's recommendations, he would raise no objections to them. Congress alone would judge the merits of the case.

The Joint Committee on the Economic Report, a creation of the Employment Act of 1946, was the first congressional committee to hold hearings on the president's message. Since the Republicans had won control of both the Senate and the House in 1946, the chairman of the Joint Committee was Senator Robert S. Taft. Marriner had often dueled with this Republican hierarch in previous years, but, despite their fundamental differences on many points of domestic and foreign policy matters, their personal relationship was marked by mutual respect.

Since the first two items on the administration's anti-inflation program dealt with curbs on consumer and bank credit, Marriner was called as the lead-off witness before the joint committee. If he had been sensitive to political currents—the climate was being roughed up in preparation for the 1948 presidential election—perhaps, as he later said, he would have "softened" his words. Since 1934, he had learned much in Washington about the legislative process. But as the head of an independent regulatory agency, he had never been a "political animal" in an electioneering sense, tailoring his utterances with an eye to their effect on voter responses on election day. Where electioneering was concerned, he did not know, didn't care to know and had no aptitude for learning when to play the fox and when the lion.

Testifying on the causes of the inflation that was then rampant—the cost of living would soon be a third more than it had been in 1945—he condemned the Democrats for removing the harness of controls, and the Democrats and Republicans alike for reducing taxes and failing to create large budgetary surpluses. He then made the case for the special reserve, but coupled it with a reminder "that the need for action on the monetary and credit front would be reduced to the extent that needed action was taken on the far more important front of fiscal policy." Where, he caustically asked, were the "budget balancers" who decried government deficits during the deflation and massive unemployment of the Great Depression, who were strangely silent when a balanced budget, to be attained by higher taxes on a booming economy, was a categorical imperative in the postwar years? How could deficits be justified when industrial production promised to surpass its wartime peak—and when employment was steadily rising—54 million jobs in 1956, 57 million in 1945, 60 million in 1947?

Marriner's testimony received wide press coverage, and more than one Washington eyebrow was raised when Senator Taft warmly complimented him on his presentation. With his presidential ambitions, Taft had a natural interest in encouraging anyone prominently identified with a Democratic administration to speak in sharp criticism of it. Yet the senator seemed to favor the special-reserve concept on its merits; enough, at least, to discomfit various bankers who appeared before the joint committee to testify against the plan. Taft's buzz-saw questions seemed designed to bring home to them a truth they had ignored—that they had no thought-out alternative plan.

While Marriner moved on to support the special-reserve proposal at a hearing of the House Banking and Currency Committee, Snyder went before the Joint Committee to testify about other items on the administration's anti-inflation program. At one point, asked what he thought of the special-reserve plan, he replied that he didn't think it would work. He neither elaborated on his skepticism nor offered a substitute proposal; yet his few words were at once converted by the press into front-page news stories bearing captions like these:

SNYDER DISAGREES WITH ECCLES ON RESERVES

SNYDER, ECCLES SPLIT ON BANK CREDIT CONTROLS

TREASURY HEAD AGAINST GIVING BLANKET POWER TO RAISE RESERVES

The stories beneath the captions implied that Snyder had lined up with the bankers in opposing the Reserve Board's proposed curbs not only on bank credit but also on consumer credit. Congress, on its part, did what came naturally to it in the face of formidable banker opposition on the one side and lack of administration support on the other. It did nothing. It neither gave the board the power to authorize a special reserve nor approved the restraint on consumer credit. In a time of retrospect, Marriner remarked:[20]

I can't say that we would have been granted the power to impose a special reserve if the Secretary of the Treasury had actively backed the Board's request, or if he had said nothing. Moreover, it would be wrong to imply that there was something insidious in his opposition to our program. Even my friend Allan Sproul, the president of the New York Federal Reserve Bank, who is the very soul of integrity, testified against the Board's program, and his stand honestly reflected the opposition of the bankers in his district to the special reserve plan. My point is, however, that I was disturbed by Secretary Snyder's failure to support the Board in the matter at issue. In the absence of anything better, the device of the special reserve was the only way the Reserve Board could simultaneously serve the Treasury's need for a stable market for government securities at existing levels and at the same time answer the President's call for a curb on the inflationary expansion of bank credit.

It is possible that a distracted President Truman may have failed to grasp what was at issue. The Cold War by now was on in earnest; the world was polarized by rival camps led, respectively, by the United States and the Soviet Union; American ships—propelled by the Truman doctrine—were carrying food, bullets and advisers to Greece and Turkey. With foreign affairs engrossing the president's attention, it is possible that he did not read the text of an official document that was issued over his name and that ran contrary to the stand previously taken by Secretary Snyder. That document was the president's Economic Report for 1947, sent to Congress in early January 1948. It stated, unambiguously, that in view of their central relation to inflation controls, current proposals for curbs on credit, "especially those which have been presented by the Board of Governors for the increase of bank reserve requirements, should be given close study by the Congress, and legislation should be enacted of a sufficiently comprehensive character to make available all the powers that may be needed."

v

The events just related ran parallel with those involving the bank-holding company bill, as drafted by the Federal Reserve Board, and introduced into the Congress in 1947. The Senate Banking and Currency Committee, after extensive hearings, unanimously reported out a satisfactory version of the measure, but leaders of the counterpart House committee said they would be willing to consider the bill *only* if it were passed by the Senate. That was the end of the matter. The bill was never placed on the Senate calendar for a debate and vote. It was pigeonholed because of the backstage opposition of John Snyder and of the Comptroller of the Currency who was subordinate to him.

In the meantime, another possibility for curbing the expansion of the Transamerica Corporation was opened up by the decision the Supreme Court had rendered on June 10, 1946, in the case of the *American Tobacco Company* v. *The United States*. The decision seemed to say that proof of abusive tactics was not an indispensable element in an antitrust case. It was enough to show that a corporation was in a *position* to exert monopolistic power. Leonard Townsend, counsel for the Federal Reserve Board, believed that, if the foregoing information was correct, it would remove the barrier cited as an impediment to an anti-trust suit against Transamerica. With this in mind, Marriner wrote Attorney General Clark on February 26, 1947, to ask if the Court's decision in the American Tobacco case "might not lessen" the department's earlier doubts "as to the ultimate success of anti-trust proceedings against Transamerica." In a brief note of reply, dated March 4, Clark said he would be glad to reconsider the case and would get in touch with Marriner "sometime soon." If conventional governmental procedures had been followed, the attorney general would have turned Marriner's letter over to the Antitrust Division of the Justice Department for interagency discussions with the legal staff of the Federal Reserve Board. In the next six weeks, however, no such interagency staff discussions were held, nor was there any further word from the attorney general.

But a chance meeting between Marriner and Clark occurred at the end of this period. "By the way," Marriner asked, "what ever happened to that letter I sent you about the possible relationship between the Supreme Court's decision in the tobacco case and the Transamerica matter?" Clark explained, "I was asked by the Secretary of the Treasury to keep him advised of any matter pertaining to Transamerica that might come to my notice as attorney general. When I received your letter, I was obligated to send it to him." Marriner promptly informed the Federal Reserve Board of this interesting fact, and with its backing, on April 15, 1947, sent Secretary Snyder a carefully worded note:

On February 26 last I wrote Tom asking whether his Department had considered the recent decision of the Supreme Court in the American Tobacco case in relation to the Transamerica matter. . . . I talked with him again about a week ago and he told me that he had asked you to consider the entire matter and to give him the benefit of your views.

While I know how extremely busy you are, I nevertheless hope that you will be able to give this subject your early consideration. The Board is very anxious to obtain a decision from Justice on this subject just as soon as possible so that it may determine its own future course of action in dealing with this vexing problem. I do not know whether Tom sent you a copy of my letter of February 26th. A copy is enclosed herewith. If there is any other information touching this matter which we can supply you, please let me know.

The letter was never acknowledged.

In the fall of 1947, the Reserve Board learned something that was not by itself unusual—that the Comptroller of the Currency was being pressured to permit the Gianninis to branch the additional banks Transamerica had acquired. However, he no longer resisted the arm twisting as in former years. In an increasing number of cases since John Snyder became Secretary of the Treasury, the Comptroller approved Transamerica's requests. The reason seemed obvious. The Comptroller's office is a bureau of the Treasury; its legal staff is directly subordinate to the Treasury's general counsel; the Comptroller's deputies are appointed by and serve at the pleasure of the Secretary of the Treasury.

Since the attorney general would act *in re* Transamerica only on the advice of the Secretary of the Treasury, and since the Secretary kept his advice to himself, what, if anything, could the board itself do in the matter?

Leonard Townsend replied with a legal brief that stressed two points. First, the Comptroller of the Currency probably did not feel justified in refusing to approve Transamerica's applications to establish more branch banks when the Reserve Board itself had not proceeded against Transamerica. Second, it was still the duty and responsibility of the board under the Clayton Act to execute aspects of national policy regarding the restraint of trade and monopolies.

Spurred by this legal brief, the Reserve Board on November 7, 1947, notified the attorney general, the chairman of the FDIC, and the Comptroller of the Currency that it had started a preliminary investigation of Transamerica to determine if there were grounds to justify Clayton Act proceedings against it. The comptroller informed the board that he had on his desk Bank of America applications to take over and convert into branches twenty-six banks under Transamerica control, along with applications by the First National Bank of Portland to do the same with ten other Transamerica-controlled banks. A further exchange of letters between the board and the comptroller produced a stand-still agreement by whose terms the comptroller would defer action on the pending applications until the board had finished its investigation and decided what its next step should be.

VI

In the third week of December, before Marriner left Washington to spend the Christmas holidays in Utah, he called on President Truman. While the relationship between the two men lacked the give-and-take intimacy of Marriner's relationship with President Roosevelt, it was friendly enough. Marriner always had ready access to Truman, and was given to understand that he possessed his full confidence. The first item of discussion was the future composition of the Federal Reserve Board of Governors, in view of the untimely death of Ronald Ransom, and the impending expiration of the term of Matt S. Szymczak. Truman agreed that Szymczak should be reappointed, and at the same time said he would not fill the vacancy created by Ransom's death without first discussing the matter with Marriner. The second issue brought forward by Marriner concerned the way his differences of opinion with Secretary Snyder regarding approaches to bank-credit controls had been treated by the press. He regretted, said Marriner, that Snyder's offhand remark at the hearing of the Joint Committee on the Economic Report chaired by Senator Taft had been amplified into a major clash between the Treasury and the Federal Reserve. As a battle-scarred veteran of press attacks, the president readily accepted Marriner's explanation about what had happened, and was neither annoyed nor disturbed by the press hubbub.

It was on this cordial note then that the two men wished each other a merry Christmas and a happy New Year. There was also a cordial Christmas note from Secretary Snyder which Marriner received before leaving for Utah.

The fine understanding between the Federal Reserve System and the Treasury Department which has made possible such a splended record of cooperation during the past year, is a source of much gratification to me. I am indebted to you for setting the tempo. You have my best wishes for a happy and prosperous holiday season and New Year.

At the time of the pre-Christmas meeting in the White House, there is no reason to believe that the president was aware that Marriner's four year statutory term as chairman of the Federal Reserve Board would soon expire, or that he knew of the board's move to investigate the affairs of the Transamerica Corporation. There *is* reason to believe, however, that soon after the meeting, people who were aware of the first detail, and had more than a bystander's interest in the second, not only brought both pieces of information to President Truman's attention but were able to influence what he did about them.

It was not a joyous holiday season Marriner spent in Utah. His wife Maisie by now was in the seventh year of her absence from Washington. It seemed best, however painful, to legally terminate a marriage that had no more life in it. By mutual consent, it was agreed that divorce proceedings would be instituted. After the first of the year, Marriner returned to Washington, where he was presently treated to a further jolt.

34. Knifed

ON THURSDAY, JANUARY 22, 1948, nine days before Marriner's term as chairman of the Board of Governors was to expire, he received a telephone call from John Steelman. Could the two get together that day? Marriner explained that he was due to be at an important meeting of the National Advisory Council but would come to the White House the next day. "All right," said Steelman, "but don't make it any later than that."

On that Friday, Steelman greeted Marriner in a friendly way and, after a brief chat about general economic conditions, came to the point. "The president," said he, "has given me a very unpleasant assignment. I am to inform you that he is not going to redesignate you as chairman of the Board of Governors. But he told me to be sure you understand that he wants you to stay on as a member of the board."

Marriner was dumbfounded. "The president has a right to designate any man he wants as chairman," he said when he finally regained his power of speech. "But when I saw him at Christmas time, he in no way indicated that I would not be redesignated. Why did he wait until nine days before my term was up? What's back of this?"

"Marriner, believe me, I don't know what this is all about," Steelman replied. "Few people stand as high in the White House as you do. This is as much of a surprise to me as it is to you and I have told you all I know." He added that the matter was "not subject to reconsideration." The president, however, would be willing to see Marriner any time he wished. When Marriner asked for the earliest possible appointment, Steelman at once called Truman's secretary and an appointment was set at the White House for ten-thirty the next morning.

When I saw the President [Marriner later recalled][21] it was obvious that he had been influenced to make a distasteful and embarrassing decision. Our meeting was an ordeal for him and for me. I assured him that I knew better than most people that the relationship between a President and a Chairman of the Board of Governors is an intimate one; that, recognizing this, I had offered to resign in 1945 so that he could fill the post with a man of his own choice. I therefore did not question the decision that had been conveyed to me, but I would be sub-human if I did not show some interest in finding out what had happened since I last saw him shortly before Christmas.

I observed that if he had advised me in December that he wanted to designate someone else as Chairman of the Board, I would have had a decent interval in which to resign from the Board of Governors and announce that I was not a candidate for redesignation as chairman. In this way, I could have saved all parties painful embarrassment. But to submit such a resignation just a few days before my term was due to end, would create the impression that I had failed at my job and was being asked to resign.

The President responded by saying that when I saw him in December, he had not thought about the matter. As for the action he later decided to take, it had nothing whatever to do with me. He wanted me to stay on the Board and would designate me as its vice chairman if I would agree. If there was some other position in the government service I wanted that was available, he would be glad to give it to me. He had every confidence in me and completely approved of my actions and those taken by the Board of Governors during my chairmanship.

He said several times: "Please stay and help me. I need your help."

"What, then, is behind this change?" I asked him.

Once again he repeated that the change was for reasons that had nothing to do with me, but were best known to himself alone. It was clear that he did not want me to know what lay behind his action. Any further questioning would serve no purpose except to prolong the unhappy interview. I told him at last that I did not know whether it would be possible for me to remain on the Board, since the whole turn of events had taken me by surprise; I would need time to get my bearings again. The President, for some reason, was anxious to have my reply as promptly as possible, and it was arranged for me to see him again on the following Tuesday, January 27. I would give him my answer at that time.

There have been times in my life when I felt cut off from all human contact, but never as completely and painfully as on the three days following this call at the White House. I knew that the decision of a President not to redesignate an incumbent to a government post was not the end of the Republic. It is an incident of the moment that is quickly absorbed and forgotten in the tidal ebb and flow of American life. Yet when *you* are that official, holding a nonpolitical office for fourteen years, you feel yourself thrust naked into public view with all eyes turned in your direction for an explanation.

Marriner did not think of himself as wedded to public office, and he was indifferent to the glamor of high places. He had stayed on in Washington at President Roosevelt's request in order to push for reformist measures, and he had stayed on at President Truman's request in order to complete tasks in hand. As a leading actor since 1934 in the struggle to govern the nation, he never sought nor secured any unwarranted personal gain from the policies he advocated. He was ambitious for power, but it was for the power to discharge his official responsibilities.

Meanwhile, he had paid a heavy personal price for the years he spent in Washington. His marriage was headed for the divorce courts, and, though he had always been a concerned father, he had little time for his children; they had come of age at a distance from him. Any divorce carries with it a sense of defeat, and so does any gulf that arises between a parent and children. But Marriner's inward loneliness on these counts was now made all the more acute by his inability to account for what lay behind the White House decision. In his business enterprises and in his approach to public problems, he had always been confident that if he probed deep beneath surface appearances, he could perceive cause and effect. But in this event, everything was shrouded in fog. Nameless and faceless forces wanted him out of the way for indeterminable reasons.

All I knew [so Marriner later recalled][22] is what my instincts told me. President Truman had been brought under great political pressure by certain interests that wanted me out as Chairman, and off the Board, and the same interests thought that if I were not redesignated as Chairman, I would promptly resign from the Board. My instincts further told me that the President was in earnest when he said that he wanted me to continue in government service. He could satisfy those who were bringing pressure on him by not redesignating me as Chairman, and he could satisfy his own desires by urging that I remain on the Board.

The range of choices Marriner faced was equally bleak. If he resigned as a member of the board—though his appointment still had ten more years to run—he would immediately satisfy his wounded pride but he would give currency to a public impression that he had failed in the discharge of his duties. If he remained on the board, he would have to swallow his pride and accept a subordinate place in an institution he had revolutionized. It was a painful prospect; for the greater part of his adult life, Marriner had always been the number one man at the head of the table of any enterprise with which he was associated. Still, if he was prepared to go along with the president's proposal, he could in all probability get a letter from Truman stating the substance of their Saturday conversation in the White House.

On the advice of friends and several Senate leaders he took into his confidence—including senators Robert Taft and Arthur Vandenberg—and after no small personal convulsion, Marriner swallowed his pride. On Tuesday morning, January 27, he called on President Truman to say that he would remain on the board, but asked that the shift be announced through an exchange of letters. One, from the president, would be along the lines Marriner had in mind. The other, from Marriner, would contain an expressed willingness to remain on the board in the capacity of vice-chairman, as Truman had suggested. The president quickly assented to the arrangement. Final texts were prepared at the White House and the exchanges were made before Marriner left there that morning. With Truman's consent, he called on Charles Ross, the president's press secretary, and turned the letters over to him.

"For heaven's sake, Marriner!" Ross exclaimed when he read the texts handed to him. "What's happened? I couldn't be more surprised. This is a mistake."

"I wish I knew what's back of this," said Marriner, "but I don't. The letters will have to speak for themselves." The letters read:

Dear Mr. Eccles:

Shortly after I became President you offered to resign as Chairman of the Board of Governors of the Federal Reserve System and said it was your feeling that the Chairman, who is designated by the President, should serve at his pleasure. I told you then and on other occasions that there was no one I desired to appoint in your place.

You will have completed your present term as Chairman on February 1, your appointment as a member of the Board continuing until 1958. As I explained to you last week, it is now my preference to appoint a new member of the Board to fill the vacancy created by the death of Vice Chairman Ransom, and, when confirmed by the Senate, to designate him as Chairman.

This decision, as I assured you, reflects no lack of complete confidence in you, or dissatisfaction in any respect with your public service, or disagreement on monetary or debt-management policies, or with official actions taken by the Board under your chairmanship. All who are familiar with your record recognize your devotion to the public welfare and the constructiveness that has characterized your leadership in the Federal Reserve System.

Therefore, I urged you to remain as a member of the Board and to accept the Vice Chairmanship so that the benefit of your long experience and judgment will continue to be available and so that you may carry forward legislative proposals now pending in Congress dealing with the important problems of bank credit as outlined in the President's Economic Report to Congress, as well as with other matters in the interest of a sound banking system and a sound economy.

Sincerely yours,
Harry S. Truman.

My dear Mr. President:

You have stated in your complimentary letter the substance of your conversation of last week. As I advised you then, I desired to have time to consider fully your decision and request. I have not altered my conviction that the Chairman of this Board should serve at the pleasure of the President, and I sought to have such a provision included in the Banking Act of 1935.

I have carefully considered your request. After consultation with close friends and associates on the Board and because of the reasons mentioned in your letter, I have decided to remain with the Board in the capacity you suggest.

Respectfully yours,
M. S. Eccles
Chairman.

When Marriner decided to remain on the board, he anticipated a scornful public reaction upon the release of the news. It would be said, he thought, that he was just another timeserver, with no independent life of his own and with not enough dignity to get out of Washington when his services were no longer wanted by the administration. He particularly expected this from the financial and business community whom he had enraged by his various stands over the years on public issues. Spokesmen for that community would lend their voices to a chorus of regret—sounding in the press and in Congress—that he had not seen fit to resign at that time.

Public reaction to the news, however, was the exact opposite of what Marriner expected. Old and implacable adversaries made common cause with old and steadfast friends in resounding praise of his governmental career and of his willingness to stay on under humbling conditions. The many kind things that were said helped alter the face of the event from a defeat to a triumph of the spirit. It was brought home to Marriner, as never before, that his strenuous efforts on one or another front of public policy in the preceding years were not without effect.

At a White House press conference following the release of the Truman-Eccles letters, the president was sharply questioned about the changes that had been announced, but none of his answers satisfied the reporters. In the absence of anything better, it was said that Marriner had at last proved to be "too much for Wall Street to swallow," and that "the president at last bowed before banker pressure." In the same breath it was said that by "insisting on a balanced budget and tighter credit policies, Eccles had foresaken his earlier position in the New Deal years and had gone over to the camp of the reactionaries." The President was alleged to be "annoyed by his consorting with Republicans like Tobey, Taft, and Vandenberg," and Eccles was supposed to have caused the "Administration considerable political embarrassment by implying that it had a full share of responsibility for failing to curb inflationary developments."

Marriner continued to remain in the dark as to which, if any, of these reasons seemed the more valid explanation of what had happened. Other political obligations might call for payoffs in the form of jobs, but in this instance, no one wanted the job for himself, and especially not in the 1948 presidential election year, when all the signs seemed to indicate that the Republicans would win the election in November. In fact, one of the White House aides who was assigned the task of finding a new chairman of the Board of Governors confided to Marriner that he had been repeatedly turned down by the likely candidates he approached. As for the nameless people who wanted Marriner removed, none came forward with substitute candidates. All they wanted was to get Marriner out.

The mysteries deepened as President Truman failed to follow through on his suggestion that Marriner be appointed vice-chairman of the Federal Reserve Board. The same sources that were behind the original decision may have reasoned that if the vice-chairmanship was withheld, Marriner would feel compelled to get off the board as he was supposed to have done in January. On April 16, two and one-half months after the offer of the vice-chairmanship had been made—by which time Thomas B. McCabe had been chosen as chairman—Marriner sent Truman a letter saying that he wished to have his name withdrawn from consideration as vice-chairman. The president refused to accept the letter because, he said, he still meant to go ahead with the original understanding. When nothing of the sort happened in the next month and a half, Marriner again wrote to the president (on May 26) and asked to have his name withdrawn, adding that he would continue to serve as a member of the Board of Governors. This time the letter was accepted. Marriner did not need a title to make his influence felt on the Board of Governors. Wherever he sat as an ordinary board member was the head of the table.

At no time did Marriner ever discover an explanation which was free from doubt in his own mind. Did Secretary Snyder simply want to get rid of his abrasive adversary? Did Snyder act as the hatchet man for the Giannini interests in California? Did the Gianninis want him out of the way in the belief that without him governmental action in the Transamerica case would die on the vine? In a presidential election year, when California was a key variable in President Truman's hopes for election, were the Gianninis in a position to demand the exile of Marriner as the price of their support of Truman—or neutrality—in the campaign? Marriner answered these questions differently at different times of his life but was never certain where the truth lay. Ironically, after years of litigation the Justice Department, which had taken over the Transamerica case from the Federal Reserve Board, finally decided to drop it. More ironically still, Marriner agreed with that decision. "There was," he said, "no way on earth to prevent the Bank of America from expanding."[23]

II

President Truman won an upset victory in 1948 in a "give 'em hell, Harry," campaign in which he blasted the Republic-controlled eightieth Congress as a "do-nothing, good-for-nothing Congress." The Democratic party regained control of the House and Senate. Yet, afterward, the only visible difference between the eightieth Congress and the eighty-first was the difference between "do-nothing" and "ho-hum." At least so it seemed to Marriner when the Reserve System's repeated requests for congressional support for its inflation control program could not pierce the wall of congressional indifference or ignorance.

In the country at large, relatively few people were aware of the running conflict between the Federal Reserve and the Treasury or grasped its direct bearing on their own and on the nation's economic well-being. The need to raise the threshold of public awareness of what was at stake and, at the same time, to resolve the conflict in ways that would serve the public interest kept Marriner in Washington when he had strong personal motives to resign and return to Utah. The need also lay behind a project he undertook at this time. He spent his spare moments—at night, over weekends and holidays —in working on what became his analytical memoir, *Beckoning Frontiers*.

Suddenly, in June 1950, the "postwar world" became the world of the Korean war. From the start, Marriner had strong reservations about America's involvement in it. He feared that the United States was stumbling into an uncharted Asian morass without reckoning the costs. He did not adhere to the civil religion which conceives of America as a steward of divine righteousness and the carrier of divine destiny. He believed there were limits to American power, and he was mindful that no nation had a built-in immunity against the ancient truths that good fortune never remains in the same place for long, and that the problems of success can be as great as the problems of failure.

Some of his reservations appeared in an article he prepared at the request of the editors of *Fortune* magazine for publication in their issue of November 1950. The entire number was devoted to the new defense program spurred by the Korean war, and all articles in it were staff written except for Marriner's signed piece devoted to its economic aspects. He analyzed in detail the terms for a manageable economic program in support of a long-range, open-ended national security policy but, at one point, interjected several paragraphs that could just as well have been left unstated without weakening the main thrust of his argument:

When it is realized that we have but six percent of the world's population and limited resources, it becomes evident that we must utilize our restricted manpower and materials most efficiently as well as make every effort to mobilize for defense all the manpower and resources of neutral nationals wherever possible. This becomes increasingly evident as we make an appraisal of our geographical handicaps, the obstacles of distance, and the potential enemy's superior numbers and position. . . .

World security depends upon our getting a better balance of power with Russia. Therefore, as soon as the Korean War is over, we should recognize the present government of China and support its membership in the United Nations, as Britain, India, and others of our friends have done. The future status of Formosa should be left to determination by the United Nations. Such action is justified because Chiang Kai Shek's Nationalist government cannot speak for China. Recognition would also help maintain the national independence of China and may prevent it from becoming just another Russian satellite. As long as we recognize Communist Yugoslavia, to say nothing of Communist Russia and her satellites, it is difficult to justify our failure to recognize Communist China before the Korean War. . . . The Korean War is only an incident in the long, hard task of achieving and maintaining peace in the world. Its termination must not prevent us from carrying out the essential long-term program. In that lies the hope, however remote it now seems, that Russia may find it in her own interest to seek a genuine peace.

In saying that "Chiang Kai-Shek's Nationalist government cannot speak for China." Marriner did not reinforce his case by drawing on his personal knowledge about how members of Chiang's immediate entourage had lined their pockets even as they wept about the "poor Chinese." For example, at the time of the Bretton Woods conference, General Lucius Clay had privately detailed for Marriner the full story of the enormous bills Chiang's associates had submitted to the White House for wartime work on Chinese soil. One such bill for $200 million was the claimed cost of building an airfield behind Japanese lines in China, for use by bombers under the command of General James Doolittle of the U.S. airforce. Even the final settlement price of $100 million was an American concession.[24]

Again, Marriner had been a member of the U.S. governmental committee which approved a grant of $500 million for use by General George C. Marshall in trying to bring the Nationalist and the Communist Chinese together. With the failure of that mission, the $500 million was deposited in New York, ostensibly to help stabilize the Nationalist Chinese yen. Yet it was not long before Chiang's intimate associates got their hands on $300 million of the $500 million stabilization fund by buying dollars with yen worth only one-sixth of their official value. Intelligence agents of the United States government who had the task of finding the missing $300 million later reported that part of the sum was used by Chiang's associates to buy apartment buildings in New York City and in Washington; part was carried as deposits to their personal account in New York and London banks; and part was used to support the China lobby in Washington, which, among other things, backed the reelection bids of congressmen favorable to and favored by the lobby.

Marriner's call for a *post*-Korea recognition of Communist China led to a telephone call from the chief editor of *Fortune* magazine. The editor explained that the defense issue was about to go to press, and that the article Marriner wrote for it was excellent except for one "small matter." Objections had been raised at *Fortune* about his lines concerning the Nationalist and the Communist Chinese. Would he be good enough to allow their deletion since they were not germane to the rest of his economic analysis?

Marriner flatly refused to permit the deletion—which he assumed had been ordered by Henry R. Luce the owner of *Fortune* and a passionate supporter of Chiang Kai Shek. The people at *Fortune,* he said, were free to reject the whole of his article; but if they published it, it must be as *he* wrote it. With a deadline at hand, it was too late for anyone else to write something to fill the space earmarked for Marriner's text. His article was published with the "objectionable" passages intact, though with a footnote in which the editors of *Fortune* registered their dissent from his views about the Nationalist and Communist Chinese. The greater part of his article was later incorporated in the pages of *Beckoning Frontiers*. After that, the same "objectionable" passages were to have a long career.

III

In the six months between June 1950 and the start of 1951, the cost of living rose 7 percent, wholesale prices 17 percent, wholesale farm prices 22 percent, textile products 32 percent, and basic raw materials 50 percent. These increases were not due to the arms program or to an excess of government spending over receipts. The volume of arms production was still relatively small, while the federal government's receipts exceeded expenditures by almost $2 billion. The price rise was mainly due to two interrelated factors, of which the first was the increased use in the *existing* excessive supply of money. Secondly, the existing supply was greatly expanded because the Reserve System was still being forced to support the government security market in line with the Treasury's cheap money policy. This entailed continued purchases by the system of government securities from nonbank as well as from bank investors, and the result was an abnormal and swift growth in bank credit. In the last half of 1950, the banking system expanded its loans and investments by 20 percent—about $10 billion—while concurrently increasing by 8 percent the money supply in the form of deposits.

The cold statistics of a hot inflationary spiral dominated the domestic economic picture by the end of 1950. But, suddenly, the economic picture was absorbed into a military and political emergency fanning outward from the far-off Korean battlefield. In late 1950, a Chinese Communist army swarmed across the Yalu River and into North Korea, caught the command of General Douglas MacArthur by surprise, and forced the American-led United Nations units into a fighting retreat down the length of Korea until a defense line was formed around "the Pusan perimeter." It was now apparent that the United States had on its hands not a "police action" but a major conflict of indeterminate length, although it was called a "limited war."

Against the background of affairs in Asia, there now began to unfold in Washington one of the more abrasive conflicts in the troubled history of Treasury-Reserve relations. The curtain raiser was a speech John Snyder made on January 9, 1951, at a luncheon meeting of the New York Board of Trade. In the course of his remarks, he announced a policy of debt management whose purpose was to free, for the duration of the Korean War, the existing pattern of rates for government securities. The Secretary said:

> In the firm belief, after long consideration, that the 2½ percent long-term rate is fair and equitable to the investor, and that market stability is essential, the Treasury Department has concluded, after joint conferences with President Truman and Chairman McCabe of the Federal Reserve Board, that the refunding of new money issues will be financed within the pattern of that rate.

Here was an attempt to present the Federal Reserve System with a *fait accompli*. Chairman McCabe had no advance knowledge of what Snyder meant to say before the New York Board of Trade, nor did he personally agree with the announced policy. Besides, the right of an official endorsement of that policy resided in the twelve members of the Federal Reserve Open Market Committee who were *collectively* responsible to the Congress, and not to the Secretary of the Treasury, for the way they discharged their statutory duties under the Banking Act of 1935.

Four days after Snyder's pronouncement, Edward H. Collins, then the chief financial writer on the staff of the *New York Times,* struck a note of protest which other organs of the press were to echo. "All that Mr. Snyder has proved," Collins wrote, "would seem to be that he is still top dog at the White House. But this was enough to convince him that he has been right all along, and all this nonsense about short-term money rates and their application to inflation was just so much highfalutin book talk, important only for purpose of theoretical debate by central banking authorities." Collins continued:

> More shocking, fundamentally, than this absurd dictum, however, was the simple fact of what seemed to be the Secretary's mission. Central banks in their general policies may from time to time make concessions to the temporary needs of the

Exchequer, but when and if they do they announce the fact themselves. In the opinion of this writer, last Thursday constituted the first occasion in history on which the head of the Exchequer of a great nation had either the effrontery or the ineptitude, or both, to deliver a public address in which he has so far usurped the function of the central bank as to tell the country what kind of monetary policy it was going to be subjected to. For the moment at least, the fact that the policy enunciated by Mr. Snyder was, as usual, thoroughly unsound and inflationary, was overshadowed by the historic dimensions of this impertinence.

While this line of criticism was being amplified by the national press and by economists generally, the Federal Reserve Board observed a discrete official silence. Alan Sproul, President of the New York Federal Reserve Bank, and the ablest man in the regional System, however, replied by indirection to Snyder in a speech on January 22 before the New York State Banking Association. The press rightly construed Sproul's guarded remarks to be a challenge to Secretary Snyder's views. Marriner Eccles was in no mood to be indirect or guarded. He was aflame with anger and was ready to scorch the earth beneath the Treasury Department and Snyder's office in it.

The opportunity to do so arose with the help of Senator Taft. After the 1948 election, Taft had reverted to being the ranking Republican member on the Joint Committee on the Economic Report. With his own game to play in connection with his 1952 presidential ambitions, he had the joint committee invite Marriner to appear before that body on January 25 in order to present the Federal Reserve's side of the case in the mounting controversy with the Treasury Department. Democrats on the committee with close ties to the Truman administration did not want Marriner as a witness. They wanted Chairman McCabe. But McCabe begged off on the ground that he would be placed in an impossible position if he testified. He could not publicly defend the Treasury's position in view of his disagreement with it. Yet he could not oppose it publicly without resigning as chairman of the Federal Reserve Board. Marriner was under no such constraints. He accepted the invitation to appear at a hearing of the joint committee, and in plain words stated why the Reserve System was appalled by the substance and implications of the policy Secretary Snyder had announced.

The tumult continued. Never before in the history of the Federal Reserve System had a president called either the Reserve Board or the Federal Open Market Committee to the White House for the purpose of discussing or influencing their policies. Finding his administration under attack from all sides, President Truman broke with precedent and asked them to meet with him on January 31. Marriner was reluctant to join the other members of his committee but consented to go with them to the White House after they agreed with the two conditions he set. They would listen in respectful silence to what the president had to say; second, McCabe alone would respond for the committee, and then only in general terms.

Immediately after the end of that meeting, the committee returned to the Federal Reserve Building to assess what had been said. All the members without exception agreed that President Truman had *not* asked the committee, either directly or indirectly, to support the policy Secretary Snyder had announced on January 18; nor had McCabe given any pledges of support for it. Marriner now suggested, and the other members agreed, that a memorandum "for the record" should be prepared. Governor R. M. Evans, aided by Samuel Carpenter, the Secretary of the Board of Governors, prepared the memorandum, and the text, subject to minor corrections, was accepted as an accurate account of the event. This done, the meeting of the Federal Open Market Committee adjourned, with the members due to meet again in two weeks.

It is necessary to reproduce only part of the long memorandum, but the document as a whole would figure in an explosive new development.

The President stated that during the past few weeks he had met with many groups in the Government because he wanted them to know the seriousness of the present emergency and to ask for their full assistance and cooperation. He stated that the present emergency is the greatest this country has ever faced, including the two world wars and all the preceding wars.

He gave a brief sketch of the difficulty of dealing with the Russians.

The President emphasized that we must combat Communist influence on many fronts. He said one way to do this is to maintain confidence in the Government's credit and in government securities.

He felt that if people lose confidence in government securities all we hope to gain from our military mobilization, and war if need be, might be jeopardized. . . .

The President said that he felt he had done a good job and wanted us to continue to do a good job in maintaining the financial structure of the country. . . . He made no mention of recent differences of opinion with the Treasury.

Chairman McCabe thanked the President for receiving us and indicated that we all share his concern for the maintenance of the Government credit. . . . He stated that the Federal Open Market Committee always carefully weighed its responsibilities to the Government and to the general economy as well and that these are statutory responsibilities which it could not assign if it would. . . .

The chairman outlined concisely some of the responsibilities with which we were charged, principally to promote stability in the economy by regulating the volume, cost, and availability of money keeping in mind at all times the best interests of the whole economy. . . . Chairman McCabe stated that with a group of men such as these composing the Federal Open Market Committee, there would, of course, be differences of opinion as to just how the best results could be obtained. The President nodded, indicating that he understood this. The chairman suggested the following procedure: that we consult frequently with the Secretary of the Treasury, giving him our views at all times and presenting our point of view strongly, and that by every means possible we try to reach an agreement. If this could not be accomplished, he (the chairman) would like to discuss the matter with the President.

The President said this was entirely satisfactory and closed the meeting on the same note as it was opened—namely, that he wanted us to do everything possible to maintain confidence in the credit of the Government and in the Government securities market and to support the President of the United States in achieving this end. . . .

Though the text lacks literary polish, it well reveals the little that actually occurred at the White House meeting on January 31. Still, around noon of the next day, Thursday, February 1, ticker tapes serving news outlets in Washington and across the nation hammered out the following story:

WASHINGTON (AP)—The Federal Reserve Board has pledged its support to President Truman to maintain the stability of Government securities as long as the emergency lasts.

White House Press Secretary Joseph Short announced this today, saying there had been reports of differences of opinion between the Treasury and the Federal Reserve Board.

"This is to quiet those rumors," Short said.

Members of the Federal Reserve Board conferred with Mr. Truman yesterday. Secretary of the Treasury Snyder did not attend the meeting.

After a brief pause, the ticker tape added a second story: a source identified only as a "Treasury spokesman" construed the White House announcement to mean that the Federal Reserve had been aligned behind the position Secretary Snyder took in New York on January 18.

WASHINGTON (AP)—A Treasury spokesman said that the White House announcement meant the market for government securities will be established at present levels and that these levels will be maintained during the present emergency.

Soon afterward, Marriner received telephone calls from Alfred Friendly of the *Washington Post,* and from Felix Belair, Jr., of the *New York Times.* Both reporters observed that the back-to-back stories on the wires suggested that the Reserve System, under pressure from the president on the previous day, had capitulated to the Treasury. Was this true? No, said Marriner, it was not. There had been no pressure and no commitments.

Friendly and Belair, in the byline stories they wrote for the next day's edition of their respective newspapers, reported that, despite the White House statement, no settlement nor even a truce had been reached in the long-standing controversy between the Treasury and the Federal Reserve over monetary and credit policies. Yet, unknown to Marriner when he gave his telephone interviews to Friendly and Belair, the Treasury spokesman's interpretation of the White House meeting was being confirmed in a presidential letter drafted in the Treasury at the direction of Secretary Snyder. The letter signed by President Truman would be hand-delivered to Chairman McCabe later that afternoon.

The next morning, an executive session of the governors of the Federal Reserve Board was held at the express request of Governor James K. Vardaman, a Truman appointee and one of his intimate friends from Missouri. Vardaman had read what Alfred Friendly had written in the *Washington Post* and demanded to know who had been the source of the story. "The information in it," said he, "could only come from someone who was present at the White House meeting."

"*I* was the source of the information," Marriner promptly replied.

"What you did," said Vardaman in response to this unexpected admission, "was inappropriate."

Marriner stood his ground. "Under normal conditions," said he, "I would be equally critical of any such disclosures. But the circumstances were abnormal. In view of what the real facts were, there was the need promptly to correct the false impressions created by the White House press release, and particularly by the Treasury interpretation of the release."

The tension in the room increased when McCabe now showed the board the text of the letter he had received from President Truman on the previous afternoon. Addressed to "Dear Tom," its key passages read:

Your assurance that you would fully support the Treasury financing program, both as to refunding and new issues, is of vital importance to me. As I understand it, I have your assurance that the market on Government securities will be stabilized and maintained at present levels in order to assure the successful financing requirements and to establish in the mind of the people confidence concerning Government credit.

I wish you would convey to all the members of your group my warm appreciation of their cooperative attitude.

Board members instantly protested that no such assurances had been given. After much discussion, the members agreed to Marriner's suggestion of what to do next. McCabe should promptly secure an appointment with the president in order to show him the memorandum Governor Evans had prepared at the request of the Federal Open Market Committee. He should also ask that Truman's letter of Thursday afternoon be withdrawn because it was in direct conflict with the version of the Open Market Committee. The two-step procedure would spare the president embarrassment since his "Dear Tom" letter had not yet been released to the press. McCabe agreed. As events proved, however, he did not arrange to see Truman that Friday afternoon on an emergency basis, but left Washington to spend the weekend at his Philadelphia home.

Meanwhile, Secretary of the Treasury Snyder also read the stories that appeared in the morning editions of the *Washington Post* and the *New York Times*. He construed them to mean that the Open Market Committee would continue to resist any pressure to support the Treasury's announced policy of "pegged prices" for government securities. He arranged for a Byzantine move to be made. On late Friday afternoon, the White House released to the press the text of President Truman's letter to McCabe—without prior notice to him or to anyone else connected with the Reserve System. By the time it was on the wires, all the members and staff of the Reserve Board, except Marriner and his secretary Va Lois Egbert, had left their offices for the weekend. Marriner also meant to leave the Federal Reserve Building once he cleared his desk of paper work, but his plans were changed by a telephone call around seven in the evening. Felix Belair of the *New York Times* was on the line, and there was an edge to his voice. "I understood you to say," he began, "that the Open Market Committee hadn't agreed at the White House conference to support the market for government securities at present levels.''

"That's right,'' Marriner replied.

"Well, then, listen to this.'' He read the text of President Truman's letter to McCabe.

"Where did you get that?'' Marriner asked. "I thought that was a confidential letter.''

"Why, the White House has just released it to the world. What have you got to say to that?''

"I don't know,'' Marriner replied. "Let me think about it. I'll call you later.''

For Marriner, the release of the letter was no chance bubble in the oceanic ebb and flow of Washington news items. It was the ultimate attempt by the Treasury to impose its will on the Federal Reserve System. If the attempt succeeded, the Federal Reserve would no longer have a say in formulating monetary and credit policies. It would lose the status Congress meant it to have as an independent regulatory agency. In its most important function—open-market operations—it would be reduced to the level of a Treasury bureau.

In pushing through the Banking Act of 1935, Marriner had not helped break the power private banking interests wielded over the Reserve System merely to see the system become a captive of the Treasury. But what could he do at once to block the Treasury's intentions? His thoughts fastened on the confidential memorandum covering the White House discussions between President Truman and the Open Market Committee. If it were released to the press, objective readers would see at once that the president's letter to McCabe in no way reflected what transpired at the meeting. To be effective, however, the text must be promptly released. But who should take the initiative in the matter? McCabe? The full membership of the Open Market Committee? McCabe was away. Besides, as the president's choice to head the Federal Reserve Board, he could not personally release the memorandum without resigning as chairman of the Board. As for the Open Market Committee, the members could not be brought together in Washington until the first part of the next week. Even then it was doubtful if they would deem it appropriate officially to authorize publication of the memorandum.

Marriner Eccles had stood virtually alone at all the critical moments of his career in Washington, and it was alien to his nature to tailor any of his public actions to a mere desire to please. Nearly at the end of his career in Washington, he was driven by the conviction that if men lose their minds as well as their souls, there would be nothing left for the times to try. In this conviction, he knew that he must personally assume the responsibility of releasing the memorandum. The logic of everything he had publicly said in recent years, months, and weeks pointed to that conclusion.

But there was a complication in the decision that was taking shape in

Marriner's mind. In the immediately preceding months, while working on his book *Beckoning Frontiers,* he had been arranging to leave government service in Washington for a return home to Utah and to his private business interests in the West. As it happened, on January 28, 1951—three days before the White House meeting—he wrote but had not yet submitted to President Truman a letter of resignation from the Federal Reserve Board. The effective date of the resignation, March 1, would mark the end of seventeen years spent in government, sixteen as a member of the Federal Reserve Board. But what if he simultaneously released the memorandum and submitted his resignation? What then? It would then appear that he was running away from an alarming situation he had precipitated. To get on with the business of immediate concern, he must postpone his resignation.

Sam Carpenter had made only one copy of the Open Market Committee's memorandum. Marriner now called him at home, to relate what he had just learned from Felix Belair. Without revealing what he wanted to do with the copy in question, he asked Carpenter where it was. It was in the latter's office. "Sam," said Marriner, "I hate to break into your plans for this evening, but I have a great personal favor to ask. Could you come to the Federal Reserve Building to pull the copy out of your files so that I can read it?" Carpenter agreed and, after an interval, was in Marriner's office. "I have one more personal favor to ask," Marriner now said, "and I hope you won't object. Can I keep the memorandum over the weekend? I'll get it back to you on Monday morning." Carpenter did not object and soon was on his way home.

Marriner then called Elliot Thurston, who long served him in the capacity of assistant to the chairman of the Federal Reserve Board. But before Thomas McCabe succeeded to the chairmanship, Marriner had arranged for Thurston to have the security of being made assistant to the board as a whole. Marriner brought him abreast of what had happened, indicated what he was of a mind to do, and asked Thurston to call him back when he had thought about a possible statement to go with the release of the memorandum.

As the hours went by, Felix Belair, who had been waiting in the Washington office of the *New York Times,* conveyed his impatience in successive telephone calls to Marriner. Had he made up his mind about what he meant to say? Not yet. In point of fact, Marriner had concluded that, to gain the maximum impact, the Open Market Committee's memorandum should be timed for release not for the Saturday morning newspapers with their reduced readerships but for the Sunday editions. Further, to command the maximum attention of official Washington, the release should not be a *New York Times* exclusive but should be made available as well to the *Washington Post* and the *Washington Evening Star,* each of which also published Sunday editions.

By eleven o'clock on Friday evening, Va Lois Egbert had typed up copies of the memorandum. Thurston had also called in to take down a statement dictated by Marriner and to receive instructions concerning the timing and distribution of the text on the following day. When all was in readiness, Marriner telephoned Belair to say that he might have a statement to make later on in the evening, but wanted to sleep on it. One way or another, he would get in touch with Belair the next morning. A night's sleep did not change Marriner's plan. In response to a telephone call on Saturday morning, Belair appeared at his apartment in the Shoreham Hotel and repeated the question of the previous day. What is your view of the president's version of his meeting with the committee as explained in his public letter to Chairman McCabe? Marriner handed him a prepared statement.

I am astonished. The only answer I can make is to give you a copy of the record of what took place at the White House meeting, as agreed upon by the other members of the Federal Open Market Committee and from which I have deleted only certain references which deal with the international and military situation. Any other comment would be superfluous. I am giving you this solely upon my own responsibility and without the knowledge of other members of the Committee. It is most unfortunate that this vitally important matter of money and credit which Congress has placed in the Federal Reserve System has been raised in a manner which only needlessly adds to the confusion.

Belair could rightly claim credit for having ferreted out the story, and he was naturally annoyed when he learned that it was not his as an exclusive. But there was nothing he could do except swallow his frustration. Copies of the memorandum and accompanying statement would be on their way to the editors of the *Washington Post* and the *Washington Evening Star,* as well as to the *New York Times.*

The texts made headline or front-page news on the Sunday press for February 4. In the newspapers around the country that carried the story, the universal judgment was that the record of what had happened at the White House did not support the version set forth in President Truman's letter to McCabe. The memorandum contained no references to the maintenance of the government-securities market at current levels, to the pattern of rates announced by Secretary Snyder or to the refunding of new issues. Instead, the record showed that President Truman declined to discuss the behavior of the government securities market and that he merely spoke in general terms about the need to maintain confidence in the government's credit. The public may not have grasped or understood all the technical details of the controversy, but it did understand the essential point—that the White House was putting pressure on a governmental agency meant by law to be independent of political influences. In consequence, public sentiment, and hence congressional sentiment, swung into a support position behind the Federal Reserve.

By Monday morning the controversy had reached blast furnace heat. Rather than wait for the scheduled meeting on February 13, McCabe convened the Open Market Committee the next day, February 6. The purpose was to consider what should be done in view of the developments over the weekend. Except for Allan Sproul, no members of the committee either approved or criticized Marriner's action in releasing the memorandum. Sproul, who approved, expressed the view that what goes on at a presidential conference should not be disclosed except by the president, but that, in doing so, the president should give an accurate report of what transpired. It was the board's memorandum and not the president's letter to McCabe that accurately reflected what actually was said and the spirit in which it was said. For this reason, Sproul continued, he was glad Marriner had acted on his own in releasing the memorandum—since the effect temporarily retrieved the place of the Federal Reserve System in the eyes of the financial community and of the general public.

Marriner voiced his regret that events on the move had reached a point where releasing a confidential document seemed absolutely essential in the public interest. He had deliberately avoided informing any other member of the Open Market Committee about what he had planned to do, since he did not want to involve anyone else in the consequences. Turning to the larger question that justified the release of the memorandum, Marriner said that he fully recognized the vital importance of carrying out a successful defense program. But it was of equally vital importance for the Open Market Committee to do everything in its power to try to prevent inflation. He added:[25]

If we fail in this task, history may well record that we were responsible in great measure for helping to bring about the destruction of the very system our defense effort is designed to protect. We should not delay action. In retrospect I think we have been derelict in not acting more aggressively, particularly since Korea. We know what *we* should do in this inflationary situation. We should publicly inform the President, the Treasury, and the Congress of what we propose to do, and then do it. Otherwise the public will get the impression that we have capitulated and lack the courage to discharge our responsibilities. If Congress objects to our actions it can change the law; but until it does that, we have a clear responsibility to check inflation—in so far as we can do this within the framework of our authority—by preventing a further growth in the supply of money and credit at this time.

The committee then agreed to two suggestions made by Allan Sproul. A letter should be sent to President Truman in order to restore the current controversy to an official context. Second, as part of an attempt to resume discussions with the Treasury about debt-management policies, a letter should be sent to the Secretary of the Treasury along the lines of the procedural points McCabe had suggested to the president at the January 31 White House meeting. Before the day was over, both letters had been drafted and approved by every member of the Open Market Committee except for James K. Vardaman. It was hoped that the White House would release the committee's letter, since it clearly explained the basis for the committee's resistance to the Treasury's policy of "pegged prices," and was also a complete answer to the president's letter to McCabe.

Later, however, when reporters pressed their questions on Truman, he replied that he had not yet seen the text of what the Open Market Committee had sent him. At the same time, White House staff members tried to get the Open Market Committee to withdraw the letter. When the committee as a whole refused to do so, administration leaders in the Congress who had long been friendly to Marriner converged on him as the key figure in the resistance. They urged him to use his influence to prevent the Federal Reserve from doing anything "to embarrass Secretary Snyder." Marriner explained that he had no desire to be vindictive. Having fought the Treasury's policies, he could not be expected suddenly to go into a reverse and to try to take the committee with him. But he agreed, without abandoning his position, to do what he could to help "save the face of the Treasury."

Consequently he worked closely with Allan Sproul in formulating a plan where the Federal Reserve would commit itself to support the pegged market for government securities up to a limit of $500 million dollars—and no more. The Treasury accepted the plan and, in doing so, let it be known that the Federal Reserve was obedient to the will of the Treasury. The case, however, turned out differently. In March 1951, when this so called "accord" went into effect, the Federal Reserve in only three days was compelled to spend all of the agreed upon $500 million in supporting the government securities market. It had thus lived up to the terms of the "accord," and cited the terms when the dismayed Treasury officials asked for continued support. The request was refused, and there was nothing more the Treasury could do about the matter. Its "face had been saved." Henceforth, the Federal Reserve ceased to be a party to the system of pegged prices, with their inexorable inflationary consequences. Marriner had won his last battle in Washington.

35. Shadows of Coming Events

FIVE MONTHS BEFORE THE EVENTS just related reached their climax, a Washington rainstorm set the stage for a fateful encounter in Marriner's life. By that time, he had lived alone in Washington for ten years and had been divorced for the last two. How he reacted to the emotional aspects of his aloneness cannot be judged on the basis of his papers. They are an open book about many matters, but one searches them in vain for material about experiences not related to business or governmental affairs.

Marriner was aware of his reserve in matters touching his emotional experiences. His friends were aware of something else, that it was next to impossible for him to engage in small talk at a social gathering. He had a dry wit, could be very funny, and delighted in a good joke even when he was the butt of one. But he had no taste for gossip or chit-chat. As these pages have indicated, his mental energy in Washington was expended—to the exclusion of virtually everything else—on fiscal, monetary and credit policies as they affected the United States and the rest of the world. When he started to talk about any of those matters, he amplified his views with an intensity of purpose that sometimes bore hard on the mood of other people at a dinner table.

Careful listeners to his comments on public issues could find their own perceptions enlarged and clarified by what he said. Leaders of the Washington press corps such as Walter Lippmann and Doris Fleeson, for example, wrote many of their syndicated columns on the basis of what they learned from him. Not everyone, however, had the patience to sit still while he negotiated the turns and returns of his own thoughts until he reached what he was aiming at all along—an exact and flashing statement which lit up the heart of a public issue. As for his relations with women, he admired those who excelled in their chosen field of work, but his friendships were with men only.

Still, it is conceivable that Marriner may have thought more about the barren regions of his private life as he drew closer to the hour of his planned resignation. He had joined the New Deal when he was forty-three years old, and now he was in the sixtieth year of his life. What would he take back to Utah? National celebrity? Yes, in abundant measure, Achievements? Yes, many of them—despite many failures not of his own making. Valiant service to the nation? Again yes. He had moved *against* the current of history, to give it a new direction it might not have taken except for the intervention of his personal thoughts and will. But what else would he carry back with him?

A proven talent for money making? Suppose that talent increased the size of his personal fortune beyond what it already was? Would money-making fill his life after his years in the thick of Washington battles for the public policies and programs he thought were right?

The answer to the question of what he would take back to Utah came into view on a day in late November 1950, when he was about to leave a Washington cocktail party in the home of Harold Rusk.[26] A driving rainstorm posed a problem for some of the departing guests who were without transportation of their own. Marriner's chauffeur was on hand, waiting to return him to the Shoreham Hotel. A woman's voice was heard saying: "Is anyone here headed for the Shoreham who can take me along so that I might get a taxi?" Marriner observed that the question was asked by an attractive, youngish woman named Sara—or "Sallie"—Madison Glassie, to whom he'd earlier been introduced by Woodlief Thomas, director of research for the Federal Reserve Board. There was a note of caution in Marriner's voice when he said to Sallie: "I live in the Shoreham and will be going there in a little while. If you can wait, I will be glad to take you."

En route to the Shoreham, Marriner, as usual, did most of the talking. It was not long, however, before Sallie's darting responses to what he was saying made him aware of something out of the ordinary. He did not abandon his caution, but with the rain beating on the windshield and roof of the car, he asked a question whose answer would determine whether he would say something more. As he later recalled it, the exchange went like this:

"Where do you live?" If the place were way out in the suburbs, he would put her in a taxi. But if it were a reasonable riding distance?

"I live," said Sallie, "along the east-west road near the Chevy Chase Country Club."

"Are you a member?"

"Yes."

"I am too . . . I've no other appointments this evening. I'll see you home."

The necessary instructions were given to the chauffeur. The ride continued, as did the questions and answers.

"What were you doing alone at the cocktail party?" Marriner asked.

"I happen to be married," said Sallie, "but am in the process of getting a divorce."

"Well, I'm ahead of you by two years . . . Any children?"

"Two."

"And you?"

"Three—all married."

In time, they reached Sallie's home, an elegant colonial mansion, 150 years old, set in a wooded grove extending over ten or fifteen acres.

"May I call on you sometimes?"

"I'd be pleased if you would."

"By the way, what's your telephone number?"

The data was supplied, and Marriner duly recorded her name and number in his pocket notebook. Sallie, at the time, did not grasp the full significance of the gesture. Years later, however, she would say: "Little red and green lights buzz on and off inside Marriner's head when a deal's afoot, and he also has a sixth sense about what *not* to put down on paper. That explains something *all* the Eccles do in a pinch. They go to the *files*. That's where TRUTH is."

There was no telephone call from Marriner in the weeks that followed. He went home to Utah for the Christmas holiday, and upon returning was immersed in work bearing on the preparation of the president's State of the Union message and the budget message, as well as the increasingly acute conflict between the Federal Reserve and the Treasury. On a day in mid-January 1951, however, Marriner glanced at his desk calendar and saw he was free that evening. So he reached for his pocket notebook, found Sallie's name and the telephone number and placed a call.

Was she free to go out that evening?

She was.

After that evening together, there was another long interval before they saw each other next. Marriner was now engrossed in work on three fronts: the final phase of the conflict between the Federal Reserve and the Treasury, the writing of a new concluding chapter for *Beckoning Frontiers* and the preparations for his impending resignation from the Federal Reserve Board. It was spring before there was another telephone call to Sallie, another evening together, followed this time by shorter intervals between meetings.

If marriage was on Marriner's mind, no hint passed his lips. He admitted that he enjoyed Sallie's company. He also valued her suggestions about the speeches he was to give. Sallie, a graduate of Mount Holyoke College and a clear-eyed observer of both the comedy and the tragedy of being human, knew that laughter could bring a person closer to what was truly serious and solemn. She had a reflective turn of mind, was fully at ease in the world of ideas about ideas, and had an uncommon grasp of the structure and nuances of the English language—a reflection perhaps of her concentration on Latin while a college student.

Something of her style can be sensed by leaping ahead to a time when she was reviewing the years of her marriage to Marriner.[27] She began by understating the range of her own interests when compared to Marriner's. "The big difference between us," she said, "is this. Marriner has a BIG THOUGHT. I have a LITTLE one. He is rejoiced by signs of wisdom in national affairs, and I am rejoiced by flowers everywhere, and by buoyant talk with happy people. Marriner seeks peace in the world. I seek something beautiful for the mantle. It is amazing that we still manage to get together occasionally." This was followed by an account, told in high glee, about how she and Marriner managed "to get together occasionally"—about the strategies she used, along with the miscarriages.

I discovered, that LOGIC is basic to Marriner. Value is LOGIC. Filling a need is LOGIC. It's that simple. Other considerations just aren't valid. "It makes no sense," Marriner would often say about my enthusiasms. But once LOGIC and REASON can be established, he is wonderfully generous. So the trick is to get your proposition under the aegis of LOGIC. Then, at least, you can get an ear and a chance "to make the case." Otherwise, its just plain "No!" Actually, it's less frustrating now than it used to be. It used to be that if I coveted a painting, Marriner would say: "There's no sense in it—you paint!" And any idea that a "Sallie Eccles and an Henri Matisse weren't the same just couldn't be explained.

Sometimes now I win, and Marriner agrees that we really needed those old French crystals on the sideboard. He's delighted to provide a necessity. He's always done that. So all I have to do is to prove the basic need for crystals. The argument need not be impressive, so long as it makes Marriner feel better about LOGIC. Once when I knew I wasn't making the case—his favorite phrase—and was a bit exasperated on that account, I said: "Well, Marriner, all right. I can't explain it. But I can tell you one thing. It makes my heart go pitter patter." To my astonishment, Marriner seemed quite shaken by this announcement, even a bit respectful. Suddenly, he decided I was quite right. The English chair was the only answer for that particular corner. Nothing else in the world would do. Naturally, I filed this unexpected success in the back of my mind for future reference, and the pitter patter business did serve me very well once more. But when I tried it a third time, I batted zero. "Well," said Marriner. "There's one thing I've learned. When your heart goes pitter patter, I'm out $3,000."

She continued with an account of how she once made a try at changing the expression on Marriner's face:

When Marriner sees someone he dislikes or distrusts, a furious expression comes over his face. So I decided to talk to him about it. I told him that his face was a dead giveaway, and he had to do something about it. He was not very receptive. "I can't help my face," said he. "Yes you can," I insisted. "The look on your face is the thought in your mind. So all you have to do is change your thinking." Then I told him about Oliver Wendell Holmes who apparently had the same problem. The procession of tragic derelicts filing before him for sentencing, when he was a judge in Massachusetts, upset and repelled him. He was afraid his face might reveal his turmoil and hurt the feelings of the defendant. So, as each one was brought forward, he momentarily closed his eyes to the human picture and said softly to himself, "Hail, Son of God." He found it very helpful. "Marriner," said I, "I think that's wonderful, and I don't see why it wouldn't be a good thing for you to try." "Well," said Marriner, "I could try, but it wouldn't work for me. If I saw so and so walk into this room, and I started off in my mind with a 'Hail, Son of . . .' you can bet your life it wouldn't be *God* I'd be thinking of."

The 1951 springtime evenings Marriner and Sallie spent together, though enjoyable, seemed to be only self-limiting events. Marriner, as usual, had many other things on his mind, including the commencement address he was scheduled to give on June 4 at the Utah State Agricultural College in Logan. He had agreed to it for a sentimental reason: Logan had been his birthplace and then his home for many years. But there was another reason.

He saw in that event the chance to deliver a "valedictory" on his Washington experiences drawing to an end and, at the same time, to identify new problems he saw emerging.

He began by cataloguing "the frightful mistakes made in the twentieth century at a time when mankind had witnessed the greatest technological and scientific progress in all history." There were, for example, the illusions and the failures of the world order which ended in the carnage of two world wars. There were the illusions and the failures of the capitalist order which ended in a devastating depression in the United States, and the spread of totalitarianism abroad. There were the illusions and failures of American domestic and foreign policy in the years immediately after the Second World War. Then, in an echo of a note he first sounded in the depths of the depression in 1931, Marriner dwelt on the common fault underlying these failures, which, he said did not "lie in our democratic institutions, nor in our ability to produce and distribute goods." It was not due "as yet, to insufficient material resources or to any lack of scientific and inventive genius." The common fault "was in our thinking." It was "our inability to deal with the basic causes of political and social upheavals abroad that led to war, in which we inevitably become involved, and to our failures at home to find any answer except war or preparation for war, to the problem of distributing our abundance." Our economic thinking had not kept pace with material and scientific progress. We were "too prodigal in diverting our human and material resources to military preparations for war and defense, and too conservative about using them to alleviate human misery on which communism and aggression both feed." In Iran, China, Korea, Indochina and elsewhere, we and other countries of the Western world blessed and backed reactionary government that lacked the confidence and support of the people. "We have failed to realize that a large part of the world is in a state of economic revolution which we view as communist-inspired and try to buy off with dollars or settle through war." We must recognize that "the communist can only exploit the conditions that will continue to exist unless we ourselves, in our foreign policy, deal with the underlying causes of a world-wide revolution."

At this point, Marriner sharply contrasted the $400 billion the nation spent on the Second World War—plus the new Korea-inspired defense program of $60 billion annually—and the relatively small costs of helping the underdeveloped world to help itself. He then turned to what he called "the most fundamental problem of all—overpopulation."

We cannot hope to improve the lot of the common man in China, India, Japan or any of the other overcrowded and underdeveloped nations of the world if the only check on the number of their inhabitants is the availability of food. The existence of large masses of people subsisting at starvation levels is an open invitation to revolution and communism, since most people will try to fight their way out of a bad situation before they will willingly starve to death. Such improvements in the standard of living as the democratic system of production and distribution of the western world might provide, would, in the absence of a positive population policy, quickly be dissipated among the rapidly increasing numbers of people.

The two basic causes of world conflict—rapidly growing population and consequent inadequacy of the means of production and distribution necessary to feed and clothe such numbers of people—must be dealt with realistically in many areas of the earth if peace is to be established and maintained. Misguided idealism must not be allowed to obscure the need for hard headed realism in dealing with the basic causes of war. While we have adapted the laws of nature to serve our own ends in the realm of the physical sciences, we have chosen to ignore or neglect such adaptation in the social sciences. It has been said: "We live in a Universe which stands for no nonsense from anyone and which orders us to play not the fool but the man in solving our problems."

The college printed Marriner's address as a brochure and distributed it widely. An influx of approving letters suggested that he had given voice to inchoate stirrings in a reflective segment of the public. In his Washington career, once Marriner deemed a particular problem to lie at the root of a cluster of other issues, he returned to it again and again at the risk of appearing to be a man obsessed. So he would return in the years ahead to the subject of overpopulation.

After the Logan speech, there were the formalities that brought Marriner's career in Washington to a close. On June 20, he wrote President Truman:

It is now more than 17 years since I came to Washington to engage in a public service that I fully intended and expected would be of comparatively brief duration. A succession of events, including the war period and the special problems of its aftermath, led me to stay on. It has been a great honor and privilege to serve my country for so many years, but now I feel the time has arrived when I can and should return to my home and private business affairs in the West. Accordingly, I am submitting herewith my resignation as a Member of the Board of Governors of the Federal Reserve System to be effective as of July 15, 1951.

Truman often could be generous toward his adversaries in public controversies, but Marriner was denied that kind of presidential dispensation. His reply was a pro-forma expression of good luck and good-bye, without a syllable of thanks for services rendered the nation. The chill in the presidential letter, however, was more than offset by the plaudits Marriner received from the nation's press when his resignation became known. Editors who had once been among his most intransigent critics joined with those who had valued him from the start in swelling a nationwide chorus of acclamation.

The *New York Times:* The grip of the Treasury on Federal Reserve policy was finally broken . . . largely because Marriner Eccles refused to relinquish the role he had assumed many years earlier as keeper of its conscience. Defying the Administration, which backed Secretary Snyder in an effort to compel the Reserve System to peg the prices of government bonds, Mr. Eccles forced this long smoldering controversy into the open by a coup that would have done credit to Theodore Roosevelt in his heyday. Public opinion, once the issue had been clearly presented, did the rest, and one of the really great victories of these times over the evil of inflation had been won.

The Washington Post: His is a record that is pretty well unique—of a man who stayed true to his ideals and beliefs, who never got softened or seduced by the fruits of office, from the day he came to Washington 17 years ago until his resignation. . . . Mr. Eccles has been a model public servant, with ability joined to probity, who has earned the respect of both friends and foes. . . .

The *Washington Star:* The qualities which Mr. Eccles has shown that he possesses are exceptional rather than commonplace. The need for them is great, especially in this day of mounting complexity in governmental operation, and it is not surprising therefore that his decision to return to the management of his private affairs has met with an almost universal expression of regret.

The *Dallas Morning News:* As Mr. Eccles returns to Utah and private life, he can look back on a long period of honest and unselfish public service, one that left a deep mark on national policies. No political crony of Mr. Truman can fill his shoes.

The Oregonian: Marriner Eccles' consistent stand against all manner of pressures entitles him to the gratitude of the people.

Life magazine: The real hero of the fight on inflation was not the administration but a man who fought it to a stand-still over a vastly important technicality: Marriner E. Eccles, ex-governor of the Federal Reserve Board. He deserves some kind of medal as Economic Man of the Year.

A few days before Marriner's scheduled departure for Utah, the top drawer of Washington's officialdom crowded into the capitol's largest ballroom for a farewell party given in his honor. A hardened New Dealer who liked big government looked at the guest list of people Marriner knew, and shuddered. "It may well be," he muttered, "that we have gone too far." But it was left for Doris Fleeson to render one of the more perceptive judgments on the meaning of the event. She wrote:

Washington crowded in to pay tribute to one of the most interesting and dedicated men—a Republican, incidentally—of the Roosevelt era. Marriner Eccles owns a secure place in American economic history. He was the great exponent—perhaps the ablest here—of the Keynes theory that government must step in and compensate for the rigors of the economic system when they inflict too great a hardship upon too many people. By a little realized irony, Mr. Eccles did not know and had never read the British economist Keynes when he began to expound Keynesian doctrine before the Senate Finance Committee headed by the late Pat Harrison back in February 1933.

The last Republican President, Herbert Hoover, was decisively defeated because during a deep depression he fought assumption by the government of responsibility for the economic welfare of the citizenry. His party has been denied power in four succeeding Presidential elections mainly because a prominent part of its leadership, especially in Congress, does not really acknowledge the thesis that flowered in the Full Employment Act passed in 1946 by the only Republican Congress since 1930—President Truman's despised 80th. Mr. Eccles seems orthodox now only because the general principles that he espoused in the thirties are accepted doctrine.

It was on that note that Marriner left Washington for Salt Lake City, where he paused for a while before going on for a vacation in Canada. And Sallie? She had left beforehand to visit friends in Seattle and then to go on to San Francisco, which she had never seen.

VI

THE PUBLIC CITIZEN

36. *Reunion*

I

WHILE IN CANADA, Marriner corresponded with Sallie, who had returned to Washington, and the correspondence continued when he was back in Salt Lake City. At one point he wrote to suggest that she join him in Salt Lake to meet the members of his family there, and to continue on with him to San Francisco, where he was scheduled to make a speech before the Commonwealth Club. "After all," said he, "you would enjoy being in San Francisco again." Sallie acted on the suggestion. She was introduced to Marriner's mother—then in her eighties—and to one of his sisters. She did not at that time meet Marriner's brothers, who were still based in Ogden. Later, at the end of the stay in San Francisco, Sallie put a direct question to Marriner.[1] "Listen," said she, "is there any meaning to these trips? Are you serious about me?"

"I had not thought about that," he said, in a distortion of the truth. The need for the distortion—to cushion the hurt of a possible rebuff—came out when he added: "I am not sure that anyone would be interested in *me*."

"Well I am," Sallie said simply, "and if you are not, it's best that we part right here."

Marriner met the challenge by suddenly asking: "By the way, when will your divorce come through?"

"Momentarily."

He was now all business. "For tax purposes," he said, "there will be a saving if we get married before the year is out."

Against the background of a happy flurry—enhanced by laudatory press reviews of the recently published *Beckoning Frontiers*—Marriner and Sallie were married in New York City on December 29, 1951, a decent forty-eight hours under the legal wire for tax purposes. They returned to Salt Lake City and moved into a large apartment in the Hotel Utah. This would become their legal residence in the years ahead although, after 1952, they maintained an apartment in San Francisco, partly for Sallie's sake and partly for business reasons.

II

If Marriner had served out his full appointed term as a member of the Federal Reserve Board, under existing law he could have at once reentered the family banking business as an operating officer of a bank. But as he had resigned long before his term was due to expire, he was required by law to wait for two years if he wished to resume work as a bank executive. No legal barriers, however, stood in the way of his filling the newly created post of chairman of the board of the First Security Corporation, the Eccles-Browning holding company. The fact that he could not engage directly in the day-to-day operations of any bank suited his personal taste. It also reduced the threat which his return to Utah posed for his brother George, who had ably served as the Eccles family chief executive officer in the banking business during the years when Marriner was in Washington.

Other benefits would flow from the fact that Marriner was thus barred from bank work by law and by personal preference. He would concentrate more of his attention on the affairs of the Utah Construction Company to which he returned as an active chairman of the board, and on the affairs of the Amalgamated Sugar Company, of which he was vice-president and treasurer, and soon president.

While still in Washington, but in anticipation of his return to private life, Marriner had taken a first step to revitalize the management of Utah Construction. The business had got off to a very fast start from a very small base in 1900; it would not have grown as it did if it had not been a highly capable heavy-construction outfit. Its character was shaped by the facts of western enterprise, with western growth all around it, and with owner-managers like Will and Ed Wattis who were accustomed to taking risks, on the basis of much experience and a tradition that went back to the opening of the West. From its early years up to 1920, Utah remained principally a builder of railroads, and some of the jobs it accomplished had all the elements of a Hollywood western. In the quarter of a century after 1920, it branched out into almost every kind of earth-moving and construction project, including the Hetch-Hetch Water Supply System for San Francisco, a Mexican railroad (its first foreign construction job), the Hoover Dam, the Alcan Highway, Navy air bases, and the United States Steel plant at Provo, Utah.

The size of these projects, however, did not mean equally large-scale profits. Utah continued to make money, but by the end of the Second World War, its earnings through heavy construction seemed to have reached a plateau. In prewar ventures, other heavy-construction companies needed Utah as a partner, but that was seldom the case by the end of the Second World War. Competition among the companies was brisk, and to the usual high risks attending a contract—based on a bid which did not provide for unforeseen difficulties—there was added the fact of postwar inflation which unhinged estimated costs. As the man who had led the fight against the Treasury Department's "chronic institutional bias toward cheap money," Marriner was particularly concerned about the effects on the Utah Construction Company if inflation were to become "a way of life" in the American economy.

In 1946, when he had not yet decided on the future policies of Utah Construction, an opportunity arose to sell about 600,000 acres of ranch land the company owned in three western states.[2] With land prices up, the directors of Utah endorsed Marriner's proposal to sell the land that year and to distribute the cash proceeds to stockholders. As this sale left the company with construction equipment as its only or principal physical assets, some of the directors thought that it might be a good time to liquidate Utah entirely; however, Marriner persuaded them to remain in business but alter the company's emphasis.

In a company annual report, Marriner was soon to write: "Your management had recognized at the end of World War II that inflation would be the inevitable result of the fiscal and monetary policies being pursued by the federal government. To offset the detrimental effects of inflation upon our general contracting business, the company has adopted a policy of devoting a part of its resources to the acquisition of basic raw materials, the ownership of which would serve as a source of profit as well as a hedge against inflation."

The first developments made in line with this new policy were based on what seemed to be sound logic. In addition to the equipment Utah had on hand, the company was also amply endowed with construction personnel experienced in moving earth. Mining was an earth-moving operation. Why not acquire some small mines where the equipment and personnel could be used? In 1946 the company acquired an iron-ore mine near Cedar City, Utah, and the main customer for the ore was initially the United States Steel plant at Provo, Utah. Two years later, Utah acquired coal deposits near Ozark, Arkansas, for which the main customer initially was the Colorado Fuel & Iron Company.

Utah had recently entered into an invaluable association with George Ishiyama, a Nisei, a graduate of UCLA and a man who early saw an opportunity to profit by helping supply Japan with the raw materials needed for her postwar economic reconstruction, at a time when Utah was seeking new customers for its iron and coal mines. Marriner was well known to an older generation of Japanese bankers, but not to those who came to the fore after VJ day. He was unfamiliar with the nonlegalistic way the Japanese negotiated business contracts. Ishiyama provided Utah's management with the knowledge it needed for a mutually profitable and felicitous relationship with managers of Japanese enterprises. Thus in 1949, when Japan's steel production did not exceed 1.5 million tons annually, Ishiyama negotiated the first contract by which iron ore from Utah's Cedar City mine was supplied to Japanese steel mills. He negotiated all subsequent contracts, making Utah a trusted major supplier of both iron ore and coal to the Japanese steel industry—whose production is now in excess of 100 million tons annually.

During this postwar period, the chief operating officers of Utah Construction were Lester Corey and his second-in-command, Allen D. Christensen. The direct attention Marriner gave the enterprise was confined to the days when he drew on his accumulated leave from the Federal Reserve Board to attend company meetings in Ogden. But the closer he came to the time of his planned resignation from the Federal Reserve Board, the more closely he examined the status of the various enterprises to which he could legally return. He concluded that the company needed an infusion of imaginative young executive talent—men who could think anew about how to advance Utah's efforts in mining, construction and land development. The interests of Marriner's own sons, Campbell and John, lay in other directions. But there was a former boyhood playmate of Campbell's, Edmund W. Littlefield, whose uncle Shepphard Mitchell, brought that name to Marriner's attention. Littlefield was the grandson (through his mother) of Ed Wattis.

A graduate of Stanford, Littlefield had worked for the Standard Oil Company of California until America entered the Second World War. After Pearl Harbor he became a lieutenant in the navy. But when Ralph Davies, the executive vice-president of Standard Oil of California, was called to Washington for wartime service in Harold Ickes' Petroleum Administration, in June 1943 Davies asked Secretary of the Navy Forrestal to release Littlefield from active duty for a dual role: as special assistant to the Deputy Petroleum Administrator, and as Secretary of the Domestic Operating Committee for petroleum allotments.

Marriner saw Littlefield in Washington several times during this period, and discussed his family interests in Utah Construction.* After VJ day, when Littlefield returned to civilian life, he continued his association with Davies—who left Standard Oil when the presidency of the company went to someone else. Davies entered the petroleum and shipping business on a large scale, and also became chairman of the Golden State Dairy Company of which he was a major stockholder. Littlefield worked with him on the affairs of the dairy company, where he held increasingly important executive positions. Laudatory reports of his performance reached Marriner. Soundings of Littlefield's possible interest in joining Utah Construction were not very promising. A direct approach was indicated, which Marriner made on January 2, 1951, after the Rose Bowl game in Pasadena, California.

He talked to Littlefield at length about the affairs of the Utah Construction Company, what was wrong with the management, what needed to be done to set it right and the promise ahead if things *were* set right. He observed that the stock in the Utah Construction, which Littlefield would some day inherit from his mother, was currently selling at only a modest price because the company's earnings were modest; but if Littlefield cast his lot with Utah and helped develop the enterprise further, he would be among the principal legatees of the profits earned. Marriner offered him the post of financial vice-president and treasurer, adding that this was only the first rung

*He did not learn until two decades later that Littlefield at the time helped abort a move among certain Utah Construction stockholders who wanted to form a voting combination strong enough to remove Marriner from any future leadership in the enterprise. Young Littlefield and his uncle, Shep Mitchell, convinced another uncle, Pat Wattis, a major stockholder in Utah Construction, that their own best interests would be served by backing Marriner fully instead of joining the proposed combination against him. The fact that Pat Wattis took the advice of Littlefield and Mitchell put an end to the anti-Marriner move.

on a ladder that could lead to the top position. Littlefield was not over-whelmed. He had much to weigh before responding to Marriner's offer. Matters were left in suspense until March, when the two men met again. Littlefield would now accept the financial post and would look forward to advancing in the management of Utah Construction—subject to one condi-tion. He did not want "to be saddled in the years ahead with operations men who owed their posts solely to the fact they they were a Corey, a Wattis, an Eccles, a Dee, and so on."

"Ed," replied Marriner, "the condition you set is precisely why I want you in the company right now, so that you can be groomed to take over all its operations. More business failures have been caused by nepotism than by adverse market conditions. I will back you to the hilt if you insist on award-ing management positions in the company to people of proven talent without regard to the family name they bear."[3] There was a handshake, and Littlefield cast his lot with Utah. Marriner, as his father had been, was generally sparing in his compliments; but in the years ahead he always used superlatives when referring to Littlefield's performance,—"a superstar," "terrific," "done a fantastic job."

III

Marriner's return to business affairs in Utah was no easier than was his readjustment to marriage after more than ten years as a bachelor. At times he was like a diesel engine hitched to a child's wagon. When he had spent seventeen years in the thick of battles for economic policies and programs affecting the entire nation and its place in the world, it was not easy to find an outlet for his immense hauling power in the context of his various com-panies. Though large, these filled but a few crannies in the nation's financial and industrial structure. Perhaps because he missed not so much the levers of power in Washington as the scope for the play of consequential ideas, he regularly converted meetings of a board of directors into a seminar of gen-eral economic conditions, with himself as the professor in the chair. Not every director, however, was an enchanted student. With a long agenda of decisions to be made, reviewed or approved, his colleagues were often impatient to dispose of immediate matters.

The impatient ones included H. A. Benning, vice-president and general manager of the Amalgamated Sugar Company. At one directors' meeting, into which Marriner had introduced a protracted discussion on money, credit, banking and fiscal policy, he was briefly interrupted by a long dis-tance telephone call which required his leaving the room. He was no sooner out the door than Benning, who was presiding, waved an agenda of items before the other directors and said: "All those in favor say 'Aye.' Those opposed, 'Nay.' The ayes have it. The meeting is adjourned." And so it did quickly, before the teacher returned.

The teacher himself had something else on his mind.

37. Strained Interlude

I

MARRINER SELDOM MASKED his reactions to public events he touched or was touched by. His habit was to speak openly about them, to admit his errors of perception and, when he changed his mind, to explain why. By contrast, therefore, his reaction to a brief episode in his life—his 1952 bid for the Republican senatorial nomination in Utah—is all the more striking. He later seemed embarrassed by the event, was reluctant to talk about it, and conveyed the impression that he wished the incident never occurred. That he was defeated does not explain his guarded attitude. He had been defeated in other matters, and readily spoke about them. This attitude could be understood if there had been something subversive about his only foray into electoral politics—as though he had tried to buy a party nomination to a seat he was not qualified to hold—or merely coveted the title of "senator" out of personal vanity.

But nothing of the kind was true. He was forthright—painfully so—in what he had to say during his brief campaign. His expenditures on a statewide political effort were, by ordinary standards, very modest, not exceeding $30,000. His qualifications for a Senate seat were acclaimed by the national press when he announced his candidacy. His lack of interest in high-sounding titles was twice underlined during the Roosevelt years, when he agreed to accept an appointment and reappointment as chairman of the Federal Reserve Board only on condition that the president would agree to back reformist legislation. It was again underlined after President Truman failed to reappoint him chairman and he remained an ordinary member of the board until he won his battle to free the Reserve System from being a captive of Treasury policy.

There are larger riddles. Though Marriner had battled Democrats as well as Republicans during his years in Washington, why did he offer himself as a candidate for a *Republican* senatorial nomination when the whole of his public career in national government had unfolded under Democratic presidents? Did he enter the Republican lists out of anger at the treatment he had received at the hands of President Truman? When the whole of his public career had been marked by his impatience with unreality, what were his grounds for believing he could win a Republican senatorial nomination in Utah? Was his motive a desire to establish his Republican credentials in order to qualify himself for a possible appointment as Secretary of the Treasury in a Republican presidential Cabinet?

The questions cannot be answered in ways free from doubt. Yet

Marriner's brief venture into electoral politics must not be passed over into silence. The event *happened* and, in happening, cast some sidelights on aspects of his character—and on American electoral politics as well.

II

The plans of any man who holds a front and center position on the Washington stage are always the subject of press speculation, and it is not beyond the imagination of reporters to invent their facts according to convenience. Yet there is reason to believe that Marriner himself, with his habit of "thinking out loud," was the source of the earliest press references, published in July 1951, to his future political plans. The common note the press struck was that he would "like to" return to Washington either as a Republican Senator from Utah or as Secretary of the Treasury in a Republican presidential Cabinet.

Many men who have held high appointive posts in Washington, where they have been shot at by the guns of legislators, would "like to" serve on the Senate side of the battles between appointive and elective officials. Yet very few of them, on leaving Washington for their home base, have actually sought party nomination to the Senate, or won such nominations, and even fewer have won a Senate seat.

As to Marriner's aspirations to the Treasury: in the years of leadership he gave the Federal Reserve Board, when the Treasury was his main adversary in policy contests, he had ample reason to wish that *he* were Secretary. Few other men in the United States had his proven qualifications for the post. Still, this doesn't mean he seriously thought he would be appointed to the job in a Republican Cabinet—at least not if the president turned out to be Robert A. Taft.

It is true that after 1948, in his search for allies in the fight against the Truman administration's inflation-generating policies, Marriner drew fairly close to Senator Taft. "I shall miss you here," the senator wrote him when Marriner resigned from the Federal Reserve Board, "but I hope I may from time to time receive very useful advice which I have frequently asked from you." Though the two men were personal friends, the fundamental differences in their political outlook and public manners made it highly unlikely that Marriner could ever hold a seat in a Taft Cabinet. Marriner was not a "party loyalist"; Taft had a burning passion for Republican party regularity. Marriner made no secret of his contempt for the Nationalist "China lobby"—which supported such political figures around Taft as Senator Joseph McCarthy. In their eyes, Marriner had committed the ultimate heresy of advocating American recognition of Communist China *after* the end of the Korean war.

Though the July 1951 press speculation about Marriner's political plans died down in the months that followed, a column Drew Pearson wrote in mid-February 1952 (following a visit to Salt Lake City, where he spent several hours with Marriner and Sallie) triggered a revival of national press references to Marriner's political aspirations.

I asked Marriner Eccles if he planned to run for the U.S. Senate from Utah. He said he hadn't made up his mind yet, but if he did it would be on the Republican ticket. That thought is very intriguing to Washington, because Eccles had been such a staunch New Dealer and was the founding father of the fiscal policies of the Roosevelt Administration.

There were two grounds for Marriner's indecision at the time. He must first know whether Arthur W. Watkins, the incumbent Republic senator from Utah, would abide by his pledge, made six years previously, to serve "one term only." A conservative and an isolationist, Watkins had strongly declared himself in favor of Senator Taft's bid for the 1952 presidential nomination. But where his own political plans were concerned, he confined himself to the evasive remark that he would reveal his intentions "to his supporters well in advance of the Utah State Republican nominating convention."

The second ground for Marriner's indecision was the mounting conflict within the national Republican party between Senator Taft's forces and the newly energized elements of- the party urging General Dwight D. Eisenhower to enter the contest for the Republican presidential nomination. Senator Taft appeared to be the unquestioned front-runner in the period prior to General Eisenhower's announcement that he was "available." As the 1952 Republican convention drew ever closer, Taft seemed to view any criticism of his conduct, even by the most solidly conservative press, as a plot to promote Democratic prospects in the election ahead. Some of his oldest and most steadfast friends came to look upon him as a spendthrift who sacrified their friendship to his passion for winning the 1952 Republican nomination and election on his own dogmatic terms. Marriner could not identify himself with Taft's species of Republicanism if it were to prevail in the convention.

All the while, Marriner, after more than seventeen years in the pressure chambers of Washington, could not find any equal sense of utility or fulfillment in the affairs of his companies. He missed the tensions that went with Washington-based struggles to govern the nation, just as Sallie missed the company of congenial Washington friends, whose counterparts she had not yet found in Salt Lake City. And so months passed by in indecision and restlessness.

On the eve of the Republican convention, Senator Watkins explained away his "one term" pledge and made known his intention to seek renomination in Utah to the seat he held. In the convention itself, he and other members of the Utah delegation stood by Senator Taft to the bitter end. It was not until July 12, a day after General Eisenhower emerged as the Republican presidential nominee, that Marriner, in a photo finish with the deadline for filing, announced his candidacy in Utah for the Republican senatorial nomination. He could, without strain, ally himself politically with General Eisenhower, something he could not do with Senator Taft. Moreover, since General Eisenhower had served the nation in a nonpartisan post under two Democratic presidents, Marriner could analogize his own position to that of the general, for he too, in times of crisis, had served in a nonpartisan post under those same presidents.

Four candidates in all filed for the Republican senatorial nomination in Utah, and the contest itself unfolded in two stages. The first came to a head on August 1, when the Republican state convention qualified two of the contenders to enter the primary. The second came to a head when votes were cast for the two qualifiers on primary day. But it was recognized all along that Watkins and Marriner were the main contenders. Their contest amounted to a replay within the Republican party in Utah, of the recently concluded Republican presidential nominating convention, with Watkins standing toward Marriner as Taft had stood toward Eisenhower. That the case was so viewed by the national press appears in a caption over a lead story in the *New York Times:*

ECCLES PRIMARY FIGHT WITH WATKINS, INCUMBENT, ETCHES ISSUE OF LIBERALS VERSUS OLD GUARD.

The next day the *New York Times,* in a follow-up editorial, observed:

There will be those, no doubt, who will say that [the primary contest in Utah] is in the nature of a local issue. But these will not be the persons who have followed Mr. Eccles' career. For the latter will tell you that no issue is a local one that involves this man, who, until his retirement a year ago, had been identified more intimately with American monetary policy than any figure of his time.

With Marriner Eccles in the race, the Utah election cannot be regarded as a local issue. It has suddenly been vested with a national interest—and, in our opinion, an interest of very substantial dimensions.

The *Washington Post* editorialized in somewhat the same vein:

Marriner S. Eccles' entry into the race for the Republican senatorial nomination in Utah will focus considerable attention on that primary battle and revive memories of the many fights he waged in Washington against Democrats and Republicans alike. All who knew the former chairman of the Federal Reserve Board know that he is first of all a fighter. What a great many people did not know was that he is also a Republican. . . . The Utah state Republican convention will be made up of the same men who instructed the Utah delegation to the national convention to vote for Senator Taft, whom Senator Watkins also favored. Undoubtedly the pro-Eisenhower men in the State Convention will try to unseat Senator Watkins, a bitter-end critic of the bipartisan foreign policy.

Since Marriner's forces got into the campaign only three weeks before the state convention met, his managers could not and did not expect him to lead in the balloting, and especially not over an entrenched incumbent senator who could count on the automatic support of the Taft-minded delegates in command of the convention. The aim was to qualify Marriner for a place on the ballot as one of the two primary finalists, and that objective was gained when the convention cast 785 votes for Watkins, and 222 for Marriner as the runner-up.

That this vote was decisively in favor of Watkins did not by itself discourage Marriner's managers as they faced the primary contest ahead. They hoped that many Utah Republicans—those who could remember the Great Depression, those who had come of age during the Second World War, and those who lived on fixed incomes—would want to be represented in Washington by a man whose battles for the public interest had made him not only a national but an international figure (see Appendix C).

Above all, Marriner's managers hoped for support from political independents and disaffected Democrats. Their support would be all the more possible because of a feature of the Utah ballot in a nominating primary. A voter did not have to be a registered party member or declare his party preference. At polling places he was handed a perforated ballot, listing on one side all candidates for Republican nominations, and on the other, all Democratic candidates. In the polling booth itself, the voter separated the ballot at the perforated seam, marked up and deposited only one part, and placed the blank part in a special receptacle. This feature could enable disaffected Democrats easily to cross party lines and to vote for Marriner, just as it would also enable independents to participate.

III

Nothing that was done on Marriner's behalf—by himself, by Sallie, by the campaign managers, old friends, new ones within the universities and in the ranks of Young Republicans—could surmount the obstacles to his winning the nominating contest.

Marriner was mindful of the help he received from many sources, and publicly acknowledged that help. At the same time, he reserved a special tribute for Sallie, saying that "if she had been the candidate, we would have won the nomination in a walk." Sallie, from all accounts, was superb in her novel role as wife of a political candidate.

The first obstacle in the way of Marriner's success was the simple fact that only in very exceptional circumstances is an incumbent United States Senator ever denied a party renomination he wants; incumbency itself gives him natural advantages that are denied a challenger. Second, what might have appeared as Marriner's natural sources of strength—his independence, his extensive experience in public affairs, his talent for economic management and for social invention, and the very acclaim he won nationally and internationally for his work in Washington—somehow made him a suspect figure in the eyes of certain clannish Utah circles. He was not "one of the boys." He was not a "safe man" whose stand on issues could be controlled in advance or at least influenced by the agents for local vested interests.

Ironically, Marriner's respect for the integrity of words also worked against him. He assumed that the first duty of a candidate for a public office was to *explain* himself. And so he did, in detail, on all the propositions comprising his personal campaign platform. Electoral politics, to him, was a branch of the teaching profession, and accordingly, the best receptions he received were from college and university audiences. Elsewhere in the state, however, more than a few listeners were disturbed by the remorselessly logical questions he asked, and by his equally uncompromising insistence in getting better answers than the simplifications that passed as wisdom in boardrooms and clubhouses. He had none of the electioneering arts that were second nature to a political leader such as Franklin D. Roosevelt.

A passage from his *Beckoning Frontiers* became one of the two main weapons used against Marriner by the Watkins camp. By wrenching out of context the lines he had written for *Fortune* magazine in November 1950 and repeated in *Beckoning Frontiers,* Watkins supporters made it appear that Marriner had aided and abetted the Chinese Communists in Korea by advocating immediate American recognition of Communist China and support for its admission into the United Nations. In August 1952, when Marriner was first hit by these distortions, he merely joked: "Nothing could please me more than to have the people of Utah read my book, *Beckoning Frontiers,* which has had numerous favorable reviews. I shall be glad to loan copies to those who are interested in getting the full picture." But the distortions continued, and he was compelled again and again to deal with the matter in the course of the contest, with a consequent cut-back in the attention he could give to other things.

The second main line of attack consisted of the orchestrated charge that he was not a Republican and thus had no right to seek the Republican nomination to the United States Senate. The same tactics were used by the Taft forces in their attempt to deny Eisenhower the presidential nomination. Marriner was not content merely to repeat what he had said when he announced his candidacy: "I have always been a Republican, my father was a Republican, my whole family were and are Republicans." He countered with a public statement which could hardly endear him to the Utah Republicans who shared Senator Taft's passion for party regularity:

Yes, I voted for a change in 1932, but so did a few million other good Republicans. . . . If that made us all Democrats, there certainly would not be enough Republicans left over to win an election. In the bottom of the depression, when this country had 10 million unemployed, millions of others on part-time work, banks failing by the thousands, I was asked by our government to accept public service. And I responded as any loyal American would in such a crisis. I became chairman of the Federal Reserve Board, a nonpolitical office on a nonpartisan and independent board which is responsible to the Congress and not the administration. There were many other prominent Republicans who likewise accepted government service. Does this service to our country in time of great need make me a Democrat? If so, many leaders of the Republican party today are Democrats, including the Republican presidential nominee—Dwight D. Eisenhower.

Most aspirants for political office tend in their remarks to become progressively more outlandish the closer they come to election day. Marriner did likewise—in the eyes of professional politicians. He insisted on speaking his mind, without regard to the number of political altars he thereby desecrated. He agreed that it would be "desirable to reduce taxes and the budget," but warned that "it would be misleading to promise such a reduction at an early date." In reclamation-minded Utah, he inveighed against the use of reclamation as a political issue, saying: "The development of our water resources should be more a question of economics and finance than of politics. Otherwise, reclamation, the very lifeblood of Utah, becomes a political football, to be kicked high or low with the turn of politics." So, too, with his expressed attitude toward defense plants. "Anyone representing the State of Utah in Washington is naturally all out for all the defense plants he can get. Yet the sites for such installations should be determined by military authorities with an eye to their relationship to the whole of the Pacific coast. Political influence should have little to do with their establishment and operation."

When the votes cast on primary day were counted, they gave the Republican senatorial nomination to Watkins by a decisive margin. There was no sour note in the statement Marriner issued the next day. "It was my good fortune," said he, "to have the assistance of my friends, old and new. To them I am grateful for their efforts in my behalf. We did the best we could in the very short time available since I entered the political race. Even though defeated I am glad I made the effort, as it gave me an opportunity to become actively acquainted with the young, vigorous and liberal group of the Republican party in Utah."

It was left to the *Baltimore Sun,* in an editorial after the primary, to sound a lament that was echoed in other organs of the press at the time.

One of the truly regrettable casualties of the last batch of Republican primaries was Marriner S. Eccles, former head of the Federal Reserve Board. In his native State of Utah, Mr. Eccles tried to take the Republican nomination away from the incumbent, Senator Arthur V. Watkins. He missed. That is too bad. . . . The reason is that Mr. Eccles is one of the smartest experts in money and fiscal policy which the country has seen in modern times. And how it needs that kind of expert! . . . He brought to the support of his views the advocacy of a precise mind and a passionate spirit. Such a man should have a place in the United States Senate and it is too bad he lost out in Utah.

After Marriner's first and only venture in electoral politics ended in defeat, he never again sought public office. He did not, however, retreat into privacy. He remained fully engaged in public affairs as a free-standing "public citizen"—as an informed critic or advocate of public policies across the board of national and international issues—though his post-Washington impact on public opinion and on officialdom cannot be precisely measured.

Marriner's impact on public policies from 1953 onward cannot be quantified, but the traits he brought to his role as a public citizen are clear-cut. They were the same as those he showed when a public official—complete self-possession, the courage to say exactly what he thought, an imperious indifference to the howl of the mob, and a will to march in advance of events in the hope of altering their direction.

In May 1954, the Korean war had only recently ended; Vice-president Richard Nixon had floated a proposal for an American bombing mission in support of the French military effort in Indochina; Secretary of State John Foster Dulles was set to walk out of the Geneva Conference called to negotiate a settlement of the conflict between the French colonial government and the insurgent forces in Indochina grouped around Ho Chi Minh. In Washington, Senator Joseph McCarthy was at the height of his bizarre power to intimidate; countless public figures were driven by fear of the man to seek safety in silence.

Marriner, in Allan Sproul's telling phrase, was not "a glossy print man." As in the past, it was time for him again to speak his view openly and roughly. He chose the occasion—an address to a meeting of the National Association of University Presidents held in Salt Lake City on May 3, 1954. In updating the argument he had advanced in his November 1950 *Fortune* article, and again in *Beckoning Frontiers,* Marriner said:

Any idea that there could emerge a victor in a war between the democratic and the communistic political systems is totally unrealistic in the light of today's weapons of mutual annihilation. . . . We should know by now that the forces of Communism cannot be contained by isolated military efforts around the world and the cost in blood and treasure in attempting to do so is formidable, endless, and futile. It would be far less costly and more successful to use our knowledge and substance to create economic and political conditions in the backward countries of the world which the Communists cannot exploit.

It is equally important that we discontinue our blessing and backing of the reactionary governments that lack the confidence and support of their people, such as Chiang Kai-shek, Syngman Rhee, the French colonial government of Indochina. We must not repeat the costly and futile mistakes of Korea by a military intervention in Indochina. Having recognized Russia and all her satellites, as well as Tito, Peron, and Franco, it would seem that the time has passed when the Communist regime of China should have been recognized by us as the ruling power which it is. Great Britain and most of the other countries of the Free World have done so long ago.

Nothing is solved by our denial of the fact that the Communist government is the government of China. In fact, our attitude toward China only serves to weld the Communist world more closely together. Realism, instead of political expediency, is sorely needed. A solution of the involved problems of Korea and Indochina, which so directly affect Red China and the Free world now being discussed at the Geneva Conference, will not be hastened by Mr. Dulles' refusal to either speak or look at Mr. Chou En-lai, Red China's premier, as reported by United Press yesterday.

We must recognize sooner or later that economic necessity is more powerful than any other force in ultimately determining the course of history. We are therefore going to find ourselves increasingly isolated from our natural political allies if we do not accept the fact that the nations of the Free World must trade with those of the Communist World, Mr. McCarthy notwithstanding. Japan, for example, cannot long survive as a free nation without such trade.

The remarks, when reported in the press, outraged the McCarthyites, the China lobby, the adherents of the John Birch Society, as well as other elements in a resurgent radical Right. But they were left frustrated. When they tried to strike back at Marriner, all the weapons of intimidation they effectively used against others were scornfully ignored by him.

A remote epilogue to Marriner's speech fell in place in 1973, when America was winding down its intervention in the Vietnamese conflict and a move was afoot to resume official contacts between the United States and Communist China. At that time, to Marriner's surprise, the passage just cited from his remarks to the university presidents in May 1954 was re-printed as a frontispiece in *The Record,* the monthly magazine of the Indus-trial Conference Board. In an introductory note to the extract, Alexander B. Trowbridge, president of the conference, first dwelt on what Marriner had foreseen two decades previously, and then, as if in a printed sight added: "How marvelous it would be if we had the capacity to identify with parallel accuracy the changes in store for us in the next twenty years!"

The older he grew, the more conscious Marriner became of the dark-ness in which even the best of human judgments often flounder. And his knowledge of the many occasions where he had seen even "enlightened" people hail a serpent as a hero seemed to reinforce a pessimistic streak in his temperament—as if he were haunted by the prospect that the world lying beyond his lifetime would consist of nothing but sandy wastes and wild beasts. Yet he did not abandon himself to cynicism. He somehow converted the energy within his pessimism into a positive force—into an urge to con-front the public and its officialdom with the hard acts of choice they would rather ignore, and to have them accept the burden of decisions which prom-ised at least a fighting chance to surmount public dangers.

In these respects, the public citizen of the post-Washington years was an extension of the public official of the Washington years—both recogniz-able in the businessman who proceeded to guide the growth of Eccles-dominated enterprises in directions and on a scale which dwarfed the achievements of 1951.

38. The Businessman Revisited

I

HAROLD BURTON, a Harvard-educated director of several Eccles-dominated companies, recalls that his father had a piece of advice for all the Burton children who would inherit his substantial stock holdings in the Amalgamated Sugar Company and the Utah Construction Company. His father, a contemporary and intimate friend of David Eccles Sr., whom he outlived by many years, said to his own children in the tone of a last will and testament: "Whatever Marriner is doing or wants to do in the companies, you are to support him 100 percent."[4] Harold Burton, the youngest of the children, did not come to know Marriner until 1951. Afterward, as the Burton family representative on the boards of the enterprises Marriner headed, he not only adhered to his father's dictum but found that other directors who were not related by blood or marriage to the Eccles family generally followed wherever Marriner led. Why? It was not because Marriner was a textbook model of an *operating* business executive. He was not thought to be anything of the kind even by his most admiring associates. "If Marriner," said one of them, "was caught in the hurly-burly of getting the laundry out, he would not get the washing in on time."

Marriner was not a rapid-fire decision maker in routine matters of business. For one thing, he was a very slow reader, though for a good reason. He meant to understand and fix in his mind all the angles and tangles of every syllable in a document before him. For another thing, he seemed to lose all sense of time when he was thinking aloud about the implications of any matter requiring his yes or no. This, in turn, could bear hard on his business associates, and especially at the end of a day when he was airing his thoughts—without any auxiliary thought of waiting secretaries, impatient wives, or commuter train schedules.

Experiences with Marriner's indifference to the passage of time when thinking out loud lay behind a condition set by Edmund W. Littlefield—about to be promoted within the management of Utah Construction at a marked increase in salary. When the terms of the new position were discussed, Littlefield did not ask for the moon but for something he valued even more. "Marriner," said he, "except in emergencies caused by earthquakes, fires, floods, or the outbreak of nuclear war, I want the right to leave my office at a quarter of six in the evening so that I can catch the train that will take me home to my wife and children."[5] Marriner readily agreed, but, as the event proved, he honored the agreement more in the breach than in the observance.

Marriner himself sensed that he was not cut out to be an operating executive. He was dependent on the exceptional managerial talents of his brother George, and of other men such as E. G. Bennett, H. A. Benning, and Littlefield. But the question repeats itself. Why, as if in response to the Burton family rule, did other directors generally back what Marriner wanted done?

The answer has something to do with Marriner's fierce honesty. He did not believe that the rules of the competitive capitalist game were promulgated on Mount Sinai. They were man-made, unstable and could be displaced in a different social and political context by other modes for organizing production and distribution. But as long as the competitive capitalist game was "the only game in town," Marriner played by its existing rules, and played hard. At the same time, however, in what appeared to be an ongoing sequel to the 1913–20 clash with his half brothers—and to what he had fought against in Washington—he was infuriated by any sign that "someone was milking the cow behind the barn." Perhaps that is why he was never invited to serve on the boards of corporations in which he was not already a major stockholder. He would not show an ounce of tolerance for any shady policies or practices forced into the open by his questions.

Still, strenuous honesty alone could not have sustained his preeminence in the governance of his diverse enterprises, any more than honesty alone would qualify a man to be a brain surgeon. What further qualities did he possess? While the shelves in Marriner's Salt Lake City office contain more than ten thick volumes of his public utterances, a "how to succeed in business" kind of speech is conspicuous by its absence. Marriner never once, in any public forum, spoke on the subject for the instruction of the young. Yet it is possible to deduce from his career several simple but powerful maxims that informed his conduct. First, he did not believe that success in management automatically purified the means by which it was achieved. In private business, as in government, he insisted on a union between power and responsibility not for any abstract textbook reasons but to safeguard the continuity of valuable institutions from the immediate present into a future lying beyond the here and the now. Whether in private business or in government, the modes of managerial action he consistently advocated called for giving the operating heads of an enterprise all the lawful means and discretionary powers they needed to discharge their defined responsibilities, while holding them strictly accountable for the uses they made of them.

Second, viewed from afar, Marriner conveyed a different impression than when viewed close in. From afar, he appeared to see things in their economic aspects alone, without taking into account the limits of economic concerns among human interests at large. He appeared to use the very word "economic" as though it were a synonym for "rational" and "intelligent"—or as "the science of rational activity" focused on the choice of means suitable to "given" ends. Viewed close in, however, he insisted on questioning the given "ends" as closely as he questioned the procedures for attaining them, and he questioned the ends *first,* before turning to the means. The proper ends to be pursued took their definition from human considerations which transcended the narrow realm of economic technique.

Third, precisely because Marriner was not saddled with the details of daily operations, he could maintain the necessary critical distance that enabled him to see—and see himself seeing—where an enterprise was tending, where it *should* go, and how best to get there. Ends and means were thus held by him in a single vision. He carried other directors along with him in formulating policies that could point a company in promising new directions because, as Littlefield put it, "we learned through direct experience that Marriner was a matchless source of wise judgments which stood up under the severest tests of time and events."[6]

Fourth, because Marriner viewed business as a "judgmental art"—not readily reducible to theories that would be true under all circumstances—he avoided the traps piled high with the broken bones of businessmen who assumed that the methods underlying their success in one line of endeavor were automatically extendable to another line. As he moved back and forth among his diverse enterprises, he viewed each as having a distinctive character of its own, and he made adjustments on the lens of his perceptions so that he could clearly see the problems special to each and correct any prior errors of judgment which he himself or someone else had made.

Finally, Marriner did not expect his operating managers to report on and justify every decision they made in the course of a day. He knew that to demand something of the sort would harm them personally and the companies with them. It would make them defensive, incline them to postpone hard acts of choice, inculcate mental habits of dependency, so they would be wholly unfit to succeed to his own position at the head of any enterprise. He gave his operating managers ample latitude in which they were free to use their own discretion about what should be done, and thereby bring to mature strength their will to decide. What he expected of them was candor in speech, and to keep him informed of all the ins and outs of the *major* decisional issues about which a chairman of the board must be informed and to which he must be a direct party.

II

Soon after Edmund Littlefield joined Utah Construction as its financial vice-president, the management of the company made a daring move in mining—the Marcona venture in Peru. The existence of an iron-ore deposit in the desolate coastal region 250 miles south of Lima was well known. Development had been started by the Peruvian government and then abandoned, and the property was put on the market for private development. An ore broker who knew that Utah was looking for West Coast iron-ore deposits brought the Peruvian prospects to the attention of Marriner, Christensen and Littlefield. On February 7, 1952, Utah signed an exploration contract with Peru, went in, test-checked drill holes that had already been made and did some further drilling of its own.

Utah was not prepared to put up all the money required to open the mine, build plants and piers, and build a small town from scratch. The Export-Import bank was prepared to help with the financing, but only if more equity capital were put in the project. And so Utah approached another mining company in southern California, the Cyprus Mines Corporation, which had cash available for investment. While the negotiations with Cyprus were going on, Utah looked for a sales contract that would return at least a portion of its first costs—something, as Littlefield put it, "like trying to have a baby with a full-grown beard." United States Steel's new Venezuelan iron ore mine was not yet in production, and Utah was able to negotiate a short-term contract for Marcona to supply the corporation's great Fairless Works near Morrisville, Pennsylvania. With immediate profits assured, Cyprus wrote a check.

Utah construction men, who had been held on a standby basis while Littlefield, backstopped by Marriner, was arranging the financing, went into action. They unloaded the first bulldozer on the beach in February 1953, and the first ore shipment left Marcona's own dock in the first week in May. Marcona turned out to be one of the great open-pit iron-ore mines in the world. The main ore body covered an area about two miles long and one mile wide, and had reserves of direct-shipping ore (averaging above 60 percent natural iron) estimated at 50 million to 100 million tons. Underlying the direct-shipping ore was the primary ore deposit, containing 50 to 60 percent iron. The proved reserves of primary ore exceeded 200 million tons.

The details of Marcona's rapid development, the rising volume of ore it shipped to international markets, the profits to Utah Construction, and the present unstable political conditions in Peru which now cloud the future of the mine lie beyond the scope of these pages. Suffice it to say that Marcona got Utah into an ocean shipping business that has been independently lucrative (though its profit levels were reduced when the worldwide recession, which started in the early 1970s, reduced the demand for the use of the cargo fleet). Utah's management knew that the sales and profitability of the Marcona operation would depend in part on shipping costs which fluctuate widely in the charter market. In response to that reality, Allen Christensen advanced the argument that, if Marcona developed its own fleet of specialized ore carriers, of which there were few at the time, Marcona would eliminate the hazards of price fluctuations, achieve new economies and shipping, and create another income-producing business.

Charles Robinson, a Utah executive and later Marcona's president and general manager, proceeded to follow through on Christensen's idea. A shipping organization called Cia was set up within Marcona's marketing division. The original cost of a specially designed ore/oil carrying fleet, starting with six ships purchased in seven years, came to $33 million.

Littlefield, again backstopped by Marriner's advice, adroitly financed the cost by several means—pledging the fleet itself as collateral, and pledging part of its charter income to back-haul oil from Sumatra.

In 1953, at Marriner's insistence, the headquarters for the First Security Corporation was moved from Ogden to Salt Lake City. The Amalgamated Sugar Company remained headquartered in Ogden. The headquarters of Eccles Investment Company remained in Salt Lake City—or perhaps, more precisely, any place where Marriner sat down to study the affairs of the company. Though the headquarters of the Utah Construction Company would not be officially shifted from Ogden to San Francisco until 1957, its main operations by 1953 were directed out of San Francisco, and these loomed ever larger in Marriner's plans for the future of the company.

Accordingly, at this time, Marriner and Sallie changed their living arrangements. While the apartment they maintained in Salt Lake's Hotel Utah continued to serve as their legal residence, they acquired a second apartment in San Francisco. Henceforth, without fanfare—one might almost say stealthily—Marriner regularly contributed 50 percent of his gross annual income to support worthy causes such as education in both communities. However, the fact that he commuted between San Francisco and Salt Lake City in connection with his business interest worked in its own way to restrict the scope of his social life in either place. Not that he felt deprived on that account. "Marriner," Sallie would say to him, "we've got to have some people over for dinner, because if we don't, we'll never be invited out." To which he would answer—and with greater emphasis as he grew older: "That suits me fine. I've got a briefcase full of work that interests me more." When she nonetheless went ahead and arranged a dinner party, she tried to conceal from him until the last moment the names on the guest list. "Otherwise," so she explained, "Marriner would appoint himself chairman of the icebox."[7] A gourmet would consider Marriner an enemy alien.

The step-by-step approach to mining deals—getting a prior commitment for a market outlet for use in helping to swing the financing—was the characteristic Utah pattern. That pattern could be seen, for example, in the way it entered the business of mining for uranium in 1954, when the company's own discoveries did not amount to very much. Other uranium prospectors with claims in the Gas Hills district of Wyoming had formed the Lucky McUranium Corporation, but they ran out of development money and had trouble finding an interested partner or investor—a common difficulty in the uranium industry's "penny-stock" era. The worth of Lucky Mc's claims was not then proved, and several hundred thousand dollars were needed for tests for a reasonable estimate of their value. After one of Lucky Mc's stockholders had discussed the problem with Marriner, and various further discussions and inspections had ensued, the geologists of Utah concluded that the financial risks involved in a Utah connection with the claim were worth taking. So the deed was done. Utah took an option on a controlling 60 percent interest in Lucky Mc's, agreed to do the development work, to try to get an Atomic Energy Commission contract and to seek the means for financing a mill.

When the ore body proved out, Utah's mining men negotiated a contract with the AEC. Financing the mine and mill and getting working capital, however, were still difficult. Aside from the fact that the money market was tight because of the 1954 recession, there was widespread skepticism among bankers about the profits to be made in uranium. Though Littlefield reminded them that sales were assured by a contract at a fixed price, the bankers were reluctant to make a loan without some sort of guarantee that Lucky Mc could produce uranium at a cost low enough to ensure a profit. The institutional lenders Littlefield approached talked about money at what was then high interest rates, and wanted 20 percent of the common stock besides.

Littlefield then went to commercial banks in San Francisco, Salt Lake City, and New York, trying to get a better deal for Lucky Mc. He finally got it after Utah entered into a fixed-price contract with Lucky Mc to open and operate the mine and construct the mill. By guaranteeing the costs in this way—though without guaranteeing Lucky Mc's loan itself—Utah made the loan bankable. In 1957, six banks put up the $10 million that enabled Lucky Mc to get into business. Success followed swiftly, and the $10 million loan was quickly retired from the profits earned. In early 1960, Utah acquired the other 40 percent of Lucky Mc at a cost of $12 million in Utah stock, and absorbed Lucky Mc into its mining division.

Utah's policy in land development was similar to its policy in mining. The company bought undeveloped properties, used its earth moving and construction capabilities to improve them and then sold the properties. Not everything here, however, went along swimmingly. The Alameda South Shore land-fill project in the San Francisco Bay area, though a notable engineering feat—some 400 acres of tidelands were converted into dry land —proved to be a project where, in words of one Utah man, the "company spent more on aspirins to cure its financial headaches, than it took in on profits." Development costs were higher than Utah had estimated. There were delays when some residents protested their loss of a waterfront; and by the time Alameda was ready, the real-estate market had softened. In addition, for the Bay Farm Alameda project of 900 acres of tideland fill, Utah bought the first of two large and expensive dredges it came to own. Viewed from a technical standpoint, they were beautiful pieces of specialized machinery, each a giant complex with an attendant machine shop. Subsequent to Bay Farm, however, they were idle much of the time, or, because they were costly to maintain even when idle, their very existence became the source of pressure to make use of the dredges on projects which were unprofitable.

The moral that project pointed up for Littlefield was to avoid in the future any large-scale "freezes" of Utah's capital. This was all the more important because construction work entails expenditures which exceed receipts until the job is near completion, and when a job takes four or five years, an inordinate amount of capital is tied up. In a company such as Utah, with many demands on its working capital, this posed a special problem.

For all this, in the decade following Marriner's return from Washington to his business affairs, Utah Construction quadrupled its annual earnings and more than quadrupled its net worth. The growth had been achieved in the face of one recession in the national economy between the years 1953 and 1954 and another recession and lingering economic sluggishness extending from 1957 to past 1960. Yet Utah's profits in 1960 rose 10 percent over 1959, while the 1959 profits were 75 percent higher than in 1958. Even so, the greatest years of growth for Utah still lay ahead.

From Marriner's standpoint, Littlefield's major contributions to the growth of Utah Construction more than confirmed the early hopes he had placed on the man. He brought Littlefield forward in two steps to head all the operations of the company. In 1957 he was made Utah's executive vice-president and general manager, and in 1960 he displaced Allen D. Christensen as president of the enterprise. Marriner remained chairman of the board. When asked at the time by a reporter for *Fortune* magazine whether *he* was the chief executive officer, he shrugged off the question with a laugh, saying "Damned if *I* know." The reporter alluded to the question in the article he wrote about Utah Construction, and answered it himself in the form of a parenthesis, "(He is)."

And so he was. The reporter, however, would have had a better story had he known of an exchange between Marriner and Littlefield at the time. The point was raised whether the phrase "chief executive officer" should be attached to Littlefield's title. "Ed," said Marriner, "I advise against adding the phrase, because it will complicate your position when you eventually succeed me as chairman of the board. *Your* successor as president, citing *your* precedent, would then expect to be designated as 'President and chief executive officer.' Where would that leave you? If you intend as chairman to be the chief executive officer as well, don't weaken your position beforehand by strengthening your title right now." Littlefield agreed.[8]

In the same year that Littlefield became president of Utah, Campbell Eccles, Marriner's oldest son, died. Marriner had suffered many blows which further impoverished his family life, including the death of his mother in 1957 at the age of ninety. He had rolled with the punches and kept the pain to himself. But this new loss was not like any of the others. In his long mourning, he seemed to his friends to be beyond consolation. He persisted in assailing himself for having spent so little time with Campbell, indeed for having failed to grasp his emotional needs, saying that he had sacrificed the possibility of a healthy father-son relationship to the demands of business and public affairs. Later on, Marriner's friends sensed that, perhaps unconsciously, he came to see in Littlefield—twenty-three years his junior—a surrogate son.

Any full-length portrait of Utah Construction's post-1960 history must be inaccurate in points of detail because of the swift-moving changes that continue to occur. All that can be indicated here is the general direction in which it evolved, and is still evolving.

It was said a moment ago that Utah's "project type" construction services lost their charm for Marriner as far back as the early 1950's—due to a progressive inflation, the increased risks and competition in the construction business and the promise of greater returns from mining. It seemed logical to consider selling Utah's construction division to some other company, especially since it accounted for one-half of Utah's overhead costs and for only one-tenth of its profits. Any move toward such an immediate sale, however, was checkmated by considerations involving Utah's long-time construction employees.

We owed [Littlefield explained] a special debt to our construction men for a way of thinking about business. They were the fellows who were always ready to *move*—to test themselves against a job, and the greater its challenges, the greater their eagerness to tackle it. They were willing to proceed with about 75 percent of the facts in hand—that's usually all they had time to get—whereas men with financial backgrounds could be paralyzed by their own analyses of the risks to be run. The construction men didn't scare easily, and they were the initial source of Utah's drive and national reputation. They were not to be cast to the wind simply because mining instead of heavy construction promised greater profits for Utah in the years ahead. If the construction division was to be sold, it must be to a firm of outstanding competence that would provide our construction employees new and broader career opportunities.[9]

But that judgment posed another problem. In order to attract a buyer of national stature, Utah must show profits in its construction division, along with project-contracts worth buying. The implied strategy—to seek new construction work with the object of profitably withdrawing from the field—was skillfully managed by Littlefield until April 1969, when Utah sold virtually all of its heavy construction assets and business to Fluor Engineers and Constructors, Inc., except the dredges, which Fluor did not want. The $10.7 million received from the sale added to the fund of capital Utah used to develop its existing mining properties or to develop new mines. Some of these as in Australia, Canada, and New Zealand, required extensive support structures—from railroads and ports to new towns—and Fluor's own gain in the sale lay in taking over from Utah the construction of such facilities. The dredges were later sold to a Japanese concern for a substantial amount.

Utah's gains from mining alone had regularly increased from one year to the next throughout the 1960s. The great leap forward, however, dates from 1969, though not without sweat and dust. Virtually all operations showed profits, but in particular areas profit levels were reduced by a variety of causes beyond the control of Utah.

First, after investing $59 million in the development of its copper mines on Vancouver Island in British Columbia, Utah in 1969 had negotiated long-term contracts calling for the sale of approximately 60 percent of the copper concentrates to one Japanese mining and smelting company, and 30 percent to another such company in Japan. But in the face of the worldwide recession in 1974–75, which led to a slack in the demand for Japan's finished industrial products, those two Japanese enterprises could not use all the copper they had contracted for—at prices to be determined by copper quotations on the London Metals Exchange. The concurrent fall-off in the demand for copper and the sag in its price cut into Utah's returns on its investment in the Vancouver Island mines. By the same token, a recovery from the worldwide recession would imply more profits from these mines.

Within the United States, meanwhile, the environmental movement directly or indirectly affected Utah's profit picture. In order to comply with newly enacted environmental protection laws, Utah spent large amounts of money for reclamation in connection with its steam coal mine located on the Navajo reservation in northern New Mexico. The environmental movement brought to a virtual halt the further construction of atomic energy plants, and thereby reduced the demand for the uranium Utah produced at its Wyoming mines.

Yet, for all this, if Utah's aggregate net profits from mining continued to soar, the main reason was the coking coal it extracted from mines at Blackwater and Goonyella, Peak Downs and Saraji, in Queensland, Australia. It negotiated long-term contracts to supply a total of 70 million tons of coking coal to Japanese steel and chemical companies. Subsequently it entered into agreements—again under long-term contracts—to supply many more millions of tons of coking coal to Japanese industrial enterprises.

Another present and prospective source of Utah's growing income was the steam coal mine on the Navajo reservation. In the late 1950's, Utah had negotiated an agreement with the Navajo tribal council and with Arizona's Public Service Commission. In return for granting Utah the right to build an open-pit steam coal mine on the reservation, the Navajos were to receive royalties on the sale of the coal and special concessions with respect to power. The state of Arizona, which was then investing $100 million in the development of its electric power facilities, was guaranteed a cheap and reliable source of fuel for the power-generating plants it meant to build. It was a "sweet deal" for everyone concerned, and it got sweeter after 1969 when the need for more power in New Mexico, Arizona, and California lay behind the move among utilities companies to build leviathan-sized generating stations close by Utah's steam coal mine on the Navajo reservation. Utah is to supply these stations with many millions of tons of coal under contracts extending over the quarter of a century ahead.

It is easy enough to observe that the company picture at the end of 1970 was a far cry from the one in 1900 when David Eccles organized the enterprise in Astoria, Oregon. But the stunning fact is, that by the end of 1970, the picture also differed radically from the one in 1951 when Marriner, on the eve of his return to Utah from Washington, prevailed on Edmund Littlefield to join the company. Utah's dividends had increased in every year of the following two decades. The value of its stock, which was first listed on the New York Exchange in 1969, had increased over sixty times.

III

The post-1951 development of the Amalgamated Sugar Company was no less striking. Viewed as a single whole, the domestic sugar industry —cane and beet alike—had been stabilized in 1934 when the Congress passed the Jones-Costigan Act whose allotment features Marriner had helped devise. Stability, however, was not another name for prosperity. In the years following 1934, most sugar beet companies in particular, lived with an unsatisfactory return on invested capital. There were three main reasons. The first was the high cost of constructing new and modernized beet sugar plants whose productivity could offset rising costs in every aspect of the refining and distribution process. Second, sugar was for many years a surplus commodity in the world market, selling at depressed prices even after the price of other commodities such as wheat, corn, and soy beans shot skyward. And, third, since farmers tended to plant more profitable crops, the sugar beet industry, taken as a whole, was dogged by the problem of contracting for adequate supplies of sugar beets.

With the growth of world population, however, and a per capita rise in the use of sugar, world consumption began to exceed the production of sugar. The result was a rise and then the recent explosion in the price of the commodity—an explosion triggered by what the U.S. Congress *failed* to do in 1974. In that year, a sugar bill, reported out by the House Agricultural Committee, died in the Senate—in line with the will of the then Secretary of Agriculture. The United States for the first time in four decades was thus left without any sugar legislation. Domestic prices and supply were entrusted to play of "world market" forces—a hazardous kind of play considering that when the American market for Cuban sugar was closed after the Castro revolution, sugar imports from about thirty nations were required to offset the lost source of supply from Cuba.

In the many years prior to the recent price explosion, Amalgamated was among the exceptions to the negative picture the sugar beet industry generally presented. It quietly and methodically strengthened every aspect of its operations. When the results were reflected in a surge in Amalgamated's fortunes, Marriner went out of his way *not* to claim a monopoly of credit for the event. As a matching piece to his stress on Littlefield's leading role in the post-1951 development of Utah, his boast was of the immense contributions made by H. A. Benning to Amalgamated's general operations, and by R. H. Cottrell, who grappled with the intricate scientific and technological problems the company faced. Marriner's personal contributions, aside from the general direction he gave to the company's policies, lay in designing financial strategies which enabled the operating officers of Amalgamated to do what they convinced him needed doing.

Small obsolete sugar factories in Utah and Idaho were replaced over a period of time by three new ones in Idaho—Twin Falls, Rupert and Nampa—and by a new plant in Nyssa, Oregon. The company was receptive to technological innovations that promised greater speed in the handling and processing of sugar beets, the reduction of labor costs, and better quality control in the production process. Some of the innovations stemmed directly from Amalgamated personnel, and some were developed by industrial enterprises serving the sugar beet industry in general. Either way, the incorporation of new technology in Amalgamated's operations often entailed heavy outlays for capital improvements. Major investments were also made in research work and in new research laboratories so as to bridge the agricultural and manufacturing aspects of the company.

What was gained from the vast expenditures on capital improvements? Several comparative figures suggest the nature of the answer. When the Logan and Ogden plants were in operation before they were shut down, each could handle no more than 500 tons of sugar beets daily. Now the smallest of Amalgamated's modernized plants daily handle 6,000 tons of sugar beets, and the largest 10,000 tons. Taken together, the factories at Twin Falls, Rupert, Nampa and Nyssa can daily process more than 25,000 tons of sugar beets.

Three more details remain to be added to this abridged account of Amalgamated's post-1951 story. First, in 1956, H. A. Benning, who had been Marriner's intimate collaborator in Amalgamated's affairs, suffered a stroke and could no longer be active in the management of the company. His successor as president and general manager was his son, A. E. Benning, who had been groomed since boyhood for a leading position in the sugar business. Some of the other directors of Amalgamated initially objected to this succession, but Marriner threw his weight behind the son, as he had bet on the father's talents years earlier. The objections dissolved when A. E. Benning advanced the interests of Amalgamated well beyond the point reached in his father's time.

The second detail concerns a gesture made at a meeting of the directors of the Amalgamated Sugar Company held on April 21, 1966, at which Marriner was present as chairman of the board. As the meeting drew to a close, Paul Ray, a director and general counsel for the company, rapped for attention and began to read from something he had written on a legal-sized pad: "This meeting marks an anniversary which should not pass unnoticed. I hope I may be indulged a few minutes to speak about our chairman. This month he is finishing fifty years of service upon this board of directors. Marriner's services to the company have been immeasurable in value and should be recognized by the board. It would be idle to try and enumerate the countless contributions he has made, but I would like to mention just a few. . . ." There followed a recital of the way he had "rescued the company from imminent financial disaster shortly after the First World War''; his role in bringing H. A. Benning into the company, "in reclaiming control of the company" from the Boetchers, in "reorganizing and recapitalizing Amalgamated" and in many other areas. All this was cast into the form of a resolution of "deep appreciation" for Marriner's "countless services to the company."

Until that moment, Marriner had lost sight of the fact that he had served on Amalgamated's board for a half-century. He had been only twenty-six years old when he joined it in 1916. And now, at the age of seventy-six, as he looked around the table while the directors unanimously approved the resolution, he realized that all the other members of the 1916 board were gone. He was the only survivor. It was good to know that his contributions to the life of the company met with favor by a successor generation of directors.

One more detail rounds out the story. At the end of January 1975, Loeb, Rhoades & Company, a leading Wall Street firm of financial analysts, made the sugar beet industry the subject of the *Research Notes* the firm sends to investors. It singled out for special mention Amalgamated Sugar, saying that it ranked third in total capacity in the industry after Great Western United and Holly. But what caught the eye of the analysts was something else. It was that Amalgamated Sugar is "one of the strongest companies financially, is generally accepted to be the best managed company in the sugarbeet industry, and has long been regarded as the most efficient company in the field." It had $35 million in fixed assets, $136 million in liquid assets, while the replacement costs of its plants was estimated at $200 million.

39. *Old Issues Revisited*

THOUGH MARRINER FOUND PLEASURE in the continuous growth of the enterprises he headed, his outlook was not limited to the bottom line on the quarterly report or annual report of his various companies. He remained firmly attached to the larger propositions that have governed his outlook since 1931—namely, that the wealth of *men* depend in the final analysis on the wealth of *nations*. In the years following his return from Washington to Utah, he stressed that point with the same high seriousness he had shown in the years 1934–51 when his direct conversational partners were presidents of the United States. He stressed it in his private correspondence with strategically placed members of the Congress, in his testimony before congressional committees, in his "question and answer" interviews for national magazines, in his many speeches before major private organizations, and in the context of the American Assembly of Columbia University, of which he was a trustee. The same outlook governed his approach to the work he performed between 1959 and 1961 as a member of the Commission on Money and Credit.

In 1950, Senator Paul H. Douglas' subcommittee of the Joint Committee on the Economic Report recommended a "thorough and complete study of the monetary and credit system and policies of the United States."[10] There was no immediate response to this recommendation, but in December 1955, Allan Sproul, then president of the Federal Reserve Bank of New York, suggested "a renaissance in the study of money and banking in general and of central banking in particular." Again there was no immediate response, though Sproul, during his sixteen years as president, had contributed more than any other single contemporary to enhancing the public prestige of the country's regional reserve system. He was now about to retire to private life in his native California, and the occasion he chose for his "valedictory address" was a meeting in Atlantic City, on May 24, 1956, of the New Jersey Bankers Association. In the final paragraphs of that address, he again dwelt on the point of his remarks in December of the previous year, urging

an inquiry into the whole intricate and complicated arrangement of financing institutions which has developed during the past 40 years and particularly during the latter half of that period.

We cannot afford much longer—or we can only afford it because we are rich—to go ahead not really knowing what to expect of our central banking system, of our commercial banking system, of our savings banks and building and loan associations, of our insurance companies and pension trusts, and of all the other bits and pieces which we are using to try to keep our production facilities and our credit facilities in balance. The task would be a difficult one. The rewards could be commensurate with the difficulties.

Marriner, since leaving Washington in 1951, had maintained close touch with Sproul, and his boundless respect for the man was in no way affected by their recurrent disagreements on judgmental issues. He cherished a photograph of Sproul on which the latter had inscribed the words: "To Marriner Eccles, who made me his friend despite myself and despite himself." He was now among the first to welcome the kind of study his friend had proposed.

The term "stagflation" had not yet been invented to describe a simultaneous condition of economic recession and inflation, but both men had been disturbed by recurrent signs of the phenomenon in the decade after the end of the Second World War. Both men knew that money and credit functioned in the national and global economy through a tangle of financial machinery, whose slightest change affected vast numbers of people. It affected what they were paid for their work, what they paid for the things they wanted, what they sold, what they invested in, their plans for retirement, and so on. Yet the public at large had no firm grasp of how the components of the financial machinery acted and reacted on each other. It had no grasp of the consequences of the tremendous expansion in government debt; of the extensive governmental involvement in direct loans, guarantees and loan insurance; of the declining significance of the commercial banks and the rapid rise of investment trusts, pension funds, saving and loan associations and credit unions.

Despite Marriner's many attempts while still in the government to restructure the mechanism for the management of money and credit in the economy, the Banking Act of 1935 had remained for two decades the only significant forward step in the institutional picture. Now he and Sproul were agreed that the national economy had outstripped many of the major assumptions underlying its monetary and credit arrangements. The Federal Reserve in particular was saddled with an increasingly difficult task when it tried, with the means at hand, to cope with the new kind of inflationary pressures that regularly broke through the surface of price stability. Whatever the Federal Reserve did invited a crossfire of criticism. When it tightened the supply of money and credit as a part of a planned curb on inflation, there was an outcry over a consequent slowing down of economic growth and a rise in unemployment. When it loosened the supply of money and credit as part of a planned spur to growth and employment, there was an outcry over the consequent increase in inflationary pressures.

Sproul's call for a monetary reappraisal was met with silence on the part of most bankers and businessmen, but generated considerable interest in academic and government circles. The difficulty lay in deciding on the appropriate vehicle or forum for such a reappraisal. The playing out of this difficulty corresponded to a pattern painfully familiar to Marriner Eccles during his own long and futile efforts to establish a rational structure for monetary management beyond the advances made under the Banking Act of 1935.

First, though President Eisenhower had ample power to appoint a monetary commission himself, the funds needed for research required congressional authorization. Also, if the resulting recommendations were to attract bipartisan support necessary for their enactment, it was important for the commission to be established by joint action of the president and the Congress. Thus, in his State of the Union message on January 10, 1957, the president suggested that Congress authorize "a broad national inquiry into the nature, performance, and adequacy of our financial system, both in terms of its direct service to the whole economy, and in terms of its function as the mechanism through which monetary and credit policies take effect."

The Senate and the House at the time were both Democratic, and the Democrats feared that if the president were allowed to appoint a commission, he would choose men who reflected his own political viewpoint. There were other complications. Some legislative leaders felt that such an inquiry was properly the prerogative of the legislative arm of the government. Others saw in such an inquiry an opportunity to earn some political capital by conducting an investigation of their own. In consequence, not only did the Congress turn down President Eisenhower's request, but various committees of the Congress proceeded to fight among themselves for the exclusive right to conduct the investigation. Amid the confusion, Senator Harry Byrd stepped in and announced that his Senate Finance Committee had unanimously determined that it would assume responsibility for the investigation and make a complete study of the whole range of interlocked matters bearing on the financial condition and financial institutions of the United States.

It soon became evident that some senators were more interested in political polemics than in an economic analysis. The committee was virtually without a supporting technical staff especially assembled for the purposes of the study. What had been billed initially as a "serious investigation" quickly degenerated into a round of political skirmishes in which economic theories were the weapons used. Little new information was developed, and Senator Byrd's investigation died in April 1958.

In the interval, however, the White House quietly expressed the hope that, after the Senate Finance Committee had finished its work, some independent nonpolitical group would assume responsibility for a serious investigation. The Committee for Economic Development responded on November 21, 1957, announcing plans for the creation of a committee whose members would be selected on the basis for their reputation for competence and objectivity.

To that end, the CED delegated to a specially formed committee of presidents of universities and major research organizations the responsibility for choosing the members of a privately financed Commission on Money and Credit. The original plan called for a commission of nine to eighteen men, experts in the field ranging in outlook from conservative to liberal, but with no organization representatives who might take doctrinaire positions. The plan was upset, however, when most of the conservatives who were invited accepted, while many of the liberals declined. To redress the balance, the selection committee issued a second round of invitations which not only expanded to twenty-five the membership of the commission but included figures prominently identified with the institutions of organized labor. It was explained at the time that unless professional labor representatives were part of the commission, the eventual report would simply be "thrown in the waste basket at the White House and in Congress."

This is not what Allan Sproul had in mind. He agreed that the collective wisdom of a large committee whose members were drawn "from all walks of life," could help out in such varied causes "as improving schools, raising money for cancer research, and fighting urban blight." But he rejected the proposition that such a committee could collectively produce an incisive report on issues of monetary and credit policy—issues which were as technically complex as they were emotionally divisive. Sproul, who was to have been a commission member, at an early hour severed his connection with the enterprise.

Marriner, having accepted an invitation to serve on the commission, stayed the full course. He thought that the work of the commission might afford him a chance to tie together the loose ends of the various policy and institutional proposals he had tried to advance as the chairman of the Federal Reserve Board.

In May of 1958, the CED announced the creation of the Commission on Money and Credit with Frazar B. Wilde, president of the Connecticut Life Insurance Company, as chairman, and with H. Christian Sonne as vice-chairman.* The costs of the three-year study—$1.2 million—were covered by grants from the Ford and Merrill foundations. Dr. Bertrand Fox, of the Harvard School of Business Administration, and Dr. Eli Shapiro,

---

*Some of the other members, in addition to Marriner, included Adolph A. Berle; James B. Black, chairman of the board, Pacific Gas & Electric Company; Henry Fowler, a lawyer and later Secretary of the Treasury; Philip M. Klutznick, a civic leader and prominent developer of "new towns;" Isador Lubin, former commissioner of labor statistics; Robert R. Nathan, former chairman of the planning commission for the War Planning Board; David Rockefeller, chairman of the board, Chase Manhattan Bank; William F. Schnitzler, secretary-treasurer, AFL-CIO; Jesse W. Tapp, chairman of the board, Bank of America; J. Cameron Thomson, retired chairman of the board, Northwest Bancorporation; Willard L. Thorp, director, Merrill Center for Economics, Amherst College; Theodore O. Yntema, vice-president and chairman of the Finance Committee, Ford Motor Company, and Beardsley Ruml of New York. There would be changes in the original composition of the commission as members resigned or died. Gaylord Freeman of the First National Bank of Chicago, for example, succeeded to the place of Beardsley Ruml.

professor of finance at Massachusetts Institute of Technology, as directors of research for the enterprise, mobilized 110 professors who eventually supplied the commission members with 11,000 pages of research papers. The members were assigned to any one of several task forces into which the commission was subdivided.

Three principal goals of special concern to the commission, having particular relevance to monetary and fiscal policies, were agreed upon at the outset. They were an adequate rate of economic growth, sustained high levels of production and employment, and reasonable stability of prices. The commission's job was not to try to make intellectual history by offering ex cathedra pronouncements on matters lying in the realm of theoretical economics. Its job was to make wise choices among existing and conflicting views, and to convert the choices into practical policy proposals bearing on the three stated goals of national economic policy.

This would have been difficult even for a small group of "disinterested" experts. It was all the more difficult for a large and diverse group containing spokesmen for entrenched institutional interests. Indeed, the sharp divisions of opinion were flagged by footnotes containing individual dissents which almost eclipsed what was affirmed, as in the instance of a member who presented a 12,000-word footnote, which eventually fissioned off into a separate pamphlet.

Each task force invested much time digesting material gathered from government and academic sources. The recommendations of the majority of each task force, along with the dissents, were then presented to the full commission, which met eleven times for week-long meetings in each month of the winter and early spring of 1960–61. Here they argued points of policy proposed by the various task forces, assessed the consistency or inconsistency among the recommendations, wrote, revised, rewrote, and again revised the document that eventually emerged as the final report.

The official release date for the final report was set for June 19, 1961, when a copy was formally presented to President John F. Kennedy in the White House. But instant criticism of its contents began several days earlier, when *Business Week* broke the embargo on the release and rushed into print with an appraisal of the 285-page report. Other publications followed, and the result of "reflex journalism" was a confusion of tongues along with cannonades from the camps of the political "right" and the political "left." In the absence of a sober analysis of what was being shot at, the press attacks contributed to a climate of negativism that made the hard work of the commission a case of love's labors lost.

On June 20, for example, the *Wall Street Journal* reported that "it is a pity that a 285-page report on which three years and $1.3 million have been spent should add up to so little of importance. And it is sadder still, for the future of the nation, that so many minds are still mired in the statist errors of the past." The more liberal *Reporter* dismissed it on a different ground, saying: "The report admirably sums up what we thought should be done ten years ago. But a lag of only ten years in economic policy may in reality be a pretty good definition of progress." *Fortune* magazine, in its July issue, was more sarcastic: "There is a lesson in this for the well-intentioned business-man who lends his name to a worthy-sounding committee." The lesson is to refuse to participate in any such public activities, as this "would allow the businessmen more time to attend to their business, which in the last analysis is probably the best cure of all for a declining G.N.P."

Marriner Eccles had his own objections to the final report, although it arrived at two conclusions that he himself had reached back in 1931. It formally stated that a "mixed governmental and private economic system best meets the nation's needs"; and that "cooperative action by government and by private enterprise were mandatory if the national economic goals of a low-level of unemployment, adequate rates of economic growth, and reasonable price stability were to be met." Other tonal aspects of the final report echoed lines of argument Marriner had often sounded in various public forums and had accented with renewed intensity during meetings of the commission. He had contended that the nation and the world were "passing through the most revolutionary phase in human history, in its science and technology, in its political, social, and economic structures"; that this reality rendered "irrelevant the Jeffersonian proposition about how government is best which governs least"; that the "critical problems rising from the worldwide revolution called for responses which could only be forthcoming from a strong central government presided over by a strong president."

A second line of argument followed from the first. "The proper func-tioning of the nation's monetary and credit machinery," said he, "was an indispensable means to the promotion of the most productive use of the nation's human and material resources." But the machinery "could not by itself successfully attain that goal." National economic policy "was an in-tegrated whole." Hence an adequate rate of economic growth, low levels of unemployment, and reasonable price stability could be attained only if something were regularly done at the presidential level—"only if monetary, credit, *and* fiscal and debt management decisions were carefully planned, reviewed, and coordinated with other major measures of both the executive branch of government, and of the independent agencies in government." Hence, too, changes in existing institutional relationships were plainly indi-cated.

The commission recommended eighty-seven major institutional changes. Many of them reflected stands Marriner had taken years earlier when he tried to change aspects of the public and private components of the nation's financial machinery. Expressed in shorthand form, the commission's specific recommendations included the following proposi-tions: Require all insured banks to be members of the Federal Reserve System. Make reserve requirements identical for all banks. Use debt man-agement as a countercyclical tool. No priority should be given to debt retirement; public debt should fluctuate in response to policies required for economic stability and growth. Use loan insurance in preference to direct government lending. Eliminate debt ceilings and interest rate ceilings for government-underwritten securities, mortgages and agricultural credit. Changes in tax structure and expenditure program should be timed to coincide with stabilization needs. Standardize the FDIC and FSLIC insurance, and administer them by one agency. Continue the FHA loan insurance program. Make permanent the home mortgage credit and FHA-certified agency programs. Permit branch banking operations in trading areas regardless of state boundaries. Extend federal charters to mutual savings banks and life insurance companies. Extend federal regulation to private corporate pension funds. Liberalize commercial banking regulations by eliminating reserve requirements on savings and time deposits, and by placing interest rate ceilings on a standby basis. Operate federal credit programs in harmony with monetary policy. Use reserve requirement changes sparingly, for long-term purposes, with consideration given to bank earnings.

The knowledge that Marriner's influence was written particularly large in the portion of the commission's report which dealt with the public sector of the nation's financial machinery was recognized in the Congress by members of the Joint Committee on the Economic Report. They invited him to come before their body on August 14, 1961, to discuss that portion specifically. This would not be the last time Marriner offered testimony at a hearing of a congressional committee. Yet what was said on the occasion amounted to a final attempt to put back into the 1935 Banking Act provisions that had been deleted at the insistence of Carter Glass. In a larger sense, what Marriner said was a coda to the many years he had spent in trying to close the gap between existing governmental institutional arrangements and the new challenges posed by changes in the realities which affected monetary, credit, fiscal, and debt-management policies.

Marriner began his testimony with a swift sketch of the revolutionary developments which had overtaken the nation and the world in the quarter of a century since the Banking Act of 1935. He then pinpointed "one of the most important recommendations made by the commission." It was that "the Congress modernize and make consistent the legislative mandates expressed in the Federal Reserve Act and the Employment Act of 1964." He argued that identical language stating that the nation's economic goals were to be a low level of unemployment, adequate rates of economic growth, and reasonable price stability should be used in these two fundamental statutes, and that the same goals should be extended to all federal agencies administering economic programs. "At the present time," said Marriner, "the Employment Act does not include stability as one of the goals, and, by its accent on full employment, invites inflation while the Federal Reserve Act contains no provisions which specifically state any of the objectives of national economic policy."

More than identical language was needed, however, to bring about the coordination of policy that could make the mandates effective. Marriner proposed, as had the commission, that "the president consider setting up a council under a chairman to be designated by him, and which would plan its work so that weekly meetings could be held of related and interested departments and agency deputies." The ultimate object of the work to be done, aided by the staff of the Council of Economic Advisors, "would be to provide the president at regular intervals with a coherent picture of how the nation's economic goals were adversely, or favorably, affected as the economic activities undertaken by different arms of the government, acted and reacted on each other."

Marriner then turned to the major instruments of monetary policy—the power to buy and sell securities in the open market, to fix discount rates, to regulate conditions of member-bank borrowing, and to change reserve requirements of member banks within the limits specified by the Congress. The commission had recommended that the exercise of these powers be confined to the Federal Reserve Board, and Marriner explained why. "At the present time," he said, "discount rates are set by each Federal Reserve Bank every two weeks by its Board of Directors, subject to review and approval of the Federal Reserve Board. Credit markets, however, are national in character, and regional differences in discount rates are ineffective as economic controls." Hence, a *national* discount-rate policy should correspond with the *national* open-market policy. To that end, "a discretionary uniform discount rate should be established by the Federal Reserve Board for all Federal Reserve banks."

A corollary followed. The existing Federal Open Market Committee, whose powers were shared by the Federal Reserve Board and by five Reserve bank presidents, should be abolished. Instead, as the commission had recommended, the functions of the committee should be vested in the board alone. "The five bank presidents serving on the existing committee," Marriner explained, "cannot be considered governmental as they are elected by the member banks, whereas the members of the Federal Reserve Board must be appointed by the president and confirmed by the Senate and make their reports to Congress." Only this would "provide a clear center of responsibility for the use of all three of the major general instruments of monetary and credit policy."

Similarly, Marriner supported a commission recommendation calling for a reduction of the existing membership of the Federal Reserve Board from seven to five, and for the substitution of overlapping ten-year terms with eligibility for reappointment in place of the existing fourteen-year terms with no reappointment. "The reduction in membership," said he, "should enhance the status of each member, and the ten-year term is a sufficient protection for independence." In a further echo of what he had tried to achieve in his draft of the 1935 Banking Act, Marriner urged—as had the commission—that the occupational and geographical qualifications for board membership be eliminated. The status instead "should stipulate that members be positively qualified by experience or education, competence, and objectivity, commensurate with the increased responsibilities they assumed in achieving national economic objectives.''

A strengthened board, however, would still be in need of channels of outside advice, broader than those in existence. But, Marriner said, an obstacle to the attainment of that objective was the current "statutory position of the Federal Advisory Council, each of whose twelve members is appointed by a respective Federal Reserve bank" and is "by custom a commercial banker." The aggregate effect made for a very narrow channel of advice. To widen it, Marriner recommended that the existing Federal Advisory Council be replaced by a new advisory body whose twelve members would be appointed by the board from nominees presented to it by the Board of Directors of the Federal Reserve banks. "At least two nominees, and not more than one of them from any single sector of the economy, should be presented by each bank. The Federal Reserve Board, itself, should make its selections in such a manner as to secure a council broadly representative of all aspects of the American economy."

The board was also in need of a stronger internal source of advice. With that in mind, Marriner argued in favor of a proposal whereby the twelve Reserve bank presidents would be constituted by law as a Conference of Federal Reserve Bank President to meet at least four times a year with the board, or as often as the board thought necessary. By the same law, the board when establishing open-market policy, discount rates, or reserve requirements would be required beforehand to consult with the Conference of Presidents. But it was not enough, said Marriner, merely to broaden the external and to strengthen the internal sources of advice. The Federal Reserve Board had a duty of its own "to keep the public informed, with reasonable promptness and in reasonable detail, of the reasons for its major policy decisions and actions in order to avoid misunderstanding and misinterpretation." He admitted, as did the commission, that this was a "delicate matter." But once the duty was recognized, "the timing and substance of such reports must be left to the good judgment of the board."

Marriner next picked up the strand of his old and frustrated effort to do something about the nation's dual banking system. His testimony on the point reads:

The strength and influence of the Federal Reserve in our economic system is closely related to the strength of the commercial banking system through which it functions. The commercial banking system has great need of modernization. It has steadily lost ground in relation to other financial institutions during the past 60 years, and especially during the last 10 years. In 1900, it represented 52.9 percent of the nation's financial assets as compared with 39.5 percent in 1958; whereas the savings and loans institutions increased from 2.6 percent in 1900 to 9.1 percent in 1958. In the interests of the economy as a whole, the Federal Reserve and the commercial banking system must both be strengthened. To that end, the commission recommends three steps which I have long advocated.

First, all government insured commercial banks should be required to become members of the Federal Reserve System. Around 6,000 of these banks are not members. Legislation requiring them to be members—or to lose the coverage of government insurance if they refuse—would be consistent with Home Loan Bank legislation which requires all insured savings and loan companies to be members of the Home Loan System. Second, all federal bank supervisory agencies should be unified by transferring to the Federal Reserve System the functions of the Comptroller of the Currency, as well as those of the Federal Deposit Insurance Company. This would greatly simplify and strengthen the examining, regulatory, and supervisory functions of the three agencies. Third, competitive relationships between the commercial banks and the thrift institutions should be improved by providing for greater tax equality.

So far, the recommendations of the commission conformed to Marriner's long-held views. But his major point of dissent, expressed in a written footnote to the report, was amplified in his testimony before the Joint Committee on the Economic Report. "I have," said he, "grave doubts whether the commission's recommendations will prove adequate to achieve the national economic goals which they seek—an adequate rate of economic growth, low levels of unemployment, and reasonable price stability." Why not?

The first of the cardinal reasons went back to his long-standing concern, first expressed at the time of the 1937–38 recession, at the dual signs of a fall-off in labor productivity and the way organized labor was pricing itself out of the market. "A special weakness of the report," Marriner told the joint committee, "is that it fails to give adequate consideration and weight to the unstabilizing effects of the monopolistic power exercised by organized labor." It was "unrealistic to gloss over the effects of its actions on prices, imports, exports, employment, rates of growth, and the deficiency in our international balance of payments." And he continued:

Organized labor represents about 25 percent of the labor force. There is a wide discrepancy between the income of the organized group getting between $3 and $6 per hour and most of the 75 percent of unorganized workers earning between $1 and $2 an hour. The disparity in the incomes of these groups makes it increasingly difficult to exchange goods and services, resulting in unnecessary unemployment. How can workers earning from $1 to $2 an hour buy or rent houses or apartments built by unions with common labor getting, in wages and fringe benefits, $3.52 per hour now and $4.02 in two years, plumbers getting $5.78 per hour now, and $7.55 per hour in two years, and other union wages in proportion?

Much has been said of the monopolistic power of business, but the real monopoly today that is creating our problems is the monopoly of organized labor. We should not tolerate private groups dominating our government and our economy by means of organized monopolies. . . . Until the government recognizes the seriousness of this situation and passes legislation which adequately deals with it, as it has with business, there is, in my opinion, little chance of meeting the nation's economic goals.

Another "special weakness of the report" was, in Marriner's view, indivisible with the first. It was that the report "did not deal more realistically with our international balance of payments problem in the light of the phenomenal recovery and great increase in the productivity of Western Europe and Japan." Wages and fringe benefits of union labor in the United States were from "two to five times that of other industrial countries." Thus, organized labor not only "drew from the economy benefits in excess of increased productivity" but undermined "our ability to compete in world as well as domestic markets," and all the more so since "productivity in Western Europe and Japan" was "rapidly increasing and approaching that of the United States." Hence the dollar "was overpriced in relation to other currencies."

There was another complicating factor:

Our failure to recognize our economic limitations has aggravated our international balance of payments. During the last fifteen years, we have disbursed over 100 billion dollars in economic and military aid, not including our own extensive military expenditures abroad. This, together with large private foreign investments and expanding foreign travel by Americans, along with the increasing difficulty of selling American goods in the world market because of the monopolistic practices of organized labor, has drastically changed the position of the Western World from one of a dollar shortage to a dollar surplus. This has deprived us of much of the economic freedom which we formerly enjoyed since we now find ourselves locked into a world situation which we can no longer control.

Marriner did not see how the United States could continue as the reserve currency country and the world banker, given its present domestic price structure. Instead, the United States should "move as rapidly as possible to transfer this responsibility to an international monetary organization where currency values could be adjusted—upward or downward—over the longer period as basic needs were determined. "Meanwhile," said he, "the radical change that had overcome the international balance of payments pictures confronted the nation with a set of hard and critical choices." On the one side, it could try "greatly to increase productivity," and to translate the gains into "lower prices and better products." If this were not attempted or achieved, then the choice on the other side pointed to "tariffs, quotas, embargoes, exchange controls, or the discontinuance of present foreign aid and defense policies."

Much of what Marriner had to say was prophetic. It also was ignored at the time. So it was with his concluding and seemingly odd remark, coming from a man who had been one of the leaders of the fight for deficit spending during the New Deal years. "I strongly feel," said he, "that federal expenditures are unjustifiably increasing in many categories. The public is not getting value received. This is especially true of the rapidly expanding and continuing foreign military and economic aid program." Soon afterward, starting with the escalation of the American involvement in the Vietnam conflict, Marriner would be among the first major figures in the business world to protest—and to keep on protesting—the failure to get "value received" in return for the lives and treasure invested in *that* foreign military-aid program.

The recommendations issuing from the commission as a whole, save for marginal exceptions, never traveled the vital distance between precept and practice. They were ignored by successive presidents and Congresses. In this way, by the end of the 1960s, the nation was left entirely unprepared to cope with the tangled factors that pulled the economy down into the worst morass since the Great Depression.

40. More Old Issues Revisited

ASIDE FROM THE TWO YEARS Marriner spent in Europe as a young missionary on the eve of the First World War, he visited Europe only four times during his long life, and it was not until the spring of 1956 that he made his first trip to the Far East. He was royally welcomed wherever he went, and was the subject of a particularly poignant tribute when he stopped in the Philippines. Here a dinner was arranged in his honor by Mike Cuaderno, the governor of the Central Bank of the Philippines. In the course of his address, Cuaderno saluted Marriner as one "of the protectors for Philippine independence and self-determination at a critical moment in the history of that nation."

In support of the salute, the host read from the text of a letter Marriner had written back in 1947, the substance of which had been crowded out of his memory by the intervention of a thousand other events. The letter, addressed to the U.S. Secretary of State and the U.S. Secretary of the Treasury, argued that the Philippine peso should *not* remain tied to the U.S. dollar as was being widely proposed at the time. The pertinent passages cited by Cuaderno were these:

My basic position is that usually it is inordinately expensive—I would say extravagant—for any foreign country to administer its currency system on a straight U.S. dollar basis, whether it uses dollars as its sole medium of circulation or issues its own currency backed 100 percent by U.S. dollar reserves.

Not only does such a system involve locking up highly valuable foreign exchange assets which might be used productively to finance imports for development purpose; in addition it deprives the country concerned of any freedom of action in managing its domestic monetary affairs. It forces a rigid pattern of monetary policy completely at the mercy of the flow of funds in the balance of payments in time of depression and leaves the country concerned without effective defense against stagnation and waste of resources. Furthermore, in the specific case of the Philippines, which is suffering budgetary difficulties imposed by reconstruction needs, it forces the country to assume burdensome external liabilities to meet purely domestic expenditure requirements. . . .

It seems to me that when the issue arises, we must give due consideration to legitimate Philippine aspirations as well as to our own business interests. Indeed, I am convinced that in the long run the interests of private American capital will be best served by a broad-gauged policy which refrains from undue insistence on narrow national self-interests at the expense of the independence and self-determination of foreign peoples.

The 100 percent dollar backing requirement for the Philippine peso was relaxed. One letter, one forcefully stated argument, one act of bureaucratic assent to the argument—and a whole nation was liberated to be the author of its own economic history. Marriner could only wish that other letters among the mass he had written were as productive of results.

Aside from the foregoing, the 1956 trip to the Far East added little to what Marriner already knew about economics of the region—based on the mass of data he had stored in his mind during his years as governor of the Federal Reserve Board and on the flood of reports related to the international operations of Utah Construction & Mining Company and the Amalgamated Sugar Company. Yet what he encountered face to face in the Far East added an emotional dimension to his previously formed convictions about two public matters both discussed earlier in these pages.

One was the need for the United States to recognize Communist China and to restore normal trade relations with her. The other was the need to face up to the "fatal dangers latent in the runaway growth of the world's population." Both convictions were fused in an article Marriner wrote for The *American Banker* on his return from the Far East. He there asserted anew that the "rate of growth of the world's population is the most vitally important problem facing the world today, and may well prove to be more explosive than the atomic or hydrogen bomb." Then, in the course of an analysis of Japan's needs for exports and the American imposed ban on trade between Japan and Communist China, he again reemphasized his old call for a more rational basis for U.S. relations with Communist China:[11]

Because of what I saw in the Orient I am more convinced than ever that the American policy of non-recognition of Communist China—and the dogmatic theories underlying the policy—are costly and dangerous absurdities. If persisted in, they are bound to lead us into a deadly trap.

Why do we insist on trying to make the world over in our own image? We should understand that economic facts make democracy, for the present, as we know it, impossible for great areas of the world. Recognition of Red China and trade with the Communist world would eliminate war tensions more than anything else. The power of modern weapons has produced a Great Power military stalemate, while in the political and economic field, the unhappy fact is being forced upon us that the world does not revolve around the United States. . . . In the final analysis it is the economic necessities of each country that ultimately determine its political course and consequently, the course of world affairs.

These views led to personal consequences. First, and most immediately, Marriner came to the front of the then small group of prominent American businessmen who were willing, by word, deed and pocketbook, to help provide leadership for the stammering population control movement. Later, starting in in mid-1965, he was foremost among those American businessmen outspoken in their opposition to the escalation of the American involvement in the Vietnam conflict.

II

In 1958, President Eisenhower appointed a nine-member committee under the chairmanship of General William Draper, Jr., to examine the United States foreign aid program. Among the various recommendations to emerge from this group, one called for the extension by the American government of assistance in population planning to friendly nations—*upon their request*. Marriner at once recognized the cardinal importance of this particular recommendation and promptly wheeled into a support position behind it. In a note of approval and encouragement sent to his friend, General Draper, he wrote:

Any foreign aid program is, at best, a stopgap unless we deal with the basic cause —which is the runaway population. Unimpeded fertility is giving the backward countries exactly what they do not need—more people—and hindering what they do need—more capital, more skills, and greater productivity. A continuation of the present combination of low death rate with high birth rate is a sure prelude to disaster. In the absence of realistic population planning, no conceivable economic aid program will change this course. Inevitably, the existence of masses of people subsisting at starvation levels invites revolution and communism.

Subsequent to the publication of the Draper committee report, nothing was done in the remaining two and one-half years of the Eisenhower presidency to spur a program of governmental assistance to nations requesting help in population planning. It was President Eisenhower's view that the American government had no responsibilities in the matter. Hope for action was revived after the 1960 election in which John F. Kennedy attained the White House to the sound of his own summons: "Let's get America moving again." Yet, in the months following Inauguration Day, though Washington was agog with the glamor and vigor of the youthful New Frontiersman, nothing moved on the front of population planning—because of a deliberate decision to do nothing. This was first made clear in May 1961 in a terse note the medical director of the American foreign aid program sent to the president of the International Planned Parenthood Federation of the Western Hemisphere. "It is the official policy of this government," the medical director wrote, "not to provide help on questions relating to population control."

Marriner was appalled by this policy. He was equally disturbed by the "do-nothingism" of the United Nations, whose own statistical reports underlined the conclusions reached in a major study: "The world population growth in the next twenty-five years, from 3 billion in 1960 to a projected 6.2 billion by the year 2000, has an importance which transcends economic and social considerations. It is the very heart of our existence." Marriner, who by now was heavily involved in the educational work of the Planned Parenthood Association, besides rendering it substantial financial support, talked ceaselessly about the "population dilemma" and railed against the timidity underlying the failure of the American government and of the United Nations to come to grips with the issue. As usual, it was his wife, Sallie, who was the first to hear the full range of his outrage over "willful inactivity" in high places. But on May 11, 1961, he had a larger audience. A testimonial dinner honoring Mrs. Margaret Sanger for her half-century of work in the cause of birth control was held at the Waldorf Astoria Hotel in New York, coincident with the opening of the Conference on the World Population Crisis. More than two hundred of the main financial backers of the movement were in attendance, and at the invitation of Lamont Dupont Copeland, the chairman of the affair, Marriner was the featured speaker.

He would not, he said at the outset of his remarks, address the audience immediately before him. To do so would amount to a case of the "convinced talking to the convinced." He would address "the people who have the power to act effectively on the population explosion—the great problem of our time—but who have thus far tried to escape and evade their obligations to act." His list of those he indicted began with the officials of the American government and the delegations to the United Nations. Next, in an expanding roll of thunder, he addressed three other groups of people "who have the power to act." They were the business community, the great philanthropic foundations who "bear a special responsibility in this crisis," and "the great Roman Catholic Church."

Taken in sequence, he appealed to the business community in its own "enlightened self-interest" to support the cause of population planning both "morally and financially." The prevailing notion that "surging populations guarantee increasing profits" was dead wrong. Such populations perpetuate poverty and "fall easy victims to the glittering but never fulfilled promises of communism." Capitalism "could not expect to survive as an island of abundance in a sea of poverty." As for the philanthropic foundations, Marriner credited them with having promoted public health services throughout the world. In consequence, diseases which once ravaged whole populations were eradicated, and health and a longer life span were substituted for sickness and early death. But in Marriner's double-entry ledger system there was a massive fact to be noted on the debit side.

In the developing countries of Asia, Africa, and particularly at this time, Latin America, from the most humanitarian motives, we have interfered with the controlling laws of nature. We have drastically lowered the death rate in these countries, but have neglected to exert a compensating influence on the birth rate. Laws of nature, however cruel, are not usually so illogical. Our policy has been to work for death control without taking the necessary steps to reduce the number of births, and so offset the consequent runaway inflation of people.

It is unpardonable irresponsibility, in the light of today's knowledge, to inaugurate programs to reduce death rates and increase birth rates without any possibility of providing for the generations so created. Misguided idealism must not be allowed to obscure the need for hard-headed realism on this point.

Marriner's major thunderclap was reserved for the Catholic Church.

He combined in it a due respect for the Bill of Rights, a blunt statement of known facts seldom mentioned in public forums, and an appeal to the church's own self-interest:

We, as a nation, will always support the freedom of worship, as we do the other freedoms. This does not mean, however, that any church should be permitted to so dominate the economic and social life of a country or a continent as to make it impossible to carry out the measures for population planning which are essential for survival.

We all know the power and influence that the Catholic Church exercises to discourage appropriate steps being taken to deal with this most basic problem—not only in the United States, but particularly in the Latin countries. Few people in public life have the political courage to challenge this opposition. However, unless this barrier is soon overcome, and the forces of the democratic world are united in facing the dangers inherent in this unchecked population surge, the free world will have lost its position to the communists.

Marriner, as usual, followed the logic of his own reasoning wherever it led, without regard to the people he might offend. And he offended many, including the editors of the *New York Times*. A day after his speech, they administered a sharp editorial rap on Marriner's knuckles, saying that he had falsely singled out the Catholic Church as one of the main barriers to the general acceptance of birth control methods. Marriner continued to press his case. Having riled the hierarchy of the Catholic Church in New York and elsewhere, he presently "balanced the ticket" by displeasing a segment of Mormon Church leaders in Utah and elsewhere.

In March, 1962, at Brigham Young University, where he had been invited to address business students on the topic of "Monetary Policy and Inflation," he announced that he had switched the topic to "The Population Problem and Education—in the United States and throughout the World." In view of what he meant to say, he should have given the authorities of Brigham Young, a Mormon-controlled institution, advance notice of his change of topic—though doing so might have put them in the embarrassing position of having to withdraw their invitation. But if Marriner could be faulted for a show of dubious manners, he could not be faulted for his resolve to talk about a subject that was now uppermost in his thoughts.

The convergence of four events accounted for his resolve. First, figures just released by the Census Bureau showed that America's expanding population was growing older and younger at the same time, with a consequent increase in the rate of dependency. By 1970, there would be ninety-one old and young dependents for every hundred productive workers between the ages of 20 and 65—in contrast to seventy-five dependent in 1962. To Marriner, this imbalance plainly spelled trouble unless the national population growth was curbed.

Then, in 1962, a statement signed by thirty-eight Nobel laureates gave a scientific imprimatur to a warning note Marriner had repeatedly struck in the preceding decade. "In spite of technological advances"—so the statement read—"the earth cannot provide much longer enough food and materials for a population that is increasing more than geometrically. Unless a favorable balance of population and resources is achieved with a minimum of delay, there is in prospect a dark age of human misery, famine, undereducation, unrest, which could generate growing panic, exploding into wars fought to appropriate the dwindling means of survival."

Also in 1962 there was the rising nationwide demand for federal aid to education, in order to shore up state and local educational institutions inundated at every level by students born during the postwar "baby boom." In addition, there was the recent creation by the Kennedy administration of the Alliance for Progress, as the vehicle for a large new program of United States aid to Latin America. Marriner agreed on the need for that program. He also agreed with President Kennedy's statement that, unless Latin America used United States aid to raise the standard of life for the mass of their people and not just for some of them, they would get no aid. But he failed to see the logic in the parallel insistence of the administration that what happened to the population of Latin America was not the business of the United States.

Much of the foregoing was touched on by Marriner in his speech to the business students at Brigham Young University. But another note he sounded was meant to, and did, strike closer to home. He had been a long-time supporter of quality in education, and had long insisted that a program of federal aid to education fell squarely within the Constitution's grant of power to the Congress to levy and collect taxes in support of "the general welfare of the United States." The need in Utah for a federal sharing of the financial burdens of education was particularly great. This was because the formation of early marriages and large families was strongly encouraged by the Mormon Church and because Utah already led the nation in stretching local tax resources to the outer limits in order to educate an increasingly large cohort of young people. Yet the political picture in Utah, like that of the Alliance for Progress, was shot through with contradictions. A significant body of Mormon opinion opposed federal aid to education, fearing that it implied federal control of local schools. But that same body of opinion was committed to bringing more and more children into the world whose education would impose an increasingly heavy burden on the state's tax base.

Marriner pointed to that contradiction, stressed the need for federal aid to education, and then came to the heart of his message. Drawing on the statistics that were available in 1961–62, he remarked:

Our life and our hopes as a national community depend on high-quality education. Yet our educational tasks cannot be adequately discharged until the population problem, in its stark reality, has been faced and brought under control.

I should think that Utah, in its own self-interest, would be in the front rank of those states which are in favor of federal aid to education, and which also favor an effective program of population planning. The figures make the case: Utah not only leads all the states in the nation in the ratio of public school enrollment to total population, but leads it by far in the number of school-age children per 1,000 of working adults between the ages of 21 and 64.

Personal income in Utah divided by the school enrollment is $7,196; in the United States as a whole, $11,179. Now there is an impressive difference. In 1961, public expenditures for schools was 6.27 percent of personal income in Utah; in the United States as a whole, only 4.2 percent. In the nation, more than 33 percent of all state and local government expenditures are for education, but in Utah, 49.9 percent is for education.

Brigham Young authorities did not publish Marriner's remarks to the business students, but the text would crop up in a different university context in Utah. As of the early 1960s, reluctance to face up to the population dilemma was not confined to governmental authorities, international agencies, or churchmen of particular creeds. The same reluctance was present among private associations which stressed their boldly independent approach to public issues in other respects.

This was brought home to Marriner at a 1962 planning meeting of the Trustees of the American Assembly. He had regularly urged that an Arden House conference of the Assembly be organized on the subject of the population dilemma, with such persistence that, whenever he arrived at a meeting of the trustees, board chairman Henry Wriston greeted him with the same question: "And how is Mr. Population Explosion today?" Yet what he urged anew in 1962 was tabled on the ground that the whole question of population control was "too controversial." This was another way of saying that the assembly should not risk offending financial supporters of its work. By year-long persistence, however, Marriner finally mustered enough support from trustees such as William Benton, John Cowles, Clifford Nelson and Alan Kline, so that an Arden House meeting on the population dilemma was set for May 1963. Professor Philip Hauser of the University of Chicago, a world-renowned authority on demography, was engaged to supervise the preparation of research papers, and the published volume that eventually emerged from the conference remains to this day the most widely read of all the books ever issued under the imprimatur of the American Assembly.

In May 1963, on the eve of that particular Arden House conference, Marriner still had on hand the unpublished text of the speech he had given fourteen months earlier at Brigham Young University. He had polished its language, tightened its structure, updated its statistical data. He had also added the word "taxes," so that the title now read, "Population, Taxes, and Education." All he needed was a public forum where it could be delivered, and that turned out to be the Town and Gown organization at Utah State University in Logan. The text was later published by the Utah State University Press as part of a monograph series issued by the university's College of Education, and was widely distributed throughout the state. The essential difference between the new version and the earlier one was that Marriner put his case more bluntly, as can be sensed from his summary statement:

If we are to *avoid* further tax increases and adequately *meet* our pressing problems of *education*—*reduce* juvenile delinquency and adult crime—overcome increasing transportation congestion—*provide* adequate hospitals and medical care, housing and recreational facilities for our teeming millions—*meet* the problem of water conservation and pollution—*reduce poverty and unemployment*—then our rapidly growing population must be curbed. This means *birth control* and not just planned parenthood, useful as this may be in many cases.

In the years ahead, increasing numbers of other people came to share those views and act on them. Thus, the expansion of the United States population slowed down to near "zero growth," while more members of the United Nations—as well as the UN organization itself—finally joined in population control efforts. Yet the years of intervening delay, and the pressures of the population born in the quarter of a century after the end of the second World War, brought hundreds of millions of the world's people to the threshold of starvation by the mid-1970s. Marriner gained no satisfaction from having been "an early warning system."

41. Vietnam

I

IN RESPONSE TO AN INVITATION issued by Joseph Fowler, Marriner came to Washington, D.C., in late August 1964 for a meeting in the Metropolitan Club of some seventy-five leading figures in the world of American finance, commerce and industry. Here, in line with a predetermined purpose, the participants pledged their personal support for the recently chosen 1964 Democratic ticket of President Lyndon B. Johnson, and his vice-presidential running mate, Senator Hubert H. Humphrey. In a related move, the participants agreed to serve as the nucleus for what was to be a nationwide "independent committee" that would seek, among other things, to raise at least $500,000 for use in connection with the Democratic presidential campaign.

The cochairmen chosen by the nuclear group for the larger committee to be formed were John T. Connor, an independent Democrat and president of Merck & Company, and John I. Loeb, a registered Republican and senior partner in the Wall Street firm of Loeb, Rhodes & Company. Three quarters of the other organizing members were Republicans either by registration or by past voting habits. They included Ford Motor Company chairman Henry Ford II, and two men who had held Cabinet posts under President Eisenhower—Robert B. Anderson, former Secretary of the Treasury, and Marion B. Folsom, former Secretary of Health, Education and Welfare.

At the end of the meeting, Joseph Fowler shepherded the participants over the distance between the club and into the White House where President Johnson was waiting to receive them. Johnson expansively thanked his visitors for their pledges of support, and dwelt on the promise he saw in them not only for victory in the impending election but for a more perfect national union afterward. Marriner could not stay to the end of the president's remarks. He was on a tight schedule, and had to catch a plane for San Francisco. He whispered his apologies to Bill Moyers, a Johnson aide, asked that they be conveyed to the president, and then slipped out of the room.

By past voting habits, Marriner, was a "broken field runner." Perhaps it would be more precise to say that he was a displaced person in the political landscape. Yet, there were several reasons why he was drawn to the 1964 Democratic presidential ticket. He had known both Johnson and Humphrey since the time of their arrival on the Washington scene, and was on friendly personal terms with them. Though he saw some worrisome aspects to their "Great Society" program, he welcomed their call for governmental action on a long agenda of the nation's "unfinished domestic business." At the same time, he believed that the approach to the nation's domestic problems advocated by Senator Barry Goldwater, the Republican nominee, amounted to a romantic throwback to the precepts of nineteenth-century "laissez-faire" liberalism—attractive in academic theory but socially and politically divisive if put into practice.

Above all, Marriner was drawn to the 1964 Democratic ticket because of his mounting concern over the American policy toward the civil strife in Vietnam. Since the Korean war, he had been unalterably opposed to any move that might again entangle the United States in an Asian conflict. He was therefore alarmed by Senator Goldwater's apparent support for a policy where the American military contingents then in Vietnam would shift from their advisory and training mission to a direct combat role, backed by the striking force of American bombers. President Johnson appeared to be a model of restraint. Marriner was particularly comforted when he heard Johnson say: "We don't want our boys to do the fighting for Asian boys. We don't want to get involved . . . and get tied down in a land war in Asia."

By long-standing tradition, presidential candidates make one of their major campaign speeches in the Mormon Tabernacle in Salt Lake City. Johnson's schedule for the event, when he arrived there on an evening in late September, called for breakfast the next morning with David O. McKay, the president of the Mormon Church, who lived in an apartment in the Hotel Utah on a floor directly below Marriner's. Then, promptly at 8:30 A.M., he would come up to Marriner's apartment for a "continental breakfast" with thirty people who had each contributed $500 to a $15,000 broadcast fund. The president shook hands with the thirty contributors and spoke to them for some fifteen minutes. When he left for his 9 A.M. speech, the group followed by bus to the Mormon Tabernacle, where they were assigned seats directly behind the president. The $15,000 collected from them was used to purchase time for an evening rebroadcast on the Intermountain Television Network of the morning speech.

II

Throughout the whole of the presidential contest, and again in the weeks immediately following Johnson's landslide victory, the Bay of Tonkin resolution, which Congress approved in the summer of 1964, seemed to be little more than a psychological gambit. Since the early 1950s, three similar congressionally approved texts—the Formosa resolution, the Middle East resolution, and the Cuban resolution—appeared to give the president a free hand to "make war" on the basis of his own judgment without a declaration of war by Congress. Except for a brief incursion in Lebanon, none of these had been followed by an actual clash of arms. Suddenly the explosive potentialities within the Bay of Tonkin resolution lit up the sky of December 1964, when American aircraft began to bomb North Vietnam in retaliation for Vietcong terror attacks on American marine bases in South Vietnam.

Early signs of public unease over these Vietnam developments took several forms. One was a pacifist-style protest parade in Washington, organized in April 1965 by the Students for Democratic Action. Another was the Vietnam "teach–in" which originated at the University of Michigan and quickly spread to some fifty other campuses. The teach-in, by its nature, expressed a spirit of hesitation between respectful inquiry and protest, and the campus setting emphasized that any objections to the Vietnam war were still mostly on an intellectual plane. It was appropriate to a period when the public at large knew very little about the origins of the conflict in Vietnam or about America's involvement in it. Dissent in Congress was as ill-formed and hesitant as elsewhere. In May 1965, when a chance arose to oppose an expanded American role in Vietnam with a vote—the issue was a supplemental appropriation of $700 million, the first of a series of presidential requests for more money for the war—only seven representatives and three senators voted against it. Senators Eugene McCarthy and Robert F. Kennedy were among those who voted *for* it.

By June 1965, the 23,000 U.S. troops in South Vietnam were fully committed to combat roles and the first waves of U.S. army reinforcements were landing in that country. Marriner was dismayed by these developments and ceaselessly discussed their implications with his friends, either in face-to-face conversations, or in letters and telephone calls. At first, most of his friends—and his business associates as well—automatically backed the line being taken by the Johnson administration. But among the few who shared Marriner's alarm was Palmer Weber, who had become very successful in the over-the-counter brokerage business in New York City. He and Marriner tied up their telephone lines for long hours, talking about what could be done to reverse the course of American policy toward Vietnam.

In early July 1965, Weber drafted a resolution whose terms called for an immediate cease-fire in Vietnam and the start of negotiations to end the conflict. He sent the draft to Marriner with some suggestions about how the text was to be unveiled in the Senate. First, Marriner was to have his friend J. William Fulbright, chairman of the Senate Foreign Relations Committee, privately show the draft resolution to President Johnson and outline certain procedural steps bearing on it. An appropriate group of bipartisan senators—three Republicans and three Democrats—would be picked to act as sponsors of the resolution. With Johnson then lending a hand behind the scenes, a drive would be mounted in the Senate to secure majority approval of the resolution. Approval would take the president "off the political hook." He could explain to the nation, and to the eavesdropping world, that in obedience to the express will of the Senate he was himself calling for a cease-fire in Vietnam and the start of negotiations.

As it happened, the resolution and the explanatory letter reached Marriner in Salt Lake City on the eve of his departure for Washington, D.C. Joseph Fowler, now Secretary of the Treasury, acting at the direction of President Johnson, had invited to a White House dinner the members of the "independent committee" of businessmen that had backed the 1964

Johnson-Humphrey ticket. As a member, Marriner was among those who accepted the invitation. Senator Ernest Gruening, the chairman of a Senate subcommittee that was conducting hearings on the "population question," had previously asked Marriner to testify. Indicating that he could not make a special cross-country trip solely for that purpose, but promising to inform Gruening when he had to be in Washington in connection with other things, Marriner agreed to come before it, if the timing was right from the standpoint of the subcommittee. In this way, it was agreed that he would offer his testimony on the morning after the White House dinner.

Before Marriner's departure for Washington, he telephoned Senator Fulbright and arranged to see him as soon as the session with Senator Gruening's subcommittee was over. He put Weber's letter and resolution into the vest pocket of the suit he wore on the plane trip to Washington. On arrival, he checked into the Madison Hotel. Being pressed for time, he made his way to the White House without changing his clothes. Some seventy other members of the former "independent committee" were on hand for the event. After cocktails were served, all were ushered into the East Room, where they were seated in three rows facing President Johnson—flanked on one side by George Meany and on the other by Walter Reuther. The full Cabinet, reinforced by White House staff members, by General Maxwell Taylor, and by the chairman of the Federal Reserve Board, William McChesney Martin, were grouped around these three central figures.

It quickly became apparent to Marriner that the "social event" was no ordinary exercise of a President paying off debts to political supporters. The object was to convert the 1964 "independent committee" into a source of support for the Johnson administration's escalation of American intervention in the Vietnam conflict.

After welcoming the guests, the President spoke briefly about the aims of American policy in Vietnam, and then zeroed in on the listening audience. Secretary of State Dean Rusk spoke about how the success of America's Vietnamese policy was vital to world peace. Secretary of Defense Robert McNamara followed with a dazzling statistical show, backed by charts and computer printouts. All went to underline the wisdom of the "search and destroy" strategy the American military were pursuing in Vietnam. Indeed, said the Secretary of Defense, "fast-moving favorable developments on the military front indicated that it would be possible to withdraw American military forces within the coming year." The technical details underlying the optimistic picture were then elaborated with the help of a large map subdivided into red, white and grey zones corresponding to the areas controlled by the North and South Vietnamese and the zones in dispute.

At the end of these presentations, Secretary of the Treasury Fowler, the master of ceremonies, spoke up to say that there was not sufficient time left for the guests to ask questions before dinner was served. He added, however, that at each table were place cards next to the name of the guest. One card was marked "writer" and one was marked "speaker." The speaker would have three minutes of time allotted to express his views. The writer was expected to write what he would have said if he had had an opportunity to speak.

The seating chart directed Marriner to table eight, and the card at his place setting was marked "speaker." He at once began to sweat. What could he say in response to the things he had just heard from the president of the United States and from his principal officers? He sweated all the more profusely as one after another of the men who also held cards marked "speaker"—seven in an unbroken row—rose to praise Johnson personally in extravagant terms, and sweepingly to endorse his course of action in Vietnam. Marriner had never before witnessed what to him was so embarrassing a mass spectacle of "apple-polishing." Further, with the exception of the celebrated witnesses before the Senate Finance Committee back in February 1933 who called for a balanced budget in the depth of the depression, he had never before heard so many captains of commerce, finance and industry united in support of what was to him a mindless public policy. When it came his turn to speak, he rose and addressed President Johnson directly.[12]

"I take it, Mr. President," he said, "that you want me to say what I think?"

"Oh, yes, of course, of course, Marriner," said Johnson.

"Well, I regret that I cannot follow or subscribe in any sense to what the seven preceding speakers have said concerning Vietnam, or what I heard a while ago from members of the Cabinet. I believe the administration's policy toward Vietnam to be based on fatal errors, and that our national interest would best be served if the administration disentangled itself from a course of action that is bound to be ruinous." Here Marriner remembered Palmer Weber's letter and draft resolution that was to be discussed with Senator Fulbright the next day, and which he accidentally had left in his pocket. He took out the documents and continued his remarks: "My own position of opposition to your administration's Vietnam policy —as well as what I think should be done to reverse it—is laid out in something which I brought with me from Utah. Let me read from the texts."

There was a stunned silence while Marriner was speaking and reading, and an uneasy silence when he was through. But then President Johnson turned to Secretary of State Rusk. "Dean," said he, "You have heard Marriner state his position. Have you any reply?"

"You have all heard my views," said Rusk, "and I have nothing more to add." The response from the group was a collective sigh of relief. As for Marriner, he had dueled with other presidents and their chief advisers over other major public policies, and had lived to see *his* judgment, and not *theirs,* confirmed by the march of events. At noon on the next day, after testifying before Senator Gruening's committee on population issues, Marriner met with Senator Fulbright and opened the conversation by alluding to the White House dinner of the previous night.

"And what did *you* say there?" the senator asked.

"I got up and read from the letter and the resolution I meant to discuss with you."

Fulbright exploded with laughter. "And what did the *boss* say?"

"The *boss* had nothing to say. He ducked behind Secretary of State Dean Rusk. Rusk also had nothing to say. His mind seemed closed to argument or persuasion."

That was the last White House function Marriner was ever invited to attend.

III

Public expression of antiwar sentiment ceased to be a student monopoly after November 27, 1965, when 20,000 people from around the country descended on the nation's capital for what was called a "March on Washington for Peace in Vietnam." The sponsors included well-known names identified with the arts and sciences and with pacifist organizations, although in the derisive phrase of Senator Robert F. Kennedy, they were viewed only as "people with picket signs and beards." Their efforts still lacked open support from a major figure in the world of American commerce, finance and industry, until Marriner Eccles came into the picture.

In the months following the White House dinner, as was his way in other matters, Marriner made double entries in the mental ledger he kept on Vietnam. He tabulated the times when the hierarchs of the Johnson administration predicted that the most recent infusion of American forces into Vietnam would prove the instrument of victory. In an adjacent mental column, he also tabulated the times when the inflated predictions burst, not in a sea of red ink, but in a sea of blood—followed in turn, by the call for still more combat troops in support of a trumpeted new strategy.

During the Thanksgiving holiday in November 1965, Marriner entered St. Marks hospital in Salt Lake City for elective surgery his physician had recommended in connection with a regimen of "health maintenance." While convalescing in the hospital, he spent many hours thinking, reading and watching TV programs about the ever-expanding American involvement in Vietnam. Television news programs, with few exceptions, struck him as being carriers of government-generated views in support of the administration's Vietnamese policy. Though his body temperature had returned to normal, his anger over Vietnam raised his psychic temperature to a boiling point. He now resolved to state publicly far more than he had said privately to President Johnson, to his Cabinet Secretaries, to his chief military advisers, to the top-ranking labor leaders and to the "independent committee" of American businessmen gathered at the White House dinner in July.

He planned a personal letter which he meant to send to the hundred United States senators and to members of the House Foreign Affairs Committee. After returning to Salt Lake City from a directors' meeting of Utah Construction in San Francisco, he was interrupted in his work on the text by the demands of business affairs, and it was not until December 22, 1965, that he finished the final draft. He realized that the draft, consisting of six pages, was too long to serve as a personal letter. It was best sent to members of the Senate and to three major committees of the House—Foreign Relations, Ways and Means, and Finance—as a statement of his personal position, covered by an attached personal note in which he explained to the recipients that he wished to share with them his thoughts about Vietnam. He instructed his secretary in Salt Lake City to put the statement and covering notes in the mail on the day after Christmas.

On the day before Christmas, Marriner left Salt Lake City to join Sallie in San Francisco. He showed her a copy of the statement he had written. She ardently agreed with his line of argument and with his decision concerning the dissemination. It was Marriner and Sallie's practice to go on December 27 to their cottage at Eldorado in Palm Desert and remain there until after New Year's. Before leaving, they happened to go for cocktails to the home of nearby San Francisco friends, Jean and George Wolfe. Sallie had with her a copy of Marriner's statement on Vietnam, and at one point asked that he read it to their hosts. George Wolfe asked to keep the statement, to which Marriner assented.

The next day, after Marriner and Sallie had left for Eldorado, George Wolfe called on a friend, the editor of the *San Francisco Chronicle,* and gave him Marriner's statement to read. "I know," he said, "that what I am about to ask you is unusual. But I also know that Marriner Eccles is anxious to get the widest possible dissemination for his views on Vietnam. Won't you publish the statement in the *Chronicle?* I'll take full responsibility if you do." The editor quickly said yes, and proceeded to publish it in unusual form. On two successive days, January 3 and 4, 1966, he devoted the whole of the "Letters to the Editor" section of the *Chronicle* to what Marriner had written. Here is a representative extract:

Under no circumstances should we escalate the war in Vietnam. Our position there is indefensible. Contrary to government propaganda, we were not invited by and have no commitment to any representative or responsible government of South Vietnam. We are there as an aggressor in violation of our treaty obligation under the United Nations' Charter. We have not observed either the letter or the spirit of our obligations with respect to our actions in Vietnam.

He then dealt with the terms of the Geneva Treaty of 1954, and the events that followed the suspension of the scheduled national elections in Vietnam, the nature of the Diem regime in South Vietnam, Diem's assassination, and the governmental instability in South Vietnam. Marriner then continued:

In this civil war between the North and South Vietnamese, we have provided large amounts of military and economic aid to the South Vietnamese, and supplied them with military advisers. But until the present administration came into office, we did not furnish American troops to help fight their war, until it was apparent they were being defeated. We have gradually taken over the direction of *their* government as well as *their* war until now it is becoming an American war rather than a Vietnamese war. Why go to Vietnam to drive the communists out when we can't get them out of Cuba, 90 miles from our shore?

The North Vietnamese supplied troops to the Viet Cong only after American troops entered the war and we commenced heavy bombing of North Vietnam and the Viet Cong. We cannot WIN. We cannot defeat people in a jungle war where the majority is neutral or against you, and it is impossible to tell your friends from your enemies. We are rapidly destroying the very country we propose to save—South Vietnam—as well as killing thousands of its men, women, and children by our incessant and heavy bombing of the Viet Cong. We are adding to our burdens tens of thousands of refuges that we must feed, clothe, and house.

Marriner then predicted that, if the war was further escalated, the United States would probably be required to go on a war footing. In any case, "inflationary pressures will greatly increase and the position of the dollar in the world market will be further jeopardized unless we bring about a balanced budget through increasing taxes and cutting back domestic programs." In his view the United States could not have chosen anywhere in the world a more difficult place to challenge the communists than a country bordering in China. How, he asked, "could we have been so blind and misinformed?" In answer to his own question, he said:

The decisions were made by the President and a handful of advisers in the White House, State, and Defense Department without debate or prior approval of the Congress. This is dictatorship that has no place in our democracy. . . . Blindly accepting the government's position in Vietnam is more senseless than blindly accepting its domestic program because mistakes in Vietnam can be far more disastrous. The real patriots today are the *members of Congress and other public leaders* who have the courage to oppose the Administration and urge it not to escalate the war but to get out of Vietnam at the earliest possible date. This would be the least costly from every standpoint—even our image and world prestige would be enhanced.

If our leaders insist on escalating this war to a finish, it is likely to be the most disastrous war we have fought, measured by financial cost, loss of life and prestige throughout the world, and the most futile.

"Peace in the world," said Marriner, "would never be brought about by aggression or by rash and inept remarks" such as had been made by Secretary of Defense Robert McNamara at the Paris Conference of NATO when he urged America's European allies "to plan now to meet a Chinese military threat to their own security within five years." The way to peace was "to recognize China and bring her into the United Nations before she becomes an atomic power in three to five years." Marriner concluded:

With all our domestic problems—pollution, mass poverty, city slums, riots in our streets, and the world's highest rate of juvenile delinquency and crime—who are we to be the world's policeman? The billions being wasted on the war in Vietnam, if used to eliminate mass poverty and illiteracy in the undeveloped countries, would do far more than aggressive military action to prevent the spread of communism.

We must recognize that it is just as important, if not more so, for the communists to save face in Asia as it is for the U.S. We should be less interested in saving face and more interested in saving lives. . . .

Previously in Washington, FBI chief J. Edgar Hoover had described the small, but highly vocal anti-Vietnam demonstrators as being, for the most part, "halfway citizens who are neither morally, mentally, nor emotionally mature."[13] No stretching machine could make the description fit Marriner Eccles—aged seventy-five, with distinguished credentials as a widely experienced public servant and as the guiding hand at the helm of major American business enterprises. Yet here this man was protesting the involvement in Vietnam with more force and more knowledge than was true of the "kids" with picket signs and beards. One should also add that he did not fit the simplistic picture drawn by Marxist-minded anti-war "kids" who ascribed American military policy in Vietnam to a "capitalist plot" whose object was to seize and exploit the raw materials available in Vietnam. Marriner, a supremely successful "capitalist" who was opposed to the Vietnam war, burst the crude frame of the Marxist picture.

While in Eldorado with Sallie, Marriner, was not aware of the *Chronicle's* publication of his statement until a friend called his attention to it. When his inquiries revealed George Wolfe's role he fully approved of his friend's initiative. Meanwhile, the two-part "Letter to the Editor" had an electric effect on a segment of opinion in the Bay Area, for in the days following Marriner's return to San Francisco he received thousands of letters voicing agreement with what he had written. Not one letter disagreed.

Beforehand, in the Bay Area, as elsewhere, people who had been nagged by doubts concerning the growing American involvement in the Vietnam conflict hesitated to voice them openly for various reasons—the constraints of simple patriotism, the fears rooted in a dependence for bread on nearby defense industries or on governmental contracts, or the timidities which could be ascribed to the overawing certitudes of the numerical majority. In Marriner's case, a minimizing bystander might say that he ran no risks—that in the new crisis facing the nation, as in the earlier one of the Great Depression, he could well afford to be outspoken. No one could "fire" him from a job, or refuse him a job he needed, or otherwise threaten his livelihood. His strong personal economic base enabled him to defy mob opinion—to take an independent stand on an inflamed public issue, knowing in advance that he could not be touched by any forces bent on punishing him. Still, there were other businessmen in the Bay Area and elsewhere in the nation who also were economically impregnable, yet did not openly challenge such tenets of majority opinion. Among major figures in the American business world, Marriner stood virtually alone when he first publicly stated what he believed was wrong with America's intervention in

Vietnam. Many people in the Bay Area who now took courage from his example and began openly to voice views like his looked to him for leadership in the antiwar cause—and he provided it.

Other responses were conveyed to Marriner by people located elsewhere in the nation. From Senator Frank Church: "You have rendered a distinct public service in having issued your statement." From Raymond P. Brandt, Washington bureau chief of the *St. Louis Post-Dispatch:* "The country owes you a debt of gratitude." From Marquis W. Childs: "Yours is the strongest and, in many ways, the most cogent statement I have seen on the whole tragic conflict." From Walter Lippmann: "Your Vietnam statement is first-rate, courageous, lucid, and very well informed. I would like to see it printed in the East, and I hope you have sent copies of it to the *Washington Post* and the *New York Times.*" General James M. Gavin: "It is a superb summary of where we are, and, in part, how we got there." Senator J. W. Fulbright: "I think it was one of the best examples of your concise and forceful prose."

President Johnson had ordered on Christmas Eve a thirty-hour bombing pause. He then extended the pause into January, while U.S. envoys were sent to several countries in a widespread diplomatic effort to open the doors to peace talks. At the end of January when the president revealed that the bombing of North Vietnam had been resumed, further escalation of the war seemed inevitable. On February 1, after a strategy meeting of Senate doves, Senator J. William Fulbright, as chairman, announced that the Senate Foreign Relations Committee, would hold televised hearings on Vietnam. Fulbright and other committee members were neither hostile to President Johnson personally nor to the broad principle of executive leadership in national security matters; but they sensed that the United States was plunging into a major conflict without being fully aware of the implications. If the hearings generated an outpouring of public sentiment against the administration's policy in Vietnam, President Johnson might refrain from further steps which the committee members feared would lead to a direct confrontation with Red China, another World War, or a nuclear holocaust.

In the televised hearings of the Senate Foreign Relations Committee, a national audience for the first time saw elected officials in a legislative context expressing doubts and airing alternatives to current American policy in Vietnam. The hearings also made visible a group of Senate Democrats, joined by a smaller group of Senate Republicans, who had begun to function as a loyal opposition. But the hearings neither generated a nationwide groundswell of antiwar public sentiment, nor did they stop the escalation of the American military involvement in Vietnam.

IV

To meet the growing manpower needs of the armed forces in Vietnam, General Lewis Hershey, head of Selective Service, had an announcement to make in the spring of 1966. Some students, he said, would have to be drafted, and student deferments would be terminated for those whose class standings were poor or who failed to reach a certain level of performance on a soon-to-be administered Selective Service Qualification Test. Campus reactions were immediate and sharp. Professors and students alike —whether prowar or antiwar—protested the use of grades for Selective Service purposes. In the case of professors, they could foresee that every examination would be another time of torment for them. If they gave a student a low mark because he deserved nothing better academically, they might be sending him on his way to war. If they gave him an unearned high mark simply to spare him from the war, they were corrupting the standards of academic excellence they professed to live by. As for students, they could foresee that every examination would be another time when they would be competing with their classmates in order to avoid the draft.

It was from that moment forward that major campuses in the United States were swept by a hurricane of demonstrations and protests—seizures of buildings, sit-ins, draft-card burnings, attacks on university officials, counterattacks by the police, riflings of files, wreckings of university structures housing some form of defense-related activity, and on and on. Meanwhile, in the ghettos of the nation's cities, the unfulfilled hopes originally aroused by the combination of Dr. Martin Luther King's nonviolent civil rights movement and the Johnson administration's announced War on Poverty formed the tinderbox for the "manifesto of the match" issued in the name of Black Power or Black Liberation. Urban life appeared to have lapsed back into a Hobbesian war of each against all as inner cities went up in flames.[14]

Marriner, meanwhile, used all means of communication in an attempt to help mobilize an informed opposition to America's ever-deepening involvement in the Vietnam conflict. In particular, he focused his attention on the business community. In successive speeches, and in full-dress interviews which were published in major business magazines such as *Forbes* and *Duns,* he spelled out the direct connection between the costs of the Vietnam venture and the growing disorder in all corners of the American economy —higher taxes, mounting budgetary deficits, surging inflation pressures, tighter money, and a worsening of America's balance-of-payments picture.

To account for all of Marriner's public utterances about Vietnam would overload this narrative with repetitive details; yet several extracts from his speech on August 11, 1967, merit attention, partly because his immediate audience on the occasion was San Francisco's influential Commonwealth Club, and partly because the substance of his remarks gave form to the felt reasons why increasing numbers of people were stiffening their resistance to the Vietnam war.

At one point, for example, Marriner asked whether the stated justification for the American involvement in Vietnam corresponded to reality. In this connection, he analyzed the administration's thesis that communism, governed at a single center, intended to conquer the world, and that it was the duty of the United States to save the world from that fate. This picture of communism as a monolithic world power, he said, did not make sense. "National rivalries divide communist states as well as democracies, and communist states are as intensely nationalistic as others. They crave independence, resent interference, and will fight against domination by foreigners—whether they be capitalist or communists."

We might as well face it: there may be more communist countries in the world, but we need not panic at this. Communist nations vary widely; each has a different version of communist theory to fit its own problems. The more of these countries there are, the greater their diversity. Communism is only part of a broad movement: the rise of desperate people in Asia, Africa and Latin America. We crush insurrection in one place, only to find a revolution—whether communist, socialist or nationalist—springing up somewhere else.

The Vietnam war, he said, was directly responsible for "the most serious economic, financial and political problems facing the nation." While citing the statistics of disorder in all sectors of the economy, he observed that the costs of the war would not end with the cessation of hostilities. Veterans costs would "grow rapidly as long as the Vietnam war lasted" and would "continue for decades." The "ultimate astronomical expense" was difficult to conceive since, "in a financial sense, a war is never over."

Marriner next frontally attacked the whole theory of United States participation in negotiations to decide the future of Vietnam. We are, said he, "an outside power, which is also true of China and the Soviet Union." Whatever negotiations go on should be among the Vietnamese themselves. "In any case," Marriner added prophetically, "the United States cannot, through negotiations, create strength for a segment of a future government in South Vietnam. The presence of the United States can only distort the true balance of force, and only a settlement representing this balance can bring about a stable government."

He recognized that it "was not easy for a proud nation to admit it has blundered, but throughout history great men and nations have gained stature by so doing." Getting out of Vietnam would "enable the United States to reestablish a friendly relationship with Russia, and thereby bring about a balance of power in the world which would tend to deter any aggressive policy on the part of China. At the same time, we should recognize China diplomatically, open our doors to Chinese trade and travel, and help bring China into the United Nations. It is dangerous folly to ignore one-fourth of the world's population as though it did not exist."

The speech, aside from its impact on the establishment in the Bay Area, was circulated across the United States, inserted into the *Congressional Record,* excerpted by the wire services, cited in editorials of major newspapers, and so on. The result was a new mound of approving mail which landed on Marriner's desk either in San Francisco or Salt Lake City. Names among the letter writers went far beyond the group of like-minded people with whom Marriner had been in contact since December 1965. They were new names, including the significant addition of those representing major business enterprises. Marriner construed this to mean that something was at last "stirring" in the nation, and he passed the fact along to encourage his old and new political friends who were now in the thick of the fight against the administration's policy in Vietnam: senators Fulbright, Morse, Hatfield, McGovern, Gruening, Church, Case, McCarthy and Percy. But the road leading to any disengagement from the Vietnam morass was still years away.

v

In Washington throughout this period, Senator Robert F. Kennedy had slowly inched away from his initial support for the administration's Vietnam policy and slowly crossed over into the anti-Vietnam camp. In late 1967, after Senator Eugene McCarthy laconically announced his candidacy for the Democratic presidential nomination in 1968, pressures on Robert Kennedy either to become a candidate in his own right or to announce his support for McCarthy increased. But he resisted those pressures until after the New Hampshire primary on March 12, 1968, where McCarthy polled a surprising 42 percent of the total Democratic vote, to 48 percent representing a write-in vote for President Johnson. Immediately afterward, Senator Robert Kennedy announced his candidacy for the Democratic nomination.

About a week before Kennedy was to address a campaign rally in Salt Lake City on March 26, George Hatch, a power among Utah Democrats and a staunch Kennedy backer, put a question to Marriner. Would he consider introducing Kennedy at the rally? The answer was yes, but on one condition. "I will introduce Kennedy," said Marriner, "provided it is understood in advance that I will not directly endorse him or in any way appear to be an active campaigner in support of his candidacy. I will merely present him to the crowd as one man among others, who appears to be qualified for the office he seeks." The condition was accepted.

In the early evening of March 26, after attending a cocktail party in the Hotel Utah held in Kennedy's honor, Marriner retired to his apartment in the hotel to await the hour when he would leave for the rally. Presently there was a knock on the door, and when Marriner opened it, there stood Kennedy with an outstretched hand. "I understand," he said, "that I am to take you in my car to the rally." This had not been "understood," but Marriner went along with the improvised arrangement.

When the car in which they were riding drew near to the hall, their further advance was stopped by an officer in command of a cordon of police. Marriner later recalled a sharp exchange that went something like this:[15]

Commander: I'm sorry Senator—and Mr. Eccles—I can't let you proceed any further.

Kennedy: Why not?

Commander: We've received a tip that a bomb has been planted in the hall.

Kennedy: (Pushing forward) Try and stop me!

Commander: Senator, it's my duty! I must!

Kennedy: Damn it! Get out of my way! If five thousand people in that hall are to be blown to bits, I intend to be among them. I'm not going to let them face a bomb while I return to the security of my hotel room.

Commander: All right. You can proceed into the hall provided you let me announce to the crowd that we are investigating a tip about a bomb being planted in the place. That will give anyone who wants to leave a chance to get out.

Kennedy: Agreed. Are you coming with me, Marriner?

Marriner: Of course.

As the two men walked onto the stage of the hall to a roar of welcome from the crowd, it might have struck some observers as being odd that Senator Kennedy, "the candidate of youth," had chosen to be presented to a Salt Lake City audience by Marriner Eccles, then aged seventy-seven. But now the commander of the police security force came forward on the stage, asked for silence, referred to the bomb scare, and suggested that those who wished to leave should do so in a quiet and orderly way. There was a gasp, a mass craning of necks, and then a brave cheer when not a person left the hall.

If there were deep ambiguities in Senator Kennedy's past record on Vietnam, there were none in Marriner's when he rose to perform his assigned function. A fragment from his words of introduction suggests the tenor of the whole:

I've been invited to meet with you tonight to introduce our distinguished speaker. I welcome the opportunity. But I am not here as a partisan. I am here as an independent. I supported President Johnson because I thought he more nearly represented my liberal economic and social views, as well as promising to keep our boys out of a land war in Asia. I worked hard—both in Utah and California—to get President Johnson back into office, and now for more than two years—largely because of his Vietnam policy—I have been working harder to get him out. I am in favor of both Republicans and Democrats who have taken a strong and courageous position against this administration's involvement in Vietnam. . . .

Increasingly, Americans realize that our intervention in Vietnam is an ill-advised, senseless and massive blunder, and that our leaders are compounding this error rather than recognizing their misjudgment and miscalculation. Fear haunts our nation—fear that there may be no limit to what a desperate leadership may do to escape from admitting its mistakes. There is a terrifying unreason about our deeds —like a deranged giant loose in the world. . . . The people of this country are afraid of their leadership. I am afraid of that leadership. I distrust its pronouncements. I distrust its goals. I question its wisdom. I deplore its sense of our country and its destiny. . . .

Senator Kennedy, who has come to my home state of Utah, offers a view of the direction in which we should move as a nation, and the concepts that should guide us along the way. He is well-qualified by family background and experience to be a candidate for a presidential nomination. May I now present him to you.

Four days later, President Johnson, in a telecast, startled the nation by announcing that he had ordered a halt to the bombing of North Vietnam and that he would neither seek nor accept the Democratic presidential nomination. With Johnson's withdrawal, the contest for that nomination ceased to be a contest over principle. It became a straightforward power struggle between McCarthy and Kennedy, two men who opposed the Johnson administration but who differed in their tactics and were agreed only in their intense dislike for each other.

Soon matters went from bad to worse in the nation as a whole—the assassination of Martin Luther King, Jr., conflagrations in the ghettos, a new pitch of violence on the campuses of major universities, the assassination of Senator Robert Kennedy, and still more deaths in Vietnam. Marriner's response came in the form of an anguished speech he gave in June 1968 before businessmen in Detroit, Chicago and New York. Along with Palmer Weber, he had previously been one of the main architects of a newly-formed national organization—Business Executives Move for Vietnam Peace. Here, at last, was a mobilization of "clout" whose effective power to influence public opinion went beyond the influence of the one-shot or episodic antiwar protest parades that were student-led. Palmer Weber had arranged the Detroit-Chicago-New York speaking tour for Marriner, and it was at his suggestion also that Marriner's remarks entitled, "Vietnam—Political Hypocrisy—A Tragedy of Errors," were published as a pamphlet and widely distributed. The pamphlet contained fervent passages such as these:

The hypocrisy of our leaders, especially those in politics, is perhaps the deepest corroding influence in our society today. As evidence of this hypocrisy, only recently, consider the nationwide climax of grief over the assassination of Dr. Martin Luther King. Walking with bowed heads in the vast funeral procession were state and national dignitaries and public officials—who just the day before his death had considered Dr. King a revolutionary, a troublemaker, a communist, and a traitor. No doubt some of the judges who sentenced him to prison twenty-two times were among those marching and delivering the expansive eulogies that went on all over the world for weeks afterwards. And now the nation is rocked by the shocking assassination of Robert Kennedy. . . .

How can our President justify calling upon us to remove violence from our hearts and mind when our hearts and minds are soaked in it daily? Violence is a way of life in the nightly fare on television. It is totally unrealistic to rise up in wrath at a single shooting when we remain relatively unshaken at mass killing. We have handed over our youth to the military to be dehumanized—and to be turned into killers. By what process, then, can we expect them to become rehumanized and to forget their familiarity with violent death and their casualness towards it?

. . . The core of the problem is Vietnam. We must get out—making the best arrangement we can. Kennedy preached this, and McCarthy still does. Rebellious students demand this. The plight of the underprivileged masses cries for it. Our rapidly worsening financial stituation requires it. Our plummeting status in the world makes it imperative. We must prepare for change at a more rapid rate than this country has ever before experienced. This is not as simple as changing another President or another party. It must be a total change of concept—a concept of our place in the world. This requires: a change of goals; a change of temper; a reeducation of our people.

Marriner's passion about Vietnam was not spent in the cry of these lines. As will be seen on an occasion in 1972 when he was the recipient of a unique award—he was eighty-two years old at the time—the heat of his protest against the whole of the American misadventure in Vietnam browned, before age did, the paper on which he wrote down his thoughts.

42. Summations

LONG BEFORE THE DISCLOSURES OF WATERGATE, Marriner was appalled by Richard M. Nixon. He had no use for him as a person, a political figure, a representative, a senator, vice-president, or as a president. In one context after another over the years, he had seen Nixon corrupt the integrity of words, had seen him stir false fears and arouse false hopes, had seen him twist and turn on policy issues.

Marriner had come to understand that every president who takes an oath to uphold, protect and defend the Constitution to the best of his ability is heavily burdened by the fact that the oath does not tell him *how* he is to do these things. He had come to understand that every president lives at the center of the fierce cross-tensions between what the law allows and what politics disallows, between the legal constraints of the presidential office and the boundless expectations of the people, between needs and resources. He had seen President Roosevelt grapple with those cross-tensions and, in retrospect, forgave the episodes marked by his escape and evasive tactics. He had seen President Truman in the same position and, in retrospect, forgave the personal hurt he had known at Truman's hands. As time separated the main thrust of their efforts from wayward incidents, he recognized that Roosevelt and Truman, each in his own way, thought of promoting the common good without regard to private or sectarian considerations.

In Nixon's case, however, cunning things seemed to be done for the sake of cunning itself, and for the moment alone. That such an unrooted man should have been raised to the presidency struck Marriner—long before the disclosures of Watergate—as a scandal of the nation's soul.

In this, as in many other matters in his long life, he was out of phase with the dominant attitude of the major figures in the nation's business community. Most business leaders were pleased to barter their political support for the Nixon presidency in exchange for the "tax breaks" they received at the hands of the Nixon administration—which escaped public notice. The "tax breaks" did in fact give them short-run advantages. Yet as Marriner repeatedly stressed, since the "tax breaks" meant greater budgetary deficits—in an economy that was expected simultaneously to support social programs of every kind and the continuing high costs of the Vietnam war—the "advantages" meant more inflation that stealthily reduced the value of the very dollars the businessmen banked.

Meanwhile, every shell fired in Vietnam cost more than the previous salvo. Within the United States, every hospital, school or road that was built cost more than the previous one. Every increase in social security benefits had its real value undercut by continuing inflation. Every weakening in the purchasing power of the dollar meant that more dollars had to be spent to compensate for the weakness, which in turn added to the inflationary pressures that again eroded the worth of the dollar.

Watching the process, Marriner was besides himself with anxiety. The unifying object of the last four decades of his life had been to help lay the foundations for a stable economic order at home or in the world arena. Now, wherever he looked in the public realm, he saw disarray, political evasion and mindless grabbing and getting. He construed all this to be a personal affront, a kind of collective mockery of the aims that gave meaning to his work in government and as a public citizen. He could say to himself that at least the private enterprises he had helped build were in vigorous health. He could say that he had previously warned against the disorders in store for the nation, that he had repeatedly urged lines of action designed to nip the causes for the disorders in the bud, that he was not personally at fault if his warnings and pleadings were ignored. But saying this gave him no consolation.

As a man born to have no peace himself, and to allow little peace to other people, he was not an easy person to be around. He tended to turn his encounters in the course of a day into a declamation about all the things that were out of joint in the world around him. It was as if he hoped somehow to ignite a self-sustaining fire in the mind of the person he spoke to, so that this person would then hurl himself into the battle to govern the nation—a battle that Marriner had been fighting since 1934.

The hope, and the driven spirit behind it, seemed only to isolate Marriner from the pattern of socializing that prevailed in Salt Lake City and San Francisco. Old friends, his comrades-in-arms in the battles of former years, were no longer nearby. Some had died; some had succumbed to the afflictions of age; others had retired to places where their interests were confined largely to the weather or their digestion. As for the social circuit in Salt Lake City and San Francisco, Marriner was not cut out to be a benign "elder statesman" who could delight other guests at a dinner party with charming anecdotes about personages and events in the historical past. He was consumed by events on the move in the present, and insisted on talking about their startling implications for the future. The more he talked, the less he was welcomed at dinner parties, the less he cared to be welcomed, the more he was thrown back on himself, and the more intense were the pressures that compelled him to talk.

He would detail the way certain basic advantages the United States had long enjoyed—access to raw materials, a large internal market, adequate capital and an industrious and educated people—had been acquired by other nations. He would detail the effects on the American economy that flowed from an end to its monopoly over these advantages; or how increasing labor costs within the United States, without a commensurate increase in productivity, were pricing American products out of world markets and out of domestic markets as well. He would detail the way in which the rise of imports overtook the volume of exports until a point was reached in 1971 when, for the first time since 1888, we had a deficit in our balance of trade—$2.7 billion in that year, and $6.8 billion in the next. He would detail the way in which the value of the dollar was eroded by the failure of the Congress and the executive to deal with the causes of inflation—a failure rooted in the fact that a consumption minded nation wanted wages to go up, profits to go up, the stockmarket to go up. If prices also went up, so what? People figured that they would take care of themselves by keeping in debt and paying off with continually cheaper dollars.

Above all, Marriner dwelt at length on the direct connection between the Vietnam war and the spreading disorders in the American economy. Some sense of what he said over and again can be gained by glancing at a representative extract of an interview published in *Dun's* in May 1970, right after President Nixon sent American forces into Cambodia. Within the United States at the time, the Federal Reserve Board was under sharp scrutiny—perhaps without parallel in its fifty-seven-year history—as it tried to cope with the worst inflation since the Korean war and the deepest business downturn since the 1950s. To assess the board's performance, the editors of *Dun's* decided to "talk with an outspoken, sharp-tongued, memory-filled man who had faced more difficult problems during his sixteen years as chairman of the Federal Reserve Board." The editors also recalled that, back in 1965, "Eccles, a pillar of the Western business establishment" was "one of the few top-level executives to speak out against the U.S.'s growing Vietnam involvement." The general tenor of the interview went like this:

Mr. Eccles, much has been said and written recently about the Federal Reserve's responsibility for our current economic problems. How much of the blame would you pin on the Fed.?

We can't lay the blame at the door of the Federal Reserve. Its overall objective is to maintain an adequate rate of economic growth, low levels of unemployment and reasonable price stability. But its principal job under present conditions is to supplement fiscal policy. The fiscal problem continued to be one of heavy deficit financing. And the Fed, whether it likes it or not, is required to provide adequate reserves to the banking system in order for the government to finance its needs, even when that is inflationary. If you want the real culprit for this country's mess, it is Vietnam, not the Fed.

You put the entire blame for our economic problems on the Vietnam war?

There is no question but that it is the principal cause.

But isn't it a fact that the causes of our recent and current economic problems are more complex and subtle than that?

As you may know, I was one of the first businessmen in this country to publicly oppose our intervention in Vietnam. As far back as 1965, I said that it would lead us into the most serious economic problems, including inflation and extremely tight money, the nation has ever faced. And under President Johnson it did. And there has been no improvement under President Nixon. . . . I think the Fed has done as good a job as it could under the circumstances. The first thing to remember is that there is a basic conflict of objectives here. The Fed wants to stop inflation, but the government doesn't want badly enough to stop the war. . . . William McChesney Martin and Arthur Burns did everything they could to prevent inflation, but how could they cope with this fiscal policy of ours?

Don't you see some light at the end of this tunnel now that several prominent businessmen who were supporters of President Nixon until recently have begun to attack our Vietnam policy?
Some. It is encouraging to see IBM's Chairman Thomas J. Watson, du Pont's President Charles McCoy and Chairman John T. Connor of Allied Chemicals, as well as Chairman Louis Lundborg of the Bank of America, and others all coming out publicly in opposition to our involvement in Indochina. . . . One reason for this happening is that the drop-off in business, the decrease in profits, and the bankruptcies are reaching down to the heart of our capitalistic system. . . .

How would you sum up your outlook for the economy?
I think unemployment will increase, inflation will continue, interest rates will remain relatively high because of the lack of liquidity, the federal and many state budgets will remain in deficit, and large deficiencies are ahead in the international balance of payments. Declines in many corporate earnings will continue, savings will remain inadequate, and housing will remain a problem. I don't think I've left anything out, have I?

Hardly. . . .

II

Aside from Marriner's election to the Hall of Fame, and the honorary degrees he received from two publicly supported universities in Utah, few of the standard public honors were bestowed on him in the course of his long life. Nor, for that matter, did he seek them. Now and again, some organization would propose to hold a testimonial dinner in his honor, but the proposal would die on the point of his blunt "no." He cherished a compliment conveyed to him in private by a person he respected, but public praise was not to his taste.

In the summer of 1971, however, he was forced against his will to go along with such a prospect. It was the practice of Governor Calvin Rampton of Utah to sponsor and organize a "Governor's Appreciation Dinner" for eminent citizens in the state. When he indicated that he wished to so honor the two Eccles brothers, George's quick assent made it impossible for Marriner to refuse without raising suspicions of some sort of family conflict.

On that night, as various speakers praised the contributions the two brothers had made to the West, the nation and the world, Marriner's face visibly creased with distress, and his lips puckered in distaste. "You would have thought," said one onlooking friend, "that Marriner was being dished up a plate of sauerkraut into which a vial of ambrosia had fallen." Toward midnight, when he was called to speak, he used a device which conveyed his wry recognition of a personal trait that often bore very hard on his family, his friends, and his associates. The device was a "prayer" ascribed to an old San Francisco doctor, and whose text had been discovered by Sallie. The audience, experiencing what literary men call "the shock of recognition," rocked with laughter as Marriner read the prayer:

Release me from the craving to straighten out everybody's Affairs. Teach me the glorious lesson that occasionally I might be mistaken. Make me thoughtful—but not moody, helpful, but not bossy. With my vast store of wisdom, it seems a pity not to use it. But thou knowest, Lord, That I want a few friends at the end.

But when the laughter subsided, Marriner compressed into a few paragraphs the convictions that had become as much a part of him as the air he breathed:

I now know, however hard we strive and fight for our principles—however fortunate we are in reaching our goals—we must, at the same time, understand that it is not forever. It may not even be for very long. What we have attained—what victories we have won—must be defended again and again. There is no static position: no guaranty of performance. This is true of a family, a business, or a nation. The freedoms we enjoy in our country were dearly bought long ago. But they are not forever, unless we make them so in each generation. . . . Every threat to our freedoms must be faced, or our liberties will slip away.

As individuals, all we can actually hope to do is to run a good race in our time—always knowing that the torch must be held high and passed on to strong hands if the forward momentum is to continue. It would seem to be a reasonable expectation to ultimately sit back and enjoy what has been accomplished. But strangely enough, the joy is not there unless we can see new leaders for the causes we have championed, rising on the horizon.

In the words that followed, this eighty-one-year-old "pillar of the Western Business Establishment" looked at "the ranks of the disturbed, protesting, critical, questioning young people" and was not horrified by what he saw. "Tomorrow's leaders," he said, "will come from their ranks, and it's up to us to identify them early, to encourage them to carry on the fight where we must necessarily leave off. When we find courage, drive, integrity, intelligence, and tough, fair minds, let us forget about long hair and unfamiliar customs. Let us accept change instead of fearing it."

Then Marriner turned to matters very close to home. In an indirect reference to his business enterprises, he observed "that the most fortunate corporation is the one which has coming up in its organization, intelligent, loyal and energetic young executives—confident of the support of their seniors. There need be no fear for the future of such a company." In a direct reference to his own family, he added that it was not enough for a family to bask in the reflected glory of a famous ancestor, while pursuing its own selfish interests. Since the "true influence, power and meaning of a family" depended on a family's contribution to the betterment of society, "each generation must reestablish the significance of the family as a force for good in its own time." But above all, said Marriner, there were some "simple truths" which stood out among the things he had learned over the past eighty years:

> You cannot operate in isolation as an individual, as a family, or as a nation. We are all involved in the world's problems. And, for better or for worse, our lives are intertwined. The good of one must be the good for all. The only true satisfaction is to feel that we have contributed in some way, however small, to the well being of others around us. If we covet honor we will never get it by serving ourselves. If we covet distinction, we will get it only by serving mankind. We are here to enrich the world. And insofar as we lose sight of that fact, we impoverish ourselves.

It was the summation of a man who accepted the facts of his own mortality, and who was busy tidying up his personal affairs in line with the precepts voiced at the governor's "appreciation" dinner.

III

It was now time, for example, to make some changes in the management of Utah, as well as in the Eccles Investment Company, which Marriner had organized back in 1915. Eccles Investment had grown from its original nine members to over ninety family stockholders, but there was no market for the stock of this personal holding company. The older the original members grew, the more the absence of that market weighed on Marriner's thoughts. At different times, therefore, a large portion of the stock held by Eccles Investment had been distributed among the stockholders. In 1970, however, the company still had substantial assets beyond the 10 percent represented by its holdings in Utah Construction and Mining. So in that year, Marriner arranged the sale of everything Eccles Investment still owned except for the Utah stock, and used the proceeds to buy still more stock in Utah, making it Eccles Investments' sole holding. He then arranged a merger of Eccles Investment with Utah. Eccles Investment was liquidated, leaving its stockholders with only Utah Construction stock, a marketable security.

As for Utah itself, in February 1971 Marriner voluntarily retired as chairman of the board of which he had been a director for fifty years. This did not, however, bring his connection with the enterprise to a close. He was named honorary chairman of the board and was reelected chairman of the executive committee. As part of the same change, Edmund Littlefield was elected board chairman and chief executive officer. The future line of succession was also indicated by the election of A. M. Wilson as president, and the elevation of still younger men to a hierarchy of posts below the level of the presidency—the youngest of these, the financial vice-president, being in his thirties. At the meeting at which the reorganization was announced and became effective, Marriner for once publicly indulged himself in a sentimental salute. "I take great personal satisfaction in these changes, for they will assure continuity and the highest competence in the company's management."

In the case of the Amalgamated Sugar Company, his personal wish to retire as the active chairman of the board encountered the resistance of younger managers in the company who insisted that he remain in that post until their own order of succession had been worked out. When this was done, he would relinquish the active chairmanship and become an honorary one.

Of all the enterprises of which he was a major architect, the one whose line of succession caused him the most concern was the First Security Corporation. When Marriner left as president of First Security in 1934 for government service in Washington, its total resources were $60 million. When he returned to Utah in 1951, they were reported as $331 million. By the end of 1974, they were in excess of $1.8 billion, while the number of banks in the First Security system had grown from 21 in 1934, to more than 128 banking offices in Utah, Idaho and the southwest corner of Wyoming.* Throughout this history of growth—which made First Security one of the most prosperous bank holding companies in a broad region extending from the Canadian border to the Arizona border—Marriner recognized the immense contribution of his brother George. He cited his brother's incisive managerial ability and remarked that "things go well when George is on the job." The problem, as Marriner saw it, was the need to strengthen the personnel structure of First Security, to bring forward talented younger men who would be delegated responsibilities and granted rewards that would encourage them to look to First Security as a place to pursue promising careers. But it was not until the spring of 1975 that he achieved what he had hoped to bring about; with the approval of First Security's board of directors, Marriner became honorary chairman of the board; George became chairman, and young Spencer Eccles, Jr.—their nephew—became president.

Arrangements for the disposition of Marriner's estate were also attended to. He would not leave matters in the air as had his father, who died without a will. Aside from provisions that were made for Sallie and for other members of his family, Marriner initiated bequests designed to encourage the emergence of young leaders of the future who could recognize, as he did, "that the good of the individual, the family, and the community was indivisible with the good of the larger national and world society." Without fanfare,

---

*In addition, First Security, as of the early 1970s, had a substantial interest in Aubrey G. Langston & Company, a dealer in government securities. It also had these wholly-owned subsidiaries: Utah Mortgage Loan Corporation, with four offices in Utah and Idaho; First Security Insurance and First Security Insurance Agency: First Security Life Insurance of Texas: First Security Leasing; and First Security Savings and Loan Association.

starting in 1970, he made a series of contributions to the University of Utah that will eventually total more than $1 million in a trust fund. The fund, administered by the trust department of the First Security Corporation, will disburse, quarterly, the income to the university for Marriner S. Eccles Fellowships. They will be awarded by a committee of deans of the University to qualified graduate students for advanced studies in economics, social studies, business, and political science. The income will not be less than $5,000 per year, per student, for as many students as the trust income warrants.

In addition, the Marriner S. Eccles Library of Political Economy is being built at the University of Utah to contain not only Marriner's personal and public papers but a special collection of reference works bearing on the era of American history in which he lived. The Roosevelt Library in Hyde Park and the Library of Congress both wanted these papers, but Marriner thought that he should leave them to the university of his home state, where in 1943 he received his first honorary doctorate along with his friend Walter Lippmann.

In 1972, Marriner created the Marriner S. Eccles Foundation, which is to receive a substantial part of his estate and whose income is to be distributed to private, nongovernmental, charitable, scientific and educational organizations located within Utah for the benefit of the citizens of the state. According to Marriner's guidelines, 25 percent of the income is to be distributed to nationally accredited universities in Utah, for libraries, special equipment and research, but not for brick-and-mortar plants, nor for salaries or other remuneration except where they are an integral part of a basic research program. Another 25 percent is to be distributed to hospitals for medical equipment, medical libraries and medical research organizations, including the University of Utah medical school and hospital, and such research projects as are associated with them. A share of 17.5 percent is to be distributed among Utah's not-for-profit, nongovernmental organizations concerned with the support of the symphony, ballet, opera, theatre, painting, sculpture, and other forms of the performing or plastic arts. Another 17.5 percent is to go to Utah's not-for-profit, nongovernmental organizations engaged in a search for solutions to basic social problems—population control, drug abuse and alcoholism. A remaining 15 percent, to be used at the sole discretion of the trustees, is to be applied to the support of other not-for-profit, nongovernmental social and welfare organizations in Utah.

In the spring of 1973, Marriner broke new ground when he established, at the Stanford University School of Business, the Marriner S. Eccles Professorship of Public and Private Management. "As a citizen," he said at the time, "I am deeply concerned that government, as well as business, attracts the high level of management needed to face and solve the country's problems wisely and effectively. We must prepare for change—rapid change —and I think our first order of priority is the training of managers capable of assuming leadership positions in both sectors." Stanford Business School dean Arjay Miller, former president of Ford Motor Co., terms the new professorship "a fitting expression of Marriner Eccles' long-time recognition of the interdependence of the public and private sectors of our economy. This is the first known professorship of its kind devoted to both government and business management, and that's no accident. Marriner Eccles has never waited on tradition, once he has been convinced of a real need."

IV

Still, Marriner's largest concern was with the state of the nation and the world around it. He expressed that concern at the age of eighty-two in what he announced beforehand would be the last public speech of his life. The occasion was an evening in May 1972, when the World Trade Club of San Francisco honored him at a dinner where he received its International Achievement Award. Marriner had been advised by friends to confine himself to some pleasantries. But he was not born to be pleasant. Because he "gave a damn" about what he saw, he didn't "give a damn" about what people thought of him personally for saying exactly what he thought.

His somber note sounded in his first words. "We all recognize that these are unusual and tragic times for anyone to be accepting an award for furthering the cause of world peace and world trade, since we have very little of either. I assure you, I would be much less hesitant about accepting an award if I could feel that I had accomplished something toward these ends." He recalled that he had worked for most of his life for measures which he believed were indispensable for a stable and prosperous society at home and a respected position abroad. Yet whether the measures concerned fiscal and monetary matters, the population dilemma, or world affairs, "a life of pressing for change" was all he "could claim credit for." He went on to observe that the dilemmas facing America had been apparent on the horizon for over a decade. Yet, through two administrations, "the wrong road was taken every time we had a chance to alter our course." We were now, in the present world crisis, confronted with the sum total of all our mistakes, which he proceeded to list:

We have "completely ignored our domestic needs" so that "we have a frustrated and angry society" in which explosive and dangerous rebellion "simmers just below the surface." We overestimated our wealth and power and spread ourselves too thin around the world, and are just now "realizing that we cannot dominate the world militarily and take care of our domestic needs as well." We took no steps to reverse the balance-of-payments deficiency, "but just watched the dollar depreciate," so that it is now "a floating currency of indeterminate value." We never "faced up to the monopoly of labor, the favoritism toward big business, and the inequities in the tax structure," failures that have "made the control of inflation impossible." We allowed "the military to become blown up into such a force that it is now our master instead of our servant. Far from being a department of defense—which we do need—it has become a political arm of the president and the delineator of our foreign policy.''

Here Marriner turned directly to the "Vietnamese debacle." He recalled his widely circulated warning back in January 1966, not under any circumstances "to escalate the war in Vietnam," since our "position there was indefensible." He then reviewed the disastrous effects that the war had had on the American economy:

Our annual defense budget has increased from $49 billion to approximately $80 billion at the present time. This is almost entirely due to the war in Southeast Asia, which has cost about $150 billion. The federal deficit during the period was approximately $90 billion. Without Vietnam, there would be a budgetary surplus of around $60 billion. The U.S. has already spent well over a trillion dollars on the military since 1946. The accumulated deficiency in our international balance of payments through 1971 was approximately $73 billion. We had a deficiency last year in our trade balance for the first time in 77 years of more than $2 billion, with an increasing deficiency this year. Previously, for a number of years this country had a trade balance surplus averaging about $5 billion. . . .

The problems of deficiencies in our international balance of payments and in our trade balance, as well as the increasingly large federal debt and the increasing cost of labor, have brought about a growing inflation in our country and made our dollar increasingly less desirable as a world currency. Since the International Monetary Fund was created at Bretton Woods after the war, the dollar based on gold at $35 an ounce has been the world currency. All other currencies were related to it. In the summer of '71, it was inevitable that the twenty-seven-year-old Bretton Woods system of fixed international exchange rates, all pegged to the U.S. dollar, would collapse. On August 15, when Nixon was forced to cut the dollar loose from gold, the old currency system died, and the dollar was left to float. Some of the other countries acted previously and others followed the dollar in letting their currencies float. Since that time, there has been no stability in the world currencies.

Marriner went on to observe that the United States had become great in world affairs because of its economic strength and not because of its military strength. If we had to "depend on the military/industrial complex for our prosperity" that would be "a profound indictment of our capitalistic democracy." No matter how much we spent for armaments, there was no safety in arms. To rely on military strength primarily, as in Vietnam, to solve political problems, is to breed violence everywhere and ultimately to destroy the foundations. of the Republic. Here Marriner added:

We are told we have to have a victory in Vietnam or there will be a "blood bath." What do you consider over 700,000 Vietnamese troops killed by us and our ally—not to mention the appalling civilian toll? Isn't that a "blood bath?" A parallel situation in the U.S. would figure out to about 6½ million young men dead. What do you think that would be called in the U.S.?

So—we have to face it! There already is a "blood bath,"—and it is our doing. We are guilty. And no amount of rhetoric about a "generation of peace" will make it go away. It will never be forgotten—or forgiven. Nor should it be.

Turning directly to the economic interests of his audience, Marriner observed that there are some obvious prerequisites for world trade. "You have to have a climate of peace. You have to have a stable currency. You have to show a capacity for behaving in a responsible way in the world arena." To maintain 2,300 military bases around the world was not conducive to world trade. Nor was world trade promoted by ringing China and Russia with nuclear installations:

World trade and world friendship go hand in hand. Neither self-isolation nor aggression can solve the acute problems that each nation shares with the rest of the world. It is one world—or no world. The raw materials of the world belong to the people of the world and must be shared through international trade and finance. . . .

One thing is certain, we have learned some important truths about ourselves in these difficult years. We have learned that we can be influenced erroneously: that our judgment and sense of fair play can be distorted. We can be fooled and confused and made uncertain.

Deep down in our hearts we know we have strayed far afield from the ideals on which this country was founded. We know that killing and carnage do not bring us honor. We know the quiet of a shattered country is not peace. We know that the prestige of the presidency and the honor of our country are enhanced in the world by integrity and stability, and we are appalled at the savagery we have unleashed on a small Asian country which has in no way offended us.

In that last speech of his life, as in virtually all the other public speeches he had given since 1931, Marriner neither aimed at nor expected immediate applause. Yet when he was through, he was surprised by the salute of a standing ovation. Not that all agreed with the substance of what he said. Far from it. A significant segment of the audience would be among the financial contributors to Richard M. Nixon's landslide reelection victory in November, partly because they agreed with his conduct of the war in Southeast Asia and partly because he was the source of the "tax breaks" they enjoyed. Yet even the people who disagreed with the critical bent of Marriner's remarks recognized that they were in the presence of a man of honor with few counterparts in American public life. They were in the presence of a man who had the moral courage to walk alone, who never made himself a slave to other people, who sought counsel in his own convictions, and spoke truths, however unpleasant, as he understood them.

APPENDIXES

Appendix A

(to chapter 16)

WHEN THE FHA PROGRAM underwent certain changes during the 1937–38 recession, the potential for new home construction began to be converted into market place realities. The provisions of the act authorizing the creation of associations to deal in FHA mortgages initially seemed destined for a stillbirth. No such associations were formed by any private financial group. The large banks and almost all the insurance companies were particularly hostile. They assumed that the whole housing program would collapse if no associations were formed to buy insured mortgages or that the depression would somehow end without further governmental intervention in the economy. Either way, they could then resume mortgage business on the customary terms calling for large down payments, high rates of interest and short maturity dates.

But when private lending institutions did nothing, the RFC created a market for FHA-insured mortgages by organizing a Federal National Mortgage Association (now known as "Fannie May" after the initials FNMA). Private lending institutions then came to see that their opposition to the whole mortgage insurance scheme was pointless. They also gradually came to see that the FHA loan was a very desirable and profitable credit instrument.

As time went on, a "strange" thing happened to the premiums the savings and loan associations paid into the Insurance Corporation of the Home Loan Bank Board. Unbeknownst to most people, lobbyists for the associations secured reductions in the premium from the original one-quarter of 1 percent of share accounts and creditor liabilities, to one-eighth and then to one-twelfth of 1 percent. The danger in this narrowing base for the insurance fund was regularly decried by Marriner, and regularly ignored. With rising property values, his warnings made him sound as though he were a common scold. Why pay attention to anything he had to say? After all, the smaller the insurance premiums, the more the associations could increase the volume of their loans. The greater the volume, the greater the earnings. The greater the earnings, the more interest on savings accounts. The more interest, the more accounts they could attract. But when property values began to decline and overextended savings and loan companies paid the price in bankruptcy for their dubious financial management, a previously unconcerned Home Loan Bank Board looked anxiously at the insurance fund that was being taxed to cover losses on savings accounts.

Another "strange" thing happened. Prior to 1934, commercial banks and loan associations each maintained a relatively static share of savings funds. Subject to regulations that did not apply to the associations, banks offered greater safety to savings funds; the associations, relatively free from regulatory requirements for liquidity, and enjoying special tax benefits besides, offered a greater return. Creation of the Federal Loan Insurance Corporation, however, upset this preexisting competitive balance. The corporation gave the associations the appearance of equal safety but did not require them to change their heavy loan policies. The associations were positioned to offer a higher return as well as what seemed to be equivalent safety.

The seeds were thus planted in 1934 for a development Marriner watched closely because of its implication for the management of money and credit. Slowly throughout the remaining years of the depression, but at an accelerating rate in the years after the Second World War, the loan associations increasingly became the place where the public preferred to entrust its savings funds. They increasingly strengthened their position as a major holder of the nation's savings and were at liberty to invest virtually all the savings entrusted to them in mortgage loans on an unrestricted basis to nonmembers as well as to members of the associations. They could not be reached by the Federal Reserve Board's monetary and credit policies, nor for that matter by the fiscal policies of the federal government. In 1960, over four hundred savings and loan institutions in forty-five major metropolitan areas, with total savings of $7.5 billion and aggregate net income after all dividends of $65 million, did not pay one dollar in federal income taxes.

Appendix B

(to chapter 17)

J. J. THOMAS, Adolph Miller, Charles S. Hamlin, George R. James and Matt Szymczak were honorable men, but none could fill the vacuum of leadership in monetary and fiscal matters in an hour of revolutionary changes. Miller, a Californian and friend of Franklin D. Roosevelt since the Woodrow Wilson presidency, had been a member of the Federal Reserve Board since its creation in 1914. As an academic economist, he had written a number of scholarly articles on monetary matters. But to judge from an appraisal once made by Benjamin Strong, Miller was "the eternal consultant and critic, never the bold and imaginative enterpriser." He was a "self-centered person," jealous of his title of governor, and inclined to "shift his position on important issues for trivial reasons."

Hamlin had been the personal secretary to President Grover Cleveland and, like Miller, was an old friend of President Roosevelt. He too had served on the board since its creation. A lawyer by training, and a diarist by avocation, he had a shrewd grasp of political issues and details of administration; personally much beloved by the technical staff of the Federal Reserve Board. Yet he had only a limited grasp of the broad issues of monetary and fiscal policy, while his desire to please tended to make him a stranger to personal audacity in thought and action. As judged by Benjamin Strong, his temperament made him "an amanuensis sort of fellow unlikely to undertake anything on his own."

George J. James, a native of Tennessee, had been a small manufacturer and merchant dealing in feed grains for horses; immediately prior to his appointment to the Federal Reserve Board, he had served as the president of a small commercial bank. As a board member, his most notable contribution to economic theory was his often voiced—but never explained—conviction that the advent of the automobile in American life was the root cause of the Great Depression.

Matt Szymczak, a Chicagoan, was the youngest member of the board and the latest addition to it. He had been a key aide to Chicago's Mayor Anton Cermak, and was in Miami with Cermak and FDR on the day when an assassin, firing at the president, killed Cermak instead. Roosevelt afterward seemed bound to Szymczak by a kind of "blood sacrament," and appointed him to fill the first vacancy that appeared in the membership of the Federal Reserve Board.

Appendix C
(to chapter 37)

MARRINER'S MANAGERS could cite, for example, what the London *Economist* had to say about Marriner Eccles in the course of its laudatory review of *Beckoning Frontiers:*

Mr. Eccles never sacrificed his economic convictions to political expediency, never expected gratitude or hesitated to criticize even his friends, and as head of an independent government agency always maintained his statutory freedom from outside influence, whether of the Administration, the Congress or the financial community.

Marriner's managers hoped, further, that his record of success at the head of far-flung private enterprises, along with his proven capacity to crack open the heart of complex economic problems, would attract the support of the Utah business community. After all, the business-minded *Fortune* magazine, in an editorial for its issue of August 1952, observed:

There was a good omen for Republican monetary policy in a story that came out of Salt Lake City the day after the G.O.P. convention ended. It was the announcement that Marriner Eccles, chairman of the Federal Reserve Board during twelve [sic] of the Roosevelt-Truman years, is running for the Senate—as a Republican. . . . During the 1940's he fought both Presidents, in a valiant effort to save the dollar, then retired in 1951, three years after Truman had eased him out of the FRB chairmanship. . . . Mr. Eccles still has to get himself nominated, and then elected, and we hope he will do both. Meanwhile, his filing as a Republican is an eloquent, expert estimate of the outlook for the dollar under a Republican administration.

NOTES

Notes

To avoid a hopelessly large number of notes, I have followed the practice of collecting the references necessary to a particular passage in a single note. As indicated in the Introduction to this biography, all quoted statements not otherwise footnoted are taken from the files of Marriner S. Eccles in his Salt Lake City office. In those instances where the documents are part of bound volumes, the volume number is indicated.

Part I. FATHER AND SON

1. Bank failures, starting in 1930, were initially confined to the Middle West and Far West. But they became nationwide in scope, bringing the total to 5,505 by March 4, 1933, representing deposits of $3.4 billion. The rate of failures accelerated in the months immediately prior to the inauguration of Roosevelt, when depositors withdrew $1.8 billion from the banks. Nevada, on October 20, 1932, was the first state to declare a bank holiday. Iowa followed on January 20, 1933, Louisiana on February 3, and Michigan on February 14. Yet the bank holidays which stopped withdrawals in one state made for failures elsewhere since the banks that had been given temporary relief withdrew funds from their correspondents in order to shore up their own positions.
2. The reference combines passages taken from Roosevelt's address from the Governor's Mansion in Albany, July 30, 1932, and from his address in Pittsburgh, October 19, 1932.
3. Senate Finance Committee, *Investigation of Economic Problems: Hearings,* 72nd Congress, 2nd Session, 1933.
4. Marriner Eccles to the author, interview, July 8, 1971.
5. Benedict Spinoza, *The Philosophy of Spinoza* (New York: The Modern Library, 1937), p. 3.
6. Eccles to the author, interview, July 11, 1971.
7. George Wharton James, *Utah: The Land of Blossoming Valleys* (Boston: The Page Company, 1922), p. 128.
8. *Utah.* The American Guide Series (New York, Oxford University Press, 1939), p. 309).
9. Family memorabilia, Eccles files, Salt Lake City.
10. Milton Friedman and Anna Jacobson Schwartz, *A Monetary History of the United States 1867–1960* (Princeton: Princeton University Press, 1963), pp. 91–3.
11. Family memorabilia, Eccles files, Salt Lake City.
12. George Wharton James, *op. cit.*
13. Family memorabilia, Eccles files, Salt Lake City.

Part II. HALF BROTHERS BUT NOT FRIENDS

1. Marriner Eccles, *Beckoning Frontiers* (New York: Alfred A. Knopf, 1951), pp. 43–44.
2. Lila Eccles Brimhall to the author, interview, July 11, 1971.
3. This historical sketch is taken from the speeches of Gaylord A. Freeman, chairman of the board of the First National Bank of Chicago. They were brought together and published as *Freeman of the First Chicago,* edited by Sidney Hyman (Chicago: R. R. Donnelley, 1975).
4. The newspaper references are taken from an unpublished manuscript by Leonard Arrington, "A History of the First Security Corporation."

5. *Ibid.*
6. Eccles to the author, letter, October 5, 1971.
7. The last depresion that was both acute and protracted occurred in the 1890s. In the twentieth century, the only time prior to the Great Crash of 1929 when unemployment exceeded 10 percent of the labor force was in 1921, when unemployment reached a high of 11.2 percent.
8. Arthur M. Schlesinger, Jr., *The Crisis of the Old Order* (Boston: Houghton Mifflin, 1957) p. 135–6.
9. *Ibid.*, p. 136.
10. Herbert Stein, *The Fiscal Revolution* (Chicago: The University of Chicago Press, 1967).
11. *Beckoning Frontiers*, p. 55.
12. Eastern institutions felt safe behind their protective layers of fat as long as they called in the obligations owed them in the South and West. But when these obligations were no longer collectible, and the Eastern creditor institutions lay exposed to the onslaught of the depression, they demanded something like the RFC and they got it later in 1931.
13. Eugene Meyer to the author, from notes taken during a conversation with Meyer shortly before his death in 1959.
14. Schlesinger, *op. cit.*, p. 113.
15. *Beckoning Frontiers*, p. 59.
16. First Security Corporation, Reports to the Stockholders for the years 1930 to 1933.
17. W. T. Foster, "Wizards with Bootstraps," *North American Review*, April 1933.
18. *Beckoning Frontiers*, p. 75.

Part III. THE STRUGGLE TO GOVERN

1. For a more detailed account of his program, see *Beckoning Frontiers*, pp. 105–13.
2. Schlesinger, *op. cit.*, pp. 195–6.
3. Charles Hamlin, *Diary*, vol. 22.
4. Robert E. Sherwood, *Roosevelt and Hopkins* (New York: Harper Brothers, 1948), p. 34.
5. *Beckoning Frontiers*, p. 120.
6. John Morton Blum, *From the Morgenthau Diaries* (Boston: Houghton Mifflin, 1959), p. 61.
7. Papers of Marriner S. Eccles, vol. 2.
8. Paul H. Douglas to the author, interview, December 28, 1974.
9. *Beckoning Frontiers*, 126–7.
10. Eccles to the author, letter, November 22, 1973.
11. Sherwood, *op. cit.*, p. 69.
12. Blum, *op cit.*, p. 73.
13. Eccles to the author, interview, June 17, 1972.
14. *Ibid.*
15. *Ibid.*
16. *Ibid.*
17. Sherwood, *op. cit.*, p. 72.
18. *Ibid.*
19. Eccles to the author, interview, March 16, 1973.
20. Cited by Gaylord A. Freeman in *Freeman of the First Chicago*.
21. *Beckoning Frontiers*, p. 58.
22. Sherwood, *op. cit.*, p. 72.
23. *Beckoning Frontiers*, p. 175.
24. Arch O. Egbert, "Marriner S. Eccles and the Banking Act of 1935" (Ph.D. dissertation, Brigham Young University, 1967), p. 10.
25. *Beckoning Frontiers*, p. 197.
26. Egbert, *op cit.*, p. 14.
27. *Beckoning Frontiers*, p. 191–2.
28. Papers of Marriner S. Eccles, vol. 3.
29. Egbert, *op. cit.* p. 25.
30. Papers of Marriner S. Eccles, vol. 3.
31. Egbert, *op. cit.*, p. 23.
32. *Ibid.*
33. *Time Magazine*, February 4, 1935.
34. *Washington Post*, May 3, 1935; *New York Times*, May 4, 1935.
35. Papers of Marriner S. Eccles, vol. 4.
36. Eccles to the author, interview, March 20, 1973.
37. Raymond Clapper in the *Washington Star*, August 2, 1935.
38. *Beckoning Frontiers*, p. 234.
39. *Ibid.*
40. *Beckoning Frontiers*, p. 246.

Part IV. IN DUBIOUS BATTLE

1. Blum, *op. cit.,* p. 356.
2. Cited in *Beckoning Frontiers,* p. 258.
3. Blum, *op. cit.* p. 357.
4. Blum, *op. cit.,* p. 358.
5. Blum, *op. cit.,* p. 363.
6. Blum, *op. cit.,* p. 280.
7. Friedman and Schwartz, *op. cit.,* p. 527.
8. *Ibid.*
9. *Ibid.,* pp. 511–34.
10. Robert Lekachman, *The Age of Keynes* (New York: Random House, 1966), pp. 126–9.
11. Blum, *op. cit.,* pp. 391–2.
12. *Ibid.,* p. 394.
13. *Ibid.,* pp. 419–20.
14. *Ibid.*
15. Sherwood, *op. cit.,* p. 210.

Part V. THE ECONOMICS OF WAR

1. *Beckoning Frontiers,* 341.
2. *Ibid.,* p. 347.
3. *Ibid.,* p. 350.
4. *Ibid.,* p. 360.
5. R. F. Harrod, *The Life of John Maynard Keynes* (London: Macmillan, 1951), pp. 599–602.
6. Sherwood, *op. cit.,* p. 340.
7. *Ibid.,* p. 402.
8. *Robert Lekachman, op. cit.,* pp. 144–60.
9. *Ibid.*
10. *Beckoning Frontiers,* p. 339.
11. Eccles to the author, interview, December 13, 1974.
12. R. F. Harrod, *op. cit.,* pp. 510–11.
13. *Ibid.* See chapter 13.
14. Eccles to the author, interview, March 18, 1973.
15. *Beckoning Frontiers,* p. 341.
16. R. F. Harrod, *op. cit.,* p. 603.
17. *Ibid.,* pp. 604–7.
18. Eccles to the author, interview, December 15, 1973.
19. *Ibid.*
20. Eccles to the author, interview, July 17, 1972.
21. *Beckoning Frontiers,* pp. 452–3.
22. *Ibid.*
23. Eccles to the author, interview, June 14, 1974.
24. *Ibid.*
25. *Beckoning Frontiers,* p. 460.
26. Eccles to the author, interview, June 17, 1974.
27. The quoted passages are taken from the remarks of Sallie Eccles on the occasion of an eightieth birthday dinner party she gave for Marriner.

Part VI. THE PUBLIC CITIZEN

1. Sallie Eccles to the author, interview, July 20, 1973.
2. The ranch land had originally been purchased by David Eccles as a breeding ground for horses needed in heavy construction work. Mechanization of heavy construction had eliminated the need for horses.
3. Edmund Littlefield to the author, interview, July 21, 1973.
4. Harold Burton to the author, interview, July 22, 1973.
5. Littlefield to the author, interview, July 21, 1973.
6. *Ibid.*
7. Sallie Eccles to the author, interview, July 27, 1973.
8. Marriner Eccles to the author, interview, July 26, 1973.
9. Littlefield to the author, interview, July 21, 1974.
10. The summary account is taken from *Freeman of the First Chicago.*
11. Marriner Eccles, "Impression of the Orient," *The American Banker,* June 1956.
12. Marriner Eccles to the author, interview, June 14, 1972.
13. Sidney Hyman, *Youth in Politics* (New York: Basic Books, 1972), p. 265.
14. See *ibid.,* chapters 1–5, for a summary account of the youth movements of the time.
15. Eccles to the author, Interview, July 25, 1973.

INDEX

Index

Acknowledgments

THESE FEW WORDS stand as emblems of the immense debt I owe to individuals for their contributions to the preparation of this biography.

From the outset, Ms. Irma Hogan, private secretary to Marriner Eccles in his Salt Lake City office, served me in outsized ways. She regularly called my attention to critically important documents in the Eccles files which I had overlooked, helped establish the links between them and other documents, and reproduced literally hundreds of texts so that I could have them before me in Chicago. I would have floundered without her support.

A matching form of assistance was forthcoming from Marvin Grandlinger, a San Francisco-based aide to Marriner Eccles. The preparation of a biography of any living subject goes hand-in-hand with irrepressible problems, and Mr. Grandlinger was a model of calm judgment and sound advice about how they could be solved. He assumed on my behalf many of the time-consuming technical tasks that needed to be discharged before these pages could be brought to the point of publication.

I benefited from another form of assistance, generously and candidly rendered by associates of Marriner Eccles either in government or in business. Among these, Allan Sproul gave form and focus to Eccles' role in the Federal Reserve System. Edmund Littlefield and George Ishiyama did that with respect to his role in the affairs of Utah International. Harold Burton was a valuable source of insight into contributions Eccles made to the growth of the First Security Corporation and the Amalgamated Sugar Company. Not least of all, Sigmund P. Harter and Joseph Rosenblatt filled in gaps in my knowledge about Eccles' place in the business community at large. All these men, of course, should be absolved from any errors of fact or interpretation I may have committed in these pages.